SMALL BUSINESS MANAGEMENT
TOOLS FOR SUCCESS

Second Edition

JIM CARLAND
JO ANN CARLAND
Western Carolina University

1998

DAME
PUBLICATIONS, INC.

Cover Design: Amanda S. Austin

Cover Photo: © **Corel Professional Photos.** Images may have
been combined and/or modified to produce final
cover art.

© **DAME PUBLICATIONS, INC.—1998**
7800 Bissonnet—Suite 415
Houston, TX
713/995-1000
713/995-9637—FAX
800/364-9757
E-mail: dame.publications@worldnet.att.net
Website: http://www.damepub.com

ISBN 0-87393-719-8

Library of Congress Card No. 97-94633

Printed in the United States of America.

You have deeply ventured;
    But all must do so who would greatly win.

                Lord Bryon
                Marino Faliero, Act 1, Scene 2

SMALL BUSINESS MANAGEMENT TOOLS FOR SUCCESS

Second Edition

ABOUT THE AUTHORS

Jo Ann and Jim Carland are uniquely suited to author a text in small business. Their academic, business, research, consulting and teaching backgrounds combine to give them unique insight into the problems and opportunities of small firms. The authors are entrepreneurs themselves. They have started seven businesses! Consequently, they have experienced the challenges of entrepreneurship and learned how the storm is weathered. They speak as doers as well as teachers and their text is founded on pragmatism.

Jim holds a PhD in Management Policy and Systems with related fields in Finance, Accounting and Economics. A Certified Management Accountant, Certified Valuation Analyst, and Certified Public Accountant, he has ten years of business experience and fifteen years of teaching experience.

Jo Ann holds a PhD in Educational Psychology with minors in Social Dynamics, Statistics and Computer Systems. A Certified Data Processing Professional and Certified Computer Professional, she has five years of business experience and twenty years of teaching experience.

Jo Ann and Jim are prolific researchers. They have co-authored more than 150 articles, papers and books and are recognized internationally as experts in entrepreneurship and small business. They have published in such prestigious journals as the *Academy of Management Review*, the *Journal of Business Venturing*, the *International Journal of Management*, the *International Journal of Small Business*, the *Journal of Small Business Management*, *The American Journal of Small Business*, the *Journal of Business and Entrepreneurship*, the *Wisconsin Small Business Forum*, and the *Journal of Business Strategies*. Jim's depth and breadth of knowledge in planning and management tools is complemented by Jo Ann's skills in teaching methodology, social dynamics, personality and computerized systems. They have consulted with more than 300 small firms on a variety of topics ranging from computer systems to management processes. They have seen business from the inside in large firms and in small firms. They have experienced the thrill of success and the heartbreak of plans gone awry in their own firms. Their long time collaborative efforts are culminated in the second edition of this text which reflects an exceptional depth of insight into small business.

SMALL BUSINESS MANAGEMENT TOOLS FOR SUCCESS

Second Edition

PREFACE

Small business has become a fixture in the curricula of colleges nationwide. The interest which has developed in this topic is gratifying in light of the significance which small business has for national and world economies and the challenging and rewarding careers which it makes possible. We are pleased to offer the second edition of this text as support for a first course in small business management.

The subtitle of this text reveals the primary focus which has been pursued in its development. As active teachers and consultants in small business, as current owners of five small businesses, and former owners of two additional small businesses, we are convinced that a primary factor in the failure of many firms is the absence of management skills and planning. The fundamental objective of this book is the development of those skills.

The text is divided into six parts. Part I is an introduction to the subject of small business management. It describes the importance of the field from an economic and innovative perspective and examines personal considerations of importance to a prospective small business owner. Personality characteristics, life experiences and their role in the establishment and success of small firms is discussed. The sacrifices required for success in a small venture are explored in depth.

Part II of the text contains the tools which are required for the successful creation and management of a small business. Each chapter in this section has been designed to stand alone so that instructors may omit any segments which are deemed to be unnecessary for a given class. In fact, instructors of advanced students may omit this entire part of the text or use sections of it for review without impairing the remainder of the book. The first chapter explains the principles of marketing which are pertinent to small firms and establishes the knowledge which will be required to complete the marketing segments of the business plan and which will be required for ongoing success in operations. The next chapter explains financial and managerial accounting. The focus is on the accounting knowledge which the chief executive of a small firm requires vice the processes which will be employed by an accountant. Despite the fact that many students in small business will have been exposed to accounting principles, experience teaches that few will have a real understanding of the relevant issues which will be required for the successful creation and management of a small firm. The following two chapters explore cost, volume, profit relationships and explains in great detail how breakeven analysis and target sales analysis is conducted. Budgeting techniques with special emphasis on cash flow budgets and their role in strategic planning is the subject of the next chapter while financial analysis is presented in the following chapter. The analysis focus is the establishment of analytical tools which are required for effective planning and evaluation in a small business setting.

Part III of the text presents the business plan. A step by step approach to the initiation of a small business is explained from a strategic perspective. From the establishment of goals and objectives through market identification, feasibility assessment, development of financing and the timing of the opening of a firm, the chapters in this section reinforce the value of planning as a key factor in the success of a small business venture. Because of their relative importance for a successful venture, separate chapters on marketing and financial planning are presented.

Part IV of the text is entitled The New Venture. Topics in legal organization and structuring and the pros and cons associated with alternative forms are covered in the first chapter in this unit. Income tax considerations and concerns are explored in depth. Issues in purchasing an ongoing business are discussed in the second chapter with special emphasis on establishing a value for a firm. The final chapter of this unit explores franchising. Pertinent factors from the perspective of both a franchisee and a franchisor are discussed as are the pros and cons of franchising.

Part V of the text is devoted to the management of an ongoing small business. Strategic management and planning techniques are stressed throughout the chapters in this section. The first chapter is an introduction to strategic management which focuses on the functions of top management in a small enterprise. The second chapter examines the management of human resources while the third chapter explains marketing management. The next chapter deals with risk management and insurance issues and discusses the effective control of risk and hazards in operating a small business. The following chapters treat special problems for chief executives of small firms. The effective use, control and management of receivables, inventory and production are explored in detail. The section closes with a chapter on financial planning which focuses on the acquisition and maintenance of adequate physical and financial resources for the operation of a small business.

The final unit in the text, Part VI, is entitled Special Topics. Any chapter in this section may be omitted at the instructor's discretion without sacrificing the integrity of the text. The content includes planning for management succession and bequeathing a small business, the potentially catastrophic effects of divorce on small firms, business law issues, international markets and opportunities for small firms and ethical issues for owners and managers of small ventures.

The text reinforces the concept of a strategic competency for a successful venture. If we examined the strategic competency of the text itself, we would identify the emphasis on tools and planning as the attributes which set this book apart from its competitors. We believe that the key to success is planning, planning and more planning. The tools we present are actually tools of planning. This text has been designed for individuals who will actually put its precepts into practice.

The depth of material in the tools chapters will permit anyone to actually apply those tools in the creation and operation of a small business. The detail in the planning chapters will enable an individual to systematically assess the feasibility of a business concept and to prepare a start-up plan. The managing chapters make the strategic issues clear and will facilitate the organization and maintenance of an effective management team in a small business.

The text has been written for individuals without experience or knowledge in small business. In addition, those concepts from other disciplines which are mandatory for success in a small business are covered in detail. These concepts include marketing, accounting, finance, economics and management. A cursory reading of the contents might lead one to conclude that redundant material was included in the text. Should that prove to be the case, segments of the text as identified above may be skipped, reviewed or minimized without affecting the remainder of the book. However, we believe that a closer examination of the contents and a reading of the chapters will lead to the conclusion that for the majority of colleges and students the redundancy is minimal. Most students struggle with the concepts and premises of marketing, finance, accounting and economics because of the orientation of those courses in most schools toward large firms. This text focuses on the aspects of those subjects which are pertinent and crucial to success in a small firm. In addition, the exposition of those subjects is precise and complete so that understanding will be facilitated.

The text is liberally supported with illustrations of concepts and approaches. Vignettes, mini cases and anecdotes are used to exemplify, reinforce and illustrate points which should be retained. In addition to supporting the education process, these examples add readability and interest. One of our primary objectives in developing this text has been to produce a book which the students will enjoy reading. To that end, simplicity and clarity of exposition, a practical orientation and a real world focus have been pursued in every chapter and in every exercise and assignment.

We have tested this text extensively in our own classes. The second edition results from four years of teaching with the first edition and incorporates comments which other users of the text have made over the years. We do not shy away from the tough topics. We introduce and explore them from a practical, straightforward perspective. We believe that inclusion of the entirety of the tools for success in small business creation and management will make this book a useful reference tool for your students in the years to come.

We invite you to test the book with your students. Further, we want to hear from you and to receive your comments and feedback. Please feel free to e-mail us at carland@wcu.edu, at any time. We will be pleased to hear from you and to have your help in improving what we have experienced as a labor of love.

Finally, we would like to thank Bill McDowell. Without his vision and perseverance, this book would not exist.

Jo Ann and Jim Carland

SMALL BUSINESS MANAGEMENT
TOOLS FOR SUCCESS
Second Edition

Brief Contents

Part Five   Managing for Success

Part Six   Special Topics

CONTENTS

Part Four   The New Venture

Part Six   Special Topics

PART ONE

INTRODUCTION TO

SMALL BUSINESS MANAGEMENT

CHAPTER ONE

SMALL BUSINESS AND ENTREPRENEURSHIP

CHAPTER OBJECTIVES

Upon completion of this chapter, you should be able to:

- Describe the impact of small business owners on the economy of a nation;

- Describe the impact which business size has on the operations of the business;

- Describe the impact of small businesses on innovation and its importance;

- Explain the personal goals and objectives involved in starting a small business and why they are important; and,

- Recognize the challenges in owning and operating a small business.

SMALL BUSINESS AND ENTREPRENEURSHIP

INTRODUCTION

When humans first began to live in groups, domesticate animals, and perform specialized tasks, small business had its origins. Today a popular definition of **business** is, *the activities of individuals or groups who are involved in developing, producing, and distributing the goods and services needed to satisfy other people's needs or desires.*[1] With a little imagination, we can visualize how business was born at the dawn of history. One individual who was especially skilled at making a particular object was pressed by other members of the tribe into the manufacture of this item for themselves. Think about one of the earliest of weapons, the sling. Making a good sling is truly an art. An individual who had mastered that art would be constantly besieged by his or her peers to make slings for them. Surely such an individual would have been paid for the slings by meat or other items: the first barter. As the size of the tribe grew, the amount of time required to manufacture slings for other people grew. Soon the sling maker became an artisan specializing in the craft and dependent for food and other items on the trade of his or her slings for those items. The sling maker was the first business owner, but was soon joined by other business people who were adept at making spears and other weapons, and clothing, etc.

When early man began to specialize and produce goods or services for others, he was in effect participating in business, and since such ventures involved small numbers of people, they were small businesses. In fact, one of the earliest known writings, which dates from 2,500 B.C., is a document concerning *money* loaned at interest.[2] As the size of the tribe increased and the demand for goods and services increased, these businesses grew. As tribes grew into nations and states, and evolved laws and rules for living, these laws had to address business. The conduct of business was important to the well being of every member of the society because each member was increasingly dependent on the producers for food, clothing, shelter and luxuries. Each nation put its mark upon the activities which we call business and enhanced the means with which business was performed, while seeking to protect people from unscrupulous business activities. One of the earliest and best known examples of such laws is a code drafted by the King of Babylon in 2100 B.C. This code contained 300 laws which were designed to protect both consumers and small business people from fraud and other unscrupulous acts.[3]

As civilizations advanced, several factors caused the number, size, and complexity of business to increase:

1. More complex goods being manufactured;
2. Problems related to shipping goods;
3. Risks associated with collecting monies for goods sold on credit;
4. The growing difficulty of communicating, frequently over long distances, with present and potential customers;
5. The increasing burden of compliance with the laws.

More and more skill in management was necessary to succeed in the enterprise of providing goods and services to others for a profit. The skill of the artisan was no longer sufficient for the success of that artisan. In today's business world, sling makers require capable managers in order to be successful in producing and selling slings.

THE IMPORTANCE OF MODERN SMALL BUSINESS

Despite the rise in complexity of business operations, not all businesses become large. In fact, most remain small. In the United States and in the rest of the world, small businesses dominate the market place for many goods and services. Further, small firms constitute the overwhelming majority of businesses in America, indeed, throughout the world. To understand the scope of modern small business, we must first define the term.

DEFINITIONS OF SMALL BUSINESS

In the United States, the government defines a business as small if it *...is independently owned and operated and is not dominant in its field of operation.*[4] This definition was used to establish whether a business could qualify for assistance under the U.S. Small Business Administration (SBA) program, which was established in 1953 to aid small businesses.

There is still no clear consensus as to one definition for small business. Even the SBA guidelines enacted by Congress and mentioned above are difficult, if not impossible to apply. To produce quantifiable guidelines for eligibility for loan and assistance programs, the SBA has developed a lengthy document, covering some 750 different industries, which delineates qualifying size classifications for firms industry by industry. These size classifications were made based on sales in some industries and number of employees in other industries. Table 1 displays a small sample of the guidelines.[5]

As the table displays, the SBA definitions vary widely. Many writers have embraced the SBA definitions, but others have criticized the wide range which the definitions permit. Frequently, a writer in the area of small business will establish his or her own definitions. Generally, most writers and researchers require independent ownership and management as part of the definition and then select some arbitrary level of sales or assets or employees.

We believe that the key distinguishing criterion of a small business is not its sales or other size indication, but its management structure. The thing that makes a small business unique and also makes it a more complex business entity to manage is the absence of a management hierarchy. As we will discuss throughout this text, small business owners do not have the luxury of a staff of specialists to assist in the planning and management of the firm. Small business managers must be generalists, rather than specialists. That makes small business management *more difficult* than management in a large firm. Throughout the text, when we refer to a small business, we will mean a business which is individually owned and which has limited management resources.

Table 1

SBA Size Standards for Qualification as a Small Business

Type of Business	Maximum Size
Advertising Agency	$3.5 Million in Sales
Furniture Stores	$3.5 Million in Sales
Insurance Agency	$3.5 Million in Sales
Meat Packing Plants	500 Employees
Hardware Wholesale	100 Employees
Metal Can Manufacturing	1,000 Employees
Mobile Home Dealers	$6.5 Million in Sales
Residential General Contractors	$17.0 Million in Sales

THE ECONOMIC IMPACT OF SMALL BUSINESS

Regardless of your definition of small business, these firms have a dramatic effect on the economy of every nation in the world. In the United States, the number of small businesses vastly exceeds the number of large firms. If one considers the tax returns filed each year with the Internal Revenue Service, there are some 20 million businesses in the United States. Of those, more than 99% would be considered small by the SBA.[6]

Many writers prefer to look at other statistics because the tax return data includes businesses which have no employees, which are hobbies rather than businesses, or which constitute part time business activities. If we look at only those businesses which have at least one paid employee, the number of firms drops dramatically, but the overwhelming majority are still small. Table 2 displays a list of the number of such businesses by industry.[7] This estimate, some five million businesses, is still dominated by small firms as more than 98% of these businesses employ fewer than 100 people. This pattern of small firm domination is repeated throughout the world. In fact, the President's Task Force on International Private Enterprise declared that *small and medium sized businesses are the heart of the private sector in most of the countries in which the Agency for International Development operates.*[8]

Table 2	
The Number of Businesses in America	
Selected Industries	Number of Businesses
Services	1,922,000
Retail	1,110,000
Wholesale	374,000
Manufacturing	327,000
Construction	597,000
Finance, Insurance and Real Estate	420,000
Mining	24,000
Transportation, Communication and Utilities	181,000
U.S. Total for all Industries	5,074,000

You must remember that 98% of businesses being small does not mean that those businesses employ 98% of the people or that they make up 98% of the sales volume. One large business can be many thousands of times larger than one small business. If we consider a breakdown by industry segment, we can see that small businesses do constitute a major force in the economy, despite the existence of giant firms. Table 3 displays U.S. employment by industry segment and business size.[9]

The data in Table 3 is drawn from the same source as Table 2. The table displays the percentage of total employment in each of eight industries provided by firms with less than 100 employees, firms with 100 to 499 employees, and firms with 500 employees or more. As you can see, if one considers small firms to be those with less than 100 employees, just over 39% of total U.S. employment is produced in the small business sector. If one broadens the definition to firms employing less than 500 employees, the small business sector produces almost 58% of the jobs in America. The number of jobs is a good proxy for the volume of goods and services produced by businesses, so we can conclude that U.S. small businesses account for about half of the employment and half of the production of goods and services in the economy.

Small businesses are even more important than the 50% figure suggests. For example, some reports suggest that small firms create jobs at *eight times the rate* of larger firms.[10] Despite that startling statistic, not all small firms grow. In fact, one estimate concludes that less than 15% of small firms account for virtually all of the jobs growth.[11] In our view, the firms that are growing strongly are created by *macroentrepreneurs*, a concept we will discuss at length in a few moments.

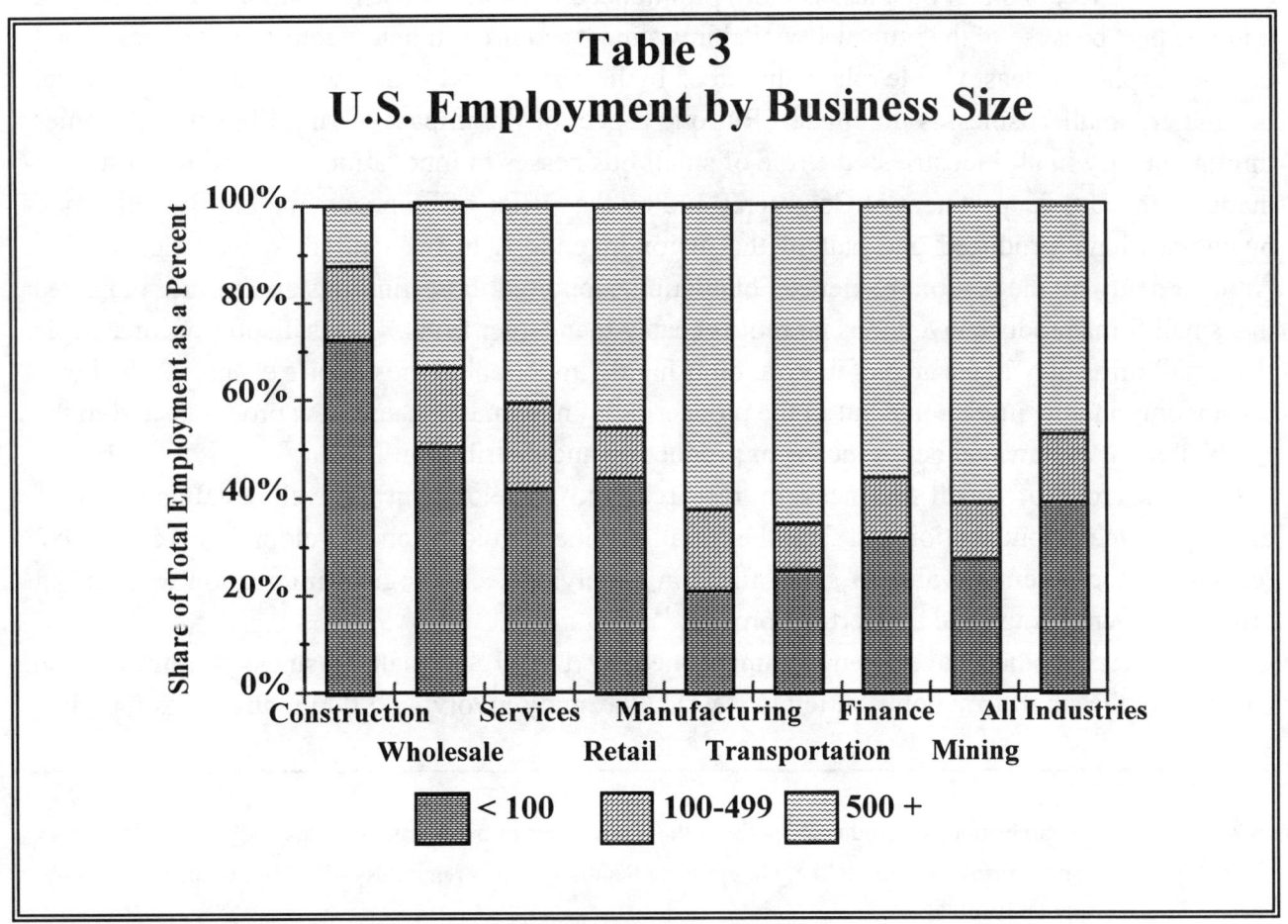

THE BACKBONE OF THE ECONOMY

From a global perspective, entrepreneurship is the backbone of our economies and the mandate for the wealth of our nations. It is at the very core of our existence. It is, at once the source of economic stability and the well spring of innovation. In the United States, small businesses are uniquely positioned to play this latter role. While large firms choose as their edict the maximization of shareholder wealth, small firms, without the specter of stock market activity and public and psychological vagaries, are able to look to the future, to innovate and to excel. Entrepreneurs are not limited by the short term vision of profits for shareholders but instead are empowered to look to the future and answer only to themselves and the new markets which they create. It is this uniqueness of entrepreneurship which we find so fascinating: its ability to provide economic stability at the same time that it propels innovation.

THE ROLE OF INNOVATION

The effect of small business is more pronounced in some industries than in others. As one might expect because of the immense capital investment required in manufacturing ventures, small businesses play the least visible role in this area. In the services industries, where capital investment is smaller, small businesses dominate. But one aspect of the impact of small businesses comes through clearly in all industries: the role of small businesses in innovation. According to studies made by the U.S. Department of Commerce and by the Office of Management and Budget, small businesses have produced one half of the major inventions in the United States since 1953.[12] Another study by the National Science Foundation supported those findings and further indicated that small firms produce inventions far more cheaply than larger firms.[13] This disproportionate role that small firms play in the area of innovation is highly important to the nation's economy. It shows up, not only in new inventions, but in the pioneering of new markets and new products, and in the establishment of new and better means of production and distribution.

The role of small business in research and development is well established as a disproportionate contribution. In fact, the Small Business Innovation Development Act of 1982 recognized the potential value of small firms in supplying technological innovation and set out programs to encourage and support the process.[14]

Several studies have been commissioned by the U.S. Small Business Administration concerning the small firm contribution to R&D. One study involving 5,000 innovations found:[15]

Small businesses produced 2.4 times the innovations of their larger cousins;

Small firms were more likely to innovate than large firms regardless of the importance of the innovation;

Small firm innovations were 4 times more likely to be privately financed;

Small firm employment was 22% more likely to increase subsequent to an innovation;

Small firms were 22% more likely to sell innovations to other businesses while large firms were 42% more likely to sell to the military and 32% more likely to sell to government; and

There is no difference in the 4.3 year delay between invention and innovation as regards small or large firms.

This disproportionate role of small business in innovations is not the result of the greater numbers of such businesses. Nor is it the result of a growth orientation. In fact, if we adjust the data to examine the number of innovations per employee, we can see a better picture of the innovative impact. Table 4 displays the number of innovations per million employees divided into groups.[16] The first group is employees in small businesses, less than 500 employees, in industries which are experiencing growth in term of total employment. This is compared to employees in large firms, 500 or more employees, also in growing industries. The second group uses businesses in industries which are experiencing a decline in growth, in terms of total employment. As the table shows, employees in small firms do produce more innovations than their counterparts in large firms, whether the industry is growing or not.

Clearly, small business involvement in R&D and innovation is a valuable commodity for the U.S. economy. In some industries, notably biotechnology, virtually all innovations arise in small firms.[17] Regardless of industry, entrepreneurs and small businesses display a strong commitment to innovation. Some entrepreneurs have a stronger commitment than others. The differences in entrepreneurial behavior and vision are the subjects of the following sections.

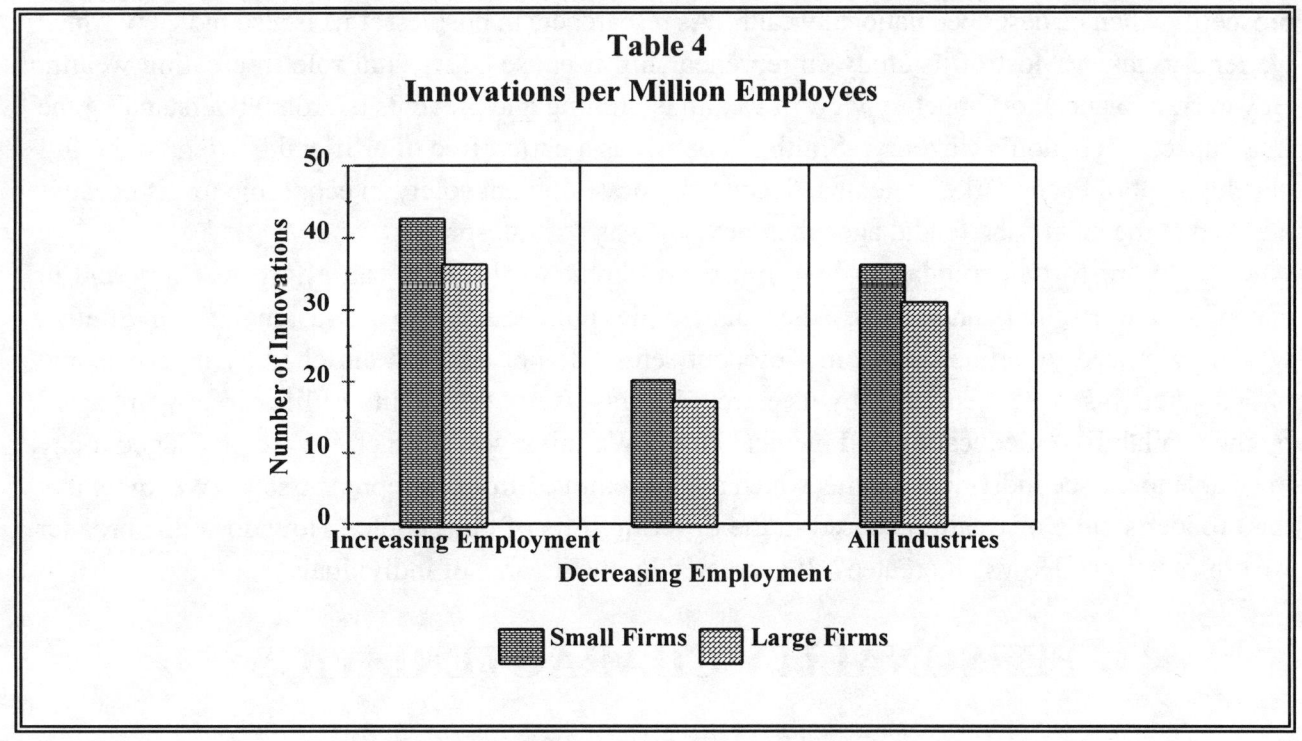

Table 4
Innovations per Million Employees

THE AMERICAN DREAM

With virtually no thought, all of us can describe people who have demonstrated dramatically different expressions of the American dream. For every Ted Turner, Bill Gates, or Steve Jobs, there are hundreds of unknowns who labor in family owned, local businesses. How can a single perspective encompass such a wide range of behaviors? Why are some driven to create new industries while others are content to keep the family business in tact, under control, at home? The answer lies in the different expressions of the dream. There is only one aspect of the phenomenon which is common to all of the unique expressions of the American dream: the dream itself.

Entrepreneurship is one of the oldest established processes of human society and it has been a driving force in the world ever since the first humans began to develop specialization of labor at the dawn of history. As the centuries pass, the importance and role of entrepreneurship grow. All that we have and all that we have accomplished owes its existence to the dreams of individuals. From the discovery and mastery of fire, to the specialization of labor, to the development of agriculture, to the invention of writing, to the establishment of civilization, to the development of the printing press, to the exploration of the world, to the industrial revolution, to the information revolution, we witness the reality of social evolution embodied in the conscious acts of individuals.

Adam Smith,[18] the father of modern economics, was writing in 1776 about economic prosperity when he described national wealth. As researchers in business, this is also the view which we tend to take. Most of us study entrepreneurship because of its vital role in creating wealth. However, a financial or monetary view of wealth is limiting and prevents us from understanding the true impact of a nation's citizenry. Smith's dream was a nation free of artificial barriers to the full development of each worker's genius. He viewed development solely in economic terms because he lived at the end of the feudal age when poverty was so widespread.

We are fortunate today to live in a far different world. We can afford to enjoy and to encourage the arts, literature, sports; a host of activities unimaginable to the vast majority in Smith's world. We need to define wealth in a broader sense. Is not a nation enriched by its artists and philosophers just as it is enriched by its entrepreneurs? Is not the quality of life directly impacted by the availability of education and medical care? We think yes. In fact, we are privileged today to be able to pursue individual dreams which are far removed from entrepreneurship. We know that the broader source of wealth is based in the differing gifts of our people. How does this broader wealth function? How is it created? It is created by the dreams of individuals.

PERSONALITY CHARACTERISTICS

Clearly, a small business venture, just like an individual life or career, is a complex function of a myriad of life experiences, perceived opportunities, individual skills, abilities, and gifts, and the dynamic environment in which these variables interact. What is the source, the basis, the foundation of an individual's foray into entrepreneurship, or any other career, avocation or pursuit? Dreams.

DREAMS AS A PARADIGM

The role of individual dreams is not just a casual insight. It can support a deeper understanding of the phenomenon we study; it can lead to a change in the paradigm of entrepreneurship. Just as dreams drive individuals into dramatically different life styles, they drive individual entrepreneurs into dramatically different expressions of entrepreneurship.

For example, we know that there are visionaries in the world; those who *see what is not there*. Visionaries exist in every aspect of modern life. They see things that no one else can see and set about proving their visions are real and true. We find them in research laboratories pursuing treatments for disease; we find them in universities seeking to expand the boundaries of knowledge in a myriad of fields and disciplines; we find them in the arts seeking new outlets for expression and communication; we find them at the forefront of knowledge throughout the world. What drives them on their quest? What is the source of their energy and inspiration? Their dreams. When one of these visionaries turns his or her interest to business, those dreams drive a very different expression of entrepreneurship; so different that we propose a new word: ***macroentrepreneur***.

MACROENTREPRENEURS

Macroentrepreneurs see their involvement with their businesses or their positions as the primary vehicle for pursuing *self-actualization*. These people may be found in a corporate environment, but the strength of their entrepreneurial drive will be so strong that they may feel frustrated by the confines of a managerial hierarchy. Disproportionately, we expect to find *macroentrepreneurs* establishing their own firms or ventures, growing those firms, taking those firms public, striving to dominate a market.

What makes *macroentrepreneurs* unique is their definition of success. Because their drive for self-actualization is bound up with their ventures, *success is measured in terms of growth and profits of the business*. Their interest is not truly monetary; rather, they see growth in profits and sales as a convenient scorecard to measure success. They truly want to dominate the arena in which they find themselves. Their lives are a constant striving for dominance.

No two *macroentrepreneurs* will be the same, but all have one thing in common: a dream, a dream to create, a dream to change, a dream to make the world different. *Macroentrepreneurs* will be innovative and creative and will be constantly striving to find new ways to translate their dreams: into new products and services, into new markets, into new industries, into new heights of growth; into new challenges, into new frontiers, into new expressions, into new insights. They may fail and fail spectacularly, but failure will not result from a lack of effort.

On the other hand, there are people who own and operate small businesses, but their behavior and their management practices leaves us wondering. Closing early, taking off to go on an unannounced fishing trip, opening late, ignoring customers, these and other behaviors are observable in the shop keepers of any small town in America. Clearly, we need a different word to describe such a dramatically different expression of entrepreneurship. We propose to call these people ***microentrepreneurs***.

MICROENTREPRENEURS

Microentrepreneurs are the individuals at the opposite pole of the entrepreneurship continuum. They have a much lower level of entrepreneurial drive and they see their business ventures as primary sources for family income or to establish family employment. They will view their businesses as important aspects of their lives rather than being consumed by those businesses. *Microentrepreneurs* will pursue self-actualization through some vehicle outside their businesses. *Microentrepreneurs* will not be found in corporate environments because they view their self-employment as a key aspect of their individual freedom and they gain self-esteem from operating their own ventures. They will not be as interested in pursuing growth. In fact, as soon as the business venture can provide a standard of living which they find satisfactory, they will be content to operate it in the same fashion throughout their careers.

For *microentrepreneurs*, success is measured by *freedom*. Operating their own businesses frees them from the pressures and demands of a career in management while it provides their families with financial support. As soon as they have reached a comfort level, being able to support their needs, they will feel successful and the focus of their lives will shift elsewhere. They will not pursue innovative or creative approaches to business. They will prefer the safer venue of tried and true techniques. They have no real interest in innovating because the higher level of energy and involvement it requires takes away from the freedom which they enjoy. No two *microentrepreneurs* will be the same, but all have one thing in common: their dreams. Their dreams are dreams of freedom, dreams of holidays and family times, dreams of vacations, and time to pursue a myriad of avocations.

ENTREPRENEURS

Entrepreneurs will have a great deal of their self-perception bound up in their businesses or positions, but they are not as consumed by entrepreneurial drive as *macroentrepreneurs*. They will be interested in profits and growth beyond that of *microentrepreneurs*. They may be found in corporate environments. The presence of *entrepreneurs* in any data set is the primary source of confusion in interpreting results. The key is that *entrepreneurs* will have a higher standard of success than *microentrepreneurs*. For each one, that level will vary. As soon as they achieve the level they require, they will shift focus outside the business, just like *microentrepreneurs*. Until that time, they will seem to be pursuing profit and growth, but that pursuit will fall short of the single mindedness of the *macroentrepreneur*. *Entrepreneurs* will be innovative, but they are more likely to pursue enhancements to established products, services and procedures, rather than seek totally new approaches. Enhancements are safer and less likely to disrupt the steady climb to perceived success which is so important to entrepreneurs. No two *entrepreneurs* are the same, but they all have one thing in common: their dreams. Theirs are dreams of recognition and advancement, dreams of wealth and admiration.

OBSERVABLE BEHAVIORS

The insight which we can gain could help to understand the behavior patterns in various individuals, the outcomes of their business lives, and the consistency with which they strive toward those outcomes. As indicated above, *macroentrepreneurs* will be highly innovative. This is an important contrast with the ingenuity which entrepreneurs will display. Innovation implies the search for that which does not yet exist, while ingenuity implies the search for improvements to what does exist. This is an extremely different orientation with dramatically different outcomes: the former produces new products, services, markets, industries, etc., while the latter results in improved products, services, markets, industries, etc. *Microentrepreneurs* will display neither innovation nor ingenuity, opting for the traditional because it takes less time away from their personal free time, the dream which really drives them. As a result, they are more likely to produce, small, stable, slowly changing, family owned businesses. A *macroentrepreneur* will never cease striving for the dominance suggested in his or her revolutionary dreams. *Entrepreneurs*, on the other hand, will be less consistent, shifting their focus outside the business as soon as they perceive that their individual goals of success have been met. *Microentrepreneurs* really only want comfort. As soon as their individual perceptions of adequate family income are met, they will shift focus outside the business.

Table 5 Entrepreneurial Dreams as a Paradigm				
Classification	Dreams	Behavior	Outcomes	Consistency
Macroentrepreneur	Dreams of revolutionary change	Innovative	New markets, services, products and industries	Never stops striving for dominance
Entrepreneur	Dreams of personal success, wealth and accolades	Ingenious	Enhanced markets, services, products and industries	Shifts interest at perceived success level
Microentrepreneur	Dreams of personal freedom	Traditional	Small, stable, slowly changing, family businesses	Shifts interest at perceived comfort level

Table 5 displays the differences which dreams can make in the expression of entrepreneurship. Note that each of the different expressions of entrepreneurship has something of value to contribute to a nation's economy. *Macroentrepreneurs* create new markets and new industries; *entrepreneurs* enhance existing markets and industries; and, *macroentrepreneurs* provide economic stability. One expression is not superior to another. All are required for economic well being, but the various approaches produce dramatically different results, both for the individuals involved and for the nation.

SUMMARY

Small business had its origins centuries ago. Even though we have progressed by boundless leaps through time because of man's innovation and use of technology, we still find that small business is the backbone of every free nation's economy. Man has evolved using the technology of his day and enhanced his achievements in his steps through time. He has learned from his errors and benefitted from his strengths, made laws for his protection and enforced them with zeal, and used his imagination to dream dreams and create new worlds for the future generations to explore and expand.

The type of person who serves as the backbone of the nation's economy and maintains the stability of its growth is the small business owner who is willing to take the risk and strive for success in an increasingly competitive environment. The small business owner is one of three types: a *macroentrepreneur* who dreams of change and innovation, of new markets, new products or services, new industries and wants to dominate his environment; an *entrepreneur* who dreams of personal success and wealth, self esteem and enhanced markets, services and products which bring their own rewards; and the *microentrepreneur* who dreams of personal freedom, family enrichment and maintaining comfort levels within as well as outside the business. Although the three types differ in desires and dreams, they complement each other in the business environment. Success is in the mind of the individual small business owner.

QUESTIONS, EXERCISES AND CASES

QUESTIONS:

1.   Who is a macroentrepreneur?

2.   Who is an entrepreneur?

3.   Who is a microentrepreneur?

4.   What is the impact of small business on the economy?

5.   What is the role of innovation in small business?

6.   What is the Small Business Administration's definition of small business and what are the implications for the future of small businesses without the guidance of the SBA?

7.   Why was it necessary to have different definitions for different types of businesses?

EXERCISES:

1.   Find several examples of profiles of microentrepreneurs, entrepreneurs or macroentrepreneurs and discuss their characteristics and their long term prospects for success.

2.   To be one's own boss seems to be the American dream for a large number of people. If you could open your own business, what would be your service or product? What would be your primary considerations from a behavioral perspective? The text should give you some pointers about the how-to start your own business, so you may want to continue this activity throughout the text as it explains about competitive strategies, strategic postures, and business plans.

3.   If you are the employer in a small business, what types of personnel do you feel that you should hire, with what skills and what salaries? You have limited resources at present but cannot do all the work alone. Who would you hire and why?

4.   After discussion of this topic in class, several groups might like to visit some relatively new businesses in the area and ask them some of the following questions. After returning, these students should make a presentation of their findings. Based upon the answers to the questions, the students might then determine if the business owner could be classified as a macroentrepreneur, entrepreneur or microentrepreneur and discuss whether they think the company will be successful or not based upon those factors which they deem important.

Some questions which might be asked are:

- When you established this company, how did you plan to make money or what did you think would make your company successful?
- Why did you start this company? What were your reasons and motivations?
- What are your present plans for making money or what do you think will make the company continue to be successful?
- What is your company's greatest advantage over the competition?
- What is your company's greatest weakness from a competitive view?
- Who or what kinds of firms do you believe are your competition?
- What are your long range plans for growth or diversification of the company?
- What are your personal goals and aspirations?
- What have you done to make your company stand out from its competition or what makes your company different from its competitors?
- Do you feel that there are any external factors which could limit your success? If so, what are they and how do you plan to overcome them?
- How much time do you spend in strategic planning? How much in day to day planning?
- What are your long term plans for the company--to make a living for your children or to go public or just to make a nice profit for yourself and your family?

CASE

Jim Reecer was a man with a dream. He had always wanted to go into business for himself. He had watched his mom and dad spend their lives slaving away in factories, just getting by but not happy in their jobs, waiting impatiently for retirement. At a very young age, Jim was determined that such was not going to happen to him. He was going to depend upon his own skills to get ahead and reap his own rewards. Enough of working and making others rich by his labor.

Jim was very good with his hands. He could not only fix what was broken, he could create masterpieces out of seemingly worthless junk. Locally he had made quite a reputation for himself not only as a handyman, but as a source for unique gifts. Having worked at odd jobs to support himself through school and having made spending money working on his hobbies, he decided that perhaps he ought to concentrate on his assets and go into business for himself.

Jim was young but not naive. He knew that to make his business a success, he would need more than just his hands. He would need a good business head, too. Jim's parents, who were quite proud of their son and his ideas, helped him to get a loan at the local bank, and find an inexpensive building not far from Main Street where he could set up shop. Jim with the help of his friends did most of the renovation of the shop and painted it in brilliant shades to not only brighten the gloom but also to draw attention to the *artwork* displayed there.

Just before opening his doors, Jim was beset by fear. How could he meet the public? He knew that people liked his work, but he had seldom sold any of his artwork or made any repairs for anyone except his friends or acquaintances and these people had come to him. He was basically a shy person and didn't like talking to strangers. He also knew that when he was working on his projects, he was totally oblivious to what was happening around him. He did not like interruptions even for such basics as eating or sleeping. What would he do? His friend, Charles, who had been enthusiastically helping him to get started, had been bubbling over for the last two hours about how he should handle the opening of his shop with a party atmosphere. He had also mentioned door prizes and balloons for the kids. Charles had thought that the shop should open with a bang and Jim had just imagined that folks would just wander in from time to time, browse and buy.

1.   What could Jim do at this eleventh hour? He wanted the shop to be a success but was beginning to see that perhaps talent was not enough. Discuss what you would do if you were he.

2.   What does this case reveal to you about starting a business of your own? Is having a competence in one area enough for success? Why or why not?

3.   From what you have learned in this chapter about behavior and small business ownership, what would be a reasonable solution to Jim's dilemma?

CHAPTER TWO

PERSONAL CONSIDERATIONS IN SMALL BUSINESS

CHAPTER OBJECTIVES

Upon completion of this chapter, you should be able to:

- Describe the personal considerations which influence people to go into business for themselves;

- Discuss the personality characteristics which are frequently cited in small business ownership literature;

- Discuss the influence of life experiences, parental influence, career displacement, and education on the development of personal values and the impact which these values have on entry into small business;

- Explain the requirements for success in the small business environment; and,

- Be aware of the reasons why many small businesses fail.

PERSONAL CONSIDERATIONS IN SMALL BUSINESS

INTRODUCTION

Beyond a simple desire to be one's own boss, what is it that makes people go into business for themselves? In 1971, Peter Kilby likened the search for an entrepreneur to the search for the heffalump which Winnie the Pooh conducted in A.A. Milne's famous book.[19] The heffalump was a large and important animal which everyone had seen. The problem was that every person who reported seeing the creature described it differently and no one wanted to admit that he did not know what it was. People who start businesses are very like the heffalump: everyone has seen them, but no one agrees on their descriptions.

A.A. Milne in his 1926 children's classic, *Winnie the Pooh*, featured a small boy named Christopher Robin and his teddy bear, Pooh, and their friends, including a small pig named Piglet. One chapter deals with Piglet's encounter with a Heffalump:

One day, when Christopher Robin and Winnie-the-Pooh and Piglet were all talking together, Christopher Robin finished the mouthful he was eating and said carelessly: "I saw a Heffalump today, Piglet."

"What was it doing?" asked Piglet.

"Just lumping along," said Christopher Robin. "I don't think it saw me."

"I saw one once," said Piglet. "At least, I think I did," he said. "Only perhaps it wasn't."

"So did I," said Pooh, wondering what a Heffalump was like.

"You don't often see them," said Christopher Robin carelessly.

"Not now," said Piglet.

"Not at this time of year," said Pooh.

PERSONALITY CHARACTERISTICS

In this chapter, we will examine some of the personality characteristics which are frequently attributed to small business owners. We will also examine the personal considerations involved in the decision to go into business and the characteristics which are associated with success. These

---

attributes include the need for achievement, appropriate locus of control, personal values, and life experiences.

THE NEED FOR ACHIEVEMENT

In a highly acclaimed work during the early 1960s, a Harvard psychologist, David McClelland, demonstrated that a high ***need for personal achievement*** was the primary factor in an individual's decision to become an entrepreneur. In several books and numerous articles, he demonstrated his precepts empirically.[20] However, in recent years the definition which he used for entrepreneurship has come under attack. His definition permitted officers of large companies and salespersons, among others, to be defined as entrepreneurs. Many recent researchers disagree with his definition and, therefore, with his conclusions. More recent writers, attempting to duplicate his findings with a more rigorous definition, have found that the need for achievement is a weak indicator of the tendency to start a business.[21] We must conclude that a link between a high need for achievement and the desire to start a business is not proven. That means that people who go into business for themselves do not necessarily have a higher need for personal achievement than other people, and we must look to other personality characteristics in order to better understand venturers.

LOCUS OF CONTROL

Other writers have attempted to demonstrate that it is an internal ***locus of control*** which is the key factor in an individual's decision to start a business.[22] According to the locus of control theory, an individual either perceives the outcome of an event as being within his or her ability to control or not. People with internal locus of control believe that they can and do control their own destinies and that luck or other external factors have no bearing.[23] Researchers have examined samples of entrepreneurs and declared them to have an internal locus of control.[24] However, recent writers, attempting to duplicate the earlier results, have disagreed with the findings.[25] Definitional issues may again be at fault. At any rate, a link between an internal locus of control and the initiation of a business has not been demonstrated, although there may be a link between successful people, both inside and outside entrepreneurial ranks, and an internal locus of control. That means that researchers think, but have not proven, that successful people in all walks of life have a belief in their abilities to control their own destinies. Such a personality characteristic seems logical for success, but we still have no further information concerning the psychology of venturers.

RESEARCH ON PERSONAL VALUES

One of the first major studies of personal values among people who start businesses was conducted in 1971. Objective tests were used to identify and measure a variety of personality characteristics. That study found that venturers scored higher on scales of *independence* and effectiveness of *leadership* than did the general population, and lower on a scale measuring the need for support.[26] This would lead us to conclude that people who start businesses have more independent minds, prefer individual action and display effective leadership. They also seem not to need support from other people for their actions or activities. These findings are very attractive, because they tend to fit the stereotype which many people have of venturers. However, the research was conducted with a small group of 40 individuals. The group they examined had been in business for at least five years and demonstrated some success. The same study disclosed a high need for achievement among the individuals making up the businesses. In short, the findings can not be extrapolated to the general population. Regardless of what we would like to believe about people who start businesses, there is very little which can be demonstrated to be believable and dependable.

A great deal of research has been conducted in an attempt to better understand the personal values of people who start businesses. Unfortunately, all of it suffers from possible criticism of definitions employed. It is very difficult to study a group of people, if no one fully understands who belongs to that group and who does not.

THE ROLE OF LIFE EXPERIENCES

By this point it must be clear that no one really knows the personal considerations involved in starting a business. Even though our knowledge of personality characteristics is thin, we do know some things. It is clear that *life experiences* play an important role in the decision to start a new business. We will examine some of the aspects of those experiences in the following paragraphs.

PARENTAL INFLUENCE

Several researchers have shown that the children of people who started their own businesses are more likely to go into business than those whose parents work at regular jobs.[27] The record is clear that *parental encouragement* and support is an important factor in the decision to start one's own business whether there is a family business or not. Parents clearly impart a value system which can make a business venture seem more or less attractive, depending upon their perspective. This has long been true for virtually every profession; venturing is no exception.

CAREER DISPLACEMENT

Several researchers in the field have examined *career displacement* factors, such as the sudden loss of a job, or a growing dissatisfaction with one's position, and the impact of support from family, friends, and associates and the existence of a mentor.[28] Most writers agree that dramatic changes in a person's life are closely linked with the decision to go into business. These range from the loss of an argument with one's superior to the loss of a country and forced immigration. It seems a sad statement on entrepreneurship that starting a business in the United States appears to be more the result of negative factors than it does positive factors. The loss of one's present position appears more likely to trigger a business start-up than does the recognition of an untapped market or the discovery of a fantastic new product.

PARENTAL INFLUENCE

Several famous and successful people made references to the effects which their parents had had on their decisions to start businesses during a survey conducted by Babson College of its Academy of Distinguished Entrepreneurs.[29]

Mr. John Johnson, founder of Johnson Publishing Company, Inc., said: "My mother was one of the most intelligent people I have ever known. She is responsible for any success which I might have had over the years..."

Ms. Mary Hudson, founder of Hudson Oil Company, said: "My mother and father firmly believed in the golden rule. They wanted for their children a good education, regular church, and success..."

Ms. Mary Wells Lawrence, founder of Wells, Rich, Greene, Inc., said: "My mother used to whisper in my ear every night, *You can do anything you want to, Mary, if you'll work hard enough..*"

Mr. Franklin P. Perdue of Perdue Farms, Inc., said: "My father established a rock solid foundation on which I could build..."

MENTORS

One positive factor which has a major impact on the decision to start a business is the existence of a mentor. A *mentor* is a person who is respected and looked up to and who plays the role of convincing, assuring and instructing. The existence of such an individual, be it family member, friend or teacher, exerts a powerful positive influence on potential ventures.[30] This is a well known fact in other cultures, especially in the Far East. Immigrants from China brought a custom called *hui* with them to the United States. Japanese immigrants brought the same custom, called *tanomoshiko*, with them. These customs involve the establishment of a pool of money made up of regular contributions from the incomes of the members of the group. The funds are loaned to new immigrants or other poor members of the group for use in the establishment of business ventures.[31] American Jewish communities have formed associations to provide free loans to help new immigrants, while Greek business owners frequently hire new immigrants and help them to start their own businesses.[32] These illustrations show that the American dream of owning one's own business are not restricted to America! They also demonstrate that positive influences can trigger the business start-up process and point educators to a role which they can assume to foster business development and growth: that of mentor to students in small business and entrepreneurship.

THE VALUE OF EDUCATION

Education and its value to a person starting a business was discussed by the people surveyed by Babson College in its Academy of Distinguished Entrepreneurs.[33]

Mr. An Wang, founder of Wang Laboratories, Inc., said: "I was fortunate to have a good education."

Mr. John H. Johnson, founder of Johnson Publishing Company, Inc., said: "Education is important if you want to get ahead. I worked hard to get a good education though I never finished my last year of college. It was best for me; I went to college to get a good job."

Ms. Mary Wells Lawrence founder of Wells, Rich, Greene, Inc., said: "My parents expected me to go to college. They wanted me to succeed."

Ms. Mary Hudson, founder of Hudson Oil Company, said: "My parents valued a good education."

Mr. Gustavo A. Cisneros, of Organizacion Diego Cisneros, said: "I am grateful for my ... education."

Others surveyed were less sure of the value of education, as these comments indicate.

Wally Amos, founder of Famous Amos Chocolate Chip Cookie Corporation, said in a speech to a group of college students: "If I had your opportunity I maybe would have started Famous Amos cookies at 25. Then again, I might not have started it at all."

Franklin Perdue, who took over Perdue Farms, Inc. from his father, said, speaking of his father: "As I got older he seemed to get smarter, and after a couple of years of exposure to college professors I decided that the best teacher I'd seen in 14 years of education was back on the farm, so back I went to finish my education."

THE IMPACT OF EDUCATION

We cannot even be sure that education has any significant impact on the entrepreneurial spirit. There are those who say that entrepreneurial abilities cannot be learned, while others say the opposite. Peter Drucker believes that entrepreneurship is a discipline and can be learned like any other.[34] Research on the impact of education on the decision to start a business demonstrates mixed results. In a 1975 study of 56 people who had started their own firms, it was found that 62% had graduated from college, while 59% reported that they had been *serious* about school.[35] All of the people in that study had survived at least five years and had at least eight employees, therefore they had demonstrated at least some degree of success. Earlier studies tended to show that people starting non-technical businesses had modest educational qualifications and often left school at an early age, though they did tend to have higher educational levels than the general population.[36] People starting technical businesses typically do have college degrees and many have graduate degrees.[37] Successful business people, like researchers in the field, do not agree on the value or impact of education.

There are some aspects of the impact of education about which we can be sure: the *requirements for success* in a business venture. If the business originators of the past have not been well educated, then the high failure rate of business start-ups is more understandable. We will talk more about the failure problem among business ventures and the impact which education can have on that problem. Perhaps we do not understand the psychology of a person who starts a new business, but we do understand what is required for that new business to be successful. That knowledge can be imparted by education.

REQUIREMENTS FOR SUCCESS

The majority of new business start-ups do not succeed. Statistics kept by a variety of sources point to alarming *failure rates*. Dun and Bradstreet reports that 50% of all new ventures fail during the first five years, with as few as 2 businesses out of 10 surviving for 10 years.[38] The overwhelming majority of these failures are caused by poor management. Almost half of the failures are attributed to managerial incompetence, while lack of experience brings the tally in the management column to 90% of all failure causes.[39] Table 1 outlines these statistics.

On the plus side, not all of the failures are bankruptcies. Many businesses are simply closed out for a variety of reasons: boredom, absence of heirs, changing competitive environments, etc. Also, failure in a business venture does not preclude an individual from trying again. Many successful business owners have had business failures before finally becoming successful.

Henry Ford was credited with putting the country on wheels, but he was a loser before that. In 1899, Ford, together with a group of associates, started a company to build custom cars. He left that business, which later failed, to start another business in 1901, which manufactured racing cars. He personally raced 90 miles per hour in one of his cars which brought him instant notoriety, but the market for racing cars was too small. That company failed. In 1903, at the age of 40, Ford began the Ford Motor Company with the express intention of building a car for the masses.[40]

Education can play an important role in reducing the failure rate of business ventures. Since managerial problems are the primary culprit, colleges and universities can attempt to provide management skills for their students. The primary purpose of this textbook and the course in which it is being used in your school is to provide those skills. Far too many people who start businesses think that all that is required is a knowledge of the product or service to be offered. Nothing could be farther from the truth. It would be closer to the truth to say that an individual need know nothing about a product or service in order to be successful in selling it. The knowledge required for success is managerial. The owner of a small business must wear many managerial hats. Large firms can and do employ specialists in finance, marketing, accounting, production, personnel and planning. The owners of small firms cannot afford such specialists and must perform those tasks themselves.

Table 1
Causes of Business Failures

Cause of Business Failure	Percentage of Failures
Managerial Incompetence	44%
Lack of Managerial Experience	17%
Unbalanced Experience	16%
Inexperience in Business Line	15%
Neglect, Fraud or Disaster	2%
Unknown	6%

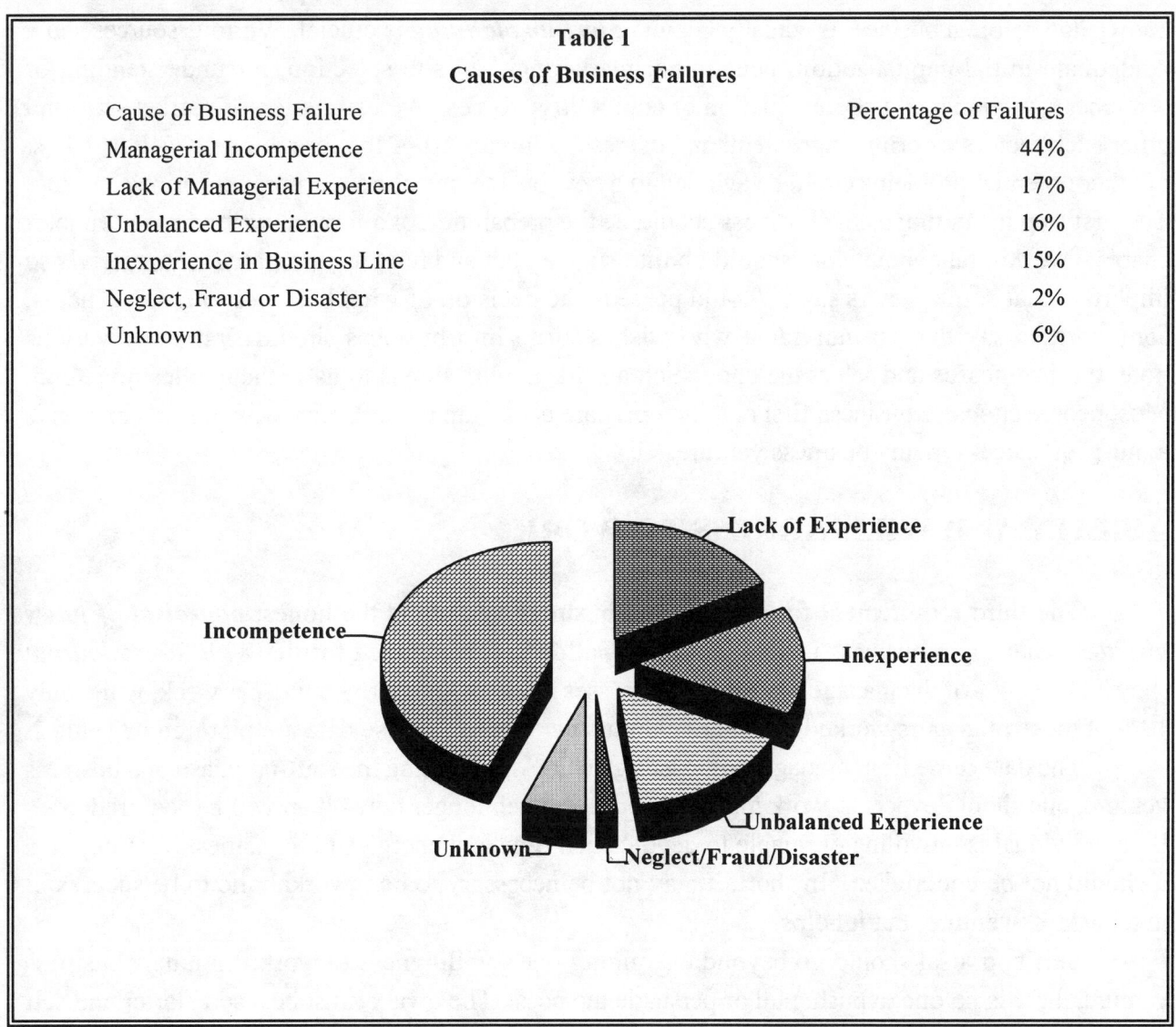

MANAGERIAL EXPERTISE

The first requirement for success in starting a business venture is knowledge of a variety of managerial functions and/or *managerial expertise* or the plan as to how to acquire them. One need not be a specialist in all areas, but one must have an understanding of a variety of areas. Such knowledge is best obtained through a combination of education and experience. That experience is gained from working for someone else. Statistics show and most writers agree that work experience is a tremendous advantage in successfully launching a new enterprise. Obviously, that experience is best if it can be gained working in a business similar to the one which is going to be launched. Even if that is not possible, some type of work experience will be an asset.

The second requirement for success in a new venture is the application of managerial knowledge before a business is actually begun. *Start-up planning* is crucial. Various sources show inadequate initial capitalization, poor initial marketing, bad site selection, misunderstanding of customer requirements, underestimation of competitive forces, overestimation of market size, and other such factors as prime ingredients in business failures. All of the foregoing as well as a host of other potential problems could be avoided in a new business venture with proper, prior planning. The first step in starting a new business should be the preparation of a formal, written plan. In later chapters we will talk about what should go into such a plan and how it is prepared. This step is so important that some writers say it should precede the decision of what business to enter. That is, some writers say that an individual who wishes to go into business should first study various potential businesses and select the one which a start-up plan shows to have the greatest potential. Most people choose a business first and then prepare a start-up plan. Either way, a start-up plan is a must for success in any business venture.

ABILITY AND WILLINGNESS TO WORK

The third requirement for success in a business venture is the honest *appraisal of one's abilities*. Starting a business is hard work. A Gallup poll conducted for the *Wall Street Journal* showed that 24% of the managers of small businesses worked 70 or more hours per week, while only 19% of those managers worked less than 50 hours per week.[41] These data are pictured in Table 2.

The data came from managers of existing businesses. During the start-up phase of a business venture, one should expect to work much harder, and much longer hours than will be required later. If an individual is unwilling or unable to devote such time and energies to a business venture, then it should not be undertaken. In short, it may not be necessary to be a workaholic to be successful in a business venture, but it helps.

Self appraisal should go beyond examining one's willingness to work. In a new business venture, there is no one to push, pull or persuade the boss. The owner must be a self starter and self motivator. Typically, self motivation requires the establishment of *personal goals* and objectives and the acknowledgment of their relationship to the business goals and objectives. The statement of these goals in writing serves as a yardstick for oneself as well as the others in a business. One's own goals and those of one's employees must support each other in order to ensure a successful work environment. This is called *goal congruence*. One should also monitor one's progress toward meeting those goals. Goals for the business will be a part of the start-up plan which we talked about above. The personal goals may encompass those, go beyond those or be entirely different. If you intend to start a business, then your personal goals should express what you expect for yourself at various points in the future: at the end of one year; at the end of five years; at the end of ten years. Such goals are not necessarily monetary in nature. They may include early retirement, more free time, careers for children, going public with the firm, etc. The establishment of such goals, preferably in writing, will give you something to work toward and make continual self motivation easier. It will also make it easier to be a finisher as well as a starter. It is equally important for a prospective entrepreneur to be an individual who finishes projects and undertakings as well as one who can start such projects.

Table 2
Working Hours of Chief Executives

Weekly Hours Worked	Small Firms	Medium Firms	Large Firms
50 hours or less	19%	13%	4%
50 - 59 hours	24%	31%	30%
60 - 69 hours	32%	39%	46%
70 hours or more	24%	16%	18%

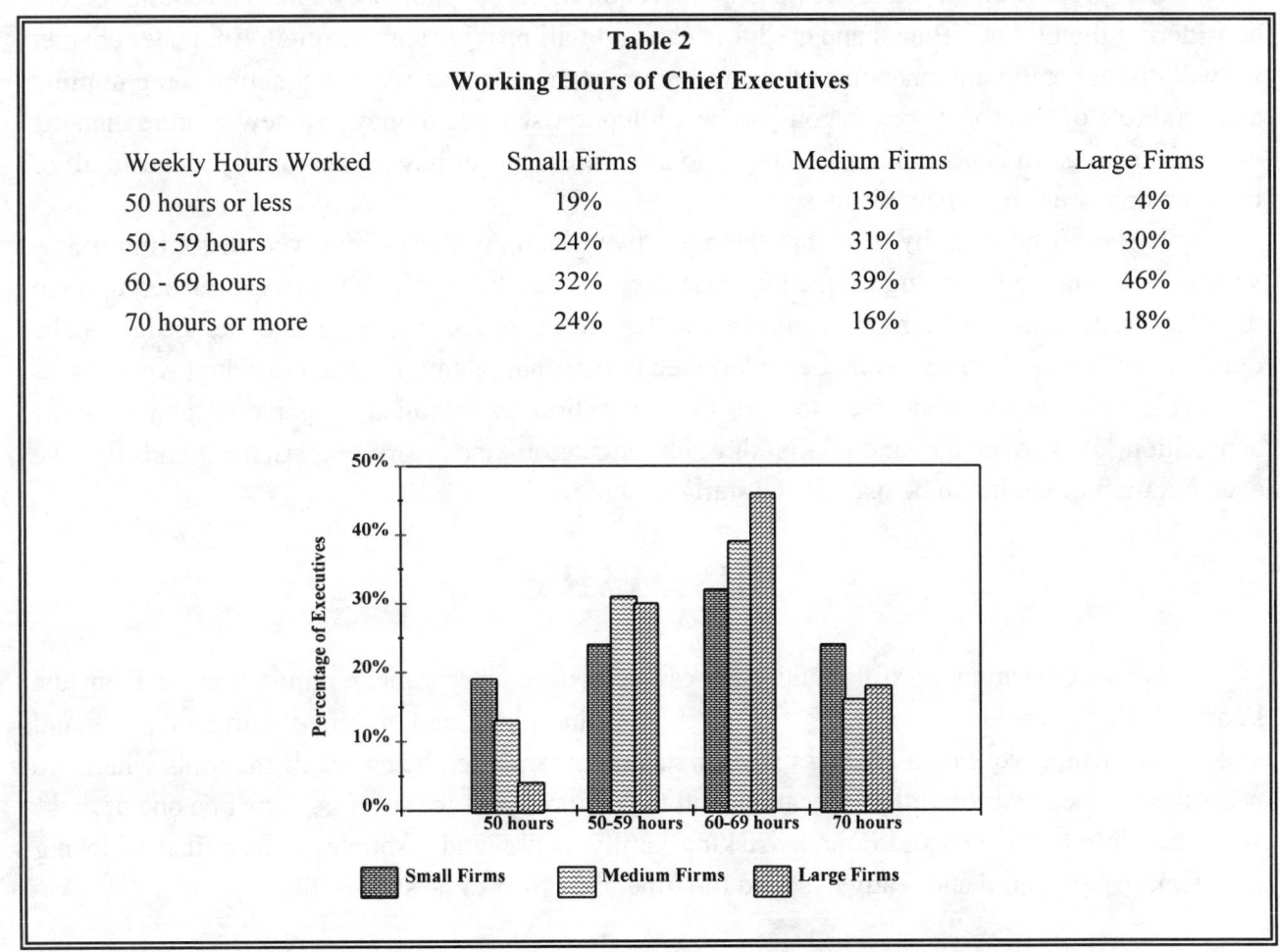

Because of the long hours and hard work which will result from a decision to go into business, health is an important personal consideration. Poor health may make it impossible for one to follow through on the commitments made in a new venture.

Perhaps the best way to perform a self evaluation is to consider oneself as an applicant for the job of manager of the proposed business. What kinds of skills, education, experience, aptitudes, attitudes and abilities would you expect of a manager for your business? An honest evaluation of oneself as applicant for that job can be enlightening.

FINANCIAL REQUIREMENTS

One final attribute which we need to discuss is wealth. Statistics show and researchers agree that the ***primary source of capital*** in a new venture is personal savings and loans from family sources. One step required in the business plan which we mentioned earlier will be the determination of start-up capital. A prospective entrepreneur should plan to have available a substantial proportion of the start-up capital required for a planned business venture before considering the plunge. Banks and creditors can and will provide some capital. In a later chapter we will discuss credit and financing of a new venture at great length. At this juncture, keep in mind a general rule of thumb: no one is going to be willing to risk more money in a new venture than the owner is risking. In general that translates into a requirement for having personally at least half of the start-up capital for a new business.

It should be clear by now that there are two planning phases involved in starting a new venture. The start-up planning for the business itself is something which we have touched upon in this chapter, but which is so important that we will devote an entire chapter to its coverage later. The other planning phase which should be undertaken is personal planning. An individual who wishes to start a business would do well to plan for that action by establishing personal goals for the acquisition of knowledge and skills through education and work experience, and for the accumulation of capital to be used in the start-up phase.

SUMMARY

To become a successful small business person or entrepreneur requires more than just knowledge of a product or service. It requires tools and planning combined with hard work and ability. If owning your own business is your special dream, then be aware of the tools which are necessary, of the need for further education, and the requirements for success. Don't be one of those who jump into a business and flounder risking family, health and resources before finally closing in defeat. Be prepared and ready to spend the time and effort to be successful.

Personality attributes which have been ascribed to small business owners are the intense need to achieve, a risk taking attitude, an internal locus of control, and higher independence and effectiveness of leadership which as we have discovered may or may not be true. Success is like the *heffalump*: everyone knows what it is but has a difficult time putting labels on it or deciding how one reaches that state.

Life experiences, parental influences, career displacement, mentors, and education have been identified by successful entrepreneurs as those factors which had the most impact upon their success, so perhaps inferences could be drawn in parallel. If you have had experiences such as those enumerated in this chapter, does that mean that you too will be successful? If you will be able to heed the warnings and **PLAN** and meet the requirements of success, no matter how difficult they may seem, success can be yours. Education is very important to your success, because it gives you the tools with which to work. Managerial expertise is essential. If you don't have it, you must be aware of your limitations and get it or hire someone with it. You must be willing and able to work long hours and hard to accomplish your goals and be able to come up with the capital requirements to get you started and on your way to success.

Sounds easy, doesn't it! If you follow the prescription to success, it will be yours. Perhaps so, but remember four out of five small businesses have to close their doors in the first five years. Remember the secret of success is always **PLANNING**. In the following chapters, we will help you to understand the important considerations in starting a small business and how each component is planned for success.

QUESTIONS, EXERCISES AND CASES

QUESTIONS:

1.   If you were about to make the decision to go into business for yourself, what personal characteristics do you have that might make you successful?

2.   What difficulties might you encounter or have to overcome because of expectations or personal values?

3.   Is the need for achievement a personality attribute necessary for success in small business? Why or why not? Locus of control? Independence? Leadership?

4.   How might the following characteristics impact success in small business: Life experiences; parental influence; career displacement; and education?

5.   List and elaborate upon the elements required for success.

6.   What is the principal cause of failure in small business?

7.   Why is capital an important requirement for start-up in the small business environment?

8.   What two planning phases are important in starting a new venture?

9.   Name several personal considerations for starting your own business.

10. Discuss the causes of business failures listed in your text.

11. What can one do to reduce the risk of failure in a small business?

EXERCISES:

Read the following profile of a start-up and list those attributes which you feel made it successful. Are there any weaknesses in the profile which might spell doom, if not handled adequately?

The Apple Seed Revisited

The Homebrew Computer Club, located in Silicon Valley, was a prime factor in the beginnings of the Apple microcomputer. Stephen Wozniak claimed that the Apple I and II were designed strictly for fun and to be brought to the club and demonstrated. The club was a loosely structured organization in early 1975, and one of the first organizations of its kind. Both Stephen Wozniak and Steve Jobs were members. They would meet, trade parts, discuss projects and problems and help each other. Wozniak passed out copies of the circuit schematics of the Apple I to members of the club and helped several members build their own machines. During the design phase of the machine, the computers were shown off every two weeks at the club meetings. Wozniak received tremendous positive feedback from the members, which he felt to be a highly motivating factor.

Jobs and Wozniak found jobs with computer firms. Wozniak went to work for Hewlett Packard and Jobs for Atari. Jobs had long wanted to start his own company. Wozniak was more interested in the technical aspects of building computers. Jobs' experience at Atari led him to believe that a fabulous market existed which no one was tapping in inexpensive personal computers. At that time there was only one personal computer in existence: the Altair 8800, based on the Intel 8080 microprocessor which sold for $370. Another microprocessor was available, the 6502, which sold for $20 and was readily available. The Intel processor was only available through distributors. The 6502 chip seemed a natural for the processor in an inexpensive personal computer. Woz used this chip and designed a circuit which had the fewest chips of any microcomputer board built at that time.

Jobs developed a friendship with Nolan Bushnell, the founder of Atari. He developed a tremendous respect for Bushnell, who advised him and coached him during the early start-up phase of Apple. Bushnell, himself a successful entrepreneur, may well have been the key factor in Jobs' decision to push Wozniak to start a company to produce and sell their hobby machine. It was an uphill battle. Wozniak was enjoying his work at Hewlett Packard and did not want to leave. In addition, he was concerned about the risk involved in starting a new venture. Jobs was relentless. He persuaded all of Wozniak's friends and relatives to call Woz up and tell him he was making a mistake. Woz was finally persuaded to make the leap from a garage project to manufacturing.

There were numerous problems, not the least of which was financial. Jobs persuaded a parts supplier to supply them on 30 day terms. They planned carefully. Production and sale prior to the parts bill due date was a must in the early days! Jobs was as meticulous as he was brilliant at marketing. He not only sold machines, he sold people on the idea that the machines were useful and necessary. Nevertheless, a great deal more money was required for the firm to really get started.

Nolan Bushnell and Regis McKenna, of the McKenna advertising agency, referred Jobs to a venture capitalist, Don Valentine. The investor was repelled by the appearance of the principals; Jobs was wearing cut off jeans and sandals and sporting a Ho Chi Minh beard and shoulder length hair the day that Valentine came to see the machine. Valentine mentioned the visit to Mike Markkula who was a 35 year old marketing manager at Intel. Markkula was intrigued and ultimately left Intel and brought $250,000 and his not inconsiderable talents to the firm. Within months, Markkula had arranged for investments by venture capitalists totaling $377,000. Now the required capital was on hand, and the company incorporated and began full scale operations.[42]

CASE

Joan McCoy was a young lady who was a very good cook. She loved making gourmet meals for friends and neighbors. Many times she would be asked to make dainties for showers and weddings and felt quite good about what she was doing. Her husband, while he wanted to encourage his wife's enjoyment, felt that when she counted her time and the massive storehouse of ingredients required by her hobby she was getting very little in return for her effort.

Jim McCoy worked as an accountant in a large textile plant and was concerned about his job. The textile industry was facing enormous cutbacks and even though he had been with the firm since graduation, he knew that he would be the first to go in a cutback in his department. Because of his job concerns, Jim was also upset about the personal expenditures at home. Joan was having a ball cooking for others and eating up the praise which came her way at each and every function where her wares were displayed and tasted. When the McCoys were financially secure, there was no problem, but now with Jim's job at risk, the extra expenses incurred by Joan were straining their already tenuous relationship.

One evening in an effort to return their relationship to an even keel, Jim and Joan sat down and discussed frankly what was happening to their marriage; to their lives and what could be done to improve the situation. Jim was worried about losing his job even though he had not been happy there for a number of years. His job represented stability and was non threatening. Joan wanted to work but her greatest asset seemed to be in feeding others. A friend, who was aware of the strain Joan and Jim were under, and who happened to be a local businessman suggested that the two open a bakery or sandwich shop. The McCoys were immediately interested. Working together in a business of their own might be the perfect solution.

After discussing what was necessary to begin with their friend, they decided to invest their savings in the start-up of a bakery. Jim because of his accounting background and a business major in college knew some of the aspects of management and marketing and therefore would handle the managerial functions of the bakery and Joan would take care of producing the goods. If the business grew, they could hire some people to help out in the cooking area. The excitement of working together and knowing that success depended on themselves alone filled all their time together. The McCoys were ready to go. They began to plan the opening of their business.

1.   What personal considerations make it reasonable to assume that if they plan wisely, the McCoys might make a success of their bakery?

2.   What obstacles might they need to overcome to ensure their successful venture?

3.   If you were the McCoys would you engage in this new venture? Why or why not?

4.   List other alternatives to actually going into business which the McCoys might pursue initially if capital were a problem.

5.   How might the McCoys raise the capital for their venture?

PART TWO

TOOLS FOR SUCCESS

CHAPTER THREE

MARKETING TOOLS

CHAPTER OBJECTIVES

Upon completion of this chapter, you should be able to:

- Explain the dynamics involved in marketing a product or service;

- Describe the marketing of a product or service by examining the who, what, when, where, how, and why of purchasing products or services;

- Discuss the factors involved in the marketing effort such as seasonality, frequency, durability, location, and buying methodology;

- Explain the three approaches to marketing: push, pull, and piggyback;

- Enumerate the advantages and disadvantages of each; and,

- Explain the requirements for doing marketing research.

MARKETING TOOLS

INTRODUCTION

This chapter will focus on the marketing tools which are required for success in a small business. We will examine why people buy things, how things are sold and the principles of marketing research. We will examine the steps which should be taken to ensure that your product or service is viable from a marketing perspective. A word of caution is necessary. Your own judgement as to the value of a product or service is not necessarily valid. Just because you would be willing to buy an item or service is no guarantee that there are sufficient numbers of people in your market area to create a successful business based on that item. Market research is required to answer that question. Further, even if there is sufficient demand for an item in an area, it will not automatically be successful. The manner in which the item is offered for sale will be a major factor in determining its success. Finally, we will address the image of small businesses and the need for consistency of approach in marketing, advertising and pricing, and talk about marketing techniques and overall strategy for small businesses. Finally, we will show how every aspect of a business must be coordinated to design an effective marketing approach.

Early in the process of starting a small business a decision must be made as to the product or service which will be offered. Many people choose a product/service based upon situations or past experience. Others discover a product or service which they think no one is addressing and for which they believe a large market exists. Both of these approaches have value. It is always valuable to have experience with the product or service which you intend to sell. This helps you to understand what is required in the production of the items and what is required to sell them. Tom Land, the founder of Land Pyrometers, one of the largest producers of industrial thermometers, avows *Business is founded on knowledge.*[43]

New products and services are valuable also as are innovative ways of making, packaging or offering existing items. If you plan to start a small business, you must be very careful during the start-up phase. All too often potential entrepreneurs take Ralph Waldo Emerson's words to heart:[44]

If a man can write a better book, preach a better sermon, or make a better mouse trap than his neighbor, though he builds his house in the woods, the world will make a beaten path to his door.

(R.W. Emerson, Lecture in 1871)

There have been many enterprises which seem to bear out the truth of Mr. Emerson's words. Consider the case of Win Schuler, a millionaire restauranteur.[45]

Located in Marshall, Michigan, a town of only 6,000 people, Win Schuler built a restaurant which served more than 500,000 patrons in 1959. Many patrons commuted 100 miles, each way, to eat at Schuler's. Another half million people ate in the three newer units in Jackson, Grand Rapids, and St. Joseph, Michigan. One patron, when interviewed, explained, *this is the place to go. The food is excellent, the atmosphere unusual, and they know how to take care of people.* Such attitudes among his customers have propelled Mr. Schuler's net worth to $3 million.

Even though it is an old story, a half million customers attracted to a town of 6,000 people certainly does sound like a *house in the woods*. Before you take Mr. Emerson too seriously, please note that Win Schuler took over that restaurant from his father. For the next 10 years, it had a lackluster history and mediocre success. Finally, he redesigned his restaurant to give it the appearance of a European Inn. The new decor, coupled with the 15 hour, seven day weeks that Schuler worked over the course of the next 10 years, transformed it into the marvel which it became. The truth is that Mr. Emerson was a bit naive. He failed to take the time factor into consideration in his advice to would-be business owners. Today we know that the world may beat a path to our door because of our superior offerings, but that without a little help from the science of marketing, we may be out of business before the world gets there! It would be closer to the truth to accept the old adage: *nothing happens until somebody sells something.*

Harley Procter, a salesman for the family candle, lard and soap company called Procter and Gamble, realized the truth of that statement in 1878. When his firm developed a new, hard, white soap, he was given the job of selling it to America. His efforts laid the groundwork for much of the consumer advertising, merchandising and marketing techniques in use today. Procter and Gamble remains one of the largest advertisers in the world, constantly renewing its faith in the sales process pioneered by Harley despite the original reluctance which the firm displayed when he proposed national advertising for what he dubbed *ivory* soap.[46] That is the point you should keep in mind in selecting a product or service for a new business. Regardless of what the item is or what its appeal may be, it must still be sold! That means that the first thing we need to do is examine the sales process so that we can better understand buyer motivation.

WHY PEOPLE BUY

People buy things for complex and poorly understood reasons. Marketers attempt to examine those reasons by looking at consumer demand from the perspective of the *who, what, when, where, how and why* of purchasing decisions. The **who** refers to the people making the purchase. This is not as simplistic as it sounds. Identification of the *who* in the purchasing decision is the first step in identifying a target market. The ***target market*** refers to the sub-group of the population to whom particular products or services are sold. It is one of the most important concepts in marketing because it serves to focus marketing activities and planning.

WHO BUYS THINGS?

Few items have universal appeal. That means that purchasers of a product or service can generally be classified as to age, sex, educational attainment, occupation or profession, family income, social status, and a host of other factors. Understanding those factors make it easier to design marketing activities which will appeal to the appropriate group. Did you ever wonder why beer producers so frequently use professional athletes to promote their products? It is because marketing research shows that the primary consumers of beer are male, aged 18 to 40, with blue collar occupations and a strong identification with physical prowess. This is not to say that all beer drinkers have those characteristics nor that such characteristics are in any way undesirable. It simply means that a large proportion of the demand for beer comes from consumers who can be impressed and influenced by the use of professional athletes as sales people.

Few people can be expected to start a new beer producing company but the process of identification of the target market is just as important for any other type of business. If you plan to open a small hardware store in a small town, you must know to whom you will be selling in order to assess the prospects for success. Who buys hardware? If we determine by marketing research that the target market is male, 20 to 50, homeowners, with middle level family incomes and strong identification with hobbies, crafts and *do-it-yourself* repairs, then finding the best location for the hardware store is a function of finding a community which has a large proportion of those kinds of people. It almost seems so trivial and obvious when you look at it that way that you might wonder why anyone would fail to consider the *who* in the purchasing decision. People make such mistakes frequently! The obvious can easily be overlooked in the excitement of starting a new business.

In the insert for the case from our files, is it clear to you why the lounge owner was having problems? He had simply failed to consider the target market when he started the business. His lounge would probably have been a smashing success had he located it in a larger city. But the people in the small coastal town in which he did locate the business never considered his lounge for anything other than a special place to go on a special occasion, and there simply weren't enough people for him to be successful based on such an infrequent patronage. His competition was successful because it was perceived as a place one could go without requiring a special occasion and therefore had people coming frequently. Sadly, the stuff that dreams are made of may not sell at a given time or place.

There is one more aspect of the *who* issue which we need to discuss. The person who buys an item is not necessarily the person who will use that item. Earlier we talked about who drank beer and we identified the consumers as predominantly male. That is true, but the purchasers of beer are predominantly female. That is because the major sales of the beverage are in grocery stores to women who buy it for their husbands.

A CASE FROM OUR FILES

We were called in as consultants by the owner of a small lounge in coastal Georgia. The owner, who was operating the lounge as a proprietorship, had been open for 6 months and had been losing money steadily during that time. The lounge was located in a small town which was 50 miles from the nearest city and which was dominated by the shrimp fishing industry. We went to see the owner at the lounge on a Friday night. It was located on the main drag, 3 or 4 miles from the center of the little town. We passed another lounge on the way out which had a parking lot filled with cars.

When we got there we were really impressed with the place. It was beautiful! The owner said he had invested $20,000 in leasehold improvements in the place. The building was well done, both inside and outside. It had a long padded bar, a carpeted floor space with circular tables and padded chairs, a hardwood dance floor and a raised stage for musicians. Live music was featured on Friday and Saturday nights. No big names, but good players who featured contemporary *pop* music. The bar served several kinds of beer on tap, wine, mixed drinks and snacks. No food was served except for a weekly oyster bash on Tuesday nights featuring fresh oysters and shrimp. Prices seemed to us to be reasonable. Not cheap, but not too expensive either. He had a bartender and two waitresses who were clean, well dressed and polite. They were all young. The bartender was wearing a tie.

There were a few customers in the lounge and they all seemed to be enjoying themselves. They were young, couples mostly, and were all dressed nicely.

The owner said that this lounge had been a dream of his for years. He had always wanted to own a really nice place, not what he called a *honky tonk*. He had finally saved enough money to make the venture, but he was not a wealthy man and he could not continue to put money into the business. He had tried all kinds of specials and all kinds of advertising, but he couldn't seem to make a profit. He had talked to customers at great length, but all of them said they loved the place and wouldn't change a thing. That's why he had called us. He was on the verge of losing the place.

We talked to him and the employees, looked at the books, watched the customers for a while and left. We told him we'd get back to him soon. On the way out of town we stopped by that other lounge we had passed to look at his competition. The place was jumping! It had a juke box, blaring so loud you couldn't hear a thing. It was packed with people, most of whom were wearing work clothes. The place wasn't nearly as nice as our client's, and honestly wasn't terribly clean. Our client's problem suddenly became crystal clear.

If you think about it you can see how the issue of who is going to buy an item is as important as who is going to use it. Most toys are used by children, but purchased by adults. Therefore success in toy sales is a function of offering toys which will appeal to both the users and the buyers. Marketing efforts need to be oriented toward both groups. Frequently, this requires different marketing approaches. Saturday morning television is saturated with toy commercials aimed at children, but marketing efforts aimed at parents and grandparents must be timed and designed differently because they do not normally watch Saturday cartoons.

Of course, it is possible to rely totally upon demand created in the primary consumer without concern for the purchaser. Such a strategy would mean that a toy maker would depend upon children communicating to their parents which toys they preferred. Toys which create a high level of desire in children probably need no other marketing effort. In recent years the *He Man* and *Nintendo* toys are a good example. Toys with a somewhat lower demand level or designed for children who cannot communicate well must have some marketing aimed at parents.

It is also possible to depend totally upon marketing aimed at the purchaser rather than the consumer. In the toy example, a company which makes educational toys might decide to direct all of its marketing at parents and ignore the children completely. The point is that a firm needs to know who buys as well as who uses its products in order to effectively market.

WHAT DO PEOPLE BUY?

The *what* of marketing may or may not be the product or service that people buy. Consider the case of a restaurant in a college town. In most college towns there is no scarcity of restaurants from which students may choose. What makes them select one restaurant frequently enough to make that business successful? Obviously food is not the only factor. A location convenient to the students will clearly be a major factor, but is there anything else? What makes you choose a restaurant when you decide to go out? Would it make any difference to your decision if you knew that you would see other students who were friends at a particular place? If you plan to open a restaurant, it may well be that what you will be selling is entertainment as much or more than food. If so, then the atmosphere which the restaurant portrays will be as important as the menu and the food preparation. Remember, Mr. Schuler's restaurant did not begin growing until he changed the atmosphere.

Consider a hamburger franchise restaurant located on an expressway. Is it food that such a place sells or is it convenience? Does it make a difference? It certainly will! Speed of service will be more important to a restaurant selling to people who are in a hurry while food quality will be more important to a restaurant selling to people who want a taste treat.

Think about what is required in a national fast food restaurant in order for it to be successful. Food quality is obviously a factor, but how strong a factor and in what fashion? When travelers from out of town stop in at a McDonald's restaurant, what is it that they expect? If you think about that for a bit, you might see that food consistency is more important than any other aspect of quality. Travelers have eaten at other McDonald's restaurants so they know what the sandwiches are supposed to taste like. So long as they are not unpleasantly surprised, the food quality will not be a factor in their decision to stop at another McDonald's in the next town or state. Some analysts think that the problems which the Kentucky Fried Chicken restaurants encountered a few years ago was the absence of consistency. Since the majority of the restaurants were franchised, the company exerted little control over them and the food ranged all over the scale in terms of taste and quality. The firm has since begun a program of acquiring more of the outlets and exerting more control over the remaining franchises. Its performance has improved since those changes were implemented.

The *what* which a business sells must be clearly understood in order to effectively market. If convenience, service, speed or other factors are more important than the merchandise, then that is what must be promoted in the marketing efforts, and also that is what is most important in the daily management of the enterprise.

WHEN DO PEOPLE BUY?

The issue of **when** people buy a particular product or service includes but is not limited to the issue of time of day. One of the major problems which a restaurant faces is the fact that people predominantly eat at set times each day. That means that the capacity of a restaurant must be adequate to handle the load during those times and yet it will have excess capacity and therefore unnecessary expense most of the time. The timing issue is closely related to the target market to which a business appeals. For instance, if a business appeals primarily to middle income, working people, its hours must accommodate the times those people have available for shopping. The issue is much broader than that. Most businesses have seasonal patterns. That means that they sell more at certain times of the year than at other times. Consider a novelty and gift shop located in a vacation resort. Such businesses frequently close after the tourist season to save money because they know that the sales volume at other times of the year are too low to cover the cost of being open. Even when the seasonality is less pronounced, it still has an effect and marketing activities need to be closely meshed with the seasonality factors of a business.

Timing the opening date of a new business cannot be accomplished without knowledge of the seasonality factor. One restaurant with which we were familiar opened its doors in June after most of the students in town had gone home for the summer. The summer school population of the town was dramatically lower than at other times of the year, as is the case in most college towns, and that restaurant sustained extreme losses throughout its first summer of operations. The business was never able to recover and closed its doors within six months.

Another aspect of the *when* issue is the frequency of purchase. People buy soap more frequently than they buy cars. That means that you sell soap differently than you do cars. Soap is a **consumable** item. That means that it is used up frequently and more must be purchased. Cars are **durable** items. They are used up over a longer period of time and are therefore replaced infrequently. The development of **brand loyalty** is a frequent strategy in the consumables industry. Pepsi wants you to always buy a Pepsi instead of a Coke and so their marketing efforts are aimed at developing that loyalty. It is much more difficult to develop brand loyalty in durables, so the producers of such items tend to concentrate on the characteristics which make their products superior in price, quality and/or performance when compared to their competitors. The same holds true for services. Tax preparation services are sold differently than are real estate listing services. The marketing approach and the timing of the opening of a business are both affected by the frequency of the purchase decision.

WHERE DO PEOPLE BUY?

Did you ever stop to consider why retail stores tend to group themselves together? The issue of *where* people buy is one of the factors behind the development of shopping centers and malls. The grouping is largely a matter of finding a location which is convenient to shoppers. As recent as twenty years ago the downtown area was the most convenient available, so retailers tended to congregate there. Suburban living patterns, two income households, and changing life styles changed all that. Now, a major social problem facing American cities is the decay of downtown shopping areas caused by the flight of retailers to malls and shopping centers located on the periphery. Another factor, which plays a role in the development of malls and shopping centers, is *derived traffic*. That means that smaller retailers tend to group themselves near large stores which draw large numbers of people. In a shopping center or mall, such stores are called *anchors*. In a shopping center, the anchor store is frequently a grocery store. They make good anchors because people use them so frequently. Location of other types of retailers close to a grocery store enhances the convenience and provides higher visibility. In malls the anchors tend to be major department stores. Such stores tend to have larger volumes of customer traffic because of the marketing efforts of the stores and the broad product lines which they offer. Location of other retailers close to such stores enhances their convenience and visibility and also frequently aids sales when those retailers offer products and services which are complementary or competitive with those of the anchors.

Location and occupancy expense are interrelated. In general, the more desirable a location, the higher the rent or purchase price of the site. Consequently, new businesses frequently choose lower rent areas in an effort to save money. That is not always wise. Although a lower occupancy expense is desirable for a new business, if there are no established traffic patterns of consumers which that business can tap, it will have to expend more marketing dollars to draw the necessary volume of people than it would have to otherwise. It may well be that the marketing costs consume the occupancy savings. We will have a great deal to say about this problem in a later chapter.

So far we have discussed the *where* issue as though it only affected retail businesses. That is not true. It also affects service businesses, wholesalers, manufacturers, and construction firms. In fact it affects every business to a greater or lesser degree. Consider a wholesaler. Location of the business itself is important because of shipping patterns and costs, but the issue of where people buy the products is still real. The difference is that now the business is one step removed from the ultimate location of the purchase. The considerations for the wholesaler revolve around the kinds of retailers which will be approached. Marketing efforts must now include the retailer.

Service businesses must be easily available to customers. Many times professionals will locate in parks with other professionals to attract their own and their competitors' customers. While the reputation of a profession or service may be a draw after a few years, new businesses must many times compete for their clients from the existing market. Service businesses must be convenient to the customers, so they must be in an easy to reach location with sufficient parking for their clientele. Notice the increase of small financial institutions and/or photo kiosks in the parking areas of supermarkets. A small local bank has a branch with all the traditional services of the large banks actually in the grocery store. The location of service companies can also be important, because of its effect on their image. Consider the potential success of a young accountant or lawyer setting up shop in a strip shopping center versus setting up shop in a professional park.

Manufacturers and construction firms have different needs. They typically sell to dealers or wholesalers, so their main concern is sufficient space for manufacture and storage. They may have the advantage of more inexpensive facilities and location, but they must consider the access to expressways, railways, and airports, etc, to ensure the movement of their products to others.

HOW DO PEOPLE BUY?

When we talk about the *how* issue, people frequently say, *why with money, of course!*, and laugh. Unfortunately, it is not that simple. People frequently do not buy with money. They frequently use credit cards or charge items on company accounts receivable. Sometimes they use lay away plans. Sometimes they borrow money. It is important to the marketing effort to understand how people will buy the product or service which you intend to offer.

One client with whom we worked sold satellite receiving dish antennae. The dishes ranged in cost from $1,500 to $4,000 including installation. When we visited with the owner of the business and asked him how people bought his antennae, he declared that he did not know. If any financing was occurring, then the customers were arranging their own, because our client required cash. He refused to examine the issue or to consider any alternatives. As you might guess, new competitors began to spring up who offered a variety of financing arrangements for their antennae and our client was forced to sell his business when his sales volume fell off. Obviously, the lack of success was not solely a function of the client's failure to offer financing, but that failure was a major factor, and it provided his competitors with a marketing approach which damaged his sales. It has frequently happened in the business arena that competitors have used financing techniques to enhance their performance at the expense of a firm who demands cash.

Many merchants detest credit cards, not just because they require special handling, but because they also cost money. The credit card firms charge merchants a fee for permitting them to accept the cards. This fee may run from 2% to as high as 6% depending on the annual volume which the merchant generates. A recent phenomena in gasoline sales involves using credit cards at the pump. It will be interesting to see which approach, cheaper gas or the convenience of credit cards, is successful over the long run.

It is certainly true that selling on credit or arranging financing for sales introduces complexity into a business' operations. There will be additional records which must be kept and collection efforts will have to be instituted. That does not mean that credit arrangements should not be considered. On the contrary, it is important to know how the consumers of a product or service will buy. Marketing activities and plans are affected by that knowledge.

WHY DO PEOPLE BUY?

In a larger sense this entire section of the chapter deals with the issue of why people buy an item. In examining the *why* we want to focus on the specific motivation of an individual purchaser rather than the characteristics of the general target market group.

You are accustomed to considering items as falling into the categories of necessities and luxuries, but if you examine an individual's purchasing pattern, such classifications are of little value in understanding the pattern. Food is a necessity, but why does an individual shop at one grocery store rather than another? Why does an individual purchase one brand of bread rather than another? Jewelry and gift shops sell luxuries, but the same questions apply. The answers are not simplistic, nor are they well known. The actual purchase decision of an individual is a psychological and sociological phenomenon.

Have you ever noticed how different producers of a product have different marketing approaches? Think about toothpaste. One producer of toothpaste touts the cavity prevention ability of its product. Another toothpaste producer touts the teeth whitening and breath freshening ability of its product. The first producer believes that people buy its toothpaste because they want to protect their teeth from decay. The second producer believes that people buy its toothpaste to enhance their *sex appeal*. Both producers are successful, so that must mean that they are both right!

The apparent inconsistency of the toothpaste companies can exist because there are two basic approaches to take when incorporating the *why* of the buying decision into a marketing strategy. The first is to attempt to discover, through market research, the primary motivations people have for buying a product and appeal to those motivations with the marketing effort. That is what the first toothpaste company has done. It attempts to appeal to the cavity prevention goal which it believes is the primary motivation for people to purchase toothpaste. The fact that it has been successful means that a significant portion of the population has been swayed by its marketing efforts.

The second approach to developing a market strategy is to attempt to create a reason for people to want to purchase a product. That means that the marketing efforts are aimed at creating consumer demand rather than tapping an existing demand. That is what the second toothpaste company has done. It has decided that a marketing campaign could be effective in making people consider toothpaste in the same light as cosmetics. The fact that it has been successful means that a large portion of the population has been swayed by its marketing efforts.

Understanding why people buy things is difficult, perhaps impossible. About all that we can do is to attempt to gain an understanding of the motivations through research. That is what the first toothpaste company did. The best understanding comes from experience. We can attempt to sell an item using a market strategy which we think appeals to the correct motivations. If it doesn't work, we can try something else. Gradually we learn about our target market and how best to appeal to them. The first toothpaste company developed and ran a variety of ads over the years, constantly changing and tuning its approach while monitoring the success of its various marketing approaches. Unfortunately, during the start-up phase of a new venture, there is no experience upon which to draw, unless there has been familiarity developed through working with similar items in another company prior to the start-up. That is the major reason that prior experience with a product or service is valuable for a new business owner. Attempting to create a demand for an item with marketing can be effective. This is the route the second toothpaste company took. However, creating demand tends to be more costly from a marketing perspective and it is definitely more risky. A much greater level of marketing is required to convince people that they will want to buy a product than is required to inform people who want to buy a product where they can get it. If the effort to convince is not effective or fails to convince a large enough portion of the target market, the new business can fail before it has an opportunity to try anything else.

HOW ARE THINGS SOLD?

There are three basic approaches which can be taken to the marketing of an item. We can call them *push*, *pull* and *piggyback*. Most marketing strategies represent one of these approaches or a combination of them. We might say that there is another approach which can be taken which is the absence of a marketing plan. If a business does no marketing, then it has made a selection of a marketing approach even though no conscious decision may have been made. If the demand for an item is sufficiently great and competition is sufficiently small, then marketing may not be required for success. Markets like that are exceedingly rare. For many years professionals such as physicians, dentists, attorneys, etc., believed that such was the case for their businesses. Professional association rules prevented marketing efforts in many cases. Now professionals are coming to realize that marketing is a necessary process for a successful business.

PUSH MARKETING

Push marketing refers to the attempt to push an item through the market. It can best be visualized from the wholesale perspective. Consider a wholesaler calling on a retailer. The wholesaler can attempt to persuade the retailer to buy its products by offering price and discount concessions which will make it lucrative for the retailer to sell the items. Such a strategy is a ***push*** strategy in which the wholesaler is dependent upon the retailer to ultimately sell the items to the consumer. The focus of the marketing is the intermediary rather than the ultimate consumer. Consider the use of private or generic labels in grocery stores. Pricing makes them attractive to the retailer and such discounts may be passed on to the consumer, thus creating a demand. These strategies frequently employ pricing policies, resupply agreements, and similar steps aimed at making the intermediary desirous of selling the items. One popular ploy has been gifts, trips and premiums for the individuals in the retail outlet who are responsible for buying from the wholesaler. Push marketing is inexpensive when compared to alternative marketing strategies and can be quite effective. It may be a more viable option for a new venture than ***pull*** marketing.

PULL MARKETING

Pull marketing refers to the attempt to pull a product through the market. This is done by creating demand in the ultimate consumers for an item. It can also be best understood by considering a wholesaler. As in the preceding section, consider a wholesaler selling to a retailer. An option which can be used as a marketing strategy is to create a demand in the retailer's customers for an item so that the retailer will wish to purchase it to satisfy its customers' needs. The focus is on the ultimate consumer rather than the intermediary. Consider the amazing success of Nintendo. Several years ago no one had heard of their electronic games and now consumers are purchasing them almost faster than the retailer can stock them. The demand for these electronic toys is causing the retailers to purchase them for their customers, many of whom are children and adolescents. This demand was created by television advertisements which were artfully done and created a sensation in the minds of the children who demanded Nintendo and Nintendo cartridges for Christmas. This strategy is an effective one if the marketing is successful, but tends to be more expensive and time consuming than push marketing. It is attractive because it permits higher prices to intermediaries and thereby enhances profit margins. It may not be a viable strategy for a new venture because of the time and expense involved.

PIGGYBACK MARKETING

One of the most frequently used marketing strategies for a new business venture is ***piggyback marketing***. This refers to the identification of a successful competitor and ***piggybacking*** its marketing efforts. This can be easily visualized by considering the motel industry. The market research which goes into the identification of a site for a motel is extensive and expensive. Location is the prime factor in the ultimate success of such a venture. You can probably remember several occasions when you have seen a small motel built close to a large chain such as a Holiday Inn. Such firms attempt to succeed by competing with the larger motel on the basis of price. The strategy they are pursuing is a piggyback strategy. The smaller inn does not expend the money for market research in site location, nor does it spend large sums in advertising. It tries to garner a section of the market attracted by its larger competitor and allows that business to do the marketing.

Piggyback marketing is one of the most viable alternatives for a new business venture. It involves building on the marketing efforts of competitors and attempting to perform some aspect of the sales process more effectively. It can be used in most industries and works equally well with services as it does with products. It is a conscious recognition of the adage that, *It is easier to take business away from an established firm than to create that business in the first place*. It is also the reason that many inventors and innovators do not do as well as the firms which follow them into the new markets which they have created.

MARKETING RESEARCH

Marketing research refers to the exploration of the who, what, when, where, how and why which we discussed in the first part of the chapter. It is not a simplistic area. There are entire curriculums devoted to marketing research in many schools, with multiple courses devoted to the development of understanding and skills. Our purposes here will be to familiarize you with the basic tenets of the science. The research can include the kind of library research with which most students are familiar and it can include the preparation and use of surveys. Finally it may involve exploration of pertinent facts directly.

LIBRARY RESEARCH

For almost all existing products or services, there exist great quantities of information in published sources. Virtually all established industries have magazines and journals which contain information of value to the businesses in that industry. Your library probably has many of these journals and can obtain through interlibrary loan others which might be needed. These journals are a priceless source of information about the markets which have been examined and identified for products or services in the industry as well as specific articles and advice about marketing and other aspects of the industry. Don't overlook general business publications or books. Journals such as the *Wall Street Journal, Business Week, Fortune, Inc., Advertising Age, Venture* and others are also a valuable source of information. In addition, you may well be surprised at the number of books which have been written about markets and industries. Scholarly journals are often gold mines of information which may be of value to a marketing effort. There are also reporting services which analyze industries and sell those reports. Your library probably subscribes to several of those such as *Value Line, Standard and Poors, Moody's* and others. Additionally, information from government agencies will be included in the library which can help with the more quantifiable aspects of a market. Census tract data is available which will not only describe populations, but family size, number of households, family incomes, retail sales, disposable income and other information which is of value in marketing. A census tract is an area of 4,000 to 5,000 people which the Bureau of the Census uses to report the results of its studies. There is also a Census of Business which reports information about businesses by census tract. Also available from government agency publications and from many local chambers of commerce are sales data for various industries and areas. This information can also be of great value in investigating a market. There may be published surveys available which contain valuable information. If these exist they can frequently be discovered through discussions with librarians, bankers, government assistance agencies, chambers of commerce, industry associations and business school faculty members. Finally, an amazing number of sources are becoming available on the internet. The census bureau, various federal agencies, numerous state agencies, and a host of private firms are producing web sites with great detail which are rich in information.

MARKETING SURVEYS

When most people think of marketing research, they think of *surveys*. Surveys can be invaluable, but they are expensive and time consuming. The preparation and conduct of a survey is an exercise in statistical sampling. That means that it can be quite complex. There are entire courses devoted to surveys in market research curricula. It is possible for a prospective small business owner to conduct an inexpensive, *rough and ready* survey to gain an understanding of some aspect of the market. Simply stopping people on the street and asking questions can provide some insight, so long as you are careful to ask questions in such a way that the listener is not led to an answer. Other surveys involve the measuring or counting of items and activities of interest. Such attempts can be valuable, but may not be reliable. The best use of such an approach is in the exploration of simple, straightforward issues such as automobile or foot traffic flows at a particular location.

FOOTWORK

One of the best and least expensive ways to conduct market research is *footwork*. By that we mean the personal investigation of a market and an area. Few people actually do much footwork when planning to start a business. Perhaps it is overlooked because it is so obvious. At any rate, there is no substitution for going out to look for and at a market. If you plan to start a business in an area, you should visit the local chamber of commerce. Not only will they have published information which may be of use, conversations with the people will provide insights and further contacts which can be explored. Discussions with bankers in the area can not only shed light on the market and its viability, but can be useful in establishing contacts which will be valuable later on in the business' life. Personal or telephone conversations with industry associations can be useful as can discussions with salespeople. Few have a better insight into the market for an item than salespeople involved in selling to businesses in the area. Discussions with the representatives of governmental assistance agencies can also be invaluable. If there is an office of the Small Business Development Center in your state, it would be a serious mistake not to discuss a business start-up with them. Other assistance agencies also exist including the Service Core of Retired Executives, Economic Development Centers, and various business development and assistance programs of state and federal agencies. Many of these have web sites and most can be located through the home page of the U.S. Small Business Administration. We will talk about these assistance sources in the financing tools chapter.

One final point about footwork deserves special mention. The existing competition for a new venture may well be the most valuable source of information from a marketing perspective available. Walk or drive through the area in which you plan to do business. Look at the yellow pages in the phone book. Talk to as many businesses as you can. Many potential competitors may be prepared to meet with you and discuss their businesses. Others may be reluctant to talk to a potential direct competitor. In either case, close observation of competitors can reveal the existence and size of a market. Observation of marketing practices of competitors can reveal how they go about attracting and keeping customers. Additionally, such observation may reveal gaps or chinks in the marketing which a new business can tap to make itself more competitive. If there are no direct competitors in an area under consideration, then examine similar businesses in other areas. The experiences which they have may not mirror that of a different area, but will certainly be useful. People in business in other areas will probably be more amenable to meetings and discussions than will potential competitors. They can be a goldmine of information about start-up marketing approaches and problems as well as a host of other aspects.

THE BUSINESS IMAGE

Nothing is more important to the success of a business venture than the *image* which it will portray to its customers. You should think long and hard about how you wish your customers to perceive your business. What do you want them to think of when they think of your business? What do you want them to think of when they see your business? You want to be distinct from your competition. What do you intend to do to make your business distinctive? You want your business to be as unique as your own personality makes you. What do you wish your business' personality to be?

Whatever image you decide to portray, you must be consistent with everything else involved in the business. You cannot send conflicting signals to your customers. Look at the case from our files. Can you guess what the store's problem was? It was inconsistency in image. The prices were those of a discount, bargain store, while the decor, stock and location were those of an exclusive gift shop. Our advice to the owner was to raise prices across the board by 25%. After considerable discussion and reluctance, she complied, and sales went up dramatically within a month; doubling within three months. The shop still exists and is now profitable. The point to remember is that all aspects of an image must be in harmony or your customers will be confused.

A CASE FROM OUR FILES

The business was a small gift shop located in a rather expensive section of suburban Atlanta. The owner, a lady in her mid forties, had called us in because she was losing money steadily and was at a loss as to the basis for the problem. The shop was beautiful. It had been in business for less than six months and was located in a shopping center with a good anchor store and excellent traffic patterns. The shop was tastefully decorated and the inventory was artfully displayed. There were plenty of indirect competitors, but no direct competitors within 10 or 15 miles of the shop. When we walked in, we were really impressed. The outside of the shop, its sign, and the shopping center in general were attractive and it was clear that there was an adequate population base to make the store successful.

At first we asked to look at advertising records and mockups, but the program looked fine, so we looked at the accounting records. One thing was puzzling; the gross profit margin had been stable at 20%. We thought that was a bit low for a gift and novelty shop, so we asked about markup policy. The owner said the policy was a 25% markup based on selling price, but occasional sales held the margin down a bit. Then we looked more closely at the inventory in the store and the prices.

We couldn't believe the bargains! The items were beautiful, including many glass pieces and art objects at prices which were well below the prices you would expect in Atlanta.

SUMMARY

Your own judgment as to the value of a product or service is not necessarily valid. Nor is demand for a product or service an automatic guarantee for success. If the demand is present, an effective marketing plan is essential.

An early step in starting a new business is selecting the product or service to be sold. Whether the product or service is chosen based upon experience or the fulfillment of a recognized niche in the marketplace, the selling of those items must take place before a business can succeed. Business seldom beats a path to the door of the new venture, so strategies must be designed to attract public attention.

In order to focus marketing activities and planning, you should examine the reasons people buy by considering the who, what, when, where, how and why of purchase decision. Marketing efforts need to be oriented toward both users and buyers. Seasonality is also a factor to be considered in the marketing scheme. Frequency of purchase is another consideration in marketing. When the product is consumed quickly, brand loyalty is a frequent strategy while in a durables industry, one tends to concentrate on the characteristics which make the product superior in price, quality, and/or performance when compared to competitors. Location is another important factor in setting up a business. To be successful one must be aware of traffic patterns as well as convenience.

How a customer buys is an important consideration. There are several methods available as in cash or credit. The why of the buying decision is to discover the primary motivations for buying a product or else to create a reason for people to want to purchase a product. The three basic approaches used to market an item are *push*, *pull*, or *piggyback*. In the push method, the focus of marketing may be the intermediary rather than the ultimate consumer and may well be a viable option for a new venture. Pull marketing depends upon consumer demand and is quite effective when the marketing is successful, but tends to be more expensive and time consuming. Perhaps the most viable alternative for a new venture is the piggyback approach. This method tries to garner a section of the market attracted by its larger competition and allows its competitors to do the marketing.

Marketing research is a science whose tenets it is well to learn. It is a method used to aid those interested in starting new ventures to discover the who, what, when, where, how and why of business. Marketing research includes a literature search in which newspapers, journals, periodicals, books, indexes, and census data are examined. Surveys also render valuable data but may be complex and time consuming. A good inexpensive method of conducting research is footwork. There is no substitute for observing for oneself.

QUESTIONS, EXERCISES AND CASES

QUESTIONS:

1.   What are the factors involved in the selection of a product or service for a new business?

2.   Examine the who, what, when, where, how and why of purchasing a satellite dish antenna? Notebook paper? Science Fiction novels?

3.   Why is brand loyalty not as important a consideration in the durables industry? There are some cases in which brand loyalty may be considered. What are they and why?

4.   List the three basic approaches to marketing and give an example of each.

5.   What source would be good for finding industry averages for comparison purposes?

6.   What are some advantages and disadvantages in library research? Footwork?

7.   Why is area selection important to the marketing plan?

8.   Why should marketing be included in the budget initially?

9.   Why are image and timing so important in marketing?

10.   Why is the marketing plan so important in the initial stage of small business management?

Define the following terms:

a. push
b. pull
c. piggyback
d. viability
e. seasonality
f. durables
g. consumables
h. image

DISCUSSION QUESTIONS:

1.   Can you foresee any problems that people like John Sculley might have had when he came from the Presidency of Pepsico to Apple Computers? Or Nolan Bushnell going from Atari Computers to Pizza? How are the industries different? If you were on the Board of Directors of a durables industry, would you hire personnel from a consumables industry or vice versa? Why or why not? Sculley appeared to have been successful while Bushnell was not. What are some of the adjustments each would have had to make? What do you feel made one successful in the transition and the other not?

2.   Why must marketing attempts be designed to appeal to both users and purchasers? Give several examples other than those listed in the text.

3.   Why are timing and image so important to a new venture? Can you give examples of your own knowledge that were either successful or unsuccessful because of the issues of timing and image?

EXERCISES:

1.   You are about to set up your own business in VCR machine and tape rental and sales. Do some of the footwork involved in setting up your own business. Find a good location available locally, find out the rental or sales price of several sites and compare them. Then go to the library and see if any industry averages are available on your product or other information is available in periodicals about the industry into which you are about to venture.

2.   Choose an area in which you are interested and develop a marketing plan according to the steps listed in the text.

CASE

The Ultimate opened its doors early last year. It was the ultimate college hangout: *the* place for good food, fun, friends, and variety. It had a menu of pizza, subs, steaks, lasagna, spaghetti, chili and hamburgers. The owner was young, local, knew everyone, and he was in heaven about his venture.

Opening week had its share of problems. Everyone wanted burgers when Todd expected the Italian cuisine to be the best seller based on his prior experience with a local competitor. He had to suggest alternatives. The help was slow, because they weren't trained, and frustrated diners with class schedules to keep had to bolt their food when it came.

The decor was romantic with red and white checkered table cloths for the booths and low lighting. Actually, there was a problem with the lighting. It was either off or on. On was very bright and off was dark. Todd wanted a romantic atmosphere for dates and dinners, so he placed filters in the light panels allowing only a very small amount of light to come through. Some of the customers were heard to remark to the waitresses that the food was very good but they wished that they could have seen it. Ordering from the menu was an adventure. Customers were seen striking matches to read. When several of the older customers asked Todd about candles, he claimed that they were too expensive and the students would swipe them.

The food was delicious and the prices were reasonable for the quantity served. The portions were large but many a diner was surprised by the low bill. The variety should please everyone. And there were specials from time to time, usually lasagna or all you can eat spaghetti. But occasionally there was ribeye steak. The only difficulty for the patrons was that they didn't know when the specials were coming. The advertisement was on the chalkboard inside the restaurant.

Newcomers were told of this great place to eat just off campus, but most couldn't find it and ended up at the Pizza Hut a few yards down the road. The Ultimate was parallel to the main drag, but you had to know it was there. It was connected to a service station and was not readily differentiated from the garage. The gas pumps and tow truck parked near by faked out potential customers.

Too soon, the school year was over. Todd was in a quandary as to whether he should close down or stay open. He didn't have the same number of customers but many of the locals were hoping that he would stay open. Professors and students with late classes went there for a while and then discovered that Todd was closing early. There was no knowing the hours. Soon he was closing at lunch and open only from 4 PM to 10 PM. Many of his best customers were no longer coming in. What could he do?

1. What are some of the obvious problems you can deduct from the case?
2. Describe the location. Why would Todd have chosen it? What are potential advantages and disadvantages for such a location?
3. Were there any inconsistencies in image both obviously and reading between the lines?
4. What was Todd's target market and how was he planning to compete?
5. Is this enterprise headed toward success or failure? Why or why not?
6. Why is marketing more than just advertising? What else is involved?

CHAPTER FOUR

ACCOUNTING TOOLS

CHAPTER OBJECTIVES

Upon completion of this chapter you should be able to:

- Explain the concept and importance of accounting;
- Describe the how and why of record keeping;
- Explain the importance of the internal control guidelines;
- Explain the role of a CPA in a small business;
- Distinguish between financial accounting and managerial accounting;
- Define contribution margin and understand its significance in decision making;
- Explain the value of contribution margins reports and what managerial information can be learned from them;
- Calculate operating cash flow and net cash flow and understand the difference; and,
- Prepare a cash flow report and be able to explain its importance in managerial decision making.

ACCOUNTING TOOLS

INTRODUCTION

Accounting has been called the language of business. In reality, it is the language of trust. The transactions which are recorded in accounting are called *debits* and *credits*. These words are derived from Latin and developed from the Roman practice of accounting. That practice, which predates the birth of Christ, used the term *credere* to describe bookkeeping entries which represented obligations of people. The interesting point is that *credere* meant *to trust*. The Romans obviously thought that the transactions they recorded were supported by trust in the people who were to repay the debts. Today, people still trust one another to honor financial obligations, and accounting has become a science in which trust is paramount. People trust the outcome of accounting: *financial statements*. People expect the financial statements to reflect the true financial condition of the firm. People outside and inside the firm trust the statements and use them to made decisions about the firm: decisions about investing in the firm; lending to the firm; buying from and selling to the firm; taxes due from the firm; decisions about pricing, cost control, expansion and growth; decisions about the performance of managers and employees. In fact, every decision made in the business world is affected by financial statements.

The problem with financial statements is that they are not automatically trustworthy. People have confidence in accounting but that confidence can be misplaced. In reality, accounting, like everything else in the business world, is a reflection of management. If management has designed a sound accounting system and installed sound accounting practices and controls, then the financial statements will be dependable and trustworthy. If management has not done these things, then the financial statements will be misleading and erroneous.

In this chapter we will present an overview of the accounting process in a small firm. Our purpose here is not to make you an accountant, but to provide you with an awareness of accounting principles and processes which are required to effectively manage a small business. The pursuit of any business is profit. Plautus said some 2,400 years ago that profit cannot exist if the outlay is too great. Accounting is the tool which is used to control that outlay.

RECORD KEEPING

The success of John D. Rockefeller is often ascribed to his *training in the points of scientific accounting at Folsom's Business College in Cleveland.*[47] Rockefeller was quoted as saying, *I knew where I stood at the close of every business day. I charted my course in figures, nothing but figures.*[48] It is clear that *figures* become increasingly important as a business grows. The larger a business becomes, the more removed its owners and managers are from the daily happenings and the more important numbers become in making management decisions. If a business is very small, then the owner/manager is intricately involved in every thing. That person makes every sale, knows every customer, writes every check and handles every piece of merchandise. Record keeping is unimportant because the owner feels the results of each day's business personally. That is only possible for extremely small ventures. As employees are added and as they take over the work, the manager begins to lose touch with the pulse of the business. Record keeping then becomes the source of the information which has been lost: the information about what happens each day.

Record keeping is simply the process of capturing every transaction which affects a business. We generally think of these transactions in financial terms, but they are not all financial. The hiring of people, recording of personnel evaluations, entering into contracts to buy or sell, capturing of names and addresses of customers, are all examples of records which must be kept. All of these things will eventually have a financial impact on the firm, but initially, many records are nonfinancial in nature. Management's responsibility is to decide what information is to be captured, when and how it is to be recorded, who is responsible for its capture and maintenance, how and to whom it is to be reported. These decisions will establish the record keeping system for the business. Because the business will be constantly changing, the record keeping system must also change. Consequently, management must always be cognizant of what is currently flowing into the record keeping system, must constantly compare that to desired information, and must make changes to the system on an ongoing basis.

Any information which you think would be of value in the decision making activities of the firm should be captured. However, the information must be captured in a form which is usable or it has no value. The proverbial *shoe box* of papers is all too common in small businesses.

The small business owner in the case note on the following page simply did not see the value in record keeping. He was probably like many other small business owners who think that record keeping is something that must be done for tax purposes. This is a common misconception. Owners who have this opinion are apt to use shoe boxes and wait until tax time to have an accountant sift through the papers and put together enough information to prepare a tax return. Such people never stop to think how much more it costs to have an accountant wade through a box of papers as opposed to using clear, clean reports from an accounting system. It is true that record keeping is required for tax purposes but that is of minor importance. The more important use is to aid managers in making decisions about the company. Records and reports are the primary tools of management. A good manager, like a good worker, keeps the tools of the trade sharp, clean and well organized.

CASH VERSUS ACCRUAL BASIS ACCOUNTING

Most businesses must use *accrual based accounting*. Under accrual accounting, after a company has gone out of business, the totals of revenues and expenses will be the same as the cash which has been received and distributed. At any point in time for an ongoing business, cash may have little relationship with profit. Revenues and expenses are recorded based on obligations to receive and pay money. The recording of the transactions is not dependent upon money changing hands. That means that **cash flow**, money moving through a business, and **profit**, the difference between revenues and expenses, are both important concepts but are not the same thing.

A CASE FROM OUR FILES

Like most of the small firms who call us for help, this client was having *cash flow problems*. Of course, inadequate cash flow is not a problem, rather it is a symptom of a problem. It cannot be corrected without discovering the underlying cause.

We asked the client for specifics about his *cash flow problem* and he told us that he could not meet the payroll on a regular basis. We went out to take a look at the business.

We were completely stymied! There was absolutely nothing we could do to even begin to help the poor guy. When we asked to see his records, he pulled out a desk drawer which was literally overflowing with papers. He said all of his bills, receipts, invoices and such were in there. He just had not gotten around to arranging them in any order. We asked about accountants, tax returns and the like. He had not gotten around to any of those things yet. He had been in business for a year and a half and knew that he was going to have to do *something soon*. Right now he was more worried about not being able to meet payroll again this coming Friday.

We had seen *shoe boxes* before, of course. Everyone who works with small businesses sees those. But this was ridiculous! We explained to him how much it would cost to have us dig through that paper morass and he quickly decided that he had better make time for a little paper work himself.

We showed the client how to set up a simple record keeping system and got him started, then we left. At that point all we could do was hope that he could survive long enough to be able to generate some financial information to use in examining the company. The saddest part of the story is that he never called us back. The business doesn't exist anymore.

Cash basis accounting systems record transactions only when money actually changes hands. That means that there are no accounts for receivables or for payables because purchase and sales transactions will not be recorded until cash flows. This can be a problem for a business. Additional records have to be kept outside the accounting system in order to know about receivables or payables. Accuracy can be a problem if the records are outside the accounting system, as they are not subject to the same controls. In addition, revenues and expenses will be recognized when cash flows rather than when the transaction takes place. This will cause a distortion in the amount of income which results, especially toward the end of the accounting period. It is simply a matter of timing; the timing of when transactions are recognized. In turn, this timing problem will distort information used for decision making purposes. You cannot decide that costs for inventory have been too high in any given month because you will not know how much was spent in that month, only what cash actually flowed out during that month.

Many small businesses use cash basis accounting despite the problems it creates. Many do it for income tax purposes because they think it results in lower taxes. This is not necessarily true. Only an accountant can examine a company's operations and determine whether cash basis tax reporting is desirable. If it is, then tax reports can be prepared on a cash basis while the company's records are kept on an accrual basis. Perhaps the primary reason for the prevalence of cash basis systems is the fact that most small business owners think accounting is hard and that accrual based accounting is harder. That is really not true but even if it were, the prevalence of microcomputer based accounting systems and their ease of use makes accrual based accounting achievable by every small firm in the land. We strongly recommend that all firms use accrual systems because of the improved decision making information which results. The tools which we present in this section of the text really require an accrual based system in order to be effective. Every owner owes an effort to learn enough about accounting to rise above the initial phobia reaction and establish a sound, accrual based system in order to improve the prospects of the operation.

INTERNAL CONTROLS

Internal controls are procedures which are designed to ensure that transactions are properly captured and handled. There are six general rules of internal control which should be followed. These guidelines are indications of work arrangements which enhance control. Table 1 displays those rules. Internal controls are the key to a successful record keeping system. They are so important, that the first step which a CPA firm performs in conducting an audit of a company's books is the review and assessment of internal control. Under established auditing standards, a CPA cannot testify to the fairness of the financial statements unless first satisfied with the adequacy of internal controls. In small businesses, internal controls must be established by the owner. No one else has enough influence in the business to make employees believe that such controls are important. That means that it is particularly important for a small business owner to understand internal controls and to be aware of them at all times.

Internal controls are the same for small companies as for large. The difference is that large companies have an accounting staff who worries about such things while the small business has no one but the owner. Some people think that controls mean a lack of trust for employees and so are hesitant to use them. But controls are for the benefit of employees, too. Strong controls protect employees from being accused of improper behavior. They also help keep honest people honest during times of trouble or great financial need. Perhaps the most important aspect of controls is that they give employees a sense of importance and value, because controls mean that their work is vital enough to merit special procedures and attention.

Table 1: Guidelines for Internal Controls

I.   Use competent well trained people.

Hiring and retaining competent, capable people is probably the most important step in internal controls. This is accomplished through the recruiting, compensation and supervision policies of the firm. These people must be well trained and their training must be maintained as duties and responsibilities change.

II.   Separate custody from record keeping.

An individual who has custody of an asset should not have access to the records of that asset. A person who is assigned an automobile should not have access to the records of that automobile and its supporting expenses; a person who has access to cash, or makes deposits in the bank should not have access to the bank statement.

III.   Separate record keeping duties.

Record keeping should be partitioned into components which support each other and those components should be handled by different people. Cash receipts should be recorded by a person who does not have access to cash disbursements and who does not prepare bank deposits. Accounts receivable posting should be handled by a person who does not have access to the general ledger nor the bank statement.

IV.   Rotate duties.

Every person performing record keeping activities should be cross trained and should be rotated between jobs periodically. Not only will this make it impossible for an individual to hide incorrect procedures, it will ensure that everyone follows established record keeping policy and encourage people to do better work. Every employee will know that his or her work will be seen by others as jobs rotate. This will encourage them to follow established practices carefully because of the pending peer review of their work.

V.   Use proofs and security measures.

Proofs are checks used to ensure accuracy. They include such things as trial balances, summary totals and cross totals and verification by others. They are of particular importance in automated systems. Security measures refer to physical protection for records and assets, restricted access, and backup provisions for record systems.

VI.   Conduct an independent review.

There should be a work review performed by an independent person at least once each year. The reviewer should be totally independent and report only to the owner. People will develop their own practices and fail to follow established procedures if they know that no one ever checks. In addition, the review will give people the feeling that their work is important to the company.

FINANCIAL STATEMENTS

The primary output of an accounting system is the ***financial statement***. This document can be prepared for any period but must be prepared at least annually at the end of the firm's fiscal year. It portrays the financial condition of the firm and details the results of its operations. An effective manager will require at least an abbreviated financial statement every month in order to evaluate and guide the firm. These are called ***interim*** financial statements because they are for less than a full year of operations. Whenever the term financial statement is used, it generally means a year end financial statement. By convention, one year is the established time period for a company's report on its performance. This is called the ***fiscal year***. That year can begin and end on any dates a firm desires. It need not correspond to the calendar year. Many companies choose a fiscal year which corresponds to the natural business year. That means that the fiscal year is matched to the seasonality of the industry. The low point in the cycle, the point at which inventories and receivables are at their lowest, is the fiscal year end. The advantage to that plan is that the physical inventory is less of a problem because inventories are at a minimum and year end close out requirements which include the preparation of the financial statements and tax returns falls at a time when normal business activities are at their lowest. In 1987 the Internal Revenue Service instituted a new rule which makes it extremely difficult for most small businesses to use a fiscal year which is different from the calendar year. The IRS wanted to standardize reporting periods which is probably beneficial to the service but their actions have forced a mismatch of fiscal and natural business years on many small firms.

BALANCE SHEET

The financial statement consists of four parts. The ***Balance Sheet*** shows the dollar value of all assets, the present value of all liabilities and the historic value of capital. Assets are divided into Current and Noncurrent categories. ***Current Assets*** are, in general, those which are cash or are expected to be converted into cash within one year. Liabilities are also separated into Current and Noncurrent categories, with the ***Current Liabilities*** being generally those which are expected to be paid within one year and ***Noncurrent Liabilities*** being those which extend beyond one year. This separation usually requires long term installment loans to be separated. The part of the principal of the loan which will be repaid during the next year is called ***Current Portion of Long Term Debt***, while the remainder of the loan is called ***Long Term Debt***. Of course, assets must balance liabilities plus capital or else an error has been made. That's why the statement is called a balance sheet. An example of a typical balance sheet is displayed in Table 2.

A CASE FROM OUR FILES

In one case, the client called us in after her head bookkeeper has been missing for two weeks. The lady had disappeared and no one knew where she had gone, not her neighbors, not her friends, no one. Our client feared the worst! The first thing we did was to check the role which the bookkeeper played in handling cash. It was an absolute disaster! This one person not only prepared the bank deposits, she reconciled the checking account statement! We couldn't believe it, but the client said she thought everything was all right because no one in the company could sign checks except herself. Besides, she had known the bookkeeper for 15 years. They were good friends! It took several days to find out how much money was missing, but when we got done the owner was sick! The company did recover, but it took more than two years to get back to the position it had before the embezzlement.

In another case, we had a trusted employee involved. This person was the chief of purchasing and didn't have access to any of the records so the owner thought he was safe. What happened was a lot of fictitious purchases to a fictitious company. Since no one else had to approve purchase orders, the cash disbursements clerk just routinely cut checks to pay for things that were never delivered. That problem was also discovered when the purchasing agent got all he wanted and left town.

We had one client who was especially upset because he was convinced that he had strong controls. The mistake he made was assigning one employee to handle the mail. We found out later that she had opened accounts at several banks in nearby towns under the same names as many of the company's suppliers. All she was doing was keeping the checks, instead of mailing them! The banks just asked for a corporate resolution to set up a business account, that was easy to supply, and the mail clerk was able to deposit checks in the business name to those accounts. Since she also opened the mail as well as taking it to the post office, she just threw the delinquency notices away. When she heard about the owner getting upset about collection calls for accounts that he had paid, she ran. By that time she had taken over a $100 thousand.

In another case we had a client who got suspicious because of one employee who didn't want to take his vacation. When the owner insisted, he left for two weeks but managed to find some excuse to come back in almost every day. Our client called us in and we checked over this guy's work assignments. He was a bookkeeping clerk who had responsibilities for accounts receivable. Every day that he dropped by, he asked the woman filling in for him whether so and so, one of the delinquent accounts, had paid yet. When she said no, he just left. It wasn't hard for us to discover that he had been taking some of the accounts off the books through the normal charge off procedure, yet continuing to call those people for payment. When they made payments, they sent checks to him and he just pocketed them. Since the accounts were no longer on the books, there was no way the payments showed up anywhere. As for cashing the checks, he had a bank account in a neighboring town under the same business name. Simple! He was just afraid that the clerk filling in would receive a payment, try to post it and find no record of the account. There was a sad aspect to this story. The bookkeeper had been with the firm a long time and was well liked and respected. He had always been honest and hard working. But his wife had come down with a horrible disease and the medical bills were killing him. The insurance only paid 80% and the other 20% was more than his entire salary. He broke down when confronted. He intended to pay the money back. He just had to have it now, to pay for treatments. It was really a sad story and the guy was really basically honest.

INCOME STATEMENT

The *Income Statement* shows the aggregate of all revenues and expenses which have occurred during the year and nets these to determine profit or loss. The *cost of goods sold* section details all the expenses of acquiring or producing inventory and subtracts that from sales to produce *gross profit*. Service firms will not include this section in their statements. The remainder of the statement organizes and subtotals expenses to highlight important costs and subtracts those to find *net income*. Note that there is no account in the general ledger for net profit because it doesn't exist until the income statement is prepared! An example of a typical income statement is displayed in Table 3.

STATEMENT OF CASH FLOWS

The *Statement of Cash Flows* shows the flow of cash through the business during the course of the year. The Statement of Cash Flows shows the flows of cash affecting the Balance Sheet which would otherwise be a static statement of position. In the past the Statement could be based on cash or based on working capital, as a company desired. *Working capital* is defined to be the difference between current assets and current liabilities, and is a representation of financial resources which can support daily operations. Recently, the *Financial Accounting Standards Board*, which sets rules for preparing financial statements, has decreed that all firms must use the cash basis in preparing the Statement.

THE ROLE OF THE CPA

Most people think of CPAs as auditors. It is true that most of the revenues of CPA firms comes from performing audits on financial statements. An *audit* is an investigation of the internal controls and record keeping processes of a business and the evaluation, testing and confirmation of the assets and liabilities of a firm. Most small businesses do not employ CPA firms to perform audits of their statements because it is generally an expensive undertaking. Every *publicly owned business*, that is a corporation whose stock is subject to control by the Securities and Exchange Commission, is required by law to have an audit performed by an independent CPA firm each year. The word *independent* means that the CPA should not be involved financially or personally with the firm being audited.

Contrary to popular belief, an audit is not designed to catch fraud. Its real purpose is to ensure that the financial statement has been prepared in accordance with the accounting principles which the profession has established. The testing, evaluation and confirmation steps are based on samples and are designed to indicate the reasonableness of the numbers.

Table 2

ABC Chemical Company, Inc., Balance Sheet

ASSETS

	December 31, 199B	December 31, 199A
Current Assets:		
Cash in Banks	$ (4,132)	$ 254
Accounts Receivable, Net	41,167	27,619
Inventory	27,629	18,849
Prepaid Expenses	12,922	2,159
Total Current Assets	77,586	48,881
Plant, Property and Equipment:		
Land	10,500	10,500
Building	74,399	74,399
Machinery and Equipment	45,249	44,349
Leasehold Improvements	21,937	20,672
Total	152,085	149,920
Less Accumulated Depreciation	(57,004)	(40,862)
Net Book Value	95,081	109,058
Total Assets	$172,667	$157,939

LIABILITIES AND STOCKHOLDER'S EQUITY

	December 31, 199B	December 31, 199A
Current Liabilities:		
Accounts Payable	$ 95,762	$ 93,237
Accrued Items	9,382	7,113
Current Portion, Long Term Debt	35,445	25,286
Total Current Liabilities	140,589	125,636
Notes and Mortgages Payable:		
Mortgage on Building	37,745	52,186
Notes due to Banks	44,789	13,651
Total	82,534	65,837
Less Current Portion	(35,445)	(25,286)
Total Long Term Debt	47,089	40,551
Stockholder's Equity:		
Capital Stock	15,300	15,300
Paid In Capital	20,573	20,573
Retained Earnings	(50,884)	(44,121)
Total Stockholder's Equity	(15,011)	(8,248)
Total Liabilities and Stockholder's Equity	$172,667	$157,939

Table 3

ABC Chemical Company, Inc.

Statement of Income (Loss) for the years ended December 31

	199B	199A
Sales	$328,590	$391,352
Cost of Goods Sold:		
Beginning Inventory	18,849	38,104
Purchases	184,645	203,340
Plant Labor	22,541	21,301
Total	226,035	262,745
Less Ending Inventory	27,629	18,849
Total Cost of Goods Sold	198,406	243,896
Gross Profit on Sales	130,184	147,456
Operating Expenses:		
Salaries - Officer	16,090	28,250
Other Salaries	12,482	14,642
Payroll Taxes	3,860	8,854
Freight Out	16,636	29,724
Insurance	8,011	7,191
Utilities	1,417	1,436
Telephone	4,737	5,281
Auto and Truck	6,665	8,613
Travel and Entertainment	9,597	6,002
Bad Debts	1,305	1,759
Depreciation	16,141	14,018
Miscellaneous	21,457	12,731
Total Operating Expenses	118,398	138,501
Operating Income	11,786	8,955
Other Expenses:		
Interest	14,549	6,885
Income (Loss) Before Taxes	(2,763)	2,070
Income Tax Provision	0	0
Net Income (Loss)	$ (2,763)	$ 2,070

The review of internal controls is the key to the audit and it is this step which is designed to ensure that the proper accounting principles are being followed and that the records are dependable. Further, this last step can be of value to a small business. An independent review of the internal controls can be revealing and can result in better record keeping and more dependable records.

CPAs perform other types of services as well as audits. They can prepare financial statements for a business without audit. This is the most frequently encountered use of CPAs by small businesses. This task simply involves taking the records maintained by employees of the firm and converting them into the correct format for financial statements. Sadly, this is one of the least valuable tasks which a CPA can perform for a small business. Any good microcomputer package can do the same thing faster and cheaper than using a CPA or even an outside accountant. The use of CPAs to prepare statements continues because most small business owners know little about accounting and are convinced that the statements are some sort of mystical, magical creation. The truth is that CPAs do not actually prepare the financial statements either! Clerks and assistants in the CPA's office will prepare the statement after which the CPA will look it over for completeness and any obvious mistakes. This is called a *review* and is simply a matter of examining the statement to determine whether it appears reasonable given the business and its background. Using a CPA for this purpose once a year should be enough! You would do better engaging a CPA to help you find a microcomputer accounting package than in preparing your monthly statements.

The best use of a CPA in a small business is as a partner to management in structuring the record keeping systems necessary to provide the decision making information which is required for effective control. CPAs call this kind of activity *management advisory services*. These kinds of services are actually less expensive than audits and when compared to the benefits to be derived in the form of faster, more accurate and useful information, management advisory services can be an extremely good buy. You need a CPA who is knowledgeable about your industry, approachable when you need advice and help, and interested in working with you and helping the business. That kind of person should not be wasted on preparing financial statements. A person like that should be used as a resource to develop and improve upon control and reporting systems of all kinds.

Another valuable role which CPAs can perform is in the area of taxation. Preparing fringe benefit packages which could minimize taxes for employees and for the firm can be complex. A CPA is a must for that kind of activity. Tax planning does not mean having a CPA prepare your tax returns once each year. Effective tax planning goes on during the year, not after the year is over. You need to involve your CPA in tax planning, you need to discuss the tax implications of any changes in the business which you are considering, you need tax advice on an ongoing basis.

THE IMPORTANCE OF CHOOSING A CPA

Whether you need an audited financial statement each year or not, a CPA can be a valuable asset in managing the business, simply because few small firms can afford to employ an CPA or other qualified accountant as a full time employee. Assistance in tax planning and management advisory services of all types can easily be justified by the benefits which they produce. One final comment about CPAs is pertinent. The largest accounting firms in the United States are collectively called the *Big 6*. These six firms control over 80% of the dollar value of accounting audits in the country despite the fact that there are thousands of CPA firms in the United States. Many people tend to think of size as indicative of competence or knowledge of accounting. Nothing could be farther from the truth. Just as your business can be a viable part of the economy and provide a superior product or service in the face of competition from giants, so can CPA firms. Many of them are small businesses as well. The CPA who will be working with you is far more important than the name of the firm.

MANAGERIAL ACCOUNTING TOOLS

As we have learned in the preceding sections, *financial accounting* refers to the activities which result in the production of the financial statement. Accounting principles dictate how those statements must be prepared. The accounting profession has developed those principles over the years with the purpose of generating statements which are general purpose. That means that the statements can be used by outsiders to support the broad range of decision making activities which those people need to make: investment, buying, selling, taxing, lending, etc. The principles are also designed to permit comparison between firms. Since every firm must use the same rules for preparation of the financial statements, then the statements of the various firms can be compared to other firms to yield a better understanding of how one firm compares to its competitors and other small businesses.

Managerial accounting uses the record keeping tools which have been developed in financial accounting, but is not hampered with any rules or principles other than those of common sense. The outcome of managerial accounting is intended solely for internal use. Managerial reports are prepared for use by the owner and other managers in the business. We can prepare reports on any area and in any format which we think is important. The only purpose which managerial statements have is the support of the decision making process. If they provide valuable information on a timely basis, then they are valuable. Otherwise, they should not be prepared.

MANAGERIAL STATEMENTS

As we indicated above, *managerial statements* are financial reports which are designed for use inside the business. There is an almost unlimited variety of such reports. Some of them are well known such as delinquency reports on accounts receivable, projected payments reports on accounts payable, and various kinds of inventory status and turnover reports. The variance reports which are used by manufacturing firms are another example as are sales by agent reports. In fact, many of the things which we talk about in this book could be examples of the application of managerial accounting to small businesses. We cannot possibly detail all of the variety of reports which are possible. Consequently, we have selected two types of reports which can be of value to any kind of small business and which are not used with the frequency which they deserve. We will concentrate on managerial reports dealing with contribution margins and on cash flow reports. Remember that there are numerous other types of reports which can be of value to a small business owner. Many of them are specific to particular industries such as inventory movement by size in the garment and shoe industry. Others may be unique to a particular small business or developed by an individual manager to serve specific needs. These reports can be ongoing, that is generated on a regular basis, or they can be the result of a special study. Time and motion studies in a manufacturing business may be performed on an infrequent basis or customer arrival patterns may be studied in a bank. Special records might be kept to monitor the results of a marketing or advertising campaign or a sale of some kind. Whenever you think that you would like to know something about a particular aspect of the business or the results of some activity, a report can be designed to capture that information. In fact, managerial reports do not have to be historic in nature. Forecasts, analyses and budgets of all types are examples of managerial reports. Reports can cover virtually any topic. The only risk is that it might cost more to accumulate the data than the information is worth. To constantly guard against that, you should always consider the use that a particular piece of information will have and what the potential value of that information might be. Comparing that to the effort which will be required to capture and compile data will give you an insight as to whether it is worthwhile to proceed.

CONTRIBUTION MARGIN STATEMENTS

Contribution margin is defined to be the difference between sales and variable costs. Variable costs are not limited to those involved in the production or acquisition of inventory. They include any costs in the business which go up and down with changes in sales. Subtracting such costs from revenues will yield an indication of the monies which sales generate for support of the business. Contribution margin concepts are used in breakeven analysis and target sales forecasting, but there are many other uses. Contribution margin can be converted to a percentage so that dollar amounts are eliminated. This permits comparison of various products, departments and divisions in a business. It also permits the examination of marginal profits and can point out weaknesses and strengths. Contribution margin can even be calculated on the basis of a scarce resource to aid in selecting where those resources can best be applied.

A *scarce resource* is one which limits the ability of the firm to generate revenues. If, for example, a service company depends upon the application of the expertise of its employees to generate sales, then employee time is a scarce resource. Such an example would be a law firm or a CPA or consulting firm. If a firm uses machines to fabricate a product, the scarce resource could be machine time. Money is frequently a scarce resource for new businesses. Whatever the scarce resource is, a firm cannot expand its sales and profit generation abilities without increasing the amounts of the resource which its possesses.

One of the best applications of contribution margin is in the form of income and expense statements reflecting margins and prepared by product, department, division, or other business segment. These contribution margin statements demonstrate the relative role the segments play in a company's profits. They work equally well for service companies, retailers, wholesalers, manufacturing, construction or other types of businesses. Table 4 displays a contribution margin statement for a small business which leases buses to musicians and groups for use in tours. In this small business, the age, condition and appearance of the buses is a major factor in success, consequently, the statement reflects margin by vehicle.

Notice that the income statement for Mountain Coach in Table 4 does not follow the traditional format. It doesn't look anything like the income statement in Table 3. The statement is designed to provide information of value to the management of the firm, not to those outside the company. The company is heavy with debt because of the loans against the buses, consequently, the ability to cover loan payments is more important than profit. Therefore, the statement highlights loan coverage ability. Notice that the contribution margin by bus, as well as overall, is extremely high. That is normal in a service industry. Nevertheless, the contribution margin did vary by bus. Can you see from the statement areas which need management attention? Is the relative value of each bus to overall operations highlighted? One important area to note is that not all expenses were allocated to the buses. This will almost always be the case for any kind of small business preparing a contribution margin statement. There are expenses which cannot be traced to the products or segments of the operation. The correct treatment of these expenses is to treat them as expenses of the firm rather than allocating them on some arbitrary basis.

Compare the service company statement in Table 4 to the statement for a retailer displayed in Table 5. This business is a convenience food store. The statement focuses on the sales and cost of sales by product groups within the business because that is the key factor for monitoring performance in a convenience store.

Notice that the percentages for the sales portion display the makeup of gross sales, while the percentage in the cost of sales and gross profit sections are based on the sales for the product group. The expense section percentages are based on gross sales. The gross profit displayed for this firm is equivalent to the contribution margin which we have been discussing because the only variable costs in the firm are product costs. This is frequently the case in small retailers. Even if there are expenses which are variable, the actual change in such expenses may be so small that it is best to treat them as fixed expenses. Hourly wages are a good example. They may seem to be variable expenses, but if your employees generally work the same hours each month, they are really fixed.

Table 4

Income and Expense Statement for Mountain Coach, Inc.

for the period 7/1/19XX - 8/31/19XX

	Bus 1	%	Bus 2	%	Bus 3	%	Total	%
Revenues	$13,020	100%	$14,130	100%	$16,200	100%	$43,350	100%
Daily Average	$310		$307		$300		$305	
Revenue Percentage	30%		33%		37%		100%	
Days Up (Down) or Idle	42 (4) 14		46 (7) 7		54 (1) 5		142 (12) 26	
Variable Expenses:								
Commissions	$ 1,302	10%	$ 1,413	10%	$ 1,620	10%	$ 4,335	10%
Repairs	335	3%	1,169	8%	1,967	12%	3,471	8%
Other Expense	537	4%	1,156	8%	168	1%	1,861	4%
Totals	2,174	17%	3,738	26%	3,755	23%	9,667	22%
Contribution Margin	$10,846	83%	$10,392	74%	$12,445	77%	$33,683	78%
Fixed Expenses:								
Insurance	1,306	10%	1,305	9%	1,305	10%	3,916	9%
Depreciation	4,688	36%	5,625	40%	4,688	29%	15,001	35%
Interest Expense	5,868	45%	7,043	50%	5,868	36%	18,779	43%
Profit Margin	(1,016)	8%	(3,581)	25%	584	4%	(4,013)	9%
Cash Flow	$9,540	73%	$ 9,087	64%	$11,140	69%	$29,767	69%
Loan Payments	9,375	72%	11,250	80%	9,375	58%	30,000	69%
Unallocated Expense:								
Tags and Taxes							985	2%
Travel & Entertainment							150	-
Miscellaneous							40	-
Professional Fees							500	1%
Totals							1,675	4%
Profit (Loss)							($5,688)	13%

Table 5
Income and Expense Statement for Convenience Food Stores, Inc.
for the nine months ended 9/30/19XX

		This Month		Year to Date	
Sales:			% Total		% Total
	Gasoline	$ 82,927	61.7%	$ 730,932	60.5%
	Groceries	16,136	12.0%	150,778	12.5%
	Tobacco	19,922	14.8%	189,224	15.7%
	Beer and Wine	11,567	8.6%	107,617	8.9%
	Sundries	3,747	2.8%	29,412	2.4%
	Gross Sales	$134,299	100.0%	$1,207,963	100.0%
Cost of Sales:			% Sales		% Sales
	Gasoline	$ 76,493	92.2%	$ 680,585	93.1%
	Groceries	12,456	77.2%	118,915	78.9%
	Tobacco	16,124	80.9%	164,679	87.0%
	Beer/Wine	9,652	83.4%	91,224	84.8%
	Sundries	1,401	37.4%	12,471	42.4%
	Total Cost of Goods Sold	$116,126	86.5%	$1,067,874	88.4%
Gross Profit:			% Sales		% Sales
	Gasoline	$ 6,434	7.8%	$ 50,347	6.9%
	Groceries	3,680	22.8%	31,863	21.1%
	Tobacco	3,798	19.1%	24,545	13.0%
	Beer/Wine	1,915	16.6%	16,393	15.2%
	Sundries	2,346	62.6%	16,941	57.6%
	Total Gross Profit	$ 18,173	13.5%	$ 140,089	11.6%
Expenses:			% Gross		% Gross
	Salaries	$ 6,783	5.1%	$ 51,397	4.3%
	Payroll Taxes	508	.4%	1,748	.1%
	Employee Benefits	460	.3%	1,843	.2%
	Rent	800	.6%	7,240	.6%
	Utilities	1,557	1.2%	13,166	1.1%
	Travel and Entertainment	279	.2%	4,397	.4%
	Management Fees	2,352	1.8%	9,674	.8%
	Interest Expense	204	.2%	1,869	.2%
	Miscellaneous	1,253	---	22,851	.2%
	Depreciation	4,471	3.3%	15,034	1.2%
	Total Expense	$ 18,667	13.9%	$ 129,219	10.7%
Net Income Before Taxes		($ 494)	.4%	$ 10,870	.9%
Cash Flow		$ 3,977	2.9%	$ 25,904	2.1%

Looking at Table 5, can you see any items which appear to need attention based on the statement? Why do you think the gross profit margin on tobacco changed so much during the last month as compared to the year to date? Could it be that a big price increase on tobacco items was implemented? That might explain the slight drop in tobacco sales as a percentage of overall sales. If there has been a price increase, then the sales bear watching!

Do you see any areas which could improve the firm's performance if sales could be increased? How about the **sundries**? These are items such as novelties which have a much higher markup than most of the items in a convenience store. The income statement makes that obvious! A small increase in sales of sundries could have a marked impact on gross profit because the contribution margin for sundries is so much higher than for the other items. Consider, a $1,000 increase in the sales of sundries will produce $576 in profits (57.6%). Groceries have the next highest contribution margin at 21.1%, but it would take an increase in grocery sales of $2,730 in order to produce $576 in profits ($576/.211 = $2,730). Gasoline has the lowest margin of all at 6.9%. It would take an increase in gasoline sales of $8,348 in order to produce that same $576 in profits ($576/.069 = $8,348). The other side of that coin is also true. A decline in sales of $1,000 in sundries would reduce profits by $576 while gasoline sales could drop by $8,348 before losing that much.

The contribution margin can also demonstrate aggregate values. For example, gasoline sales had a 6.9% margin on total sales of $680,000. If prices could be increased enough to provide a 1% increase in the margin without losing sales, then the effect would be to increase profits by $6,800. That's well over half the $10,870 profit which the firm is currently generating. It may be hard to raise those prices without losing sales however, even though we are talking about only a 1% increase. Remember that the contribution margin ratio is directly affected by selling price. That means that a 1% increase in selling price will produce a 1% increase in contribution margin if the variable costs remain the same. Gasoline sales through convenience stores tend to be highly competitive. Consider the impact of raising the price and losing sales. As we saw earlier, a loss in gasoline sales will not have a pronounced effect on profits until a major loss occurs. However, if people stop coming to buy gas, they stop coming to buy other things. How much of our sales of other items might we lose if we have a decline in gasoline business? Unfortunately, that potential cannot be calculated, it can only be estimated subjectively.

Quantitative techniques can only provide so much information. The owner/manager must constantly be aware of the nonquantifiable elements in any situation. Nevertheless, the contribution margin can be a useful tool. It can be used with historic numbers or forecasts or a combination. It can provide a monitoring device for use in measuring progress toward objectives and trends in performance. It can also function as a planning device for use in marketing, pricing, inventory stocking, and a host of other planning activities. Finally, the contribution margin can function as an analysis tool for use in comparing products or business segments as well as breakeven analysis and target sales analysis.

A CASE FROM OUR FILES

The client was a building contractor. He had called us in because he said he was *working himself to death and not making any money.* He wanted to see if we could find what he was doing wrong. He had plenty of jobs, won most of the bids he entered and did not have the capacity to handle any more work. Nevertheless, his profits were never more than modest.

That comment about winning almost all of his bids made us very nervous.

The first thing we asked for was to see his books and records. Even though he had been in business for 9 years and was known as a successful and competent builder in the area, all he could show us was the financial statements prepared by his accountant for each of the previous year ends. He had no interim statements.

We explained that we had to see something in order to evaluate his bidding process and get some feel for his profit margins. He showed us a drawer full of file folders. He had one for each job he was working and one for each job he had finished since last year. These were the records which he gave to the accountant once each year to prepare his financial statements. As bills came in, he filed them in the folder for the appropriate job. The system worked pretty well for material expenses, but there was absolutely no record of how much labor was expended on a particular job. That meant that we could not determine the contribution margin of any given contract.

We asked how he went about preparing the labor portion of his construction bids. He explained that he estimated the material and then added 25% to that number to arrive at labor estimates. The material was relatively easy to estimate and those records that he did have, indicated that he had been doing an admirable job of estimating material costs in the past. He added that he was sure that the labor was being covered or else he wouldn't be making any money! His overhead was virtually nil; his own time being the primary component. The firm was profitable, but not in the same profit league as its competitors.

Since the client's records were of no value, we asked for and gained access to the bidding records of a state agency which our client and his competitors frequently serviced. Fortunately, those bids were a matter of public record. Our client was absolutely appalled to learn that he had won his last three bids with that agency by a 25% to 40% margin. In every case his bid was substantially lower than his competitors.

The solution to his problem was now obvious.

Take a look at the case from our files on this page. Do you see the solution to the contractor's problem? Clearly his bids have been much too low. Since he has not been capturing labor costs by job and had been properly estimating material requirements, he was underbidding labor expenses. By instituting a managerial accounting system which captures all costs by job the contractor will be able to gain expertise in labor estimation which will allow him to increase his profits. The consultants were nervous about his winning too high a percentage of his bids. That fact would indicate that the contractor was *leaving a lot of money on the table.* If he had been generating similar cost estimates as his competitors, then one would expect him to win some bids and to lose others dependent upon the inconsistencies of the estimation process. This small business owner was apparently consistently underbidding the real cost of construction.

CASH FLOW STATEMENTS

Both of the income statements which we discussed in the previous section displayed cash flow numbers as well as profits. That was no accident. We have mentioned the value which cash flow has for a business several times. If you simply remember that *profit* is always a historic indication of the difference between revenues and expenses over some arbitrary period of time, then you will understand that profit cannot be used to pay bills or purchase items because **there is no cash there!** Only cash can be used to purchase items or pay bills. Profit is valuable for only two reasons: profit enhances a small business' borrowing power and financial strength because analysts use it as a major factor in evaluating firms; profit is valuable because it is a source of cash flow.

OPERATING CASH FLOW

What is the difference between profit and cash? The difference is in timing. Remember that in order to achieve a consistent evaluation of performance over time that we recognize revenues and expenses at times other than when cash changes hands. That means that cash flow and profit will not be the same thing. Consequently, we must examine the cash flow of the business as closely as we do the profit.

Think about revenues first. As sales are made, accounts receivable are created unless the sale is made for cash. Of course, that portion of sales which were made for cash represents *cash inflow*. In some businesses virtually all sales may be for cash while in other businesses virtually all sales may be on credit. The rules of recognizing revenue say that an entry for sales must be made whether the cash is collected or not because an *account receivable* is a valuable asset given in return for the product or service delivered. Except for a small portion of accounts receivable which will be lost in the form of bad debts, the accounts represent cash which will be collected in the future. When the accounts are collected, they will represent *cash inflow*. That means that we can convert the revenues for a given period of time to cash inflow by adjusting for accounts receivable. The beginning and ending balance of accounts receivable is the key. If the beginning value of accounts receivable is larger than the amount of accounts receivable outstanding at the end of the period, then there must have been more cash inflows than there were sales. Consider an example. Assume that accounts receivable at the first of the month were $1,500, sales during the month were $4,000 and receivables at the end of the month were $1,000. There were no charge offs of bad debts during the month. Total cash inflows for that month must have been the entire $4,000 in sales plus $500 of the receivables which were outstanding at the beginning of the month. Since there were no charge offs of bad debts, the decline in the balance of receivables must mean that we collected more money than was charged. It doesn't matter whether the sales were all for cash or all on credit, the total amount of money collected had to be $4,500. If all of the sales were on credit, then the initial accounts receivable of $1,500 would have been increased by the $4,000 in charges. That would have been a total of $5,500 in receivables. The only way that the $5,500 of receivables could have been reduced to $1,000 at the end of the month would be if $4,500 worth of payments were received. If there had been any charge offs, we would have removed them from consideration because they were not collected. Now, the rule is: add any decrease in accounts receivable to sales to arrive at cash inflow. Reverse the direction of change of receivables and you will see that an increase in receivables during a period must be subtracted from sales to arrive at cash inflow.

Cost of goods sold represents an expense, but not a ***cash outflow***, or all the cash flowing out of the business. Cash is involved in the purchase of inventory. If any inventory items are acquired on credit, then ***accounts payable*** will be involved just as accounts receivable were involved in sales. Cost of goods is also affected by changes in inventory levels. If we buy more than we sell, then inventory will go up. That must mean that more cash was expended than the cost of goods would indicate. If we sell more than we buy, then inventory will go down. That means that we used less cash than the cost of sales would indicate because part of the expense is coming from inventory which had been bought in a previous period. All this means that we must adjust cost of sales for both accounts payable and inventory changes. To convert cost of goods sold to cash outflow, we must add any decreases in accounts payable and add any increase in inventory which has occurred during the period. Increases in accounts payable or decreases in inventory are subtracted.

The remaining expenses are converted to cash outflow by examining any accrued items which relate to the expense. For example, insurance expense is converted to cash outlay by examining the prepaid insurance account. Prepaid insurance is an asset. If the prepaid account has increased, then the amount of that increase must be added to insurance expense to arrive at cash outflow. A decrease must be subtracted. If there is an accrued liability, then it will behave opposite to assets. For example, if there is an accrued wages account, then any increase in that account must be subtracted from wage expense to arrive at cash outflow. A decrease is added. Liabilities behave in an opposite direction from assets because they are opposite in nature. If an asset increases, it means that cash has been expended to invest in the asset. If a liability increases, it means that cash has not yet been expended.

As you can see, the process of item by item inspection can become tedious. The solution is to begin with income and convert it directly into cash flow. We will focus on operating income first. ***Operating income*** is the profit which results from the day to day operations of the business. Any unusual items or money made or lost on sales of plant assets or money from investments should not be included. Only those revenues and expenses which relate directly to the operations of the business should be included in the calculation of operating income. In this way we will arrive at a number which represents the earnings power of the firm. The important thing about ***earnings power*** is that it is a representation of performance which can be expected to continue in the future.

To find operating income we subtract from sales the cost of sales, selling expenses and general and administrative expenses. Any items of *other revenues* or *other expenses* are ignored.

Table 6

Operating Cash Flow

I. Find Operating Income
   - A. Operating Revenues
   - B. Less Cost of Sales
   - C. Less Selling Expenses
   - D. Less General and Administrative Expense

II. Adjust Operating Income for non cash expenses
   - A. Add Depreciation Expense
   - B. Add Amortization Expense

III. Adjust Operating Income for changes in Current Liabilities
   - A. Add Increases in Accounts Payable
   - B. Add Increases in any Accrued Liabilities
   - C. Subtract Decreases in Accounts Payable
   - D. Subtract Decreases in any Accrued Liabilities

IV. Adjust Operating Income for changes in Current Assets
   - A. Add Decreases in Accounts Receivable
   - B. Add Decreases in Inventory
   - C. Add Decreases in Prepaid Expense items
   - D. Subtract Increases in Accounts Receivable
   - E. Subtract Increases in Inventory
   - F. Subtract Increases in Prepaid Expense items

V. The result is Operating Cash Flow

Remember that interest expense is not an operating expense either. *Interest expense* results from debts which the management has decided to undertake and therefore are not a function of operations. Consequently, the operating income will be before taxes and interest expense. This is sometime referred to as *EBIT*, earnings before interest and taxes. After operating income has been determined, we will convert it to operating cash flow by adjusting for the timing differences we talked about above and adjusting for any items of expense which do not consume cash. Principal among these is depreciation expense. We have already discussed how depreciation expense reduces profit but does not affect cash. Amortization is another such expense. In reality, it is a type of depreciation. We generally term the depreciation of such assets as leasehold improvements and other intangibles, *amortization*. An *intangible* is an asset which is not a visible part of the business. For example, leasehold improvements belong to the landlord, not to the business. Table 6 displays the adjustments. *Operating cash flow* may well be the most important number in a business. It reveals how much cash is being generated by the ongoing activities of the business. This is the cash which must be used to pay bills, purchases assets, make loan payments, etc. The process of generating operating cash flow appears involved, but is actually simplistic. Most people find that this is an excellent application of a computerized spread sheet program. At any rate, operating cash flow should be calculated every time profit is calculated. That means at least monthly!

From month to month the changes in the items which affect operating cash flow are frequently minor. Accounts receivable, payable, inventory, prepaid items and accruals frequently change only a small amount. Consequently, many firms use a short cut method to arrive at an approximation of operating cash flow. This method is to simply add depreciation back to operating income. That is what was really done in Tables 4 and 5 to arrive at the number called cash flow. This short cut is acceptable if the amount of error is small. If there are large changes in any of the other components, then the longer version should be used.

One of the best uses of operating cash flow is a comparison to loan payments. Only the interest portion of loan payments shows on the income statement as an expense, but both the principal and interest portions of the payment consume cash. Examination of the operating cash flow demonstrates how easily, or with how much difficulty, a firm can meet its loan payments. The financial statement in Table 4 made that comparison. As the *operating income* is an indication of future earnings power, the *operating cash flow* is an indication of the future cash generation capabilities of the firm.

NET CASH FLOW FROM OPERATIONS

Just as net profit is different from operating profit, net cash flow from operations is different from operating cash flow. To find this number we must begin with the net profit and adjust for any items which do not affect cash. Table 7 displays the process. As you can see, the process is very similar. The difference is that we do not restrict adjustments to items associated with ongoing operations. The *net cash flow from operations* is a valuable indication of the liquidity of a firm. *Liquidity* is the ease with which a firm can meet its obligations. This number is an historic one and will not be as representative of the future as the operating cash flow was, but it is a better indication of the performance of the firm during the time period under review.

NET CASH FLOW

You may have noticed that the process of generating net cash flow from operations is the same as would be followed in preparing a statement of cash flows. The process is identical and the conversion of the net cash flow from operations into net cash flow occurs in the statement of cash flows. ***Net cash flow*** should always equal the difference in the cash balance at the beginning and end of the period. If it does not, an error has been made in calculation. Of course, if there should be a net loss instead of a net profit, then the very first number in the table will be negative and must be subtracted to arrive at Total Sources of Cash.

Table 7
Net Cash Flow from Operations

I. Find Net Profit
  A. Total Revenues
  B. Less Total Expenses
  C. Less Income Taxes
  D. Less Unusual and Nonrecurring items

II. Adjust Net Profit for non cash expenses
  A. Add Depreciation Expense
  B. Add Amortization Expense
  C. Add any other expenses which did not consume cash, i.e., *loss on sale of noncurrent assets*
  D. Subtract any revenues which did not generate cash such as *gain on sale of fixed assets*

III. Adjust Net Profit for changes in Current Liabilities
  A. Add Increases in any Current Liabilities
  B. Subtract Decreases in any Current Liabilities

IV. Adjust Net Profit for changes in Current Assets
  A. Add Decreases in any Current Asset except cash
  B. Subtract Increases in any Current Asset except cash

V. The result is Net Cash Flow from Operations

The net cash flow calculations show where every dollar that flowed into a firm over a given time period came from, what every dollar that flowed out was used for, and the effect on cash of these flows. This can be a powerful tool in evaluating the effectiveness of the management of cash. It also demonstrates the role which capital investment and debt played in financing the firm's activities during the period. Finally, the schedule shows the acquisition, disposition and financing sources for productive assets. Lenders are particularly interested in such information because it can be an indication of the ability of the firm to repay credit. Net cash flow is an historic representation and as such is not a good tool for judging future cash flow potential. Nevertheless, it is a good report card for management. Lenders are fond of saying that managers are like leopards and seldom change their spots. That means that a good manager will probably go on being a good manager in the future, while a poor manager will probably go on being a poor manager. The net cash flow schedule is one device for determining the category in which a manager should be placed. By monitoring the cash flows month to month, an owner can make adjustments which will result in being considered a good manager. If you wait until the year is over before calculating any the flows, it will be too late to change anything.

The effective management of cash is one of the most important of all management functions because cash flow is the life blood of any business. In a later chapter we will discuss forecasting cash flows and talk about how it can be managed in a more ***proactive*** manner. That means making adjustments before something happens rather than after it happens. The continual monitoring of all three types of cash flow which we have discussed is the best approach to self evaluation. You will find that cash flows are frequently quite different from profits at any level. The continual monitoring of cash flow will prevent profits from obscuring the cash resources which are so important to your firm's survival

SUMMARY

Accounting was established by the early Romans and was based on the trust which businesses felt in the honesty of people who owed them. Today that trust is still implicit in the accounting function. People expect financial statements to reflect the true financial condition of a company.

In reality, accounting is a reflection of management. If management has designed a sound accounting system and installed sound accounting practices and controls, then the financial statements will be dependable and trustworthy.

In extremely small businesses, record keeping is not as vital because the owner is aware of money flowing in and out of the business. However with the addition of employees, the record keeping process becomes essential to help management stay knowledgeable and to provide a basis for decisions.

Two types of accounting techniques discussed here are cash based accounting and accrual based accounting. Small businesses should use the accrual methodology because of the demand for the generation of financial information necessary for decision making. Under the cash method, revenues and expenses are recorded only when cash changes hands. Under the accrual method, revenues and expenses are recorded whenever an obligation to receive or pay money arises, regardless of whether the money changes hands. This method results in a more systematic and accurate measurement of a firm's activities over time and is the preferred approach. However, under accrual accounting, a company can show a profit but have serious cash flow problems.

Internal controls refer to techniques used to safeguard assets and records and ensure that transactions are properly recorded and the accounting process properly managed.

The role of the CPA is to be a partner in management not simply a preparer of financial reports. That role involves tax consultant, management advisory services, tax planning, fringe benefit preparation and advisor about internal controls whether from a manual or automated perspective.

Financial accounting refers to the activities which result in the generation of the financial statement. Accounting principles dictate how these statements should be prepared and are general in nature so that different companies may be compared along appropriate lines.

Managerial accounting uses the record keeping tools developed in financial accounting and is used internally in the generation of reports for decision making. Examples of managerial reports are delinquency reports, projected payment reports, and inventory turnover and status reports.

Two such reports of real value to a small business are contribution margin reports and cash flow reports. One of the best applications of the contribution margin is in the form of income and expense statements reflecting margins and prepared by product, department division or other segment. This contribution margin statement demonstrates the relative role the segment plays in the company. The contribution margin report can provide a monitoring device to measure progress toward objectives; can function as a planning device; and can be used for comparing product and development as well as breakeven analysis and target sales analysis.

A scarce resource is anything which limits a firm's ability to generate sales and profits. It is frequently money for a new small business, but can just as easily be the time of expert employees, machine time or any other factor. A firm cannot expand its sales and profits without increasing the amount of the scarce resource which its possesses.

Cash flow reports demonstrate the amount of cash available to the company to pay bills or purchase items. Involved in cash flow statements are operating cash flows and net cash flows.

The effective management of cash is one of the most important of all management functions because cash flow is the life blood of any small business. The continual monitoring of cash flow will prevent profits from obscuring the cash resources which are so important to your firm's survival.

QUESTIONS, EXERCISES AND CASES

Questions:

1.   Define the following terms: Accounting, Profit, Cash Flow, and Auditing.
2.   Why is accounting called the language of trust?
3.   Why is record keeping so important to a business?
4.   State and explain how you would set up internal controls in a small business. Give specific examples.
5.   What task do CPAs usually perform for a small business and what service would be better done for the business?
6.   What is the purpose of an Audit?
7.   What is the difference between financial accounting and managerial accounting?
8.   What is one of the best applications for the contribution margin?
9.   How are the two income and expense statements in Tables 4 and 5 different and why?
10.   Why is cash flow more important to the survival of a company than profit?
11.   How does one find operating cash flow and net cash flow?
18.   What is a scarce resource and what is its significance to management?

CASE 1

Jason Trevor was a true artisan. He had shown his work all over the country and had gained acclaim for his unique designs. Jason had taken up the art of pottery from his grandfather. He had watched the old man lovingly create works of art with his hands. He could make the most simple and utile object a masterpiece in Jason's eyes. So he taught his craft to his young grandson mostly because he loved having the boy around, not with any thoughts of preserving his skill for posterity.

Jason was a fast learner and learned to innovate himself. He went to art school and studied other art techniques, but he still preferred to use those techniques learned at his grandfather's wheel. After college and much recognition of his talent, Jason decided to go into business with his pottery. His work seemed to be in great demand and he had been offered some sizeable dollar figures for his pots. Or so he thought. What could be simpler? He had a wheel, a storage area and his own talents. He was willing to work and the business would indeed be a success.

A year into his business, frustration took its toll on Jason. He had seemingly hundreds of orders. More than he could possibly fill within the time allotted. He had just received notice from the bank that his account was overdrawn by his last order from his supplier and he was exhausted. What was he going to do?

1.   What was the *scarce resource* which bounded the firm's ability to generate income?

2.   What kinds of managerial reports would have been valuable in controlling the firm? When could they have been generated and how?

3.   What problems can you foresee for Jason's company and why? What can he do about it?

CASE 2

Geraldine Franks was relieved. She had made a decision about her accounting situation. When she had decided to open her own small office supply company, she had consulted a CPA and found that record keeping could be an expensive proposition. The CPA had suggested that he could do more for her than just preparation of financial statements, but she wasn't interested at this time. Now Geraldine had the answer. Yesterday, she had been approached by a computer salesman who claimed to specialize in accounting packages for small companies. The computer could do all the accounting needs of the company and there would be no need for a CPA claimed the salesman.

The computer system was installed and Geraldine felt that all five of her employees should know how to operate it, but she, herself, was too busy to find time for the training. After all, that's why she had employees, because she couldn't do everything!

The system was a success. The employees loved it. She had chuckled about all the game playing that had occurred after hours on the system since the salesman had thrown in a couple of games with the purchase. He claimed that the games would overcome resistance in the employees in learning to use the computer and that it had!

All the employees had access to the system and Geraldine wondered what she had done without it. Bob Grant especially seemed to enjoy it. Although Susan Winters was the bookkeeper, ever time she had a problem, she called Bob to help her. He was much more technically oriented than she, she insisted. Bob had even come in on nights and weekends to work on the computer.

Two years went by and Geraldine's future didn't look as rosy. She knew that business had picked up. Even an idiot could see that now there were more customers dropping in and she had several large clients which she didn't have last year. What was wrong? The cash flow wasn't there. Then the bank called and said that she was overdrawn. This couldn't be happening to her. What could she do?

1.   What do think might be happening? What could be done to discover what was happening?

2.   What internal controls may have been violated?

3.   What common sense control was violated?

4.   What should Geraldine do?

5.   What could the CPA have done for her had she consulted him even after the purchase of the computer system?

CHAPTER FIVE

BREAKEVEN ANALYSIS

CHAPTER OBJECTIVES

Upon completion of this chapter, you should be able to:

- Explain the principles of cost-volume-profit analysis;

- Perform breakeven analysis for a new venture;

- Perform target sales analysis; and,

- Describe interrelationships between cost, volume and profit factors.

BREAKEVEN ANALYSIS

INTRODUCTION

The financial planning which is required in a new venture start-up includes an assessment of the feasibility of the business. A major factor in feasibility is the prospects for financial success. ***Breakeven analysis*** examines the relationship between cost, volume, and profit (CVP), and it is a technique which permits the examination of financial feasibility. This concept is applicable to many more situations than a business start-up. CVP analysis can aid in determining whether a new product or market area should be added or deleted, whether a new plant, division or department should be added or deleted, the relative importance of various aspects of a business to its profitability, and much, much more. CVP is one of the most versatile and useful tools available to a small business owner. In this chapter, we will examine CVP tools with particular emphasis on breakeven analysis.

BREAKEVEN ANALYSIS

No business should ever be started without a breakeven analysis. It is really impossible to determine the viability of a new venture without investigating the volume of business which will be required for the venture to survive. Once that is determined, we must think about the probability that the venture can produce that volume. There are three steps involved in breakeven analysis. First, we have to estimate the fixed costs which we are going to have. Then, we must estimate the variable costs as a percentage of sales. Finally, we must calculate the breakeven point, the sales level which is required to cover all costs.

In the accounting chapter we talked about fixed and variable costs. Fixed costs are those that do not change immediately as sales change. These are things like the rent, utilities, salaries, insurance premiums, and so on. Variable costs are those that do change immediately when sales change. For many businesses, virtually all the costs are fixed except those costs for replacement inventory. If you pay sales commissions, those will be variable, but most of your costs will not be. For some businesses selling services rather than products, there might be no variable costs at all.

BREAKEVEN ILLUSTRATION

The best way to understand CVP analysis is to begin with a simple illustration. Let's examine an illustration of a breakeven analysis for a new venture. We will assume that we want to start a hardware store. Following is an illustration of the process.

ESTIMATING THE FIXED COSTS

First, we visit a lot of hardware stores and we do a layout for our store, then we find a building to rent which fits our needs and is located in a good place. From the real estate agent, we find out that we will have to sign a three year lease at $2,000 per month. That will be $24,000 each year. We'll have to make two payments in advance.

The agent also said that we would probably have $180 per month for utilities. That's $2,160 each year.

We call the telephone company and find out that the telephone is going to cost $40 per month, plus long distance calls. We don't expect a lot of long distance calls except for calling suppliers to make orders, so we guess that we'll average $20 per month. That will make the annual cost about $720.

We call an insurance agent and we get an estimate for insurance of $2,200 per year.

We call an equipment supplier and find out that we can lease all of the display racks and bins, counters and everything else we need. They want three payments in advance, then the lease will be $300 per month, or $3,600 per year.

We call an office supplier and find out that they can sell us the computer, the software and the cash register which we need. They want a down payment of $500, then they will finance the rest for us and the loan payments are going to be $190 per month. That will make the annual cost $2,280.

We're going to need one additional person to work in the business with us during the whole time the store is open, 10 hours per day, 6 days per week. We will need a second person during the evening hours and on Saturday. That's five hours per day plus 10 hours on Saturday. That means a total of 95 hours per week or 4,940 hours per year. If we use part time people, we can get them for $5.50 per hour. That means that the payroll will be $27,170 per year. We talked to an accountant and we know that we will have to pay payroll taxes of about 10% on the salaries. That will make the salary cost $29,887 per year. We decide to round that to $30,000.

We are going to have to draw $20,000 per year out of the business for our living expenses. If we took a job rather that starting this business, we would make more, but that's the minimum we can live on at first.

We call several hardware suppliers and we estimate that we will need $30,000 of inventory when we open the store. That's a start-up cost, but we will need to borrow a large part of it.

We call a sign company and we find out that putting up the kinds of signs we want on the building will cost $2,000.

We call a contractor and talk about leasehold improvements we want made to the building. They are going to run $11,000.

We check with the state department of revenue and our business license will cost $50.

We have to make deposits on the water and the electricity. Those will be a total of $200. We have to have the phone installed and that will cost $300.

We ask an accountant about taking care of payroll and filing sales tax returns and state and federal income tax returns. She says it should run about $1,500 each year.

We're sure that we overlooked something, so we decide to add another $150 each month to our costs, just in case. This will be $1,800 per year.

Now, the start-up costs are the advance rent payments, the down payments, the leasehold improvements, the sign, the deposits and the initial inventory. That's a total of $48,950. We will want to make sure we have some cash to carry us for a few weeks, so we add $5,000 to the start-up costs to make $53,950. We have saved $10,000 and we have to borrow the rest. We call a bank and found out that if we are approved for a loan of $43,950, the loan payments will be $980 per month, or $11,760 per year.

Looking at the fixed costs for the year, we add up all the costs including the loan payments. That comes to $100,020, or rounding off, $100,000 per year. That's our estimate for the annual fixed costs for the hardware store.

Now that we have the fixed costs, we need to think about variable costs. Those will change with small changes in sales volume. Since we are not going to pay any commissions, our only variable cost will be for replacement inventory. We talked to hardware store owners in various cities, we talked to the hardware suppliers, and we looked up hardware stores in the library and read about them. Our best information is that most hardware stores have a gross profit of about 35%. Gross profit is the difference between sales and the cost of the inventory. For example, if we buy a power saw for $40 and sell it for $62.50, then we will make $22.50 over the cost of the saw. That would be a gross profit of 36% ($22.50/$62.50). We would say that the gross profit margin is 36% on the saw. This also means that the cost is 64% ($40/$62.50). If we buy #8 wood screws for $.01 each and we sell them for $.02 each, we will make a profit of $.01, or 50%. The cost would also be 50%. Each product that we sell will be the same. There will be different gross profit margins on different products. When people say that the average gross profit for the hardware store is 35%, they mean that the average of all the gross profit margins on all of the products we sell is 35%. This also means that the average cost for the inventory will be 65% (100%-35%).

Think of the margins as the money you get to keep. If you sell $100 worth of products and you paid $60 for those products, you get to keep $40. That's a margin of 40%. The rest of the $100, the $60, is cost for the inventory; we can't keep it. We have to use that money to buy replacement inventory. If we don't buy new products to replace those we sell, we will soon run out of inventory. So, the sales we get must cover the replacement cost of the inventory, then we can keep the rest. If we expect an average gross profit margin of 35%, that means that we expect to keep 35% of our sales. That's $.35 out of each $1.00 or $35 out of each $100 of sales.

To continue with the illustration, we will estimate that the gross profit margin for our hardware store will be 35%. Since we have no variable costs except inventory, the gross profit margin will tell us all we need to know. How much do the sales have to be to breakeven? Remember, we have to have $100,000 to cover the fixed costs, and we get to keep 35% of our sales. If we sell $100,000 worth of products, we will have $35,000 which we can use to cover the fixed costs (35% X $100,000). That's not enough. If we sell $200,000 worth of products, we will have $70,000 which we can use to cover fixed costs (35% X $200,000). That's still not enough. What we need is to find out the level of sales that will give us $100,000 to cover fixed costs. Notice that we have been multiplying the sales by the margin to show us how much we can keep. To find out how much the sales have to be to cover a particular level of fixed costs, we go the other way. That means that we divide the costs by the margin.

$$35\% \times \text{Sales} = \$100{,}000$$
$$\text{Sales} = \$100{,}000/.35$$
$$\text{Sales} = \$285{,}714$$

The sales we need to cover $100,000 of fixed costs are $285,714. That's the breakeven point. If we sell $285,714 worth of products and we make a gross profit margin of 35%, we will have gross profits of $100,000 (35% X $285,714). Since the fixed costs are expected to be $100,000, then the hardware store will have zero profits and zero losses. It will break even. The way we found that breakeven point was just to divide the costs by the margins.

ERRORS IN THE ESTIMATE

There is a dangerous problem here for business owners. The breakeven point is an ***estimate***. An estimate means that the number is wrong. What is even worse, we don't know how wrong it is. The only way that the hardware store will have exactly zero profits and zero losses at sales of $285,714 is if it has exactly $100,000 in fixed costs for the year and exactly 35% in gross profit for the year. It is far more likely that the store will have a little more or a little less than $100,000 in fixed costs. It is far more likely that the store will have a gross profit margin of a little more or a little less than 35%. Look what happens if we're off a bit in our estimates.

Let's say that the hardware store has to have a lot of sales to get people to come into a new place and to take business away from the competition. That could mean that we have to price everything a little less than the competition. If we do that, then our gross profit margin will be less than 35%. That was the ***average*** for hardware stores. If we have lower prices, we will have a lower gross profit. That's because our costs for the inventory items will be the same as everyone else. Remember that power saw we bought for $40? The saw sells for $62.50 in the hardware store down the street. During our sale to attract customers, we find that we have to sell it for $58.50. That would give us a gross profit of $18.50 or 32% ($18.50/$58.50). If we assume that we will have similar prices throughout the store, we will have an average gross profit margin of less than 35%. Look what happens if we get the forecast for fixed costs right, but the gross profit margin is actually 32%.

$$32\% \text{ X Sales} = \$100,000$$
$$\text{Sales} = \$100,000/.32$$
$$\text{Sales} = \$312,500$$

The last breakeven point was $285,714. The new forecast is $26,786 higher. Now, what if we missed the fixed cost estimate as well? What if we find that we can't get along with the number of employees we had planned? If we find that we have to have another person for the entire week, 60 hours, and we pay that person $5.50 per hour, we are going to need another $17,160 in salary plus the 10% payroll taxes. That means that the fixed costs will be closer to $119,000. If we use that number to calculate the breakeven and use the lower gross profit margin in the calculations, we find a new beak even point, $371,875. The first breakeven point was $285,714 and the second was $312,500. This new number is $86,161 higher than the first and $59,375 higher than the second.

$$32\% \text{ X Sales} = \$119,000$$
$$\text{Sales} = \$119,000/.32$$
$$\text{Sales} = \$371,875$$

What is the *real* breakeven point? Sadly, we won't know what the real number is until the year is over. Then we can look at the actual results. What we want to do now, is to make two forecasts. The first forecast is based on our ***best guess*** of what the fixed costs and profit margins will be, $285,714. The second forecast should use higher estimates for fixed costs. What do you think the outside estimate for the costs will be? How high can they go? Think about each number in the estimate and consider how much higher it might be. Then, use a lower profit margin. How much lower is it likely to be? Use these ***pessimistic*** forecasts to make another estimate, $371,875. The real breakeven point is likely to fall somewhere between the two extremes. Now we have a good planning tool. We have a range of estimates for the breakeven point.

Our example is not yet complete, however. We don't go into business to break even. We want to make a profit. How can we estimate the sales required to produce a profit?

PRODUCING A PROFIT

If we sell more than the breakeven point, we make a profit. After you pass the breakeven point, the gross profit becomes ***real profit***. If we expect a gross profit margin of 35% and we think that it will take $300,000 in sales to break even, then everything over $300,000 produces a profit. Suppose we sell $400,000 of our inventory. That's $100,000 more than the breakeven point. The gross profit on that overage is $35,000 (35% X $100,000). That is the money we really get to keep. We've already covered the fixed costs with the first $300,000 in sales. Anything more is profit.

We can actually build in a target level of profit and find out what the sales have to be to produce that. Think about the hardware store again. Let's say that we expect $119,000 in fixed costs for the year and we expect to have a gross profit margin of 32%. We have $20,000 built in to the fixed costs for our personal living expenses, but that's the minimum amount on which we can live. We really want to make much more than that. In fact, we might say that it's not worth the problems of starting the business unless we can make $100,000 per year. Since we have $20,000 built in to the fixed costs, that would mean that we want to have a profit of $80,000. How much would the sales have to be to produce that much? We can use the same relationship we demonstrated for the breakeven calculation to estimate the sales required for any given level of profit. With this data, fixed costs of $119,000, gross profit level of 32%, and a desired profit of $80,000, it looks like this:

$$32\% \times Sales = \$119,000 + \$80,000$$
$$Sales = \$199,000/.32$$
$$Sales = \$621,875$$

In order to have a profit of $80,000, we would need sales of $621,875 assuming that our estimate of fixed costs and gross profit margin are good guesses. Now, we really have some good data for planning. We're really not willing to start this business unless it can produce more than $622,000 in sales each year. That's our target sales; the level of sales we really want to achieve.

THE EFFECT OF ADDITIONAL VARIABLE COSTS

In the hardware store example, we said that the only variable costs we would have would be to buy replacement inventory. What if that weren't true? What if we decided to pay the employees a sales commission? In addition to their salaries, we decide to pay a commission of 3% on every dollar of sales they make. We think this might be a good incentive to make them sell more. On the other hand, the sales commission means that we lose another 3% of each dollar of sales. With a gross profit margin of 32%, we were losing 68%. Now, we're losing 3% more. That means that we will get to keep 29% (32% - 3%). The breakeven point will rise to $410,345:

$$29\% \times Sales = \$119,000$$
$$Sales = \$119,000/.29$$
$$Sales = \$410,345$$

When we used the 32% margin, the breakeven was $371,875. The sales commission will raise the breakeven by $38,470. The commission will also raise the sales required to give us that $80,000 profit. The old target sales were $621,875, but the commission raises it by $64,332.

$$29\% \times Sales = \$119,000 + \$80,000$$
$$Sales = \$199,000/.29$$
$$Sales = \$686,207$$

Many businesses have variable costs like that sales commission. For example, many retail shops, especially those located in shopping malls have their rent based on sales. It is common for malls and shopping centers to charge you a flat amount each month for your rent and then to add on an extra charge of 2% or 3% of your sales. If you buy a franchise, then the franchisor will probably charge you a franchise fee which is a percentage of your sales. We'll talk about franchises in a later chapter. Right now, you just need to know that it's an arrangement that lets you use another company's name. In a franchise, you might have to set aside a flat percentage of sales to cover advertising costs as well. Many of the fast food franchises charge a franchise fee of 3% or 4% of sales and then require you to put another 3% of sales into advertising.

If you have variable expenses other than inventory costs, then the breakeven and target sales are calculated the same way. We just want the percentage of sales which you get to keep. We divide that into the estimate for your fixed costs or fixed costs plus profit to find the breakeven point or the target sales.

There are actually other expenses which have a variable nature, but which are treated as part of the fixed costs. For example, the electricity bill is made up of two parts. You are charged a flat rate each month plus a charge for each kilowatt of electricity you actually use. That means that part of the electricity bill seems to be a variable cost. We ignore things like that because the electricity bill really won't change with small changes in your sales volume. You have to have the lights on the entire time that the store is open regardless of what you sell. What we really want is to identify those costs that will change with small changes in sales and call those variable. Then we want to know what those variable costs are as a percentage of sales. The rest of the sales we get to keep. If there are no variable costs besides those associated with inventory, then we call the part we get to keep the gross profit margin. If there are additional variable costs, then we call the part we get to keep, the contribution margin.

Just because a business sells services rather than inventory doesn't mean that it has no variable costs. There may still be commissions such as in a real estate agency. The labor costs themselves might be variable as in a construction company. If any costs vary with small changes in sales volume, then we want to identify those as variable costs and turn them into percentages of sales so that we can find the contribution margin.

The danger here is to assume that some kinds of costs *will* vary. For example, let's consider the case of a garage. If you run a garage and you pay the mechanics on an hourly basis, then their salaries may be variable. If you send people home when there is no work to do, or stop their wages when they are not working directly on a repair job, then the wages are a variable expense. However, it must be a real situation. Most garages actually pay mechanics flat salaries even though they may be stated as hourly wages. What actually happens is that the mechanics work harder or slower as necessary to fill up the day and take care of the work that must be done. Since skilled mechanics are hard to find and hard to keep, you can't afford to send them home when business falls off for a short while. That means that their wages are really a fixed cost.

In some businesses, especially those that employ low skilled people, the employees will be sent home or docked if they are not actually working. Fast food restaurants frequently handle their people that way. In other businesses, like construction companies, people are hired for a particular job. When the project is finished, the job is over and wages stop. For those businesses, the wages are variable costs.

The important point is to separate the costs so that the fixed costs will be properly estimated. In fact, if you have any doubts, it's usually better to treat a cost as though it were fixed. The most conservative approach to breakeven analysis is to have more fixed costs rather than less. That way, you are less likely to underestimate the breakeven or target sales. For that reason, if a cost is hard to identify as variable or it's hard to determine what percentage of sales the variable cost will be, just add it to the fixed costs. The only error that can result is an overestimate of the breakeven and target sales. Since it is an estimate that we are making, we're not interested in trying to find a right answer. That can't happen. What we want is to make a forecast that is useful.

ADDITIONAL USES OF CVP ANALYSIS

CVP analysis has many uses other than finding breakeven points or target sales for a new venture. We can use it to help decide whether to open a new location, add a new line of merchandise, drop a line of merchandise, or almost any kind of business decision. The key relationship is simply that cost divided by margin yields sales. Let's say that the sales representative from the telephone company comes into our hardware store. She wants to sell us advertising in the Yellow Pages of the telephone book. For a half page ad on the same page as our listing, it's going to cost $6,000 per year, but they will add it to the telephone bill so that it will be easy to pay. Should we buy the advertising? If we know that our contribution margin is going to be 29%, then we can make an informed decision. Think about how much business the ad will have to bring to us in order to pay for itself. It looks like this:

29% X Added Sales = $6,000
Added Sales = $6,000/.29
Added Sales = $20,690

The calculation says that we will have to gain an extra $20,690 in sales from the yellow pages ad in order to pay for the ad. If we expect to make a profit on the ad, we will have to sell more than that. If the average customer spends $20, that would mean that the ad would have to bring us 1,034 customers whom we would not get without the advertisement ($20,690/$20). Do you think that is likely to happen? If you have doubts, then buying the advertising will not be a wise decision.

The key concept is that of added sales, or incremental sales. We can think of the additional expenditures in isolation. We ignore the established costs and the established breakeven point. We examine the added costs alone and look for additional sales required to cover those costs.

GENERALIZING FROM THE EXAMPLE

In the hardware store example, we demonstrated how CVP analysis works and how it can be applied to a small business. That illustration was somewhat simplistic to help you get the big picture of how CVP works and how it is used. We may be faced with using CVP in a more complex situation. In that case, we need to understand the relationship between costs, volume and profit to use the tool properly. In the following sections, we will examine the elements and their relationship.

FIXED COSTS

We said that a fixed cost did not change as sales change. In reality, no costs are absolutely fixed. Everything changes. To be more exact, we should define a *fixed cost* as one which is not expected to fluctuate with changes in sales volume over a relevant range of activity. Consider, for example, the salary for a supervisor in a manufacturing firm. That salary would be a fixed expense because it will not vary as sales vary. Now the aggregate of salaries for all line supervisors will also be a fixed cost but only so long as sales do not drop below the point at which one of the shifts would be shut down to save money or above the point at which another shift would have to be added to produce the volume necessary. All fixed costs are like that. If we think about fixed costs in the form of a graph in which the costs are related to the volume of sales, it would look like Table 1.

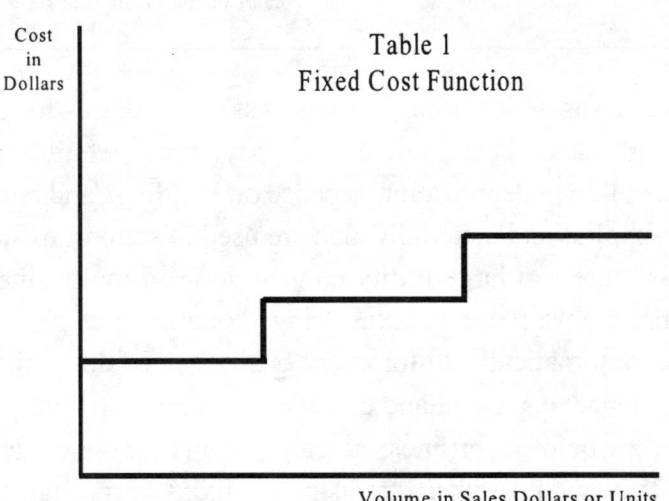

Cost in Dollars

Table 1
Fixed Cost Function

Volume in Sales Dollars or Units

The graph shows a step function, so called because of its appearance, and demonstrates that fixed costs cannot be changed in small pieces. We cannot hire 1/4th of a supervisor or buy ½ of a machine.

The range of expected sales activity is usually not a large change from the established sales level. That is, we do not normally face a situation in which we expect to lose a large percentage of sales, nor one in which we expect our sales to double or triple. Therefore, the expected activity frequently falls on a single stair step of the fixed cost function and the rest of the graph can be ignored. This expected level of activity is called the ***relevant range***. Table 2 shows how the relevant range can be used to make fixed costs look like a straight line. This is done for simplicity, but remember, if the assumption of activity within the range is invalid, or if the relevant range of activity falls across a step in the fixed cost function, then much of the breakeven analysis must be changed to reflect the real expectations.

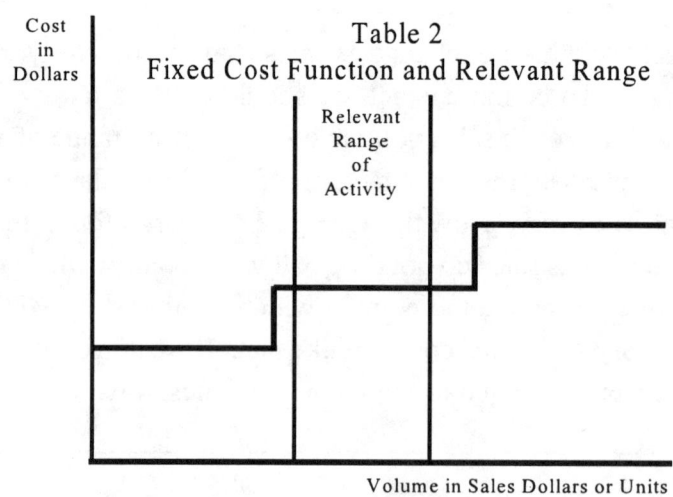

Table 2
Fixed Cost Function and Relevant Range

Examples of fixed costs which occur in a business are: salaries for officers, office workers, and others paid on a straight salary basis; rent or lease payments on buildings or equipment, unless that lease is tied to sales volume; depreciation expense on buildings and equipment, unless it is tied to units of production; supplies and material which are used to support office, sales and production efforts; utilities, unless there is a large utility consumption in the business based on volume of production; insurance premiums, property taxes, fringe benefits, etc. Notice that a lot of expenses can be fixed, but are not automatically so for every business. To determine fixed costs, an owner must examine every cost which can occur and consider whether it will vary as sales do. Imagining every cost which can occur before a business actually begins can be difficult. Most people add a hedge factor, because they would rather overestimate fixed costs than underestimate them for breakeven purposes. The best approach is to generate a range of fixed cost forecasts.

VARIABLE COSTS

As we mentioned, *variable costs* are those which do vary directly with sales levels. For a retailer or wholesaler, these can be easy to identify because they will be costs of the inventory, freight expenses for the inventory, sales commissions and the like. For a service firm, there may be very little in the way of variable costs if the people providing the services are paid on a salary basis. If they are paid hourly, or by the job, then most of the expenses may be variable. For a manufacturing firm, the variable costs may be more difficult to identify. These costs will *not* generally be perfectly proportionate to sales because of *economies of scale* as volume increases. Remember that there will be price breaks for purchasing larger quantities of items. Table 3 displays a graph of variable costs.

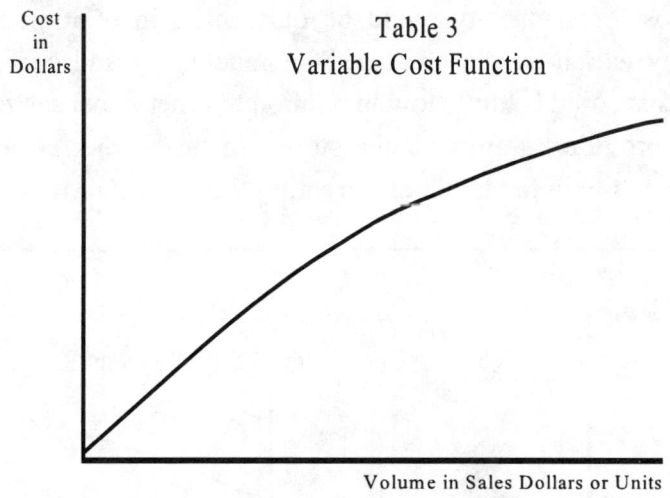

Table 3
Variable Cost Function

Cost in Dollars

Volume in Sales Dollars or Units

Notice that the cost curve is generally so gradual in terms of its change that over the relevant range of activity, it is practically a straight line. This allows us to pretend that the line is straight just as we did for fixed costs. Table 4 displays that assumption. As was the case for fixed costs, each expense which a business experiences must be analyzed to identify the variable elements.

In many cases a cost behaves as a variable cost but is so insignificant in amount that it is not worth the effort of tracing the cost to sales or keeping the records necessary to be able to treat the cost as variable. An example might be the cost of lubricants for the machines in a manufacturing company. Clearly, such costs will be affected by the amount of run time of the machines which is a function of sales. Nevertheless, if the amount of fluctuation of the cost is extremely low in relation to other variable costs, then little value will accrue to its capture and treatment as a variable cost. In such cases, it is generally wiser to treat the cost as though it were fixed.

MIXED COSTS

Many costs really have elements of both a fixed and variable nature. These costs are called *mixed costs* and examples include rent when it consists of a minimum amount plus a percentage of sales, utilities expense when a minimum fee and a usage charge occur and expenses of that nature. Mixed costs are especially hard to allocate to either the fixed or variable cost pools.

There are two ways to handle mixed costs. The first method requires the costs to be decomposed into a fixed portion and a variable portion. This method should be used when the mixed costs are significant when compared to other costs in the business. The second method is to simply classify the cost as fixed or variable. This method should be used when the cost is insignificant in amount when compared to other costs. The choice of fixed or variable classification is purely arbitrary and will have little impact on the breakeven if the costs are truly insignificant. Remember that the significance is not decided in terms of dollars, but in relation to other expenses. For example, the mixed cost of electricity could be quite high in relation to other expenses in a manufacturing company which uses a great deal of machinery and equipment which consume electricity. That same cost could be quite low in relation to other expenses for a retailer whose only use of electricity is to provide lighting for the store. In the former case, decomposition of the expense would be wise, while in the latter case treating the cost as fixed would be appropriate.

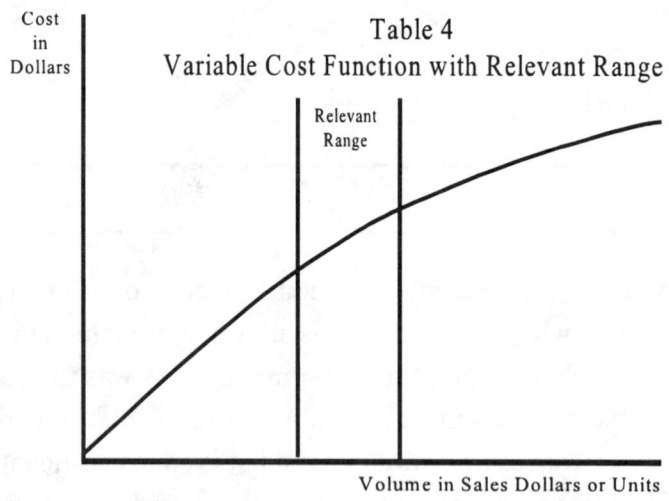

Cost in Dollars

Table 4
Variable Cost Function with Relevant Range

Relevant Range

Volume in Sales Dollars or Units

REVENUE

Revenues are also a function of sales volume, but, like variable costs, the relationship is not perfect. The more you sell, the more revenues you will have. However, just as economies of scale result in lower variable costs as volume increases, lower unit prices occur as volume goes up and purchasers receive volume discounts and economies of scale. That means that the true relationship when plotted on the cost/volume graph is a curve which is slightly concave in an upward direction. Table 5 displays a graph for revenue. The relevant range of activity is also shown on the graph.

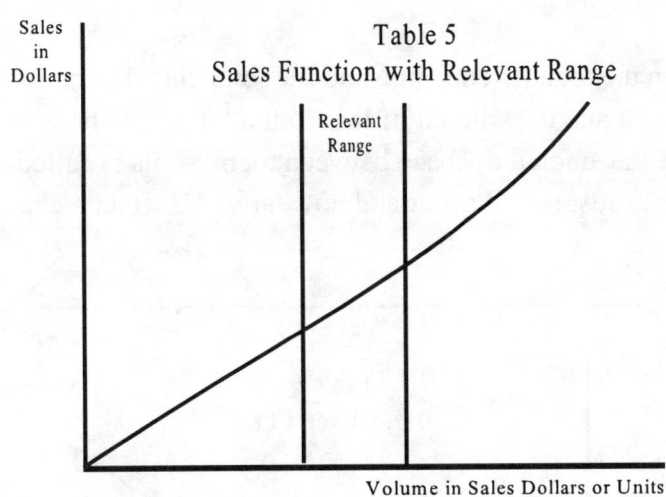

Table 5
Sales Function with Relevant Range

Using the same reasoning as we applied to variable costs, we can treat the revenue function as though it were a straight line since it virtually is straight over the relevant range of activity. This simplifying assumption can permit the graphing of all three curves on a single chart.

THE BREAKEVEN CHART

Table 6 shows the three lines superimposed. This is the classical illustration of the cost, volume, profit relationship. The graph assumes that the fixed cost line is straight and runs across the entire range of volume as a flat line. The same assumption applies to the variable cost line and the sales line. Notice that the variable cost line begins at the point at which the fixed cost line intersects the cost axis. This means that the total costs appear on one line. The variable costs are actually the amount between the total cost line and the fixed cost line. Now, we have one line for total costs and one line for total revenue. The point of intersection between the two line is the **breakeven point** for the company.

We know that these lines are not truly straight, and we know that they really do not run across the entire range of sales volume as they are depicted in the breakeven chart. The reality is that the relationship between the revenues and the costs look very much like the chart displays if the activity level falls within the relevant range. Outside that range, the breakeven chart is completely useless. Nevertheless, the graphical portrait of the relationship does help to explain the function. At a glance, we can see what happens as sales volume rises, moving to the right along the graph. We can also see what happens when sales volume falls, moving to the left along the graph.

OPERATING LEVERAGE

The area between the total revenue line and the total cost line is the amount of profit to the right of the breakeven point and the amount of loss to the left of the breakeven point. The slope of the two lines will dictate the amount of space between them. This is called *operating leverage* and displays how fast profits or losses will occur and how large the effect a change in volume will have on profits or losses.

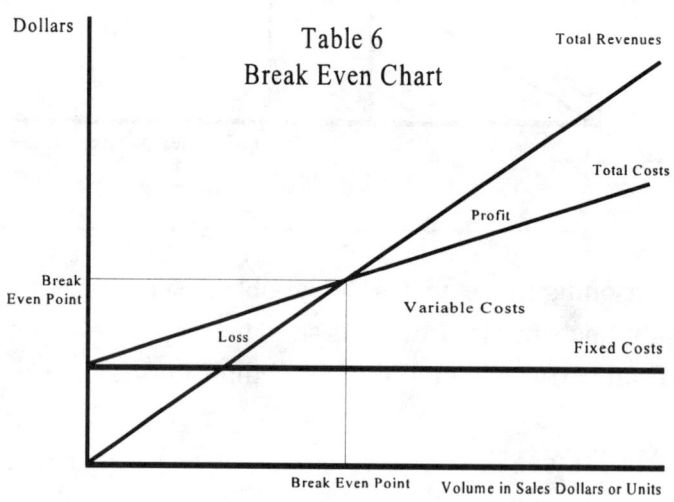

Table 6
Break Even Chart

In general, the larger the proportion of variable costs which a firm has, the lower will be its operating leverage. The higher the proportion of fixed costs which a firm has, the higher will be its operating leverage. A business with a high operating leverage will reap substantially greater benefit from an increase in volume than will a firm with a low operating leverage. There is a down side to this relationship since high operating leverage will also create larger losses faster if a decrease in volume occurs. The reverse situation holds for businesses with lower operating leverage. Table 7 displays a breakeven chart for a company with high operating leverage. Table 8 displays a breakeven chart for a company with low operating leverage. The two types of firms are frequently referred to as *capital intensive* or *labor intensive*, since labor tends to be a variable cost and capital tends to be a fixed cost.

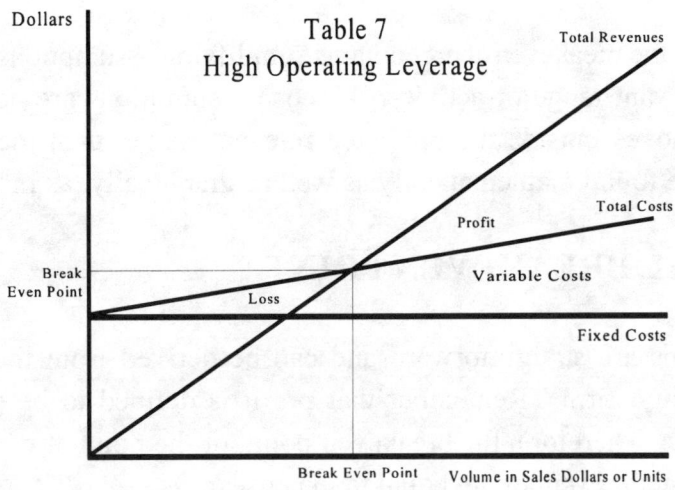

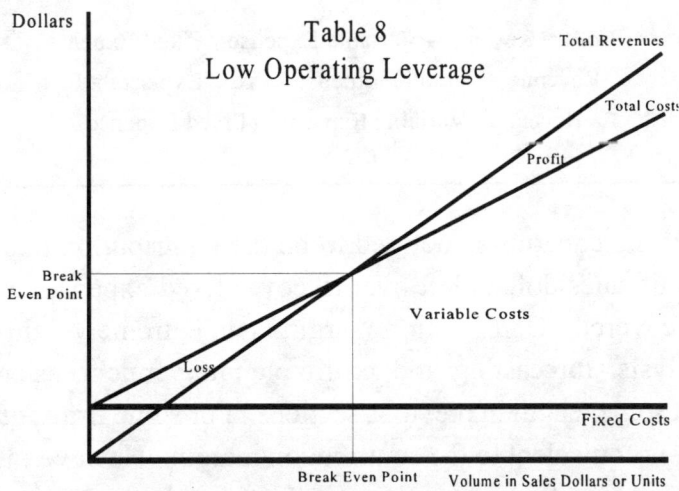

A lower operating leverage carries less risk. Of course, risk and return usually occur in a trade-off relationship. That is, higher risks are associated with higher returns while lower risks are associated with lower returns. That is the case with operating leverage. The higher leveraged firm has more risk because its fixed costs must be covered whether or not sales are made and it will incur greater losses if sales fall below the breakeven point. However, after the breakeven point has been reached, the higher leveraged firm will produce more profits, faster. Nevertheless, for a new business venture, lower risk and more flexibility are desirable. Consequently, most small business start-ups should choose to structure themselves with a relatively low operating leverage. This is accomplished by committing to as small a level of fixed costs as possible, even though the resulting variable costs are higher as a result. After a business is firmly established, it can always increase its operating leverage.

Remember that the breakeven chart contains simplifying assumptions about cost and revenue behavior over the relevant range of activity. If those assumptions are not valid or if the actual volume of the firm moves outside the predicted relevant range, then the chart is invalid. The breakeven point can be found mathematically as well as graphically, as in the hardware example.

MATHEMATICAL BREAKEVEN POINT

The calculations are straightforward and can be derived from the relationship of costs, revenues and profits in a firm. Remember that profit is defined to be the difference between revenues and expenses. Therefore, the breakeven point, or the point at which profit is equal to 0, must be the point at which revenues are equal to expenses.

Profit = Revenue - Variable Expense - Fixed Expense

Revenue - Variable Expense - Fixed Expense = 0

Revenue - Variable Expense = Fixed Expense

The left side of the equation is defined to be the contribution margin. The ***contribution margin*** is the amount of sales dollars left over to cover fixed expenses and provide profits after variable expenses are covered. Contribution margin is an extremely valuable concept because it makes breakeven analysis, forecasting and profit planning much easier. We have discussed contribution margins at some length in previous sections. For some firms, gross margin, or the sales less cost of goods sold, is equivalent to the contribution margin. However, that is not automatically the case. If a retailer or wholesaler has no other variable costs in the business except for inventory, then gross margin and contribution margin will be the same. If there are variable expenses, like sales commissions, then they must also be considered to find contribution margin. In a service company there is no cost of goods sold, so contribution margins are much higher; in some service companies, they are 100%!

Contribution margin is the difference between revenues and variable expenses. Look what happens if we convert the contribution margin equation. Remember that contribution margin divided by revenue is equal to the contribution margin ratio. So, we divide both sides of the contribution margin equation by revenues. Now, we substitute contribution margin ratio for the term on the left side. You see that substitution in the third step of the following calculations:

Contribution Margin = Revenue - Variable Expense

Contribution Margin/Revenue = (Revenue-Variable Expense)/Revenue

Contribution Margin Ratio = (Revenue - Variable Expense)/Revenue

Contribution Margin Ratio X Revenue = Revenue - Variable Expense

These calculations tell us that at the point where profits are equal to zero, the difference between revenues and variable expenses is equal to the contribution margin ratio multiplied by the revenues. These are the revenues at the point of breakeven; the breakeven sales volume. This means that breakeven revenues multiplied by the contribution margin ratio will always equal the contribution margin or the difference between revenues and variable expenses. Keeping this in mind, we can substitute contribution margin in the breakeven equation and solve for the breakeven revenues.

Revenue - Variable Expense = Fixed Expense

Contribution Margin = Revenue - Variable Expense

Contribution Margin = Fixed Expense

Breakeven Revenues X Contribution Margin Ratio = Fixed Expense

Breakeven Revenues = Fixed Expense/Contribution Margin Ratio

Usually, the breakeven point is preferred in terms of sales or revenues because most firms have a mix of products. However, a breakeven point in terms of units is sometimes desired. A firm may deal in a single product or a calculation may be needed for one division or department which deals in one product. The breakeven point can be converted to units by dividing by the price per unit or by direct calculation with a slightly different formula. Remember that the contribution margin is equal to fixed costs at the breakeven point. If we convert to the contribution margin per unit, then the equation looks like this:

Contribution Margin = Fixed Cost

Sales in Units X Contribution Margin per Unit = Fixed Cost

Breakeven Sales in Units = Fixed Cost/Contribution Margin per Unit

Actually, either breakeven point can be converted into the other. Breakeven sales can be found by multiplying breakeven units by the selling price per unit, or breakeven units can be found by dividing breakeven sales by the selling price per unit.

TARGET SALES

As we discussed in the hardware store illustration, in cost, volume, profit analysis, we are frequently not interested in the point at which an operation will breakeven. Rather, we are interested in the volume required to produce a particular profit. If we remember that the breakeven points are simply the points at which profits are equal to zero, then the formulae can be generalized to include profits in the calculation.

The formulae for target sales are exactly like the ones for breakeven points. There is no need to memorize two sets, since the breakeven calculations are a special case of the target equations in which the desired profit is 0. The advantage of the more general formulae is that it can be used to find a breakeven point or to determine the amount of sales required to achieve any level of profit which might be desired.

As was the case with the breakeven point, target sales can be expressed in units by dividing the result of the target sales calculations by the selling price per unit. Target Sales can be calculated directly by using the contribution margin per unit instead of the contribution margin ratio.

Here are the relationships:

$$\text{Profit} = \text{Revenue} - \text{Variable Expense} - \text{Fixed Expense}$$

$$\text{Revenue} - \text{Variable Expense} - \text{Fixed Expense} = \text{Profit}$$

$$\text{Revenue} - \text{Variable Expense} = \text{Fixed Expense} + \text{Profit}$$

$$\text{Contribution Margin} = \text{Fixed Expense} + \text{Profit}$$

$$\text{Target Sales X Contribution Margin Ratio} = \text{Fixed Expense} + \text{Target Profit}$$

$$\text{Target Sales} = (\text{Fixed Expense} + \text{Target Profit})/\text{Contribution Margin Ratio}$$

$$\text{Target Sales in Units X Contribution Margin per Unit} = \text{Fixed Expense} + \text{Target Profit}$$

$$\text{Target Sales in Units} = (\text{Fixed Expense} + \text{Target Profit})/\text{Contribution Margin per Unit}$$

COST, VOLUME, PROFIT FLEXIBILITY

The CVP formulae are extremely flexible. The equations which we have derived for breakeven and target sales are actually functions of cost, volume, profit relationships. These relationships can be for an entire business, for a division of a business, for a department of a business, for a product of a business, for a sales territory, etc. All that is required is the capture or estimation of revenues and costs for the entity, area, division, or product under analysis. The CVP relationships can be based on forecasts for use in planning or can be calculated using historic results for use in analyzing and evaluating performance. The difference is simply in whether the numbers used are actual or forecasts. The relationships can be calculated for any time period: one year, one month, one quarter, etc., by simply insuring that the numbers fit into the appropriate time horizon. In short, cost, volume, profit analysis, of which breakeven analysis is a special case, is one of the most powerful planning and management tools available to any business regardless of its size.

ASSUMPTIONS OF THE MODEL

We have already discussed the fact that breakeven analysis or CVP analysis assumes that revenue and cost curves are linear. That is, that the curves are straight lines. The amount of error which results from that assumption is generally small so long as the curves approximate a linear function over the relevant range of activity and so long as activity remains within that range. The formulae will yield answers whether the assumptions are violated or not. That is the problem! Unless an owner examines the numbers and forecasts carefully, he or she may never realize that the results of analysis are invalid!

There are other assumptions incorporated into the CVP models. Foremost among those are the assumptions that product mix will be constant. *Product mix* or *sales mix* refers to the proportions of sales which are represented by the various products or services which a business offers. Since few companies have only a single product or service, product mix assumptions are a major limiting factor on CVP analysis. Specifically, the models assume that if three products make up the sales, then the percentage which each product constitutes of the total sales volume will remain constant over time and over changes in aggregate sales. This assumption will almost always be invalid. Nevertheless, as long as there are no major shifts in product mix over the period under analysis, the results of CVP analysis will be valuable as the amount of error will be not be major.

Additional assumptions of the model are that sales prices per unit will be constant over time and over changes in volume as will variable costs per unit. That seldom, if ever, is true for any business. Also, the models assume completeness. That is, the analysis assumes that all costs and all revenues have been captured and have been measured accurately or, if forecasts are used, that the forecasts are accurate and complete. From a practical perspective, that assumption is also frequently invalid.

USE OF THE MODEL

The solution to the problems with erroneous assumptions is twofold. First, multiple calculations should be made using a variety of bases and estimates for the revenues and costs. The range of answers which results will not only indicate the area into which actual performance is likely to fall, but will show the sensitivity of the model.

Understanding sensitivity is particularly important. If a large change in the CVP answer occurs when a small change is made in one of the inputs, then the model is particularly sensitive to that item. Determining which numbers have the greatest impact on the results is called ***sensitivity analysis***. Owners must be especially careful of errors in items or estimates to which the model is especially sensitive.

The second approach to minimizing problems with erroneous assumptions is so simple that it is frequently overlooked. It is simply to be aware of the limitations of the model. One should never say, *My breakeven is...* One should say, *My breakeven appears to lie between ... and ...* If owners would continually keep the limitations of CVP models in mind, then they would be less likely to make mistakes in using the results of the models. Actually, this is a good idea regardless of the tools being used.

There are very few *facts* in business. Almost everything involves estimates of one type or another. In that way a business cannot be quantitatively run. The way small businesses operate, little can be expected to be perfectly accurate or perfectly representative. Consequently, a healthy dose of doubt about all numbers is a valuable asset.

On the following pages are four different examples of breakeven analysis. The first example is a manufacturing firm which handles a single product. The second illustration is a retail start-up in which the contribution margin is unknown. The third example is a service company. The fourth example is a manufacturer producing three products under an estimated sales mix.

Breakeven Analysis, Example 1

We are considering a start-up of a small manufacturing firm which will produce a single product. We have prepared engineering specifications for the product, and estimates for operational costs. Our planning and budgeting efforts have resulted in the following estimates for the various costs of operation and production:

Selling Price per Unit:		$12.50
Fixed Costs for the First Year:		$125,000
Variable Costs per Unit:	Direct Labor	$ 4.95
	Raw Material	2.35
	Variable Overhead	2.20
	Total Variable Costs:	9.50
Contribution Margin:	Selling Price per Unit	12.50
	Variable Cost per Unit	-9.50
	Contribution Margin per Unit	$ 3.00

Contribution Margin Ratio   =   Contribution Margin per Unit/Selling Price per Unit

= $3.00/$12.50 = .24 or 24%

Breakeven Points:

Breakeven Point in Sales = Fixed Costs/Contribution Margin Ratio

= $125,000/.24

= $ 520,833

Breakeven Point in Units = Fixed Costs/Contribution Margin per Unit

= $125,000/$3.00

= 41,667 Units

In order to make $25,000 in profit:

Target Sales in Dollars = (Fixed Costs+Target Profit)/Contribution Margin Ratio

= ($125,000+$25,000)/.24

= $ 625,000

Target Sales in Units = (Fixed Costs+Target Profit)/Contribution Margin per Unit

= ($125,000+$25,000)/$3.00

= 50,000 Units

Breakeven Analysis, Example 2

We are considering the start-up of a small hardware retail store. A small retailer of this type has insignificant variable costs outside of the cost of sales because there are no sales commissions. That means that the gross profit margin is virtually the same as the contribution margin. Further, since the hardware industry is well established, pricing and inventory costs can be expected to be outside our control. That means that gross profits should be virtually the same for most small hardware stores. Consequently, we can use the industry average gross profit margin ratio as a proxy for the contribution margin ratio. We found this average in *Robert Morris Associates Statement Studies.* Our planning and budgeting has resulted in the following estimates for the first year:

Fixed Costs for the First Year: $ 72,000

Industry Average Gross Profit Margin: 35%

Breakeven Calculation:

Breakeven Point in Sales = Fixed Costs/Contribution Margin Ratio

= $72,000/.35

= $ 205,714

In order to make $20,000 in profit:

Target Sales in Dollars = (Fixed Costs+Target Profit)/Contribution Margin Ratio

= ($72,000+$20,000)/.35

= $ 262,857

Breakeven Analysis, Example 3

A start-up of a small service company is being proposed. This company will be a real estate broker. Commissions which the firm earns will be 6% of selling prices, but those constitute gross sales for the business. The agents will receive ½ of the sales commission and there are no other significant variable costs, consequently the contribution margin ratio will be 50%. Planning has resulted in forecasts of rent, utilities, advertising, clerical salaries, totaling, $57,000. The owner wants to be able to take a $30,000 draw out of the business.

Breakeven Calculation:

Breakeven Point in Sales = Fixed Costs/Contribution Margin Ratio

= $57,000/.5

= $ 114,000

In order to make $30,000 in profit:

Target Sales in Dollars = (Fixed Costs+Target Profit)/Contribution Margin Ratio

= ($57,000+$30,000)/.5

= $ 174,000

Property Sales Required at 6% Commissions:

Breakeven Sales/.06 = $114,000/.06 = $1,900,000

Target Sales/.06 = $174,000/.06 = $2,900,000

Breakeven Analysis, Example 4

We are considering a start-up of a small manufacturing firm which will produce three different products. We have engineering specifications for each product. Our planning and budgeting efforts resulted in the following estimates for the various costs of operation and production for the first year:

		Product 1	Product 2	Product 3
Fixed Costs:				$250,000
Variable Costs:				
	Direct Labor	$5.25	$4.00	$4.75
	Raw Material	2.46	2.03	2.19
	Variable Overhead	2.00	1.75	1.90
	Total Variable Costs	$9.71	$7.78	$8.84
Selling Price per Unit:		$14.50	$12.75	$13.00
Contribution Margin per Unit:				
	Selling Price per Unit:	$14.50	$12.75	$13.00
	Variable Costs per Unit:	-9.71	-7.78	-8.84
	Contribution Margin per Unit:	$ 4.79	$ 4.97	$ 4.16

Product Mix Estimate:

Percentage of Sales from Each Product:	40%	30%	30%

Contribution Margin Ratios:

Contribution Margin per Unit/Selling Price	4.79/14.50	4.97/12.75	4.16/13.00
Contribution Margin Ratios:	33%	39%	32%

Weighted Average Contribution Margin:

Contribution Margin Ratios X Sales Percentage: $(.33 \times .40) + (.39 \times .30) + (.32 \times .30) = .345 = 34.5\%$

Breakeven Calculation:

$$\begin{aligned} \text{Breakeven Point in Sales} &= \text{Fixed Costs/Contribution Margin Ratio} \\ &= \$250,000/.345 \\ &= \$724,638 \end{aligned}$$

In order to make $30,000 in profit:

$$\begin{aligned} \text{Target Sales in Dollars} &= \text{(Fixed Costs+Target Profit)/Contribution Margin Ratio} \\ &= (\$250,000+\$30,000)/.345 \\ &= \$811,594 \end{aligned}$$

CVP ANALYSIS FOR THE NEW VENTURE

One of the pre-venture planning steps is the forecasting of expenses. In order to perform breakeven analysis for the start-up, those expenses must not only be identified and forecast, but classified as fixed or variable. Any mixed expenses must be disposed of, and selling prices must be developed. Once that is done, breakeven analysis and the more general CVP analysis can be performed for the new venture.

Variable expenses can either be predicted on a per unit basis or in the aggregate based on total expected sales. Either approach will permit the calculation of the contribution margin ratio. Fixed expenses must always be predicted in the aggregate since they can never occur on a per unit basis. Aggregate sales can be predicted or average unit selling prices, whichever is preferred. If unit selling prices and unit variable costs are used, then one must be careful of sales mix problems. When more than one product or service is involved, an average unit contribution margin must be calculated which takes into consideration the sales mix. It is also possible to use an industry average contribution margin if data is not available. This can be especially valuable when planning a start-up, which has no history upon which to draw.

CVP analysis for a new venture involves the calculation of the range of breakeven points which are deemed possible as a result of the planning, determining whether the target market area will support the required level of sales, and deciding whether the firm will be able to garner the required sales. The last decision is frequently a subjective one, but the proportion of the market which will have to be captured will certainly influence any lenders who may be approached. The best situation is one in which only a very small percentage of the potential market is required for breakeven. If a substantial proportion is needed, the risk is higher because it will be more difficult to wrest away the business from entrenched competition.

One question which frequently comes up during breakeven analysis is what happens when a brand new product or service is being offered so the size of the market cannot be determined. Actually, that happens very infrequently because most products and services will have near substitutes if not direct competitors and the market for the substitutes can be used as a proxy. In that rare situation where the offering is completely new and without substitutes, the evaluation becomes completely subjective. Nevertheless, the higher the breakeven point, the more difficult it will be to convince a lender or investor that the venture is viable. That will be true in every situation. The lower the breakeven point, the less risk is involved in the venture.

CVP ANALYSIS: PLANNING AID

CVP analysis is not just useful for assessing the viability of a new business venture. It can be a useful aspect of planning in an ongoing operation. It can be used to evaluate ideas and plans for new market areas, products, departments, divisions, plants or services. It can be used as an aid to budgeting as target sales can be generated from desired profit levels. It can be used in pricing decisions or in budgeting fixed costs. It can be used in monitoring and evaluating performance. It can be used to support credit requests or investment proposals. It can be used to identify the effects of changes in prices and costs on a firm's profitability.

There are three examples of the application of CVP on the following pages. These examples show some of the flexibility of the concept. The first example concerns setting prices for a new venture. The second example concerns changing prices as a result of increases in fixed and variable costs. The third example concerns target sales to produce a level of profits which is expressed as a percentage of sales.

CVP analysis is built around the concept of contribution margin ratio which is one of the most important from a small business perspective which we can identify. If the accounting system is properly structured, a regular report can be prepared each month depicting the contribution margin ratio for a firm. Few tools can be as useful for monitoring performance, for giving advance warning of impending problems, or for comparing products, departments and divisions to each other. A strong business is one in which the contribution margin ratio slowly grows over time. A stable business is one in which the ratio is constant. A declining ratio is an indication of potentially serious problems unless action is taken.

Few financial tools are as versatile as cost, volume, profit analysis. A prospective small business owner would be well advised to master the techniques.

CVP Analysis, Example 1

A firm is faced with setting prices in a market in which the sales volume in units can be predicted with a high level of confidence. Planning and budgeting efforts have produced estimates for the various costs of operation and variable cost for producing the product. The fixed costs are estimated to be $175,000 for the first year, and variable costs are estimated to be $125 per unit. The firm believes that 5,000 units of the product can be sold if the price does not exceed the level established by its competitors, which is $250. The firm desires a profit of $200,000. What should be its selling price?

Target Sales in Units = (Fixed Costs + Target Profit)/Contribution Margin per Unit

Contribution Margin per Unit = Selling Price per Unit - Variable Cost per Unit

Target Sales in Units = (Fixed Costs + Target Profit)/(Selling Price per Unit - Variable Cost per Unit)

5,000 Units = ($175,000 + $200,000)/(Selling Price - $125)

5,000 Units = $375,000/(Selling Price - $125)

5,000(Selling Price - $125) = $375,000

Selling Price - $125 = $375,000/5,000

Selling Price - $125 = $75

Selling Price = $75 + $125

Selling Price = $200 per Unit

CVP Analysis indicates that the firm can undercut the established price substantially and still achieve its profit goal. Before finalizing a price, a range of values for the selling price should be calculated using the best, worst and most probable estimates for fixed and variable costs.

CVP Analysis, Example 2

A firm which has established fixed and variable costs expects to experience an increase in both over the next year. The firm is considering a price increase to offset those increases. The established costs and selling prices are as follow:

Fixed Costs:	$225,000	Selling Price per Unit:	$330
Variable Costs per Unit:	$215	Established Sales Volume:	3,000 units

Fixed costs are expected to rise by $5,500 and variable costs are expected to increase by $5 per unit. What price increase will be required in order to maintain the established profit level?

Contribution Margin per Unit = Selling Price - Variable Cost = $330 - $215 = $115

Total Contribution Margin = Sales Volume in Units X Contribution Margin = 3,000($115) = $345,000

Established Profit = Total Contribution Margin - Fixed Costs = $345,000 - $225,000 = $120,000

New Fixed Costs = Old Fixed Costs + Increase in Fixed Costs = $225,000 + $5,500 = $230,500

New Variable Costs = Old Variable Cost + Increase in Variable Cost = $215 + $5 = $230

Target Sales in Units = (Fixed Costs + Target Profit)/Contribution Margin per Unit

Contribution Margin per Unit = Selling Price per Unit - Variable Cost per Unit

Target Sales in Units = (Fixed Costs + Target Profit)/(Selling Price per Unit - Variable Cost per Unit)

3,000 Units = ($230,500 + $120,000)/(Selling Price - $230)

3,000 Units = $350,500/(Selling Price - $230)

3,000(Selling Price - $230) = $350,500

Selling Price - $230 = $375,000/3,000

Selling Price - $230 = $116.83

Selling Price = $116.83 + $230

Selling Price = $346.83 per Unit

CVP Analysis, Example 3

A small business stocks a large number of inventory items. Its contribution margin ratio has held stable at 30%. Its fixed costs are $325,000 per year. If it wishes to make a profit equal to 10% of its sales, how much must it sell?

Target Sales = (Fixed Cost + Target Profit)/Contribution Margin Ratio

Target Sales = ($325,000 + .10 X Target Sales)/.30

.30 X Target Sales = $325,000 = .10 X Target Sales

.30 X Target Sales - .10 X Target Sales = $325,000

.20 X Target Sales = $325,000

Target Sales = $325,000/.20

Target Sales = $1,625,000

SUMMARY

There are three steps involved in breakeven analysis: estimating the fixed costs; estimating the variable costs; and calculating the breakeven point. Fixed costs are those which are not expected to fluctuate over the relevant range of activity. They include such items as salaries, rent or lease payments, utilities, supplies, insurance, property taxes, etc.

Variable costs vary directly with sales volume and include such items as inventory expense, freight expense and sales commissions.

Mixed costs are those which have elements of both fixed and variable nature. These may be treated as fixed or variable costs or decomposed into their fixed and variable components.

The relevant range of activity is established by the upper and lower levels of sales volume which are expected to occur. One of the limiting assumptions of CVP analysis is that revenues, variable costs and fixed costs are linear functions within the relevant range. Revenue is a function of sales volume.

Cost, volume, profit analysis, of which breakeven and target sales analysis are special cases, is one of the most powerful financial and planning tools available to the management of any business regardless of its size. It is especially valuable to a small business in which mistakes in judgement can be disastrous. Assumptions of the CVP model are that revenue and cost curves are linear, that the product mix is constant, and that sales prices per unit will be constant over time as will variable costs per unit. However, these assumptions may be false.

The solution to the problem of erroneous assumptions is twofold. First, one should prepare multiple calculations employing a variety of bases and estimates for revenues and costs. This will result in a range of solutions and will also reveal the sensitivity of the model to changes in the various inputs. Recognition of the relative sensitivity of factors will provide owners with a better understanding of the potential effects of errors in the inputs.

The second approach to minimizing problems with erroneous assumptions is so simple that it is frequently overlooked. Owners should simply be aware of the limitations of the model. Such awareness will prevent blind dependence on the solutions to equations which are really meant to be aids to decision making, not decision values.

CVP Analysis has applications beyond those of assessing feasibility in new venture creation. It can be useful in planning in an ongoing operation, in evaluating ideas and plans for new market areas, products, departments, divisions, plants or services. It can be used in budgeting, pricing, monitoring and evaluating performance, supporting credit and investment proposals and in identifying effects of price, cost and volume changes on profitability. CVP is perhaps the most important tool available to a small business owner.

QUESTIONS, EXERCISES AND CASES

Questions:

1.   What are the steps in breakeven analysis?
2.   Distinguish between fixed, variable and mixed costs.
3.   How would you handle a mixed cost?
4.   What is operating leverage and what is its significance for a small business?
5.   How are target sales predicted?
6.   What are some of the applications of CVP analysis?
7.   What are the assumptions of the CVP models?
8.   What is sensitivity analysis and why is it valuable?

Exercises:

1.   A start-up of a small boutique is being considered. There are virtually no variable costs expected beyond those associated with the inventory. Planning has resulted in the following estimates:
     Fixed Costs for the First Year: $40,000
     Industry Average Gross Profit Margin: 50%
     Calculate the breakeven point in sales dollars.
     Calculate the target sales necessary to produce a profit of $20,000.

2.   A start-up of a manufacturing firm which will produce three products is being considered.
     Planning has resulted in the following estimates for the first year:
     Fixed Costs: $350,000

Variable Costs per Unit:	Product 1	Product 2	Product 3
Direct Labor per Unit	$5.25	$6.00	$4.75
Raw Material per Unit	2.46	3.03	2.19
Variable Overhead per Unit	2.00	3.75	1.90
Selling Price per Unit	15.50	22.75	13.00

What is the contribution margin per unit?
If the firm expects an equal proportion of each product to be sold, what will be the breakeven point in sales dollars? What will be the breakeven point in units? How many units of each product will be sold?
If the sales mix is expected to be 25% of product 1, 40% of product 2 and 35% of product 3, what sales level will be required to produce a target profit of $30,000?

CASE

Marilyn is considering opening a small boutique with unusual gift items. Everyone loves her original ideas for parties and meetings. But she is very concerned about the risk. Marilyn has a friend who started a bridal shop several years ago and she almost lost her home as a result of its failure. Everyone had thought a bridal shop was a good idea as well, but most of her friends didn't need her services and neither did enough people in her small town. She had used her house as collateral and when the sales didn't come, the bank wanted its collateral. She had finally worked out a payment plan for the business, but it was taking her ten years to pay for her mistake.

Marilyn did not want the same costly mistake to happen to her. She had heard from a consultant who presented a seminar on starting businesses that you should always perform a breakeven analysis before investing your money, so she decided to perform one.

First she considered all of the fixed expenses for the first year:

Lease (store)	$ 8,400.00
All utilities	2,400.00
Insurance	1,200.00
Salaries (self)	20,000.00
Fringe benefits	3,000.00
Miscellaneous	1,200.00
15% of salaries	
Total Fixed Costs	$ 36,200.00

Variable Cost Estimates for the First Year:

Total Variable Cost Ratio	64%
(From *Robert Morris Associates*)	
Contribution Margin Ratio	36%

Calculate the breakeven for Marilyn and advise her as to whether she should open her boutique.

Are there fixed costs which Marilyn may have overlooked? If so, what are they? (Hint: How many hours do you think the shop should be open? Can Marilyn handle that alone?) Recalculate the breakeven using the new fixed costs. What is your recommendation after the recalculation? What could Marilyn do to make her dream come true?

CHAPTER SIX

BUDGETING TOOLS

CHAPTER OBJECTIVES

Upon completion of this chapter you should be able to:

- Explain the value of budgeting;

- Identify the key aspects of financial performance;

- Explain how budgets serve as objectives and controls;

- Describe why continuous budgeting is important;

- Explain the concept of sensitivity analysis and its role in budgeting;

- Generate a sales, purchases, expense, cash flow, and capital budget;

- Discuss the value of pro forma income statements; and,

- List the factors involved in buying or leasing for capital investments.

BUDGETING TOOLS

INTRODUCTION

Budgeting is the process of predicting costs, expenses, revenues, cash flows or investments. It requires us to look into the future and make guesses about what we expect to happen and then to make plans accordingly. The architect who is building a house must first predict what the house will look like based on the land which is available for its construction. The land will constrain the house both in size and appearance as the architect strives to make the house complement the site. After the house has been visualized, then the requirements for its construction are laid out; this is the model. Finally, costs of that construction are estimated. There is an additional step which is seldom included because it is so obvious. The costs have to be examined to determine whether we can afford to build the house. When we apply this process to business, all of the financial flows which are being budgeted must be subjected to evaluation. The owner of a small business will be especially interested in whether the budget is feasible and viable given the financial position of the business. One of the most useful applications of a budget is the determination of whether a business can absorb the costs and cash outflows which are required in the plan. Knowledge of inadequate funds in advance of the occurrence is invaluable. It permits a manager to change the plans or to make arrangements to raise the necessary capital. In this chapter we will examine the process of budgeting in a small business with emphasis on operating budgets, cash flow forecasting and capital budgets.

THE BUDGETING PROCESS

Budgeting is the process of predicting and planning for the future. A budget is both a forecast of what you expect to happen and a goal toward which you will work. It is both a planning tool and a control tool. Budgets are not as widely used in small businesses as they should be, because many people consider them to be complex and difficult. They are neither, although they can be time consuming. Every large business in the country uses budgets extensively. The budgeting process may well be the most useful managerial tool which exists. It certainly merits the attention of anyone who intends to own a successful small business.

The key aspects of **financial performance** are cash flow and profitability. Both of these can be budgeted as part of the process of preparing the supporting budgets for a cash flow forecast. The process is to prepare a sales budget, purchases or production budget, and expense budget. The information on these budgets can then be combined to yield a cash flow forecast, and a pro forma income statement. ***Pro forma*** simply means a forecast or estimate. If we add last year's financial statements to the information, then a pro forma balance sheet can be prepared as well.

Another major aspect of financial performance is the acquisition and use of long lived assets. Managing this process is facilitated by capital budgeting techniques. Under ***capital budgeting***, long lived assets or plant assets are examined in terms of their return on investment to determine which assets will be most valuable to the firm.

BUDGETS AS OBJECTIVES

Since the numbers used in a budget are predicted in the future, those numbers form objectives of our desires for the future. For example, when a ***sales budget*** is prepared it includes a forecast of sales for some specified period in the future. Those sales are an objective for the firm. They should be predicted based on a realistic assessment of what is reasonable and obtainable in the future. Every budget should be prepared the same way. The ***expense budget*** will form objectives for the various costs in the firm just as the ***purchases budget*** will form an objective for the cash outlay associated with inventory.

Since every budget forms objectives for the firm, the owner must be intimately involved. In this book we will talk a great deal about the strategic planning process and how the owner must prepare goals and objectives for the firm on an ongoing basis. We indicated that those objectives should be quantified whenever possible. Budgets are a sound way of preparing quantified objectives. However, you must be careful to be realistic and reasonable. A budget cannot simply be plucked out of the air. It must be based on reality. That means that everyone who has any knowledge which may be of value should be involved in the preparation of the budget. Input from the lowest levels in the firm should be solicited as well as from all managers. The final choice of budgets to be used is the decision of the owner, but you will find that budgets prepared without participation from the staff will be less accurate and less useful.

BUDGETS AS A CONTROL

Budgets constitute benchmarks for comparison purposes. The actual sales achieved in a given month can be compared to the budgeted sales for that month to determine how well the firm is progressing toward its objectives. The budgets for expenses can be used in comparison to actual numbers to calculate variances. ***Variances*** are frequently used when talking about manufacturing firms, but variances can be calculated for any type of business. In essence, they are simply deviations from budgeted figures.

In order for budgets to be useful as a control device, there needs to be input from everyone who will be expected to conform to the budget. As we said above, this participation helps to make sure the budget is reasonable. In addition, participation in the preparation of the budget will make people more willing to accept the budget as a control device. If people have no input to the budget, it is easier to dismiss it as unrealistic. If they have assisted in its preparation, they are more willing to accept the budget as attainable and to gear their efforts toward achieving the numbers.

There is one danger in preparation of the budget by lower level employees. That is the risk of *slack* being incorporated into the budget. It could be possible for people to overestimate costs and underestimate revenues in order to ensure that the budget will be met. Such deliberate misstatements are called **slack**. When budgets are used as a control, this is a particular problem because people may naturally try to influence their future evaluation by making the budget easy to achieve. However, if no input to the budget is sought from lower levels, people may feel antagonistic and may refuse to accept the budget as realistic. The result is an extreme lowering of morale. The best solution to this problem is the proper use of budgets in a control mode. Budgets should never be used as a *club*. Everyone should recognize that striving toward the objectives established by the budget is what is important and that achievement of the budget is not an absolute necessity. It is far more important to put forth a determined effort and have it fail than not to budget at all. After all, budgets are forecasts and therefore cannot be consistently achieved over time. Deviations from the budget can occur as the result of a variety of factors both inside and outside the firm. Consistent failure to achieve a budget does signal serious problems, either in control or in budget preparation, but isolated variances are not automatically bad.

CONTINUOUS BUDGETING

Forecasting is a difficult process initially for a small business. As experience in the business grows and experience in forecasting develops, the process becomes easier and more accurate. For this reason, the strongest approach to budgeting is to continuously prepare forecasts. A **continuous budget** is prepared for 12 months, month by month. As each month goes by, the corresponding month of the budget is compared to actual results. Then, the remaining 11 months of the forecast is revised to incorporate what has been learned. Finally, a 12th month is added to the forecast. The result is a constant focusing on the budget and a continuous forecast of a full year of operations. You will find, that the closer an event is, the more accurate you can be in the forecast. That means, the next 3 or 4 months of the budget will be more accurate than will be the 11th and 12th months of the forecast because they are closer to the present. Revising the budget each month will provide you with a continuous planning horizon of several months of strong data and several months of weaker data.

Over time your forecasting skills will increase as will the accuracy. In addition, the continuous emphasis on budgeting which will occur will keep management attention focused on the budget and its achievement rather than focusing on day to day management. From this perspective, a budget can help in making managers into planners and can allow a firm to *proact* rather than *react* to changing conditions. **Proact** means to act in advance of the occurrence of an event and is the strongest type of management action. It is much easier to walk into a bank and arrange for a short term loan to cover a cash deficiency which is going to occur in 3 months than it is to obtain a loan to cover a cash shortage which has just been discovered. It is simply good management to anticipate the future.

SENSITIVITY ANALYSIS

Every budget is an estimate of future events. That means that every budget will contain some error. Consequently, it makes sense to analyze a budget to determine those factors which have the major influence. *Sensitivity analysis* is the process of examining the effects which changes in various components of a budget will have on the overall budget. The process involves calculating the budget using a range of estimates for the various factors. For example, various estimates of sales, variable and fixed expenses could be used to determine the effect which each of those factors has on profit. Understanding what the major components of a budget are, will help in examining the source of deviations from the budget and will also identify the important areas for management's attention.

The preparation of multiple budgets can be laborious and time consuming. Consequently, an automated approach can be a valuable aid. Spread sheet programs for microcomputers were designed with sensitivity analysis in mind. They permit a forecast to be prepared and then to be subjected to a series of *what if* questions to determine sensitivity. With a few keystrokes, you can examine the results of a 10% decrease in sales on profits, or the impact of a 5% increase in fixed expenses on cash flow. In addition, such programs make continuous budgeting and budget revision a simple process. In fact, most businesses could probably justify a microcomputer for use in budgeting even if it were not used for record keeping or other activities.

THE SALES BUDGET

As we indicated above, the first step in the budget process is the preparation of a sales budget. This means that sales for the next year must be forecast, month by month. This is not only the first step in the budget process, it is the most difficult. Sales forecasting can be complex, especially for a young firm with little history. Predicting the seasonal patterns which will affect the monthly sales can also be difficult. Many large firms have complicated computer simulation models which are used to predict sales. Most small businesses cannot afford such devices and, consequently, use an arbitrary growth percentage to predict sales: *Sales will increase by 10% next year!* This is not a good method because it simply assumes that next year will be just like the last year with small growth. If the budget is to be a useful tool, one which a manager can actually use to support decision making, it must be based upon an honest attempt to predict the future.

SALES FORECASTING

If a company has an established sales history, then sales should be forecast based on that history and changes which are expected to occur. Historic sales by month should be converted to percentages of the yearly sales. This will show the seasonality of sales. Now the sales trends from year to year can be examined and used to forecast sales for the next 12 months. Remember, don't simply add a percentage. Look at the change in sales over the years and consider what happened to affect those sales. Was there a change in competition or the opening of a new store or market which influenced sales? What caused the sales to change each year? Then think about what you expect to happen this year. Are you opening new markets or stores? Will there be new products or a change in the competition? Are there any economic conditions or other factors which will affect sales? Will sales go up or will they go down? Do you plan any changes in the marketing: new sales people, higher commissions, advertising campaigns, etc. The human brain is a remarkable model builder. If you consciously examine past trends and expected changes in your business, you will be amazed at how well you will be able to forecast sales. The secret is to ensure that you don't overlook important factors which will affect performance.

After you have made a forecast of the dollar volume of sales for the next year, you must convert it to monthly figures. This is done by examining the historic monthly percentages and changes which may affect them over the next year. The process is the same as predicting sales. What were the trends in monthly sales over the years; what caused those trends; what do you expect to happen next year which will affect them? The end result should be a forecast of the percentage of sales which you expect to occur each month. The monthly sales forecast is now found by simply multiplying the percentages by the forecast for the year. Table 1 displays an example of the process.

The sales forecast will be adjusted at the end of each month under continuous budgeting principles. At the end of January, 1997, the actual sales for January will be compared to the budget, $10,350 in the example. Now, if the sales were higher than the budget and we expect that trend to continue, we would increase the sales forecast for the remaining 11 months. We might also decrease the sales forecast, if the experience for January indicated that we should, or we might change the forecast for February and March and leave the rest of the forecast intact. After we have made adjustments which are necessary, sales for January, 1998 would be forecast using the same principles we have discussed and we would again have a full 12 months of sales predictions.

SALES FORECASTING FOR A NEW BUSINESS

How do we prepare a sales forecast if we do not have any historic results to examine, or if the history is too short to see any trends, or if the economic or other conditions have changed so much that historic results are no longer valid? In such cases, the sales forecast must be based totally on expectations.

Table 1
Sales Forecast Using Historic Results

	1993	1994	1995	1996	Projected 1997
Total Sales:	$155,000	$180,000	$175,000	$225,000	$258,750
% Change	---	25%	<3%>	29%	15%

Using actual sales for 1993 through 1996 and expectations for changes during 1997, sales are forecast to be 15% higher than 1996 sales.

	1993	1994	1995	1996	Projected 1997
Sales Percentages:					
January	2%	4%	4%	4%	4%
February	4%	4%	4%	4%	4%
March	4%	4%	4%	3%	3%
Total	10%	12%	12%	11%	11%
April	3%	3%	2%	2%	1%
May	3%	3%	3%	2%	2%
June	4%	3%	3%	4%	5%
Total	10%	9%	8%	8%	8%
July	5%	4%	5%	6%	7%
August	7%	9%	11%	13%	15%
September	13%	14%	14%	16%	17%
Total	25%	27%	30%	35%	39%
October	14%	14%	15%	16%	16%
November	25%	24%	22%	20%	19%
December	16%	14%	13%	10%	7%
Total	55%	52%	50%	46%	42%

Using actual percentages for monthly sales for 1993 through 1996, and expectations for changes during 1997, monthly percentages are forecast for 1997. The 1997 Sales Forecast of $258,750 can be converted into a monthly sales forecast by applying the percentage forecast.

The following numbers have been rounded to the nearest $10:

January	$10,350	May	$ 5,180	September	$43,990
February	10,350	June	12,940	October	41,400
March	7,760	July	18,110	November	49,160
April	2,590	August	38,810	December	18,110

In some retail industries, industry averages for sales per square foot of display space are available. *Dollars and Cents*, a guide to shopping center averages is published tri-annually by the U.S. Urban Land Institute. Your reference librarian can guide you to other publications which include such data. Sales forecasts can then be prepared using the industry averages and the square footage of your store. If such data is not available for your industry, a good approach is to examine inventory turnover averages for the industry. These are also available from many published sources. Using the industry average and your initial inventory stock level, you can predict sales for the year. Don't forget to adjust for the markup. Consider an example. Assume that the industry average is an inventory turnover of 3.5 times and that you will be using a markup of 50% of cost. A cost markup of 50% is equivalent to a markup based on selling price of 33% (50%/(100% + 50%)).[49] You should compare your markup plans to industry averages for gross profit to be sure that they are reasonable. If your initial inventory investment is $100,000, then an inventory turn of 3.5 would yield a sales forecast of $525,000 ($100,000 X 3.5 = $350,000; $350,000 X 50% = $175,000; $175,000 + $350,000 = $525,000).

After the sales forecast for the year has been prepared, you must convert it into a monthly forecast. Again, this is best done using industry averages for seasonality. Frequently, such numbers are available only on a quarterly basis. If that be the case, you should make a guess about how each month of the quarter will fall out and expect to have to make significant adjustments to the forecast as actual results are accumulated for comparison purposes.

If no industry averages are available which you can use for sales forecasting purposes, then the initial sales budget will be largely guesswork and therefore subject to great error. In such a case, you should make an initial forecast based on your best guess and monitor the actual results closely with the intention of making major adjustments to the forecast during the course of the year.

CREDIT SALES

Once the sales forecast has been prepared, the next step is to predict the percentage of sales which will be made on credit. In many industries this is simple because virtually all sales will be for cash, as in the case of a restaurant, or all will be on credit, as in the case of a wholesale supplier to other firms. In most industries, sales will be a mix of cash and credit sales. It is important to be able to isolate credit sales because we are going to want to predict the cash inflows which will result from sales. That means that we must predict cash collections from accounts receivables and add that to cash sales in order to determine the cash inflows in any given month.

If we have a history to draw upon, then credit sales percentage can be expected to continue its historic trends unless there are conditions or changes which will affect it. We will want to examine historic sales to determine both the percentage of sales which have been made on credit and to determine when those accounts receivable are actually collected. The historic collection experience plus the credit sales percentage is then applied to the sales forecast to arrive at a forecast of cash inflows from sales month by month. Table 2 illustrates an example of the process using the sales forecast developed in Table 1.

Table 2
Cash Inflow Forecast Using Historic Results

	1993	1994	1995	1996	Projected 1997
Cash Sales Percentage:	45%	38%	37%	36%	35%
Credit Sales Percentage:	55%	62%	63%	64%	65%
Collection Experience					
Percent of credit sales:					
Paid within 30 days:	50%	52%	50%	51%	50%
Paid within 60 days:	40%	36%	40%	39%	40%
Paid within 90 days:	9%	10%	8%	9%	8%
Uncollectible:	1%	2%	2%	1%	2%

Cash Inflow Projections for 1997 (rounded to nearest $10)

	Actual Sales from 1996			Projected Sales for 1997		
	October	November	December	January	February	March
Sales:	$36,000	$45,000	$22,500	$10,350	$10,350	$7,760
Cash Sales:						
1997 @ 35%				3,620	3,620	2,720
Credit Sales:						
1996 @ 64%	23,040	28,800	14,400			
1997 @ 65%				6,730	6,730	5,040
Collections:						
50% within 30 days (.50 X last month)				7,200 (.5 X 14,400)	3,365 (.5 X 6,730)	3,365 (.5 X 6,730)
40% within 60 days (.40 X 1 month ago)				11,520 (.4 X 28,800)	5,760 (.4 X 14,400)	2,690 (.4 X 6,730)
8% within 90 days (.08 X 2 months ago)				1,840 (.08 X 23,040)	2,300 (.08 X 28,800)	1,150 (.08 X 14,400)
Total Cash Inflows (Cash Sales + Collections)				$24,180	$15,045	$9,925

The remainder of 1997 would be forecast in the same fashion.

Notice in Table 2 how the cash inflows exceed sales significantly in January, declining to just slightly over sales in March. This is an illustration of the cash to cash cycle: converting cash into assets which are converted back into cash. Because credit sales must be collected before the cash is available, cash inflows lag behind sales. This can cause great difficulty since stocking for major sales months frequently must take place at a time when cash inflow is low.

CREDIT SALES FORECASTING IN A NEW BUSINESS

If there is no reliable historic data to use in predicting credit sales and collection periods, we must fall back on industry averages. The percentage of credit sales is generally available from industry averages, but collection experience is not. However, accounts receivable turnover rates are generally available and these can be used to forecast collections. Consider an example in which the industry average for accounts receivable turnover was 8 times. This is equivalent to 45 days (360 days/8 = 45 days). If the turnover is 45 days, that means that the average account is paid within 45 days or roughly half the accounts are paid prior to 45 days and half are paid after 45 days. If the normal credit terms in the industry are 30 day terms then we can assume that the accounts are paid evenly over the days prior to and after 45 days. That would mean that about half of the accounts can be expected to pay in the first 15 days of the month following the month of sale. The other half can be expected to pay during the last 15 days of that month and into the second month following the sale. That would mean that the majority of accounts are collected during the month following the sale. To be conservative, we can allow for a loss percentage and spread a portion of accounts over into the second and third month following the sale. This will provide a beginning point for the collection forecast and we will anticipate the need to make adjustments as experience is gained over time. The process is the same no matter what the turnover rate is. If the industry average was a 60 day collection period (6 turns in a year), then we could expect half the accounts to pay prior to 60 days and half after 60 days. If they were evenly spread, that would mean half in the month following the sale and half in the second month following the sale.

If there is absolutely no experience or industry averages, then a good starting point is to assume that collections will be slightly longer than the terms being offered. If you will be offering 30 day terms on the accounts, then collections will probably be somewhat longer than 30 days. In that instance, a 45 day collection period would make a good starting point and we would expect to make adjustments to the forecast as experience is accumulated.

ACCOUNTS RECEIVABLE

In addition to predicting sales for the year and sales by month, the sales budget also contains information to predict accounts receivable at any point in time. The balance in receivables is credit sales which have not yet been collected. Table 3 calculates receivables at March 31, 1997.

Table 3
Accounts Receivable Calculations

Projected Sales for 1997

	January	February	March	Total
Sales:	$10,350	$10,350	$7,760	$28,460
For Cash	3,620	3,620	2,720	9,960
On Credit	6,730	6,730	5,040	18,500

Collections:	January	February	March	
50% within 30 days (.50 X last month)	$7,200	$3,365	$3,365	
40% within 60 days (.40 X 1 month ago)	11,520	5,760	2,690	
8% within 90 days (.08 X 2 months ago)	1,840	2,300	1,150	
Total Collections				$39,190

By March 31st, all receivables will have been collected except those related to sales in March, February and January because experience shows 98% of sales being collected within 90 days. Examining the calculations, remove collections which come from months prior to January.

Collections:	January	February	March	
50% within 30 days (.50 X last month)	---	$3,365	$3,365	
40% within 60 days (.40 X 1 month ago)	---	---	2,690	
8% within 90 days (.08 X 2 months ago)	---	---	---	
Total Collections				$9,420

To calculate the receivables balance at March 31st, add up the credit sales for January through March, add up the collections of those sales and subtract.

Credit Sales for January through March	$18,500
- Collections during January through March	9,420
Accounts Receivable at March 31, 1997	$9,080

Another approach is to use beginning accounts receivable, total credit sales and total collections to arrive at ending accounts receivable. The beginning receivables balance can be found from the general ledger or from a previous forecast. It is simply uncollected receivables.

Accounts Receivable at December 31, 1996	$29,770
+ Credit Sales for January through March	18,500
Total	48,270
- Collections during January through March	39,190
Accounts Receivable at March 31, 1997	$9,080

The process illustrated in Table 3 is used to estimate the receivables balance at any point in time. Notice that the percentage of uncollectible accounts, 2% in our example, will remain in accounts receivable. If we wish, an adjustment can be made to remove the uncollectible accounts from the receivables balance by subtracting the percentage of loss which is expected from the receivables. Generally, the loss percentage is so low that the error is insignificant; especially when we remember that the numbers are forecasts and estimates which will be subjected to adjustment at the end of every month. Table 4 displays the finished Sales Budget.

Table 4
The Sales Budget for 1997

	Jan	Feb	March	April	May	June	July	Aug	Sept	Oct	Nov	Dec	Total
Sales	10,350	10,350	7,760	2,590	5,180	12,940	18,110	38,810	43,990	41,400	49,160	18,110	258,750
Cash	3,620	3,620	2,720	910	1,810	4,530	6,340	13,580	15,400	14,490	17,210	6,340	90,570
Credit	6,730	6,730	5,040	1,680	3,370	8,410	11,770	25,230	28,590	26,910	31,950	11,770	168,180
Collections:													
50%	7,200	3,365	3,365	2,520	840	1,685	4,205	5,885	12,615	14,295	13,455	15,975	
40%	11,520	5,760	2,690	2,690	2,020	670	1,350	3,360	4,710	10,090	11,440	10,760	
8%	1,840	2,300	1,150	540	540	400	135	270	670	940	2,020	2,290	
Total	20,560	11,425	7,205	5,750	3,400	2,755	5,690	9,515	17,995	25,325	26,915	29,025	165,560
Total Cash													
Inflow	24,180	15,045	9,925	6,660	5,210	7,285	12,030	23,095	33,395	39,815	44,125	35,365	256,130

Accounts Receivable at December 31, 1996	$ 29,770
Credit Sales during 1996	168,180
Total	197,950
Collections during 1997	165,560
Accounts Receivable at December 31, 1997	$ 32,390

THE PURCHASES BUDGET

The *purchases budget* is based on inventory. We use the inventory turnover ratio and the gross profit margin along with a sales forecast to predict desired inventory levels. Consider an example: Assume that the inventory is expected to turn over 8 times in one year. That will mean that the inventory at the end of each month should be sufficient to cover the next 45 days or 1 and ½ month's sales (360 days/8 = 45 days). Now the ending inventory for any month is simply the cost of goods sold for the next 1 and ½ month. If the gross profit percentage is 30%, then the cost of goods sold must be 70%. Using this approach we can estimate the necessary ending inventory balance for any month end. All we need are the sales forecast, the gross profit percentage and the inventory turnover. Let's look at an example. Using the sales numbers from the previous example, it looks like this:

	January	February	March
Sales	$10,350	$10,350	$ 7,760
Ending Inventory	9,960		

Ending Inventory for January at Retail = February Sales plus ½ of March Sales
Ending Inventory for January at Retail = $ 10,350 + 3,880 = $ 14,230
Ending Inventory for January at Wholesale = 70% (February Sales plus ½ of March Sales)
Ending Inventory for January at Wholesale = 70% X $ 14,230 = $ 9,960

Sales forecasts come from the Sales Budget. The gross profit and inventory turnover figures can be estimated based on historic averages or can come from industry averages. If we use historic averages, we must remember to adjust for any conditions or changes which are expected to affect the numbers during the coming year. Since the inventory budget will also be used for control purposes, the numbers we select for gross profit and for inventory turns should also reflect our desires for the year. Be careful to ensure that the resulting ratios are reasonable and attainable. If you have averaged an inventory turnover of 6 times and you wish to increase it, it may not be reasonable to expect a doubling. An increase to 7 or 8 turns may be more attainable. Gross profits are a result of both cost and price, so be sure to take into consideration expected changes in your merchandise or production costs as well as any changes you plan for your selling prices.

PURCHASES

Once an inventory budget has been prepared, the forecast of purchases follows from the relationship between beginning inventory, purchases, and ending inventory. It comes from the cost of goods sold schedule of the traditional income statement:

	Beginning Inventory
+	Purchases
	Cost of Goods Available for Sale
-	Ending Inventory
	Cost of Goods Sold

From a budgeting perspective, we are interested in establishing the amount of purchases which a business should make, given a desired level of ending inventory. The relationship presented above, can be restated to provide a formula for the determination of purchases. We can omit the intermediary subtotal for cost of goods available for sale and note that beginning inventory plus purchases minus ending inventory equals cost of goods sold. Beginning inventory is known from the prior period's ending inventory. Ending inventory can be established from the desired inventory turnover ratios. Cost of goods sold can be estimated from the average gross profit margin. With these givens, we can restate the relationship to produce a budget for purchases:

	Cost of Goods Sold
-	Beginning Inventory
+	Ending Inventory
	Purchases

If we use the numbers from the previous examples, the purchases forecast is calculated as displayed in Table 5. The example assumes an inventory turnover of 1 and ½ months or 8 times per year and a gross profit percentage of 30%. The beginning balance for January comes from the general ledger entry for ending inventory at December 31 of the prior year. The beginning balance in inventory for all of the other months is the ending inventory estimate from the previous month.

Table 5

The Purchases Forecast

	January	February	March	April	May	June
Sales	$10,350	$10,350	$7,760	$2,590	$5,180	$12,940
(Drawn from the Sales Forecast)						
Cost of Goods Sold	7,245	7,245	5,430	1,810	3,630	9,060
(70% of Sales)						
Ending Inventory	9,960	6,335	3,625	8,160	---	---
(70% of the next 1 1/2 Months Sales)						
Beginning Inventory	10,870	9,960	6,335	3,625	8,160	---
(Last Month's Ending Inventory)						
Cost of Goods Sold	7,245	7,245	5,430	1,810		
- Beginning Inventory	10,870	9,960	6,335	3,625		
+ Ending Inventory	9,960	6,335	3,625	8,160		
Purchases	$ 6,335	$ 3,620	$ 2,720	$ 6,345		

The remaining months of the forecast are estimated in the same fashion as shown for January through April in the Table. The Purchases Budget is not yet finished, however, because we need to know the cash disbursements which we will be making. To make that estimate, we must add to the purchases data information about the timing of cash outflows to pay for those purchases. That forecast is the subject of the following section.

CASH DISBURSEMENTS

Cash disbursements are simple to forecast. We need only know the terms which our suppliers require for payment. If our suppliers require 30 day terms, then the purchases for any given month must be paid during the following month. If our suppliers offer 2/10, net 30 terms that means that a 2% discount will be available for payment within 10 days. In that case, the payment of purchases must be made within 10 days of receipt in order to get the discount. If we intend to take all discounts, then the disbursement for any month will be equal to 2/3rds of that month's purchases plus 1/3rd of the previous month's purchases. That is assuming that purchases are made evenly throughout the month. The 2/3rds comes from an assumption that those purchases made during the first 20 days of the month, or 2/3rds of the month, must be paid during that month. Those purchases made during the last 10 days of the month, or 1/3rd of the month, will be paid during the following month. By the same reasoning, terms of 2/15, net 30 would result in the payment of half of each month's purchases during the month plus ½ of the previous month's purchases.

ACCOUNTS PAYABLE

Accounts payable can also be predicted using the purchases budget in the same manner as accounts receivable were predicted using the sales budget. Payables are simply purchases which have not yet been paid. Therefore, the balance of accounts payable at any point in time is the total of beginning payables plus purchases less payments. If we put it all together, the final Purchases Budget will look like the one displayed in Table 6. The budget uses the sales data from the previous examples of Sales Budgets and assumes that the disbursement for purchases will be made on 30 day terms. That means that cash outflow will follow purchases by one month. The budget also assumes a gross profit level of 30% and an inventory turnover rate of 8 times per year, 45 days, or 1 and ½ months.

The Purchases Budget is now complete. Notice that it shows the total for cost of goods sold for the year and the ending inventory value for the year as well as purchases and payables. Notice also, that sales forecasts were required for January and February of 1998 in order to complete the inventory budget for December. That's because December's ending inventory is a function of January and February sales.

Finally, the accounts payable at December 31, 1997, is found by taking the beginning accounts payable figure, adding purchases, and subtracting cash payments for purchases during the year. Since the budget in this case assumes payment for purchases within 30 days, the ending accounts payable is simply the purchases for December.

Table 6

The Purchases Budget for 1997

	Jan	Feb	March	April	May	June	July	Aug	Sept	Oct	Nov	Dec	Total
Sales	10,350	10,350	7,760	2,590	5,180	12,940	18,110	38,810	43,990	41,400	49,160	18,110	258,750
CofG	7,245	7,245	5,430	1,810	3,630	9,060	12,680	27,170	30,790	28,980	34,410	12,680	181,130
EI	9,960	6,335	3,625	8,160	15,400	26,265	42,565	45,280	46,185	40,750	16,845	12,495	---
BI	10,870	9,960	6,335	3,625	8,160	15,400	26,265	42,565	45,280	46,185	40,750	16,845	---
CofG	7,245	7,245	5,430	1,810	3,630	9,060	12,680	27,170	30,790	28,980	34,410	12,680	181,130
-BI	10,870	9,960	6,335	3,625	8,160	15,400	26,265	42,565	45,280	46,185	40,750	16,845	---
+EI	9,960	6,335	3,625	8,160	15,400	26,265	42,565	45,280	46,185	40,750	16,845	12,495	---
Pur	6,335	3,620	2,720	6,345	10,870	19,925	28,980	29,885	31,695	23,545	10,505	8,330	182,755
Disb	7,250	6,335	3,620	2,720	6,345	10,870	19,925	28,980	29,885	31,695	23,545	10,505	181,675

	Jan 1998	Feb 1998
Sales	11,900	11,900
CofG	8,330	8,330

Accounts Payable at January 31, 1997	$ 7,250
+ Purchases during 1997	182,755
- Payments during 1997	181,675
Accounts Payable at December 31, 1997	$ 8,330
Alternatively:	
December Purchases	$ 8,330
Accounts Payable at December 31, 1997	$ 8,320

Legend:		
	Sales	represents the sales forecast for each month
	CofG	represents the cost of goods sold
	EI	represents the ending inventory
	BI	represents the beginning inventory
	Pur	represents the amount of purchases
	Disb	represents the amount of cash disbursements

THE EXPENSE BUDGET

The expenses of a firm can be classified as either fixed or variable as we discussed in the breakeven chapter. Variable expenses are budgeted as a percentage of sales. Using historic averages or industry averages adjusted for changing conditions expected in the coming year, a percentage is developed for every variable expense in the firm. This percentage is applied to the sales forecast to estimate variable costs month by month. Disbursement for these expenses is generally in the month in which they are incurred. Any deviations from that practice should be incorporated into the budget. For example, advertising expense is frequently a variable cost. Advertising may require quarterly payments to be made to an advertising agency. In that case, disbursement should not be forecast in the month in which the expense is incurred.

Fixed expenses are budgeted on a month by month basis and are derived from the estimates made for each individual fixed cost. Since these costs frequently follow a disbursement pattern which is different from the month in which they occur, care must be taken to estimate the disbursement properly. For example, property taxes are frequently shown as a monthly expense but paid annually; insurance expense is generally shown as a monthly expense but disbursement occurs in semiannual payments. In addition, some types of fixed costs do not involve cash and therefore should not be shown in the disbursements sections at all. Depreciation is the major cost of this type. Be sure to pay particular attention to taxes. Income taxes are frequently paid on a quarterly basis but because of accounting differences, tax expense may not be the same as cash outflow for taxes. In addition, payroll taxes on employees must be paid quarterly, but are withheld from employee salaries with a matching contribution by the employer on social security taxes. The withholdings are generally shown on a monthly basis, even though the deposit is made quarterly.

Finally, there are cash requirements which are not expenses and therefore have not been budgeted in any of the previous sections. For example, loan payments include interest expense and principal. The interest is an expense, but the principal portion of the payment is not an expense although it does require cash to be paid. The interest expense should have been included in the fixed expense section of the budget. Adjustment for disbursement requires that the interest expense be added back and the full amount of the payment be deducted. If we purchase a long lived asset of any type, its cost will be spread over a period of years by charging depreciation expense. However, cash outflow will be required at the time of purchase. This obligation has not been captured. Consequently, a final section in the budget is needed to take into consideration transactions which are not expenses, but which require cash.

If we prepare a budget which takes all of this into consideration, it will look like the exhibit in Table 7. The example assumes known percentages for variable expenses and disbursement for all variable expenses in the month in which they are incurred. If we total the rows of expense data, then in addition to showing monthly expense, we will have an estimate of expenses for the year. This information can be used to prepare an income statement for the entire year or for any time period desired.

THE CASH FLOW BUDGET

Each of the budgets which we have discussed has contained a section dealing with cash inflows or cash outflows. That's because **cash flow** is the most important factor in the life of a business. If we combine all of the cash flow data from the previous budgets, we can forecast cash flows for the business on a month by month basis. Table 8 illustrates a cash flow forecast.

Table 7						
Expense Budget for the first 6 months of 1997						
	January	February	March	April	May	June
Sales Forecast	$10,350	$10,350	$7,760	$2,590	$5,180	$12,940
Variable Expenses:						
Commissions @ 3% of Sales	310	310	230	80	155	390
Advertising @ 3% of Sales	310	310	230	80	155	390
Freight @ 1% of Sales	100	100	80	25	50	130
Total Variable Expenses	720	720	540	185	360	910
Disbursements:						
Advertising	850	---	---	625	---	---
Other Variable Expenses	410	410	310	105	205	520
Total Disbursements	1,260	410	310	730	205	520
Fixed Expenses:						
Salaries	2,100	2,100	2,100	2,100	2,100	2,100
Rent	800	800	800	800	800	800
Utilities	300	300	250	250	200	200
Insurance	150	150	150	150	150	150
Depreciation Expense	500	500	500	500	500	500
Interest Expense	100	100	100	100	100	100
Other Fixed Expenses	200	200	200	200	200	200
Total Fixed Expenses	4,150	4,150	4,100	4,100	4,050	4,050
Disbursements:						
Insurance	900	---	---	---	---	---
Other Fixed Expenses	3,400	3,400	3,350	3,350	3,300	3,300
Total Disbursement	4,300	3,400	3,350	3,350	3,300	3,300
(Omit Depreciation and Omit Interest)						
Other Cash Disbursements:						
Purchase Fixtures	---	---	250	---	---	---
Purchase Equipment	---	2,000	---	---	---	---
Pay Income Taxes	---	---	---	3,100	---	---
Loan Payments (Principal & Interest)	180	180	180	180	180	180
Total Cash Requirements	180	2,180	430	3,280	180	180

Table 8
Cash Flow Forecast

	Jan	Feb	March	April	May	June	July	Aug	Sept	Oct	Nov	Dec	Total
Sales	10,350	10,350	7,760	2,590	5,180	12,940	18,110	38,810	43,990	41,400	49,160	18,110	258,750
Cash	3,620	3,620	2,720	910	1,810	4,530	6,340	13,580	15,400	14,490	17,210	6,340	90,570
Credit	6,730	6,730	5,040	1,680	3,370	8,410	11,770	25,230	28,590	26,910	31,950	11,770	168,180
Collect	20,560	11,425	7,205	5,750	3,400	2,755	5,690	9,515	17,995	25,325	26,915	29,025	165,560
Total Cash Inflow	24,180	15,045	9,925	6,660	5,210	7,285	12,030	23,095	33,395	39,815	44,125	35,365	256,130
CofG	7,245	7,245	5,430	1,810	3,630	9,060	12,680	27,170	30,790	28,980	34,410	12,680	181,130
-BI	10,870	9,960	6,335	3,625	8,160	15,400	26,265	42,565	45,280	46,185	40,750	16,845	---
+EI	9,960	6,335	3,625	8,160	15,400	26,265	42,565	45,280	46,185	40,750	16,845	12,495	---
Pur	6,335	3,620	2,720	6,345	10,870	19,925	28,980	29,885	31,695	23,545	10,505	8,330	182,755
Disb	7,250	6,335	3,620	2,720	6,345	10,870	19,925	28,980	29,885	31,695	23,545	10,505	181,675
Var Exp	720	720	540	185	360	910	1,265	2,715	3,080	2,900	3,440	1,265	18,100
Disb	1,260	410	310	730	205	520	3,750	1,550	1,760	4,915	1,965	725	18,100
Fix Exp	4,150	4,150	4,100	4,100	4,050	4,050	4,000	4,050	4,050	4,100	4,100	4,100	49,000
Disb	4,300	3,400	3,350	3,350	3,300	3,300	4,150	3,300	3,300	3,350	3,350	3,350	41,800
Total Cash Out	12,810	10,145	7,280	6,800	9,850	14,690	27,825	33,830	34,945	39,960	28,860	14,580	241,575
OCF	11,370	4,900	2,645	(140)	(4,640)	(7,405)	(15,795)	(10,735)	(1,550)	(145)	15,265	20,785	14,555
Other Cash Needs	180	2,180	430	3,280	180	180	180	180	180	230	230	230	7,660
NCF	11,190	2,720	2,215	(3,420)	(4,820)	(7,585)	(15,975)	(10,915)	(1,730)	(375)	15,035	20,555	6,895

Legend:

Sales	represents the sales forecast for each month
Cash	represents cash sales
Credit	represents sales on credit
Collect	represents collection of credit sales
Total Cash Inflow	is the total of cash sales and collections
Var Exp	represents variable expenses
Disb	represents payment of variable expenses
OCF	represents operating cash flow
NCF	represents net cash flow
CofG	represents the cost of goods sold
EI	represents the ending inventory
BI	represents the beginning inventory
Pur	represents the amount of purchases
Disb	represents the amount of cash disbursements
Fix Exp	represents fixed expenses
Disb	represents payment of fixed expenses
Total Cash Out	is the total of operating disbursements
Other Cash Needs	are cash outflows for other disbursements

The information contained in the cash flow forecast can also be used to generate a proforma income statement. We will talk more about that in a minute. Notice how the cash flows are highlighted for both operations and overall. That's because the *operating cash flow* is the cash which is generated by the day to day business. If we examine that number separately from the *net cash flow*, which includes all cash transactions, then we can obtain a feel for the firm's ability to support itself.

The forecast shows negative cash flows for a significant period. Negative cash flows are not unusual. In fact, almost every business which experiences seasonality in its sales pattern will have negative cash flows. How can a business survive such flows? Obviously, it must obtain the necessary cash to be able to continue functioning until the positive flows begin. The only source for such funds is money which the firm saves to cover its needs or money borrowed from a bank on a short term basis. Because of limited capital, most small businesses try to cover their negative flows with bank loans.

THE CASH BUDGET

To the cash flow forecast we must add information about the cash held in the business. Cash is held in the form of checking accounts or in cash drawers or savings accounts. A minimum level of cash should always be maintained. Cash must be held to cover the operational needs of the business and to provide a safety cushion in the event of unforeseen problems. Some businesses also hold a certain level of cash for speculative purposes; an opportunity to make a large purchase of inventory at favorable prices might occur if cash is available. Every business should establish a minimum level of cash which it desires to keep on hand at all times. Once this is done a cash budget can be prepared using the cash flow forecast.

If we assume that cash shortages will be made up by advances against a line of credit at the bank and that the credit will be repaid out of excess cash, then we can proceed. The beginning cash on hand figure comes from the records or from a previous forecast. Table 9 displays an example of a cash budget using the data from the cash flow forecast in the previous example. Interest on the line of credit is assumed to be 12% per year or 1% per month and the desired minimum cash level is assumed to be $5,000.

The cash budget not only shows coverage of negative cash flows but shows when large excess cash flows will occur. That permits a manager to plan for the investment of excess funds as well as arrange coverage for cash shortfalls. The *cash budget* is an outstanding device to support loans and lines of credit with your bank. Bankers are much more inclined to handle the short term needs of a business when a cash budget has been prepared to show when those needs will occur and when the advances can be repaid. In addition, the cash budget permits a manager to proact: make plans in advance, rather than to react to a situation when it occurs. All of the effort which we have expended in the budgetary process is easily justified by the cash budget. It may be the most useful of all managerial tools. With practice and experience and a monthly review in the form of continuous budgeting, you can become adept at forecasting. Clearly, it is difficult to forecast 12 months in advance, but forecasts for the next two or three months are easier. Even if the budget is only accurate for two months, it can provide advance information which is invaluable.

Table 9
The Cash Budget

	Jan	Feb	March	April	May	June	July	Aug	Sept	Oct	Nov	Dec
Beginning Cash	5,900	17,090	19,810	22,025	18,605	13,785	6,200	5,025	5,010	5,080	5,005	5,004
+ Net Cash Flow	11,190	2,720	2,215	(3,420)	(4,820)	(7,585)	(15,975)	(10,915)	(1,730)	(375)	15,035	20,555
Subtotal	17,090	19,810	22,025	18,605	13,785	6,200	(9,775)	(5,890)	3,280	4,705	20,040	25,559
+Loans	---	---	---	---	---	---	14,800	10,900	1,800	300	---	---
-Repayment	---	---	---	---	---	---	---	---	---	---	13,800	14,000
-Interest	---	---	---	---	---	---	---	---	---	---	1,236*	686**
Ending Cash	17,090	19,810	22,025	18,605	13,785	6,200	5,025	5,010	5,080	5,005	5,004	10,873
Loan Balance	---	---	---	---	---	---	14,800	25,700	27,500	27,800	14,000	---

* $14,800 X .01 X 5 months + $10,900 X .01 X 4 months + $1,800 X .01 X 3 months + $300 X .01 X 2 months   = $1,236
** $1,000 X .01 X 6 months + $10,900 X .01 X 5 months + $1,800 X .01 X 4 months + $300 X .01 X 3 months   = $ 686

Total $1,922

Legend: Beginning Cash — represents the month beginning balance of cash on hand and in banks
Subtotal — represents the subtotal of beginning cash and net cash flow for the month
Loans — represents the amount borrowed from the line of credit during the month
Repayment — represents the amount repaid on the line of credit during the month
Interest — represents the amount of interest on the line of credit for the month
Ending Cash — represents the month ending balance of cash on hand and in banks
Loan Balance — represents the balance owed on the line of credit at the end of the month

PRO FORMA STATEMENTS

The budgets which we have discussed contain all the information required to prepare a pro forma income statement and balance sheet for the business. All that is needed is last year's financial statement. The ***income statement*** can be projected from the sales budget, the purchases budget, and the expense budget. The cash budget is needed for interest expense. The income statement in Table 10 is a composite of the previous budgets.

Preparing a pro forma balance sheet requires last year's statement. The changes which have been made in asset and liability accounts will show on the various budgets. Every budget will be involved and numbers from each will be required to complete the balance sheet. Table 11 shows a balance sheet incorporating information from the operating budgets displayed in previous examples. The balance sheet for 1996 is the actual historic statement from the firm's records. The balance sheet for 1997 is a pro forma statement.

Table 10
Pro Forma Income Statement for 1997

Sales			$ 258,750
Cost of Goods Sold			181,130
Gross Profit			77,620
Selling Expenses:			
Commissions	7,760		
Advertising	7,760		
Freight	2,580		
Total Selling Expense		18,100	
Administrative Expenses:			
Salaries	25,200		
Rent	9,600		
Utilities	2,800		
Insurance	1,800		
Depreciation	6,000		
Interest Expense	1,200		
Other Expense	2,400		
Total Administrative Expense		49,000	
Interest on Line of Credit		1,922	
Total Expenses			69,022
Income before taxes			$ 8,598
Income Taxes			3,100
Net Income			$ 5,498

We have now completed the coverage of all the operational budgets. At this point, the process of preparing these budgets and reviewing and modifying them each month probably seems like an overwhelming task. Especially for the owner of a small business who is also beset with daily operational issues! It is true that the monthly maintenance can be time consuming, but these budgets constitute planning activities. Their use can make the difference between a business which fails or is only moderately successful and a business which is dynamic and vibrant. There is no substitute for planning! Further, one of the most important tools of planning is budgeting, especially cash flow budgeting.

Table 11

Pro Forma Balance Sheet

Assets:	12/31/96	12/31/97	
Cash	$ 5,900	$ 10,873	1
Accounts Receivable	29,770	32,390	2
Inventory	10,870	12,495	3
Total Current Assets	46,540	55,758	
Equipment and Fixtures	19,000	21,400	4
Accumulated Depreciation	(6,500)	(12,500)	5
Net Investment in Equipment	12,500	8,750	
Total Assets	$ 59,040	$ 64,658	
Liabilities:			
Accounts Payable	7,250	8,330	6
Notes Payable	13,200	12,240	7
Total Liabilities	20,450	20,570	
Stockholders' Equity:			
Capital Stock	15,000	15,000	
Retained Earnings	23,590	23,590	
1997 Income	---	5,498	8
Total Stockholders' Equity	38,590	44,088	
Total Liabilities and Net Worth	$ 59,040	$ 64,658	

1   Ending Cash Balance for December from Cash Budget

2   Accounts Receivable Balance from Sales Budget

3   Ending Inventory Balance for December from Purchases Budget

4   Equipment of $2,000, Fixtures of $250 shown purchased on Expense Budget during the first half of 1997, $150 of fixtures purchased in the second half of 1997 as shown by the increase in Other Cash Requirements on Cash Budget

5   Depreciation of $6,000 from Pro Forma Income Statement

6   Accounts Payable Balance from Purchases Budget

7   Notes Payable reduced by $80 principal payment each month for 12 months. The loan payments shown on Expense Budget were $180 per month; the interest expense was $100 per month; meaning that $80 per month was a principal payment

8   Income from Pro Forma Income Statement

At first glance, these budgets and forecasts seem to be a great deal of work. Fortunately, there are automated systems which can take much of the pain out of the budgeting process. Microcomputer spread sheets are ideal for the preparation of the budgets which we have discussed in this chapter. They can make modification each month a quick, easy task.

LEASE OR BUY

The final topic which we want to discuss in this chapter is the lease or purchase decision. In capital budgeting decisions, the lease or buy issue is an important one. In general, it costs more to lease or rent an asset than it would to buy it. That's because the owner of the asset is making a profit on the lease. Since the entirety of lease payments can be tax deductible, it is possible for individuals or firms in high tax brackets to come out better with a lease than with a purchase. Small businesses are seldom in such tax brackets. Consequently, for the vast majority of small firms, leasing is a more expensive option.

That doesn't mean that leasing should not be considered for a small business. It can have major advantages. One of the advantages which leasing can provide is the reduction or elimination of initial costs. Almost any thing you buy must have a down payment in order for a bank to consider financing. Down payments are frequently 20% or more. Most leasing plans require at most, two payments in advance. For a small business with limited resources that can be a major factor!

Another factor which favors leasing is the credit strength of the firm. Leasing companies, because they are obtaining larger returns, frequently have lower standards than a bank would for a loan of the same amount. They are willing to accept a higher risk. That means that it is possible for a small business to obtain a lease for an asset when a bank would refuse to finance it.

The term of a lease can be an advantage. This is especially true when a building is involved. If you buy a building and the location turns out to be less favorable than you thought, you may have a difficult time selling it. If you lease a building, you are locked in for the term of the lease, but moving at the end of the lease is a simple process. Term advantage may not exist for equipment and machinery. Most firms offering leases on these assets desire terms which will ensure that they recoup their investment in the asset fully. That means that lease terms are frequently similar to loan terms and can not be canceled. This is especially true for equipment which has limited sales appeal such as heavy machinery or for machines which are subject to technological obsolescence such as computers.

Finally, if a lease is properly structured, it will not show on the balance sheet of a business. This is called *off balance sheet financing* and permits a business to acquire assets without damaging its ability to borrow in the future. This is a sensitive issue and many leases will not qualify for such treatment. Many leases, called *financing leases*, are structured in such a fashion that the transaction is closer to a loan than a lease. Accounting principles require leases of this type to be shown on the balance sheet exactly as though they were loans. Consequently, if you are considering a lease for this reason, it is mandatory for you to obtain advice from your CPA before entering into the lease.

There is a tremendous range of types and terms of leases offered which can confuse the decision. That means that any major purchase should be carefully evaluated by a professional in order to obtain the most beneficial structure. Your CPA should be consulted on any transaction of significant size before you enter into a contract.

Breaking a lease can be a serious problem. In general, there is no way to get out of a lease prior to its expiration except through contractually permitted means without seriously damaging the firm or risking litigation. That means that you should never enter into a lease agreement without a clear understanding of the terms of the contract, especially those terms which relate to early termination. Always be sure that the term is reasonable given your plans for the business.

SUMMARY

Budgeting is the process of predicting costs, expenses, revenues, cash flows or investments. Since budgeting is the process of predicting and planning for the future, it is a tool vital to the success of small businesses and yet is one frequently not used because of the time it can consume. The key aspects of financial performance are cash flow and profitability and the acquisition and use of long lived assets. Budgets should be prepared to support the prediction of cash flow and that information used to produce a pro forma income statement.

Budgets have many uses. They can be used to formulate the objectives of the company. Based upon a realistic assessment of what objectives are possible, the budget can be designed to serve as a method of quantifying those objectives.

Budgets may also serve as controls for comparison purposes. The amount of deviation from a budget is an important bit of information in controlling the assets of a company. Participation in generating the input for a budget is important in itself a useful technique. People can make work those ideas which they developed. Beware, however, that slack is not introduced into the budget which means that the budget will always be met. Since a budget is a prediction, it may not always be met. Isolated variances are not automatically bad however, But continued deviations from the budget should denote problems in budgeting either in the preparation or control and suggest reevaluation.

Forecasting is difficult initially but experience makes the process easier. A continuous budget is best with month by month evaluation. This enables a business to proact rather than react to changing conditions.

Sensitivity analysis is the process of examining the effects which changes in various components of a budget will have on the overall budget. The process involves calculating the budget using a range of estimates for various factors.

Since the preparation of multiple budgets can be time consuming, an automated approach can be valuable. Spreadsheet programs for microcomputers were designed with sensitivity analysis in mind so that quickly one can examine what effects various changes can have on the budget.

Sample budgets for sales including sales forecasting, credit sales and accounts receivable were introduced; as were budgets for purchases, production, expense, and cash flow. Finally, the lease or buy decision was discussed.

Budgeting is a time consuming task but the value gained by planning for the future cannot be equaled. If you do not want to do the work yourself, hire an accountant with microcomputer knowledge and let him or her do the work. But as the owner/manager, you must know what is input and be able to evaluate the output. Management truly makes or breaks the business because management alone can impact the business by the decisions made. Each manager must plan, staff, direct, control and supervise and do all these jobs effectively. Budgeting gives a manager the most knowledge and with knowledge comes success.

QUESTIONS, EXERCISES AND CASES

QUESTIONS:

1.   Why is budgeting important?
2.   What are the key aspects of financial performance?
3.   How can budgets serve as objectives and controls?
4.   Why is continuous budgeting important?
5.   What is sensitivity analysis and when is it used?
6.   How can budgets best be generated?
7.   What is the first step in the budgeting process?
8.   Why is the prediction of cash inflow so important to a small business?
9.   How does one generate a sales forecast for a new business?
10.   What must be captured to generate a sales budget?
11.   Why is the knowledge of credit sales important?
12.   What must be prepared before a forecast of purchases can be calculated?
13.   Why are discounts important to the success of a company?
14.   What must be captured to generate a purchases budget?
15.   Why are some cash disbursements not considered expenses?
16.   Can a company ever have negative cash flow and survive? If so, how?
17.   What do pro forma income statements tell you?
18.   Why is budgeting important even to a new business?
19.   What are the advantages of buying capital improvements?
20.   What are the advantages of leasing capital improvements?
21.   Who is ultimately responsible for the success of a small business and why?

EXERCISE:

We have prepared a sales forecast for next year for the Second Venture as indicated below. Credit is extended on 30 day terms; 10% of sales are for cash; 50% of credit sales are collected in the month following the sale; 30% are collected during the second month following the sale; and 10% is received in the third month following the sale.

Prepare a cash collections forecast for the first six months of the new year.

October Sales		$ 13,000
November Sales		25,500
December Sales		37,000
Sales Forecast:		
January	5.0%	$ 12,500
February	4.0%	10,000
March	4.5%	11,250
April	6.5%	16,250
May	9.5%	23,750
June	10.0%	25,000
July	11.5%	28,750
August	8.5%	21,250
September	7.5%	18,750
October	6.0%	15,000
November	11.5%	28,750
December	15.5%	38,750
Total	100.0%	$250,000

Inventory is purchased on 30 day terms and is generally paid for in the month following the month of purchase. The gross profit margin is expected to average 30% next year and we plan to have enough inventory on hand at all times to cover the next two month's sales. Ending inventory at 12/31 last year was $15,500. Prepare a forecast of cash outflows for purchases for the first six months of the new year.

Advertising is planned to be 3% of sales and will be paid for in the month incurred. Salaries and wages are fixed at $5,000 per month. Rent is $500 per month and utilities are expected to be fixed at $150 per month. Insurance payments of $250 will be due in March and June and income tax deposits of $400 must be made in January and April. Depreciation of $300 will be charged each month and loan payments of $290 will be due each month. Prepare a forecast of cash outflows for expenses for the first six months.

We plan to keep a minimum of $5,000 in the bank account at all times and the balance at the end of December last year was $5,500. Prepare a complete cash flow forecast predicting amounts of excess cash and cash needs for each of the first six months of the new year.

CHAPTER SEVEN

FINANCIAL ANALYSIS TOOLS

CHAPTER OBJECTIVES

Upon completion of this chapter, you should be able to:

- Explain what financial analysis is and why it is valuable to small business management;
- Describe the techniques of financial analysis, their strengths and weaknesses;
- List the areas of financial performance which financial analysis is used to evaluate;
- Explain how financial analysis fits into the month end planning and budgeting process;
- Perform a financial analysis;
- Use financial analysis to evaluate the effectiveness of past decisions and actions;
- Use financial analysis to guide development of changes in operations and policies; and,
- Use financial analysis in the development of new budgets, forecasts and plans.

FINANCIAL ANALYSIS TOOLS

INTRODUCTION

One of the best and least understood tools of management is *financial analysis*. The *financial position* of a firm at any point in time is a result of the actions and decisions its owners/managers have made. Consequently, financial analysis provides a *report card* for management; a method for evaluating how well or poorly management has performed. Perhaps the primary reason that financial analysis is so infrequently used by small business owners is the difficulty of self evaluation. None of us likes to hear criticism or to admit failure. But management, like medicine, is not an exact science. In actuality, there are no right or wrong decisions: some decisions are simply better than others. *Financial analysis* is a tool for evaluating the results of decisions. It provides a device for determining what was done well in the past and what to do differently in the future. It can demonstrate strengths and weaknesses in a firm.

Financial analysis can and should be an underlying support for planning activities. Planning which does not take into consideration financial strengths and weaknesses, which does not incorporate the effects of past planning activities is not really planning at all. It is simply hoping: hoping that things will proceed as desired. That's a poor substitute for the truth.

Financial analysis is a device for determining the truth about the firm. That truth is found by examining things as they really are, not by fooling ourselves into believing what we would prefer things to be or what they appear to be. In this chapter we will discuss the basics of financial analysis. We will present the processes of ratio analysis and trend analysis and talk about industry averages. The focus will be on using financial analysis to support management decision making activities.

TECHNIQUES OF FINANCIAL ANALYSIS

The *financial statement*, as we discussed in the financial accounting chapter, consists of the income statement, balance sheet, reconciliation of net worth and statement of changes in financial position. These reports are the chief indicators of financial performance over the last year. In addition, interim income statements and interim balance sheets should be prepared at the end of each month and are a valuable addition to financial feedback. These statements can tell a great deal about the financial well being of a company. However, much information is contained in the statements which is not readily visible. Analysis is required to learn the maximum amount from them. That is what financial analysis is all about.

In the accounting chapter we displayed various managerial statements which contain percentages for the various items on the statement. This avoids the confusion which typically follows when dollar levels are examined and is called ***component percentage analysis***. It provides a methodology for examining the relative relationship between items on a statement and over time. It is generally the starting place for financial analysis.

The most well known technique for detailed examination of the financial statements is ***ratio analysis***. Various items from various statements are divided by one another to yield a ratio. These numbers can then be used to evaluate various aspects of financial position. Ratios may be expressed as numbers or percentages. Again, they provide a methodology for examining relative relationships between items and over time.

An aspect of financial analysis which is frequently overlooked because it is so obvious is called ***trend analysis***. This simply involves comparing component percentages and ratios to those for previous periods. The longer the time period, the better the trends in items can be identified. Trend analysis is possibly the most revealing of all analytic tools, but requires a greater understanding of the relationship between items on the statements than the other tools.

Industry comparison is another well known aspect of financial analysis. It involves comparing ratios and component percentages to averages compiled from other firms in the same industry. It is the most dangerous of all the tools in financial analysis because it leads to absolute conclusions. Either a number is better or worse than the industry average and therefore good or bad. In fact, the term ***industry norm*** is frequently heard when talking about industry averages. The problem is that there is no *normal* or standard ratio for any business. Not only that, there is no way to obtain true averages of ratios and percentages. One of the authors served on the Robert Morris Associates Statement Studies Committee for two years. That is an association of commercial banking officers which publishes a book of industry averages each year. The financial statements which are used to prepare the averages are obtained from the member banks in the Association. Unfortunately, human nature affects the process. Specifically, some banks submit statements only from the financially strong customers because the officers do not want to admit that they have made loans to weak firms. Some people think that the vast majority of the statements submitted for compilation have been subjected to such screening either deliberately or unconsciously by the officers. Add to that the fact that only firms who were borrowing from the banks were included in the sample and you can see how the averages would be skewed. Many industry associations also compile averages. Those are also beset with problems because the source of data is from members. Not only is the membership of the association not necessarily representative of all of the firms in that industry, but financial statements are obtained from the members on a voluntary basis. Again, human nature will prevent most of the weaker firms from submitting their statements. Dun and Bradstreet industry averages are similarly skewed because the sample from which the averages are prepared tend to be the stronger firms. Another problem with the averages is the classification of the firms themselves. In reality few firms are identical to others which are classified in the same industry. Not only do the firms differ by size but their markets, products and strategic postures differ. We have talked at great length about the differences in firms which result from the posture which their managements choose. Industry averages make an attempt to incorporate these postures into the classification scheme, but due to the great variety of approaches which exist, the averages are flawed.

All of this is not to say that industry averages should not be used in financial analysis. They should be used whenever possible, because they add more information. The point is that they should not be considered the only tool in analysis nor the most important. They are simply another piece of evidence. So long as you keep in mind that a deviation from an industry average is not automatically good or bad, they can be quite useful. They can give you a feel for how the stronger firms with similar competitive environments are performing and how your company compares.

The techniques of component percentages, ratio analysis, trend analysis and industry comparison are collectively called *financial analysis*. None are used in isolation. As we discuss analysis, we will talk about information gleaned from all of those sources at once because they support each other during evaluation. In other words, the evaluation of financial data involves examining the results of all of these techniques.

FINANCIAL PERFORMANCE

There are generally four areas of financial performance which are of interest when examining the financial well being of a firm. These areas are: *liquidity*, which refers to the ability of a firm to meet its maturing obligations; *activity*, which refers to the effective utilization of a firm's assets; *leverage*, which refers to the appropriateness of a firm's debt level and its ability to handle that debt; and *profitability*, which refers to the cost/revenue relationships of a firm. We will talk about each of these areas separately and then discuss the overall evaluation of a business.

LIQUIDITY

Liquidity refers to a firm's ability to meet its maturing obligations. Those are the debts which must be paid within the next year. We say that a firm is liquid if it can handle its short term debts without difficulty. The best known measure of liquidity is the *current ratio* which is calculated by dividing the current assets by the current liabilities. Remember that current liabilities are those which must be paid within one year while current assets consist of cash and those other assets which are expected to be converted to cash within one year such as accounts receivable and inventory. If we had $10,000 in current assets and $5,000 in current liabilities, the current ratio would be 2 (10,000/5,000 = 2). This ratio tells us that the firm has twice as many current assets as are normally expected to be required to cover existing current liabilities. Another ratio which is sometimes used by firms with high inventory levels to measure liquidity is the **quick ratio** which is calculated by subtracting inventory from total current assets and dividing the result by current liabilities. This ratio is sometimes called the **acid test** and is an indication of how easily a firm can meet its existing obligations if it is unable to sell any of its inventory.

There are numerous ratios which can be used in the evaluation of liquidity. For example, for firms with high inventory levels, the **inventory liquidation ratio** can be calculated. It is found by subtracting *quick assets* such as cash and accounts receivable from current liabilities. The result is divided by inventory and expressed as a percentage. It tells us what proportion of inventory must be sold in order to cover maturing obligations. It can be especially useful when compared to an activity ratio for inventory movement.

Many ratios are industry specific. That means that special ratios are developed for particular industries. This is true for liquidity and for all of the other categories as well. For example, banks and finance companies are dependent upon the collection of their loan portfolios for liquidity. Consequently, a ratio called the **loan liquidation ratio** is an important one. This ratio represents the average collection period of various categories of loans. It is calculated from information which is not included in the financial statements. It represents the ratio between the total amount of principal payments received during a period to the average amount of loans outstanding during that period.

ACTIVITY

Activity refers to the utilization of a firm's assets. A firm which normally extends 30 day terms to its customers would expect its accounts receivable to *turn over* 12 times per year if all of its customers paid their bills exactly on time. Of course, all the bills are not paid on time, and having a large part of a firm's resources tied up in accounts receivable is expensive. A measure of how effectively accounts receivable are being managed is the calculation of the actual **accounts receivable turnover**. Dividing total credit sales by the average amount of accounts receivable yields the ratio. If a firm had $100,000 of sales on credit and an average of $10,000 in accounts receivable, then the accounts receivable turnover would be 10 (100,000/10,000 = 10). If we wished to examine the turnover in terms of days, we could divide the factor into 360 (360/10 = 36) and find that on the average our customers pay their bills in 36 days. That would be a fantastic collection rate if our terms were 30 days, but a poor collection rate if our terms were to require payment within 7 days. Consequently, the **accounts receivable collection period** must be compared to a firm's credit terms in order to be of value.

Another asset which is of extreme importance to many firms is inventory. The turnover period for inventory can be calculated to aid in measuring how well this asset is being managed. The **inventory turnover** can be found by dividing the total cost of goods sold by the average inventory. If firm has $50,000 in cost of goods sold and an average of $10,000 in inventory, then it has an inventory turnover of 5 (50,000/10,000 = 5). Like the accounts receivable turnover, this ratio can be converted into days by dividing it into 360. In this example, the inventory turnover period would be 72 days (360/5 = 72). That would be a poor turnover rate if we were dealing with perishable goods, but it would be fantastic if we were dealing with new cars.

Turnover rates can be calculated for any asset. Firms with high levels of fixed assets, such as manufacturing firms, would be interested in how well those assets are supporting sales. The fixed asset turnover could be calculated by dividing sales by the average investment in plant, property and equipment.

Assets exist for the purpose of supporting sales. Consequently, their effective management should be reflected in sales. The overall performance is measured by the ***total asset turnover*** and is found by dividing sales by the average total assets owned. Later on we will discuss how this ratio can be coupled with a profitability ratio to better evaluate the firm.

One note of caution is due here. All of these ratios have used average asset levels. Frequently, that is a difficult number to find. Most people simply take the beginning and ending balances of the assets from two balance sheets and find the average by adding the two together, then dividing by two. Some error is included in that, but that is the method used for most industry averages and so comparison to those will be impaired if we use another method. If there is a major shift in asset levels during the period, then the average will not be representative. In such cases, it may be wiser to use the ending value for the asset rather than an average. There are no hard and fast rules about financial analysis. The approach to use is the one which works best in your situation.

LEVERAGE

Leverage has to do with the debt level of a firm. From a simplistic point of view, there are only two kinds of money in the world: ours and everyone else's. Leverage is an indication of the proportion of assets and resources which are acquired by a firm using money contributed by owners compared to money contributed by others. One measure of leverage is the ***debt to assets ratio*** found by dividing total liabilities by total assets. The ratio is normally expressed as a percentage. If total assets for a firm are $250,000 and total liabilities are $175,000, then 70% (250,0000/175,000 = .70) of the firm's assets are provided by debt and 30% (100% - 70%) are provided by the firm's owners or its own capital. The higher the debt ratio, the greater the risk to which the firm is exposed.

Alternately debt can be divided by net worth to yield the ***debt to worth ratio***. In this example, the ratio would be 2.33 (175,000/(25,000 - 175,000) = 2.33). This ratio indicates that 2.33 times as much debt as capital has been used to acquire the firm's assets.

Other ratios which are important when evaluating debt are indicators of coverage. The ***interest coverage ratio*** is calculated by dividing the income before interest expense and taxes by the total interest expense. This tells us how well the interest charges on debt are being covered by the firm's profits. Since obligations can take the form of leases as well as loans, the ***fixed charge coverage*** is a valuable ratio. It is calculated by dividing the income before interest, lease payments and taxes by the sum of interest expense and lease payments. These same ratios can be calculated on a cash basis to yield more information. Operating cash flow before loan payments and taxes is divided by total loan payments. Leases can be included by dividing the operating cash flow before loan and lease payments and taxes by the sum of loan and lease payments. The larger these coverage ratios are, the stronger the debt position is.

PROFITABILITY

Profitability measures include the **gross profit ratio** and the **Contribution margin**. Other ratios of importance include the **net profit ratio** calculated by dividing net income by sales and the **return on investment ratio** or *ROI* found by dividing net income by net worth or total capital. One item of caution is required when examining the *ROI*: leverage affects the ratio. Actually the area of analysis called **leverage** takes its name from the impact which debt has on the *ROI*. In the budgeting chapter we discussed the impact which debt has on the *ROI*.

Component percentages are another device for evaluating profitability. The ratios which the various expenses have to sales can display the effectiveness of cost control measures as well as revealing the proportion of sales required to support the various activities within the firm.

Some of the strongest profitability evaluation processes involve more than simply ratios. There are dozens, perhaps hundreds of different ratios which can be calculated in the analysis of a firm's financial well being. Many are industry specific as we mentioned earlier. Regardless of how many or what kinds of ratios are calculated, examination of the ratios in isolation is weak. A better analysis involves examining the ratios and percentages over time.

TREND ANALYSIS

When we examine the financial statements of a firm, we are using historic data in the analysis. What is really important is the future: how can a firm be expected to behave in the future; what income levels and *ROIs* can be expected next year. Although we cannot predict the future, we can examine **trends** in the ratios over time as one indication of what can be expected to happen. For example, we could calculate key ratios in each of the four areas for the financial statements prepared at each of the last three year ends. It would be more revealing to see that the current ratio has moved from 1.0 to 1.5 to 2.0 over the last three years than it would be to know that the current ratio was 2.0 on December 31st.

Trend analysis also aids in evaluating past performance and financial condition. If we instituted a new policy of inventory control at the beginning of last year, then we should see an improvement in the inventory turnover ratios for that year compared to the previous. If that did not materialize, then the changes may not be working as they should. If we changed pricing policies, then we should see a difference in the component percentages on the income statement.

In terms of financial health, the trends can reveal just how strong or weak we are. A poor liquidity position would be of less concern if it were an unusual case, but if the firm consistently has a poor liquidity, then it may be weaker than the ratios reveal. A strong gross profit margin would reflect an even stronger business if it were consistently strong over time. If we have had a poor gross profit margin in every year but the last, then chances are that the firm has changed its pricing and cost control policies but did so to correct a weakness.

Trend analysis can be useful because potential problems might be revealed before they become problems. If the accounts receivable collection period for the last three years has been 45 days, 50 days, and 55 days respectively, then one could conclude that a problem is developing in the collection of receivables. If the gross profit margin has declined from 25% to 24% to 23% over the last three years, then it would be wise to examine pricing and product cost patterns now to ward off a more serious problem in the future. Trend analysis can highlight such potential problem areas.

Trend analysis can also demonstrate patterns which can be expected to prevail in the future. The longer the trend, the more reliable it can be expected to be, within certain limits. If the contribution margin has been constant for several years, then we can probably count on its being constant in the future. Of course, we must take economic factors and other conditions into consideration, both in the past and expected in the future. If a trend line includes years of economic hardship or economic booms or periods of prosperity, then the trend is less valuable for prediction of the future. We would expect, for example, housing starts, or new construction, to suffer during a recession and can be expected to jump considerably at the end of a national recession. Obviously, a downward trend in the ratios of a construction company is less revealing if those trends occur during times of economic recession than they would be if housing starts had been growing. Trends must always be adjusted for expectations in economic conditions and other factors which might have a bearing. We would expect an American firm which has been competing heavily against a Japanese firm to experience more favorable financial performance after a strict import policy has been adopted by the US Congress. Trend analysis requires considerable knowledge about the industry and the economy in which a firm operates as well as the policies and practices in force in the firm in order to be as effective as possible.

INDUSTRY AVERAGES

Another step in financial analysis which is useful in determining a firm's well being is comparison of the ratios to averages of other firms engaged in the same general business. As we have discussed, such averages are called *industry averages* and are available from a variety of sources. Trade associations frequently compile average statistics for key ratios from financial statements of its members. These averages are then made available to its members for use in their analyses. It is more revealing to know that the average current ratio in our industry is 2.0 while our current ratio is 1.5 than it is to be totally ignorant of the industry's pattern.

Average ratios are calculated in various industries by the *Dun and Bradstreet Corporation* and by the *Robert Morris Associates*, which is an association of bank lending officers. These organizations sell publications of industry averages. Some governmental agencies also collect and publish industry averages. For example, the *Urban Land Institute* publishes a triannual survey of shopping malls which contains a wealth of average ratios compiled from stores located in the nation's shopping centers and malls.

As we mentioned earlier, whatever source of industry averages is used, you must be aware that they are simply averages and not indications of desired or proper ratio levels. For example, economic fluctuations can occur regionally without a great deal of effect on national compilations. We have discussed other types of bias which can creep into the calculations. If an organization depends upon voluntary submissions of financial statements for the averaging process, then it is likely that firms with less desirable operating results will not be represented. Consequently, industry averages are useful only as one of several tools to be applied in the analysis process. They should never be considered benchmarks or desired ratio levels.

Another word of caution is important concerning industry averages. Conditions change from year to year. Consequently, the results of a year's operations must be compared to industry averages compiled for that specific year. This is especially important if significant economic or other factors have changed.

Another evaluation technique is the comparison of percentages and ratios to those of a competing firm or firms. This approach tries to gain information about the financial position of a firm relative to specific competitors. This is a popular technique for evaluation of publicly held companies, but is less valuable in the small business arena. Publicly held firms are required by the *Securities and Exchange Commission* to publish their financial statements and so they are available to anyone who wishes to review them. Most small businesses are privately owned and so financial statements are not available. Bankers can and do use this approach to compare customers within the same industry, but it can be difficult for you to obtain the information on a competitor. If a firm has cooperated with the Dun & Bradstreet company while it was conducting a credit review, then financial statements can be obtained for a fee from that source. Otherwise, direct comparison may not be possible.

Trend analysis can be conducted with industry average ratios and percentages to determine how a firm compares over time. This can be a valuable technique, especially when you consider that the bias which exists in industry averages probably makes them higher than is really the case. With this in mind, it would be more valuable to know that the current ratio started out below industry averages three years ago and has climbed to equal the average for last year than it would be to look at last year alone.

PUTTING FINANCIAL ANALYSIS TO WORK

Now that we have talked about the various techniques, how can they be used to evaluate your firm's progress and financial position? The best approach is to evaluate the various aspects of your firm's performance at each month end. The budget process requires you to review each month's results and modify the remaining months of forecast under continuous budgeting. That is the time to perform financial analysis. Don't just look at the month's performance: analyze it, then adjust the forecasts and budgets and make whatever policy changes or decisions which seem appropriate. In the following sections we will illustrate how that process can function. The secret is consistency. You must make the monthly review of your business a habit. It must become a part of the planning activities. If you view those planning activities as the most important part of your function as the owner of a small firm, you will find yourself miles ahead of the competition and able to set and achieve goals and objectives.

It will be hard work. There will be many times when it seems impossible to find the time. Just think about all those firms which have failed and all those firms which eke out a subsistence income. The difference between those firms and a strong healthy business is good management. Good management means planning. Planning requires financial analysis.

SALES AND EXPENSES

Since sales or revenues are the basis for everything in a business, it makes sense to start analysis there. The first step is to calculate vertical and horizontal component percentages. ***Vertical percentages*** are found by simply dividing every item on the income statement by net sales or sales less returns and allowances. ***Horizontal percentages*** are found by dividing each item on the income statement by the same item on last year's statement. If you are looking at a monthly interim statement, then you should use last month's figures. If your business has seasonality factors, then you should use the same month in last year rather than last month. For example, January should be compared to January rather than to December. This displays how things have changed since the last statement in real terms rather than in dollar amounts. For example, if sales were $50,000 last period and are $55,000 this period, then the horizontal percentage would be 110% ($55,000/$50,000). That says that sales are 10% higher this period than they were last. If salaries this period are 97% of last period's salaries, then salary expense was down by 3%. Do this for each item on the statement. Now examine the horizontal percentages over time. If you have kept the prior analyses, that simply means adding another column of data. Incidently, spread sheet programs are ideal for this process. If you have an accounting package which is able to generate a file readable by a spread sheet package, then you won't even have to reenter the data. After the horizontal percentages have been prepared, consider why the changes took place. What happened to make sales go up or down? What did you do last month or last year which is reflected in the changes? Are the changes good or bad? What are the trends like? Is the seasonality factor the same? Did you have any marketing or advertising programs in effect last period? Did those programs work? Do you need to change your advertising approach? Did you make any pricing changes? What were their effects? Do you need to make pricing changes? Are things moving in the direction which your goals and objectives desire? What changes in operations need to be made?

Consider the vertical percentages and compare them to the last period's percentages. Remember the effect which pricing has. If you sold the same number of ball bearings this period as you did last, but sold them at a higher price, then sales will have gone up, but the increase will be in dollars only. Remember that every item on the statement will be affected because each is divided by sales. The variable expense percentages, especially the gross profit margin, should stay constant over time unless there has been some change in the relationship. If the gross profit margin has gone down, then it can only be a result of a decrease in costs of sales or an increase in prices. Which was it? Look at all of the variable expense items. What are their trends over time? Is the contribution margin flat? What have you done the last month or last year which should have affected the numbers? Did your actions have the expected effect? Do you need to make changes in the future? If variable cost items go up and prices stay the same, then the percentages will go up and the contribution margin will decrease. This is not a trend which can be tolerated for long. Obviously, the desirable result is for all variable expense percentages to stay flat or decrease over time. Is this happening?

Examine the fixed cost percentages. Fixed costs should stay the same in dollar amount over time unless changes are made. That means that an increase in sales should result in a decrease in the fixed cost percentage. Did that happen? Did you take any actions last month or last year which should have affected the fixed costs? Did the desired result occur? Are there changes you need to make? One of the major problems which small business' experience during periods of rapid growth is control over fixed costs. Frequently, they act like variable costs. That is, the fixed cost percentage stays flat. If that happens, then the firm will eventually find itself in serious trouble. The first time that sales growth slows down, those rising fixed costs will consume the firm's cash flow at an alarming rate. Fixed costs must behave like fixed costs. Look at the changes from a horizontal basis. What caused the changes which you see? Are the changes permanent? Have they resulted in increased capacity or are you simply paying more for the same thing?

Compare results to the budget. What did you forecast for sales, variable and fixed expenses? How far off were the forecasts? What caused the deviation? Do you need to make changes? What will happen next month? Are any of the relationships in the budget different? If the variable costs have changed their relationship to sales, then the budget will have to be changed to reflect the new percentages. If fixed costs have changed, that will have to be reflected. Do you plan any changes in marketing, pricing, cost control or other areas which will affect the forecasts? What objectives or goals should you set for next month and for the future?

Compare the component percentages and ratios to industry averages. Are you stronger or weaker than the average? Are there factors in your strategic posture which explain the difference? For example, if your quality is consistently higher than your competitors that could explain a higher cost of goods sold ratio. What has been the trends in the averages? Have your trends been moving in the same direction? Are you satisfied with your position relative to the averages? Will your banker be satisfied with your position? Are there any factors which the banker should understand as supporting detail for the financial data?

PROFITS AND ROI

The gross profit, contribution margin, operating profit and net profit margins will have been calculated as part of the component percentages. You should calculate the return on investment (net profit divided by net worth). You should also calculate the total asset turnover (sales divided by total assets). This last ratio is used to calculate the return on total investment under the *DuPont method*. This means multiplying the total asset turnover by the net profit margin. The result will be net profit divided by total assets which represent the total investment in the firm. It can be calculated directly, however, that would cloud the components of the ratio because return on total investment is a combination of an activity and a profitability ratio. It looks like this:

Return on Total Investment = Total Asset Turns X Net Profit Margin

ROTI = (Sales/Total Assets) X (Net Profit/Sales)

Using both ratios in the calculation will reveal which part of the operations are weak or strong. Pricing and cost control actions will be reflected in the profit margin. The effective use of assets will be reflected in the asset turns. Even if the profit margin is strong, the return on total investment can be weak because of poor asset management. The DuPont evaluation will disclose any such problems.

After the numbers are calculated, look at the trends. Gross profit and contribution margin should be constant unless there have been variable cost increases which have not been reflected in pricing or a change in the pricing policy. Operating profit reflects the effect of fixed costs on the contribution margin. Net profit reflects the impact of interest expense and other revenue or expense items on the operating profit. The operating profit is more important because it is the profit which can be expected to continue in the future. What happened? Were the results as you had anticipated? How did they compare to the budget? Were there any unusual items which affected net profit? Will these recur in the future? How do the numbers compare to the budget? Are there changes which you need to make in operations? Were the returns on investment and total investment acceptable? Were they within your goals or objectives? Did debt leveraging affect the *ROI*? Was the asset turnover satisfactory? How do the returns look over time? Are they going up or down? Why are they moving? What can you do to make the returns better?

Compare the numbers to industry averages. Are you satisfied with your comparison? Are your trends comparable to the trends in the averages? Are differences between your ratios and the averages reasonable when you consider the unique aspects of your business? Will your banker agree?

CASH FLOW

In a previous chapter we discussed cash flow and how it can be calculated from an income statement and balance sheets. Operating cash flow, net cash flow from operations and net cash flow should be calculated and converted to percentages of net sales like all of the components of the income statement. Horizontal analysis should be conducted for each number. Now, examine the trends. Cash flow tends to be much more volatile than profit figures because the accrual accounting methods used to calculate income smooth out much of the timing problems. That means that you should not expect cash flow to follow profit nor to reflect smooth percentage relationships. Nevertheless, if there are significant deviations from the cash flow forecast, you should investigate to determine the cause.

Cash flow is the life blood of any business. Consequently, no analysis is complete without a detailed consideration of cash flows. Were they higher or lower than expected? What caused the deviations from budget? Calculate the accounts receivable turnover ratio and see if any changes in the collection rate has occurred. Does this change account for the deviation in cash flows? Have you changed the process of paying accounts payable? Were there any significant accrual items in revenues or expenses which affected the cash flows? Were there any unexpected inflows or outflows of cash? What about debt? Did you borrow any additional funds or repay any loans which you had not anticipated on the forecast? Is the cash flow acceptable? Do you need to make any changes in operations? What modifications need to be made to the cash flow forecast?

If industry averages exist for cash flow, then you should definitely compare your results to them. The analysis should proceed just as for the previous areas. Unfortunately, such averages are frequently not available although sometimes sufficient detail will be given to allow estimates to be made for industry average cash flow. For example, net profit plus depreciation can be a close approximation to cash flow from operations in a stable industry.

ACTIVITY AND LIQUIDITY LEVELS

Calculate the component percentages for the balance sheet. That means that each item on the balance sheet should be divided by total assets to yield a percentage. In addition, horizontal analysis should be performed on each item. Calculate the turnover rates for receivables, inventory, fixed assets and total assets. Calculate the current ratio and if inventory is present, calculate the quick ratio and the inventory liquidation ratio. Calculate ***working capital***. It is simply the difference between current assets and current liabilities. Convert working capital to a percentage of total assets. Examine the trends and compare the balance sheet to the proforma balance sheet developed in the master budget.

Have the components of current assets or liabilities changed? What do those changes mean? If inventory moved from 40% to 45% to 50% over a three year period, then that could be disturbing, especially if horizontal analysis showed total assets to be rising during that same time period. Why would the inventory percentage go up? Has the inventory turnover ratio changed? If the investment in inventory goes up without a corresponding increase in sales, then the turnover ratio can be expected to go down. The same is true for all of the asset turnover items. The desired results are flat or increasing turnover rates.

The investment levels will change in horizontal terms as sales grow. They must in order to support higher levels of sales. In terms of component percentages, however, the relative investment in the various assets should remain basically level. Any shifts in investment should occur only as a result of changes in your policies or procedures. If you change the inventory policy, then its ratio to total assets can be expected to change. If you make a significant new investment in fixed assets, then its ratio to total assets can be expected to change. If you make no investments in fixed assets at all, then its ratio will still change because of the effects of depreciation. As more depreciation expense is recorded on existing assets, the investment level in fixed assets will shrink. That should show in the horizontal as well as vertical percentages. New purchases are required to keep the investment level. Since fixed assets are acquired in large chunks, its ratio to total assets can be expected to be more volatile. That means that you must determine whether the changes in the investment level are in accord with your plans.

Are the trends in activity levels and liquidity levels good? What actions did you take last month or last year which affected those trends? Were your efforts successful or do you need to try something else? Are there any seasonality factors? Were there any changes in the credit card sales or collection periods? How about credit sales as a percentage of total sales, were there any changes there? Are these changes expected to prevail in the future? Did short term loans go up due to cash flow deficits which are expected to reverse themselves next month? Do you need to make changes in the operations to improve the trends? Are there any problems developing? What about working capital? Is it satisfactory? What trends have accounted for it? Have you borrowed any money which affects the current liabilities? Are there any maturing notes or loans which will affect it next year? Have there been any loan repayments which you had not anticipated during the budget? What adjustments do you need to make in the budget to bring it closer into line for the next period?

Do you have a revolving line of credit? How much of it have you drawn and how much is left? If unused credit exists, it can form a major portion of the liquidity of a firm. When must it be paid out and what is the renewal date? Will you be able to handle the pay out? Is your financial strength such that the renewal of the line will be approved by the bank?

Compare your percentages and ratios to the industry averages. How does your firm compare? Are the trends in your numbers consistent with those in the industry? Can you explain the differences in terms of the differences in your operation? Are you satisfied with your position relative to the industry averages? Will your banker be satisfied?

DEBT MANAGEMENT

The debt ratio, debt to total assets, will have been calculated as part of the component percentages on the balance sheet. You should calculate the debt to net worth ratio. If yours is a firm with a significant long term debt level, then it could make sense to calculate the ratio of long term debt to net worth. In addition, interest and fixed charge coverage ratios should be calculated both normally and under the cash approach.

Now examine the trends in ratios and percentages, both horizontal and vertical. How do the numbers compare to the pro forma balance sheet in the master budget? Are the trends consistent with your actions and objectives? Did you make any significant loans or loan repayments? Are these reflected in the trends? What are the up coming maturity dates of the loans? Are you going to be able to handle them? Are the coverage ratios satisfactory? How about on the cash basis? Were you delinquent on any payables or lease or loan payments during the last period? Do you expect any changes which will affect the coverage in the future? Are any of the loans on a floating rate basis? Were there any changes in those rates which you had not anticipated? What do you think they will do in the future? Is the balance between short term and long term debt acceptable? Are there any expansion plans for the future which will require more debt? Will the firm's financial position be such that the loan requests will be approved? Is the debt level unduly influencing the return on investment? Should you make any changes? What adjustments should you make to the budget for the next months? Do you have compensating balance requirements or other special requirements to support your loans? Compensating balances are deposit levels which are required by a bank as part of the loan agreement. In addition, all kinds of other requirements can be made part of a loan agreement, from minimum levels for current ratios to limitations on overall debt levels. If any such requirements exist you should ensure that you are in compliance and that no circumstances exist which will damage that compliance in the future. Finally, is your financial position such that you will be in a stronger bargaining position with respect to terms and rates on loans? Should you consider renegotiation with the bank now? Do you have room to add more debt? Will you be able to finance expected growth through debt? Should you consider seeking investors and searching for alternative debt sources?

Compare your ratios and percentages to the industry averages. How do you look? Are you satisfied with your debt trends when compared to debt trends in the industry? A fact of life is that bankers will compare your ratios to industry averages as part of their evaluation of any loan proposals. That means that you should be aware of and able to explain and justify any significant deviations from industry averages before you make a loan application. Remember that the averages may be skewed high or represent firms which are truly not comparable to yours because of size, market or other factors. They may also fail to reflect economic or competitive factors which are local or regional in nature and they are frequently too old for real comparison to current data because of the lag time required for publication. Unfortunately, you may have to justify one or more of these factors to a lender unless you have cultivated a deep understanding of your business in that lender. Consequently, you should always be aware of significant deviations from industry averages and be prepared to explain them.

STATEMENT OF CASH FLOWS

In a previous chapter we discussed the statement of cash flows. This statement details the sources and uses of cash during a period. The analysis needs to extend to this statement as well. Preparation of the statement of cash flows is part of the annual financial statement. Analysis involves converting all numbers on the statement to percentages of total sources of funds. This requires dividing each item on the statement by total sources of funds and comparing those percentages to the percentages from previous statements.

The statement of cash flows is not normally prepared as part of interim or month end financial statements. An easy approach to the preparation of a sources and uses of cash analysis for month ends is to simply compare two balance sheets. Each item on the balance sheet for this month end is subtracted from the same item on last month's balance sheet. The difference shows the movement of funds through the balance sheet. This is sometimes called the *rough and ready* approach or **sources and uses of cash**. Every increase in a liability or capital account and every decrease in an asset account is a source of funds. Decreases in liability or capital accounts or increases in asset accounts are uses of funds. In order to separate sources of cash from operations, the changes in retained earnings or owners' capital accounts and the changes in accumulated depreciation are listed separately because these changes will be equal to net profit plus depreciation for the month. The total sources must equal the total uses. The numbers on the sources and uses are converted to percentages of total sources just as in the previous case and compared to percentages from prior periods. Table 1 illustrates the process and Table 2 displays the resulting report.

Once the percentages have been prepared, the analysis examines where money came from and where it went. Remember that short term financing should generally be used for short term assets while long term financing should be used for long lived assets. Is that what happened? Where did the majority of the funds come from? How much came from operations? What are the trends? Is this period consistent with previous sources and uses of funds? What happened to create the differences? Did you have any plans in effect which should have affected the results? Were the

Table 1

Sources and Uses of Cash

	This Period	Last Period	Sources	Uses
Cash in Banks	($ 4,902)	$ 204	5,106	
Accounts Receivable	37,876	18,662		19,214
Receivables from Officers	3,291	8,957	5,666	
Inventory	27,629	18,849		8,780
Prepaid Expenses	12,922	2,159		10,763
Total Current Assets [1]	76,816	48,831		
Land [2]	10,500	10,500		
Building [2]	74,399	74,399		
Machinery and Equipment [2]	28,527	28,527		
Leasehold Improvements	21,937	20,672		1,265
Furniture and Fixtures [2]	3,972	3,972		
Vehicles	12,750	11,850		900
Accumulated Depreciation [3]	(57,004)	(40,862)	16,142	
Net Book Value [1]	95,081	109,058		
Other Assets	770	50		720
Total Assets [1]	$172,667	$157,939		
Accounts Payable	$ 95,762	$ 93,237	2,525	
Accrued Items	9,382	7,113	2,269	
Current Portion, Long Term Debt [4]	35,445	25,286		
Total Current Liabilities [1]	140,589	125,636		
Mortgage on Building	37,745	52,186		14,441
Notes due to Banks	44,789	13,651	31,138	
Total [1]	82,534	65,837		
Less Current Portion [4]	(35,445)	(25,286)		
Total Long Term Debt [1]	47,089	40,551		
Capital Stock [2]	15,300	15,300		
Paid In Capital [2]	20,573	20,573		
Retained Earnings [5]	(50,884)	(44,121)		6,763
Total Equity [1]	(15,011)	(8,248)		
Total Liabilities and Stockholder's Equity [1]	$172,667	$157,939		
Total Sources and Uses			62,846	62,846

1   Sources and uses are not calculated for subtotals or totals
2   No Change
3   An increase in accumulated depreciation is a source of funds
4   Current Portion, Long Term Debt is ignored because it is included in Long Term Debt
5   Since there is a net loss, it is a use of funds

results as expected? If a firm consistently acquires funds from debt, it will eventually have problems. Operations should be a major source of cash most of the time. Was this the case for your firm? Do you need to make any changes in operations for the coming months?

The firm in the tables had some problems during the period under analysis. The majority of funds came from long term debt (55.5%) and were used to acquire current assets (69.1%). If that were to develop into a trend, the company could find itself in trouble because the current assets would be consumed and the debt would still remain thereby placing a burden on future operations. The key question is always where did the majority of cash come from, and where was it used.

OVERVIEW OF FINANCIAL ANALYSIS

The steps of financial analysis are displayed in Table 3. This process should be followed at the end of each month as part of the planning and budgeting activities. As the table shows, the calculations are easily produced by a spread sheet.

Table 2 Sources and Uses of Cash				
	Sources	%	Uses	%
Operations:				
Income	(6,763)	(12.1%)		
Depreciation	16,142	28.8%		
Total from Operations	9,379	16.7%		
Cash in Banks	5,106	9.1%		
Accounts Receivable			19,214	34.3%
Receivables from Officers	5,666	10.1%		
Inventory			8,780	15.7%
Prepaid Expenses			10,763	19.2%
Accounts Payable	2,525	4.5%		
Accrued Items	2,269	4.0%		
Total Current Items	15,566	27.8%	38,757	69.1%
Leasehold Improvements			1,265	2.3%
Vehicles			900	1.6%
Other Assets			720	1.3%
Mortgage on Building			14,441	25.7%
Notes due to Banks	31,138	55.5%		
Total Noncurrent Items	31,138	55.5%	17,326	30.9%
Total Sources and Uses of Cash	56,083	100.0%	56,083	100.0%

Table 3

Financial Analysis

I.   Prepare month end (or year end) financial statement
    A.   Income Statement
    B.   Balance Sheet
    C.   Statement of Changes in Financial Position or Sources and Uses of Funds Statement

II.   Convert each statement to component percentages
    A.   Divide each item on income statement by net sales
    B.   Divide each item on balance sheet by total assets
    C.   Divide each item on Changes or S&U by total sources

III. Calculate horizontal percentages
    A.   Divide each item by itself for the last period
    B.   Use last year's statement for year end statements
    C.   Use the same month from last year for monthly statements

IV.   Calculate key ratios
    A.   Liquidity
        1.   Current Ratio: Current Assets / Current Liabilities
        2.   Quick Ratio: (Current Assets - Inventory) / Current Liabilities
        3.   Inventory Liquidation: (Current Liabilities - Quick Assets) / Inventory
    B.   Activity
        1.   Receivables Turnover: Sales / Average Accounts Receivable
        2.   Inventory Turnover: Sales / Average Inventory
        3.   Fixed Asset Turnover: Sales / Average Fixed Assets
        4.   Total Asset Turnover: Sales / Average Total Assets
    C.   Leverage
        1.   Debt Ratio: Debt / Total Assets
        2.   Debt to Worth: Debt / Total Net Worth
        3.   Interest Coverage: Profit before Interest and Taxes / Interest
        4.   Fixed Charge Coverage: Profit before Interest and Lease / (Interest+Lease)
        5.   Cash Coverages: Operating Cash Flow before Loan and Lease Payments /
                                                Payments on Loans and Leases
    D.   Profitability and Cash Flow
        1.   Gross Profit Margin: Gross Profit / Sales
        2.   Contribution Margin: Contribution Margin / Sales
        3.   Operating Profit Margin: Operating Profit / Sales
        4.   Net Profit Margin: Net Profit / Sales
        5.   Return on Investment: Net Profit / Net Worth
        6.   DuPont Ratio: (Sales / Total Assets)(Net Profit / Sales)
        7.   Operating Cash Flow: Operating Cash Flow / Sales
        8.   Cash Flow from Operations: Cash Flow from Operations / Sales
        9.   Net Cash Flow: Net Cash Flow / Sales

The ratios in Table 3 are not an exhaustive list. You should add any industry specific ratios which are important for your business or any other ratios which you consider valuable. In addition, the contents of the income statement should be managerially oriented. That means that fixed and variable costs should be identified and separated so that a contribution margin can be calculated on the face of the statement. Any items which are of particular interest to you on the income statement or balance sheet should be included.

Notice that the comparison is made to prior year end statements when we are analyzing year end statements. If a month end or quarter end statement is being analyzed, then the comparison should be made to the same period in prior years so that the seasonality of the firm will be reflected. You can also make the comparisons directly to the previous month. This can be a valuable technique to evaluate decisions made last month at the earliest possible date. The only danger is that you must be sure to keep in mind the impact of seasonality on the numbers.

Table 4 describes the month end routine which you should establish. Such a system will keep you on track and help you to see changes which you need to make before problems develop.

In order to develop and maintain good relations with a banker, it is a good idea to furnish a copy of your month end analysis to your lender. This will not only serve to keep that individual up to date with your operations, it will force you to do a complete job of analysis each month because someone outside the firm will be seeing it.

Communication of the results of analysis, budgeting and planning should occur inside the firm. If you have managers in the firm, they should assist in the process and be aware of how the company stands and what it needs to do for improvement. Staff and employees also need to be aware of the firm's position, although detailed knowledge is not generally important. It is important for the staff to understand the reasonableness of the plans and budgets so that they will support the firm's progress.

Table 4

Month End Analysis Routine

I.   Perform Financial Analysis

II.   Examine Trends for all ratios and percentages

III.   Compare ratios and percentages to budgets and plans

IV.   Consider the impact of past actions/need for future actions

V.   Evaluate the firm and its strengths and weaknesses

VI.   Make decisions about changes in operations/policies

VII.   Prepare new budgets and forecasts and make new plans

SUMMARY

One of the best and least understood tools of management is financial analysis. The financial condition of a firm at any given point in time is a result of the decisions and actions of its owner(s), consequently, financial analysis provides a report card for management.

The financial statements consist of the income statement, balance sheet, reconciliation of net worth and the statement of changes in financial position and are prepared at the end of each fiscal year. Interim statements are prepared at the end of each month and tend to be less complete than the annual statement. If interim statements are analyzed, they should be compared to the same month in the prior year as well as last month. The techniques used in financial analysis include component percentage analysis or vertical analysis and horizontal analysis.

Ratio analysis is the best known technique of financial analysis. It involves dividing various items on the statement by other items to highlight and reveal relationships. There are literally hundreds of ratios which can be calculated. Many are useful only in specific industries.

Trend analysis involves comparing component percentages and ratios to those for previous periods. The longer the time period, the better trends can be identified. This is the most useful of all financial analysis techniques because it can highlight problems before they develop.

Ratios and percentages can be compared to industry averages. This is a well known financial analysis technique, but is less valuable than is popularly believed. Industry averages tend not to be representative of the entire industry and they tend to represent stronger companies and are therefore probably skewed higher than the real average. You should be very careful when using industry averages because of these problems.

Financial performance is divided into four areas. Liquidity refers to a firm's ability to meet its maturing obligations. Activity refers to how well a firm is employing its assets. Leverage refers to the proportion of debt which is involved in a firm's financial structure. Profitability refers to pricing and cost control policies of a firm.

Before analysis, you should be sure that the statements are in a form which separates fixed and variable expenses and highlights contribution margin. Then you should calculate the various cash flow figures including operation cash flow, cash flow from operations and net cash flow.

If you are examining an interim statement, the statement of cash flows is not normally a part of the package. The process of preparing a rough and ready sources and uses of cash statement is outlined in Table 1 and Table 2. The financial analysis process is outlined in Table 3, and the month end analysis routine is displayed in Table 4.

A microcomputer with a good spread sheet program can make the preparation of the numbers fast and simple. This will free time for thought and interpretation. Financial analysis is part of any sound planning program and cannot be overlooked if you wish to maintain a strong, vibrant company.

QUESTIONS, EXERCISES AND CASES

QUESTIONS:

1.   What is financial analysis?

2.   Why is it important to study and understand financial analysis for a small business owner/manager?

3.   What are the techniques of financial analysis?

4.   What are the areas of financial performance?

5.   Which technique is the most useful? Which technique is the least valuable?

6.   What are the disadvantages of industry averages?

7.   Name at least 2 ratios in each of the four performance areas.

8.   How many ratios are there? Which should you use for your business?

9.   What do ratios reveal?

10.   How does cash flow compare to profit?

11.   What is the DuPont Ratio?

12.   How often should you perform financial analysis on your own business?

CASE

The following are financial statements for a retail card and gift shop. The business was begun four years ago in a downtown site but moved to a mall location two years later. That move resulted in a tremendous increase in sales but also a major increase in rent expense. Rent went from $100 per month to $300 per month plus 2% of sales in excess of $25,000.

As a result of the higher sales level, the owner began to take a small salary of $6,000 per year out of the business. Three months before the end of its last fiscal year, a new location became available and the company moved from its central location in the mall to a location at the end of a wing.

This resulted in a decrease in rent, but sales dropped by one half in the last three months compared to the same quarter last year. Rent dropped from the $300/2% level to $200 plus 2% of sales over $25,000.

Pictured on the following pages are financial statements for the first four years of the company's life. The owner needs to increase her salary to at least $12,000 and would like to go on up to $20,000 as soon as possible. Right now she is wondering whether the business will ever be able to support her.

Analyze the financial position of the firm and make recommendations.

Balance Sheets				
	199D	199C	199B	199A
Cash	$ 762	$ 830	$ 159	$ 202
Receivables	829	486	565	323
Inventory	17,556	24,063	6,474	5,031
Total	19,147	25,379	7,198	5,556
Leasehold Improvements	4,991	4,991	4,991	4,991
Equipment & Fixtures	10,890	10,890	8,108	8,108
Accumulated Depreciation	(10,593)	(8,869)	(5,642)	(2,488)
Net Fixed Assets	5,288	7,012	7,457	10,611
Notes Receivable	1,579	1,579	---	---
Deferred Interest	3,921	4,192	---	---
Other Assets	99	98	176	481
Total Assets	$30,034	$38,260	$14,831	$16,468
Accounts Payable	9,952	13,705	4,313	1,055
Notes Payable	---	---	3,074	1,901
Accruals	456	713	254	215
Current Portion Long Term Debt	5,456	4,264	---	---
Total Current Liabilities	15,864	18,682	7,641	3,171
Long Term Debt	23,212	22,919	---	---
Due to Shareholders	---	---	19,611	19,611
Current Portion Long Term Debt	(5,456)	(4,264)	---	---
Total Long Term Debt	17,756	18,655	19,611	19,611
Common Stock	4,500	4,500	4,250	4,250
Retained Earnings	(8,086)	(3,577)	(16,671)	(10,564)
Total Equity	(3,586)	923	(12,421)	(6,314)
Total Liabilities & Equity	$30,034	$38,260	$14,831	$16,468

Income Statements

	199D	199C	199B	199A
Gross Sales	$46,983	$51,377	$13,231	$11,382
Returns	541	445	---	---
Net Sales	46,442	50,932	13,231	11,382
Beginning Inventory	24,063	6,474	5,031	---
Purchases	18,164	34,696	9,686	10,576
Ending Inventory	(17,556)	(24,063)	(6,474)	(5,031)
Cost of Goods Sold	24,671	17,107	8,243	5,545
Gross Profit	21,771	33,825	4,988	5,837
Salaries	12,458	6,926	2,292	6,505
Rent	3,740	4,164	1,200	1,000
Advertising	1,628	1,930	1,434	2,141
Utilities	1,117	1,212	1,563	---
Taxes & Licenses	1,091	1,159	208	703
Repairs & Maintenance	663	234	265	102
Depreciation & Amortization	1,514	2,227	2,604	2,089
Travel & Auto Expense	689	373	261	---
Supplies	560	745	676	---
Insurance	304	236	246	---
Other Expenses	383	801	44	3,424
Total Expenses	24,147	20,007	10,793	15,964
Interest Expense	2,133	699	301	437
Income before Tax	(4,509)	13,119	(6,106)	(10,564)
Income Tax	---	---	---	---
Net Income	($4,509)	$13,119	($6,106)	($10,564)

* Note: Record keeping in the first year failed to separate many expense categories. Consequently, the *other* category of expense seems excessive.

PART THREE

PLANNING FOR SUCCESS

CHAPTER EIGHT

THE BUSINESS PLAN

CHAPTER OBJECTIVES

Upon completion of this chapter, you should be able to:

- Explain the importance of each step of the business plan;

- Describe why personal goals and objectives must be considered in business ventures;

- Discuss the importance of establishing business objectives;

- Explain the significance of strategic issues and how they impact business;

- Identify the requirements for success as outlined by the planning stages;

- Identify the distinctive competence of a business; and,

- Plan for the physical and capital requirements for a business venture.

THE BUSINESS PLAN

INTRODUCTION

Julius Caesar's famous quotation, *Veni, vidi, vici,* comes from his report to the Roman Senate about 47 B.C. of his successful campaign against the Gauls. Caesar had crossed into what is now modern France with a force of troops vastly outnumbered by the fighting forces in Gaul and faced with a territory larger than Italy in which those forces were deployed. Through superior military strategy and tactics, Caesar was successful in subjugating the territory and adding it to the Roman Empire. His report of that success was boastful and vain and lacked details, but his letter contained the essence of the desires of all individuals who set out to start new businesses. He simply said, I came, I saw, I conquered. That, in essence, is what a successful new business venture must do. It must establish a presence in the target market area, examine the characteristics of the market and the competition in that area, and effectively employ strategies and tactics which will establish the venture as a permanent force in the area. The most important consideration for the success of a business is the plan which it will follow in its campaign. That plan is the subject of this chapter.

OUTLINE OF THE BUSINESS PLAN

The first step in preparing a business plan is the establishment of business objectives. These objectives must not be vague or general. They must be concrete, specific and quantifiable. These objectives will be used to measure the progress which the company has made, therefore they need to be as detailed as possible. The personal objectives of the owner may or may not be a part of the business objectives, but they too should have been examined and recorded as part of the evaluation process in the decision to start this business. Table 1 displays an outline of the entire process.

Although the steps in the business plan are listed in a sequential order in the diagram, many of the steps will be performed simultaneously. The important point to remember is that each of the steps must be performed prior to the actual start-up of the business and the results of each of the steps must be written down in the planning document. The location of the steps in Table 1 simply indicates the point at which an absolute final determination of each aspect of the plan is required relative to the others.

Upon completion of the business plan a prospective owner will have a written document which will guide the business through its start-up phase and will provide a tool for the monitoring of the progress of the venture. Remember that the plan will inevitably require adjustment as the start-up proceeds. Changes will have to be made as new knowledge is gained and as plans are proved untenable. This is to be expected and is not a sign of failure. Changes should be made in writing to the plan so that the document can continue to provide a benchmark for the evaluation of progress.

TABLE 1

THE BUSINESS PLAN

I. Establish Personal Objectives
    A. Determine your objectives presently
    B. Determine where you wish to be in 5 years
    C. Determine where you wish to be in 10 years

II. Choose a Product or Service
    A. Evaluate the marketability of the product/service
    B. Determine feasibility of product/service

III. Select Market Area
    A. Evaluate market area
    B. Determine feasibility of market area
    C. Evaluate the competition

IV. Establish Business Objectives

V. Determine Business Strategies
    A. Determine distinctive competency
    B. Prepare marketing plan

VI. Establish Timetable

VII. Determine Human Resource Requirements

VIII. Determine Physical Resource and Capacity Requirements

IX. Select Site

X. Determine Capital Requirements

XI. Prepare Forecasts and Budgets
    A. Sales Forecast
    B. Marketing Budget
    C. Operating Budget
    D. Capital Budget
    E. Income Statement
    F. Balance Sheet

XII. Perform Breakeven Analysis

XIII. Evaluate and Modify Plan

XIV. Locate and Obtain Capital

XV. Implement the Plan

XVI. Evaluate Progress

FEASIBILITY

The first three steps of the business plan actually revolve around the feasibility of the venture. The examination of personal goals and objectives serves two purposes. It forces a prospective owner to examine whether he or she is personally willing to pay the price of success in this new business and forces a recognition of what that price will be. We talked about the long hours which successful business owners work in the introductory chapters. We also discussed the characteristics required for success. Sadly, the price of success in a new venture can be quite high in personal terms. It must be something which one wants and wants greatly. A cover story article in *Inc.* was *Divorce* and the upshot of the story was advice to business owners that to plan for a divorce may ruin a marriage, but not to plan for it may destroy a company.[50] The fact that the publishers of that magazine thought the story to be worth front cover pictures is noteworthy. Starting a new business is a very serious step. Don't consider taking that step without first carefully examining your personal goals and objectives.

Product or service viability is not synonymous with salability. In order for a product or service to be viable, there must be a demand for it and it must be feasible to produce and sell it. That means that *viability* is a function of the market and of the costs of production and the sales price obtainable for the item. The first part of the question is answered through market research. The second part of the question involves break-even analysis. Break-even analysis shows in the Business Plan as one of the last steps. That is because one of the last steps is the calculation of the final break-even characteristics of the organization, but a rough estimate of the break-even is required at this stage when product/service viability is being examined.

The actual calculation of a break-even point is a simple arithmetic solution. In a previous chapter we presented a complete review of the techniques. As we discussed, if we are assessing the viability of a product or service, then we need a rough estimate of what the fixed costs and variable costs will be. The *fixed costs* are not as hard to calculate. They include such things as rent, salaries, insurance, and utilities. *Variable costs* are the costs of actually producing the product or service. If the business is to be a retailer, then variable costs are the costs of inventory. Estimates of the variable costs may be very difficult to make, especially in the case of a manufacturing company. Estimates of selling prices which will be possible may also be difficult. The variable costs need to be expressed per unit or per dollar of sales. This allows the contribution margin to be calculated. The *contribution margin* is simply the amount of money left over to cover fixed expenses after the variable costs have been paid. In terms of one unit of sales, the contribution margin is the amount of the sales price left over after paying for the unit. The contribution margin is usually expressed as a percentage of sales. Dividing projected fixed costs for the first year of operations by the contribution margin yields an estimate of the dollar volume of sales which must be generated for the business to break-even and avoid a loss. Since all of the numbers are estimates, it is wise to make several calculations using a range of estimates for each variable from pessimistic to optimistic.

The final determination of viability of a product or service frequently comes down to a subjective determination as to whether the sales level required to break-even can be achieved in a given market area. At this point in the planning process, the prospective business owner must decide whether he or she believes that there is a high enough probability for success of a given product/service in a given market area to continue the planning process. If the decision is positive, then the remaining steps of the business plan should be addressed. The original rough estimates of break-even and product/market viability should be reassessed continuously during the planning process as new and more accurate information is obtained.

In the marketing tools chapter we discussed the technical aspects of marketing in a small business enterprise. Because of the relative importance of marketing to a successful start-up, we will dedicate the entirety of the following chapter to the issues of product or service selection and the preparation of the marketing plan. For now we will assume that the prospective small business owner has already made a product/service and market area selection.

BUSINESS OBJECTIVES

As we indicated earlier, the business objectives must be concrete and specific. They should address where the business should be in terms of sales, profits and market share at the end of the start-up period and at the end of each of the next 3 to 5 years. If there are other key aspects of the business' success, then they should be included in the objectives as well. For example, the product mix might be considered important for a retailer or wholesaler who plans to expand the lines and number of products offered during the earlier years of the venture. If so, then objectives should be established for the product mix. If the number or skill mix of the employees is important, as in the case of a service business offering professional services, then the personnel levels and skills should be part of the objectives. The point is that the objectives must address the key aspects which will determine the success or failure of the business. Such concerns are called *strategic issues*. Successful management of strategic issues will mean that the firm survives; unsuccessful management of strategic issues will spell doom for the business.

STRATEGIC ISSUES

As we discussed in the prior paragraph, strategic issues are the life or death issues for the firm. Setting objectives for the firm actually requires that the owner recognize the strategic issues for his or her business. What is it that a business must do in order to ensure its survival? The issues will be different for different businesses. For example, in a restaurant which caters to a local market, a strategic issue will be the establishment of repeat patronage. Does that sound obvious? Most strategic issues are like that, but sometimes the most obvious things are the most difficult to see.

A CASE FROM OUR FILES

We were called in as consultants because the store was losing money. It was a small grocery store located in a predominantly rural area in Southern Georgia. It had been in existence for almost 20 years and had always been profitable until the last two years. The owner had inherited the place from his father 5 or 6 years ago.

We visited the store and talked to the owner and looked at the financial statements. The statements showed a steady decline in sales starting about 18 months prior to our visit. Losses had begun to be recorded about 12 months prior and the store was now in serious trouble from the standpoint of its ability to survive.

The owner said everything had been going fine until a Piggly Wiggly opened up down the street and killed his business. We checked on that, but the Piggly Wiggly was a bit higher priced than our client's store and it had been in existence for a little over two years. At least 6 months of that time our client had done all right, so that didn't make any sense. We checked for other competitors, but there really weren't any significant changes in the competitive picture during the 18 months of the sales decline.

When we toured the store, we found the problem. But even then we couldn't get the client to see it. The first clue was a mess in the lower shelves of the pet food section. Several bags had apparently been torn because there was a lot of dog food on the floor and on the shelves between the bags. We didn't figure it out immediately, but when we got to the meat section, there wasn't a lot of meat on display in the coolers and several of the packages were torn and discolored. The store really wasn't dirty enough to explain that and some other torn packages which we saw and so we were really puzzled. Then we noticed a gap between the ice cream cooler and the adjoining shelving and took a peek in there. That's when we saw it.

It was a rat trap! Not a mouse trap, a rat trap. You could have caught rabbits in that trap!

We asked several of the employees whether any customers had ever complained about rats. The response was that only one or two had ever reported actually seeing a rat and only one had ever left because of it. Apparently one lady had left a full grocery cart sitting in the aisle and departed the store in rather a hurry.

We confronted the owner with the problem, but he said that couldn't be it, because they had about gotten rid of all the rats. It seems that a delivery truck had backed into the warehouse door one day a couple of years ago and the door had never closed completely since. As soon as the rats had been noticed, having apparently come in the door crack from a nearby creek, they had fixed the door and started trapping the pests. Most were now gone, so the owner said. Besides the health department hadn't noticed anything.

We asked about a professional exterminator service, but the owner said they were too expensive. Besides, the one firm he had talked to had wanted to fumigate the place and that would have meant that he would have lost a fortune in meat and produce!

Can you believe it! In the interest of saving a few dollars in the short run, the owner was killing his business! And somehow, we just couldn't make him see it.

The determination of strategic issues for a business frequently revolves around the image which a company wishes to portray. The marketing image is one of the strategic issues for a firm.

If, for example, a business is to have an image of high quality, then not only must the proper appearance be maintained in the business and in its dealing with the market, but the owner must pay attention to the competitors to ensure that no one usurps the image in the market area. If the image is to be one of low price, then the same rules hold true. Not only must everything in the business be consistent with the established image, but the business must continue to portray that image when compared to its competitors. This requires a close and continuous monitoring of the competing firms in the market area.

Consider the case from our files of a small grocery store in southern Georgia as described by an independent consultant. The Case Note is a true but sad story. The grocery store ultimately failed. Its owner had not paid attention to a strategic issue. Shoppers in a grocery store demand a clean facility and one which is not infested with rodents or insects. The moral of the story is that a business owner who would be a success must determine what it is that the market demands and provide that demand consistently and constantly.

BUSINESS STRATEGIES

Business strategies are the plans which are made to obtain the business objectives. After the strategic issues have been identified and goals and objectives have been established, then an owner must decide what is to be done to achieve the objectives. These strategies are statements about the image or other aspects of the business which will dictate how the firm is to be managed. The day to day management of the enterprise will be conducted in accordance with the strategies. For example, our grocery store owner could have established as one of his strategies the maintenance of a clean store. From an operational perspective, daily management would have to ensure that attention was paid to that detail. The strategies actually become objectives for the operational management. Frequently, a strategy will dictate what must be done before a company can open its doors.

DISTINCTIVE COMPETENCY

Development of the business strategies essentially revolves around the establishment of a distinctive competency and plans to maintain that competency. A *distinctive competency* is the primary thing which makes a firm stand out from its competitors. You might think of it as the thing which a business does best. As we discussed in a previous chapter, every business must have something which distinguishes it from its competitors in the minds of the market. Without some distinguishing characteristic, a business then becomes just like its competitors and there is no reason for a consumer to select one firm over another. Think about it from your own buying perspective. Why do you choose the businesses that you use? What makes them stand out in your mind?

We remember one business owner who objected to advertising in the Yellow Pages of the telephone book. When we questioned him on that oversight, he replied that consumers had already made up their minds to buy before they went to the Yellow Pages. Consequently, he believed, they used the Yellow Pages to simply shop price. Since his business did not compete on the basis of price, he felt himself at a disadvantage when faced with such callers and preferred to spend his available advertising dollars in ways which would bring customers directly to his business before they decided to buy or at least before they decided to shop prices. We had to admit that his approach made a lot of sense.

The distinctive competency which Federal Express developed was that of an extremely high level and speed of service. When the US Post Office responded to pressure from Federal and other overnight delivery services by installing its own high speed service, Federal was able to survive despite having higher prices than the Post Office because of its image and its continuing efforts to maintain that image. The Post Office doesn't come to your door to pick up your packages: Federal does. Nike has a very different distinctive competency. It makes the best shoes for various sports. It has succeeded in maintaining this image despite the fact that it does not make the shoes it sells. The distinctive competency can be based on service or on product or on any number of other factors including price, location, hours of operation, breadth or depth of product line, or simply the friendliness of the employees. A friend of ours remarked the other day that he frequented a restaurant in town because the people there all knew him by name and were so very friendly. He commented that he was fearful of taking any of his luncheons elsewhere because he did not want to damage the business of his friends. We can expect few customers to develop that high a degree of loyalty, but it illustrates how a simple thing like consistently cheerful, friendly employees can actually be a distinctive competency.

When developing the distinctive competency for your venture, be sure to consider the role which pricing plays. It is possible for the competency to be based on price. Charles Schwab founded a discount brokerage firm and quickly became the largest such firm in the United States.[51] Even though you decide not to compete on the basis of price, if your prices are not competitive then the distinctive competency becomes even more important. Your customers must have something for which they will be willing to pay a higher price. That something may be service or convenience or atmosphere, but it must exist. This points out the importance of knowing what your competitors prices are on a continuing basis. This is not to underestimate the value of added factors. We are familiar with a restaurant and inn whose distinctive competency is actually that it has the highest prices in town. It is located in a town with a high volume of tourist trade and has developed an image of an extremely luxurious inn with an exceptional restaurant. That image is actually at odds with the facts as the inn is neither as new nor as luxurious as are several others in town and the restaurant, although quite excellent, is seldom recognized by the local populace as among the finest. Nevertheless, the business is quite healthy and vibrant and consistently sells its patrons on the belief that they are frequenting the finest establishment of its type in the region.

MARKETING PLAN

The marketing plan is a natural outgrowth of the prior steps of the business plan. In the following chapter we will talk about the pre-venture marketing research which must be conducted and discuss the development of a start-up marketing plan which will address the advertising to be conducted prior to and subsequent to opening a new venture. We will talk about marketing strategies for the opening period and steps which should be taken to ensure that the members of the target market are informed as to the existence of the new business. In this chapter we will focus on the development of a marketing plan which will encompass the entirety of the first year of a business' life. This plan must address the transition period to normal business operations as well as consider the long term marketing strategies. We simply cannot say too much about the need for careful planning in the marketing area.

If special or promotional activities or prices are planned as part of a business' opening, then a problem is sure to occur which must be dealt with in the plan. What happens when the special prizes or prices or features are discontinued? When should they be discontinued and what marketing strategies should be pursued thereafter? A new grocery opened recently in our town. Its opening was well promoted for several months in advance and its initial pricing was truly amazing. The early marketing efforts were an astounding success. Virtually everyone in the market area shopped at the store during its two week *grand opening sale*. But since then the parking lot has been sparsely occupied. Clearly a great deal of money was expended on the start-up marketing efforts in the form of prices well below costs as well as advertising, but the on-going marketing has been lackluster and the prices have leaped to the highest level of any store in town. After several months it does not appear that the new store has garnered a significant share of the market. This failure is not simply due to price, although that has had an effect. The failure is primarily due to the assumption which the management made, that the initial marketing efforts were all that would be required. As soon as the market place recognized their existence and saw their facility, they were certain that success would be theirs. This has not been the case for our new grocery store and it seldom is the case for any new venture. The marketing plan must address the *post opening blues* and include steps to minimize the problem and to smooth the transition to normal business operations. Such plans must focus heavily on the distinctive competency. Hopefully, the start-up marketing has been prepared with the distinctive competency in mind so that those efforts will not damage the firm's strategies. Our new grocery store might have done better with less impressive sales prices during its grand opening if it intended to offer consistently higher prices than those of its competitors. The contrast would then not have been as great when the sales prices were removed. If the start-up marketing has been well planned, then the phase-in of normal operations should be associated with continuing marketing and advertising efforts which focus on the firm's distinctive competency. The purpose of the start-up marketing is to let everyone in the target market know that you are there. Ongoing marketing is designed to make customers continue to do business with you over the long term.

Like the start-up marketing plan, this aspect of the overall business plan should have a budget. We will talk about all of the budgets later on, but the actual preparation of the marketing inputs to the budget have to be associated with the marketing plan itself and so it is done as a part of the preparation of the plan itself.

TIMETABLE

The *timetable* refers to the establishment of dates for the beginning of the pre-venture advertising, the completion of all the opening requirements, the opening date, the end of the start-up marketing phase, the dates when key people will be placed on the payroll, dates for the remainder of the staff, and the date for the start of completely normal operations. Many new venturists neglect this phase of the plan because it is so difficult to complete. If there are construction aspects to the opening of the business, whether the building of a new facility or the completion of leasehold improvements, you will quickly learn that the estimate for completion of construction activities is frequently a complete guess. Many other of the time factors will be difficult to estimate as well. For example, the arrival date for the first inventory shipment, the installation date for telephone systems, the arrival of fixtures and furniture, among a host of other details will be difficult to estimate. Nevertheless, the timetable should not be neglected. The process of developing a timetable will be of immense value even if every date in it turns out to be wrong. Preparing the timetable will force you to make a written list of every aspect of the start-up phase of your business. Simply preparing the list is of value. Until you have actually done it once, you would be amazed at how many details are involved in the start of a new business and how easy it is to overlook things that you need to do.

Other aspects of the timetable are less difficult to determine because they are planned. These include the duration of the start-up marketing program, its beginning and ending dates, personnel requirements and the beginning of normal operations. You should give considerable thought to the establishment of this part of the timetable. Budgetary restraints will play a role, of course, but other factors such as the level of established competition, the dispersion of the target market and the difficulty of reaching that market will also affect the planning. A retail business with a small market area and a low level of established competition will not require an elaborate pre-opening marketing campaign, nor will a wholesale business which will depend on sales calls to make its presence known to the market. On the other hand, a retailer or service firm facing deep, entrenched competition or a widely dispersed market area may well be better served by extensive pre-opening advertising and a lengthy period of specials or promotional activities after its opening. Personnel needs prior to opening will be a function of the amount of work which must be done prior to opening the doors and how much of that work you can do personally. Staffing requirements at and after opening are largely determined by the human resource planning which we will discuss more fully in the following sections.

After the timetable has been established, you must remember that it is a planning document and therefore subject to change. As new and better estimates of dates for the various activities are known, the timetable should be updated. If experiences during the opening make clear that the transition to normal operations should be postponed or accelerated, then those changes should be made. By the same token, as activities are discovered which were omitted from the original timetable, those items should be added. The timetable, like all planning documents, should be continuously updated as new knowledge and experience is gained.

HUMAN RESOURCES

Human resource requirements refers to the number and skill levels of the personnel which will be involved in the business. The planning for personnel needs should encompass the entire first year of the operations of the venture. Thereafter, human resource planning should be a permanent part of the planning activities of the firm. We will discuss ongoing human resource needs in a later chapter, but start-up needs are addressed in this section.

For most types of businesses, the people employed by the businesses are the most valuable asset of the business. Competent, capable people are an absolute must for success in any venture. Remember that human resources refer not just to clerks and laborers, but to management people as well, including the top management. Your own skills and abilities should be assessed as part of this process. If there are managerial skills which you lack, then plans should be made for the acquisition of people who can shore up your inadequacies.

Don't forget to consider outsiders when you consider human resource requirements. Many small business ventures use an independent accountant to handle bookkeeping needs initially and almost all ventures require an attorney. These people are part of the human resource requirements of the firm as are the employees and must be planned for and budgeted just as the employees are.

The first step in human resource planning is the preparation of an organization chart. You may have been exposed to such charts in previous courses. If so, you know that an ***organization chart*** is simply a diagram of all of the positions within a firm with lines connecting positions to other positions which will be responsible for supervising their activities. The organization chart will simultaneously establish all of the positions which will exist in a business, identify all of the management functions which will require people, and establish the ***chain of command*** in the business. The *chain of command* describes who reports to whom and who has the power to make specific decisions. Be sure to specify numbers of people and salary levels as you build the chart.

As management people are hired, you should reexamine the organization chart. Get their input and make changes. All of the employees will have to function within the organizational hierarchy so it makes sense to gain their acceptance of what that hierarchy will be and what their own roles in the company will be.

COMPENSATION

Few things are as difficult to plan in a new business start-up as are salary levels. Because of the uncertainty surrounding the new venture, we are fearful of a large number of high salaries because of the effect that has on the breakeven point of the business. At the same time, we want to have the best people available for the jobs and so we want to offer compensation levels which will attract the best and most competent. One factor to keep in mind is that compensation includes other things than salaries. The compensation package needs to address fringe benefits such as life, health and disability insurance, vacation and sick leave, and retirement plans. When Social Security payments are considered, currently running 9.1% of the salary, the fringe benefits can easily become a highly significant part of the compensation package. Costs of 30% and higher for fringe benefits as a percentage of salaries are not uncommon. Nevertheless, such offerings are or will be demanded by the employees if you are to be able to attract and keep good people.

One aspect which can work to the benefit of the business is the establishment of a substantial portion of the compensation package in the form of profit sharing or bonus plans. This is especially true for managerial positions, whose occupants will feel better able to affect the performance of the company. Bonuses can be established and keyed to performance levels of the business which have been expressed in the objectives of the firm. The payment of these bonuses should then be accompanied by performance levels which makes the payment feasible. Bonuses can also be paid in stock, if the corporate form of business has been selected, or in the form of stock options. A portion of the bonus can be deferred for a period of time to encourage employees to stay with the company. Don't make the mistake of assuming that such deferrals can save the company cash outflows, however. To protect the employees and the firm, deferred compensation plans must be meticulously prepared and should be funded through a trustee. Discussions with an accountant or the trust officer of a bank can help to ensure that the plans are properly prepared and maintained and that they produce the best tax treatment possible for the firm.

Remember to include your own compensation when planning this phase of the business. Your own salary should be the minimum required for maintenance of your family until the business has established itself in the market place. You can provide substantial deferred compensation for yourself keyed to the performance of the firm, but you should be careful not to overburden the cash flow of the business. In addition, the compensation level you establish for yourself and any other owners of the firm will have a significant effect on the salaries which you pay to the other employees. In general, people will be more satisfied with less current salary and more deferred compensation if they see that you are leading the movement.

The actual level of salaries and other compensation which you offer will be a function of the standard of living in the area in which your business is located. To determine what is or is not acceptable for individuals with various skill levels, you may explore employment agencies, employment security commissions or industry associations. Don't forget to look in the newspaper at job listings. You may also try to find out from similar businesses or competitors in the area what their salary levels are, but expect some of those people to be reluctant to talk to you. Employment agencies or commissions can also give you an idea of the people currently available with specified skills and what they are likely to request as starting salaries. These organizations can also help you in recruiting.

RECRUITING

Where do you find the people you need? As we mentioned in the previous paragraph, employment agencies and security commissions can help. Ads in the newspaper can also be of value, but don't overlook your own contacts and those of the people going into the venture with you or already hired. One of the key aspects of the recruiting process is the determination of the responsible parties for hiring decisions. In a venture with a very small number of employees or one with few management positions, you may do all of the interviewing and hiring personally. In a venture with several management positions or a large number of people, the interviewing and hiring may be delegated to the other managers. In a very large venture, a personnel department may be planned. You should decide who will be making the hiring decisions for each position before the interviews begin.

Interviewing is an art. How to determine in a short period with a few questions and an employment application which people will be best suited for the business is difficult and fraught with error. You should decide what questions will be asked on the employment application and prepare that document in advance. Application forms can be dangerous if they include questions which you cannot ask. We will discuss this point at length in the human resource management chapter. For now, we will focus on the interview. You might consider interviewing with some of your competitors yourself to determine how their interviews are conducted. You should make a list of questions which will be asked during the interview. These may vary by the position involved. Such questions should go beyond qualifications and experience. You are going to be concerned with how well the people mesh into an effective force, how well they get along with each other and the image which they will portray to your customers. Questions concerning reactions to working with a new and as yet unproved business are not inappropriate nor are questions concerning reactions to deferred compensation plans. You should plan to have time during the interview for the applicant to ask questions as well. The kind of questions asked can sometimes be more revealing than the answers to your own questions. Remember, just because you decide that you want to hire a particular applicant does not guarantee that the individual will choose to accept your offer. The applicant will be assessing you and the planned venture as well as considering the compensation package offered. With key positions, especially managerial positions, you may need to negotiate with an applicant. Such factors as degree of autonomy and authority as well as compensation may be negotiated. Remember that the people you hire will have a major effect on the ultimate success of the business. Be sure to read the human resource management chapter before you begin to recruit and interview people.

PHYSICAL RESOURCES

The size of the facility which your business will require is really not decided in the sequential fashion which the Business Plan indicates. Everything which has been discussed about the new venture to this point will affect the requirements. Site selection is properly considered during the marketing research phase. At this point a prospective business owner must make a conscious decision about the size and characteristics of the physical facility which will be required. This decision will be affected by the amount and variety of inventory which you intend to display and to store, by the number of people who must be housed, and by the growth expectations for the business. Far too many new businesses simply go to real estate agents and find a place to rent which they believe they can afford. This is absolutely the wrong way to go about obtaining physical resources. The first question which any real estate agent will ask is: *How large a place do you need?* Until you can answer that basic question, there is no need to begin looking for a facility.

The first step in planning for physical resources is the determination of the relative importance of those resources. If the new venture is to be a retailer, for example, and it plans to piggyback its marketing by locating near a major competitor, then the physical resources will be of prime importance. In such cases it is possible for a business to gear its size, number of employees and inventory levels to a facility which is available in a Mall or other prime location. It is also possible for the physical resources to be of lesser importance, as in the case of a wholesaler who will be making all contacts with customers in their places of business through sales personnel. Service businesses can experience both conditions as well. A construction firm may have a low level of importance attached to the physical resources, while a firm of attorneys may require a prestigious address in an established office building to support a desired image. Whether customers will be coming to the business or not is a major factor in the relative importance as is the requirement for the physical handling of goods. In the former case, even though customers never frequent the business, location on or near major transportation arteries may be crucial.

If the physical resources are to be a crucial aspect of the business, then budgetary restraints may be the only other factor required for consideration before searching for a facility. Otherwise, consideration should be given to the area which will be required for display and storage of inventory, for the conduct of the business, for the housing of the staff and for expected growth in all of those areas. Regardless of whether you buy, build or rent a facility, expansion of the capacity of the physical resources will not be easy. Even in the case of a rented facility, an increase in space will not be easily accomplished without a move, and lease terms can make moving prior to the expiration of a lease an exceptionally expensive operation. Consequently, you will want to ensure that the initial facility has room available for some amount of growth, even though you will not use that space initially.

One of the more difficult areas in space determination is that required for the display of inventory. Too much or too little inventory displayed in an area can damage the image of the business in the eyes of its customers. Without a great deal of experience, planning the right square footage for a given dollar value of inventory is challenging in the extreme. One approach is to use sales per square foot statistics and inventory turnover statistics from industry associations or governmental publications and work backwards to determine the space requirements. It works this way. Assume that the average sales per square foot in your industry is $400 per year and that the inventory turnover average is 4 times per year. Now, if your markup is 50% based on selling price (100% based on cost) then you will be averaging $50 of inventory per square foot ($400 X .5 = $200 and $200/4 =$50). Now you can use inventory stocking plans or sales forecasts to determine the display area requirements. Plans to sell $500,000 in the first year would require a display area of 5,000 square feet ($500,000 X .5 = $250,000 and $250,000/$50 = 5,000). Sales per square foot averages are available from many industry associations or in governmental publications like the *Dollars and Cents* published by the Urban Land Institute and containing averages for shopping centers and malls for a variety of retailers. Assistance in finding such references is available from librarians or from governmental assistance programs like the Small Business Development Centers.

Storage area estimates for a retailer or a wholesaler or any type of business are much easier to estimate. The physical size of items to be stored dictates the overall size of the facility, but don't forget to consider handling requirements and storage weights. If mechanical equipment is to be used, the storage facility must accommodate such, and floor strength characteristics must be sufficient to handle the planned weight of the goods. In addition, if any air conditioning or heating is required for special types of inventory, that too must be considered.

Space requirements for a manufacturing firm can be extremely difficult to estimate. In essence, a production operation must be laid out on paper to obtain space requirements. This layout process is discussed in the production chapter. Construction firms must consider storage space for tools and equipment. Repair facilities must allocate space for such storage as well as the repair operation itself. Motels must determine the size of the rooms to be offered and then calculate the number of rooms based on sales projections.

Restaurants have special problems in space estimates. Seating capacity will in large measure dictate the maximum sales volume possible and is therefore crucial to the operation. Plans for required seating capacity is usually estimated by calculating the turnover expected during each meal to be offered and working backward from sales forecasts with average tickets. The turnover expected will vary greatly depending upon the type of restaurant and the target market. Average sales tickets can be calculated from menu prices or using averages from publications.

The budget is a very real factor in the selection and acquisition of physical resources. The first issue is whether you will buy and/or build or lease the facilities. The latter choice is generally less expensive in the short run, while the former is less expensive in the long run. Many business cannot consider buying because of their location requirements, i.e., the need to locate within a shopping center or mall. If there is a choice, you should recognize that financing of the acquisition or construction of a facility for a new and unproven business can be difficult. We will talk more about this in the financing plan chapter of this section of the text. Until then, just be aware that the more money you have to borrow during the start-up phase of the business, the more difficult it will be to obtain that money.

There is another advantage to leasing beyond that of reduced up-front capital requirements: flexibility. Although, you will generally have to sign a lease agreement, the term will generally be 1 to 5 years. At the end of the lease, or earlier in some lease agreements when you can find a replacement for your business, you have the option of moving. If location is not a critical issue for your particular type of business, this may not be a valuable advantage. If location is important, the flexibility may be a large advantage, because your early experience may well show that your initial location decision was not as good as it could have been. Also, if growth outstrips expectations, it is possible for your business to outgrow the facility. It is also possible for a target market to shift its desires concerning location. In either of these instances, the ability to reevaluate the site and change if necessary could be valuable. Of course, it is also possible that a particular business has no choice but to build a facility because there are none available with the desired features.

CHOOSING A SITE

Occupancy expense is a function of location as well as size of the facility. There are tradeoffs between cost and location. However, less expensive locations are not automatically better locations. A more expensive site might well be worth the difference in cost. This consideration is important and should be examined during the market research phase of the initial planning. These issues are covered in depth in the market planning chapter. Although it appears late in the Business Plan, it is entirely possible that the site selection has been completed at a much earlier stage in the planning. If it has not been done, then now is the latest time possible for the final determination.

During the market research and earlier phases of the planning process, several alternative sites should have been selected and examined. Information about costs and/or lease terms and provisions and facility size and characteristics should have been developed and recorded. Demographic factors which will affect the business should have been examined. Now that the decisions concerning the physical resources required have been made, the final selection among those alternatives is possible. Recognizing that no site will be perfect, you should choose the one which has the best combination of factors among those available.

Site selection is more than the location of a building. It also involves the selection of the geographic region, city or town in which the business will be located. Far too many small business owners simply choose to locate their businesses near their homes without giving any further thought to the process. Demographic and growth patterns may make location in your home town undesirable. Large firms spend a great deal of time and energy in selecting the locations for their operations. There is a good reason for this and small business owners would be well advised to consider them. We will examine the site selection issue in greater depth in the following chapter.

CAPITAL REQUIREMENTS

At this point in the preparation of the Business Plan, you will have finished the majority of the inputs required to determine the capital requirements for starting your business. You have determined how much the facility and physical resources are going to cost, what the personnel costs are going to be, prepared a start-up marketing budget and explored the inventory costs and other expenses of operating the business.

In the financing plan chapter of this section, we will examine the preparation of the capital requirements and the acquisition of start-up funding. In general, the *capital requirements* will include all of the out of pocket costs of acquiring the physical resources of the business, the expenses which will be incurred prior to the opening of the business, initial advertising and marketing costs, and three to six months of operating expenses.

COMPLETING THE PLAN

The final steps in the Business Plan cover budgets, breakeven analysis, and plan modification. In previous chapters in the Tools Section of the text, we discussed breakeven analysis and budgeting in depth. Budgets must be prepared for marketing and operations. Forecasts must be prepared for sales and cash flows. Finally a capital budget must be prepared which will detail the funds required for launching the new venture.

These steps are actually performed during the preparation of the earlier aspects of the plan. The forecasts and budgets are constantly revised as the plan develops and more information is gained. An initial breakeven analysis is performed and then retested as the forecasts and budgets are updated. Consequently, the process is *iterative*, that is, one which is repeated each time new and more accurate information is obtained. As the budgeting, forecasting and financial analysis evolve, the business plan is evaluated and revised. The location of the steps at the end of the plan indicate that the revisions must be finalized before the plan is complete. Once that has been done, the start-up capital can be located and the plan implemented. However, the business plan is never actually finalized. As the plan is implemented and throughout the first year of operations, progress should be evaluated and the plan should be modified. Planning is an ongoing aspect of any successful business. As soon as the time period covered by the start-up plan is over, a new plan must be developed. The most important task of the owner/manager of a small business is planning.

A DIAGRAM OF THE BUSINESS PLAN

Exhibit 1 is a diagram or flowchart of the planning process for starting a small business. As you can see, the elements are the same as described in the previous sections, however, the diagram can show that many steps are performed simultaneously. Notice that the establishment of personal objectives, business objectives, and strategies are linked by a feedback loop. Plan modification and progress evaluation are also included in the loop. This means that the process is iterative or repetitive. It is obvious that if a breakeven analysis shows the business failing, something must be changed in order to proceed. The same thing is true for every aspect of the plan. If the strategies developed are not acceptable to the owner, then either the personal or business objectives must be changed and all aspects of the planning revised.

The loop between business objectives and strategies is an extremely important segment of the process. The objectives, you remember, tell you where you want to be and the strategies say how you plan to get there. That means that both objectives and strategies must be well developed. It also means that the supporting aspects of timing, site, people and equipment must be able to support the strategies which you will pursue.

Every aspect of the plan is important, and all are interconnected. The exhibit makes it possible to visualize the process and also provides a way to manage it. The format of the exhibit is actually that of a PERT chart (Program Evaluation and Review Technique). That means that it shows the completion points of the steps that must be conducted in the start-up plan and it also shows which steps are dependent on others for completion. If you follow the diagram in completing a business plan and check off each item as it is completed, you will be less likely to omit a major step that will slow down the process. You should keep a written record for each step in the diagram. Record your original ideas and all revisions you make. Estimate how long you think each step will take and record the estimated completion dates for each point in the diagram. As you complete steps and change estimated completion dates, record those on the chart as well. That means planning to use the plan! It will also mean a more effective plan and a more workable planning process.

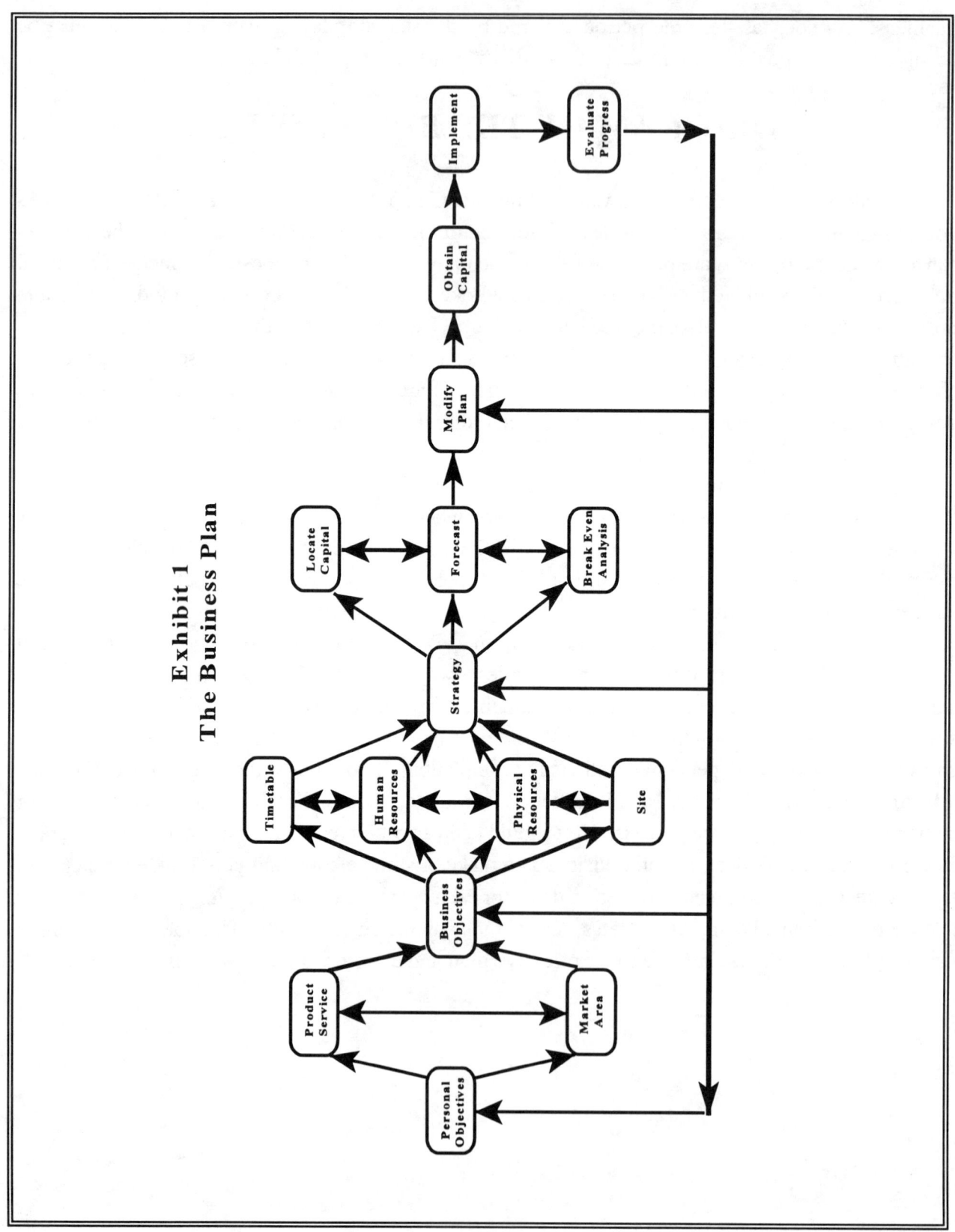

Exhibit 1
The Business Plan

SUMMARY

The steps of the business plan, outlined in Table 1, define strategies for the success of a small business venture. They include the statement of personal as well as professional goals and objectives. The plan addresses the feasibility of the concept through market research, proceeds through the selection of a product or service and a market and site. A timetable is specified as are the human, physical and capital requirements. Forecasts, budgets and breakeven analyses are prepared repeatedly throughout the planning stage and the plans are modified as appropriate.

Strategic issues which are those concerns which dictate the life or death of a firm need to be identified. The prospective owner must establish goals and objectives for the business in light of these issues. Every business must identify a distinctive competency; which is what distinguishes it from its competitors.

Forecasts, budgets and financial feasibility are iterative steps performed throughout the preparation of the plan, but they must be finalized and the final modifications made to the plan before capital can be located and obtained. After the start-up plan is completed, capital is obtained and the venture is launched, progress must be monitored and the plan revised to reflect actual results.

Planning is an ongoing process. A successful business always has a plan. As soon as the start-up plan is complete, a new plan for continued operations must be developed. The most important task of the owner of a small business is planning.

QUESTIONS, EXERCISES AND CASES

QUESTIONS

1. Describe the purpose of the business plan.

2. Why are personal goals and objectives important in business ventures?

3. What is the importance of establishing business objectives?

4. What is the significance of strategic issues and how do they impact business?

5. What are the requirements for success in the planning stages?

6. What does distinctive competency mean? Give an example.

7. How does one plan the physical requirements of a business?

8. How does one plan the capital requirements of a business?

9. What is the most important consideration for success?

10. What are business strategies and why are they important?

11. What is the purpose of the marketing plan after the initial phase of planning and opening the doors?

12. To what does the timetable refer?

13. What is the first step in human resource planning?

14. What is the difficulty in deciding upon salary levels?

15. What is the first step in planning the physical resources?

16. Why is location of less importance to certain types of businesses?

17. What other considerations should be given to a location other than site?

18. How can one determine the space requirements for inventory?

19. What are three ways to obtain facilities?

20. What are the inputs required to determine the capital requirements for starting your business?

21. Define breakeven, fixed costs, variable costs, and strategic issues.

ACTIVITIES

1. You have decided to open a small craft shop. Draw up a business plan for your new business. Include in this plan all the steps as required by the business plan outline.

   (This activity may best be done as a group project if only limited time is available or it may be ongoing as more is learned about the process in later chapters.)

2. Visit a small business in your community and ask the owner(s) how the venture came about, whether planning is conducted, how and by whom. Try to determine the strategic competency of the business.

   (You might also assign groups to various types of small businesses and have them present to the class the most important aspects of their planning especially noting how the emphases may change according to industry. This activity will especially point out the lack of planning which takes place in some small businesses.)

CASE

Al Kitchen was excited. He was going to own his own business just as soon as he got all the paperwork squared away. He was young and enthusiastic and had his whole life ahead of him. Just a few short weeks ago, he had said good bye to Uncle Sam and when he couldn't find a job immediately that appealed to him and for which he was qualified, he decided why not start his own business and be his own boss.

He had always enjoyed cooking and his grandmother had passed down several recipes which were out of this world. That's what gave him the idea one day when he came home early from job hunting and had some delicious home cooking waiting for him to ease his troubled spirits. And it

---

had! It had given Al this wonderful idea about what to do with his future. The job hunting was not going well and he had to do something soon because he needed to support his wife and little boy.

He started making his plans. There was a new mall going up outside of town and all the spaces had not yet been leased. He would go talk to them and see what he could do. After all if he only served soup, it couldn't be too expensive a proposition, could it? And, too, there wasn't any other place like this in town, so it was bound to be successful. He would start small and then grow.

Al decided to make this a family business. His sister and wife would help him out with the cooking and waiting on tables. He could also cut down on expenses by using paper and plastic products rather than dishes that had to be washed. If things went really well, he would expand to sandwiches and hire someone to take over for his wife from time to time.

Al had already contacted the mall officials to inquire about leasing possibilities and had learned that the only site he could afford was the one that leased for $10 per square foot and measured 500 square feet in the shape of an ell in an interior corner of the mall. He was to sign the lease quickly if he was to get the space because the mall manager was anxious to have all the floor space assigned within the next few weeks. Al was tempted to go ahead and sign the lease right there on the spot rather than risk losing out to someone else. He had $5,000 mustering out pay from the service that he had put in the bank when he got home, but his wife had made him promise not to sign anything until they had had time to discuss it more fully.

When Al got home full of visions of grandeur and dreams of making this small area just the beginning, he and his wife sat down and started discussing how much money would be needed in addition to the lease payment. There was kitchen equipment to lease, paper products and supplies to buy, operating expenses, and leasehold improvements and furniture. Since this was a new mall, there had been no other tenants in this space before and he needed to start from scratch.

After a very confident trip to the bank, he was declined the $20,000 loan he requested. It seemed that the loan officer didn't share his dream of success. The loan officer had asked him some searching questions about things he had never considered. The one that bothered him most was about breakeven analysis. The banker asked how much soup Al had to sell to breakeven. This had him worried. The banker had suggested that he call an assistance agency which gave that kind of advice free. Al called the Small Business Development Center and decided that before he gave up his savings, he would go see those people. He would see whether they thought he could be successful and find out exactly what his breakeven was. Surely, they would see how great his idea was and maybe they would even help him get a loan.

1.   Should this young man continue with his dream?
2.   Look at the outline for the Business Plan and discuss which steps he has at least considered even informally.
3.   Discuss which steps he needs to consider more fully.
4.   Which steps has he left out altogether?

Al received help from the SBDC in developing estimates for the expenses which the business would incur in its operation. They also established forecasts for prices and average ticket levels for the customers. The forecasts are listed below.

Examine the information and prepare a breakeven analysis for the operation. Be sure to calculate breakeven in sales dollars and in number of customers. Also calculate the breakeven in sales and number of customers per day. This will help in determining reasonableness and attainability of the forecast. On the basis of your analysis, do you think the venture is feasible?

Average Ticket per Customer	$ 2.50	
Fixed Cost Estimates for the First Year:		
Lease (store)	$ 5000.00	
Lease (kitchen equipment)	2400.00	
All utilities	2600.00	
Insurance	1500.00	
Salaries (wife & sister)	12000.00	
Owner's Draw	20000.00	
Fringe benefits (15% of salaries)	4800.00	
Total Fixed Costs		$ 48300.00
Variable Cost Estimates for the First Year:		
Food (industry average)	60% of sales	
Paper & utensils	$.10 per customer	
Variable Cost Ratio	$.10/$2.50 = 4%	
Total Variable Costs	64% of sales	
Contribution Margin		36%

CHAPTER NINE

THE MARKETING PLAN

CHAPTER OBJECTIVES

Upon completion of this chapter, you should be able to:

- Explain the steps in starting a new venture;

- Describe the trade offs in site selection;

- Explain the importance of image and timing in starting up a new venture;

- Prepare a start-up marketing budget; and,

- Frame the marketing steps into a viable plan of action.

THE MARKETING PLAN

INTRODUCTION

In this chapter we are going to assume that you are planning to go into business. We will examine the steps which should be taken to ensure that your product or service is viable from a marketing perspective. The marketing considerations covered in this chapter will be those involved in the start-up phase. The on-going marketing considerations will be discussed at greater length in a later chapter. Here we will focus on the steps one should take to establish the existence of a market for a product or service and the initial marketing plan. One word of warning is valid at this point. *Your own judgement as to the value of a product or service is not necessarily valid.* Just because you would be willing to buy an item or service is no guarantee that there are sufficient numbers of people in your market area to make a business based on that item successful. Market research is required to answer that question. Further, even if there is sufficient demand for a particular item in a particular area, it will not automatically be successful. The manner in which the item is offered for sale will be a major factor in determining its success. You can't just open a store. You have to sell your products.

THE FIRST STEP

As we have discussed, the first step in starting a new business is the establishment of personal goals and objectives. The prospective small business owner should determine why he or she wishes to start a business and what the desired outcome of the venture should be. The prospective owner should evaluate his or her skills, strengths and weaknesses and determine what the price of the venture will be in terms of personal time, effort and dedication. In the introductory chapter we discussed the characteristics of a successful venturist. If any of those are missing from your personality or if you are unwilling to pay the price in terms of time and effort, then the best decision may be not to start a new business, or to wait until required skills or abilities can be gained. Once the decision has been made and you have recorded your personal objectives, then you can proceed to the next step. The entire business plan was displayed previously. The marketing portion of the business plan is reproduced in Table 1. The table indicates that the evaluation of the product or service and the evaluation of the market area are separate steps. We show it that way to emphasize the importance of the evaluation of both the offerings and the area in which the offerings are to be sold. In practice, however, the two aspects are generally evaluated at the same time. In the later sections of this chapter, we will discuss the evaluation simultaneously.

Table 1
The Marketing Plan

II.   Choose a Product or Service
        1.   Evaluate the marketability of the product/service
        2.   Determine feasibility of product/service

III.   Select Market Area
        1.   Evaluate market area
        2.   Determine feasibility of market area
        3.   Evaluate the competition

The first step in the marketing plan is the selection of the product or service which is to be sold. As we discussed in the previous chapter, many people choose a product based upon situations or past experience. Others discover a product or service which they think no one is addressing and for which they believe a large market exists. Both approaches have value. Experience with the product or service which you intend to sell helps you to understand what is required to produce the items and what is required to sell them.

STEPS IN DEVELOPING A MARKETING PLAN

We previously outlined the marketing process in great detail. We discussed the who, what, when, where, how and why of the buying decision. We explored the importance of identifying *who* the consumers of the product or service are; *what* it is that they are really purchasing; *when* the purchase transactions take place for our product or service; *where* the sale actually occurs; *how* the sales transaction is handled; and, *why* a consumer would wish to buy our product or service. We explored the three basic approaches to marketing: push marketing, pull marketing and piggyback marketing strategies. In *push* strategies the focus is on encouraging the intermediary supplier rather than the ultimate consumer to stock our goods; in *pull* marketing the focus is on persuading the ultimate consumer that he or she desires our products or services for some specific reason; and, in *piggyback* strategies we allow a competitor to create and attract a market which we will try to take away on the basis of price or some other factor. In addition, we discussed the techniques of marketing research and we stressed the importance of the business image and the need for consistency. We discussed the concept of a distinctive competency which will set our business apart from its competitors: a factor which our customers will think of when they think about our business. Now that we have a basic understanding of the marketing process, we need to discuss the steps in developing the marketing plan for a new business venture. Table 2 presents those steps in outline format.

Steps one through five of the plan are iterative. That means that the venture should not be initiated nor the marketing plan finalized until products and/or services and the market area are deemed to be viable based upon the market research.

Table 2
The Marketing Plan

1. Select products or services to be offered;
2. Select the area in which the business is to be located;
3. Conduct market research;
4. Examine products or services and area for viability;
5. Change products, services or areas as necessary;
6. Select alternative sites for the business;
7. Establish pricing strategies and policies;
8. Establish promotional strategies;
9. Establish the budget for start-up marketing;
10. Determine the image to be portrayed;
11. Make the final site selection;
12. Establish the marketing plan.

PRODUCT/SERVICE SELECTION

Most people select a product or service with which they have experience or for which they believe an untapped demand exists. The market research is made simpler in the former instance, but is still required. In the latter instance potential difficulties exist resulting from lack of familiarity with the items which are to be offered for sale. It is always better to have experience with an item when possible. If not possible, then the acquisition of people with appropriate experience should be a high priority. Starting off in a new venture with a product or service with which you have no experience and without knowledge in the firm from other sources makes the venture more risky and success more difficult to obtain. If you intend to start such a venture, be especially sure that the market research has been well and thoroughly done!

Stories abound about fortunes made by the inventor of a new product. The truth is that many inventors and innovators are not successful. We just don't hear about the failures. If your product or service is a new one for which a market does not really exist, then be forewarned that success in a business based on that item will not be easily achieved. The real success stories for new items frequently involve a venture which has been well funded and in which talented people in a variety of areas have been recruited. The days of a single inventor being able to start a million dollar business on a shoe string are gone forever: if they ever existed!

AREA SELECTION AND MARKET RESEARCH

The ***market area*** is that geographic territory from which you can expect sales to come and is a part of the site selection process. Most people starting a new venture do not pay enough attention to the issue of area selection. All too often the area chosen is simply the one in which the originator lives at the time. The area chosen will have a profound impact on the ultimate success of the company. As the market research should show, the size and viability of demand for the offerings of a new business vary by geographic area.

We are familiar with a small business which failed in its first year of operation because it located in an area without consideration of economic prospects in that area. The story is presented in the case from our files.

A CASE FROM OUR FILES

The business was located in a rural county in North Carolina which had one major employer. That employer was a paper mill which had been in existence for more than 40 years and had more than 5,000 employees. For more than 10 years the paper mill had been coming under attack because of water pollution claims. In fact, the Environmental Protection Agency (EPA) had threatened to close the plant just last year if it did not reduce the level of its discharges into the local river. Political pressure had been brought to bear, the plant spent considerable dollars in pollution control, and the EPA was appeased for the time being.

Our client decided to go into business in his hometown without consideration for any other details, never thinking about the potential impact of a failure of the paper mill. He had been in business less than six months when the EPA hammer fell. Pressure from environmental groups had been building and the EPA acted to require that the mill update its pollution controls further. The management of the mill declared it was not economically feasible to upgrade such an old facility and dramatically reduced its operations to those which could meet EPA standards. The result of this cut back was a lay off of more than 3,000 workers. In a county with a population of 30,000 people and virtually no other industry which could absorb this lay off, the effects were devastating. Our client was only one of many small firms to fail in the ripple effects.

Obviously, no prospective small business owner would start a business in an area experiencing economic problems unless the business was such that it was proof against the ripple effect of a major upsurge in unemployment. Nevertheless, all the signs indicated that a negative ruling from the EPA was highly possible. In fact, one could say that the signs made it clear that some major change would be occurring, the unknown factor being its timing. Our client simply failed to consider the possibility. In fact, he failed to consider any possible change in the local economy.

The story serves to reinforce the need to examine an area in terms of its future economic and demographic characteristics as well as its present. There are a host of publications available which can provide insight into the area selection process. The Census Bureau publishes manuals which contain not only the basic demographic data about every area in the country but also include a host of business factors as well. The Small Business Administration also produces publications designed to help in area and site selection. In fact, all of the states have a business development office whose function is to provide information to prospective business start-ups within the state. These offices collect business and demographic data which can be of assistance not only in choosing a state in which to locate, but a region within that state as well. Most of this information is available free or at a small charge. Contact your local SBA office or the SBA office or Census Bureau in Washington, DC, or the office of business development in each of the respective state capitals. Local chambers of commerce frequently collect data of interest to small businesses and are always happy to assist a prospective new business. One of the publications available from the SBA is a compilation of statistics which show the number of people which are needed in an area to support a particular kind of business. Combine that information with a population count from the Census Bureau and you will have a much better idea of the potential viability of an area.

In order to make maximum use of data about an area, you need to know the characteristics of your target market. We discussed these concepts in a previous chapter and we indicated that *target markets* are classified according to age, sex, income, occupation, family status, etc. *Demographics* are more than population counts. Census data and data available from state and local sources will also include income and other factors. That means that a firm understanding of target market will make the utilization of demographic data more effective. Remember the example of the lounge owner in a previous chapter. In that case the owner had located a bar with an exclusive image in a small town which did not have the population of higher income people needed to support the venture. The company failed but could well have been successful if located in a city with a larger population of more well to do people.

AREA SELECTION AND COMPETITION

One of the prime factors involved in area selection is the existence of direct competitors. A *direct competitor* is one with which you will be competing *head to head*; one who carries the same basic items or provides the same basic services as you will. *Indirect competitors*, on the other hand, will offer competition for some items which you carry, but not all, or will offer competition for the dollars which your customers can spend. An example of the latter situation is the competition offered to a movie theater by an arcade. Both offer entertainment and are therefore competitors for the entertainment dollars of the market area, but they are not direct competitors because they offer different kinds of entertainment.

Contrary to the usual first impression, it is easier to start a business in an area which has direct competition than in one which does not. Piggyback marketing strategies are possible in such areas, whereas they are not in areas without direct competitors. To be successful in an area in which direct competitors exist, you need only do a better job than the established firms. To be successful in an area in which no direct competitors exist, you must create a market. That may be simple in the case of a product or service which a community has long desired, such as a theater in a small town which prevents people from driving to the city. On the other hand it may be quite difficult. The establishment of a microcomputer retail store in that same small town could be a risky venture!

A CASE FROM OUR FILES

The client came to see us and wanted help in starting a new business. He had found a vacant lot on the edge of town which was available at a good price and which had good highway access. He wanted to buy that lot and build a roller skating rink. Now, you must realize that this fellow was from an extremely small town in rural Mississippi. The town had a population of about 5,000 people and was located some 60 miles from a city of 75,000. In the city there were two roller skating rinks and both seemed to be surviving.

Our client was convinced that a skating rink would be successful in his home town because so many of the local high school kids drove to the city on weekends to skate. Not only would he be closer, he could considerably undercut the prices charged in the city as well.

The guy had done some research and knew what it would cost to build a rink the size he desired as well as pave the parking lot, put up a sign and other costs. Together with the cost of the land, he needed $250,000. He wanted us to help him put together an SBA loan package to get the money because his local bank had said no to the loan.

We didn't like the idea at all. In the first place, we just could not believe that the folks in that small town wanted a skating rink. There was one big plant in town which employed most of them and the local economy was not strong. In the second place, the client had no conception of breakeven. He was sure that he would have no problems because his wife and children were going to work in the rink, and he would run it on week ends when he was off work from the plant. That meant low overhead, plus he would be able to keep his job until the place was established. We forced him to do some cost estimation for operating the rink and to forecast his own salary and then we prepared a breakeven analysis.

The major fixed cost was the loan payment, but it was so high that he would have had to have 250 skaters a week to cover it. We just didn't think that was feasible long term in his town. He wouldn't believe us. He got someone else to help him and now there is a nice new building with hardwood floors for sale.

Another case from our files illustrates the right way to do things. This client wanted to start a restaurant. The people in this case went about site selection the right way. They located in a different state from their home but spent several months locating the right spot. That effort and the other start-up planning that they conducted was well worth while. They were easily able to outdistance the established competition because they understood their target market and organized the business to attract the market. The business actually was selling entertainment, but making money on pizza and beer.

A CASE FROM OUR FILES

A young couple just out of college called us up and asked for help in starting a restaurant. They said that they had selected our town because it had a large university which was growing and would provide a steady source of new patrons. Plus, it was in the sun belt and had liberal liquor laws. We talked about what kind of restaurant they wanted and they said they hadn't decided yet. They wanted to look at the local competition and locations which might be available.

We found several good places located close to the university, several within walking distance of some of the larger dorms. We also found that there were 18 pizzerias in town, that being the single largest type of restaurant. Our clients checked out every one of those, and all seemed to be doing fine. Our clients decided to go with pizza and beer. They settled on a place, leased it, and put $20,000 into leasehold improvements. The place was built for students! They had three different rooms set up, each with a juke box and lined with booths. The only tables were long ones down the center of two of the rooms. The third room had arcade games between the booths.

Inside three months, they had surpassed their sales forecast for the year! The place was a resounding success! That was three years ago and now they have three restaurants and two arcades scattered about the edges of the campus. For two kids in their twenties they are an impressive pair!

MARKET RESEARCH AND AREA SELECTION

The kind of business you intend to start has an effect on the area required. As you can see from the pizza example, access to the target market and a market of sufficient size were the primary criteria. For a manufacturing business, area requirements could include a ready supply of labor and access to transportation networks. For a construction company, area requirements might be major population growth which would drive new home construction. For a wholesaler, access to manufacturers or jobbers, and to retail customers could be the primary consideration. For other firms, the regulatory environment could be a key. One client of ours selected the Atlanta, Georgia area to start a local delivery trucking company. The city required trucks delivering within the city limits to have a permit, and the city was extremely reluctant to issue new permits. That meant that established firms held a strong competitive position. Our client located a small trucking company whose owner wished to retire, bought the firm to obtain access to the delivery permit, and established a highly successful operation.

In all cases the area to be considered must be researched to determine its suitability for the venture. We mentioned the use of Census Bureau, SBA, state business development offices and local chambers of commerce as sources of information about an area. Don't overlook the possibility of personal research. In the pizza example, the owners conducted a survey of the established competition by personally visiting every pizza restaurant in town. They looked the place over, bought dinner, watched the customers, evaluated the service, hours, location and menu of every competitor. As a matter of fact, they continue to do this on a regular basis today! There is no substitute for personal investigation.

The process of market research to determine area suitability starts with an understanding of the venture which you will begin and the characteristics of the target market which you wish to tap. Once that has been determined, you know what kinds of information about an area you require. That makes your research more effective and improves your ability to interpret all types of data, including information from published sources.

Don't overlook general information about an area. It is easy to get lost in demographic detail and overlook pertinent information such as number and stability of employers, economic conditions and prospects for future growth. Strong insight into the viability of an area can be obtained by investigation through the local employment security commission. Not only can this agency help you find prospective employees, it can give you information about unemployment levels, skill levels of the work force, nature and number of employers in the area, and a host of other factors.

The local zoning board can also be a goldmine of information. Not only will it be able to show you where various types of industry can be located, it can show you concentrations of potential competitors. The zoning board can also give you insight into locations which may be suitable for your business. That can avoid problems like those of one owner who bought land and built a grocery store based on traffic count data and accessibility. After construction was under way, he learned that the city limits were about 1,000 feet short of his location which meant that he must operate under county laws. The county prohibited the sale of beer and wine! This was a major setback because the other grocery stores in town could sell beer and wine giving them a competitive edge.

In a previous chapter we talked about marketing strategies. One of those approaches was piggybacking. If you intend to locate close to competitors to benefit from their draws, be sure that those competitors are strong. One company we know of established an inexpensive motel across the street from a Holiday Inn in an attempt to siphon off business based on price competition. Less than a year later, the Holiday Inn was sold to a discount hotel chain which changed its name and reduced its rates! Piggybacking is especially popular as a strategy for location within a shopping mall. Research is required in this instance to determine the viability of the mall and the traffic patterns within it. Some locations in malls have better traffic patterns than others.

MARKET VIABILITY

To assess the viability of a new venture, we must evaluate the market for a product or service. We must conduct market research and compare the market information with the financial needs for the new venture. In simple terms, ***market viability*** means the ease with which a new company can sell enough to make a profit in a specific area and location. We discussed mathematical techniques of break-even analysis in a previous chapter. Those tools can be useful in determining viability, but they will not provide an ultimate answer. In essence, the assessment of viability is the judgment that a sufficient market demand exists in the area for the offerings of a business to make that business successful. In the case of a business whose market area is not constrained by its location, such as a mail order business, the viability of an area will be based on other success factors. These might include access to shipping, warehousing or suppliers, or they could be such factors as regulatory environment, labor pool and conditions, etc.

Viability is often a subjective evaluation. That means that it cannot be computed mathematically, but is a matter of judgment. Breakeven analysis can tell you how much you have to sell, but the determination as to whether that number can be achieved remains a judgement call. Market research can help to make that judgement stronger. For example, if you know that a population base of a certain level is required to support your business, it is easy to determine whether such a population base exists in a given area and location. To do that you must accumulate the information.

The best approach to market research is to make a list of the factors which will be important in making your business successful. Be specific and make the list as complete as you possibly can. Then make a list of potential areas for location. You can make the initial list based on areas in which you would like to live. Research each of the success factors for each of the areas. Assess the market viability and eliminate areas. Once a viable area has been found, repeat the process with locations within the area. Remember that if an area is not deemed to be viable, then a new area or new products or services should be selected and the process of market research and evaluation repeated. Until you feel comfortable with the probability of success in an area with a particular business configuration, you should not proceed with the business venture.

ALTERNATIVE SITE SELECTION

The selection of the actual location of a business within the market area has cost/benefit tradeoffs. That means that some sites will cost more, but may be more valuable from the perspective of the amount of business which can be expected to occur at that site. The business site is more important for some types of businesses than it is for others. If the business is one in which customers will be expected to come to the business location, then the site is obviously more important than it would be if sales people were to be used who call on customers at other locations. It is very difficult to make the evaluation as to a particular site, especially when there are limited funds as is usually the case in a new venture. Traffic patterns, both automobile and pedestrian, as well as public transport access, ease of access, visibility, makeup of the surrounding area and a host of other factors play a role in the relative worth of a business site. A good starting point is to look for where the competition is located. As we indicated above, site selection can be piggybacked just like marketing strategies. Footwork should also be used. Get out and look at alternatives sites. Draw up a list of the sites which you are considering and record their good points and their bad points. In other words, use the same procedure we outlined above: list desirable factors, list alternative locations, research the factors for each location. Remember that a more expensive location should not be automatically eliminated. Consider as many alternatives as you can before making a final selection. The site you finally select is going to be with you for a while. Make sure it is the right one for your business.

One final point needs to be made about site selection. When we talk about the marketing plan, we are going to be discussing the image which you wish to portray to your customers. The site which you finally select is a major part of that image. If you are opening a professional services business, then a prestigious address may be required to support such an image. If you are opening a discount retail business, an address in a shopping mall could be a disadvantage because it carries with it the image of expensive stores. The final decision about the location which you will acquire cannot be made until you have finalized the image for your business.

FINAL SITE SELECTION

As we mentioned earlier, the final site selection should include consideration of the image as well as the cost/benefit tradeoffs which you should have analyzed for each of the alternative sites. If none of the sites seem to fit, then more should be sought until you are well pleased with the result. It is an expensive process to relocate a business. Lease terms frequently make it impossible during the first year.

Be sure to allow for change or growth in your business in the site selection as well. Try to visualize what the business will be like in a year or two if it is successful. One liquor store with which we worked had selected a fine site in a shopping center, but located in an inner space thereby eliminating drive-up service options. When the business grew and customers began to desire drive-up service, the business was forced to relocate. The landlord required a substantial sum for early release from a five year lease. That penalty could have been avoided, because at the time of the original lease, a corner location was available for a small additional rental. Our client had tried to save a few dollars and ended up spending much more. The moral of the story is, don't think about minimum needs, think about what you really need, and might really grow into, when you are trying to make the site selection.

PRICING AND PROMOTIONAL STRATEGIES

How much is a product or service worth? There is no answer to this question. As we discussed in previous chapters, we can't even be sure we know what it is that a customer is buying when they purchase goods and services from us. In the pizza example, the customers appeared to be buying entertainment rather than pizza. The restaurant was one in which all their friends hung out, consequently, it became the place to go. Obviously, this would not have happened if the customers felt that prices were too high. On the other hand, mink coats are not sold in department stores. People who purchase such items expect a level of service from the sales staff which is inconsistent with department stores. Furthermore, they don't expect to find a discount mink coat. Clearly, a furrier can have a sale on furs and can have success with that sale, but the items are sold differently and price is less of a factor than with many other goods.

Cost is really not an important consideration in pricing, contrary to popular opinion. Prices can be perceived by customers as low even when mark ups are quite high. Consider the case of expensive jewelry. Mark ups of 300% are common, although customers may still perceive these as low. On the other hand, grocery store mark ups tend to be extremely low on staple goods, 10% to 15%, but customers still make price comparisons and may perceive these prices as high. As you can see, it is customer perceptions which make prices high or low, not costs!

How many times have you heard people say that prices must be high enough to at least cover costs? In previous chapters we learned that there are many different types of costs. It is true that no business can sell for less than variable costs over the long term and be successful, but as long as variable costs are covered, fixed costs can be absorbed by volume sales. This may not even be as static as it sounds. When Texas Instruments was a young, entrepreneurial venture, it got into the calculator business. Competition was quite heavy. TI grossly undercut the prices of all of its competitors, but they responded by cutting their prices as well. TI recognized that its labor force was becoming more proficient at manufacturing calculators, remarkably so, and decided to capitalize on that learning curve. They actually priced calculators below their own costs in anticipation that those costs would drop as volume of sales went up and labor continued to improve its efficiency. The strategy worked; competitors did not feel able to match the extremely low prices; volume did grow and efficiency grew with it; TI was able to establish a major market share in calculators and become profitable as manufacturing costs dropped.

None of that helps in establishing initial prices or promotional strategies for a new venture. Then how does one go about it? The first step is to assess the competition. There are three basic pricing strategies: ***pricing at the market***, ***pricing below the market***, or, ***pricing above the market***. We will discuss these approaches in detail in the marketing management chapter. For now, recognize that ***pricing below the market*** implies that a major aspect of your business will be price competition. That is, you will be attempting to win business based on having a lower price. ***Pricing above the market*** implies that you will be striving to win business based on quality, image, location, service, or other factors. ***Pricing at the market*** implies that you will be striving to remove price considerations from the purchase decision. In other words, you will not want price to be a factor in the customers purchase decision.

Each of the approaches has advantages and disadvantages. However, pricing below the market can be dangerous for a new venture because established competitors can retaliate by lowering their prices as well in an attempt to force out the new company before it has a chance to get established. If the start-up can weather such a storm as Texas Instruments did, then this could be a viable strategy. But, if a venture is weak financially, as most are, and cannot afford a battle with established competitors, pricing below the market can be risky.

Pricing above the market also carries significant risk. If the firm is unable to establish in the minds of its customers a belief that the higher price is justified by quality or other factors, the business may not be able to establish itself. Nevertheless, during the early months of a new venture, customers tend to be more cognizant of prices because they have not yet established an image of the business in their minds. Furthermore, all of the customers have been purchasing from other firms and are therefore aware of price discrepancies. An established business is more likely to be able to price slightly above the market without its clientele realizing that fact than is a new venture.

As you can see from the foregoing, the least risky pricing strategy is to price at the market. This infers that competition will be based on other features than price. Be aware that when we talk about market price there are fluctuations which result from image differences. In other words, there are multiple prices for a product or service in the market place. For example, men's suits have an established price range in department stores. They have another established price range in discount stores. Tax preparation services have an established price in CPA firms. They have another established price in accounting firms and still another in tax preparation chain stores.

When you set out to establish the market price for your goods or services, you must be sure to examine competitors with the same approach or image as that which you will be pursuing. Of course, that implies that the image of the business will be established before its pricing policies. That is the case with much of the marketing effort because consistency of price, location, hours, service, promotion, etc., can only be obtained if each is consistent with the image of the business.

There is one other point about pricing which must be made. If you will carry multiple products or services, all must be priced consistently. You cannot be lower than the market in some areas and higher in others because your customers will be confused by the differences and will not be able to formulate an image of your business in their minds. This confusion may not be voiced, but it will exist and it will cause many customers to feel uncomfortable with your business.

Promotion strategies cannot be set until pricing strategies have been established, both of which must follow the image of the business. ***Promotion*** is more than advertising. We will talk about initial advertising in the next section and we will talk about it in more detail in a later chapter. At this point we need to focus on non-advertising aspects of promotion. These include signs, layout, point of sale promotional pieces, letter, notes or cards to be mailed to customers periodically, special events and sales, to name a few. Every aspect of your business which is or which can be seen by customers is an aspect of promotion. It is no accident that sales people in multiple industries send their customers birthday cards; retailers send customers private announcements of sales; people in services businesses send newsletters, etc. All of these efforts are oriented at obtaining and maintaining visibility in the eyes of the customer. You want your present and prospective customers to think of your business often and in a positive light. When they are ready to buy, you don't want them to shop! You want them to call you!

Effective promotion requires constant planning. Before the venture is established, you should consider various approaches to obtaining visibility, ensure that they are consistent with the image you want to portray, and establish a time table for their execution. One locally owned furniture store with which we are familiar has a sale every single month. Each sale has a different name and each promises huge discounts off the manufacturer's retail price. The truth is that the store is actually a discount furniture store and the prices offered are those the store would charge anyway. Nevertheless, the sales do work! The store sells the vast majority of each month's volume in the week long sale. Furthermore, the constant exposure from sales promotions makes the store's name a household word.

MARKETING BUDGET

People frequently think of the start-up capital requirements for a new venture strictly in terms of what it will cost to acquire any initial inventory, equipment, supplies, etc., and what will be required to cover initial operating expenses for some period of time. That is not adequate. The start-up budget must include monies for the start-up marketing and the operating expenses must include an allowance for ongoing marketing expenditures as well. Obviously funds will be limited, but inventory, equipment, supplies, leasehold improvements, and the like will not be valuable to a company which has no customers. Marketing is expensive, but it is also vital.

Discussions with advertising agencies can be valuable. Such firms are expensive, which may be why few small business start-ups use them, but you should at least investigate the possibility of employing an agency and discussing what kinds of start-up advertising campaigns they suggest. Talk to more than one agency and discuss agencies with other business owners, with bankers, with the chamber of commerce and others. The selection of a good agency could be a valuable step in the marketing plan. If you decide not to go with an advertising agency, let that decision be the result of conscious thought: not the result of a failure to consider the alternative.

If you decide to handle your own marketing, then talk to the various media representatives in the area and get circulation or coverage data as well as prices. Don't overlook outdoor advertising or direct mail. You should explore the cost of mailing lists and printing costs for brochures. The Chamber of Commerce can give you ideas about sources of mailing lists as can other businesses, bankers, state and federal assistance offices, etc. In addition, most larger communities have directories available which list the names and addresses of the population. The Chamber can help you with that as well.

The start-up marketing budget is really the result of planning the initial advertising and estimating its cost. The start-up operating budget, which we will discuss in a later chapter, recommends the incorporation of some *slack* in case you have overlooked or underestimated some expenses. This is also a good idea for the marketing budget. Once you have estimated the requirements, add some more in case you have overlooked something, or in case a second advertising push is required to get the business rolling.

THE BUSINESS IMAGE

As we have mentioned repeatedly, nothing is more important to the success of a business venture than the image which it will portray to its customers. You should consider carefully how you wish your customers to perceive your business and how your business will be distinct from its direct and indirect competition. Whatever image you decide upon, you must be consistent with everything else, especially, the advertising. In large measure, the advertising approach which you take initially in a new venture will set the tone for the image which the business will have in the minds of its customers.

THE MARKETING PLAN

The start-up marketing plan includes much more than the initial advertising. The plan should address the opening date, the initial marketing budget, start-up advertising and its media, and beginning promotional plans. The purpose of the plan is to gain rapid recognition among the target market and to persuade potential customers to examine the offerings. Frequently, an advertising campaign will be accompanied by sales prices, contests or prizes or other attention gainers. The plan should allow for a time table for the various aspects of the start-up of the venture. All aspects of the start-up must be coordinated. Staffing concerns are not the least of these. One restaurant with which we are familiar, held its grand opening after much start-up advertising and promotional coupons, but neglected to train the temporary waiters and waitresses who were hired to handle the expected opening night crowds. The expected crowds did appear, but the staff confused the orders, forgot to replenish the salad bar, and became exasperated and distraught. Many of the customers left, vowing never to return. Everything had been done perfectly and the advertising and promotions had attracted tremendous attention. One small detail, the training of six temporary staff members, turned the grand opening into a catastrophe from which the business may never recover.

GENERALIZING THE MARKETING PLAN

The process which we have described in this chapter for developing a start-up marketing plan apply to any type of venture. Service businesses tend to overlook some aspects of the process because theirs is a venture which depends upon people rather than things. This is a mistake. It may be true for a particular type of business that some aspects of the start-up are less important than others. For example, site location may be less important to a firm which never expects customers to come to its offices. This does not mean that any of the steps are unimportant or that any should be skipped. Only by systematically proceeding through the process can the pitfalls of starting a business be minimized. Just as in meeting people, first impressions are hard to change, the first impressions which customers develop of a new business are hard to overcome. The only way to ensure that those impressions are positive is to plan.

SUMMARY

The first step in starting a new business is selecting the product or service to be sold. The product or service can be chosen based upon experience or to fulfill a recognized niche in the marketplace. In either case, strategies must be designed to attract public attention.

The steps in the marketing plan are outlined in Table 2. The steps in the plan are generalizable to service and other types of businesses as well as the traditional retailer. Some steps will be more important for a specific business than will be others. Nevertheless, none of the steps can be omitted or else the prospective business owners risks initial mistakes which can be costly and difficult to correct in the future.

QUESTIONS, EXERCISES AND CASES

QUESTIONS:

1.   Why is your own personal judgement about the marketability of an item invalid?
2.   List the steps in starting a new venture.
3.   Why is the evaluation of personal goals and objectives the first step in starting a business?
4.   Discuss and/or review the who, what, when, where and how of the marketing process.
5.   Name and describe the three approaches to marketing.
6.   How does market research affect the success of a new product/service in its selection?
7.   What is market area and why is its selection important?
8.   What is the difference between direct and indirect competition?
9.   Why is your choice of products/services and market area iterative?
10.   What are some of the considerations in determining site selection for your business?
11.   Why is a marketing budget important and what areas should you examine in determining your marketing alternatives?
12.   List and explain the components of the marketing plan.

Define the following terms:

1.   market area
2.   direct competitor
3.   indirect competitor
4.   market viability
5.   image

EXERCISES:

1.   Take a look in your neighborhood. Observe several businesses to see if they have a marketing plan which is observable. If they advertise, rate the methods used. In conjunction with deciding about marketing plans, evaluate the image, location and product/service. Do these attributes indicate planning or happenstance?

2.   Are there any new businesses starting up in your town? What types of activities can you see which would indicate a market strategy? Do they have a market plan? What observations can you make about their activities? What would you do if you were they?

CASE

Mark Davis was a conscientious young man who was determined to be successful. He wanted to set up a really neat bar in the university town which he had adopted. He had gone to school there and was finishing up his MBA. This was where he wanted to stay. After having spent nearly six years in this town as a student, he knew that there were few places that students could really go and have fun. The town was progressive in the sense that the sale of beer/wine/liquor was possible, but the only places in town where one could go and drink on the premises would be classified as "joints". Mark had visited some of these places with some friends and found them to be a bit rough. The customers were serious drinkers and didn't much cater to the younger crowd who wanted music and fun.

Mark decided to approach this decision to open a pub realistically. He wanted to create an atmosphere where students could meet or date and dance, listen to music and relax, but he wanted to be successful most of all. He visited the nearest Small Business Development Center and asked for their advice about starting his business. He needed to make a loan, acquire a site, hire some people, and do some marketing. He worked with the consultants assigned to him and everything was looking good. His case worker told him that his success would depend upon how well his initial marketing campaign was carried out and whether he could get some capital. So Mark began to do some planning.

1. What kind of site do you think Mark should find?
2. What external or legal constraints might Mark have in starting a bar?
3. What kinds of planning should Mark do to see if the bar itself is a viable alternative?
4. Who would be Mark's competition?
5. How would Mark build an image for his bar which would accommodate drinks, snacks and dancing which would be more pleasing to him?
6. What would probably be his target market?
7. Prepare an initial marketing plan for Mark's business.
8. Obtain cost estimates for the locations which you consider appropriate for such a business and estimate the cost for the promotion and advertising plans that you have prepared for the business.

CHAPTER TEN

THE FINANCING PLAN

CHAPTER OBJECTIVES

Upon completion of this chapter, you should be able to:

- Explain that financial planning includes consideration of risks to which firms will be exposed, its required performance levels for solvency, start-up capital requirements, and plans for obtaining that capital;

- Determine capital requirements for a new venture;

- Find sources of funding;

- Identify assistance agencies; and,

- Draw up a loan proposal.

THE FINANCING PLAN

INTRODUCTION

The financial planning which is required in a new venture start-up includes the start-up capital requirements and plans for obtaining that capital. We will address each of these areas in this chapter. As these topics are discussed, remember that we are still in the planning phase and these considerations are part of the business plan which we have been discussing in this part of the text. These are the final considerations before embarking on a new venture start-up, but they are no less important than the market considerations or other aspects of the business plan. In fact, the capital needs determination and acquisition may well be one of the most important aspects of starting a new business because undercapitalization is one of the major factors in business failures.

CAPITAL REQUIREMENTS

If you were to conduct a poll of owners of small businesses and ask them to list the major mistakes they made during the start-up phase, the number one item on that list would likely be starting with too little capital. Start-up capital is hard to get. When people have made their minds up to do something they are hard to discourage. Consequently, the vast majority of small businesses are begun undercapitalized. That is a major mistake. Many ventures are unable to recover from that mistake and ultimately fail. Many other ventures find their growth severely restricted and their prospects doomed to mediocrity because they haven't enough capital to establish the business.

If the financial portion of the pre-venture planning is done properly, determining the capital required for start-up is not difficult. Table 1 is a checklist of some of the items which must be reviewed and estimated in determining the capital requirements for a successful start-up. Please note that the list is not necessarily complete. It is intended to suggest the kinds of things to be considered.

Notice that several of the items required to perform capital needs assessment come from the forecasts and budgets. This is the area frequently overlooked in capital planning. It is not enough to have sufficient capital to open the doors of a new venture. You need enough capital to carry the operations of that venture to the point it becomes self sustaining through its cash flow generation. In general that takes between 3 and 6 months of operating expenses on hand in the form of cash at start-up or set aside in committed lines of credit from a lender. The best determination comes from looking at the cash flow expected from the sales forecast and operating budget. That is why the first item on the list of determining capital requirements is a sales forecast! Until you know what your expectations for sales are, you cannot determine the kinds of facilities, personnel and other requirements which you will need.

Table 1

Determining Capital Requirements for a New Venture

I.   Prepare a Sales Forecast

II.   Determine Cost of Production and Supporting Assets
  A.   Cost of land and building, if applicable
  B.   Cost of machinery and equipment
  C.   Cost of furniture and fixtures
  D.   Cost of telephones and communications equipment
  E.   Cost of computers and information systems
  F.   Ensure that all costs include delivery/installation
  G.   Investigate cost/availability of used equipment
  H.   Investigate construction costs
  I.   Investigate leasing costs

III.   Determine Cost of Inventory and Supplies
  A.   Initial inventory requirements and cost
    1.   Enough initial inventory to support the inventory turnover expected
    2.   Cost should include freight
  B.   Initial supplies required
    1.   Production supplies
    2.   Office supplies
    3.   Janitorial supplies

IV.   Determine Start-up Marketing Costs
  A.   Initial promotional expenses
    1.   Signs, point of sale displays
    2.   Promotional materials, premiums, gifts
    3.   Special events and demonstrations
  B.   Initial advertising costs
    1.   Media costs
    2.   Direct mail, mailing lists, printing and postage
    3.   Flyers and their distribution
  C.   Initial price concessions, discounts and sales

V.   Determine Operating Requirements
  A.   Fixed Costs
    1.   Occupancy expense

V.   Determine Operating Requirements (continued)

     A.   Fixed Costs (continued)

          2.   Salary and personnel expense

          3.   Fringe benefits for personnel

          3.   Insurance premiums

          5.   Rental or lease expense, if any

          6.   Computers/information systems maintenance

          7.   Communication expense; telephone, fax, etc.

          8.   Repairs/maintenance/upkeep expenses

          9.   Property and other taxes

          10.   Licenses and fees

          11.   Professional fees

               a.   Accounting

               b.   Legal

               c.   Other

          12.   Franchise fees, if any

     B.   Variable Costs

          1.   Production costs

               a.   Raw materials

               b.   Direct labor

               c.   Variable overhead

          2.   Inventory replacement expense

          3.   Commissions

          4.   Freight expense

          5.   Variable rent/lease expense, if any

          6.   Variable Franchise fees, if any

          7.   Marketing and advertising expense

     C.   Estimate fixed costs for a full year using a monthly forecast

     D.   Estimate variable costs as a percentage of sales

     E.   Determine required cash on hand and in banks to support operations

VI.   Calculate the Required Operating Capital for Start-up

     A.   A minimum of 3 months of operating expenses

     B.   Preferably sufficient capital to carry the firm until cash flow forecasts are predicted to become self supporting

     C.   Don't forget to include monthly payments on loans which the business will have

VII.   Add requirements for production and supporting assets, inventory, marketing, cash and operating capital to determine total start-up capital required

COST OF PRODUCTION AND SUPPORTING ASSETS

During the process of site selection, a prospective business owner should be gathering information about costs of facilities. Comparison of costs of acquiring or leasing various facilities and equipment should be a routine part of site evaluation. The key here is to establish a complete list of specifications for the business. How large must the facility be; what kinds of machinery, equipment, furniture, fixtures, etc., will be required; what kinds of computing equipment and software will be required; what other assets are needed; how much will it cost to deliver and install these assets; should new or used items be acquired; should they be purchased, constructed or leased? Don't forget office equipment and initial supplies, telephones, supplies for the rest rooms, etc. Preparation of a complete list makes the process of contacting real estate agents, equipment suppliers, vendors, etc., more productive. The list of items in the table is by no means complete. It is a sample of the kinds of considerations which must be made. The complete needs of a new venture are determined by the characteristics and plans for that venture in its specific product/market.

Cost estimates start with real estate agencies which specialize in commercial properties or with agencies which handle the accounts of malls, shopping centers, office buildings or specific sites of interest. From this point, contact suppliers or vendors of the types of equipment you need. A copy of the yellow pages and a few telephone calls should get you started. Be sure to ask vendors who might handle items which they do not carry. In smaller towns you may have to search for suppliers in nearby cities. Call several vendors for each item on your list and be sure to check on the availability and costs of used equipment at the same time. Watch for advertisements for store sell outs in which the fixtures and furniture will be sold. Equipment and furnishings are expensive. A little shopping around can save a great deal. Be sure to look into the possibility of construction. One restaurant owner we know hired a local contractor during the off season to build booths and tables. The result was an attractive alternative which cost 25% of the price of new tables and chairs.

INITIAL INVENTORY AND SUPPLIES

One area in which initial cost estimation presents difficulties, especially for retailers and wholesalers is the determination of initial inventory requirements. Industry averages for the percentage of total assets which inventory represents is a good starting place for the calculation of start-up inventory. Factors which influence the decision include lag time for receipt of inventory after purchasing, the risk of obsolescence and the risk of stock outs. Obviously, if new inventory items can be acquired in a short time from a reliable vender, then the amount of inventory to be carried at start-up is less important than it would be if it took weeks to get the items. In the latter case, it could be dangerous to stock too little inventory. Also, if there is little risk that the inventory items which are purchased will become worthless if not sold, then the amount acquired is of less import than would be the case if unsold inventory had to be ultimately written off as a complete loss.

In that case, it could be dangerous to stock too much inventory. Stock out problems affect the decision in the same fashion. If you don't have the items which a customer wants, will you lose that customer completely? Will you damage your ability to sell to that customer in the future? If the answers to these questions is no, then the risk associated with too little inventory or too narrow product lines is lessened. These factors must be balanced against a need to minimize the initial cash investment in inventory.

If there is little risk associated with underestimating the start-up inventory, then the major factor in deciding the amount may well be to acquire sufficient inventory to ensure that the facility looks good. In a retail business, if the store looks understocked, people will form an opinion about the store which may be detrimental to its image. Of course, the opposite can be true as well: a store which looks cluttered because it has too much inventory crowded into too small a space will give consumers a poor image of the business. To aid that problem, industry averages about inventory levels per square foot of space can help, but nothing is superior to planning the display of inventory. Part of the start-up planning should be the determination of how inventory is to be displayed and how much space it will take up in display.

If there are significant problems associated with under stocking or incomplete stocking of inventory, then deciding on the correct initial supply will be of major importance. The key factor will be determining an inventory policy which will be consistently followed and which will be used in budgeting purchases. The inventory policy should be stated in terms of sales. Assume, for example, that you determine that sufficient inventory should be carried to provide one and one half month's sales at all times because of the lag time for resupply and the risks of obsolescence and stock out. If the cost of goods sold percentage is expected to be 50%, then the initial and continuing inventory levels should always be equal to 50% of the sales forecast for the next month and a half. This approach makes the sales forecast even more important but it will prevent unrestrained purchasing from depleting the resources of the firm. The inventory policy should be adjusted as experience is gained, but changes should be carefully assessed before being implemented. We will discuss this process at some length in a later chapter.

Whether or not there will be inventory requirements, most start-ups will have to deal with initial supplies. As we indicated in the previous section, you need to make a list. How about office supplies, janitorial supplies, etc. Call several office supply firms and explain your needs. They will not only be able to provide price quotes, they can help you determine what items you will need and how much you should purchase initially.

START-UP MARKETING COSTS

Most people think about the costs of the initial advertising campaign which will be run to announce the opening of a new business, but few people remember to budget for items like premiums which will be given away to customers. If you are going to provide pens, pencils, windshield scrapers, kitchen mitts or lollipops to people during your grand opening, someone has to order and pay for those! What we need here is another list. It seems like we are *listing you to death*, doesn't it. Unfortunately, no one can expect to remember all of the details associated with a business start-up. You simply must make lists! The costs of signs, printing, special events like radio shows on site or demonstrations, are all readily available if you simply look. The secret is remembering to look. Lists help you remember.

We have talked in previous chapters about the initial advertising you intend to pursue. As you investigate advertising agencies and media availability, be sure to accumulate cost data as well. Your new venture will have trouble reaching customers if they don't know you exist.

One aspect of start-up marketing costs which is frequently overlooked is the cost of price concessions. If you will be offering special prices, discounts or sale items during an opening period, be sure to include an estimate for this cost. Preparation of a sales and cash flow forecast is generally based on pricing policies which will be pursued in the business. Significant deviations from those prices will damage the forecasts unless you take those prices into consideration. This cost may not be an out of pocket expense unless your initial price is below variable cost, but it will impact forecasts and cash flow.

We need to make a point about initial sale prices while we are on this subject. If you start a business with a sale, when the prices go back to their real levels, your customers may react adversely. This is especially true if there is a major difference between sale prices and regular prices. Your customers may develop a perception that your prices are higher than the market when in fact that is not so! In general, we discourage start-up sales for this reason. Customers will generally be curious about a new venture and will be attracted to it simply because it is new. That means that a sale may not be needed.

OPERATING REQUIREMENTS

The list of fixed and variable costs in Table 1 is a representation of the kinds of costs which must be considered in start-up planning. Some of these items may more properly be termed mixed costs in that they have both fixed and variable components. We discussed these costs in a previous chapter and described how they must be handled. Mixed costs must either be classified as fixed or variable if the amount of error from that treatment is not significant. Otherwise, they must be decomposed into fixed and variable components and be budgeted in that fashion. For example, a part of the occupancy expense is costs of utilities. Heat, light, water, etc., may be virtually fixed for some companies like retailers and service firms, but variable for other companies like manufacturing firms. Communication costs usually consist of a flat fee each month plus charges for long distance calls. If a company has few such calls, its communication expense should be treated as fixed. If it has many long distance calls, its communications may be better budgeted as variable.

As in the previous cases, the table is representative of the kinds of operating costs which may occur, but each venture must establish for itself the kinds of costs which it will face. If you do not have experience with the kind of business which you are starting, this can be a difficult job. The best approach is to think through every aspect of what the company will be doing each day. What is required to support those activities in terms of facilities, personnel, supplies, etc? How will the costs of those activities behave in relation to sales? Make another list! Now you can set about obtaining estimates for the costs.

Industry averages from published sources or industry trade associations may be helpful in making these cost estimates, but great variation between companies is the rule. That means that a lot of leg work will be required to obtain sound estimates for these expenses. Remember that it is better to estimate too high than too low. A pleasant surprise is better than an unpleasant one at the end of the month.

In a previous chapter we described how these expense forecasts should be made monthly and yearly, with variable expenses being set as a percentage of sales and fixed as a set amount each month. We described the preparation of a monthly and annual expense forecasts based on the sales forecast. We also talked about the minimum cash on hand required to support operations. We want to have enough cash on hand at start-up to cover at least 3 and preferably 6 months of operations. In fact, what we really need is enough cash to carry the business until the point at which cash flows are expected to become self supporting. The preparation of a cash budget will predict when this point will occur.

All of this information will ultimately be used in preparation of a loan request, so be sure to keep supporting estimates, quotes and details to show to the lender. You also need to be careful not to overlook anything and to prepare estimates properly. If a prospective lender discovers significant omissions or errors in any of these forecasts, then loan prospects will be dim. Consider the case from our files on the following page.

TOTAL START-UP CAPITAL

Addition of all of the elements which we have discussed in the preceding sections will produce a forecast of the capital needs of the new venture. There is one further problem, however, which complicates the forecast. If you intend to borrow funds, as most new ventures do, you will need to include loan payments for the first several months in the start-up capital needs. Obviously, that means that you need to know how much money to borrow, but the amount you borrow changes the amount you need. The solution is to accumulate all the capital requirements and then add the prospective loan payments for a variety of borrowing amounts. This will result in a range of estimates, of which you should take the largest as your capital forecast. As we mentioned in the previous sections, it is better to err on the side of conservatism.

A CASE FROM OUR FILES

We were called in to help obtain financing. Our client had done a fine job of start-up planning, but he had made one small mistake. The business was to be a service company involved in selling advertising for cable television stations in a 300 mile radius. The prospective owner was convinced that cable operators did not have the time, staff or expertise to find local advertisers for the slots which were reserved for local use. He proposed using a staff of sales people to locate advertisers and sell advertising contracts. He would also have facilities for filming commercials. It sounded like a fine idea to us.

He had decided that a computer print out from a spreadsheet would impress lenders. Unfortunately, he didn't know anything about computers, so he hired a young man who was a student in computer science at the university to prepare spreadsheets for all of the income, expense and cash flow forecasts.

When he presented his loan package to the bank, the loan officer asked several pointed questions about expenses which had been forecast. Apparently, she didn't like the answers she got, because the loan request was denied. We asked to see the forecasts. The forecasts had been prepared on a month by month basis for three years. It was obvious that all of the expenses on the forecast had been classified as fixed, because none of them fluctuated as sales growth occurred. We found that hard to believe. In the first place, that meant that all sales people would be salaried and that no additional sales force was planned as growth occurred. In the second place, it assumed that most of the commercials were going to be prepared by advertising agencies or other outsiders, because there were no added costs in the firm to support growth. Our client had apparently thought that questions like that were considered by the young man who prepared the forecasts. At any rate, no one had addressed them in the forecasts. We showed him how to fix the forecasts.

That one mistake caused a real problem because there was only one bank in town who was really interested in lending to small firms with good ideas but limited capital and that bank had already said no! It also refused to reconsider the loan. None of the other banks would give us the time of day! Since the venture was of an entirely new type in their experience, and since our client had little money, they weren't interested. We never did find debt financing from any source. The client finally had to bring in some partners and ultimately lost control of the venture. We still believe that a mistake in the forecasts caused that!

SOURCES OF FUNDING

After you have determined how much capital will be required to undertake a new venture you must set about finding the necessary funding. For a new and untried business this can be a major problem. Especially, if the venture is being initiated by a new and untried business owner.

PERSONAL SOURCES

The first place to look for funding is personal savings and assets. People are fond of telling stories about million dollar companies which were started on a shoestring; stories about people who started with nothing and became rich. The truth is that such stories tend to be greatly exaggerated. One successful business owner who seemed to typify the rags to riches stereotype once confided his story to us. The following case from our files contains his story.

A CASE FROM OUR FILES

I like to talk about immigrating to this country 50 years ago with two dollars in my pocket and a head full of dreams. Now I own a string of restaurants and everybody thinks I became rich overnight! They all forget that I slaved for 20 years saving every dime until I got enough money to open my first restaurant! It was another 10 years of 18 hour days for that to become successful enough for me to expand. I am very grateful for the opportunity which exists in this country and I am proud to be a citizen and I am proud to have my own business. But I did work for it!

Few lenders or investors will be willing to risk their funds in a new venture in which the owner/manager does not have a significant investment. The inescapable reasoning is that if times get tough, as they probably will, an owner without much to lose may be inclined to give up and walk away. If that owner stands to lose his or her life savings and family home, then that person is much more inclined to stay with the venture and make every effort to make it succeed. An unwritten rule of thumb which many lenders quote says that one should never lend more than half of the start-up requirements to a new business. Whether such a rule is followed or not, it is clear that everyone you approach for funding is going to be deeply interested in how much of your own money is tied up in the venture. One word of caution is important here. If your own investment in the business is not cash from savings but is actually cash from loans which must be repaid, then the amount of cash required for that repayment must be considered as part of the operating requirements for the business in addition to everything else. Otherwise, you can find yourself unable to meet payments on those debts because the business is not generating enough cash to cover your living requirements and also pay back the loans.

Another prime source of capital for a new venture is family, friends and business contacts. If such people are willing to make an investment in the venture, it can decrease your ultimate borrowing requirements. Many potential business owners are reluctant to approach family and friends because of a fear of rejection or because of fear of failing those close to themselves. If you intend to be successful in a business venture, then the first fear must be overcome. If you do start a business, then you will be faced with rejection repeatedly. You might as well get some practice now! The latter fear may be very real. If you don't believe that your family or friends can afford to assume the risk involved in your new venture, then it may be better not to approach them. If you are going to be constantly concerned with the repercussions of failure for those close to you as well as its impact on your own situation, then your judgement and your ability to manage the business may be adversely affected. On the other hand, if you truly believe that the venture entails tremendous risk, then perhaps you should reconsider your decision to begin! If you do obtain financing from family or friends, be sure to cover the arrangements in writing. Paul Margolis told a story about how loans from his family used to start his business became a nightmare in family squabbling after his business became successful. The fight was over how much of the business his family owned.[52] His experience was not unique.

INVESTORS

Before we talk about finding investors, we need to say a few words about investment instruments or securities. Securities do not necessarily have to be common stock. Securities may also be: preferred stock, which has a specified dividend rate and may have conversion or repurchase provisions; bonds or debt instruments, which can have conversion features or can be secured by mortgages or liens on assets; partnership certificates, which may have risk limitations; or special classes of common stock, which may have special participation features or restricted voting rights. In general terms, a *security* is simply an instrument which outlines the details of an investor's interest in a business and the obligations which that business has to the investor. Since they can be quite complex, most small business owners considering the use of securities as an investment vehicle should obtain legal and professional assistance at an early stage.

There are special provisions in the regulations of the Security and Exchange Commission which permit small business to solicit investors. The SEC oversees the securities markets and has the power to regulate virtually all public offerings in the United States. Its rules are quite complex. No one should consider attempting a public offering, regardless of its size, without the aid of an attorney experienced in SEC matters. Frequently, the assistance of a CPA firm will also be required to prepare and certify forecasts. Because of the difficulty involved in skirting SEC registration and disclosure requirements for new businesses and the difficulty in complying with those rules and the expense involved, few small business ventures actually obtain funding from this source. There are added problems: after professional assistance has been obtained and an offering properly structured, it still must be sold. That means that a local stock brokerage firm or similar agency must be obtained to actually find investors in the securities. Needless to say, such assistance is not without expense. From a practical perspective, few small business ventures can expect to obtain capital from public offerings of securities. Data about small company public offerings which is quoted in support of the rapid growth of such financing arrangements generally includes data for all offerings, not just start-ups, and frequently classifies businesses as small based on quite large net worth levels. If you plan to start a venture which you believe will be large enough to consider a public stock offering, then we recommend early exploration of the issues with an attorney.

Instead of a public offering, a private placement of securities may be a much more viable option for a small business. There are numerous investment groups, some formal, some informal, which exist for the purpose of finding investment opportunities for members. These groups are generally made up of well to do individuals who are looking for larger than average returns on their investments. The formal groups may hire professionals to seek out and screen investment opportunities or may use a local stock brokerage firm or bank for the same purpose. Informal groups may be nothing more than a group of friends or coworkers who meet on call to discuss a potential investment which has come to the attention of one of the members. Frequently, access to an investment group can be obtained from local stock brokerage firms, bankers, business consultants, or private financial planning firms. These groups may prefer to specialize in loans or in equity investments or in a combination. They may prefer investing in a particular industry or desire a particular kind of security, such as real estate. They may have minimum and/or maximum investment amounts which they like to consider. Generally, a successful approach to one of these groups will require professional assistance in preparing and structuring an investment proposal.

VENTURE CAPITALISTS

Venture capitalists are firms which specialize in investing in new venture start-ups. These firms frequently structure their own investments by specifying percentages of ownership required and taking a combination of equity and debt securities. Venture capitalists also frequently offer managerial assistance. Such firms frequently desire to handle the entirety of outside investment which will occur in a new venture to protect their position relative to other investors. The investment contract may have restrictive covenants to ensure that position. Frequently, venture capitalists will require stock options as part of the deal which can be exercised at a future date should the business become a major success. There have been cases in the past in which venture capitalists used options to take control of a business after it had survived its start-up problems. Venture capitalists may also be willing to provide funding on a continuing basis as a business grows and requires more capital. They frequently desire a voice in management to protect their interests.

The public library is the best place to find venture capitalists. Since there are over 500 firms in the United States, there are numerous directories of investment capital firms published. Your reference librarian can point you to the correct directory for your needs. Many venture capitalists specialize in a particular industry or in a particular market or geographic territory. For example, some limit their investments to high technology industries, while others are interested only in ventures which will provide real estate as collateral. The directories will indicate such preferences if they exist and will also explain the minimum and maximum requirements of the firms.

Venture capitalists frequently have minimum and maximum investment amounts which they will consider. The minimums may seem quite high. Many venture capitalists feel that an investment of less than $500,000 is not justifiable because of the expense of reviewing and analyzing the investment. Consequently, venture capitalists are frequently a viable option only for a small business start-up which doesn't plan on being a small business for long! By that we mean, a new venture which consists of a local restaurant or retailer will not generally be able to approach a venture capitalist. Such firms are more interested in ventures which project tremendous growth in the short run and which plan on rapidly becoming national in scope.

If your venture is one which you believe would attract a venture capitalist, then you should be aware that the analysis of your venture or its business plan will focus heavily on you and your background. Venture capitalists will be interested in determining whether your venture is viable and whether you are qualified to manage the venture. We recommend that you communicate directly with a venture capitalist before preparing an investment proposal. You will find a wide range of requirements for the proposal, consequently, it is best to tailor the package to the specifications of the venture capital firm who will be reviewing it. A word of caution is due here. According to an article in the *Wall Street Journal*, 95% of applicants for venture capital investment are declined.[53] That doesn't mean you should be discouraged from seeking the investment: just don't spend any of the money until you have it!

SMALL BUSINESS INVESTMENT COMPANIES

Small business investment companies, or SBICs, are public or private firms which are licensed and regulated by the U.S. Small Business Administration under the Small Business Investment Act of 1958 to provide capital for small businesses. In 1969 a new type of investment firm was created especially to aid minority owned firms. The *Minority Enterprise Small Business Investment Companies*, or MESBICs, are also licensed and regulated by the SBA but generally require 51% ownership of any small business seeking assistance to be minority held or held by socially or economically disadvantaged individuals. A list of SBICs and MESBICs can be obtained from the local office of the Small Business Administration, through the National Association of Small Business Investment Companies located in Washington, D.C., or from the SBA web page (www.sbaonline.sba.gov). These firms are truly venture capitalists operating in a more regulated environment so you can expect much the same situation as discussed in the preceding section. One major difference is that SBICs and MESBICs typically have lower minimum investment levels, making them a more viable option for truly small start-ups.

ASSISTANCE AGENCIES

There are a variety of local, state and federal assistance agencies which can be of value in obtaining start-up as well as continuing funding for small businesses. An example of local assistance is the *Local Development Company* (LDC) program. The federal government provides assistance in the form of loans to LDCs who frequently have favorable lending terms and rates to aid small business start-ups. Requirements for assistance vary greatly. To determine whether your community has established an LDC, contact your local bankers or city or county offices. Other forms of local assistance can come from loans or grants made to cities by the U.S. Department of Housing and

Urban Development which are used by the cities to finance small businesses which will aid the local economy. City offices are the source of information about the existence of such programs in your local area.

About half of the states have agencies which provide loans to small businesses. Some of these have special provisions such as a requirement for matching funds from other sources. To determine whether your state has such a program contact the bureau of commerce or office of business development or similar agency in the state capital. Such agencies can also identify other state assistance programs which may exist.

The federal government has numerous loan and assistance programs which are designed to aid small businesses. Many of these have special emphasis on start-ups. In fact, there are some 350 assistance programs. The programs are offered through the departments of Commerce, the Interior, Housing and Urban Development, Farmer's Home Administration, the National Science Foundation and the Small Business Administration. There is actually a bewildering array of programs which is poorly publicized and, consequently, frequently underutilized. The government publishes a list of agencies and their programs. The *Catalog of Federal Domestic Assistance*, is available from the U.S. Printing Office in Washington, D.C.

One of the best places to determine the existence of a program which could be of value to you in a particular venture is to contact the local office of the *Small Business Development Center* (SBDC). SBDCs are an assistance program of the Small Business Administration and now exist in every state. They are generally established as joint programs with state university systems. SBDCs provide counseling and consulting services of all types for small businesses, generally without charge. If an SBDC exists in your state, you should definitely contact them for aid in preparing the business plan as well as information about loan and investment programs. The Small Business Administration in Washington maintains lists of SBDC offices around the country and these are shown on the SBA web page.

The *Economic Development Administration* (EDA) is a branch of the U.S. Commerce Department located in Washington, D.C. The EDA has a loan program which exists to aid businesses in geographic areas of the country which have been identified as economically depressed. The loan process is highly complex and the application is quite involved. To determine whether your area qualifies and to obtain assistance in preparing loan packages, you should contact the nearest EDA office. The location of the offices can be obtained from the Washington headquarters of the EDA.

The *Farmer's Home Administration* (FmHA) has a loan program designed to aid the development of businesses in rural areas. Small towns with populations of less than 25,000 people can generally qualify for FmHA assistance. The program is one of loan guarantees rather than direct loans and therefore requires a local bank's participation. Consequently, your best source of information about FmHA loans will be from local participating banks. You should contact several local banks to find one which is willing to participate in the guarantee program.

SMALL BUSINESS ADMINISTRATION

The SBA is probably the best known assistance agency for small businesses in the United States. It offers a broad range of counseling and consulting programs through SBDCs, mentioned above, and through *Service Corps of Retired Executives* (SCORE) and other programs. These consulting activities are generally without cost to a qualifying small business. Information about such programs can be obtained through the nearest SBA office or the SBA web page.

The loan assistance programs of the SBA have fallen under a great deal of criticism recently due to cost overruns and excessive losses. Consequently, the loan programs have been sharply curtailed. For all practical purposes, the direct loan program has been eliminated for small businesses. There remains a direct lending process, but it is restricted to disaster assistance and special programs. The SBA does still have a loan guarantee program, although the amounts of the guarantee have been reduced. The guarantee will now generally be a maximum of 80% of a qualifying loan with the participating bank assuming 20% of the risk. There are maximum loan amounts and maximum loan terms which vary depending upon the use of loan proceeds and the collateral assigned. The application package is lengthy and involved.

The SBA loan guarantee program is designed to reduce the risk of default to a participating bank thereby encouraging banks to make loans which they might not otherwise consider. Since the program now revolves around bank participation, the best source of information about SBA loans is your local banker. A *bank certification program* has been developed which permits selected banks to process the entirety of an SBA loan guarantee package independently. These are several hundred banks in the United States which have been certified. Non-certified banks can participate by routing an application package through the local SBA office for approval. You may need to check with several banks in your area to find one which has been certified or one which is willing to participate in an SBA guaranteed loan. A call to the local office of the SBA should help in finding certified or cooperative banks. Although the program has several attractive features from the perspective of a bank, some banks prefer not to participate due to the reporting requirements of the SBA. One word of caution is necessary at this point. SBA guaranteed loans generally carry restrictions against the acquisition of additional debt prior to repayment and frequently require blanket liens on all assets. Consequently, you need to be especially careful to make sure that the start-up capital is sufficient before accepting an SBA loan. Future access to debt will be difficult!

BANK AND OTHER FINANCING

Throughout the preceding sections we have ignored local banks as a source of start-up capital. This is not because banks do not make start-up loans to small businesses; in fact they make many such loans. Banks tend to be more cautious in lending in a start-up situation. Finance companies and insurance companies also make business loans and may be more willing to accept a start-up loan than banks. Insurance companies, however, generally require stable collateral for a loan such as real estate.

Table 2 recaps all of these potential sources of capital which we have discussed in this chapter. This list is by no means exhaustive, but it does illustrate the range of funding sources which exists.

Table 2

Potential Sources of Capital

1. Personal funds and savings
2. Family and friends -- Loans and investments
3. Partners -- Friends and business associates
4. Private investors -- Need professional assistance to find
5. Venture capitalists -- More than 500 appear in published lists
6. Small Business Investments Companies (SBICs) and Minority Enterprise SBICs
    Both SBICs and MESBICs are chartered by the SBA;
    Check with SBA for lists and addresses
7. State sources -- Check with business assistance office
    Local Development Companies
    Industrial Development and Business Development Agencies
8. Federal sources
    Small Business Administration
    Department of Housing and Urban Development
    Department of Commerce--Economic Development Administration
    Farmers Home Administration
    More than 350 assistance programs
    Published directory available from Printing Office
9. Banks--Independent, SBA Certified, SBA participating
10. Insurance companies
11. Finance companies
12. Public or private stock offerings--Require professional assistance

---

THE LOAN PROPOSAL

Regardless of where you locate financing, a *loan proposal* will be required which spells out the total capital involved in the start-up, the amount requested from the lender, the use of the funds, the terms of repayment, the collateral available, and the source of repayment. Table 3 displays the contents of a typical loan proposal.

Table 3

The Loan Proposal

I. Amount of Loan Requested
    A. Total amount and sources of all capital
    B. Uses for loan proceeds
    C. Repayment terms desired for loan

II. Assets of the business
    A. Value of all assets presently owned
    B. Value of assets to be acquired
    C. Assets pledged as collateral to others
    D. Assets available and offered as collateral for loan

III. Personal Assets of Owners
    A. Listing of all owners of the business
    B. Personal financial statements for all owners
    C. Listing of managers of the business
    D. Resumes for all owners
    E. Personal guarantees offered by the owners

IV. Forecasts
    A. Sales forecast and supporting data
    B. Income statement forecast and supporting data
    C. Cash flow forecast and supporting data

V. A Summary of the Business Plan
    A. A description of the business and its products/services
    B. The target market and market research data
    C. The breakeven analysis
    D. The distinctive competency and market strategy

The information required in the loan proposal is in essence a shortened version of the business plan. The proposal must be as short as possible without omitting pertinent information which may be of value to the lender in reaching a decision. Once the proposal has been completed, you should arrange to present it to the lender in person, if possible. Most lenders will have loan committees which will actually make the decision, however, a lending officer will generally present your proposal to the committee and make a recommendation. If you make a good presentation displaying an open, confident attitude and a professional demeanor, that can go a long way toward assuring that the lending decision is on your side.

Whether you intend to obtain credit from a bank or not, it is a good idea to establish a banking relationship and to discuss your venture with a banker. Even if you do not solicit bank loans for start-up purposes, you will probably have recurring needs for loans in the future. Obtaining lines of credit for operating purposes and loans for expansion purposes will be enhanced if your banker is knowledgeable of the business from its inception. As we discussed when describing the search for an attorney and accountant, selecting a banker should take some thought. Convenience of branch locations is of less importance than is developing a relationship with lending officers who understand your business and are willing to assist it in its growth and development.

SUMMARY

The vast majority of small businesses are begun undercapitalized. Many are unable to recover from that mistake and ultimately fail or find their growth severely restricted as a result.

If the financial portion of the pre-venture planning is done properly, determining the capital required for start-up is not difficult. Table 1 in the text is a checklist of some of the items which must be reviewed in determining capital requirements for a successful start-up. Note that in addition to the capital required to open the doors of a new business, 3 to 6 months of operating expenses should also be on hand in cash or set aside in committed lines of credit.

After determining capital requirements, finding funding can be a problem for a new and untried business. Prospective business owners should look to personal sources, family, friends and business associates first. Investors, public or private can be pursued, but professional assistance is frequently required to gain access to such funds. Venture capitalists, SBICs, MESBICs and local, state and federal assistance agencies can be explored. The federal government has more than 350 different loan and assistance programs designed to aid small businesses.

Banks are a prime source of credit for small businesses, both initially and on a continuing basis. It is a good idea to establish a sound working relationship with a bank early on in a new venture, whether or not start-up financing will be sought. The business plan, when completed, will yield the information necessary to prepare loan and investment applications and proposals, regardless of the source of funding sought.

QUESTIONS, EXERCISES AND CASES

QUESTIONS:

1.   Why are capital needs determination and acquisition perhaps the most important aspects of starting a new business?

2.   What does the acquisition of capital entail?

3.   What are the capital considerations in determining the cost of production and supporting assets?

4.   What are the capital considerations in determining the cost of inventory and supplies?

5.   What are the capital considerations in determining operating requirements?

6.   How much capital is required at start-up and why?

7.   What factors influence the initial inventory requirements?

8.   What are the tradeoffs between low initial inventory and initial cash investment?

9.   Why should you plan your displays of inventory before purchase?

10.   Discuss the possible sources of funding and include the advantages and disadvantages of each source.

11.   Why are public offerings not a good method for obtaining funding for a new venture?

12.   What are the advantages and disadvantages of dealing with a venture capitalist?

13.   How does one find a venture capitalist?

14.   What are the major components of a loan proposal?

15.   Why are relationships with attorneys, accountants, bankers and other professionals important in starting a new business or maintaining an existing one?

Define the following terms:

1. start-up capital

2. undercapitalization

3. securities

4. preferred stock

5. bonds and debt instruments

6. partnership certificates

7. common stock

8. venture capitalists

EXERCISES:

1. Visit or call several of the assistance agencies listed in the text and determine the level of funding which might be received or determine if you qualify for any assistance.

2. Visit a venture capitalist and determine the expectations and support of that group or individual for your potential enterprise.

3. Develop a loan proposal for a new start-up and take it to your local bank and see what the lender feels are its strengths and weaknesses.

CASE

Trax & Trux, a new skateboard and bicycle outlet, opened its doors two weeks before Christmas. Barb and Don were excited about their new venture. As in all small towns, a large number of people had dropped in just to check out the shop. The kids were all excited and started revamping their Christmas lists on hearing of the new enterprise. Skateboards were back in and freestyle bikes were the most popular items on the lists that year.

Many parents, eager to finish their shopping, and thrilled that there was a place in town which sold such items, rushed to make purchases only to find that the store had been opened with a very modest inventory. There were five freestyle bikes in pink with sold signs pinned to them and no complete skateboards. You purchased the assembly as well as the deck, wheels, trucks, clouds and decals. Most parents were at a loss. They had written down specific detail about the boards, knowing full well that only someone who knew boards could help them. Yet they remained unconvinced that assembly would result in the desired product.

Several inquiring minds asked the owners why they had decide to open a board and bike shop and they replied that there was a market in this area for replacement parts for these items and they had spent a great deal of time and energy on their son's behalf in trying to supply his needs.

The demand was indeed in the area but the frustration was also present. Parents needing Christmas toys had to resort to a larger town sixty-five miles away because Trax and Trux was an almost empty building. Replacement parts were possible but not that complete, perfect dream for Christmas morning.

Several months later, there was an exceptional amount of inventory. So much in fact that it was difficult to walk into the store without knocking against ice skates, jams, vans, and almost any part you could imagine. But Christmas was over!

1.   What do you think customers felt at the lack of inventory at the opening?
2.   Why do you think that the owners opened their doors when they did?
3.   How well do you think the store is doing today and why?
4.   Why do you suppose the situation ends with the statement "But Christmas was over!"?
5.   Do you think that there might have been a problem with start-up capital? Or do you think there was another problem entirely?
6.   What aspect of planning may have been short circuited in this case?
7.   What should have been done and what might still be done to cause the business to succeed?

PART FOUR

THE NEW VENTURE

CHAPTER ELEVEN

BUSINESS FORMATION AND TAX ISSUES

CHAPTER OBJECTIVES

Upon completion of this chapter, you should be able to:

- Distinguish between the legal forms of business and know the advantages and disadvantages of each;

- Explain the alternatives to originating your own business;

- Explain the requirements for a Subchapter S form of corporation;

- Explain the tax differentiations between S Corporations and Partnerships;

- Evaluate the organizational issues in establishing a new venture; and,

- Describe the federal income tax responsibilities of a small business enterprise.

BUSINESS FORMATION AND TAX ISSUES

INTRODUCTION

In this chapter we will address the legal form of business and the pros and cons of the alternative forms. We will also discuss alternatives to starting an independent business from scratch. The approach you take in initiating your new venture is important because it will follow you throughout the life of the business. Finally, we will examine federal income tax issues of concern to any small business venture. Many of the topics which we will discuss in this chapter are quite complex. Frequently, we will recommend the retaining of professional assistance to ensure that pertinent factors are considered before a decision is made. The expense of such assistance is easily justifiable because of the far reaching implications of the decisions which must be made in starting a new venture.

THE LEGAL FORM OF BUSINESS

There are three forms of business: the proprietorship, the partnership and the corporation. It is important to understand how each is treated from a legal perspective as well as from an income tax perspective in order to properly choose the form which you will use for your new venture. Laws, including tax laws, recognize entities and endow them with rights, obligations and responsibilities. The entities recognized do not include businesses. The ***entities*** are simply natural persons or corporations. There are complicating factors involved such as the existence of fiduciaries which can represent other entities and therefore have rights and obligations as well. Natural persons are simply people. ***Corporations*** include, but are not limited to, business corporations. Non-profit organizations, charitable organizations and foundations are also corporations. ***Fiduciaries*** are such things as estates and trusts or individuals acting on behalf of others.

PROPRIETORSHIP

The simplest and easiest business to form is a ***proprietorship***. Its popularity rests with its simplicity. A proprietorship is simply an individual who conducts a business. If that individual uses his or her own name in the name of the business, then all that is required to start the venture is opening the doors for business. If the owner does not use his or her name for the business, it is still a simple start: all that is required is the filing of a declaration of identity of ownership with the local court house. That document simply establishes a public record demonstrating who the individuals are behind the fictitious name of a business. The filing is simple and inexpensive. From a legal perspective or a tax perspective, proprietorships do not exist. The individual who owns the business is a natural person and, therefore, the business is simply treated as an extension of that person. This has far reaching implications.

All entities have obligations under the law to behave in a rational manner and to refrain from injuring other entities. In the event that another person or entity does sustain injury, either physical, mental or financial, then the law provides recourse to the injured party through litigation. The injured party can sue the responsible party for damages. If the injured party wins the suit, the court can award damages from the responsible party's property. Since there is no difference under the law between a proprietorship and its owner, that means that if the business loses a suit, then the property of the owner is available to the courts for awarding to the damaged party. Personal assets do not legally exist separate from business assets.

From an income tax perspective, a proprietorship pays no tax. The owner of the business simply declares business income and expenses on his or her personal income tax return. Since the owner is the taxpayer, salaries or draws paid to the owner by the business are not expenses of the business. The taxpayer will simply pay tax on the amount of profit whether or not any of those funds have been removed from the business. The filing usually requires a special form to be attached to the return; a *schedule C* in the case of a business, other forms are required for investment property or farm income and expenses. This means that the profits of the business are taxed at the personal income tax rate in effect for the owner considering all other income and deductible items. Of course, losses from the business can reduce the personal income tax of the owner, but problems can develop if losses continue over an extended period.

The Internal Revenue Code incorporates a rule concerning losses from a business activity called the *Hobby Rule*. Under the *hobby rule*, a business which does not make a profit in three out of five years is in danger of being adjudged a hobby instead of a business, in which case the losses would not be deductible on the taxpayer's return. It is not as simple as that statement makes it sound because many taxpayers have fought hobby rulings in Tax Court and won by demonstrating that the business was a legitimate venture which was striving to make a profit. The rule exists to prevent people from deducting the expenses associated with activities which are not truly of a business nature. One of the tests which the Tax Court has used to determine whether the intent exists to make a venture profitable is whether its affairs are conducted in a business-like manner. This means, among other things, the existence of separate bank accounts, accounting records and the like. To take the step of incorporating a venture is definitely evidence of a business-like manner.

We can find little to recommend the choice of the proprietorship form of business. As we will discuss later, the taxation issue is not really a problem because there is a filing selection which corporations can elect to be taxed in the same manner as the owners are taxed. It is true that no form of business is as easy to start as the proprietorship, but that simplicity is more than offset by the problems involved. First there is the lack of a legal liability limit. Some would argue that the liability issue can be resolved through insurance, but that is only partially true. In the event of a serious litigation, modern courts might well award damages far above the limits of insurance coverage. It is true that not even a corporate veil can protect an owner's personal assets in the event of a truly flagrant act of negligence. We will talk more about that in a later section. Perhaps the most important drawback to the proprietorship form of business is the requirement to pay personal taxes on all of the profit regardless of the amount of draw which an owner makes. This can and does result in a penalty for the retention of profits in the business. In order for long term success to be achieved, most businesses need to reinvest at least some portion of profits back into the business to fuel growth and enhance borrowing power. This is best achieved through the corporate form of business. Furthermore, the corporate form can provide opportunities for stock funded profit sharing and ownership plans. In general, we believe the corporate form to be *superior to the proprietorship.*

PARTNERSHIPS

A *partnership* exists when two or more people go into business together without filing for a corporate charter. There should be a contract which spells out the rights, powers and participation of the partners in the firm. Although it is possible to start a partnership without such an agreement in writing, it is not wise. Consider the experience of the partners in the case from our files.

A CASE FROM OUR FILES

We had worked with the business before it was established, helping to complete the business plan, finding financing and setting the business up, so we had established a relationship with the two owners. That's why they called us six months later to say that things weren't going so well. The business was owned by two young and very talented women. They produced stained glass art objects, lamp shades and windows. Their work was exceptional. We knew of several churches and restaurants which had used their work and several gift shops that carried their art objects. The business was strictly wholesale and contract oriented. There was no attempt made to get into retailing.

We had tried to persuade the owners to incorporate the venture at the outset, but they refused. They wanted to share 50/50 in every aspect of the enterprise and for some reason felt that a corporate form would damage that sharing. They were the best of friends and trusted each other implicitly, they said. Furthermore, they had the utmost respect for each others talents and abilities. We tried to say that none of those facts were in dispute and that the managerial functions would proceed better under the corporate form, but they would have none of that. It wasn't the cost of incorporating which deterred them. Looking back on it, it seems that they were unwilling to assign the office of president to one and vice-president to the other, silly as that sounds.

CASE continued

When we went out to see them, we found that they were not being consistently profitable despite the fact that they had more work to do than they could handle. They had hired three people to assist with the work, but none of them were talented enough to handle a job alone. One of the partners had to do the design and layout for every piece. We looked at the books and nothing terribly amiss jumped out, although expenses did seem to be running a little more than the projections and sales a little less. We asked them to be more precise about the problems they were having and the major factor appeared to be inadequate cash flow. They couldn't be more specific.

We toured the shop, and noticed that supplies and inventory seemed to be quite high. In fact, so much stuff had been bought that there wasn't room to store it all and glass and other supplies were stacked against the walls all around the production area. When we commented on that, the well cracked and the whole story came tumbling out.

It seems that the two partners who had had such a close and trusting relationship six months ago now couldn't stand each other. There had never been a decision made about who would be responsible for any particular aspect of the business, so one partner had taken it upon herself to acquire a large quantity of inventory when a *deal* surfaced. The other partner was angry about that, saying that the business had not had sufficient cash to handle that purchase. Not to heap the blame on one individual, the second partner had incensed the first with a bid on a large church. The first partner was convinced that the bid was below costs and that the size of the contract was such that the business could not sustain the loss. After that came out, things really got bad. They were even angry at each other over failures to take appropriate turns at posting to the books and cleaning up the workshop!

There really wasn't much we could do except try to point out how crucial it was for them to work out responsibilities for each other and reduce those to writing. One person had to have the ultimate responsibility for the various aspects of the business and had to be held accountable for her performance. We suggested that they consider incorporating the business and assigning offices, powers and duties to each other. They said they would consider it, and we left feeling quite sure that they wouldn't.

Sadly, we were right. Less than three months later the business shut down. One of the partners had left town, with all the cash in the bank according to the other partner. At any rate, what had great promise as a strong, viable business had gone down the tubes. The worst thing about it was that there was a market for the product and the people were able to penetrate that market. The cause of the failure had nothing to do with sales or business -- it was all in not understanding the establishment of authority and responsibility.

When two or more people go into business together, it is an absolute certainty that problems will develop between them. The only unknown factor is *when* those problems will surface and *how severe* they will be. More than one business has been destroyed by disagreements among its owners. The only way to minimize the effect of future disagreements is to firmly establish at the outset what each owner's role will be in the organization. In a partnership, this can only be accomplished through a contract. Such a requirement makes the partnership of virtually equal difficulty level with the corporation in terms of formation. Therefore simplicity of formation is not an advantage for the partnership form of business.

From a legal perspective, a partnership carries some special problems. If the contract establishes equal power in the organization, then any partner can bind the others. In fact, unless the partnership agreement explicitly restricts the powers of a partner, that partner can bind the others without their knowledge or consent. That means that if a partner enters into a contract with someone outside the firm, then the other partners are bound to live up to the terms of that contract. In the absence of a partnership agreement, all partners are considered to be equal and to have this binding power. In fact, even if a partnership agreement expressly restricts a partner's power, that individual might still be able to bind the organization. Since outsiders are not privy to the contents of a partnership agreement, the courts have held that the actions of a firm are the important factor in dealings with the public. If a partner acts as though he has authority to bind the organization and the other partners permit that impression to exist in the minds of the public, then that partner can bind the others. It's called the ***doctrine of ostensible authority*** or ***apparent authority***. If someone enters into an agreement with a partner in a firm and does so in good faith, assuming that the partner has the power to speak for the firm, then the courts may enforce the provisions of the contract even if the partner did not have the power to speak for the firm. If the courts believe that the partner consistently displayed apparent authority which a reasonable person would have interpreted as binding authority, then the contract will be considered valid. Clearly, such a possibility is not a recommendation for the partnership form.

Income taxes for the partnership form of business are similar to those for a proprietorship. The business pays no taxes, but the partners must declare on their personal returns their share of profits or losses and pay taxes on those sums personally. As in the case of a proprietorship, any salaries or draws made by a partner are not deductible by the business. Additionally, the owners must pay tax on all profits, whether or not they are withdrawn, resulting in the same penalty for accumulating profits in the firm as for a proprietorship. The partnership must file its own tax return, but the return is simply an information return. The partnership filing declares who the partners are, what the taxable income of the business was, and how much each partner should declare on his or her personal income tax return. The amount reported on the partnership return must agree with the amounts declared by each of the partners on their personal returns.

A partnership form of business tends to increase the friction between the owners, especially if the partnership is an equal one simply because the issues of relative power of the individuals in the firm are not clearly resolved. For that reason alone, we cannot recommend the partnership form. For some types of ***professional businesses***, such as physicians, lawyers and accountants, the partnership form is the only one available. The rationale behind the rules is that a professional is selling his or her advice, skills or knowledge, therefore, that individual should not be able to avoid responsibility for that advice by hiding behind a corporate shield. All of the states have passed professional association acts which permit such firms to be taxed as though they were corporations. If the venture you intend to start is such a professional organization, then be aware of the potential problems in management which so often arise in partnerships. The best plan to prevent problems, is to structure the business as though it were a corporation. That includes the establishment of individuals in the firm with specified powers and limitations, the appointment of a chief executive officer and establishment of a chain of authority and command. It also includes the establishment of a board, made up of the partners, who will act as a board of directors to oversee the chief executive officer and other members of management. Voting rights on that board for each partner should be part of the plan. This entire structure should be created by the partnership agreement and enforced through everyday management. Nothing short of an established and accepted chain of authority and command can forestall the managerial problems inherent in the partnership form.

CORPORATIONS

It should be clear before we begin to discuss the corporate form of business, that it is our preference for any venture in which it is possible. As we mentioned in the prior section, some types of businesses cannot legally choose the corporate form. In addition, there are special cases in which the corporate form is not advisable. Most of these revolve around income tax issues and generally affect ventures which are expected to produce losses instead of profits. Consequently, we will not delve into such ventures in this book, since they involve highly technical issues and are more properly considered in the realm of investments rather than management.

Corporations are created by filing a charter with the Secretary of State's office in the state in which the business will be operated. If the business will operate across state lines, then the filing generally must be done in the state in which the business will call home and which houses the headquarters of the venture. The charter is really not difficult to prepare and file. Most people starting a new venture do engage attorneys for the purpose of preparing the charter and establishing the business. An attorney is not required, nor are legal skills necessary to prepare the charter or any of the other documents involved in setting up a corporation. Nevertheless, an attorney will be required from time to time during the business start-up and later on during the business operations. There will inevitably be contracts involved which an attorney must prepare or should review for any business. Legal fees for chartering a corporation vary considerably depending upon competition among attorneys in a particular area and upon the complexity of the corporation being established. Nevertheless, legal fees for chartering a corporation are not unreasonable considering the difficulty of the preparation of the filings by a novice. Consequently, we recommend that an attorney be engaged to prepare and file the charter and to handle such other needs as may arise. We do recommend that you talk to several attorneys before choosing one. You should not only ask about chartering fees, but investigate legal specialties, background and experience. Above all, you should determine whether the attorney is truly interested in you and in your business.

TAX ISSUES IN BUSINESS FORMATION

Some people criticize the corporate form of business because of the income tax treatment of such entities. They claim that the corporate form leads to ***double taxation***. That is the corporation must pay income taxes on its profits and the owners must pay income taxes on the salaries they draw and on any dividends they receive. This is true, but is less of a problem for small ventures than it seems on the surface. First, a corporation does pay income taxes on its profits. The tax structure is similar to that of the personal income tax rules in that income is taxed on a sliding scale. Table 1 displays that scale as well as the individual tax rates for comparison purposes. Remember that salaries paid, including salaries paid to the owners of the business, are deductible expenses for the corporation and taxable income to the owner. That means that the income which an owner derives from salaries for services rendered to the business will not be taxed twice, but will be taxed at personal income tax rates when the money is received. Dividends paid by corporations are not deductible expenses and therefore are subject to double taxation, the corporation pays income tax at corporate rates, then the recipient pays taxes again at personal rates. Nevertheless, there are two approaches which an owner can take to minimize the effects of double taxation.

ELIMINATING DOUBLE TAXATION

The best known of the tax saving steps is the chartering of the corporation under a special provision in the Internal Revenue Code called ***Subchapter S*** which permits a qualifying corporation to be taxed as though it were a proprietorship or partnership. We will talk about that in the next section. The other approach is to simply utilize the salaries, bonuses and fringe benefits provided by the corporation to its employees as the sole source of income to the owners and thereby avoid dividends entirely. So long as an owner is careful about the structure and amounts of salaries, bonuses and fringe benefits, all of the items will be deductible expenses to the corporation thereby eliminating double taxation. In fact, it is even possible for tax free income to come to an owner which is also deductible for the corporation. Health insurance premiums and life insurance premiums, with certain restrictions, are an example of a fringe benefit which is tax deductible for the corporation but non-taxable to the owner. In other situations, income can be provided which is tax deferred. For example, qualifying pension plans are tax deductible to the corporation but non taxable to the owner until such time as the cash is received. It is also possible to minimize the overall tax bill by manipulating the amounts which will remain for corporate tax purposes and the amounts which will have to be taxed personally through a year end bonus. Since personal income and corporate income are taxed at different rates as displayed in Table 1, adjusting the amount which will fall into each category makes good sense.

Table 1
Income Taxation Rates

Corporations

Taxable Income	Taxation Rate
$ 50,000 or Less	15%
$ 50,001 - $ 75,000	25%
$ 75,001 - $100,000	34%
$100,001 - $335,000	39%
$335,001 or more	34%

Individuals (Married, filing jointly)

Taxable Income	Taxation Rate
$ 40,100 or Less	15%
$ 40,101 - $ 96,900	28%
$ 96,901 - $147,700	31%
$147,701 - $263,750	36%
More than $263,750	39.6%

Competent tax advice is required for success in maneuvering through the tax rules. The general rule is that an expense must be ordinary and necessary to the business in order to be deductible. Just what falls into those categories can be surprising. A good CPA or tax advisor is a must if a business owner expects to minimize taxes. As we discussed above, when we talked about the selection of an attorney, the selection of the tax advisor should be approached carefully and methodically. One final point: please don't construe our comments about taxation as being critical. We are not condoning tax evasion; that is illegal. We do recommend tax avoidance when possible. A former Justice of the U.S. Supreme Court, Justice Learned Hand, wrote:

> *Over and over again courts have said that there is nothing sinister in so arranging one's affairs as to keep taxes as low as possible. Everybody does so, rich or poor, and all do right, for nobody owes any public duty to pay more than the law demands: taxes are enforced exactions, not voluntary contributions. To demand more in the name of morals is mere cant.*[54]

SUBCHAPTER S CORPORATIONS

As we mentioned earlier, one method of avoiding the double taxation issue is to charter a corporation under Subchapter S of the Internal Revenue Code. Such a corporation is generally exempt from taxation, except for certain tax preference items. In order for a corporation to qualify for S status, it must be a ***domestic corporation***, which simply means that the company was chartered in the United States. It must also have 35 or fewer shareholders, none of whom can be corporations or nonresident aliens. It is important to note that married shareholders are treated as a single person regardless of their stock ownership proportions. The firm can only have one class of stock, although differences in stock voting rights are allowed. Certain types of firms are precluded from S classification including financial institutions and most insurance companies as are corporations which already enjoy another favorable tax treatment or which have tax sheltered income. The firm's income must not be from passive sources. If more than 25% of the corporation's gross receipts are from rents, royalties, interest, dividends, annuities or gains on sales of securities, it will not qualify for S status. All shareholders must agree to the election of S status which can be revoked in future years if a majority of shareholders desire.

S corporations pay no federal income taxes. Most states also recognize S corporations for state income tax purposes. The firm is required to file a tax return which details all corporate activities and identifies shareholders and their shares of corporate income. The shareholders must report their shares of corporate income on their personal returns and pay taxes on those amounts at their respective taxation rates. This is the same requirement for a partnership. The two types of organizations are treated similarly for tax purposes although there are significant differences.

S corporations carry all of the benefits of ordinary corporations. They are not treated differently under the law in any way except taxation. Consequently, they can be a viable vehicle for elimination of the double taxation problem caused by dividends paid to owners without having to resort to the partnership form. There are even some distinct advantages which the S corporation has over partnerships in that some fringe benefits which have favorable tax treatment are available in S corporations as they are in C corporations (normal corporations) while they are not available for partnerships.

CHOOSING THE FORM OF BUSINESS

We believe that the corporate form of business is superior to proprietorships or partnerships. Consequently, we recommend that the corporate form be selected whenever possible. If S status is being considered by the new venture, then that possibility should be discussed at length with the tax advisor. S status is not automatically superior. There are issues such as desire to retain funds for future investment which must be considered. Under S status, as in a partnership, all income, whether received by the owner(s) or not, will be taxed. Therefore, retaining funds in an S corporation can result in paying taxes on funds which have not been received. The issue can be quite complex and really requires expert assistance in weighing the pros and cons of the election.

FEDERAL INCOME TAXATION ISSUES

Federal income tax laws apply to small businesses in two ways. First the business or its owner(s) or both are subject to taxation on income. Secondly, the business must collect income taxes for the federal government on all employees. In fact, all businesses except sole proprietorships must obtain from the IRS an *Employer Identification Number* (EIN). This number serves the same purpose as the Social Security Number for individual tax payers and for sole proprietorships. That is, it provides the IRS with an identification device to ensure that all taxpayers are included on its roles. Acquiring an EIN is simple; one call to the IRS will result in your being sent an application form which, contrary to the typical IRS form, is not difficult to complete. Unfortunately, handling the tax paying and tax collection responsibilities is more complex.

ESTIMATED TAXES

Virtually all small businesses, regardless of type, must file a declaration of estimated income tax liability and pay toward that liability during the year. The *estimated tax payments* play the same role as withholding on employee paychecks. That is, it provides the government with progress payments toward the tax liability during the year. A business must forecast its income, estimate its income tax liability and file a declaration by April 15th of each year. The taxes must be paid at the time of declaration or in four installments on April 15, June 15, September 15 and January 15 (December 15 for corporations). The business will settle up with the IRS at its normal tax time, usually March 15 since virtually all small businesses must now use calendar years for tax purposes.

If the estimated taxes paid are substantially less than the real tax liability, the business may be subject to penalties. If the tax payments were equal to the amount of last year's tax liability or are at least 80% of this year's tax liability (90% for corporations), then there will be no penalty.

DETERMINING TAX LIABILITY

In general, small businesses must include income from all sources in their calculation of gross income. From this may be deducted expenses which are *ordinary and necessary to the operation of the business*. Table 2 displays a list of income and expense items which are typical for a small business.

The table is by no means an exhaustive list, but is representative of the approach to business income determination. If the business is a proprietorship, then these income and expense items will be shown on Schedule C of the owner's personal income tax return. If the business is a partnership, then these items will be reported on *Form 1065* which also discloses the individual partners' names and shares of the income for reporting on their personal returns. If the business is an S corporation, these items are reported on ***Form 1120S*** which also discloses owners and income shares. If the business is a corporation, these items are reported on ***Form 1120*** and the corporation will pay taxes on the income shown.

Table 2
Computation of Business Income

Gross Income:
- Receipts from sale of products or services
- Interest, Rents, Royalties
- Gains from sale/exchange of property
- Other income

Minus: Expenses and Deductions:
- Cost of Goods Sold
- Salaries and wages to employees
- Salaries to Officers (for corporations)
- Professional Fees
- Rents, Repairs and maintenance
- Bad debts (If accrual method is used)
- Advertising
- Pension and profit sharing contributions
- Employee benefit costs
- Taxes, Interest, Insurance
- Charitable contributions
- Losses from sale/exchange of property
- Depreciation, Amortization
- Travel and Entertainment Expenses (limited)

Equals Business Income

Most of the expenses of a business are easily justified as ordinary and necessary to the operation of the business. There are a few exceptions which we need to talk about. We will examine these in the following sections.

DEPRECIATION

Long lived assets, those expected to last more than a year, must be deducted over several years. This practice is called ***depreciation***. The time period and amount no longer has any significant relationship to life expectancy, however, because the ACRS (***Accelerated Cost Recovery System***) must now be used to calculate depreciation. There are four life categories: 3, 5, 10 and 15 years. Table 3 displays the amount of depreciation charges which can be used for the first three of these. Personal property items like automobiles, light trucks and tools go in the 3 year category. Personal property items like office furniture, fixtures and equipment go in the 5 year category. Real property items like mobile homes go in the 10 year category. Real property items like buildings go in the 15 year category. It is true that straight line depreciation can be used in lieu of the ACRS, but this is seldom desirable because it will reduce the amount of the deduction in the early years. Since money has time value, the next best thing to tax deduction is tax deferral.

Table 3			
Accelerated Cost Recovery System			
	3 year property	5 year property	10 year property
year 1	25%	15%	8%
year 2	38%	22%	14%
year 3	37%	21%	12%
year 4		21%	10%
year 5		21%	10%
year 6			10%
years 7-10			9%

Total cost of the asset without regard to salvage value is multiplied by the percentage from Table 3 for the respective year in which the asset has been owned to arrive at the depreciation amount. In general, a business can deduct the full cost of depreciable assets purchased each year up to $10,000. This only applies if the business buys less than $200,000 worth of depreciable assets during the year. This last exclusion is designed to prevent large firms from taking advantage of the deduction.

Amortization refers to the depreciation of an intangible asset. Small businesses most frequently have amortization for leasehold improvements. These costs are generally deductible over the term of the lease.

TRAVEL AND ENTERTAINMENT EXPENSES

Travel must be reasonable in amount and must be required in the business. That means that you cannot fly first class unless you can demonstrate some business reason which justifies the extra expense. All expenses associated with travel are deductible, including meals and lodging if you or your employees travel away from home overnight, although deductions for meals are limited to a percentage of the cost.

Entertainment of business clients and customers is one of the areas which has been heavily criticized as a tax loophole. Consequently, new tax laws have significantly restricted what is deductible and when. Professional assistance is required in planning for entertainment deductions.

OWNER COMPENSATION

The amount which you choose to pay yourself in a corporation can present tax problems if the IRS considers the amount to be *excessive*. The IRS permits deductions for salaries that are *reasonable*, but it will treat compensation in excess of that as dividends and subject to double taxation. Large, unplanned year end bonuses are especially suspect to the IRS. That means that you should plan early, set your salary and bonuses early in the year and keep records which substantiate those decisions. Professional tax advice can help in this regard. With proper planning and record keeping you can justify large salaries.

SMALL BUSINESSES AS TAX COLLECTOR

As we mentioned earlier, any business which has employees must calculate and withhold income taxes from their paychecks. These funds must then be paid to the government. This is an extremely important and sensitive area. We have had experiences with several small business owners who actually went to jail for failure to deposit tax withholdings from their employees! The government does not consider that to be tax evasion; it is theft! Proper planning and controls are important in tax withholdings.

Calculating payroll tax withholdings is beyond the scope of this book. It is a lengthy and complex process and requires professional assistance to organize and plan for the proper calculation, record keeping and report generation.

Payroll withholdings are involved with federal, state and sometimes local income taxes. Withholdings are also required for Social Security taxes, which must be matched by the employer. Furthermore, federal unemployment taxes must be withheld as well. In some states, state unemployment taxes must also be withheld, while in other states these taxes must be paid entirely by the employer.

A report must be prepared which details the amounts withheld in each of the categories for every employee and this report must be filed with the federal and state taxing authorities. In addition, payment of the amount of the withholdings plus the employer's share of social security must be paid to the federal and state departments of revenue. These reports and payments are required at least quarterly for most small businesses.

There are numerous microcomputer based payroll systems available which can calculate payroll taxes, print checks, keep appropriate records, and print necessary reports and forms. Any business which has more than a few, stable employees, would be well advised to consider purchasing such a system. The record keeping can rapidly become an expensive, time consuming problem. Of course, if you do consider acquiring a system, it would be wise to have a professional examine the system to ensure that it will handle your needs and is justifiable.

SUMMARY

There are three organization forms which a business may use: proprietorship, partnership and corporation. Proprietorships and partnerships do not have a legal existence separate from their owner(s). They pay no taxes. Their assets are available to creditors and successful litigants as are the personal assets of their owners. Personal assets of owners of corporations are only exposed in the case of gross negligence.

Professional organizations cannot adopt the corporate form, however, all states do recognize a professional corporation which has the same tax treatment as a corporation but is legally a partnership.

Corporations cannot deduct dividends when calculating taxable income while individuals receiving dividends must pay taxes on them. This results in double taxation. Using salaries or bonuses or fringe benefits instead of dividends can help avoid this problem but professional assistance is required to avoid potential IRS claims of excess compensation.

S corporations are taxed in the same fashion as a partnership but have all of the legal treatment of regular or C corporations.

Income taxation and tax withholding issues generally require professional assistance due to their complexity and potential impact. Thus the advice of your attorney and/or accountant can help you determine the most appropriate form for your small business and the best method for receiving the most benefits from that business. So plan ahead and take advice.

QUESTIONS, EXERCISES AND CASES

QUESTIONS:

1.   Name the three forms of business and give a brief analysis as to how each is treated.

2.   What are the different types of corporations?

3.   What is the simplest form of business to start?

4.   In what ways can a proprietorship be dangerous? A partnership?

5.   What is the hobby rule?

6.   What is the primary cause of conflict in a partnership?

7.   What is the doctrine of ostensible authority?

8.   What form of business is available to professionals? Why?

9.   Why is the corporate form of business preferred?

10.   What is double taxation? How can it be minimized?

11.   What is excess compensation?

12.   How is depreciation calculated?

13.   In what way is a small business a tax collector?

EXERCISES:

1.   Ask a lawyer and a tax advisor to come to class or to a club meeting and discuss the options available for starting a real or contrived business situation.

2.   Find in your community owners of each of the types of businesses and ask them how they arrived at the decision to become a proprietorship, a partnership or a corporation

CASE 1

Bill and Diane ran a small photographic studio. It was run out of their apartment and they decided that this would be a partnership in which they would share everything 50/50. They were reasonably successful and the business grew. They needed more space. The apartment was too small for themselves, their three cats and the dark room. Most of their business was outside. They handled school pictures, weddings, parties and studio shots. They also liked to take nature shots for themselves, frame them and give them to family and friends as gifts.

The couple were quite happy until a former roommate of Bill's moved in with them. He was also into photography and helped with the business. The extra hand increased business, but clear lines of responsibility and recompense had not been drawn as happens with friends. The three shared the apartment, the work, the recreation. Yet Gene wanted more. Gene began to develop a relationship with Diane which Bill did not suspect. Diane, who was thrilled with the attention of someone besides her husband who found himself taking on more and more responsibilities at work, fell for the attraction.

Bill came home late one Friday night to discover that Diane had left him for Gene and had taken all the money from the business checking account with her. Gene and she were going to set up a shop of their own.

1.   Breakups in partnerships can occur with regularity. Are there any more serious ramifications when the partners are married?

2.   What should or could have been done to save this company and this relationship?

CASE 2

Bryan was a recent graduate of a regional university who decided to start his own business. He felt that there was a demand for a computer center store in the town to sell hardware, software, peripherals, supplies and customized work. To start his business, he was advised to do a marketing plan to see if the area really could support such an endeavor. He claimed to have done such a study, but the results were never available for perusal. He was also asked to do a breakeven analysis on his products/services to see again whether he could be successful in the area. He was asked to establish who his competition was and how serious they were. Then it came to the capital.

Bryan had an original plan to secure his start-up capital. He identified ten professors, some of whom he knew well and some with whom he was only familiar, but according to his plan, each professor would invest $10,000 in his company. This would give him $100,000 in capital and eliminate the need for a loan. His pitch included the comment that if the company failed, no one could lose more than 10% of his or her original investment.

1. Would you invest in this business? Why or why not?

2. What type of organization would you select if you did invest?

3. Expound upon Bryan's business plan. What troubles you as a potential investor?

CHAPTER TWELVE

BUYING A VENTURE

CHAPTER OBJECTIVES

Upon completion of this chapter, you should be able to:

- Evaluate a small business venture;

- Describe the two ways to buy a business;

- Explain the complexity in valuing a business;

- Define rules of thumb and understand their limitations;

- Describe the process of normalization of financial statements;

- Identify expense preference behavior;

- Define goodwill;

- Describe sustainable competitive advantage and excess earnings; and,

- Define a fair price.

BUYING A VENTURE

INTRODUCTION

The alternative to starting a business from scratch is to purchase one. The business which you purchase can be an independent venture or it can be a franchise. How do you decide which approach is the best? It may seem that most of what we have discussed in the prior chapters concerns starting a totally independent business from scratch. Actually, the planning steps which we have discussed are relevant no matter what kind of business start-up is contemplated. In this chapter we will address alternatives to the independent start-up and how planning is important in those cases. In this chapter, we will address purchasing a business. The following chapter will be devoted to franchising, because it is an option, whether a business is bought or started anew. Keep in mind that all of our comments in this chapter are relevant to the purchase of a franchise or an independent business.

THE BUSINESS PURCHASE

Many people who start in business do so by buying an existing business. The reasoning is that an existing business has an established customer base and reputation in the market area. It has also survived the start-up phase and is therefore less risky than starting a new business from scratch. These things may or may not be true. All too often a small business is sold because its owners cannot make ends meet and selling is the only alternative to bankruptcy. Consequently, one of the primary interests you should have when considering the purchase of a business is why the owner wants to sell. If the business is not doing well, then you may be better advised to start a duplicate business from scratch. Of course, if the business has some asset, franchise or license which you want, then you may have to purchase it anyway. In that case, however, the value of the business cannot be much more than the value of the asset which you want.

If the business is doing well, then why does the owner want to sell it? It may take some research to find out the answer to this question. Financial statements and statements made by sellers must necessarily be suspect. Talk to competitors, bankers, suppliers and customers. Make sure you establish a satisfactory reason for the sale before you proceed.

The biggest disadvantage in buying a business is the tendency of the purchaser to overlook all or part of the start-up planning. Buying a business does not remove any of the requirements for pre-venture planning. In fact, buying a business adds an additional step to the process in that the price for the business must be evaluated to determine its fairness.

In some industries, buying an existing business may be the only viable alternative. For example, local trucking permits may be extremely difficult to obtain in a city. There may be a territorial franchise restriction which prohibits entry into a particular market. In other cases, liquor licenses may be difficult to obtain. In such instances, buying an existing business is the only entry into the market, but these purchases are not really of on-going ventures so much as they are purchases of selling rights. In other instances, it may be that the attraction which a business has is its location and purchasing the business is the only way to obtain that location.

If you are considering buying a business, you should be sure to carefully evaluate what you are buying. Outside of the situations mentioned above, the purchase of a small business may well provide little more than the physical assets of the business and any time left on a lease. Sellers of small businesses are fond of speaking of goodwill as a major asset of the business. **Goodwill** is actually an accounting term which is used to describe the portion of the purchase price of a business which exceeds the value of its assets. Sellers frequently use the term to refer to some nebulous level of market acceptance. Is there such a thing, and if so, is it transferable? Goodwill does exist in the economic sense but it is a difficult concept to handle in small firms. In general, it refers to some sort of advantage which a small business has over its competitors. Many people think of it as customer loyalty. But, in the case of a small business, if there is any loyalty developed in a customer group that loyalty is apt to be directed at the owner(s) of the firm rather than at the firm itself. In that case, transfer of the loyalty may not be possible. We will address the issue of goodwill in more depth in a few minutes.

METHODS OF BUYING A BUSINESS

There are two ways to buy a business. Its assets may be bought, or the business can be bought as a going concern. In the former case, the purchaser simply acquires the physical assets of the firm and starts a new business which owns those assets. In the latter case, the business continues with new ownership. The difference is that purchasing a going concern means assuming the liabilities of the business as well as the assets. As you can readily see, that could be dangerous since all of the liabilities of the business might not be disclosed, or even known, by the seller. Purchasing the assets of a business is generally a better idea because any debts to be assumed must then be spelled out contractually and any liens which exist against the assets can be readily determined.

USE OF PROFESSIONALS

You should retain an attorney or a business broker to handle the actual sale itself. An attorney will collect the purchase price from the buyer and hold it in escrow for the seller until such time as clear ownership rights in the assets being acquired can be transferred to the buyer. Both parties are protected in such a situation. No sale or purchase of a business should be considered without the use of an attorney or broker.

There are business brokers in many communities who handle the listing and sales of businesses in the same manner as real estate agents handle the sale of homes. The involvement of a broker in a business purchase can bring substantial benefits. In the first place, the broker tends to be more knowledgeable about the competitive environment and can better advise a seller or buyer as to realistic values for a firm. Further, brokers must operate in a reputable fashion in order for their own firms to succeed. This means that a broker will be concerned about having a satisfied buyer as well as a satisfied seller. Of course, you should satisfy yourself that the broker is indeed reputable. Check with the Better Business Bureau, check with local bankers and ask for references to other businesses sold. Most business brokers truly are ethical and responsible.

A broker can advise buyer and seller of the proper procedures to follow whether assets are being sold or whether a going concern is being sold. The broker can handle the sale through an escrow account or can refer you to an attorney experienced in such matters. This is important to ensure that buyer, seller, suppliers, creditors, customers and other parties are properly protected and the transfer of ownership is properly handled.

A consultant can also be a valuable asset when purchasing a business. An individual who is skilled in small business valuation can aid in determining whether a particular price is appropriate. Furthermore, a competent consultant can aid in determining whether the purchase is a good idea in general terms. The consultant can aid in identifying advantages and disadvantages of purchasing a particular business or of purchasing in general. As in the case of a broker, you should satisfy yourself that the consultant is knowledgeable and capable. Check with bankers, the Better Business Bureau and with former clients. If there are business brokers in the community, be sure to check with them as well.

Assistance programs such as the Small Business Development Center, sponsored by the SBA, can also be of value. In the financing plan chapter, we talked at some length about assistance programs available, what they are, how they are located, what benefit they can serve, etc.

VALUING A SMALL BUSINESS

Valuing a business is one of the most complex actions which anyone can undertake. All too often, one finds experts who provide a cursory overview of the issues and declaim that the value should be simply X% of the gross or net revenues. This technique is called a ***rule of thumb*** and is not generally acceptable as a valid appraisal technique. There is a rich literature in business appraisal and, like generally accepted accounting principles, there are established techniques which must be followed in order to produce a valid appraisal. The actual techniques of valuation are beyond the scope of this book, however, we will discuss the general approaches.

RULES OF THUMB

As indicated above, a rule of thumb is a guideline which suggests that a business of a particular type can be valued by multiplying its revenues or its cash flows by a factor which is drawn from industry observation. For example, a restaurant might be valued at 3 to 6 times the annual cash flows which it produces for its owners. The selection of the actual factor will vary based upon an expert's subjective assessment of the strengths of the particular restaurant. There are reference books which report rules of thumb for various kinds of businesses, but the application of these rules in a real situation is complex and requires a great deal of judgement and experience.

Rules of thumb can never provide the kind of insight into a business value as can be gained from other techniques. The range of variation in businesses, their market areas, their competitive posture, and a host of other factors, makes any general rule dangerous at best. At worst, rules of thumb can be extremely misleading.

One note of caution is worth noting at this point. Business brokers may provide extremely valuable services in the purchase of a business, but their opinions as to value are frequently based upon rules of thumb. Unless the broker has a deep background in business valuation and is a true expert in that practice, you would be well advised to find another expert to perform a better appraisal.

COMPLICATING FACTORS

Valuation is complicated by the existence of expense preference behavior. In fact, the first step in any appraisal must be the examination of tax returns, accounting and bank records, and financial statements to identify such items. The requirement is to produce an adjusted set of statements which are economically sound and are defensible from the perspective of industry norms. In addition, the appraiser must examine the national industry and economy, and the local economy and the local market, and the competitive mix in which a business exists, perform a financial analysis to identify strengths and weaknesses, and form an opinion as to the future prospects for the business. This knowledge is essential to establishing a defensible expectation for growth, or the lack of growth. Further, such knowledge is vital in determining capitalization rates which will be used in calculating values.

In essence, to arrive at a business valuation requires the identification of sustainable trends in cash flows available to business owners, calculation of an appropriate capitalization rate which incorporates the risk free rate plus premiums for various types of risk and liquidity, and application of the rate to the expected cash flows. Values for assets owned by the business may or may not be determined and added to the capitalization of cash flows, depending upon the situation. The actual calculation of value is simple, but every step of the process requires the application of judgement and experience. Consequently, appraisals conducted by different experts can vary tremendously.

CAPITALIZATION OF CASH FLOWS

The most frequently encountered approach to business valuation is the capitalization of cash flows. The justification is simply that the primary value of a business is the cash flows which it generates for its owners. There are three commonly used approaches: capitalization of earnings method, excess earnings treasury method, and excess earnings reasonable rate method. The methods are similar. To value a business using capitalization of cash flows, one:

1.	Normalizes the income statements and balance sheets
	(This involves removing expense preference items)
2.	Estimates future income
	(This is actually the estimation of future cash flows available to the owners)
3.	Establishes a capitalization rate
	(This is an interest rate which incorporates the level of risk which the particular business will face in its future operations)
4.	Capitalizes the estimated future cash flows
	(This involves dividing the estimated income by the capitalization rate)
5.	Adds the value of any excess assets
	(This involves assets which are not essential to the operation of the business)
6.	Adds the value of capitalized cash flows to the value of excess assets to determine the value of the business.

EXPENSE PREFERENCE BEHAVIOR

Expense preference behavior refers to the tendency of owners of businesses to minimize personal income positions through various benefit expenses. It also refers to the tendency to manage overall taxes by shifting income from the company to the individual owners to result in a lower overall tax burden.

To determine the actual earnings of a closely held business, one must examine the sources of income and expense items in comparison to normally expected, economic conditions. Nonoperational items are removed if the resulting income is to be used in valuing the business or in determining future expectations for the business. If the purpose of the adjustment is to determine family support which the business generates for its owners, then nonoperational items should be included if they are recurring in nature.

Adjustments to the expense items are based on examination of the actual transactions and comparison to industry averages. Frequently occurring adjustments are displayed in Table 1. The most frequently encountered adjustment to an income statement is owner compensation. Table 1 details some of the ways in which owners take compensation which is hidden in the financial reports. The appraiser's job is to identify expense preference items and remove them.

Table 1
Expense Preference Items

To normalize the income statements of a closely held business, an appraiser must consider:

- adjusting inventory to replacement cost or market value
- adjusting depreciation methods to eliminate accelerated depreciation charges
- investigating leases to determine whether they are actually purchases and adjusting accordingly
- investigating capitalization versus expensing policies for inventory and fixed assets and adjusting accordingly
- investigating the timing of revenue and expense recognition for year end items, for long term contracts, and for installment sales, and adjusting accordingly
- removing nonrecurring revenues and expenses
- examining owner compensation to adjust for:
    - fringe benefits, including automobiles
    - deferred compensation plans, pension plans, profit sharing plans, etc.
    - director's fees
    - travel and entertainment expenses
    - insurance coverage
    - vacation homes, cafeterias, or special amenities and facilities
    - rental income on assets owned by the business owners

In a closely held business of any kind, expense preference behavior is commonplace. Owners of businesses quite naturally seek minimization of income tax liabilities. CPAs and tax advisors make careers out of helping such individuals avoid taxes. In some cases, the expense preference behavior violates tax law, but even when the steps taken are legal, the result is a failure of net profit or taxable income to adequately reflect the earnings which occurred.

Expense preference behavior includes a variety of techniques including: perquisites, or special benefits, in lieu of salary; accelerated depreciation; deferral of revenues; deferral of compensation; loans to and from a business; and a host of other practices. Unraveling the real earnings power of a business venture requires an expert who is knowledgeable, not just about taxation issues, but particularly about small business practices.

In virtually every case in which we have been involved, we have seen businesses taking expenses for travel and entertainment beyond that required in the normal conduct of business; providing cars through rental or purchase for owners who seldom actually travel to conduct business; renting buildings and other assets from owners at rental rates in excess of established levels in the area; etc. All of the aforementioned practices can be justified from an income tax perspective, but their impact is to produce more income for the business owner than is displayed for tax purposes.

Virtually all business owners employ accelerated depreciation techniques. These practices inflate expenses in the short term, thereby reducing tax obligations. Some business owners charge what should be personal expenses to the business, again reducing its taxable income. These charges can range from insurance premiums on personal assets, to telephone bills, to charge card payments. Other owners take merchandise from the business for personal consumption. The result is an inflation of the cost of goods sold. Still others, especially in businesses handling large amounts of cash, fail to record all revenues. Some owners are able to defer the recognition of revenues for the business due to accounting conventions. This is especially prevalent in contracting and contract accounting. Others are able to establish deferred compensation and pension plans which produce higher expenses in the short term and translate into greater benefits for the owner in the long term.

Most experts in small business recognize that the true test of earnings power of a business for its owners is the cash flow which that business produces and which it can sustain. Identifying that cash flow requires a careful examination of tax returns, accounting records, bank records, etc., and comparison to industry averages and established norms. The result can be the identification of earnings which are considerably higher than that reported as net profit on a tax return.

Such an examination is required whenever an individual has an ownership interest in a business, regardless of whether that interest is large or small. It is also required when an individual has a family relationship to the owner(s) of the business. In one case with which we are familiar, an individual owned only 5% of the stock of a closely held corporation, but was receiving substantial expense preference treatment. We have seen a situation in which the majority of the stock of a company was being held in a trust for eventual distribution upon the death of the owner. This process was designed to minimize estate taxes. Meanwhile, however, the heirs of the owner worked in and managed the business, and provided substantial expense preference items for themselves despite the fact that they did not own the business.

NORMALIZING FINANCIAL STATEMENTS

With closely held businesses, the reported income and balance sheet figures often result from an aggressive income tax strategy rather than from economic conditions. Consequently, income statements and balance sheets frequently do not reflect the economic reality under which the firm is operating. Adjusting the statements is generally required to produce data which can be used to determine actual earnings of the business and the real financial position of the business.

Table 2 displays the approach which an expert takes to normalizing the income statement and the balance sheet of a closely held business. The normalized income statements and balance sheets are used to establish value for the business. As you can see from the table, the process requires a great deal of experience and judgment.

Table 2
To Normalize an Income Statement

1. Eliminate non-operationally related items

    (These are expenses or revenues which are not directly related to the day to day business operations)

2. Adjust for expense preference behavior

    (Discussed above)

3. Adjust any expense items which are understated to industry averages

    (If the business is spending dramatically less for rent, etc., than its competitors, this must be investigated, and may be adjusted upward if an expert believes that to be appropriate)

4. Recalculate income before taxes

    (Taking into consideration changes which might have been made)

5. Calculate cash flow available to the owners in each year

    (This is cash which is available, whether it is withdrawn or not)

To Normalize Balance Sheets

1. Identify any nonessential assets and remove them from the balance sheet

    (The value for these assets may be an issue for further action, but such value does not affect the appraisal of the business)

2. Determine the market values for all remaining assets and replace the book value with the market value

    (This may require an appraisal by a specialist)

3. Examine all liabilities to determine that they are liabilities of the business rather than the owners, remove any personal liabilities

4. Verify the current value of all remaining liabilities

5. Recalculate equity to reflect the difference between normalized assets and liabilities

Once the financial statements have been normalized, the appraiser will use the adjusted statements to evaluate the company and to prepare forecasts of its future earnings. Even though this process is complex, the problems of valuation extend beyond these issues. One of the most serious issues in valuation is the existence of goodwill.

THE ROLE OF GOODWILL

Numerous articles and books have been written on the subject of valuation of the small business. The processes of determining values for assets or future income streams or cash flows as described in this chapter are well established in the literature. However, the issue of goodwill remains a problem. ***Goodwill*** is well established in the economic sense. It is defined as a ***sustainable competitive advantage***. The practical application of that definition to a specific small business setting is not well established. From a valuation perspective, there are three significant problems surrounding goodwill in a small business. The first problem is ascertaining that a competitive advantage exists and identifying what it is. Secondly, the possibility of transferring the competitive advantage to a new owner/manager must be addressed. Finally, the economic value which the identified advantage creates must be determined.

Goodwill has traditionally been associated with a higher level of earnings than would have existed in the absence of the intangible resource.[55] That means that some aspect of a firm's reputation, location, or strategic posture causes it to experience higher earnings than a similar company in a similar market which does not possess the same advantage. Clearly, if a company possesses such a resource and if that resource is sustainable and transferable, that company should have a higher value. If the higher earnings are not expected to continue, then goodwill cannot be said to exist. If higher earnings are expected due to a temporary competitive example, like the printing company in the discounted cash flow section, then they can be considered in the valuation, but they are not truly goodwill in the economic sense.

If we accept the premise that goodwill constitutes a higher level of earnings, then the issue becomes the identification of a basis for the existence of goodwill. If excess earnings truly exist, they must result from a competitive advantage which is sustainable.[56] That means that the advantage will not disappear. The only way such an advantage can be expected to continue in the face of competitive pressure is if it results from a ***distinctive competency***.[57] Otherwise excess earnings will quickly evaporate as competitors move to copy the posture of a more successful firm. We have talked at great length about distinctive competencies in previous chapters. It is an aspect of business which a firm performs in a manner superior to its competitors, which makes a firm stand out from its competitors; which gives it a competitive edge; which increases its earnings potential.

There have been many categories of distinctive competencies identified in small businesses.[58] These range from the knowledge or skill of the owner to the reaching of an untapped market niche. ***Sustainability*** is a function of the competitive environment. As such, it must be assessed on a case by case basis by examining the probability that competitors will not or can not duplicate a specific competitive edge in a specific firm.

The source of a distinctive competency is a major factor in using it to evaluate goodwill. If the competency is not transferrable to new owners, then it should not be considered in determining firm value. Consequently, in the case of a firm which is experiencing excess earnings, goodwill should be assessed if a distinctive competency can be identified which accounts for the excess earnings, which is sustainable, and which is transferable to a new owner. We worked with a client who experienced this problem first hand, and with catastrophic results. The story is contained in the case from our files.

A CASE FROM OUR FILES

Our clients were a young couple who were extremely excited about owing their own business. They called us in after six months, but they were in such deep trouble, that there was little we could do.

Our clients had purchased an established campground. They used everything they had saved and everything they could borrow to make the purchase. The campground had been in business for more than 20 years. It had been extremely successful and it had a high level of repeat clientele, despite the fact that it was unaffiliated with any group or chain. Its owners, a couple in their 60s wanted to retire, so they put the campground up for sale.

Our clients bought the campground in January and spent the rest of the winter working hard to get ready for their first camping season. In late March, their first customer drove into the campground, pulling a camping trailer. They were so excited, that they both ran out to greet the customer.

The customer stopped his car and rolled down his window. Our clients gave him a huge smile and welcomed him to their campground. With a puzzled expression he asked, "What happened to Jack and Linda?" Jack and Linda had been the owners for the last 20 years. Our clients explained that Jack and Linda had taken a well deserved retirement and they were now the proud owners. Their first customer spoke softly to the woman in the passenger seat for a second, then turned back and said, "Well, have a nice day." He turned around and drove away.

That happened with such regularity over the next three months, that their business was doomed. Even those campers who chose to stay, made comments about Jack and Linda, and a number of those left after a single night. We tried to explain the problem to our clients, but they were so upset that it really didn't make sense to them.

The campground was not really in a good location and it did not really have any competitive advantages. The grounds were old, there was no swimming pool, hot tub, or other amenities. They were not affiliated with any camping organization or listed in any camping resources. In short, the campground had only one asset that had made it successful: the close relationship its prior owners had developed with a repeat clientele. When Jack and Linda left, they took that asset with them.

EXCESS EARNINGS

Excess earnings can be defined as those profits which exceed industry average performance. The utilization of trade association or *Robert Morris Associates* or other sources of averages permits the identification of a firm which has demonstrated excess earnings as well as identifying the value of those earnings.

Once the existence of excess earnings has been demonstrated, the distinctive competency which is the source of those earnings must be identified. Finally, the sustainability and transferability of the distinctive competency must be investigated. The key is identifying the distinctive competency itself. If that can be done, then it is not difficult to determine whether that competency will disappear when the ownership changes. Identifying the competency may require the use of a professional.

If goodwill value exists for a firm, it should be capitalized separately and added to the value determined previously. The process simply involves using discounted cash flow techniques for the amount of excess earnings which have been identified. The problem is complicated by concerns about how long the excess earnings are expected to exist; for several years or forever. Furthermore, you must decide whether the earnings are expected to be constant in terms of dollars, constant as a ratio of earnings, or growing over time. As you can see the use of a consultant or professional can be a real asset in establishing a value for goodwill.

DETERMINING THE PRICE

Retaining an expert to establish a value for the business you intend to buy is clearly the wisest course of action. Buying a business is a life changing event. It could be one of the most important actions of your life. It just makes good sense to learn all you can about a business before you make such a serious commitment. Nevertheless, you should remember that the actual sales price of a business will be a negotiated price agreed upon by the buyer and seller. Seldom will that price be the same as the value established by your appraiser. The valuation techniques provide a starting point for the negotiation process and they help you to understand what it is that you are buying and what you will be facing in taking over the business.

A *fair price* for any business will be one with which both buyer and seller are pleased. The valuation techniques are simply tools to aid you in arriving at a range of selling prices which you would be willing to accept. Another tool which can be of use in determining price is planning. As we mentioned earlier, a major problem with purchasing a business is the tendency to overlook the need for planning. Consider how much better prepared you would be in evaluating a business purchase opportunity, if you knew what the initial investment and expectations for a new venture were. If you prepare a business start-up plan as described in the planning section, you will be able to compare purchase price with investment cost. Furthermore, you will be able to compare established sales and profit levels to projected levels. If you add to this information the range of values generated above, you will be an extremely well informed buyer. There can be no better way to decide whether purchasing or starting from scratch is the preferable option.

SUMMARY

The steps in the planning process for a new venture are equally applicable to a situation in which an existing business or franchise is being purchased. In addition to those steps, an evaluation of the business must be performed for comparison to the purchase price.

The purchase of a business may not be a wise decision despite relative value or price. A business is often sold because its owner(s) are having difficulty. On the other hand, buying a business may be the only option available because of location, licenses, permits, franchise agreements, etc. All this simply means that planning is even more important than it is ordinarily.

A business may be purchased as a going concern or its assets may be acquired alone. The latter is preferable because no debts will be assumed beyond those spelled out in the purchase agreement. In any case, a professional, either a business broker or an attorney, should be used to handle the transaction.

We described the complexity of valuation and explained the limitations of rules of thumb. We talked about cash flows as the most important determinant of value and we discussed expense preference behavior and normalization of financial statements. We examined the capitalization of cash flows as the best approach to determining value.

Goodwill in the economic sense is defined as excess earnings which result from a sustainable, competitive advantage. This means a distinctive competency. In order for goodwill to be an appropriate part of the valuation, the distinctive competency must be transferable to the new owner.

Finally, we discussed the importance of planning. In order to make an informed decision about purchasing a business, we should know what the alternative costs would be to establish a similar business from scratch.

QUESTIONS, EXERCISES AND CASES

QUESTIONS:

1.   Discuss the advantages and disadvantages of buying a business as opposed to starting one from scratch.
2.   Define goodwill in the accounting sense.
3.   Define goodwill in the economic sense.
4.   When should goodwill be used in the valuation process?
5.   What is the danger of purchasing a going concern?
6.   Why is the value of the business not necessarily the price?
7.   Explain why cash flow is the life blood of every business.
8.   What is a rule of thumb and what are their limitations?
9.   What role does a business broker play?
10. What kinds of professional assistance can be valuable and why?

ACTIVITY:

1.   Assume that you are going to purchase an existing movie theater or other small business in your town. What is the distinctive competency? What would be the probable goodwill factor in that purchase?

CASE

A local karate school seemed to be taking the town by storm. The sudden proliferation of movies dealing with the study of karate and the wider goals of self discipline and self confidence provided a ground swell of appeal to not only future karatekas but to the parents as well. Riding on this wave of sudden popularity, many schools sprang up. Many black belt students who had worked under other teachers suddenly decided to go out on their own. The needs were not great. A large empty building with mirrors would suffice. The *Kar Ren Dojo* opened its doors on just such a shoestring and began attracting students by the score.

The building had belonged to Randy's family and he was a second degree black belt. He had large numbers of students vying for his attention and no one was too young or too old to learn. Randy had a better rapport with the young kids than with his older students but soon the classes were so large that he had to break them apart in order to handle them. He handpicked several students for rapid promotion and began letting his senior students take on some of the responsibility for teaching the classes. The students were proud and a steady source of free labor.

The success of the studio was evidenced by the new Porsche Randy was driving and the expansion of the dojo into a weight and exercise facility. A new dojo was opened in the neighboring town, 20 miles away, as demands and dreams drove expansion. Yet suddenly Randy was facing financial difficulties and decided to sell his business. One of his senior students who had taken on some of the responsibilities of teaching was interested in purchasing the studio. Jack had never seen the books but he knew that the school had been growing steadily since his first entry into the school. So he was sure that success could be his. After all, he had become the primary instructor as Randy had turned more and more of the teaching responsibilities over to him. Should he buy the business?

Things to consider:

The primary building belonged to Randy's father, who had owned it for more than 25 years, the last five of which it had been vacant before Randy installed his school and fixed the place up. Randy's father was willing to lease it to the new owner for $500 per month as part of the sale of the business. Utilities for that building averaged $100 per month and it contained 2,400 square feet, with 1,000 feet in karate floor, 1,000 feet in weight training floor, and the rest in bathrooms and office. The parking lot, which was gravel, could accommodate 20 cars.

The secondary building was leased, with three years left to run on the lease at $600 per month. Utilities for that building averaged $200 per month. The building contained 2,200 square feet with 200 feet in changing rooms and bathroom and the rest equally divided between weight area and karate floor by a central partition. The building was 10 years old, but in excellent condition and located on the main thoroughfare of town with room for 15 cars to be parked in the paved lot.

Both sites had weight and exercise equipment which was being paid for with a $25,000 loan from the bank in Randy's name. The equipment was less than one year old and had cost $35,000 initially. About half the equipment was located in each of the two buildings. Monthly payments on the loan were $575.

There were no employees.

There were presently 150 karate students paying $35.00 per month for three one hour lessons per week. The students were divided into beginner and advanced classes: one group for children under 16, and one group for adults. Consequently, four classes per week were taught in each of the two facilities. Since all of the karatekas were students or employed elsewhere, all classes took place after 3:30 PM. There were slightly more students in the older facility than in the newer one.

There were 15 weight students who worked out an average of five times per week. These students paid a membership fee of $25.00 per month. There were 5 students in the newer building and 10 in the original location.

1.   Why do think that Randy wants to sell his karate school?
2.   What do you think that Randy's turning over his teaching duties indicates?
3.   What is the impact of the leases on the buildings?
4.   What would a buyer of the business gain?
5.   What do you think would be a fair selling price for the business?
6.   How would your value for the business compare to the costs of starting such an operation from scratch?
7.   What would be the competitive issues in beginning a new karate school in the same town as Randy's business?
8.   Would you recommend that Jack buy the business?

CASE CONTINUATION

Jack bought the business with very little forethought, convinced that he had to act fast before someone else snapped up the opportunity. He quickly discovered how hasty he had been. Randy had kept little or no records. Many of the students were behind in their payments for lessons. In light of the new knowledge, Jack thought that the initial decision to sell might have been encouraged by the threat of Randy's losing the Porsche to the bank. To top off his problems, Jack discovered that many of the young kids who had been the cornerstone of the school were dropping out. Even some of their parents seemed to have given up on the school.

1. What do you think Jack should do now?
2. Was the original purchase of the business a good idea in retrospect?
3. Would the start-up of a competing business have been preferable to purchasing this one?
4. Can the business be saved? How?

CHAPTER THIRTEEN

FRANCHISING

CHAPTER OBJECTIVES

Upon completion of this chapter, you should be able to:

- Explain the pros and cons of franchising as an alternative to starting an independent business;

- Evaluate a franchise contract and know the prominent issues which should be included in it;

- Explain how the business plan must be modified to consider a franchise operation; and,

- Explain the benefits of franchising to the franchisor.

FRANCHISING

INTRODUCTION

The alternative to starting a business from scratch or purchasing an independent venture is to acquire a franchise. Many prospective business owners believe that a franchised business is superior to an independent operation because of the advertising, managerial, financial and accounting support which is provided by the franchisor. As we will discuss in the following sections, this is not automatically true. There is a great diversity of services offered by firms to their franchisees as well as a broad range of fees charged for these services. In addition, the amount of freedom and independence of action permitted to franchisees varies. There can be advantages to franchising. It is certainly one of the most popular methods of beginning a business in the United States today and its popularity is on the increase. However, there are no guarantees in a franchise just as there are none in an independent business. The prospective franchise owner must perform the same planning steps discussed in the planning section or else risk failure in the new venture.

FRANCHISING

A *franchise* is a business which has a contractual relationship with another business in which marketing and management services are provided in return for initial and on-going fees. Franchises are independent businesses but the public tends not to be aware of that fact. This lack of recognition is in large part a function of the blurring of ownership which occurs in the national chains. For example, most of the fast food chains have both franchises and company owned stores in the operation. The public generally cannot tell the difference between the two. The company owned stores are simply additional outlets and are managed and staffed by company employees. The franchises are independently owned and managed although the name over the store is the same as for the company.

Franchises are neither automatically better nor worse than an independent business. Like most decisions in the business world, and in every other world, it is a matter of evaluating the best option for your individual situation. Franchising is rapidly becoming one of the most popular approaches to starting a business in the United States.

The franchising arrangement is spelled out in a *franchise contract* which establishes the rights and privileges of the *franchisee*, which is the independent business, and those of the *franchisor*, which is the sponsoring business. Franchise contracts can be established between any firms regardless of the type of firm or the industry.

TYPES OF FRANCHISING ARRANGEMENTS

Manufacturers or producers can enter into franchising relationships with wholesalers. This is frequently done in the soft drink industry in which the bottlers of soft drinks are franchisees and the producers are franchisors. The overwhelming majority of soft drinks in the United States are handled under franchise relationships.

The franchisor can also be a wholesaler while the franchisee is a retailer. Hardware stores, supermarkets, convenience stores and department stores are frequently set up under franchise contracts.

The manufacturer can also enter into relationships with retailers. The vast majority of gasoline sales and new automobile sales are handled under franchise arrangements. In fact these two types of franchises are so prevalent that they account for the vast majority of total franchise sales of all types in the United States!

Service companies can also enter into franchising relationships. Restaurants are an excellent example as are hotels and motels. Printing services are a new and rapidly growing example of franchising in the services industries.

Regardless of the industry, franchising works in the same way. The franchisor charges an initial fee and collects a fee on a continuing basis often called a ***royalty fee***, frequently tied to sales volume, in return for marketing and management services. You must take the cost of start-up plus the ongoing royalty into consideration when deciding upon the opportunity presented by the franchise. Can the costs be justified when compared to the benefits received? Table 1 displays a sampling of the up-front capital required to start a franchise for various companies.[59] The franchisee receives a license to operate under an established business name in an assigned geographic area. Training is frequently offered initially and on an on-going basis. In some instances, financial assistance may be provided in the form of enhanced access to bank loans or venture capitalists or extended payment terms. Notice that the range of types of businesses as well as franchise cost is extreme. *Entrepreneur* magazine produces an annual list of 500 franchises complete with rankings and ratings.

LOWER FAILURE RATES

Many supporters of franchising point to a lower failure rate for franchises than for independent business ventures. That lower rate, they say, is a result of the marketing/management expertise and training which is offered by the franchisor. In reality, the lower failure rate of franchises is a result of the screening which takes place by the franchisors. Most of the larger, more successful franchising businesses have a major screening effort which is applied to applicants for franchise contracts.

Table 1

Minimum Franchising Costs Excluding Real Estate Costs

Category	Franchisor	Minimum Investment	# Franchises
Apparel	T-Shirts Plus	$111,700	113
Automotive	Maaco Auto Painting	$185,000	471
Automotive	Valvoline Instant Oil change	$91,000	86
Automotive	Novus Windshield Repair	$26,000	2,169
Beauty & Health	Merle Norman Cosmetics	$6,500	147
Beauty & Health	Pearle Vision Inc.	$150,000	501
Building Products	Paul W. Davis Systems	$39,500	242
Business Services	Padgett Business Services	$47,500	343
Business Services	Sunbelt Business Brokers	$10,000	71
Business Staffing	Interim Personnel	$55,000	275
Children's Businesses	Tutor Time Child Care	$172,000	229
Fast Food	Bruegger's Bagels	$269,900	147
Fast Food	Kentucky Fried Chicken	$975,000	5,774
Fast Food	Dunkin' Donuts	$221,600	4,231
Fast Food	Burger King	$360,000	7,167
Fast Food	Papa John's Pizza	$168,500	704
Fast Food	Subway	$64,300	10,890
Restaurants	Country Hospitality	$606,000	249
Restaurants	Applebee's Neighborhood Grill	$1,700,000	476
Home Improvement	Kitchen Tune Up	$13,300	297
Home Improvement	Norwalk Furniture	$200,000	35
Maintenance	Chem-Dry Carpet & Drapery Cleaning	$19,000	4,147
Maintenance	Merry Maids	$21,800	971
Pet Businesses	Petland	$156,500	146
Photography	Moto Photo Inc.	$169,800	371
Real Estate	Home Team Inspection Service	$16,500	155
Recreation	Kampgrounds of America Inc	$105,000	531
Recreation	Putt-Putt Golf and Games	$120,000	254
Retail	ColorTyme	$256,200	323
Retail	Wicks N Sticks	$178,600	189
Services	Together Dating Service	$88,000	131
Services	Complete Music	$17,500	124
Services	One Hour Martinizing Dry Cleaning	$165,000	824
Training	Sylvan Learning Centers	$78,500	529

First, such applicants are required to have a minimum level of capital. This one requirement probably accounts for the major reduction in failures, because independent small businesses have no such requirement and almost universally go into business with inadequate capital. In addition, the franchisors require a knowledge base which must be demonstrated from business experience or developed in company training programs. Even if there were no capital limitations, this requirement would have a far reaching impact on failures as the stereotypical small business venturist knows little or nothing about managing a business. Table 2 displays failure rates for restaurants as measured by businesses with Small Business Administration loans over the most recent period available. The table contrasts failure rates for franchised restaurants to independent restaurants.[60]

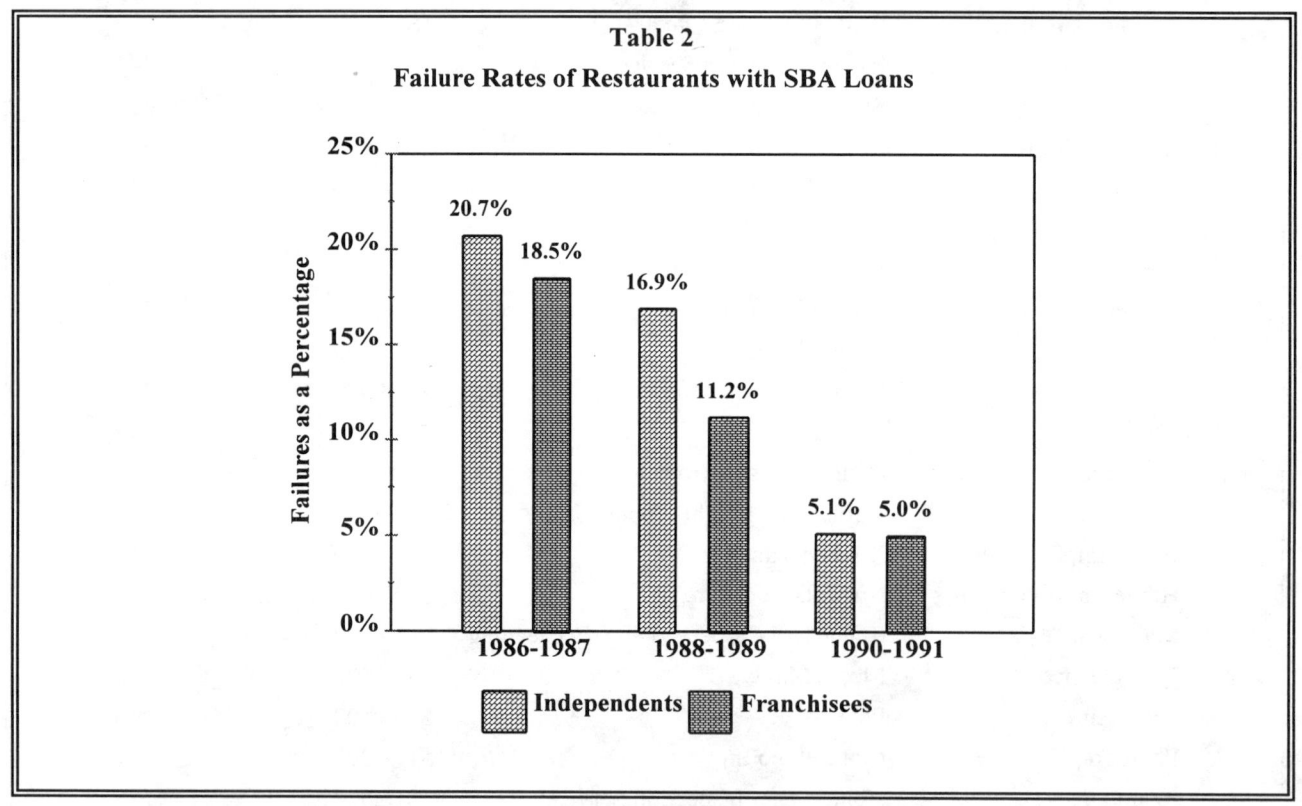

Table 2

Failure Rates of Restaurants with SBA Loans

Clearly, the on-going marketing and management assistance which is provided by successful franchisors is valuable, but it is not a panacea for all ills. The rash of failures of Kentucky Fried Chicken outlets which occurred some years ago is a prime illustration. Several of the major franchisors have modified their strategies in the last few years to concentrate on more company owned stores because of increasing problems with control over franchised stores. For example, Ryan's Steak Houses stopped accepting new franchisees in 1993. Whether this will become a trend, only time will tell.

In some industries there has been a tremendous growth in franchising, while in other industries franchising has declined. Nevertheless, franchising constitutes a major force in the economy. Table 3 displays the percentage of franchised businesses and franchising sales over the most recent 20 year period available.[61] This rapid growth in some areas has led to many cases of outright fraud and thousands of small investors have been lured into investment in small ventures which promise tremendous yields from franchising. Clearly, franchising can be, but is not guaranteed to be, a viable alternative in a new venture.

Table 3
Franchising Percentages

	Franchised Businesses			Franchising Sales		
	1970	1980	1990	1970	1980	1990
Retail Sector	**83.5%**	**71.1%**	**63.5%**	**89.8%**	**87.2%**	**85.1%**
Auto and truck dealers	9.4%	6.7%	5.2%	49.1%	42.8%	50.6%
Gasoline stations	56.0%	35.8%	21.0%	24.5%	28.1%	16.1%
Restaurants	8.2%	13.6%	19.2%	3.8%	8.7%	10.7%
Convenience stores	2.2%	3.5%	3.3%	1.4%	2.3%	2.0%
Nonfood retailers	7.7%	8.0%	10.2%	11.0%	3.1%	4.0%
Other Sectors	**14.6%**	**28.9%**	**36.5%**	**10.2%**	**12.8%**	**14.9%**
Business Services	2.7%	9.2%	12.6%	0.6%	2.0%	2.7%
Total	100.0%	100.0%	100.0%	100.0%	100.0%	100.0%

EVALUATING FRANCHISE ALTERNATIVES

How do you decide whether a franchise is the right option for you? The first step should be the weighing of the advantages and disadvantages for your particular situation. If you plan to open a fast food restaurant which will depend on one-time business from travelers for its sales, then the national marketing and advertising of a franchisor may be invaluable. If you plan to open a restaurant which will depend upon repeat business from an established clientele, then marketing support from a franchisor may be of limited value. If you have few management skills, then the management services provided by a franchisor may be more attractive than they would be if you were confident in your experience and abilities. In some industries you may have little choice. If you intend to open a soft drink bottling company or a new car sales lot, you may be forced to enter a franchise relationship in order to gain access to inventory. If there is a choice, then the relative value of franchising depends heavily on the strategy which you intend to pursue in your business and the skills which you will bring to the business. Completion of the business plan which we discussed in the prior chapters will help you determine the strategies and skills and will provide a basis for weighing the benefits of franchising for your particular situation.

A CASE FROM OUR FILES

The client was a small hardware store which had been franchised by one of the national chains. He called us in because after a year and a half he was still losing money. He was behind in his payments to the bank, and he needed more cash to buy lawn care inventory for the spring season.

We went to see him and looked the place over and examined the books. His sales had grown from about $150,000 the first year to what looked like a $180,000 pace for the second year, but his losses looked like they were going to be even greater in the second year.

The owner was really upset because he said the franchisor had assured him that a store his size should do $250,000 easily. The worst part was that the franchisor had forecast a 40% gross profit level. He was actually getting a 27% gross.

We looked at the breakeven for his operation and found that he would be making money now if he had that 40% gross which he had expected. With a 27% gross his sales would have to exceed the $250,000 which the franchisor had indicated could be expected from his store. Since he had no control over the cost of the inventory, other than minor influences which would result from better inventory management, he would have to raise prices to drive the gross up. He felt like, and we agreed, that raising prices would not be possible due to the competitive environment.

The end result was that the owner was faced with an impossible situation. There was no way he could drive sales up to breakeven levels without a major infusion of cash to expand the operations and there was no way to get the cash required from a lender due to the performance on the start-up loan. The only option was to find a private investor and give up a portion of ownership. He didn't find that a particularly attractive alternative nor did there seem to be time to find an investor given the pressure which the bank was bringing to bear.

The owner was able to find a buyer for the business, but at a much reduced price. The sale covered the existing debts on the business, but did not recover any of the initial investment or recoup any of the losses which he had sustained. It was really sad. We felt like the whole thing could have been avoided with a little attention devoted to planning up front and a careful analysis of the forecasts.

At an early point in the consideration of a franchising relationship, the franchise contract should be scrutinized. We highly recommend the use of an attorney in evaluating any franchise contract. In addition, franchising arrangements frequently are accompanied by forecasts of sales and profits which really require expert analysis as well. A qualified CPA or accountant should be engaged to analyze any financial forecasts or cost estimates. Although the use of specialists will cost money which you might think could better be used to start the business, these expenditures could be invaluable in evaluating the franchise and could well assist in obtaining financing for the venture if the franchise agreement is in fact accepted. This is especially true in the case of forecasts. People tend to be overly impressed by sales and profits projections when they are formally presented and are presumably based on the performance of similar firms. They should not be! Forecasts are simply that: guesses about what might happen. Every business is different as is every market area. Therefore, projections based on the performance of other firms in an industry are not necessarily reliable. In fact, such forecasts tend to be slanted toward the upper end. Consider which firms are used to prepare averages for costs and sales. The firms which fail are not around to have their financial performance included in the averages. Therefore, the calculation of averages is really an exercise in examining those franchisees which were successful. How can the averages of those firms be expected to represent a new and untried venture? Frequently, they do not.

Table 4

FTC Disclosure Requirements for Franchises

The business experience of the franchisor and its affiliates;

The business experience of the franchisor's officers, directors, and management personnel;

The lawsuits involving the franchisor and its officers, directors, and mangers;

The bankruptcies involving the franchisor and its officers, directors, and managers;

The initial franchise fee and other payments;

The continuing payments required;

The quality restrictions on goods and services and purchase restrictions;

The financial assistance available;

The restrictions on the sale of goods or services;

The restrictions on the customers;

The territorial protection;

The conditions of repurchase, refusal of renewal, transference and termination or modification by either party;

The description of training programs;

The involvement of celebrities and public figures;

The assistance in site selection;

The statistical data about the franchise including present and future projections, terminations, nonrenewals and repurchases;

The financial statements;

The personal participation in the operation by the franchisees;

The statement of earnings and the basis for those claims;

The listing of other franchisees.

The story of the hardware store owner from our case files has been repeated countless times. The problem seems to be that everyone thinks of McDonald's when they think of franchises and assume that if there were a chance of failure, the franchisor would not approve the venture. That is just plain not true. Pre-venture planning is as important in a franchise as it is in an independent venture. The responsibility for success always rests with the owner of the business.

All this is not to say that franchising is a bad thing. If it were, there wouldn't be so many franchises in the country. It may well be that a franchise is the best option for you in your new venture. You should simply be sure to analyze the franchise opportunity carefully.

The Federal Trade Commission requires all franchisors to disclose a wide variety of information to potential franchisees prior to the completion of a franchise contract. That information is displayed in Table 4 and should be examined carefully as should the financial statements of the franchisor. It would be a good idea to have your CPA analyze the data as well.

There are a number of excellent sources of information about franchising available. The federal government publishes a handbook, the *Franchise Opportunities Handbook,* which contains useful information on hundreds of franchisors. In addition the International Franchise Association (IFA) publishes the *Franchise Opportunities Guide*, which is a detailed listing of more than 5,000 franchisors. The IFA has more than 600 members who must subscribe to a code of ethics in franchising, therefore members are less likely to be involved in fraudulent or improper conduct. The American Association of Franchisees and Dealers (AAFD) maintains a web page:

---

www.aafd.org

The web page will allow you to gain access to a wide variety of information about franchising in general as well as specific franchisors. The AAFD charges a small fee for its publications, but can be a goldmine of information for prospective franchisees.

Of course, one of the best sources of information about a franchisor is existing franchisees. As indicated previously, the franchisor must provide you with a listing of franchisees. Call a number of them and ask about the franchisor. You will find that most of these people will be happy to discuss any problems they might have experienced.

What we have been saying in the foregoing paragraphs may sound like franchising is not a good idea. That is not necessarily the case. For many small business owners, franchising is not only a viable alternative, it is the best approach to starting a business. The point that we want to make is that franchises differ in terms of what they have to offer and the level of support they provide. If you are thinking about buying a franchise, it just makes good business sense to be careful and to investigate the deal throughly. Table 5 is a list of questions and points which you should consider in evaluating any franchise arrangement.

Table 5

Franchise Evaluation Questions

What is the expiration date of the franchise contract? What happens when it expires? How are renewals handled? What aspects of the franchise agreement can be expected to change when it comes time to renew the contract?

How strong financially is the franchisor? How long has the company been in business and how many franchisees are there? Will the company give you a list of franchisees to call? What happens if the franchisor should fail or go out of business? What assets will belong to whom in that event?

What information is contained in the disclosure statement? Remember that this statement is required by law. Consider having a professional evaluate the disclosure statement for you.

What are the termination and transfer provisions of the contract? (There has probably been more litigation on this one aspect of franchising than any other. Courts have traditionally upheld the franchisor's rights to terminate contracts.) Do you have the right to sell the franchise to a third party? What are the restrictions on transfer?

What are the territorial limits of the franchise? Is the market within that territory adequate to support the projections of the venture? What is the competition within that territory? Can you expect to compete successfully with the established firms?

What are the purchase restrictions of the franchise? How much of the materials which you will use must be purchased from the franchisor? How do prices for these materials compare to other vendors? Are there restrictions on carrying competing lines of merchandise? Are these onerous?

Does the franchisor control pricing? If so, are prices competitive? Does the franchisor control hours of operation? Are they reasonable? Are there other restrictions placed on operations? Are they reasonable? Do the expense estimates adequately consider operating restrictions?

Does the franchise contract contain quotas? Are they reasonable? What happens if a quota is not met? Are there grace periods? Do quotas have escalation clauses for the future?

What are the record keeping requirements? Do expense forecasts adequately cover the record keeping and reporting costs? Will any special equipment be required to comply?

What training is provided by the franchisor? Are there requirements for employee training as well as management? Is the training on-going? Are the costs included? What happens when employees turn over? Can new employees be trained? How much does that cost?

Table 5

Franchise Evaluation Questions (Continued)

How well known is the franchisor? Is the name important to your venture? Is the image of the franchisor consistent with the image which you intend to portray in your business?

What is the track record of the franchise? How many failures occur and why do they occur? What happens if a venture fails? What assets will belong to whom in the event of a failure?

What advertising is provided by the franchisor? Will it be effective for your business? Will it reach your target market?

What financial assistance is provided by the franchisor? Will they co-sign notes at banks? Will they permit deferred payments on franchise fees or other start-up costs? Will they aid in the establishment of credit lines with suppliers? If a new building is required, will they assist in the design and construction and/or the acquisition of fixtures and furniture?

What other services are provided by the franchisor? Are site analysis or location analysis services provided? What kinds of market research data or services do they provide? What kinds of on-going management assistance is provided? Are there analytical reports available on your financial statements? If so, when?

What are the fees, up-front and continuing? Are they consistent with the level of support which you will be receiving? Are there any hidden costs, such as escalated prices for supplies which must be obtained from the franchisor?

Do you meet the franchisor's requirements for a franchisee? Did they check you out fully? Do they have requirements beyond financial requirements to be a franchisee? If so, are they reasonable? Are you and the franchisor jointly satisfied with the probability of success for the venture?

Are you satisfied with the role you will play as a franchisee? Is the autonomy which you are giving up acceptable to you? Will you have sufficient latitude in management to be able to adapt to local conditions as they develop?

What about opportunities for growth? You probably will not be permitted to expand outside your assigned territory, so can you obtain additional territories if you wish to grow?

What are the aspects which the franchisor is bringing to you which you do not have and cannot obtain yourself? What does your attorney think of the contract? What does your CPA think of the financials? Are you satisfied that the franchise will return real value? Will you be happy running this franchise?

THE FRANCHISOR

One final topic which we need to address concerning franchising is the perspective of the franchisor. Frequently, small business venturists are heard to say, *This is just our first store! Wait 'till this one is on the ground and we'll go national!* What they mean is, they will franchise the concept. Franchising does contain benefits to the franchisor. Among these are speed of expansion, minimization of capital requirements, and reduction of labor and management requirements. There are also disadvantages to the franchisor. Profits tend to be greater with company owned outlets than they are with franchises. In addition, control is greater over company owned stores. If consistency is of great value in the successful approach to the customer, then company owned stores are superior. Some analysts declare that Kentucky Fried Chicken problems came from a lack of consistency. It is clear that consistency is of prime importance in the fast food industry. Food doesn't have to taste good: the advertising will convince people that it is, so long as the food tastes the same in all of the restaurants. If it varies, all of the restaurants will suffer, not just the offending location. McDonald's has been more successful than most franchisors in enforcing consistency and all of the terms of its franchise contracts, but the firm works very hard at that and employs a staff of field inspectors to ensure compliance with service, production and cleanliness requirements. That level of supervision is beyond a small franchisor. Nevertheless, franchising is an attractive alternative for a small business because of the reduced capital requirements of expansion. If you are considering that approach, be aware that the selection of the franchisees is of paramount importance. You can't simply give a franchise to anyone who has the money to buy it. You must try to select people who will portray the image which you desire for the company or all of the outlets will suffer.

SUMMARY

A franchise is a business which has a contractual relationship with another business in which marketing and management services are provided to return for initial and ongoing fees. The arrangement is spelled out in a franchise contract which establishes the rights and privileges of the franchisee, which is the independent business, and those of the franchisor, which is the sponsoring business. Franchise contracts can and are established between manufacturers, wholesalers, retailers, service and other types of firms in all industries.

Franchises generally have a lower failure rate than independent businesses because of the screening of applicants by the franchisors. Generally, a minimum level of initial capital is required which tends to deter undercapitalized firms from going into business. Ongoing marketing and managerial assistance may be provided. Such assistance can be of value but does not replace the need for planning and management by the franchisee.

The first step in determining whether a franchise is the right option for a new business start-up is the weighing of advantages and disadvantages for a particular situation. The franchise contract should be carefully examined by an experienced attorney and a CPA should review financial forecasts or cost estimates provided by the franchisor. The business plan, described in the planning section, is applicable to a franchise decision and is equally important as it is for an independent venture.

Table 5 displays a list of questions and points which should be considered in addition to the normal planning steps when analyzing a franchise opportunity.

Franchising may be considered as a strategy for any venture and does embody many benefits for the franchisor. Among these are speed of expansion, minimization of capital requirements and reduction of labor and management costs. On the reverse side, profits tend to be greater with company owned operations than with franchises. Control over franchises is also more difficult, making the choice of franchisees an important part of a successful franchising venture.

QUESTIONS, EXERCISES AND CASES

QUESTIONS:

1.   What is the most popular method for starting a business in the U.S. today?

2.   Name several types of franchising opportunities.

3.   Why is there a significantly lower failure rate among franchisees than among independent start-ups?

4.   Briefly list the steps used in evaluating a franchise relationship and choose the one which you feel is of the most concern to you in making that determination and explain why.

5.   Give some reasons why you might want to become a franchisor and also indicate some of the pitfalls.

Define the following terms:

1. franchise
2. franchise contract
3. franchisee
4. franchisor

EXERCISES:

1.   Visit several franchises in your area. Then try to visit those same franchises in nearby communities and indicate whether you find consistency of product/service, location, and image in the different areas.

2.   As a class project, investigate the possibility of purchasing a franchise. Decide upon the one which interests you and then contact the franchisor for details of that contract. Decide how you would improve upon the conditions of your chosen product/service and find out what benefits you would receive from the franchise as opposed to becoming an independent competitor.

3.   Go to your library and check the *Franchise Opportunities Handbook* published by the U.S. Department of Commerce and make a list of the various franchise opportunities which might do well in your area and discuss those findings in class. Were you in agreement?

CASE

Several investors met at the home of one of the more prominent townspeople. They were interested in bringing some type of eatery to the area. Presently, the competition consisted of two restaurants: a Hardee's and an old Inn which served country style meals which were rather expensive for everyday fare. The investors were friends who saw that there was an opportunity in this town for some sort of franchise. They were not inclined to invest in another typical fast food place with hamburgers as the only fare, so they contemplated other possibilities.

Discussion ranged far and wide and a committee was formed to investigate the availability of franchises. When the report came back, there was only one viable option--a steak house. Seafood was out because most restaurants who allowed franchising also had bars and the county prohibited liquor licenses. Other franchises either did not fit the bill or were too expensive for our investors.

Some planning was discussed, a site was selected and several members consulted industry averages for steak houses and the decision was made. Someone had suggested a traffic count to ensure that there would be significant exposure to their facility at their chosen location. This too was undertaken. Counting cars which crossed the intersection seemed like a really good idea and the result of the count was astounding. It seemed as if everyone in the county passed that spot every day of the week. What could be better?

The investors made their decision and purchased the franchise for the steak house. They had the facility built in conformance with the terms of the contract and were almost in business. First, they had to hire a manager. All of our investors had full time jobs in the area and were not interested in the management duties themselves. A manager was hired and dreams of success followed.

Unfortunately, those dreams turned sour quickly. They found that they were not thrilled with the food or the service at their restaurant and many of their friends were complaining. The manager was fired and he took the help with him. So a simple fix was not possible. A replacement was quickly found, a new staff hired, and the quality of food and service seemed to be improved. Then the kitchen caught on fire and there were expenses to refurbish. The return on investment planned for by the participants was clearly not going to materialize. In fact, the returns began to look negative. There was also no steady flow of traffic as indicated by their study. They learned that the corner at which the traffic count was made was a major intersection; one which many of the same cars passed repeatedly in a day's time. That explained the error in the count and suggested to the investors that other problems might exist which they did not know about. Consequently, the investors decided to hire a consultant to examine their operation and offer advice.

1.   If you were the consultant called in on this case, what would you do to try to discover any problems in the operation of the restaurant?

2.   What problems might you foresee with the manger/investor relationship?

3.   What should the franchisor have done before allowing this franchise to be bought?

4.   What steps could be taken to improve the operation? What steps could be taken to improve the return on investment?

PART FIVE

MANAGING FOR SUCCESS

CHAPTER FOURTEEN

THE MANAGEMENT PROCESS

CHAPTER OBJECTIVES

Upon completion of this chapter, you should be able to:

- Explain what management is and does;

- Distinguish between management of large and small businesses;

- Distinguish between the job descriptions of owners in each type of business;

- List the three functions of management;

- Explain the three levels of management and their functions;

- Develop goals, objectives, and strategies;

- Discuss the reason for organization charts;

- Explain the why and how of time management;

- Explain the importance of planning your time; and,

- Describe what consultants can do for you.

THE MANAGEMENT PROCESS

INTRODUCTION

In 1748, Benjamin Franklin said to a young tradesman, *Remember, that time is money!* Old Ben's words of advice ring clearly down the centuries. Time truly is money because it is time which a manager uses to guide and direct a business. Statistics compiled by Dun & Bradstreet suggest that 90% of all business failures are a result of management problems.[62] Success in business is largely a result of success in management. Knowledge of a product or service is not sufficient to build a business based on that product or service. The Dun & Bradstreet figures demonstrate that! You must also have knowledge of how to run a business. That's what this chapter is all about. We will explore what is involved in management and provide you with some guidelines for developing an effective approach to running your business.

ISSUES IN MANAGEMENT

In simplest terms, **management** is the process of deciding what tasks are to be done, assigning responsibility for doing those tasks to someone, and checking to be sure that the tasks have been done satisfactorily. It sounds quite simple when we talk about it in those terms, but in a small business setting the process of management is not simple at all. Consider the differences between small businesses and large businesses for a moment. The major difference between the two groups is not sales volume or number of employees or any of the more visible aspects. The major difference is in depth of management. In a large business the **Chief Executive Officer** (CEO), the individual with overall responsibility for the management of the firm, has a staff which can assist and advise in a large variety of functional areas. In addition, the CEO has managers at various levels in the organization who actually run the company on a day to day basis by carrying out the instructions of the CEO and other managers above them. In a small business, the owner is the CEO and is frequently alone in the management ranks of the firm or at best has only limited assistance from other managers in the organization. Therefore, the small business owner has a far greater range of activities competing for time and attention and far greater pressure from the day to day problems involved in running the business than does the CEO in a large business. A CEO in a large firm has a specialist in risk management, in personnel, in accounting, in production, in computer systems, in marketing, etc. In a small firm, the owner generally has no such specialists yet has the same responsibility for managing the same areas. In a large firm, the CEO does not meet with high schoolers selling ads in the annual or spend an hour with an unsatisfied customer or interview prospective employees or take telephone calls from people selling yellow pages ads and display counters or fill in behind the cash register when lines back up. In a small firm, the owner does all those things and more and still must retain responsibility for overall management of the firm. In a larger sense, the problem of management in a small business is an exercise in time management.

Perhaps you have read that the functions of management consist of planning, organizing and controlling. That is generally a correct view and correlates with the simplistic process which we outlined above. *Planning* in an ongoing business means deciding where the business is going and what is to be done to get it there. That means setting goals and objectives for the business and deciding on strategies which will advance the firm in the right direction. *Organizing* means structuring the people in the firm to perform what is necessary to carry out plans and delegating responsibility and authority. *Authority* to make decisions flows from the top levels of management. Individuals expected to carry out the strategies of the firm must have the authority required to permit that process. *Responsibility* is being held accountable for assigned tasks. Responsibility cannot be delegated, but rather flows from the delegation of authority. People who have been given power must be accountable for their use of that power and for the results of its exercise. *Controlling* means establishing a system of feedback which will permit the progress of the firm toward its established goals and objectives to be evaluated and adjustments made to keep the firm on track. How all of these things are done is the subject of the following sections.

MANAGEMENT LEVELS

The management in a firm can be classified according to its focus and level of involvement with each of the functions of planning, organizing and controlling. All managers are involved with all functions, however, managers at various levels must devote more time to one function than to another. We can say that a manager focuses on the function which demands the most time. The most senior level of management, frequently called *top management*, may consist of a single person or several people who are delegated authority to run the company by its owners. In the case of a corporation, this process is formalized along the lines of an election. Shareholders vote for and elect a board of directors to run the company for them and the board of directors elects officers to run the company for the board. The single individual with overall authority is called the Chief Executive Officer. In some large organizations, the process of management has become so complex that an office of the CEO has been developed which has two or more occupants who share the authority. In other firms, a *Chief Operating Officer* (COO) is added to function as the number two person in the organization and relieves the CEO of some of the duties of running the firm. Frequently in a large firm, the board of directors will take an active role in managing the firm. In a small firm, the directors generally are also the officers of the firm. Regardless of the size of the firm, the top management has overall responsibility for the company. Top management is expected to do the planning for the firm and to develop *strategies* for running the organization. A military analogy can make the process more understandable. Top management consists of the General and the General Staff of a military force. The goal of the force is to win a war or battle. The General Staff decide what the objectives of the force will be, the capturing of a hill or town in enemy territory. The staff also decides what the strategy will be to achieve that objective. That could be the use of air strikes to weaken the position, followed by an armored assault supported by infantry to secure the objective.

The next level of management in a firm is called *middle management* and consists of those managers who are responsible for translating the plans and strategies of top management into actions. Following the military analogy, the middle managers are commanders of the units to be used in the attack. They decide the **tactics** to be used. The air commander will decide what kinds and numbers of aircraft will be used, the kinds of ordinance or bombs and missiles to be used, the specific targets of the strike such as artillery emplacements and other details of the strike. Commanders of the armor and infantry forces will coordinate the attack with the air commander and decide what forces will be used, the order and direction of the attack and other details of that type. There may be multiple levels of middle managers, some of whom report to other middle managers, but the basic function of the group of middle managers is the development of tactics which will carry out the strategies established by top management.

The very lowest level of management in a firm is the *supervisory level*. Managers at this level supervise the employees who actually do the work in the organization. These managers are hired and supervised in turn by managers above them in the organization. In the military analogy, supervisors are the junior officers who command the people involved in the attack. They are responsible for carrying out the tactics developed by the middle managers. They tell the people what to do, when and how to do it and oversee the performance. Their primary focus is *operations*.

All of the officers in a military unit will be involved to some degree in all of the functions of the unit. That is, junior officers may attend strategy meetings with the general staff and may be asked to provide information on the state of readiness of troops under their command, suggestions as to strategies or tactics to pursue, etc. The general staff and senior officers may also become involved in the operations by suggesting or directing actions to junior officers. Nevertheless, the primary responsibility of each of the levels does not change. The general and the general staff must think primarily of objectives and strategies and not allow themselves to become overly involved with tactics or operations. Otherwise the development of strategies will suffer.

Table 1 is a diagram of the levels and duties of management in an organization. The diagram makes it seem that there are clear cut distinctions between the levels and functions, but that is not the case. Just as in the miliary analogy, the levels and actions of management frequently overlap. In fact, in a very small business, there may be a single individual who is responsible for performing all aspects of the management. Even in large organizations with many management people, the functions can overlap because managers can have multiple assignments. Finally, managers at every level have input to decisions made at every level.

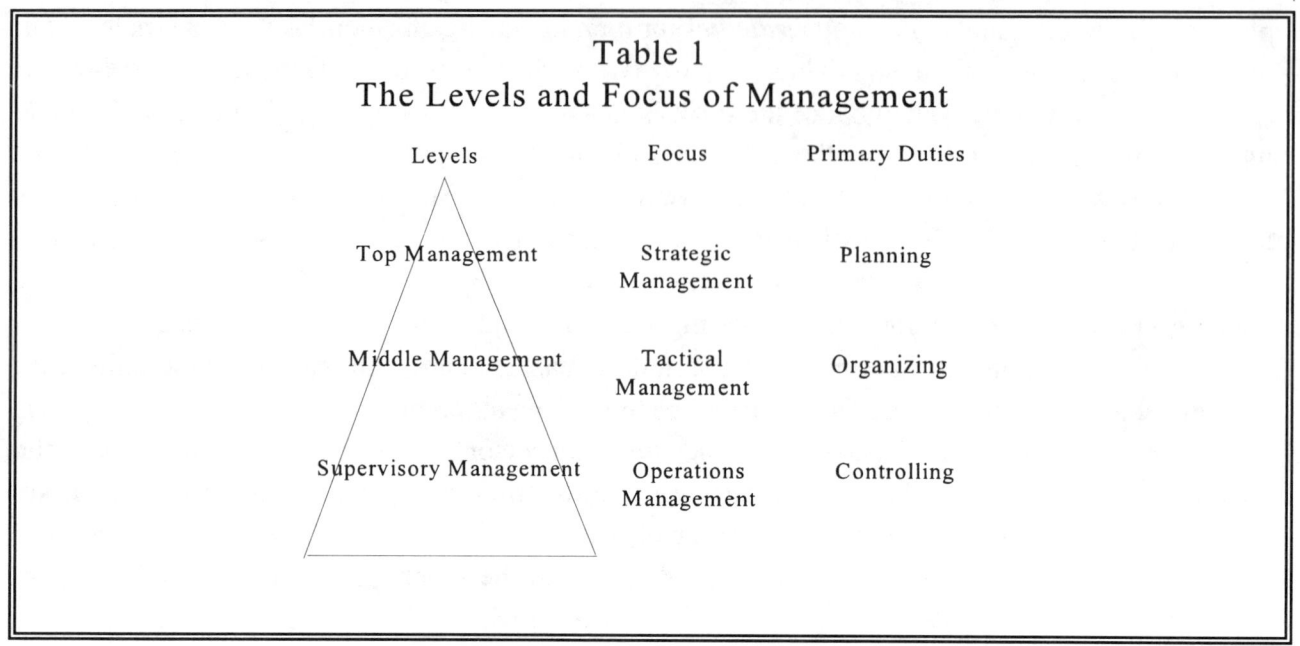

Table 1
The Levels and Focus of Management

Levels	Focus	Primary Duties
Top Management	Strategic Management	Planning
Middle Management	Tactical Management	Organizing
Supervisory Management	Operations Management	Controlling

THE DUTIES OF MANAGEMENT

The duties of management spelled out in the table can overlap tremendously not only because the assignments of managers can overlap, but because the duties influence each other. The influence runs up the scale because top management must know what the organization's resources and capabilities are in order to form strategies, and runs down the scale because tactical and operations managers must react to rapidly changing conditions in carrying out their duties without having the time or opportunity to obtain decisions or involvement from higher levels. Nevertheless, the paradigm makes a convenient tool for the discussion of management and we will discuss each level individually in the following sections.

STRATEGIC MANAGEMENT

Top management in a small firm is simply the owner. The owner is responsible for what we like to call the strategic management of the firm. *Strategic management* consists of the establishment of goals and objectives and strategies of the firm. This is the planning activity. We will examine each aspect individually in the following sections. Keep in mind that everyone in the organization must know what the goals, objectives and strategies are for the firm at all times. Since everyone in the business is necessary to advance the firm toward its goals, then everyone must know where it is going in order to be able to do a good job. In fact, if everyone does not agree with the goals and objectives, the actual success of the firm is threatened. Much has been written about *goal congruence* which simply means that the goals and objectives of the managers of the business are consistent with the goals and objectives of the business itself. If this is not the case, then managers are apt to guide the firm toward their own goals, consciously or unconsciously, rather than toward the business goals. Encouraging participation and input to the goals and objectives of the firm from all levels in the firm is a good tool for minimizing this problem.

Goals

The *goals* of the organization are the long range conditions which the owner wishes to achieve. The goals may be such things as taking a business *public* (that means making it a publicly owned corporation), expanding its geographic territory, achieving pre-eminence in a particular market, diversifying the product/service offerings, or any of a host of other achievements which the owner(s) desire. *Goal setting* means deciding what you want the business to look like in 5 years, in 10 years, or even longer into the future. Goals do not have to be financial or even quantifiable. A goal could be the development of a reputation for exceptional quality or service to the community. Goals may be quantifiable such as $1 million in sales in 10 years or 25 outlets in 5 years or operations in 5 states within 5 years. A firm may have as many or as few goals as the owner desires.

Goals must be obtainable in the environment in which the business must operate and sufficiently detailed to permit objectives and strategies to be formulated from them. For example, it would make little sense to develop the goal of becoming the world's largest company. Such a goal would not aid in guiding the company at all. It might very well make sense to develop a goal of becoming the major supplier of widgets in the United States market or of obtaining the largest market share of gadget sales in the Southeast. The purpose of having goals for the company is to establish the direction in which the firm is to move and to develop a measure of success. After all, what is success if it is not the achievement of established goals?

Goals should constantly be reviewed and modified or upgraded as conditions change. We mentioned the need for goals to make sense in the business environment. That environment is changing constantly. In the last few years there has been a major push from the federal government to deregulate various industries. A few years ago, interstate banking was not possible, airlines were heavily regulated as was trucking and various types of freight. Changes in the laws and regulations governing these and other industries have changed the environment dramatically. Furthermore, there is a ripple effect on suppliers and firms which deal with deregulated firms so that regulatory change affects thousands of small businesses as well as the large. Such change will continue to be a fact of business life. Goals must be adjusted to take into consideration the changes as they occur. Many changes have to do with consumer groups. Age, education, income and other demographic factors of the consumer group for any product or service change constantly. Consumer tastes fluctuate widely, frequently reversing trends or directions. Markets appear, age, change, dry up and reappear making established goals meaningless. In addition, major shifts in the competitive situation can be expected. New firms will come into existence; old firms will exit the market; established firms will change their marketing plans; in short, the competitive situation will be different every year. Goals must be changed to recognize all of these changing conditions in order to remain viable.

Many people overlook the impact that the regulatory changes can have on small business because they think of effects only in terms of giant corporations. That is a mistake! Consider the effect of the change in interstate banking laws. A few years ago small local banks had little to fear from competition from large out of state banks because they were protected by regulations. That's no longer true! Even when the regulatory change affects only big firms, small businesses are impacted as well. What happens if import restrictions on automobiles are eased? American automobile manufacturers will sell less cars. That means that they will buy fewer materials and components. Each of the automobile companies purchase items from literally thousands of small businesses, all of whom will be affected. Regulatory changes can also have an indirect effect. If automobile workers make up a significant portion of the market for a small hardware store, then a layoff or cut back will have a dramatic effect on the hardware store as well.

All regulatory changes are not necessarily negative. Most regulations in reality serve to reduce competition. As regulations and restrictions are eased, competition tends to increase and many firms suffer. In the long run, however, the increased competition will frequently be good for the industry and increased opportunities will develop. Entrance barriers to industries can be lowered or eliminated by regulatory changes, making it possible for new firms to enter or small firms to grow.

Local, national and international economic conditions also play a major role in determining the environment in which a business must exist. Everyone knows how recessions affect the general business condition in the U.S., but too few people understand how inflation in other countries can affect U.S. businesses. In addition to the impact on prices, inflation in a country affects the value of that country's currency in international exchange. For example, after enjoying a lengthy period of extreme success in U.S. sales, Japanese firms are now experiencing problems because of the rising value of the Yen in terms of the U.S. dollar. For the first time in recent memory, Japanese companies are no longer price leaders in the U.S. In the area of microcomputers and their components, automobiles and a host of other manufactured products, Japanese imports are suffering when compared to domestic producers. Should the trend in Yen/dollar exchange rate reverse itself, U.S. producers will find themselves suffering. Just as we discussed above, the effect of imports on the U.S. economy will have a *trickle down* impact on thousands of small businesses. Consequently, the world economic condition affects small businesses in the United States just as the domestic economic conditions.

The U.S. economy is a *cyclic economy*, as are most economies in the world. That means that it is constantly going up and down. In the last 100 years, the U.S. has experienced more than 40 recessions. Of course, each recession was followed by a recovery period. That works out to an average of one economic shift every two and a half years. That's only an average; the time between recessions has varied greatly over the years. Nevertheless, if you intend to be in business, you must be prepared to deal with economic shifts: they are virtually inevitable.

All of this talk about the environment should make it clear that a major requirement for effective goal setting is a good intelligence gathering process. In order to set goals, you must know what the environment in which you operate is and what it can be expected to do over the short and long term. Both threats and opportunities will occur to a business as a result of environmental changes. Your goals should take both into consideration. You must stay abreast of the environment by reading business and trade journals and by listening and talking to other people in your market area. Constant awareness of what is going on and its potential effect on your business will make you better able to make and modify goals for your business.

Objectives

After goals are established for a business, objectives should be set. *Objectives* are simply intermediary goals. They provide a road map of how to get from here to there. If one of your goals is to become known for exceptionally high quality, then one of your objectives could be a quality control program which reduces defective output by 5% next year and by 10% within 5 years. Unlike goals, objectives need to be highly specific. The purpose of objectives is to establish *benchmarks* against which the firm's progress toward its goals can be measured. Therefore, objectives should be quantified whenever possible.

Multiple objectives and multiple levels of objectives are appropriate. Just as you can have many goals, you can have many objectives. As in the case of goals, the only rule is that objectives should be consistent with each other. You can also have several levels established for each objective. Like the example above of reducing defective output, objectives can be established with higher performance levels required over time. Each objective should be obtainable and should be designed to provide progress toward one or more of the firm's goals. They should be reviewed and modified regularly. When the goals change, the objectives will probably need to be changed. Even when the goals do not change, objectives should be modified to take into consideration the company's progress. Each time we compare the firm to objectives all future objectives should be reviewed. Changes should be made in the levels desired or in the objectives themselves. It is a never ending process.

Strategies

Strategies are the plans for achieving objectives. Once we have determined where we want the company to be at a given point in time, then we must decide how to get the company there. The most important strategy is the distinctive competency which we discussed in the previous unit. Needless to say, the distinctive competency must be consistent with the firm's goals and objectives.

Other strategies exist, however, aimed at achieving objectives. So long as they are consistent with each other, a firm can have multiple strategies. A firm which has an objective of taking away market share from a class of competitors may establish a strategy of maintaining prices at or below those competitors at all times. A firm which wishes to increase the level of repeat business may have a strategy of contacting past customers with advertising data every six months.

Objectives are the desired ends or outcomes; strategies are what you intend to do to achieve the outcome. Objectives are *what*; strategies are *how!* The strategies can be highly specific like the ones mentioned above or they can be more general. For example, a general strategy could be *to grow through acquisitions*. That would mean that the firm would focus on purchasing other businesses. Business policy textbooks talk about **generic** or general strategies which firms can pursue regardless of the industry in which they compete. Table 2 is a list of the most frequently cited generic strategies. The table also displays examples of more specific strategies which are applications of the broader thrust.

The list in Table 2 is by no means complete. There are as many different strategies which can be pursued as there are businesses to pursue them. The only determination as to whether a strategy is appropriate for your business is whether it will help move the business closer to the objectives which you have established. One word of caution is due here. In a small business, the owner will frequently be alone in the top management or will have very few assistants at that level. Consequently, the more strategies the company has, the more difficult it will be to manage them. It is wiser for a small business to select a small number of goals, objectives and strategies and pursue them well than to develop large numbers and pursue them haphazardly.

TACTICAL MANAGEMENT

The middle management levels of a firm are responsible for the *tactical management*. That is, middle managers must implement the strategies developed by top management. This is the organizing function of management. In general terms, it means telling people what to do. Top management ensures that middle management know and understand business goals, objectives and strategies. Top management then assigns appropriate middle management personnel responsibility for carrying out specific strategies. The middle managers then decide how best to carry out the strategies. They break the strategies down into specific tasks and assign people to carry out the tasks.

Of course, the top management, the owner in a small firm, is also involved in organizing. The owner engages in organizing when he or she decides which middle managers to employ for a task. The owner is organizing when deciding on the number and skill levels of employees to be hired. Middle managers must also be engaged in planning. Not only do they have input to the planning process, they must plan how best to carry out strategies. Nevertheless, the primary focus and consequently, the primary time consumer should be strategic management for the owner and tactical management for middle managers.

Table 2
Generic Strategies

I.   Concentration on a single business
     A.   Create more uses for product/service
     B.   Use advertising
          1.   To stimulate demand
          2.   To promote more uses for product/services
          3.   To attract new groups of users to product/services
     C.   Find new markets
     D.   Find new channels of distribution

II.   Vertical integration
     A.   Backward: Acquire sources of supply
     B.   Forward: Acquire distributors and vendors

III.   Related diversification
     A.   Acquire businesses in your industry
     B.   Acquire businesses in related industries

IV.   Unrelated diversification
     A.   Acquire businesses in different industries
     B.   Build a portfolio of businesses

V.   Retrenchment, turnaround and repositioning strategies
     A.   Retrenchment
          1.   Raise prices to reduce demand/raise profits
          2.   Reduce the scale of operations
     B.   Turnaround
          1.   Change the distinctive competency
          2.   Change management personnel
     C.   Repositioning
          1.   Withdraw from some markets/products/services
          2.   Enter other markets/products/services

VI.   Abandonment, divestiture and liquidation strategies
     A.   Sell off assets/divisions/businesses
     B.   Sell the business itself

VII. Combination strategies
     A.   Mix strategies from the other groups
     B.   Match strategies from the other groups

Tactics are specific actions and activities which are designed to further strategies. Consider a strategy to use advertising to stimulate demand. Tactics to enable that strategy to be implemented would include the determination of appropriate advertising media, the design of advertising messages and appeal, and the timing of the advertising. The marketing manager would have to develop a budget to be approved by top management and assign people to complete the various tasks. Notice that successful completion will require intelligence gathering about the most effective media and the characteristics of the target market. That knowledge would have to be continually updated through monitoring of the effects of advertising and the changes in the target market composition and motivation. As you can see, it's simple to say *stimulate demand*, but carrying out that charge is complex and time consuming.

OPERATIONS MANAGEMENT

Operations managers are the direct supervisors of the people who will carry out the work. We commonly think of assembly line workers in a manufacturing firm and the line supervisors when we think of *operations management*. Such supervisors are indeed operations managers, but other types of positions qualify also. For example, the first level of management in an accounting firm supervises people. Frequently, middle managers also have operations responsibilities. For example, the marketing manager we talked about above may be responsible for performing or overseeing the performance of much of the advertising work as well as developing the tactics to be used. In such a case, the advertising manager would also be an operations manager. Any person who must actually control the completion of a task is an operations manager. The key word is control.

Control is the management function which is used to keep employees on track as to the tasks they must accomplish. In a manufacturing firm, control of an assembly line means achieving the production levels required while maintaining the quality of output at acceptable levels. It also means cost containment to budgeted levels. A lot has been written about control, especially in the area of employee morale. Everyone knows that employee morale is affected by the supervisory managers and that high morale means not only high worker satisfaction but high productivity and quality as well.

Every manager in an organization has control responsibilities in that people report to every manager. The owner manages people through the chain of command. Furthermore, the owner is responsible for control because he or she must set up and enforce the system which permits people to control other people. In fact, this is the major problem which small business owners face in day to day management of the enterprise. Far too many owners of small businesses get caught up in operations and fail to spend the necessary time on planning. It is an easy thing to do because the outcome of planning is nebulous; hard to see and understand. The outcome of operations management is direct and immediate. Many people find that operations management is more enjoyable and more rewarding because of the immediate feedback and the ability to see a tangible result from the work.

Planning, on the other hand, tends to be dull and have results that are difficult to trace back to plans and which are frequently delayed for months or years. In addition, in a small business, there is no one to oversee the planning function. There is no one to say, *you have not reviewed your goals, objectives and strategies this week*, or *you have not done your professional reading today*. No one knows whether the planning is being done properly and in a timely fashion. No one knows, that is, until the business gets in trouble!

The lack of management depth in small firms frequently means that the owner is heavily involved in middle and supervisory management duties as well as top management duties. Because the organization and control functions have to be performed in order to get through the day, it is easy to let those functions take priority. That is a major mistake! It is like driving a car. You can concentrate on the road, on steering, braking, accelerating, etc., but unless you know where you want to go, map out a route to get there and monitor your progress toward the destination, you will never get there! You may enjoy the drive and you may control the car quite well, you may even make progress in that miles are put behind you; but you cannot achieve your destination.

ORGANIZATION CHARTS

The most famous aspect of management is the ***organization chart***. This is a series of boxes connected by lines which spell out how the various management positions in a firm relate to each other and establishes the chain of command. ***Chain of command*** simply means how the power of the owner is delegated throughout the organization, who should report to whom in the organization and who supervises and evaluates whom in the firm. You should establish an organization chart for your business before it is started and you should evaluate the chart periodically and change it when necessary. Table 3 is an example of an organization chart. The chart shows only job titles, but in a real situation, names of managers holding those positions should be shown as well. The table is not intended as a recommendation. It is simply an illustration. There is no such thing as a standard organization chart. What is appropriate for any business is a function of the owners and managers of that business and the environment in which it competes.

Every business must have an organization chart because if it does not have an official chain of command established, then an unofficial chain will develop. If people do not have a clear cut idea of what they are responsible for, who they report to, and how they fit into the organization, then inefficiency will develop, duplication of jobs will occur, and morale will suffer as will the business itself. Just as everyone in the organization should know and understand the goals, objectives and strategies of the firm, everyone should know and understand the organization chart.

The organization chart is simply a visual representation of the organizational structure of the business. In addition, a written job description should be developed for each position so that every manager understands the requirements of every position in the company. Just as the organization chart should change as the business changes, so should the job descriptions. This will permit the structure of the business to conform to the environment in which it operates.

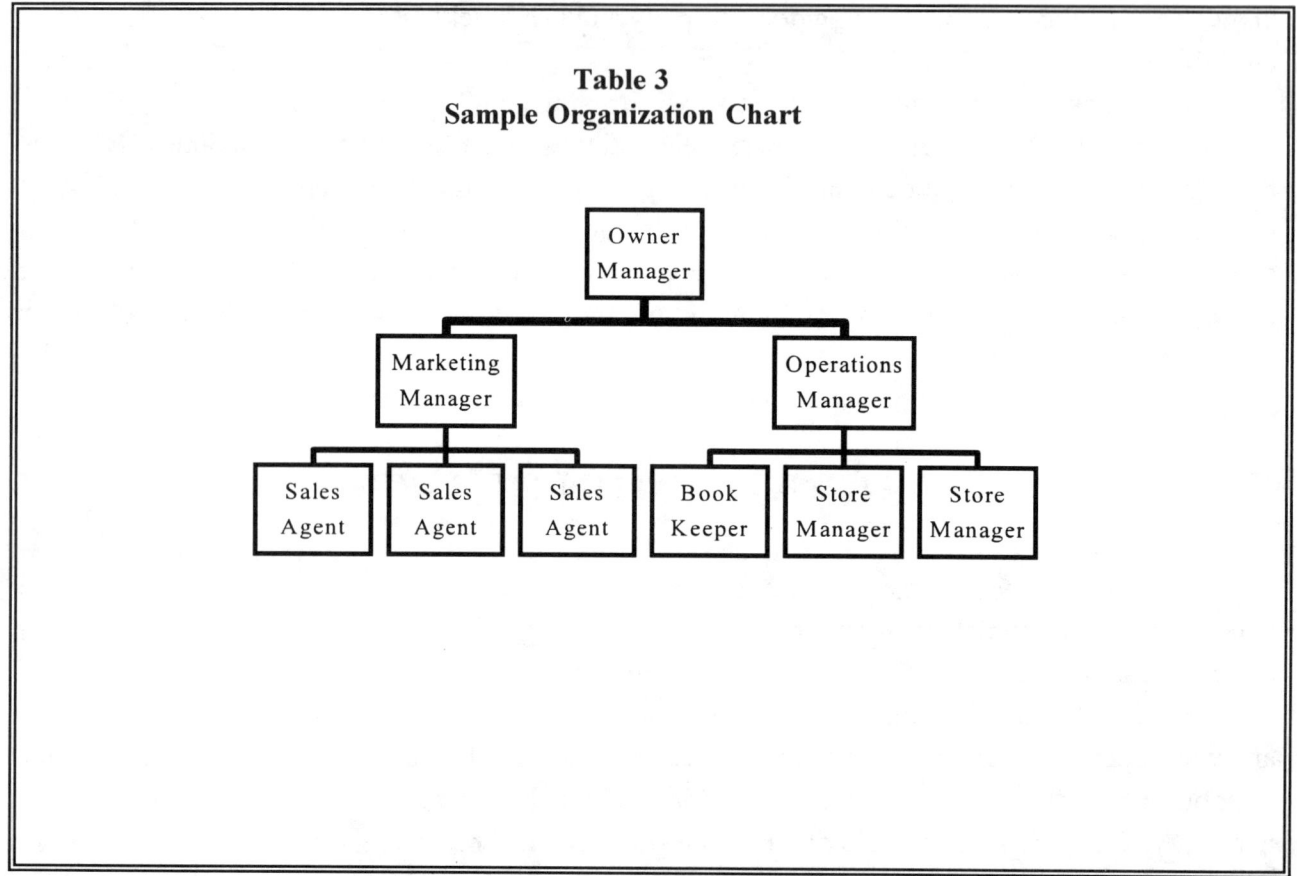

Table 3
Sample Organization Chart

Keeping up with the structure of the organization seems like a lot of work. It is! But it is also vitally important. In one of the most famous books on management ever written, Alfred Chandler explained that the structure of an organization follows the strategy which that organization is pursuing.[63] That follows from an understanding that any plan must be implemented in order to be effective. Even the best plans will fail if their implementation is poor. The implementation of a plan occurs through the structure of the organization. You must put into place people and systems to carry out the strategy and implement the plan. The inescapable conclusion is that, in order to have an effective management, the structure of the company must receive attention equal to that which strategy receives. Like most things in the small business world, the structure of the organization is also the responsibility of the owner.

TIME MANAGEMENT

From what we have discussed in this chapter, it is already clear that the owner of a small business is a very busy person. As we have indicated previously, the planning activities are the ones which typically suffer if there isn't enough time for the owner to get everything done. That is a serious problem. The only solution to the problem is to plan the planning activity. Although it sounds repetitious, it is quite simple. You must decide when you will do the planning necessary to keep the business on track. In fact, you need to decide how all of your work time will be spent.

Small business owners putting in work weeks of 60 to 70 hours are not unusual. Usual or not, a work week that long presents problems. Every one gets tired. When you are tired, your thinking and decision making power are affected. Therefore, excessive working hours may get things done, but get them done poorly. The obvious solution is to reduce working hours to something closer to a normal work week and still get everything done. But how can that be accomplished? Consider what it is that consumes an owner's time.

Numerous surveys have been conducted to analyze how managers, especially CEOs, spend their time. All of the research indicates that most time is spent in oral communication. Everyone knows how ineffective meetings can be, but that seems to be no deterrent to their use. The telephone is also a major time waster. How can you control this problem? The simple fact is that you must cut off discussion. The conversations and discussions occur with employees, with suppliers, with customers and with other interested parties either individually on the telephone or in meetings. All individual and telephone discussions should be prefaced with a statement like *time only permits 10 minutes today.* Then stick to the limit! When the time you have allocated expires, whether a resolution is achieved or not, you must end the conversation with a statement that time is now up! If further discussion is required, you can continue it another day. The secret is to enforce the time limit! Very few people will be offended by that so long as you tell them up front what the time limit is and so long as you are consistent in enforcing the limit. People will be offended if you are not even-handed and consistent in limiting your time.

Meetings are a special problem. Not only do they waste owner time, they waste time for every manager in the meeting. A meeting with 10 management people in it which lasts 2 hours has just used 20 hours of management time: half of a work week! Since the managers tend to be the highest paid employees in a business, that 20 hours could be exceptionally expensive. Not only that, the alternative uses to which that time could have been devoted could far outweigh the results of the meeting. The first step is to reduce the number of meetings to the absolute minimum. Not all meetings can be eliminated, but those that can be, should be. Before it starts, a time limit for the meeting should be established as well as an agenda for the discussion. If it is important enough to have a meeting, then it is important enough to do it right! A chair for the meeting should be established in advance, either on a permanent or rotating basis. That individual should take responsibility for planning, organizing and controlling the upcoming meeting. The subjects to be discussed at the meeting should be planned in advance and distributed in the form of an agenda. People who will be expected to present information or arguments should be notified and a time limit for their presentations established in advance. Then the chair of the meeting should moderate all discussion by limiting each person to 5 minutes or so for presenting his or her position and by cutting off debate when it is unproductive. As in the case of limiting conversations, this will not cause a problem if everyone understands the rules up front and they are consistently enforced.

Some people have developed *cute* ploys to limiting meetings such as holding them at 4:00 on Friday afternoons, 7:00 on Monday mornings, over lunch, over breakfast or dinner. None of these ploys really work well: they simply result in animosity among the people at the meeting. There is no substitute for a professional approach and a no-nonsense management of the meeting itself.

There is one final point which needs to be made about meetings. It is popular to establish a regular meeting for the purpose of communicating or updating or informing people of current issues. That is only a good idea if the meetings are infrequent! Daily and weekly meetings are largely a waste of time. People just won't prepare for meetings when they occur that frequently.

PLANNING YOUR TIME

Planning your work day is simply a matter of continuously scheduling your activities. A calendar with sufficient space to record activity reminders for a month at a time is a valuable tool as is a daily calendar with sufficient space to detail each day's activities. You should set aside time for the planning, reading and comparison of results to objectives each week. Try to make those activities as important as attending meetings! When you are unable to complete the day's requirements, which will happen more frequently than anyone would like, be sure to carry those things which have not been completed to the next day.

Keeping a constant list of what you must accomplish is the key to never forgetting an important task. The first thing you should do each morning is review the activities planned for the day and assign priorities to the tasks. Work on completing them in the order of priority during the day. The last thing you should do each day is review the day's activities, mark off the tasks completed and prepare a new list for tomorrow adding those things which were unfinished today. Sound cumbersome? It really isn't. With a little practice you will find the process becoming second nature and time management will no longer be a problem. Just remember, being a manager means managing yourself as well as managing the company. You cannot expect to be able to manage a company successfully if you cannot manage your own time. All it takes is a little foresight and a commitment to utilize your most important resource wisely. You wouldn't spend your money flippantly, so why spend your time that way? Your time is much more valuable than money!

OUTSIDE ASSISTANCE

Throughout this chapter, we have discussed the problem with the owner of a small firm having to cover a much broader range of activities than a CEO in a large firm and the lack of specialists and assistants to aid and advise. Due to the limited financial resources in a small firm, this is not a problem which can be expected to go away. It is a recurring problem which will complicate management until the firm has grown sufficiently to be able to employ the necessary staff. One approach which has been taken by many small business owners to reduce the problem is the use of outside consultants. In previous chapters, we mentioned several sources of outside consulting services which could be used in structuring the start-up plan. We need to mention those sources again here because they are also available to assist an ongoing business.

Free assistance in a wide variety of areas is available from programs of the US Small Business Administration (SBA). Those programs include the Small Business Institute (SBI), the Service Corps of Retired Executives (SCORE) and the Small Business Development Centers (SBDC). In fact, the SBA now has a web page which makes it easy to examine the full range of assistance programs which are available. The address is simply:

www.sbaonline.sba.gov

SCORE is perhaps the most famous of the governmental assistance programs. It has been around for a long time and has a long track record of successes. In essence, the SBA assigns an individual who is a retired business executive to a small business seeking assistance. Access can be had through the nearest SBA office. The executive volunteers his or her time. Consulting engagements can be short lived or very long lived and are available in a variety of areas.

The SBDC program is one of the best assistance avenues for small businesses. There are SBDCs established in every state. SBDCs are sponsored by the SBA but also receive funding at the state level. Offices are established at universities and many states have branch offices established across the state. Free consulting is available on a wide variety of topics and is provided by students who work within the SBDC under the supervision of permanent staff members. The SBDC program has established an excellent record. If one is available in your area, we highly recommend your exploration of services available.

All of the assistance programs described in the preceding sections can be accessed through the local field office of the SBA. Generally a telephone call will be sufficient to initiate the contact. If you do not know the location of the local office, a telephone call to the SBA home office in Washington, D.C., will result in that information, or you can check the SBA web page.

In addition to the assistance programs, consulting can be obtained from individuals and firms on a fee basis. There are numerous management consultants in practice in the United States ranging from firms of one or two people to gigantic corporations. Many accounting firms also offer management consulting services. The fees these consultants charge vary greatly, from around $50 per hour to as much as $500 per hour. Fees can also be established by the day, by the week or by the job. Annual retainer fees are offered by many consulting firms. The number of consultants has been growing in recent years indicating that more and more businesses are utilizing their services. Small businesses can benefit from management consultants, as well as large companies, but frequently avoid them because of the expense involved. That could be a mistake. A good consultant, hired for the right reasons, can save the firm more money than the fees charged.

How do you determine whether a consultant is good? Unlike many other professionals, there are no licensing procedures for management consultants. That's also true for financial planners who are specialists in the consulting field. That means that virtually anyone who wishes can set up a consulting business. Consequently, there is a broad range of expertise and experience among practicing consultants. You should explore the background and credentials of any person you are considering hiring as a consultant to ensure that the person has experience and knowledge which can be useful to your business. That's true whether the individual is alone in a part time consulting business or whether the consultant is being provided by one of the *Big 6* accounting firms. Ask for references and check those references. If it is a large firm, ask who will be involved with your business either directly or indirectly and find out about their backgrounds. Remember, whether it is a large or small consulting business you are considering, it is an individual or a few individuals who will be looking at your business. The expertise of those individuals is the prime consideration. All the high powered backup in the world won't help if the person in your shop is unable to find the pertinent facts to relay to that backup! Ask for the names of businesses similar to yours with which the consultant has worked and call those businesses. Check with the Better Business Bureau in your town to see if anyone has registered a complaint about the consultant. Finally, talk to the individual. Does the person try to impress you by using professional jargon or by talking over your head? Does the person seem genuinely interested in your business and in making a contribution to your business? What does the consulting contract look like? Is the person willing to spell out in writing what will be done and when? Do you think you can work with this person? Remember, you will have to manage the consulting engagement just as you must manage the business.

How do you decide when you need a consultant? Consider the kinds of things which a consultant can do for you. Table 4 is a partial list. In reality, the list is almost endless. The table is provided to stimulate your imagination about useful applications of consultants.

As Table 4 makes clear, consultants can be used to do anything which managers or other employees in a firm can do. They are especially useful in planning start-ups, and expansions and in assessing problems, but don't overlook their usefulness in day to day management. A long term relationship with a competent management consultant can be a valuable aid to any small business owner.

Table 4

Areas in Which Consultants Can Provide Assistance or Guidance

- Start-up plans for new businesses, products/services/markets

- Expansion plans for existing businesses

- Goals, objectives, strategies; short and long term

- Organizational structure and job descriptions

- Systems for accounting, record keeping, reporting, accounts receivable and payable control, budgeting, pricing, cost control, internal control, computerizing, etc.

- Human resources planning, training, recruiting, evaluating, reporting, supervision, fringe benefits planning and evaluation, pension plans, stock plans, etc.

- Financial plans, capital budgets, cash flow forecasts and analysis, loan applications, cost analyses, profitability analyses, division/department effectiveness, financial analyses, pro forma statements, tax planning, bids preparation and evaluation, etc.

- Marketing plans, advertising plans, promotional plans, evaluation of markets, target markets, market trends, customer satisfaction, new markets/products/services, budgets and media for marketing activities, etc.

- Production plans, plant layouts, workflow analysis, time/motion studies, distribution and storage analysis, equipment evaluation, automation plans, etc.

- Training for managers, in management, motivation, specialized areas, etc.

- Risk management planning, evaluation, assessment, etc.

- Inventory policy, purchasing, turnover evaluation, economic order quantity, control, etc.

SUMMARY

Management is the process of deciding what tasks are to be done, assigning responsibilities for doing those tasks to someone, and checking to be sure that the tasks have been done satisfactorily. However, the process is not simple in small businesses because of the depth of management. The owner of a small business is often alone at the helm and must perform all the tasks and accept all the responsibilities personally.

Management consists of planning, organizing and controlling functions. These functions include the tasks of deciding where the business is going and how to get it there; structuring the people to perform their duties and delegating responsibility and establishing a system of feedback for evaluation purposes.

Management can be divided into three levels with appropriate responsibilities attached. Top management deals primarily with strategic issues and decisions which have far reaching effects. That person has the life or death of the company in his or her hands and so must plan for and make decisions that will ensure its success. Middle management is involved primarily with tactical issues which means that this level must take the plans of top management and translate them into actions. The lower level of management is supervisory. Here the daily operations are overseen. All levels, functions and duties of management overlap.

Strategic management consists of the establishment of goals, objectives and strategies for the firm. The goals of the organization are the long range conditions which a company wishes to achieve. They should be specific, written, quantifiable, if possible, and reviewed and evaluated frequently.

Objectives are intermediary benchmarks which provide checkpoints for measuring progress toward goals. They too should be quantifiable. Strategies are plans for achieving the objectives. The most important strategy is that of a distinctive competency. That is, what do I do best and differently than my competitors.

Tactical management is concerned with carrying out the plans of top management. Tactics are specific actions or activities which are designed to further strategies.

Operations managers are the direct supervisors of people who will carry out the work and assure the completion of a task.

The organization chart is the tool used by management to establish the chain of command in an organization. This graph shows the delegation of power to specific individuals and dictates who should report to whom. This assignment of responsibility is important and job descriptions should be included to avoid later conflicts.

In order to effectively plan, organize, and control, management at all levels must be cognizant of time constraints. As we have emphasized earlier, management works long hours, but to be successful those long hours must be effective. Planning your time and staying with the time allocations is a must. Time truly waits for no man nor does your business thrive without constant surveillance.

There are many assistance agencies, both from profit and nonprofit consultants, who can help in a variety of ways. Several of those agencies are the SBI, SCORE, SBA, SBDC or private firms. Listed on Table 4 is a summary of consulting activities which are available to you from the above sources. Don't be hesitant to ask for aid in any of these areas, for your foresight will pay handsomely in the future.

QUESTIONS, EXERCISES AND CASES

QUESTIONS:

Define the following terms:

1.   Planning
2.   Organizing
3.   Controlling
4.   Organization chart
5.   Goal
6.   Objectives
7.   Strategies
8.   Tactics
9.   Responsibility

Answer the following questions:

1.   What is the purpose of having a Chief Executive Officer and what does he or she do?
2.   How is the CEO different from the COO?
3.   What is strategic management?
4.   Do all businesses use strategic management? Why or why not?
5.   How do goals and objectives differ?
6.   Why should goals change?
7.   What is tactical management?
8.   What is operational management?
9.   Why is time management important?
10.   What can consultants do for a business?

EXERCISES:

1.   In a role play methodology, have a member of the class act as a consultant to two or three others and have that consultant discuss the goals, objectives, strategies, and tactics of the new venture being considered and have the consultant draw up an organization chart.

2.   Do some investigative work and discover if there are assistance agencies in your neighborhood and what types of assistance they can give.

CASE

Eileen Johnson was hired on as the secretary for the Accounting department at ABC Associates. ABC Associates was a consulting and financial planning firm for area businesses. Ms. Johnson was hired by the manager as his secretary and the office secretary. There were five consultants in the department who would need different types of prospecti typed from time to time and various letters. Ms. Johnson was extremely efficient and everyone in the firm thought very highly of her skill and resourcefulness.

However, problems began to arise as the year continued with finding letters untyped or work parceled out to the secretarial pool whose members did not know the proper format nor the deadlines. When the consultants would complain to Ms. Johnson that the work was not done in a timely fashion nor properly, her response would be that she was sorry that as the manager's secretary, her time was his and that she was glad to help the others when time permitted, as it had in the beginning, but that now she had to get the other secretaries to share the load. After all, it was not her job to do all the work.

Several of the consultants approached the manager about the attitude of the departmental secretary and he would nod his head and continue on his way. Now a new development caused some worry to the consultants who had previously had a secretary who was not as sharp as this one but one who always managed to get the work done. The new development was that Ms. Johnson would come in very early before the office opened to get her day started because she was an early riser and liked to be at work early. The only problem was that the office was open from 9 to 5 and because she had arrived at 7:30 and had taken no lunch, she would leave at 3:30 or 4:00 when the manager was making his own calls on clients and so was not in the office. This meant that the consultants who were expecting late clients or paperwork prepared at a later time in the day would have to do it themselves or not get it done on time.

Because Ms. Johnson was such a personable lady, most of the consultants truly liked her, but their jobs were being made impossible to do. So several of those close to her made suggestions as to what the problem might be. She claimed that she had no problem. She was hired as the manager's secretary and so as long as he had no complaints, everything was okay. If she was efficient enough to get her work done early, then she deserved the time off. What could be done?

1.   What is the real problem in the above case and how could it easily be fixed?

2.   What part does management play in the dilemma faced by the other consultants?

3.   Is it a disservice for the manager to allow the secretary to labor under false impressions?

4.   If you were the manager in the above situation, how would you handle it?

5.   If you were the consultants in the above situation, how would you handle it?

6.   If you were the secretary in the above situation, what would you do?

CHAPTER FIFTEEN

HUMAN RESOURCES MANAGEMENT

CHAPTER OBJECTIVES

Upon completion of this chapter, you should be able to:

- Explain the importance of human resource management;
- Explain how to recruit the best people for the job;
- Specify the advantages and disadvantages of promoting from within;
- Evaluate the advantages and disadvantages of finding individuals outside the firm;
- Conduct an effective interview;
- Explain the value of on the job training programs;
- Distinguish between democratic, autocratic and participative supervision and know where you stand in these typologies;
- Specify the whys and wherefores of compensation policies;
- Explain how fringe benefits can be made to work for the employer as well as the employee;
- Describe the importance of good employee relations and how this relationship reflects upon the success of the company;
- Demonstrate the importance and methodology of performance evaluations; and,
- Explain the legal restrictions involved with recruiting and promoting personnel.

HUMAN RESOURCES MANAGEMENT

INTRODUCTION

The employer of people exercises power over those people. Benjamin Disraeli said, ... *all power is a trust -- that we are accountable for its exercise...* In Disraeli's words, with power comes a public trust and duty. It is well to heed his words, because people are the greatest asset of any business and are the vehicle through which that business achieves success. Effective management of that asset is difficult whether a business has 5 people or 50,000 people, but the kinds of problems which occur are different in small businesses.

The owner of a small firm is frequently the personnel officer as well and must oversee all the aspects of human resource management *personally*. In addition, the impact of personnel problems is greater in a small business. If a large firm loses a skilled worker or a senior manager, little damage may occur, because there are many other employees and managers who can step in to take up the slack, at least until a replacement can be found. If a small firm loses even one employee, the business can suffer for weeks or months because there is no one else in the firm who can take over the duties without other duties suffering. The problem is even worse with management personnel. Losing one manager in a small firm could mean that half the management staff is lost!

On the other hand, a small business has some advantages over large firms in personnel management. The employees of a small firm tend to feel a closer relationship to other employees and to the business simply because of the scale of the operation. Many of the problems which occur in a large operation are a result of the employees feeling unimportant; like tiny cogs in a big wheel. In a small firm, such feelings are easily eliminated and employees have no difficulty seeing the effect of their labor on the well being of the business. Nevertheless, the owner of a small firm must be cognizant of the needs of the employees in order to take advantage of the potential value of the scale of operations. In this chapter, we will discuss the management of people in all of its aspects from recruiting through training, to supervision, to compensation, to employee relations.

RECRUITING

Recruiting is the process of locating and hiring people for positions within a firm. There are two places to look for people: inside the firm and outside the firm. We will address each of these sources in turn, but first we need to discuss job specifications. You cannot recruit a person for a job unless you have a firm idea of what is required to perform that job.

JOB DESCRIPTIONS

Most *job specifications* used, in recruiting, list educational requirements and work experience desired in a potential employee. How are such things determined? In some jobs, special training is required which makes educational specifications easier. Most of the time, however, education is not that closely linked to job performance. Some large firms make it a habit to recruit MBAs for management positions and to require BAs for all other positions except unskilled labor. The theory is that although there may be little of direct benefit to the firm from the education, the fact that the individual completed the education is valuable as a screening device. Finding and hiring a person is difficult and time consuming. The situation is infinitely worse if you hire an individual who cannot do the job or who leaves shortly after having been hired. Then you have to start the hiring process over and you have to live with the consequences of having had an incompetent person in the job. Therefore, any steps which you can take which will more effectively screen potential employees are worthwhile. Educational requirements are frequently used as a screening device.

Experience requirements largely serve the same purpose: i.e., increasing the probability that an employee will be able to competently perform a job. The number of years of experience required is totally subjective. The theory is that the longer the experience, the greater the level of knowledge in the field and the greater the probability that the individual will be competent. Of course, it is entirely possible, and frequently happens, that neither education nor experience have anything to do with potential job performance. Nevertheless, education and experience requirements are almost universally used in job descriptions. One frequently hears recent college graduates lamenting the experience requirements cited on job announcements. *How do they expect me to get experience if no one will hire me without experience?* they complain. Good point, and one which you should keep in mind. Hiring a new graduate without experience may be a bit more risky than hiring someone older and with more experience, but giving a chance to a new grad could result in an exceptionally loyal, dedicated employee. Also, inexperienced people tend to be cheaper than old hands, at least, initially.

We consider the best approach to job description to be simply to use the internal job description which we talked about in a previous chapter. If you will recall, we indicated that part of the organizational structure planning was the development of organization charts and the writing of specifications for every position in the firm. If you have done this, then finding an employee is greatly simplified because you will have a firm understanding of what the individual must be able to do. If you are filling a vacancy, then the first step should be a review of the position description. It is easier to make changes in positions when they are vacant, consequently, when replacing an employee, the first step should be the determination of what the new job should look like. Once the written description is firmly established, an announcement of the position can be developed by simply summarizing the duties and requirements of the job. The only addition required in the announcement is generally working hours/arrangements and a salary range which can be expected;

minimum and maximum salaries, bonus or commission levels, overtime hours expected, or other indications of compensation. If you wish to add educational and experience requirements to the job announcement, we recommend that the wording indicate desired levels rather than required levels so that you will not unduly restrict potential applicants for the job. With the completed job announcement in hand, you are ready to begin searching for a person to fill the position.

There is just one more problem. The Equal Employment Opportunity laws makes it illegal to discriminate against job applicants based on age, sex, color, race, national origin, religion, etc. The problem is that if you are accused of discrimination you must prove that you have not done so! Furthermore, you aren't even supposed to ask the kinds of questions that lead to discriminatory practices. For example, you can't ask about religion. But if you are accused of discrimination based on religion, it would be helpful to know whether any of the people you have hired held religious beliefs in common with the accusing party. You can't know that. So what do you do? In the first place, professional assistance may be required in planning the personnel activities and record keeping. In the second place, you should keep a record of why you hired who you hired and why you didn't hire other applicants. In other words, be able to prove that the person you did hire met the job qualifications better than any of the other applicants. This generally means keeping notes based on interviews, reference checks, etc., as well as specific job qualifications for each position.

PROMOTING FROM WITHIN

When we think about recruiting, we seldom think about looking inside the firm but that is really the first place we should look. If there are people inside the firm who can do a job, then we should consider those people for the job. ***Promoting from within*** can be valuable because it encourages the other employees in the firm by demonstrating advancement possibilities. It can also be valuable in that the present employees have a track record and you can have a good idea of how well they might work out in new positions. Hiring outsiders is always a risk, because you can never be sure how capable they are until you have seen them work. Also, hiring from within can speed up the replacement process and shorten the training period. You don't have to waste time by going outside to search for people and the insiders already have an understanding of the business and may have an understanding of the job itself. There are also potential problems.

Hiring from within generally means that a second vacancy is created in the form of the job which the person promoted originally held. There have been cases in which people were not considered for promotion because their employers did not wish to search for replacements or because they were doing exceptionally well in their present positions. An oversight like that is not good for morale in general. In a small firm everyone will know about it and be affected by it. If you intend to have a policy of promoting from within, it has to be an even-handed process and you must accept the necessity of filling another position vacated by the promotion.

Hiring from inside will only work if the person selected to do a job is truly competent. Other employees will know how capable a person is and will feel betrayed if a job is given to an individual who is not competent to perform it. That means that seniority within the firm cannot be used as the basis for promotion. Problems can also develop if there are multiple people who are capable of performing a job or believe that they are capable. The individual(s) not selected for a job may feel animosity toward the one promoted. Friends and supporters of those not selected can feel the same way. Consequently, the effectiveness of an insider can be damaged before that person starts the new job. Both of these possibilities can be alleviated to a large degree if the process of filling a position from within is formalized. Everyone should know about the job and its requirements and have the opportunity to be considered for the job. Maximum input to the selection decision should be obtained from managerial people in the firm and from those employees who will be directly affected by the new job. A list of potentially qualified people should be prepared and those individuals should be interviewed. Selection of the one to be promoted should be made carefully. Then, everyone should know who was chosen for the job and why.

There is one major risk associated with promoting from within which we must mention. Just because a person has done a good job in one position does not guarantee that he or she will do a good job in a more responsible position. This is called the ***Peter Principle*** and is easiest to understand using a military example. In the old days in the military, if an officer had been a good captain, that person was promoted to major. The promotion was not based on the ability to perform the duties of a major, but on past performance as a captain. The really damaging part of the peter principle is what happens next. Now if the person does a poor job as a major, then he or she is not promoted, but is not demoted either! The person stays an incompetent major when he or she would be effective as a captain. This process has been termed ***promoting to the highest level of incompetence***. Fortunately, the military is more enlightened these days and seldom experiences such problems, but many businesses continue to practice a similar promotional policy. The difference in businesses is that an individual who is doing a poor job in a new position generally leaves the firm, voluntarily or otherwise, thereby leaving two positions to fill: the old position the person held and the new position as well. The moral is: be careful when you promote from within because if you choose a good employee for a job that person cannot do, you will lose a valuable employee and gain an incompetent one at the same time. This is another reason why seniority with the firm should not be used as the sole criterion for promotion. Maximum emphasis should be placed on your evaluation of an employee's ability to do the job in question.

OUTSIDE SOURCES

How do you go about finding an individual outside the firm to fill a job position? There are several ways to make contact with such people. The best known is probably an employment agency. There are two types of employment agencies: private and public. ***Public employment offices*** are operated by the State government and are affiliated with the United States Employment Service. Branch offices are located in most of the larger cities in the nation. The services of the public offices are free. They maintain lists of people and summary data about their abilities and will furnish names of people with particular job skills which you might specify. They will also keep an announcement of your position on file and compare it to new people as they come into the office. They will actively recruit for you in some situations. Public employment offices can be an excellent source of employees, but generally are more valuable in finding entry level or lower level employees and less valuable in finding senior level or more responsible employees. Nevertheless, you should always check with the local employment office whenever you have a vacancy. In fact, registering a job vacancy with the employment office is required in some states.

Private employment agencies perform the same kind of services as public agencies, but charge a fee. They will actively recruit for you based on the skills or experience you describe and screen applicants for you. The fees charged can be quite high and are frequently a percentage of the starting salary of any person they find for you. These fees can be paid by the employee or by the employer. As you might expect, success is generally improved when you agree to pay the fees. Many applicants specify to the agency that they are interested only in seeking *fee-paid* jobs. Many employment agencies specialize in certain types of jobs and advertise in publications which appeal to selected groups of people. Such agencies are especially good at finding people who are already employed but are unhappy with their employment or looking for a more responsible position because they tend to have a national scope. These firms, frequently called *Headhunters*, will solicit applicants on a national basis. Because of their expense and the expense associated with bringing in an applicant from out of state for an interview, such agencies are generally valuable for senior level positions or highly skilled positions for which it is difficult to find qualified applicants.

If you are willing to recruit directly, an excellent source of employees is schools, colleges and universities. Many institutions have placement offices which keep resumes on file of recent and potential graduates and which arrange interviews between students and employers. Even if no placement office exists, contact with students interested in jobs is simplified and guidance counselors, teachers and staff can be approached and asked about prospective applicants. Schools can also be valuable sources of part-time or temporary employees as well as full time people. Many schools have cooperative education or internship programs whereby students can obtain credit for a semester of work in a business, and businesses can obtain low cost temporary help and an opportunity to evaluate potential employees before they are actually hired. We highly recommend the use of Coop programs both to students and to businesses.

The most obvious way to find job applicants is to advertise positions in the local newspaper. To that should be added advertisements in trade journals and publications which will appeal to the kind of people you are interested in hiring. This is a highly popular recruiting tool, but results in the consumption of a great deal of time. Such advertisements frequently result in large numbers of applicants. Someone must wade through the applications to select those who will be interviewed.

The applications are frequently so sketchy that you must have the applicants come in to fill out more complete forms or to be interviewed in order to determine their relative skills and value. Consequently, if the owner of a small business does not have help in processing applications and does not have time available to handle them personally, this form of recruiting should not be used.

Finally, applicants can be obtained for job positions by asking the present employees for recommendations. This simple process, frequently overlooked, can be highly successful. In addition, if files are kept on former employees and job applicants, then you may be able to fill a position from that source. All applications for employment should be kept with those which you think might be of value filed separately. Scanning those files could lead to a quick solution to a vacancy. Also, former employees who were valuable may be enticed to return, if not on a permanent basis, then on a temporary or part time basis to take the pressure off finding a new employee. Temporary work may be especially attractive to retired employees.

There are several temporary help agencies, such as Kelly Services and Manpower, which can provide people on a part time or full time, temporary basis. Although such firms generally have a contract with a stiff penalty for hiring away temporary workers, the use of temporary help could smooth the process of looking for a new employee. Temporary employees are generally considered for covering vacation times of regular employees or for a short term project of some type, but they can be valuable in other ways too. If you can take more time for the search, then the probability of finding the right employee is increased. Temporary workers can give you that time.

EVALUATION OF APPLICANTS

Regardless of the source of applicants for your job, you will have to evaluate the people and choose that person whom you consider to be the best person for the job. Generally, the evaluation will be based on written documents and interviews.

Application Forms

Most employers require an ***application form*** to be completed. However, discrimination laws have made application forms dangerous. For example, Table 1 displays the contents of an employment application which was actually in use by a small business with which we worked a few years ago. The form is filled with questions that are potentially dangerous to the employer. The rules don't make clear that no questions may be asked which are not ***bona fide occupational qualifications requirements***. The use of standard forms with a standard group of questions makes it easy to violate that principle. The solution to the problem is simply not to use a standardized application form. This would be extremely difficult for a large firm, but presents little problem for a small business which does not hire that many people, that often.

Table 1 Sample Application Form		
OUR COMPANY NAME	Date:	
Position Desired:	Salary Desired:	
Personal Information:		
Name:	*Age:	*Sex::
Address:	SSN:	
	Phone:	
*Marital Status:	*Dependents:	
*Hobbies:	*Height:	*Weight:
Educational Information: List all schools attended, starting with the most recent		
School Name, Address	Dates Attended	Degree Earned
Work Experience: List all jobs held, starting with the most recent		
Employer Name/Address	Duties	Dates
References: List three people who are knowledgeable about your abilities		
Name/Address	Occupation	Phone
List below any information which you think may be important to your application.		
* These questions are clearly illegal unless you can establish a bona fide reason for them related to the job.		

Using the job description which we talked about in the last section, draw up a series of questions which you will want answered by any applicants based specifically on the job description. That will not only make the application form more valuable, it will be safer! Additional information about the applicant will be developed in the interview. That data, discussed in the following sections, should be added to the application form. Furthermore, you can always ask applicants to prepare a ***resumé***. That way, the applicant decides what information to give you, although you must still be careful not to allow any potentially illegal bias, such as age or sex or dependents, to affect the decision.

Many texts criticize the use of resumes because they will not contain information applicable to a particular job. This is true, however, what the applicant chooses to include on a resume may well provide insight to the person's abilities in general.

The Interview

The owner of a small business is frequently involved in all interviews. Other managers may also be involved or may be used to screen an initial group of applicants and narrow the field to a small number before involving the owner. In any case, every person who will be interviewing prospective employees should develop an outline to guide the interview. Remember, the ultimate purpose of the interview is the selection of an individual from a group of people who will be valuable to your firm. How can you fairly evaluate the applicants if you ask all of them different questions? Clearly, no two interviews will be exactly alike because the applicants' responses to questions will affect the flow of the discussion. Nevertheless, all interviews should cover the same basics and follow the same general pattern in order to maximize comparability between applicants.

An interview guide sheet should be developed which contains additional data about the applicant and which has basic questions to guide the interviewer. Here you must exercise extreme caution! Just as the questions asked on an application form can violate discrimination laws, so, too, can oral questions. You must not ask questions which are not related to the job under consideration. You must also be careful not to phrase questions or to make remarks which could be considered to be discriminatory. For example, questions about previous job duties or responsibilities might be acceptable, but questions about the employment status and record of a spouse are not! Nor should you use terms or job titles which are discriminatory. Busboy and girl Friday are out as are references to the girls in the office or the boys in the mail room. This is not really bad, because if you clean up words, references and vocabulary, you will find that you impact the way you and those around you think about such things at the same time. One question which you could ask during the interview is *why did you leave your last job?*

Notes concerning applicant answers to questions, appearance, questions asked by the applicant, etc., should be made either during the interview, or immediately following the interview. Some people prefer to concentrate on the applicant during the interview and make notes as soon as it is over but before the information can be forgotten. Others prefer to tape record interviews. This last approach is seldom of real value from a practical perspective because no one ever gets an opportunity to listen to the tapes! The questions which you intend to ask should generally be designed to put the applicant at ease initially, to evaluate the quality of the applicant's background, and to make a judgment as to how well the applicant will fit into the business and the position. Be sure to keep the entire interview short!

To start off the interview, many employers like to explain a few aspects of the company, its history, details of the job, policies of the firm concerning employment, promotion, fringe benefits, etc. This serves as small talk to set the applicant at ease, consequently, it should be very short: no more than 2 or 3 minutes should be used. Following the lead in, general questions can be asked as we discussed above. Again, this section of the interview should be extremely short! Finally, questions of a more specific nature can be asked. These questions should deal with knowledge about the field or industry or job; ability to relate to other people; take and follow instructions; or other information which you deem pertinent to the position. Be sure that the questions are pertinent! The interview should close with the applicant being offered an opportunity to ask questions. During this part of the interview, you should pay very close attention to the applicant, because the kinds of questions asked can tell you as much about the person and his or her concerns as the answers to your own questions can.

The notes from the interview should not only deal with the answers to questions, but should also record the results of your observation of the applicant. The individual's dress, manner, carriage, posture, etc. You should also note the way in which the applicant answered your questions: i.e., hesitantly, confidently, shyly, boldly. Did the responses indicate that the applicant had thought about the questions in advance? Did the applicant express himself or herself well? Did the applicant seem knowledgeable about the work required? Do you believe that the applicant will be able to do the work? Will the applicant be able to fit into the company and get along well with other workers? What was your overall opinion of the applicant?

Armed with the information gathered from the application and from the interview, you are still not ready to make a selection. You should discuss your findings with others who interviewed the applicants and form a consensus opinion about each. You should then narrow the field by eliminating those applicants who are clearly not qualified. Be sure to keep notes explaining why these people were eliminated from consideration. The references and former employers of the remaining applicants should be called or written. Education should be verified by transcripts directly from the schools. Police checks and credit checks may be appropriate, but be sure that the applicant knows you intend to make such checks and has given permission to make them. Many people fail to follow up on these simple checks because it's too much trouble. That is a mistake! Just a few telephone calls can help you make a more informed selection.

Former employers may be a problem. As we will discuss later in the chapter on business law, most employers are reluctant to reveal anything more than dates of employment. There is a good reason for that, and we will recommend that you follow the same procedure. Ours has become a *litigious* society. That means that people are suing people right and left! Information given to a prospective employer is potentially dangerous to the company giving that information. Consequently, you can expect little to come of calls to employers. Of course, you should still verify employment and dates, but to obtain further information by phone or letter will probably be fruitless.

You can and probably should ask those individuals who are in the final group of consideration to provide letters of recommendation from previous employers and supervisors. If the individual gives permission, then the legal aspects are safer. Be aware that no one will ask for a reference from an individual whom they expect to write a poor one! Nevertheless, the letters will at least demonstrate that someone at the previous employer thought highly of the applicant. Be sure to call the letter writers to ensure that they did indeed write the letters and did say what the letters contain.

Does all of this sound like a lot of work? It is! But the people you hire are the most important aspect of your business. They will make the difference between success and failure. That means that you should do it right!

IMMIGRATION REFORM AND CONTROL ACT

There has been a change in legislation which has far reaching implications for small business employers. The ***Immigration Reform and Control Act of 1986*** makes every employer, including small businesses responsible for verifying that all people hired are either U.S. citizens or are aliens legally authorized to work in this country. In order to comply with this law, you must complete a report on every person you hire within three days of employment. This report is a one page document, called an ***I-9 Form***, and is available from the Immigration and Naturalization Service (INS) offices around the country. The form can also be obtained from the U.S. Printing Office in Washington, D.C. The form has a section for the employee to fill out which indicates his or her citizenship status. Then, you as the employer are required to examine documents or identification provided by the employee to see if they appear to be genuine. Then you complete the bottom of the form, sign it, and keep it on file in case the INS or the Labor Department ever asks for it or comes by for an inspection. If they do decide to inspect you, they are required to give you three days advance notice. Nevertheless, it is wise to comply with the law even though you may never be called on to prove that you have.

The Act also makes it illegal to discriminate against an applicant because of citizenship status or national origin. In this regard, it is one more aspect of potential discrimination which you must watch. Unlike the other aspects, this law will provide information for its own enforcement since you must keep the forms on file. Be sure to keep records on applicants whom you did not hire so that you can demonstrate that citizenship status had nothing to do with the hiring decision.

TRAINING

Virtually all employees will require some kind of training after they are hired. In addition, most employees will require additional training as the business grows and changes to permit them to adapt to those changes. Training is as important as recruiting to a business. The most competent, capable employees in the world cannot be expected to perform a job which they don't know how to do. All new employees should be given an orientation program, regardless of training which is planned. The orientation should involve explaining the business and its operations as well as personnel, compensation and fringe benefit policies. Any working, safety or production rules should also be carefully explained. Finally, the new employee should be given a tour of the operation and introduced to coworkers and managers. Then the training program can begin.

In small businesses, training generally is conducted in the form of *on the job training* or OJT, because of the expense involved in outside training. OJT can be formalized and a structured program developed to expose a worker to all aspects of a job. OJT can be completely informal in that another worker is assigned to help a new worker when necessary. Most frequently, OJT follows a middle path in which a new employee is assigned to observe other workers for a time, then is observed by others for a time. In manufacturing enterprises which use assembly line production, a new employee can disrupt the work flow. Consequently, training generally takes place on dummy equipment or at idle or off times to achieve a minimal level of competency before injecting the new person into the assembly line.

There are advantages to OJT. One of the major advantages is the opportunity for a new employee to develop familiarity with the people, the business, the customers, suppliers, the operation and layout at the same time that job training takes place. Many people think that OJT is less expensive. That is not necessarily the case! The major expense associated with OJT is lost productivity on the part of workers involved in the training of a new employee. The cost of that loss can be high!

One word of caution is important concerning OJT. There are disadvantages. One of the foremost of these is the dilution effect which job turnover has on training. Consider an example. Assume that a new microcomputer system is acquired and the vendor comes in to perform training for the clerk who will be operating the system. Now six months later, that clerk gives notice of leaving and you have a new person trained by the old clerk before he or she can leave. The training cannot be as sound as the training which the first clerk received because the clerk's level of understanding of the system cannot be as great as the understanding of the system trainers. Now assume that six months later, the second clerk decides to leave and we repeat the process: a third clerk is trained by the second clerk. Now the third clerk's understanding of the system cannot be as great as the second's, which was not as great as the first clerk's. The knowledge is diluted with each turnover in the position. Think how little a person might know who was trained by the fifth clerk!

Another disadvantage associated with OJT is that it can never advance employees beyond the levels of understanding or ability which are possessed by the employees doing the training. That means that if you want to introduce a new practice or work technique, you must introduce another training technique.

Training can take place inside or outside the work place. It can be used for new employees or continuing employees, managers or selected groups of people. You can bring in consultants and/or trainers to conduct seminars, short programs, in depth programs or demonstrations. These can be conducted during or after working hours. These same training opportunities can be offered outside the work place if desired. Training can also take place outside the work place in the form of scheduled seminars, programs, short courses or in depth courses offered by schools, colleges, universities, trade associations, consulting or training companies. The training can be directly job related, can be oriented toward developing superior working habits, can be indirectly related or totally unrelated to the job. Even programs which are unrelated to job performance can impact that performance by increasing employee satisfaction and morale or by preparing employees for more responsible jobs.

Many companies have programs in which they offer to pay the tuition and fees of employees who continue their education at local colleges and universities. Some firms even permit flexible working hours so that employees who wish to do so can take courses during the day instead of being limited to night courses. Other firms pay a portion of the tuition and fees for such students. Although such education is frequently not directly related to job performance, companies justify it by expecting employees to become better prepared for more responsible positions within the firm or to learn more logical, analytical, and decision making skills. In fact, some employers simply use it to single out employees who are self-motivated, ambitious and willing to work for advancement. Completing a college degree or a master's degree in night school while holding down a full time job is a noteworthy achievement. It could be well worth the investment in education to be able to single out employees who have the ability required for that accomplishment.

Training is well understood in large firms in which it is frequently formalized and continuous. Small firms all too often overlook its value, overestimate its cost, or simply fail to think about it at all. In a dynamic society such as ours, training can be the key to translating competent, capable people into competent, capable employees and maintaining them as such.

SUPERVISION

Perhaps you have had other courses in which supervision philosophies were discussed. A great deal has been written on the subject. Basically, the issues revolve around the degree of participation which is permitted to employees in the management process. At one end of the spectrum is the organization in which the owner makes all decisions individually and independently.

That owner has a totally ***autocratic*** style. At the other end of the spectrum is the owner who delegates the maximum number of decisions to the lowest levels possible within the organization and solicits maximum input from the maximum number of people in the organization on those decisions which cannot be delegated. That owner has a totally ***democratic*** style. Of course, few managers actually fall at either end of the spectrum, rather they are somewhere between the extremes. Like most aspects of business, there are pros and cons for both ends of the spectrum.

Autocratic managers can typically react faster to changes, problems or opportunities in the environment but must expend great energies on obtaining intelligence about what is going on and/or structure the firm to provide maximum input. Most small businesses start out with an autocratic management simply because there are few managers and employees and the owner must make all decisions personally. Democratic managers generally have higher employee morale because the people feel closer to the firm and more able to influence its development. Reaction time may be slowed, but the quality of decisions can be increased and the effectiveness of implementation of decisions is much greater. People naturally work harder if they understand why they are doing something or if they can see the direct benefit of their labor. Larger firms typically develop a more democratic style simply because the span of control is such that one individual cannot keep up with everything that is going on in the business. There is a limit to the number of people or activities which any one person can oversee. When that point is passed, others must be brought into the process to prevent the business from suffering.

There is no best style of management: businesses and their competitive environments vary so greatly and the quality and ability of managers vary so greatly that one approach cannot satisfy every situation. Nevertheless, in general we can say that the more employees and managers a business has and the more complex its operations are, the more democratic its management should be. Many small business owners have difficulty with this transition. The stories about entrepreneurs who are forced out of their companies after the business has been successfully established and has grown, frequently overlook the problems which were developing because of the entrepreneur's inability to share management control with other people. If a business intends to grow and become a major force in its industry, the management must also grow.

One of the complicating factors in management is that different people prefer different levels of supervision. That means that some of your employees will work better in an atmosphere of freedom and will prefer maximum autonomy. Other employees will prefer close supervision and little autonomy. In order to minimize the impact of personnel differences on the firm's effectiveness, you should be aware of the management style which you have developed for the firm and discuss it with applicants during the interview process to determine whether they can accept that style or not. You should also make plans for the change in the management style by training people to accept higher levels of responsibility and then establishing those levels as the business and the talents of its people grow.

The vehicle for establishing the management and supervision styles of your business is the organization chart and job descriptions. Everyone in the business should understand the chart and his/her place in it. Your plans for changing the structure should also be well established and well understood. In this fashion, employee supervision will be more effective.

COMPENSATION

Employee compensation consists of two forms: direct and indirect. ***Direct compensation*** includes salary or wages, bonuses, commissions and fees. Salary is used to describe a base pay rate which is not geared to hours worked. Wages are generally hourly based pay rates. The difference is that hourly employees are subject to minimum wage and overtime pay rules while salaried employees are generally exempt from those rules. Federal labor laws require all hourly paid employees to receive pay premiums for work beyond 40 hours per week. The requirement is, in general, for a premium of one half the pay rate, hence the term ***time and a half***. Wages can also be based on production. In a ***piece-rate*** shop, employees are paid a set amount for each item they complete. Such wages are still subject to minimum wage and overtime requirements, consequently, the record keeping system must permit wages to be calculated on an hourly basis as well as by production to ensure compliance with payroll regulations. Wages also can be based on a combination of hours and production. In manufacturing, production standards are frequently established. When the amount of output exceeds the production standard, employees receive a higher wage rate or an additional wage based on the number of units produced above the standard.

Other types of income include the bonuses, fees and commissions we mentioned previously. Bonuses are generally cash or property awards granted because the businesses have achieved a certain level of success, or passed some benchmark. Bonuses are intended to reward employees for their role in making a business successful. Profit sharing plans usually use a bonus based on the amount of profit the business produces. Other types of bonuses may be paid simply to enhance employee morale. Christmas bonuses are generally of this type and frequently consist of a gift of food in addition to, or in lieu of a cash bonus. Fees can be paid for all kinds of activities. For example, a fee can be paid for each sales prospect developed by employees who are not employed as salespersons. Commissions are generally linked to sales and provide a vehicle for paying people based on the amount of business they create. Commissions can have steps so that percentage rates increase as the volume sold increases. Salaries and commissions can be linked so that a base rate is paid plus a commission for all sales or for all sales produced over a specified level. As you can see, the variety of calculation bases for direct compensation is almost unlimited. Of course, we must make one comment here, compensation from all sources must be based on work and must not be discriminatory. The rule is equal work for equal pay, despite the historic tendency to pay women less than men. Not only is that practice dangerous from a legal perspective, it is dumb from an employment perspective. Half the potential employees are women. If you discriminate against them, you will be denying yourself access to an extremely valuable pool of prospective people.

Indirect compensation consists of fringe benefits. Many small businesses fail to adequately explain fringe benefits offered to employees despite the fact that such benefits constitute a highly significant proportion of overall compensation. Fringe benefits consist of a variety of items like those listed in Table 2. As you can see from the table, the variety of indirect compensation which can occur is limited only by imagination, as is the case with direct compensation.

Table 2

Employee Fringe Benefits

- Pay for vacations and holidays
- Life and health insurance plans
- Pension plans
- Plans which result in financial incentives
- Dental insurance plans
- Education support for employees
- Education plans for the children of employees
- Stock option plans
- Use of automobiles or reduced lease costs for automobiles
- Use of vacation homes or facilities
- Trips, vacations, or travel expenses
- Housing or rental support
- Moving expenses and home sales assistance
- Credit union services and loans
- Reduced cost cafeterias
- Gymnasium facilities
- Recreation and leisure time activities and facilities
- Employee discounts

The purpose of compensation is to attract, satisfy and keep competent and capable people. Consequently, the compensation policy which a company pursues is a major component of human resource management. The problem is that if the compensation policy is not considered adequate by the employees, they will leave the firm; while, if the compensation policy is too liberal, the firm's profits and prospects for survival will be damaged. How do you determine how much is enough? Before we address that question, consider the value of the various forms of compensation.

Compensation can be monetary or nonmonetary. Frequently, compensation can be structured so that it is not taxed to the employee, or at least, taxation is delayed until some time in the future. That can be a valuable situation.

Consider life and health insurance. The premiums which the company pays for such insurance are tax deductible by the company, but the benefits are not taxable to the employee so long as certain conditions are met. If the employee is in a 30% marginal income tax bracket, then the insurance premiums paid by the company are worth 30% more because they are not taxable.

Another way of looking at it is to examine the alternative. Instead of paying insurance premiums, the company increases the employee's pay by the amount of the premiums. There is no difference to the company in this situation at all. The only change from the company's perspective is where the money is sent. There is a big difference to the employee! Suppose the company withholds the premiums from the employee's pay and uses it to purchase the same insurance coverage as before. Now the employee would have to pay 30% income taxes on the amount of the premiums and would really only have 70% of the money left. If you wanted to provide the same amount of after tax income and benefits, the company would have to increase the amount of the payment. The increase would be more than 30%. If the insurance premiums were $50, then the amount of pay which would result in having $50 left after tax would be $71.43 ($50/.70 = $71.43) which is almost 43%! The insurance benefits can not only save the employee money, they can save the company money!

Many types of nonmonetary compensation can result in similar situations. For example, a company car can be provided. If personal use of the car is possible, a lease payment must be charged to the employee, but it is possible to structure such a payment far below the cost of leasing if the employee were to arrange it personally. The effect on after tax benefits is the same as in the case of the insurance premiums.

Monetary compensation which is delayed can also have a beneficial income tax treatment. For example, pension benefits properly structured will not be taxable to the employee until after retirement. At that time, the individual's income tax rate and liability can be expected to be lower than during the working years making the after tax benefits of the pension payments much higher. Now you can see why indirect compensation, nonmonetary compensation and delayed compensation are so popular!

Obtaining favorable income tax treatment of the various forms of compensation is a complicated business. Professional help is mandatory to ensure that the desired results occur. Your CPA can help you in setting up what is needed and in monitoring rule changes by the Internal Revenue Service to make sure that the desired results will continue. The outcome of the compensation tax planning can be highly favorable results for both the company and the employees.

An added benefit of structuring compensation so that it receives favorable tax treatment is the effect on employee turnover. If employees understand the total compensation package, then they will think about the overall impact of changing to a new job with another firm rather than the more visible stated pay rate. That will reduce turnover. In addition, delayed compensation plans of all types can be made contingent on longevity with the company. That means that leaving the firm can result in the loss of accumulated benefits. It is common, for example, to make pension benefits subject to loss in the event of an employee's departure from the firm. There are rules governing this process as well, so you must obtain professional assistance in structuring the plan, but the result can be an encouragement to employees to stay with the company.

As in the case of nontaxable compensation, the key is in ensuring that employees understand the total compensation package, its true value in after tax terms, and the effects of departure from the firm on that package. The initial orientation of new employees should cover that information, but constant reappraisal is necessary as well. At least once each year, every employee should be informed in writing of the total compensation package, its after tax effects, and amounts held for future release. This communication could be prepared as part of the W-2 data at the end of the year or communicated in an annual employee performance appraisal, but it must be done or the impact of the compensation program on employee turnover will be damaged.

As you can see from the foregoing discussion, it is generally wise to structure a compensation program so that its after tax benefits are maximized. But that still doesn't solve the problem of determining how much you should pay employees. That determination requires a thorough understanding of the market for the services which your people provide. Just as market forces affect the selling prices of the goods and services your company provides, market forces affect compensation programs. Skills that are in high demand cost more, while skills which are in high supply cost less. It's the old economic law of supply and demand applied to the labor force. If there are not enough people qualified to operate a particular piece of machinery to meet the demand for such skills, then those people will be paid more than other types of employees. If there are far more people with clerical skills than are needed to fill the available jobs, then those people will be paid less than other types of employees.

You will be able to gain a great deal of insight into the relative supply and demand of the various types of labor you use in your company during the recruiting process. The number of applicants you receive for a particular job and the salary levels requested by those applicants will give you that insight. In addition, the compensation levels of your competitors can give you insight into what your levels should be. In general, the minimum compensation levels which you will be able to offer and still attract and keep people will be those which your competition offer. It is just like your prices! You will have difficulty offering your products/services at higher than the prices offered by your competition: compensation works the same way. Just as you can manipulate prices by offering other benefits to customers such as service levels, convenience, higher quality, etc., you can affect compensation levels by offering added benefits to employees.

Determining the compensation levels of your competitors involves obtaining industry average data, joining industry and trade associations and asking people you meet at gatherings, watching job advertisements in the newspaper and trade journals, asking your employees, etc. Since compensation levels are constantly changing in response to changing conditions, keeping up with the market for labor is an ongoing process.

One of the best ways of differentiating your compensation policies from those of your competitors is to tie a large portion of income to the performance of the company. This approach will permit the company to pay higher compensation amounts when it can more easily afford to do so while simultaneously giving employee morale a boost by allowing employee performance to affect pay levels.

There are sound arguments to support such an approach. First, basic compensation levels can be set much lower than the competition would normally allow. That can help the firm's cash flow, especially during its early days. Second, employees feel closer to the firm and more a part of the operation and therefore tend to do a better job because they know that their paychecks will be directly affected by how well the company does. In such situations, the employees tend to make every effort to see that the firm does as well as possible. If they are successful and the company is successful, they will make more than they would have with a competitor firm and their morale will be higher. Third, when the higher payroll costs occur, the money is available to cover them because the firm's profits have been leveraged up. It won't hurt the firm to pay higher than the going rate for compensation. In addition, those higher levels will permit better and better employees to be attracted and maintained which should facilitate the continued growth and success of the firm.

Of course, such a program has to be designed in such a fashion that the employees perceive it to be fair and equitable. You cannot assign the major share of profits to officers or managers of the company and expect the other employees to applaud the program. With careful planning, a sound program can be developed using fees, profit sharing, bonuses, commissions, and other devices tied to company benchmarks which will result in the desired growth. Of course, the employees will have to be kept informed of the progress of the company toward the benchmarks. They will also have to have input into the development of those benchmarks so that they will consider them to be reasonable. The result will be a more participatory management overall. There is one potential problem.

Everyone is happy with a compensation plan tied to company performance so long as that performance is good. A major problem will develop if the company begins to falter as a result of shifts in the market, changes in competition, variations in demand, or any other factor which the employees consider to be beyond their ability to influence. In that situation, the employees will leave. Their departure will be at exactly the wrong time for the firm because it will be fighting for survival. Consequently, good planning to keep the company out of such a situation and fast reaction to the development of such a situation is necessary to make the compensation plan work. In addition, the employees require knowledge about what is going on in order to encourage them to assist in combating environmental problems.

The value of a compensation plan tied to performance is generally greater at higher levels of responsibility within the firm because such people feel more capable of influencing the performance. Nevertheless, it can have value at all levels if a conscientious effort is made to demonstrate to employees at all levels that their performance does reflect on the company. A good way to approach this is through involvement of employees in stock ownership. A portion of the compensation package can be devoted to stock purchase to facilitate the plan. The result can be employees who think more like owners of the company than like employees whose efforts are insignificant. In a firm with which we are familiar, a janitor of some 30 years seniority was a major stockholder of a class of nonvoting stock. No one in the company was more concerned about the company or aware of its situation than was that janitor. As you can guess, the offices of the company were among the cleanest in town!

A great deal is involved in establishing a compensation policy for a small business despite the fact that the number of employees will be small in relation to other firms. If the business has a union, then the process involves negotiating a compensation plan with the union representatives, but little is really different. There are situations in which the relative power of a union is so great that it exceeds the power of the management of the firm, but even so an equitable compensation policy can be developed so long as an adversary relationship is avoided. Fear of unions frequently causes managers of small businesses to forget about employees until union contract renegotiation time comes around. A sound compensation program with genuine interest and concern for the employees of a company will eliminate virtually all union problems. In fact, such a program will frequently result in the absence of a union because workers will not feel the need for one.

Table 3 is a summary of the steps required to establish a compensation plan which we have outlined in the foregoing sections. Remember that there is no one way to approach compensation. What is right for a particular company is what works for that company.

A major portion of the time of the owner of a small business will be spent in managing people because people are the most important assets of any business. Consequently, it makes sense to spend the time and energy to develop and maintain a sound compensation policy. It will make the job of managing people easier and more rewarding.

EMPLOYEE RELATIONS

Employee relations refers to the interaction between and among the employees and managers of a firm and its owner. As we discussed in the preceding sections, a sound compensation program will go a long way toward establishing sound employee relations. Nevertheless, compensation is not the entirety of the game. Let's consider what is at stake for a few minutes. The employees of the firm, including the managers other than the owner, are the people who make the firm function and carry out the strategies of the top management. Not only must those people be competent, capable, satisfied with the compensation plan and knowledgeable of the company's needs and plans, they must want to work and see the company succeed. A desire to push the company forward is not automatic. That desire will in large measure come about through the interaction with other people and with the owner.

Table 3

Steps in Planning a Compensation Program

Step 1: Determine what the going rate for compensation for each position in the company is among competitors. Keep track of that information as it changes over time. Sources are industry averages, contacts in industry and trade associations, advertisements for positions in newspapers and journals, job applicants and present employees.

Step 2: Structure the compensation package with major portions of income tied to performance of the company. Fees, commissions, bonuses, profit sharing plans, etc., are vehicles for payment. Employees must understand the plan, have input to it, receive reports on progress and feel capable of influencing the performance of the company.

Step 3: Structure a major portion of the compensation package with favorable tax treatment through the use of nonmonetary compensation, fringe benefits and deferred compensation plans. A professional will be required to assist in completing such a plan.

Step 4: Defer a portion of the compensation and tie its eventual receipt to continued employment with the company. A professional will be required to assist in completing such a plan.

Step 5: Ensure that every employee understands the complete compensation package. Make a part of the orientation of new employees familiarization with the compensation plan. Make an annual report to all employees of the total compensation which they are receiving, the after tax benefits of the compensation and the amounts deferred and contingent on continued employment with the company.

The major component of a healthy interaction between people, regardless of what those people are doing, is communication. **Communication** is bi-directional. That means that communication requires both listening and speaking. Effective communication in a company takes effort on the part of the owner and every manager in the company. There must be a genuine desire to communicate on the part of every person in a position of responsibility in the firm. Most importantly, the owner must initiate and maintain support for effective communication. Without visible support on an ongoing basis from the owner, nothing will actually happen regardless of instructions or orders. Communication results from an attitude and attitudes can only be influenced by example. It's a situation of leading versus directing. You can tell people where to go and what to do, but you cannot tell them what to think about the actions. There is an old adage about a man dragging a long chain down a dusty road. When asked by a passer-by why he was dragging the chain, the man responded, *Have you ever tried to push a chain?* His cryptic response works well in the arena of human emotions. You cannot push opinions and attitudes, but you can influence them by example.

Communication between managers and employees must take several forms. First, managers must direct employees to complete assigned tasks. That involves telling employees what to do, how and when to do it. In order for that communication to be effective, the employees must be willing to accept the direction and must understand the instructions. This form of communication is well known and well practiced. The problem is that the effectiveness of this form of communication is affected by the other forms.

Second, managers must inform employees as to the quality of their performance. That means both praise for tasks well done and criticism for poor performance. There should be more praise than criticism and the praise should be specific, pointing out the situation of the business and the effects on that situation which the employee's actions have had. This is one of the difficult aspects of communication for managers because they simply forget to offer the positive feedback. Negative feedback is easy to remember, but in order for a manager to remember to praise good performance, that manager's attitude toward employees must be one of constantly seeking positive feedback opportunities. This second aspect of communication is highly important because it will affect the first aspect. In order for employees to be willing to accept direction, they must feel that their efforts are recognized and appreciated. Otherwise, any compliance they make with assignments will be grudging, unenthusiastic and uninspired.

The third form of communication involves managers listening to employees. In order for this form to be effective, the listening must be genuine, the atmosphere must be open and encouraging, and the manager must take action when valid points are raised. Employees all wish to have an opportunity to talk about the tasks they are to be assigned. They need to have input to the decision as to what those tasks will be, how and when they are to be completed. They need to feel that they are part of a team, lead by the manager, but a team rather than a machine to accomplish some task. No manager can *fake* interest in or a concern for employees. Such interest must be genuine or employees will sense the reluctance and withdraw into themselves. Without effective listening on the part of a manager, the effectiveness of the first form of communication is damaged. As in the last case, enthusiastic response to direction cannot be expected unless employees feel that they will be heard and understood when they communicate to their managers.

The final form of communication which we will discuss is communication between employees. People who work together form a social group. The overall effectiveness of the group is largely a function of the group dynamics which is affected by the communication within the group. If one or more members of the group feel ostracized from the group, the effectiveness of the group will be damaged. Every member must feel valued and respected by the other members and must feel able to communicate with the other members in order for the group to be effective. This form of communication is extremely difficult for a manager to manipulate. You cannot tell the members of a working group to respect each other nor even to talk to each other. A manager can influence this form of communication by example. By insuring that every member of the group is aware that the manager considers every member important and by encouraging every member to communicate with the manager freely, an atmosphere of mutual respect can be fostered. It takes genuine interest and concern on the part of the manager and constant attention to group interactions.

A CASE FROM OUR FILES

Our client was the manager of a branch office of a small bank. He had a serious personnel problem arise which he did not know how to handle.

A young man, the manager had little experience in direct supervision, but was concerned and hardworking and was aware that the internal strife in his branch was affecting its performance.

It seems that two tellers, who worked side by side on the teller row, had gotten angry at each other. The manager had been unable to find out what the cause of the conflict was, but had been informed by one of the other tellers that the two had been friends for years prior to this argument.

At any rate, the conflict seethed for a week or two and then flared into the open on a day when the lobby was filled with customers. One teller threw a savings passbook at the other! In loud voices, each declaimed that she would never speak to the other again! The manager quieted them down, apologized to the customers and somehow got through the day.

Repeated efforts at discussing the problem with the two tellers and reconciling them were fruitless. True to their words, each refused to speak to the other, despite the proximity of their work stations. Within a week, the entire office was suffering. The balancing rate of every teller in the branch went down. Tempers got short and arguments flared with no apparent reason. Several customers actually remarked to the manager that something was amiss.

The manager discussed the situation with his boss, but got no help. *These things happen, just ignore it* was the extent of the advice he received.

After three weeks a new head teller was brought into the branch. An experienced teller with ten years of experience with the bank, she had been on maternity leave during the time that the explosion took place. The day after she came back to work she went into the manager's office and asked him what had happened between the two feuding tellers. He explained.

The head teller waited until the lunch break when the branch was closed and everyone was balancing their cash drawers and loudly dressed down the two truants. She said that she was ashamed of both of them for acting like children rather than the capable, competent adults everyone knew them to be. She pointed out how their feud was affecting the rest of the tellers because everyone was afraid of taking sides and losing the respect of the other person.

It turns out that the head teller knew just what to do! The branch was back to normal within a day and the two former enemies were friends again. One of them even apologized to the manager, who just continued to feel helpless.

So far we have talked about communication as though it were between managers and employees. In reality the same conditions prevail for communication between managers and the owner. Like employees, managers are people too, and have the same needs and desires. Effective communication, in all its forms, must take place at every level within the organization in order for the firm to advance and succeed.

There is one aspect of human relations which is unique to a small business. Only in a small firm can all of the employees develop a personal relationship with the owner. Although such a relationship can be healthy and result in a more highly motivated staff and can foster the development of communication throughout the firm, there is one danger. If employees feel able to *jump the chain of command* and bring problems or ideas directly to the owner rather than working through the organization chart, then the effectiveness of the managers can be undermined. It is important for employees to feel that they can come to the owner if a manager is unwilling to listen, but if employees are permitted to bypass managers, then an atmosphere will develop in which managers will have no power or authority.

By the same token, if one of the employees is a personal friend or family member of the owner and consequently is perceived as enjoying special privileges, then the authority of managers over that person will be damaged as will the morale of the business in general. If you intend to be the owner of a business, then you must be prepared to undertake a very special position with respect to the people who will work for you. The slightest sign of favoritism or special treatment toward one employee will affect the others tremendously. The slightest indication that a manager does not truly hold authority will result in damaging that manager's effectiveness. The owner must always be available when the need is genuine, must be even handed and fair with all employees and managers, must be seen to support the decisions and actions of managers, must lead by example, but must never appear to be used by any of the employees or managers for personal advancement. It is a difficult trust, but one which only the owner can undertake.

PERFORMANCE EVALUATIONS

In the preceding sections, we talked about the need for both positive and negative feedback in maintaining effective employee relations. That need is critical in day to day supervision, but requires a more formalized system to solve the long term needs. Every employee, regardless of the level of responsibility, should receive a formal evaluation of his or her performance at least once each year. The evaluation should be performed by the immediate supervisor of the employee. If that supervisor should change during the course of the year, evaluations should be required on all people supervised before the change takes place. The evaluation should be discussed with the employee and the report and the results of its discussion with the employee made a permanent part of the employee's record.

The evaluation should consider the quantity and quality of work performed, dependability, cooperation and job attendance, achievement of objectives set for the employee, overall effectiveness of the employee and suitability for pay raises, advancement or promotion. As a part of the evaluation, objectives should be discussed for the employee for the coming year and those which both supervisor and employee agree upon made part of a work plan for the next year. Each evaluation should take into consideration the objectives which were established for the year and progress made toward those as well as the working record of the individual during the year. It will be difficult for managers to perform these evaluations initially, but with experience will come confidence. The formalized procedure is mandatory if you expect to recognize the strengths and weaknesses of the work force. Everyone, including managers should be subjected to the process. The owner should perform an evaluation of himself or herself as well.

Should any employee disagree with the evaluation of his or her performance, then that person should be given the opportunity to discuss the evaluation with the next highest level of supervision. If a resolution cannot be achieved after discussing the evaluation with the owner, then the employee should be offered the opportunity to make a written attachment to the evaluation form for inclusion in the personnel file. The discussion of the evaluation is as important as its preparation. Every employee is entitled to know what the supervisor thinks of his or her performance, good or bad, and to be informed of the specifics of actions which are considered positive or negative. The process of discussion will also be good for the supervisor in that it will force him or her to think carefully about each employee and that person's performance and overall value to the firm. Supervisors will be more aware of employee performance on a daily basis if they know that they will have to evaluate that performance and face the employee with the evaluation at some point.

There will be a natural tendency to avoid confrontations, so supervisors may be tempted to evaluate everyone highly. To counteract that tendency, the system should require each supervisor to rank the employees under his or her supervision in order of value to the firm. An alternative would be to establish a budget of pay raises to be distributed based on employee evaluations so that supervisors will be more inclined to rank people fairly so that pay raises will be distributed fairly. A part of the evaluation of each supervisor should be an examination of the evaluations which that supervisor has prepared. All management personnel should be constantly aware of the need to fairly and critically judge the performance of people they supervise at all times. If at all possible, the owner should personally review every employee evaluation before it goes into the personnel file. If any questions arise, the owner should discuss them with the supervisor and, if unsatisfied, with the employee. The evaluation forms should be used in all pay raises, advancements and promotion decisions in the firm. In that way everyone will come to know the importance of the process. Remember, people are the primary asset in the business, therefore, employee performance appraisals are in large measure an appraisal of the business itself.

SUMMARY

People are the greatest asset of any business and can influence its success or failure. They are even more important to a small business with fewer employees because it will be affected greatly by the loss of a valued employee or the selection of incompetent personnel.

There are advantages and disadvantages to promoting from within. Benefits may be derived from the recognition of an existing employee's skills and from demonstrating advancement possibilities to others in the firm. However, it also means creating an additional vacancy. The hiring must be fair and the person in the new position must be competent or friction will occur. Don't use seniority as the sole criterion or you may find yourself a victim of the *Peter Principle*, that is, promoting someone to the highest level of his or her incompetence.

Be objective and fair in hiring. State the criteria and evaluate the applications according to qualifications and in the best interest of the company. Then after the selection process is complete, be sure that everyone is aware of who was chosen for the job and why. Keep records showing why every applicant was denied or hired to protect yourself from discrimination suits.

Outside sources for recruitment include both public and private employment agencies. Other sources are schools, colleges, and universities, professional conferences and advertisements, and cooperative education programs. Part-time employees from temporary employment agencies or from your own or other retired persons can help fill employment gaps.

Decide the jobs and the criteria for holding them before you begin the interview process. Make up a specific application form for that job which will garner you the desired information and comply with Equal Employment Opportunity laws.

Control the interview. Keep notes. Don't hire on the spot. Check references and verify information provided.

Almost every job requires some on the job training. Be aware of who is going to do the training so that the new employee does not receive fourth hand knowledge. Training may occur both in the company on company time or outside in programs and seminars set up for that purpose.

Autocratic managers have little or no input to the decision making process so react more quickly whether positively or negatively to situations. Democratic managers assure participation and while the decision may be delayed, there is typically a consensus and therefore, a rallying effect.

Compensation may be direct or indirect and its purpose is to attract, satisfy, and keep competent and capable people. It may be monetary or nonmonetary and can often with professional guidance be designed to benefit both employer and employee from a tax perspective. It can be tied to performance which will not only boost employee morale but also attract other high achievers to your company.

Employee relations depend upon bi-directional communication. Just as employees need to receive reinforcement for a job well done or instructions for improvement if poorly done, managers must receive feedback. They, too, must listen to employees' suggestions and complaints and strive to do better. Communication is valuable between employees so that close ties will result from a close working situation.

Employees should be cognizant of the lines of communication through the chain of command and not disrupt that chain.

Performance must be evaluated according to a formal plan. The evaluation should cover all employees and managers and should consider the quantity and quality of the work performed, dependability, cooperation, job attendance, achievement of objectives and eligibility for raises or promotions.

QUESTIONS, EXERCISES AND CASES

QUESTIONS:

1. Why are human resources so important to a company?
2. What are two methods for recruiting people?
3. What are the advantages and disadvantages of promoting from within?
4. How does one go about finding potential employees outside of the firm? What are several sources for applicants?
5. What are the key elements of a good interview?
6. Why is on the job training an important concept? What are the pros and cons of OJT?
7. Distinguish between an autocratic and democratic method of supervision. Which would you prefer if you were an employee?
8. What are direct and indirect compensation categories?
9. How can fringe benefits be established which can benefit both employer and employee? Give an example.
10. How does a good employee relationship reflect upon a company? Give several examples.
11. How should one evaluate one's employees?
12. What are the legal issues involved with recruiting?
13. How do discrimination laws affect small businesses?
14. How do Immigration laws affect small businesses?

EXERCISES:

1. Using role play, have a manager interview three prospective employees for the same job. Have two applicants be from within the company and the third outside. Establish a format and then evaluate the applicants and make a selection. Be sure to include in the role play methods of compensation. The manager must have given some thought to the role as must the applicants. This activity could be good practice for both future managers and employees.

2. Have two role play situations in which one manager is an autocratic supervisor and the other is democratic. The situation is as follows: the manager has just learned that a new company is coming into town which markets the same product as you do. You had not previously heard of this company and it will be operational within the month. What should your company do about the new competition and how would each type of supervisor handle the situation.

CASE

John Davison is sitting at his desk long after hours and pondering the situation. He has been deluged all day with complaints about his long time friend, Bob James. He knew Bob had not been doing his job well in some time, but he felt a certain amount of loyalty. After all, Bob had started with him when it was a two man operation. John as the President and Bob as the Marketing vice-president had run the company during the hard times during its start-up. Bob was a super salesman and had been for a number of years. He had really brought in the sales for their little company.

John had given him the responsibility over the marketing department in fact as well as title five years ago when the company grew to the point that it had enough salesmen on staff to merit real supervision. He couldn't very well hire someone in over the head of his old buddy, so he had given the management post to Bob along with a well earned raise. Things had gone smoothly for a couple of months while Bob was training his staff. He could demonstrate his sales techniques and explain why certain ploys worked and others didn't. But times were changing and the business was changing.

Meanwhile Bob, too, sat mulling over how times had changed. Bob was still a cracker jack salesman. Now his duties were different. Bob had begun to change but not really. He was still a go-getter when he could teach or sell but supervising people was a different ball game. Bob knew in his heart that he was making problems for the company, because not only had sales fallen off, the working environment of his department had the people in it walking on rice paper. He knew the fault was largely his. He just couldn't bring the excitement to bear on someone else's successful closure of a difficult client. It was an ego thing and he knew it. He knew that his staff could see through his false congratulations and felt that he was second guessing their efforts when in reality, he was envying the fact that they were out of the office selling. He was a people person. He could sell fireplaces to the underworld, but he could not manage people.

Bob was getting more and more unhappy and it was revealed in the office. He was not offering managerial support to his staff and his people were having verbal warfare when in the office. Just as it takes a special personality to be able to sell well and enjoy it, those same egos needed stroking for work well done. When there was no one who would do the job, those same egos tried to assert themselves with each other. Chaos was the result. Bob pulled himself out of his chair and decided that tomorrow he would try harder to enjoy pushing paper instead of pushing products. If only he could get some of that old excitement back. He hated to admit it but he hated coming to work in the morning because it was the same old hassle. Oh well, his friend John had given him this responsibility, so he couldn't let him down. So tomorrow would be another day.

John drew a big sigh and decided that he was going to have to do something. He had controlled the petty office jealousies himself for a while, but this was getting too big. Sales were falling off and infighting had made the office a battleground. He knew that deep down the fix involved a change for Bob, but could he do this to a friend? Perhaps if he hired a consultant to look at the situation, he could find a different solution to the problem. Maybe he wasn't being objective. Maybe he too was succumbing to the bickering within Bob's department. Maybe he wouldn't have to fire or demote his friend. Since he felt unable to make the decision, he called in a consultant.

1. If you were the consultant above, what would you do first?

2. What do you see is the real problem causing the ill health of the company? Could one man be responsible?

3. What are the several alternatives available to John? to Bob?

4. Why do you suppose sales were falling off? How could that be remedied?

5. What do you think the consultant recommended?

6. What would be your recommendation and why?

CHAPTER SIXTEEN

MARKETING MANAGEMENT

CHAPTER OBJECTIVES

Upon completion of this chapter, you should be able to:

- Identify the factors which affect the purchasing decision;

- Describe the impact of advertising and pricing on the marketing effort;

- Distinguish between product/service advertising and image advertising;

- Identify and employ marketing techniques and evaluate their effectiveness; and,

- Explain how the marketing strategy makes everything in the small business come together.

MARKETING MANAGEMENT

INTRODUCTION

Marketing is frequently confused with advertising. Since Shakespeare's day the focus of the sales effort has been on praising the goods or services held for sale. Marketing is much more than advertising. It is true that part of any marketing effort is the planning and execution of effective advertising, but marketing must go far beyond advertising in order to be effective. The goal of *marketing* is to sell goods or services. These things are actually sold through a coordinated effort which includes every aspect of a business' operation. Effectiveness will be more determined by the degree of coordination than it will by any advertising efforts which may be undertaken.

We talked about marketing in a previous chapter in the start-up section of the text. We will begin this chapter with a brief overview of the key marketing aspects which we discussed at length previously because those concepts are important to any marketing activity. In previous chapters, we were concerned with start-up marketing efforts for a new venture. Here we will focus on how those factors are important in an ongoing business. We will follow that with a discussion of advertising and pricing, and talk about marketing techniques and overall strategy for ongoing businesses. Finally, we will show how every aspect of a business must be coordinated to design an effective marketing approach.

FACTORS AFFECTING THE PURCHASING DECISION

PRICING

If you ask an average person what the main input to the price of an item is, that person is likely to answer cost. As a matter of fact, the main inputs to price are demand and competition. Clearly, you cannot sell items for less than their variable cost, at least not for long, but you must keep in mind the purpose that price serves. The *price* of an item is designed to sell that item just as is every other aspect of marketing. A fair price cannot be defined. You may have heard it said that a *fair price* is one in which both the seller and the buyer are happy. That is a rather simplistic view, but it does recognize that the buyer has no interest in the cost of the item to the seller. The buyer's sole interest is in acquiring a desired item at a price with which he or she is comfortable. The first part of that interest is demand. The buyer must first desire the item or there will be no purchase. The second part is price. What basis does a buyer have for judging prices? The only basis is the price charged for similar items by competing firms. Consequently, demand and competition are the main ingredients in setting price.

SUPPLY AND DEMAND

Demand can be a difficult concept. The demand for a particular item can go beyond the physical product itself. **Demand** can include such elements as entertainment in that the shopping experience can be as much a part of the customer's desire as ownership of the item itself. Many restaurants, especially catering to young adults, sell entertainment in the form of opportunities to meet and mingle with friends and peers as well as food. Stores selling designer clothing for women may well be selling the opportunity to model various clothes as well as the clothes themselves. Demand can also include such aspects as convenience, both in location and hours of operation, service, advice and counseling, and a host of other factors which can be far afield from the item being sold.

Economists have a theory of price and demand which says that demand is affected by price in an inverse fashion. Further, they explain that the availability of an item is positively related to price and that where supply and demand meet, **market price** is set. The relationship is most easily seen graphically. Table 1 displays a traditional supply and demand curve.

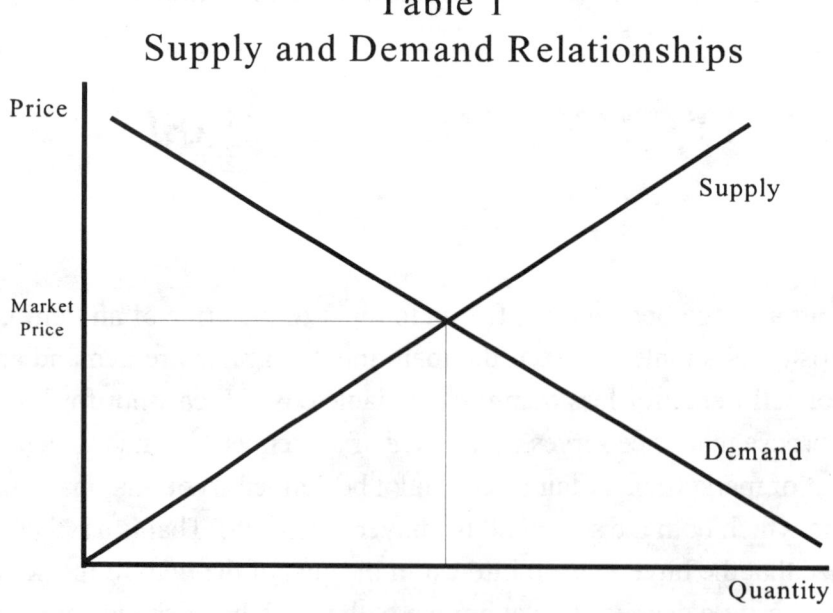

Table 1
Supply and Demand Relationships

The table shows that as price increases, the quantity of an item which is demanded will decrease. The reverse is true, as price decreases, the quantity demanded will increase. **Supply** works opposite to demand. As the price which an item will bring increases, the quantity which is supplied by firms increases. As the price declines, the quantity which firms will supply also declines. At the point of intersection of the two lines, equilibrium is reached. For a true commodity item, one which does not differ between suppliers or manufacturers, the point of equilibrium is the market price. Not every item has a downward sloping demand curve, although most items do. Virtually everything will have an upward sloping supply curve.

There are several problems with translating the economic theory into practice. First, it is extremely difficult to identify all of the elements of demand for most items. We have already talked about that problem. Further, even if we know that an item has a downward sloping demand curve, we seldom know how steep the slope is. The steeper the decline, the faster demand will fall off as price increases. It is difficult to identify for any given item how fast that tradeoff will occur. Additionally, the theory assumes knowledge on the part of consumers and suppliers. From a practical perspective, few customers truly know what the prices available from various competitors are at a given point in time, while few suppliers truly know what the demand for an item is at a given point in time. Nevertheless, the theory is quite valid and can easily be demonstrated to hold in the aggregate. That means that nation wide, over the entire range of the market for any given item, the price-demand tradeoff can be expected to be true. What it does not mean is that a small business should strive to offer the lowest possible prices.

THE ROLE OF COST

We mentioned above that you cannot sell products or services below variable cost, at least not for long. In a previous chapter, we talked about fixed and variable costs at great length. Review that section if you need to, because we are now going to examine the impact of cost on price.

For a retailer or wholesaler, the cost of acquiring inventory is a variable cost and there are frequently no other significant costs involved. If there are significant variable costs, like sales commissions, these must be added to purchase prices to arrive at total variable cost for each item sold. For a manufacturing company, the cost of production does include fixed and variable components, but the fixed components must be removed so that we can examine the variable costs only. Now, assuming that we have isolated the variable costs of products which we sell, the impact on price is a function of desired profit plus variable costs.

If, for example, you wish to sell an item at a price which will result in no profit at all, but will not lose money, the price would simply be equal to the variable costs of the item. Obviously, the fixed costs of the business are going to have to be covered before breakeven can be achieved, but that could be done with sales of other products. If you price the item at less than variable cost, the company will lose money with every item sold. Remember that the ***contribution margin*** is the proportion of the price which is left over after variable costs are covered to contribute toward the coverage of fixed costs and ultimately, profits. If there are no other variable costs outside purchases, then the contribution margin is the same as the gross profit margin.

If you want to make a 25% contribution margin on the item, its price would be:

$$\text{Price} = \text{Variable Costs} + 25\% \text{ of the Price}$$
$$\text{Price} - .25 \times \text{Price} = \text{Variable Costs}$$
$$.75 \times \text{Price} = \text{Variable Costs}$$
$$\text{Price} = \text{Variable Costs}/.75$$

This procedure can be used to arrive at price estimates based on industry average margins or target margins established by the owner. For example, if the *Robert Morris Statement Studies* showed that hardware stores had an industry average margin of 30%, then the business might decide to establish prices for all items stocked by dividing their costs by .70. Of course, if competitive pricing disallowed such prices, some adjustments would have to be made. Nevertheless, the contribution margin approach can be used as a starting point for setting prices.

For service companies, the process is exactly the same, but the variable costs are those which are a result of delivering the service. If we have a television repair shop, the variable costs will be labor and parts. A pricing policy will probably be established in which customers are charged the wholesale or retail price for parts used plus a set rate for each hour of labor involved. Deciding on the price to charge for parts would be handled in the same fashion as for a retail company because the repair shop is really selling these items. If the shop wanted to make a 20% margin on labor costs, the rate per hour would simply be the average wage rate divided by .80. The process of price, variable cost, profit trade offs is the same whether we are handling products or services.

Some service companies may think that they have no variable costs at all. For example, an accounting service company may have only salaried people who are paid the same whether they are posting client books or not. In a case like that the cost of employee time is still germane to the pricing decision. The salaries of clerks really is variable because there are only so many clients which they can handle without increasing the size of the staff. Such a service company must establish an average wage rate per hour for its clerks and treat time posting records as a variable cost. Time spent doing other things should be treated as a fixed cost. If the company truly has no variable costs, for example a dance studio in which the owner teaches all the classes, then pricing becomes a function of fixed costs and desired profits.

In the breakeven analysis chapter, we spent a great deal of time discussing target profit levels for the business as a whole. We explained how the cost - volume - profit tools could be used to set prices which will result in achieving a desired level of profits for the business. These tools use the relationship between sales, fixed costs, variable costs, and desired profit. Using this tool requires estimates to be made for fixed costs, for variable costs as a function of sales and for desired profits. The relationship looks like this:

Sales = Fixed Costs + Variable Costs + Desired Profit

If there are no variable costs, they drop out of the equation. For example, consider the dancing studio which has no variable costs and total fixed costs of rent, utilities, etc., of $19,000 per year. If the owner wants to make $25,000, then total sales must be:

Sales = $19,000 + $25,000 = $44,000

If the owner can teach three classes per week, each with 10 students, then the total charge per student per lesson must be:

Price = $ 44,000/(3 classes X 10 students X 50 weeks)
Price = $ 29.33 per student per class

Obviously, $29 per class could be extremely high, depending upon where this business is located and what its competitors charge. Nevertheless, the calculation shows the owner that more classes or more students will be required to achieve the desired level of income. The minimum charge required to cover fixed costs with the projected enrollment is:

Price = $ 19,000/(3 classes X 10 students X 50 weeks)
Price = $ 12.67 per student per class

The CVP tools can also be used to find potential profit at established price levels. Assume that research shows that dance studios in the area charge an average of $10.00 per student per lesson. With no other instructors except the owner, sales will have to be:

Sales = Fixed Costs + Variable Costs + Desired Profit
Sales = $ 44,000
Sales = Classes X Students X Weeks X Price
Classes X Students X 50 weeks = $ 44,000
Classes X Students = $ 880

This shows that three classes per week would require 293 students each to make the desired profit of $25,000. Again, that is impossible. If we decide to use other instructors who will be paid $25.00

to teach each class, then the equation will change. Assume that each class will be held to 10 students. Then, at $10 each student, each class would produce $100 in sales and $75 in contribution margin after instructors are paid. The total number of classes required to achieve target profit would then be:

Classes X $75 X 50 weeks	=	$ 44,000
Classes	=	$ 44,000/($ 75 X 50)
Classes	=	11.7 or 12 Classes per Week

As you can see, CVP techniques can be valuable in pricing decisions as well as the breakeven calculations in which they are better known. Don't forget that cost is only one aspect of the pricing decision. By far the more important aspect is competition.

PRICING STRATEGIES

There are three basic approaches to setting the price for a product or service. These are strategies of *pricing at competitive levels*, *below competitive levels* or *above competitive levels*. We might also call these market levels. Remember that when we are discussing the competitive or market price for an item, we are talking about near substitutes as well as exact substitutes. That means that the market for housing includes rental units as well as units for sale and the market for clothing includes discount houses as well as exclusive department stores. Food markets include convenience stores, grocery stores and supermarkets. Accounting and tax services include CPA firms and noncertified accountants or bookkeepers; single practitioners and nation wide chains. The *market* simply means any source which a consumer can utilize to satisfy the basic demand for an item.

PRICING ABOVE THE MARKET

Firms who consistently *price above competitive levels* must cultivate an image of providing a high level of quality and service and appeal to a target market which has a demand for those things. For example, a men's clothing store which charged high prices would locate in an expensive area, such as a mall, would spend a great deal of money on store decor and amenities, would carry brand names which had a reputation for high quality and would carry the latest items in men's fashions. That store would also have to employ sales people who were well dressed and courteous and would have to have a large number of sales people to ensure that a customer never lacked for assistance while shopping. Sales people would be trained to note and remember customer's names and to use them when possible. In addition, services such as store charge accounts and private sales might be offered and a full range of clothing items might be offered. The key aspect is for such a store to cater to a target market which demanded special treatment and high quality. That means that for such a store to be successful, there must exist a market in the area with those demands. An exclusive men's store would not be successful in a small town or a rural setting in which the population had a low to middle socio-economic level. It might very well be successful in a large city. The key point is that a firm which intends to pursue a pricing strategy of higher than the competition must be sure that sufficient demand exists in the target area to support the firm. Secondly, the firm must be sure that all aspects of the operation are coordinated in fostering an image which is consistent with the pricing strategy.

Consider the consequences of inconsistency. If a store were to foster the image of high quality and high service but failed to charge higher prices, the customers would probably harbor beliefs that the merchandise was not of the expected quality or was made up of *factory seconds*, those items which failed quality control inspections at the factory. That is not to say that some people object to low prices. A sale in an expensive store can be just as successful as in any other store, but the long term image of high quality cannot be maintained without a price differential. The reverse is also true: high prices alone will not create the desired image. If service levels and store decor are not consistent with the prices, then customers will feel that those prices are unjustified.

PRICING BELOW THE MARKET

Pricing below the market refers to a consistent policy of offering prices below competitive levels. Sales or other short term price reduction or discount plans are not part of this strategy. A firm which consistently prices its products or services below market levels is basically attempting to compete on the basis of price. This can be a lucrative strategy if an established demand exists for the products or services being offered. It is especially strong when used for items which consumers believe to be commodities. A *commodity* is any product or service which is basically indistinguishable from seller to seller. When consumers believe that to be the case, the primary difference between sellers becomes price. Items such as food, especially meat and produce, and other items which do not have a major brand image such as lumber, hardware and home repair items, automobile accessories and repair parts, etc., have been successfully marketed on a commodity basis. Services, such as plumbing, appliance repair and household maintenance can also be perceived as commodities. Any commodity item can be effectively sold using price as the principal vehicle of competition.

Goods and services are not permanently fixed as commodity items. Stock brokerage services were long considered to be above price competition and firms competed on the basis of advice, financial analyses and other services provided to buyers. Recently, brokerage services have been successfully marketed on a commodity basis with low cost or fixed cost brokerage fees. A strong inroad has been made recently by *generic* drugs. Many firms have succeeded in using price as a competitive edge in the pharmaceuticals industry which was long thought to be price insensitive. Of course, other firms have been successful in eliminating the commodity image. Chiquita brand bananas are the classic example of a commodity product being endowed with a brand image. Sunkist oranges are another example, however, many such efforts have failed, ranging from attempts to establish brand images for lobsters to tomatoes.

If a firm decides to pursue a strategy of below market prices, that strategy must be effectively coordinated with all other aspects of the operation. Customers will simply refuse to believe that low prices are being offered in plush surroundings. It makes good sense to structure the firm on a low price image anyway, because the lower prices will create smaller contribution margins. That means that higher fixed costs will be more difficult to absorb.

PRICING AT MARKET LEVELS

The most frequently observed practice among small businesses is ***pricing at market levels***. Marketers call this strategy ***Follow-the-Leader***. A firm pursuing this strategy attempts to price its goods and services at or near levels created by its competition. The objective is to remove price from the purchase decision so that the firm can compete on some other basis. This is somewhat of a middle ground to the above and below market pricing strategies which we have discussed so far.

Pricing at the market has the advantage of flexibility over the other two approaches. That means that it is much easier to change the image of a firm when it is not an image keyed to price. Remember that we have stressed the difficulty in changing a firm's image. It can be done and sometimes must be done because of changes in demand, changes in the market area, demographic, competitive, economic or other factors. The most difficult image to change is that of an above or below market price supplier.

There are other advantages as well. Profit margins under market pricing can be attractive. Such a firm is neither plagued with the low contribution margins of a below market firm or the high fixed cost levels of an above market firm. This also can translate into less risk. Remember that the higher the fixed costs in a firm, the higher the risk because breakeven points will be leveraged higher. There can also be great risk in a below market firm because there is less room to absorb sudden increases in costs due to the lower contribution margin.

PRICE COMPETITION

One of the most difficult aspects of a market price strategy is maintaining information about the state of the market. If you intend to use market pricing, then you must ensure that prices stay at market levels. Those levels can and do change over time, sometimes rapidly. You must spend time in gathering information about competitive prices in your area on an ongoing basis. Of course, the same should be done regardless of what pricing strategy you decide to use. It's just plain good sense to know what the competition's prices are at all times whether you plan to meet those prices or not.

Many firms constantly strive to avoid competing with other firms on the basis of price. They attempt to create situations in which customers will buy from them regardless of price. For a small business, this is not generally wise. Whether we understand the degree of its influence or not, the price of an item does affect demand. Further, price is never judged in a vacuum. It is a relative concept. A firm can have a 300% markup based on cost and still have a product or service which is perceived as low priced. Many items of jewelry fall into that category. A firm can also have a 10% markup based on cost and be perceived as having high prices. Many grocery items fall into that category. Since customers do not have knowledge of costs, they must make their evaluations based on prices at similar firms for similar items. That means that competition determines what is a high or low price.

The really important aspect of the pricing decision is to ensure that it is consistent with the image of the business as established by the rest of the operations. In order for that to happen, a firm must consciously decide what its image will be and what its prices will be simultaneously. That requires knowledge of prices charged by the competition at all times and requires constant attention to prices of individual items to ensure that they stay in the range dictated by the overall strategy of the firm. That does not mean that prices are changed every time that costs change. Frequently, that cannot be done. It means that prices are changed every time the market price changes.

If costs increase while market prices do not, profits will certainly suffer, but to key prices to costs only will result in customer dissatisfaction. Consider a situation in which costs are rising faster than market prices. Every firm in the industry will be affected. Someone must lead the other firms in raising prices before the market price can be set at a new and higher level. What will consumers think about the company who leads the price increase? Even if every other competitor follows suit with a price increase, the first firm to raise prices will experience negative reactions from consumers. It is possible to be placed in such a squeeze between costs and prices, that some ill will is to be preferred to a continuation of the situation. Nevertheless, you should always keep in mind the consequences of deviating from your established position relative to established market prices.

ADVERTISING

Advertising is the most visible part of the marketing operation of a firm. The average person is bombarded with advertising every day. Television, radio, print media, direct mail, billboards; advertising is everywhere! Despite the broad range of media, there are really only two types of advertising which a firm can do: ***product/service advertising*** and ***image advertising***. Both are aimed at selling. That's what advertising is: a sales pitch! We want to design advertising that will make people want to buy from us.

PRODUCT/SERVICE ADVERTISING

Much of the advertising which you see is aimed at promoting a particular product or service. That's because it is easier to sell a specific item: you can talk about that item's features, its price, its desirability, etc. This can be broadened to advertising which is aimed at several items at once. For example, several items might be placed on sale and advertising used to promote that fact. It can be highly specific. It may take several commercials or advertising spots to convey the entire message on a single product.

The outdoor advertising efforts of Burma Shave are a classic example. Numerous signs located alongside the highway were used with each sign containing a few words of the overall message. These signs would appear sequentially some distance apart with the effect of drawing a traveler's attention to what were at first meaningless phrases in an attempt to find out what the message was. The advertising was so effective that the company has recently begun to use it again. Regardless of how specific or general, regardless of the media used, advertising for a product or service is the easier approach because we are dealing with something tangible. As you will see in the next section, there can be some spill over between the two types of advertising, but the primary objective of *product/service advertising* is to create a desire in the minds of the customers for a specific item.

There is also a risk associated with product/service advertising. If the advertising is successful and a demand for an item is created, there is no guarantee that the customers will use our business as the source of supply to satisfy their demand. Most large firms attempt to create a brand image which distinguishes their wares from competitors. Most small businesses are unable to use such a strategy, as we discussed in previous chapters, because of the cost and time that creating such an image requires. Consequently, for a small business, creating a demand for an item can carry great risk because people may decide to buy the item from a competitor or to acquire a near substitute.

Frequently, price of an item is used as part of the advertising in an attempt to channel demand to a specific company. Consider a grocery store advertising its meat. If the advertising is effective, people seeing it will buy more meat but not necessarily from the store doing the advertising. You can attempt to isolate the demand through a variety of techniques including reduced prices or sales, coupons, trading stamps, etc. Another device for isolating the demand is through image advertising either in conjunction with the product/service advertising or in separate advertising efforts.

IMAGE ADVERTISING

In *image advertising*, we are promoting the reputation and image of the firm rather than the products or services of that firm. There can be a mingling of the two types of advertising in that some aspects of the products in general may be a part of the image promotion. For example, the image advertising could stress product/service quality, price, availability, etc. Nevertheless, the primary objective of image advertising is the establishment of a specific set of beliefs about the company in the minds of its customers. The primary benefit is the isolation of demand. That means that we wish the demand for items created through product/service advertising to benefit our firm rather than our competitors.

In order for image advertising to be effective, the strategic posture or competitive image of the firm must be consistently established throughout all phases of the operation. If the image we wish to portray is one of high quality, high service, then the firm must be structured so that this is always the case. If the image is one of low cost, no frills, then the firm must be consistent with that image in all of its phases. Some form of image advertising is valuable in any promotional activities not only because it helps localize demand but because it forces a firm to analyze its image and consciously consider cultivating that image over time.

ADVERTISING MEDIA

Media refers to the vehicle used to deliver an advertising message to customers. Television, radio and newspaper advertising spring to mind immediately, but there are many other types of media. In fact the array of advertising media available is staggering. Table 2 lists some of the kinds of advertising outlets which exist.

Table 2 is by no means a complete list! In fact, the type of media which can be used is limited only by your imagination. Be careful to think any unusual steps through carefully. Perhaps you have heard the story about the enterprising grocery store owner who decided to promote his sale of turkeys at Thanksgiving time by dropping a number of live birds from a helicopter hovering over the shopping center parking lot. The way the story goes, the store owner failed to realize that only wild turkeys can truly fly. The domesticated variety can only fly straight down! Such a promotion would be likely to upset people whose cars were parked in the lot and enrage the local chapter of the SPCA, not to mention the fact that the turkeys would be a bit unhappy also.

The problem from a marketing perspective is the selection of a media which will provide maximum penetration of the target market for the dollars expended. It is not enough for a large number of people to be exposed to the advertising; what is required is the exposure of a large number of people in your target market. For example, television is generally considered to have the broadest penetration of any type of advertising media because such large numbers of people watch it. However, if your customers seldom watch TV, it may not be appropriate for your advertising.

The problem is complicated by the timing and location issue. In TV and radio advertising, the time of day and the day of week is a factor in the effectiveness of the advertising. Commercials during the middle of the day on TV may be most effective if the target market is primarily homemakers, but commercials during sports games may be more appropriate for some products or services. Can you guess how many beer commercials air during the weekdays? How about beer commercials during ball games?

Table 2

Advertising Media and Outlets

Television (don't forget cable TV carriers)

Radio

Newspaper (don't forget school papers)

Outdoor:	Billboards	
	Transit:	Buses, Cabs, Trains, Personal Automobiles
	Houses	
	Barns and Barn Roofs	
	Fences	
	Flyers for Car Windshields	
	Hand Bills passed out to pedestrians and shoppers	
	Sandwich Signs carried by individuals	
	Airplanes towing signs	
Indoor:	Signs and Placards and Posters:	Grocery Stores/Store Windows
	Card Racks:	Welcome Centers and Rest Areas
		Tourist Bureaus and Chambers of Commerce
		Hotels, Restaurants
	Point of Sale Displays	
Demonstrations:	Product or Service Demos:	In your shop
		On street corners

Magazines

Trade Journals

High School Annuals

Programs for ball games

Gifts, Premiums:	Balloons, Pens, Umbrellas, Seat Cushions, T shirts and	
	Sweat Shirts, Cups, Hats, Almost anything you can think of	
Special Events:	Radio Shows	
	Celebrities	
	Ball Games and Competitions:	Basketball games with the players riding mules
		Our guys against their guys
Sponsoring:	Charity events	
	Fund raising events	
	School and amateur ball teams, clubs, groups, etc.	

Yellow Pages

Radio commercials during the 6:00 AM to 8:00 AM period and 4:00 PM to 6:00 PM period are best for catching people on the way to and from work, but may not be as effective as late night broadcasts depending upon the target market. Of course, the variety of radio stations, rock to classical, complicate the issue even more. Most radio stations have viewer profiles which can aid in targeting your message, but that presupposes that you know who your target market is.

With print media, location and timing are still issues. The Sunday newspaper gets a larger readership than any other day of the week, while location of the advertising within the paper can affect the likelihood of a member of the target market seeing it. With magazines and journals, location of the advertising is also a factor. It is no accident that the back cover of a magazine is the most expensive advertising spot. In addition, the size of the advertising and its location on the page, as well as its wording and layout, can affect its likelihood of being read.

Almost every type of media is affected by timing or location issues. Even flyers placed on car windshields can be more effective at certain times, such as on pay days of major employers in the area. In addition, all media is affected by the design of the advertising itself. Surely you have noticed that some billboards draw your attention while you can drive by others without being aware that you have passed them.

The various combinations of all of the factors of timing, location, advertising design and type of media are almost limitless. How can you wade through all this to find the best way to spend your advertising dollars? Actually, what is required is more an understanding of your target market than of advertising. If you fully understand who your customers are, what their habits and preferences are, where and when they work and where and when they play, then you can begin to plan the best way to reach them. The more detailed your knowledge about your target market, the more effective your advertising can be. However, the less you know about your market, the less effective it will be. This is also true when applied to developing the proper image for your company. The more you know about a market to which you wish to appeal, the more effectively you can design a strategic posture or business image which will appeal to that market.

Be careful! The advertising and image selection and design must appeal to your target market, not to you! The biggest and most frequent mistake made by small businesses is the confusion of the preferences of the owner with the preferences of the customers. You must put yourself in the shoes of your customers; you must develop a keen understanding of them and of the people and businesses which you wish to cultivate as customers.

How many times have you seen commercials in which the owner of a small business uses his or her children in the spot? What purpose can that serve? The answer is that it serves self satisfaction, not customer satisfaction. Advertising will not automatically attract customers. In fact, it can do the reverse. Poor advertising can discourage would be customers and drive away existing customers. In a recent election in our home town, there was a run off required between two candidates vying for a position on the county school board. One candidate, who happened to be the incumbent in office, received about 49% of the vote in the first election, while his nearest competitor in a field of five people received about 20% of the votes cast. During the campaigning for the run off, the leading candidate used a flyer with a photograph and covered virtually every car windshield in the county with those flyers. Unfortunately, the photograph was unflattering, to say the least. The quality of reproduction was poor and the candidate appeared haggard and unshaven in the flyer. To top that off, the flyer carried virtually no message: no statement of position on any issue was made. The flyer simply exhorted the reader to vote for the candidate because he had experience on the job. Can you guess what happened? On election day, the incumbent was soundly defeated. We'll never know whether he would have won if that flyer had not been circulated, but we can say that it certainly did not aid his campaign! The same thing can and does happen to businesses. Poorly designed, poorly planned advertising can be worse than no advertising at all.

You must also be careful about what your advertising promises. Recently, a local grocery store displayed a special price on T bone steaks on its marquee. Several customers were heard to complain upon entering the store, that the special price was for steaks which had turned dark while fresher steaks were displayed side by side with the sales meat which looked better but was priced higher. The store probably lost many customers permanently as a result of that mistake.

Sometimes difficulties with promises can be more subtle. A local automobile dealer is well known in the community for his television commercials in which he always displays several used cars with special prices. The dealer does the commercials personally and always ends the spot by saying, *Come and see me and let's make a deal*. After observing several years of highly successful operations using those commercials, another dealer in town decided to use the same approach. He began to air TV spots in which he displayed used cars with special prices and ended the commercial with an exhortation to *Come in and see me for a real deal*. After a few months of those spots, the dealer was reduced to the level that he could no longer afford TV commercials at all. It seems that a customer walking on his lot could never see the owner at all! Every customer was met by sales people and the owner took no part in the sales effort at all. In the case of the successful car dealer, virtually every customer would at least see and speak to the owner and a large number of them would be handled personally by the owner. The hidden promise in both of the commercials was an opportunity to bargain directly with the owner rather than a sales representative without the power to *deal*. Only one of the dealers was living up to that promise!

The image which your business has and wishes to portray must also be clear in the advertising. If the advertising works and customers are attracted to the business, they must not be surprised. If they are led to develop one image of the business through the commercial and discover another image when buying from the firm, they will become confused and may well cease to be a customer. The image is affected by the choice of media as much as it is by the design of the advertising itself. We cannot make absolute statements about the superiority of various media. It depends upon your target market. For some markets, flyers could be considered in poor taste and therefore never used by a *quality firm*. To some markets, direct mail could be *high class* while to others it could be a nuisance.

So far, it seems that everything we've said about advertising is negative. So what can you do? You must choose the advertising media, timing and location with care; you must approach the design and layout of the advertising with care; and you must get as many people involved in determining the advertising approach as you can. Sales people can be especially helpful since they deal with the customers which you wish to reach and persuade. Make sure that everything is consistent with the market you wish to reach and with the image you wish to portray and then, *keep records*.

Much of the knowledge about what kinds of media, timing, location, design, etc., are effective for a particular business must be gained on a trial and error basis. All advertising is aimed at increasing sales. If it works, that should happen. If something works, keep doing it! If it doesn't work, stop doing it. If you are trying something new, try to add a feature which will make capture of the effectiveness more direct. For example, a new radio commercial might be used which encourages listeners to mention a DJ's name in order to receive a free gift or a special discount. The gift can be a ball point pen with your firm's name emblazoned on it. The point is that knowledge of the effectiveness, or lack of it, of a particular advertising approach is valuable. A small discount to a customer for clipping a coupon from a newspaper or magazine can be well worth the cost because it will tell you how well the advertisement worked.

With or without some sort of direct measure or feedback of that type, you must have a feel for what the sales should be without advertising in order to judge its effectiveness. That means budgeting. In an earlier chapter we talked about sales forecasting and budgeting. You must develop a history of sales and make forecasts of sales trends in order to determine whether your advertising is having any effect on those sales. Some sort of yardstick is necessary for measurement, otherwise, you will not be able to separate the forest from the trees! Remember the old tale about the security guard who suspected an employee of stealing something from the warehouse? The fellow appeared several times during the day at the gate with a wheelbarrow full of sand for use in the cement mixers and each time the guard carefully searched through the sand. He found nothing, but some days later discovered that several wheelbarrows had been stolen! The morale is that the more obvious a thing seems to be, the more it disappears. If you fail to keep careful records, fail to make sales forecasts, fail to use feedback devices, fail to monitor the results of advertising, you can never know whether your money is being wasted.

SHOULD YOU USE AN ADVERTISING AGENCY?

Advertising agencies exist because the selection of media, timing, location, design and appeal is so complex that many firms prefer to employ professionals to handle the work. Should you consider using an advertising agency? The answer is maybe. Remember that the primary knowledge required for a successful advertising campaign is knowledge about your target market. No advertising agency has that knowledge. A good agency can have tremendous knowledge about advertising, the kinds and numbers of people who can be reached with various approaches and can have creative people who are capable of outstanding design and layout work. No agency can have a knowledge of your business image or of your operations. That means that if you are willing to spend the time necessary to make the people in an advertising agency knowledgeable about your firm's operation, its target market and image, and if you can find an agency which is willing to spend the time necessary to learn the necessary information about your firm, that agency can be valuable. Without the investment of time on the part of both firms, no effective advertising can be expected to result. The things which an agency can bring to you are knowledge of the advertising business and creativity.

Most of the fees which an agency earns are based on a percentage of media costs. That means that it is possible for an agency to overemphasize the standard approaches of television and radio because those will produce higher fees. Also, advertising agencies vary greatly in skill, knowledge and creativity. Agencies are mostly small businesses, and have the same problems that any small business has. They are selling the advertising expertise and creativity of the staff. Consequently, the quality of the service is a function of the competency of the people. If you choose to use an advertising agency, you should be sure that you can develop a relationship with the people in the firm which can be mutually satisfactory. You will need an agency which takes an active interest in your business and is willing to learn about it and its market. You will need an agency which will be open minded about budgetary matters. You will need an agency which is willing to work within your budgetary restraints and is willing to grow with you.

Hiring an agency does not absolve you of the record keeping responsibility. You must still keep records to determine whether the advertising is effective. There is an added factor when an agency is involved. If the advertising is consistently ineffective, you should probably consider changing agencies. In short, it's even more important to keep records when you are using an agency to determine how effective they are in addition to how well various advertising approaches work.

MARKETING TECHNIQUES

Marketing techniques are plans or devices which are designed to sell products or services. Advertising is an example, but is not the only method of promoting sales. Marketing techniques can range far afield from advertising and may result from managerial actions and strategic plans. Virtually anything which has an objective of increasing your sales or of obtaining additional customers can be thought of as a marketing technique.

SALES APPROACH

The approach you take to the sale of goods and services is a marketing technique. Do you use commissioned sales people or salaried; do you use a direct mail approach or have a store; do you use telephone sales efforts or personal calls? There is an almost unlimited variety of **sales approaches** which can be used. From door to door sales to warehouse showrooms; from part time sales people to highly trained professionals; from independent sales representatives to salaried employees; the variety is limited only by your imagination.

How do you decide what sales approach to use? As in the case of the advertising media problem, it is based on knowledge of the target market to which you wish to sell and the image of the business which you wish to portray. You must select an approach which you believe will give you maximum coverage of the market and a competitive position. Frequently, an innovative approach can be valuable because it can make you stand out from your competitors. You must temper your approach with knowledge of the industry. In some industries, the sales approach is so thoroughly entrenched by tradition that it is virtually impossible to change it. For example, college textbooks have traditionally been sold by providing *examination copies* to professors in the hopes that they will adopt the books for use in their classes. This can be a highly significant expense. Recently, several small firms which have tried to penetrate the textbook market have attempted to change the sales approach to one which requires a professor to purchase or return examination copies within a certain time if the books are not adopted for use in a class. Many professors have reacted unfavorably to this change because it requires them to review a book quickly in order to avoid being billed for it. That can be a problem given the other demands on time which they experience. Consequently, the firms using the new sales approach are significantly less competitive. Whether there will occur a shift in the sales approach over time cannot be predicted as yet. Many other industries have similar restrictions on the sales approach which have developed over time and which can limit the success of innovative approaches.

COMPENSATION

There is another aspect to the sales approach which the customer does not see: the compensation of employees. The sales people can be paid salaries or commissions or some combination of the two. When you are deciding on the sales approach to use, you must also decide on the compensation approach to use for sales people. Generally, when sales people have the opportunity to increase their pay by increasing sales, they can be expected to produce more. Promotions which give away prizes, trips and vacations for achieving established sales levels can be valuable in motivating sales people as can be bonuses and other forms of recognition. The recognition need not always be monetary. In the life insurance industry, for example, top sales people qualify for membership in the *Million Dollar Round Table* or some other *club* for high producers. This membership, which may be displayed on business cards, provides recognition and status for excellent performance. Recognition can frequently be worth more than money as an incentive. This is especially true for higher paid people.

ADVERTISING

We have talked at length about advertising, but we have not discussed its use as a marketing technique. What we mean is the coordination of advertising with operations, conditions and other marketing techniques. How do you decide which items to advertise when you are planning product/service advertising? One approach is to select items which you believe will appeal to the target market at a particular time, i.e., turkeys at Thanksgiving, toys at Christmas, swimsuits in the summer, etc. Another approach is to choose items which are not selling well when compared to other items. Still another approach is to choose items which make you stand out from your competition: items which they do not carry or which are rare or difficult to find. Still another approach is to choose some staple or basic item which has continuous appeal to the market. Yet another approach is to choose items whose suppliers will provide co-op advertising support, which means that they will pay part of the cost of advertising. As you can see, there is a large number of approaches to deciding what is to be advertised! That decision must be made just as the decision about the advertising itself.

In addition, you must coordinate advertising with the rest of the firm's operations. It makes no sense to promote an item which you do not have. If you are experiencing a strike or work slow down, advertising may well be wasted until the problems are settled. On the other hand, if you are expecting a major shipment of some item to come in next week, advertising for that item could be most appropriate. In addition to internal factors, you must also coordinate advertising with conditions outside the firm which could affect it. For example, launching a major advertising campaign the week following large lay offs of people in your target market would be a waste of advertising dollars. In a college town advertising must take into consideration semester breaks and other times when students will not be in town if they are included in the target market. In a farming community, advertising would best be geared to harvest times and could well be affected by extremes in weather.

Other marketing techniques need to be considered as well. Advertising efforts must be coordinated with sales people so that it will assist their sales efforts. In addition, everyone in the business needs to be aware of advertising campaigns so that they can capitalize on those campaigns and so that feedback information about the effectiveness of the campaign can be captured. Advertising must be coordinated with sales and must take into consideration any premiums being offered.

One final word is necessary about advertising. Never overlook the value of the free advertising which comes from *word of mouth*. If your customers are pleased with you and satisfied with their purchases, they will inevitably talk about your firm to their friends, neighbors and business associates. If they are displeased with you, they are even more inclined to talk about your firm. That means that you should always be aware of the satisfaction level of your customers and strive to keep it high. No advertising which you can buy will be as effective as customer endorsements and nothing can be as damaging to your firm as customer criticism.

PREMIUMS

Premiums are gifts, discounts or coupons which are given for purchasing an item. These can range from trading stamps given by a grocery store to dishes given by a bank for new savings deposits. If premiums of any type are used, the advertising should promote the premium offers and should make sure that customers understand the premium program. If customers do not understand the basis for the awarding of premiums, they can become angry and the program can backfire, alienating customers rather than attracting them. In addition, premiums can be costly. Consequently, careful records should be kept concerning the effectiveness of premiums. Added costs of the premium program should be compared to increases in contribution margin which result from the program. Increase in sales is not enough: the increase in contribution margin resulting from sales growth is the profit gained from the program and that must be compared to the cost of the premiums and the cost of any advertising associated with the premium offer. Don't make the mistake of believing that all sales which occur during a premium campaign result from the premium technique. Just as in the case of all other advertising approaches, you must compare sales results to sales trends and forecasts to identify real new business which you would not have received without the premiums. It is even more important in this case because of the added costs.

SALES

Everyone understands sales and how advertising is needed to promote sales. What is less obvious are the various reasons for a sale. Sales can be used to get rid of unsalable items. Have you noticed sales items which were marked *buy one, get one free*? That sales technique will get rid of more items than would simply marking every item down to half price. Another reason for a sale is to attract people into the business. If some items are on sale while others are not, perhaps people can be encouraged to buy some of the regular items. This is the philosophy behind *loss leaders* or items which are actually priced below cost. Sales can also be used to attract members of the target market who have not yet become customers or who are unfamiliar with the firm. Still another reason for a sale can be to simply make money. Have you noticed any firms which seem to have a perpetual sale going? As soon as one promotion is over, another starts. Some firms, especially those which choose discount pricing strategies, use sales as their primary sales approach.

If a sale is used for any purpose other than disposing of stale or slow moving merchandise, then you should be aware of the costs and benefits of those sales just as you should be for any other marketing technique. The costs of the sale are reduced or lost contribution margins on the items marked down as well as any advertising associated with the sale. Gains from the sale arise from increases in the overall sales of the firm and the contribution margin which results from those gains. That means that you must compare sales to trends and forecasts as we have discussed in the prior sections. You must be able to tell whether your sales are working or not. Careful record keeping is the only way to make that determination.

BUDGETING

We have talked about budgeting for the firm as a whole and about developing the budget for start-up marketing. Ongoing marketing also requires a budget. Because no firm has unlimited resources, you must plan how much you intend to spend on marketing efforts. Some firms do this by designating a percentage of gross sales for marketing expenditures. Percentages from 1% to 5% are not uncommon under this approach. When the sales forecast and the expense forecast are prepared, the dollars budgeted for marketing will be a part of the overall budget. Other firms plan marketing campaigns and forecast the actual costs of those campaigns as part of the budgeting process. Still other firms, probably the majority of small firms, do no planning at all and simply spend money haphazardly. There is absolutely no way that any business can expect to maximize the yield from its marketing dollars if it does not budget those dollars and plan where and how they are to be spent.

Once a budget has been prepared, then you must decide how the money is to be spent. That means apportioning the dollars to various advertising campaigns and media and to other marketing techniques. How you decide how much to apportion to each marketing effort on an ongoing basis is largely dependent upon your record keeping. The most effective techniques should have the most dollars apportioned. Nevertheless, you should always strive to set aside part of the budget for continued experimentation. The marketing techniques which work are bound to change over time with the changing characteristics of your market, competition and other factors. That means that you must always be trying new approaches. Since the changes will generally occur slowly, it makes sense to spend the majority of the budget on tried and true techniques. But because the change is inevitable, some dollars must always be used to test new and potentially better techniques.

STRATEGY

In this and all of the other chapters in the book we have stressed planning and strategy development. That's because planning is the single most important function of a successful management. The planning and strategy development must be done for the firm as a whole. It cannot be accomplished *piece meal*. That means that the owner and top managers of a small business must be *generalists* and must constantly strive to view the firm as a single functioning unit. The strategy development must include marketing strategies, of course, but those strategies must make sense in light of all other strategies in the firm. The long term and short term goals and objectives for the organization must impact the marketing strategy, just as it does every other aspect of the business.

PUTTING IT ALL TOGETHER

There is a difference about marketing strategy, because this is the place where every thing in the business must focus. Regardless of what kind of business or industry we are talking about, its long term success will in large measure reflect the success of the marketing strategy. Every business must sell before anything else can happen. Consequently, every aspect of the business is directed to that end: selling products and services. The overall business strategy must also be directed toward selling the firm's wares. This is true regardless of the size of the business.

Marketing is not something which is considered after everything else has been determined. It is an intricate part of the overall strategy development and planning of the firm. Marketing is really the place where everything in the business comes together.

SUMMARY

Pricing is a very important marketing concept which the novice quickly equates with cost. However, the main inputs to price are demand and competition. Both are difficult concepts to measure. There are three basic approaches to setting the price for a product or service. These strategies include pricing at competitive levels, below competitive levels or above competitive levels. Firms who consistently price above competitive levels must cultivate an image of providing a high level of quality and service and appeal to a target market which has a demand for those things.

Pricing below the market means that a firm consistently prices below market level in the form of recurring sales or discounts. The most frequently observed practice among small businesses is pricing at market level meaning that the firm is attempting to price its goods and services at or near levels created by its competition. Whatever the strategy, the strategy must remain consistent with the image portrayed in order for the firm to enjoy success.

Advertising is the most visible marketing operation of a business. Advertising has many media and typically is aimed at promoting a particular product or service. The objective of product/service advertising is to create a desire in the minds of the customers for a specific item. However, the associated risk is that the customer will buy our advertised product/service but from someone else.

In image advertising, we are promoting the reputation and image of the firm rather than the products or services of the firm. As long as the image and advertising remain consistent, the element of risk is minimized.

Media refers to the vehicle used to deliver an advertising message to customers. The media used for advertising is limited only by the imagination, however, the problem comes in selecting the medium which will provide maximum penetration of the target market for the dollars expended. Yet the various combinations of all of the factors of timing, location, advertising design, and type of media are almost limitless.

Nevertheless, beware! Poor advertising can be worse than no advertising. Be sure that the advertising campaign will appeal to your customers not you personally. Your preferences may not be congruent. Also be careful about advertising promises and be sure that the advertising is consistent with the firm's image.

In order to help you to assess the effectiveness of the advertising, keep records. Know what works and what doesn't. An advertising agency may be beneficial if you are unsure about what will work for you, however, this approach is more expensive yet it can be effective. If you choose to go this route, establish a good relationship with your agent and keep records about the campaigns.

There are several other marketing techniques besides advertising which a business may pursue. The approach you take to sales is one technique. Another technique is the use of premiums such as gifts, discounts or coupons. Keep records to see what works. To learn why sales work is another marketing technique. The reasons for a sale may be to get rid of unsalable items, to attract new customers as well as regular customers and to make money.

Just as budgeting was necessary in start-up planning, it is important in ongoing marketing efforts. Don't spend advertising dollars on impulse but plan for the expenditures. Many firms designate a percentage of gross sales for market expenses while others forecast the actual cost of marketing campaigns as part of the budgeting process. If you have kept careful records, you should know which marketing techniques are the most cost/benefit justified.

Since planning is the single most important function of management, the development of effective marketing strategies should be of primary concern. Marketing is not something which is considered after everything else has been determined. It is an intricate part of the overall strategy development planning of the firm. Marketing is really the place where everything in the business comes together.

QUESTIONS, EXERCISES AND CASES

QUESTIONS:

1.   How is advertising different from marketing?

2.   What are the factors involved in the purchasing decision?

3.   What is the purpose of loss leaders and premiums in marketing?

4.   Describe the supply/demand/pricing cycle.

5.   What are the three approaches to marketing and which is the better approach for small businesses and why?

6.   Why is image advertising less risky than product/service advertising and why?

7.   What are the various marketing techniques one can use in small businesses to enhance the marketing effort?

8.   Why is it better to plan and to budget rather than react in marketing?

9.   Is it better to use an advertising agency than to do your own, why or why not?

10.   Why is it said that the marketing effort brings together the planning and development function of a small business?

EXERCISES:

1.   You are going to open a leisure dining restaurant in a medium sized college town. Create a marketing budget for that entreprise. Perhaps talking to some existing businesses in the area such as Applebee's might give you some ideas.

2.   Discuss in class the best and worst commercials you have recently seen and indicate whether they are engaging in product/service or image advertising. Which commercials are most memorable and why? Which type of advertising do you prefer?

CASE

Let's revisit the karate school we talked about in a previous chapter prior to its sale: back to the reasonably good times in the beginning. Randy has commented to us in passing that now things are really going to get hot. "What do you mean?", we ask.

Randy's excited. We had just passed a young man in the doorway and had assumed that he was a supplier of some type, because he was just putting away a check and some papers. Randy was so pleased he had to share his good fortune and we were the recipients of his news.

"I just bought a listing in a directory which is going to be placed in hotels, resort areas and rest areas in a two hundred mile radius! Do you know how many resorts there are in this area? And think of the Blue Ridge Parkway! Business is going to boom now!"

Obviously he was thrilled. We didn't know what to say. We were his customers or at least our sons were and although he knew that we were professors, he had never asked our opinion about anything and seemed reluctant to do more than tell us what he had done and never ask us what he should do.

"Oh, is that the only advertising you're doing?" we asked unenthusiastically.

"Well, you know that the paper carries a special now and then. But it only comes out once at week and I haven't gotten much response from those ads. I have been offering a special, you know, the first two lessons free or a free *gi* with the introductory lessons. I've been alternating the ads. You know, that's a real deal. Those *gis* cost about twenty dollars for the inexpensive ones."

Sensing our lack of enthusiasm, Randy quickly changed the subject and had to go work out with the kids. What could we do? We wanted the dojo to be successful because not only was Randy a great young man, we wanted to continue our boys studies, not just for the self defense, they were learning, but for the self confidence and self discipline that were already becoming obvious to us. Other parents had agreed with us that while they were glad that their kids were learning to defend themselves, they were more excited about the philosophy that was being taught. Many of us had gone to the karate tournaments and seen the violence taught by the other schools and were truly indebted to Randy for not teaching that type of behavior.

Advertising can be a variety of types as you have discovered in your reading. You can have the soft sell of McDonald's or the hard sell of some of the automobile manufacturers, but you don't need an advertising agency to tell you what appeals to you.

1.   Think about this business and what sort of image it wants to portray. What elements would appeal to the most people? Would it be appropriate to ask his students exactly why they had chosen to study with him rather than several other schools in the area?

2.   Who is Randy's target market? Why were we not excited about the $150 he had just spent on the directory listing? What is the target market of the directory?

3.   Since the newspaper is a weekly paper rather than a daily paper, what other advertising means might Randy have chosen?

4.	What was Randy really selling? What is his distinctive competency? Do you think that he knows?

5.	Develop a marketing plan for Randy's dojo. Notice that there are two locations for Randy's business: one is his home town and the other is a college town nearby.

Note: In the home town, there are about fifty percent of the students from the local school systems, mostly junior high students. The other fifty percent are young men and a few young women who are employed in the area. There are several policemen, a couple of postmen, some mill workers, and a few white collar junior or middle managers. In the college town, almost ninety percent are from the university with the other ten percent from the local high school.

Would the same marketing efforts be appropriate for both locations? What would the difference of appeal be in the two locations? What types of marketing would be appropriate in each location? Is Randy adequately tapping the market at either place? What can he do?

6.	You have been hired as a consultant. You have been told that there is $250 maximum for the effort. What marketing plans can you come up with? Present your plans to the class.

CHAPTER SEVENTEEN

RISK MANAGEMENT

CHAPTER OBJECTIVES

Upon completion of this chapter, you should be able to:

- Explain that financial planning includes consideration of risks to which firms will be exposed;

- Describe the importance of risk management;

- Evaluate the four major risks in a business;

- Describe how insurance can be used effectively and its limitations; and,

- Prepare a risk management contingency plan for a small business.

RISK MANAGEMENT

INTRODUCTION

The financial planning which is required in a new venture start-up and as part of the ongoing management includes consideration of the risks to which the firm will be exposed. In our society, we seem to be infatuated with the concept of risk. Far too many would be business owners take Kipling's words to heart.

If you can make one heap of all your winnings
And risk it all on one turn of pitch-and-toss,
And lose, and start again at your beginnings
And never breathe a word about your loss.
. . . .
Yours is the Earth and everything that's in it,
And -- which is more -- you'll be a Man, my son!

IF by Rudyard Kipling

In business, well informed and capable managers never assume unexamined risk. It is certainly true that risk is involved in all business. What is not true is that owners of small businesses enjoy taking risks. In this chapter, we will talk about business risks, insurance and risk management. We will explore the sources of risks and methods of minimizing the exposure of a firm to those risks.

RISK MANAGEMENT

When most people think about risk management, they think of ***insurance***. ***Risk management*** is much more than just an insurance program. You must first realize that not everything can be insured. In order for a risk, or hazard, as insurance companies are fond of calling them, to be insurable, it must be possible to identify that risk, calculate the amount of loss that can occur, and spread the risk over a large number of people. Identifying a risk means an unambiguous statement of the potential loss. For example, a building can be insured against fire, but not against *everything*. Calculating the potential loss requires knowledge about the dollar value of a loss. It would not be possible to insure a business against the revenues lost from a downturn in the economy. ***Spreading the risk*** is a requirement which insurance companies have for underwriting a risk. Insurance companies can exist only because they have a large enough base of policy holders so that premiums received for coverage will in the long term exceed the amount of losses which will occur. That means that a circus high wire walker or a daredevil who jumps motorcycles over buses will have trouble obtaining insurance coverage because there just aren't enough people doing those things to spread the risk.

Even if it were possible to insure against everything that could happen in a business, it would still not be feasible for a small business due to the amount of insurance premiums which would have to be paid. *Risk management* is the science of identifying the risks inherent in a business venture, taking steps to minimize those risks as much as possible, insuring those risks which are appropriate to insure, and preparing a contingency plan to deal with potential losses. So you see, risk management is planning!

IDENTIFYING RISKS

There are four major groupings of risk in a business venture. These are risks associated with operations, property, customers and employees. We will address each of these independently and present some ideas for minimizing them.

OPERATIONAL RISKS

Operational risks are generally not insurable. These risks include the risk of recession, changes in markets, product obsolescence, changes in competition, death or loss of key employees, and risks of that nature. In other words, these are risks associated with the normal operations of a business. Effective operational risk management requires being aware of the kinds of environmental changes which can affect the business, structuring the business to avoid as many of these effects as possible, preparing a plan for dealing with those environmental changes which cannot be avoided, monitoring for the occurrence of those changes and reacting quickly to implement the plan when they do occur. This all sounds quite mystical, but it is really simple and requires nothing more than common sense.

Diversification

Diversification is probably the best protection against product obsolescence and can also protect against recessions and market and competition changes if the diversification is well planned. Obviously, a company which has multiple products and multiple markets is safer from environmental changes than a one product - one market company. Small business owners frequently fail to consider diversification because they think it is only something which large firms do. They think it means acquiring other companies, branching out into other countries, entering into new product/service markets, or strategies of that nature. All of those moves are, indeed, diversification strategies, but small businesses can diversify along more modest lines with a little planning.

A small business with which we are familiar got started a few years ago in a cut and sew operation. The company started out bidding for contracts to make ladies' dresses. After a few months, the owner began to pursue contracts for other types of ladies' apparel. Then the company went after jeans and men's slacks. During this time, the company was also gaining experience cutting and handling various types of materials. After about three years, the company was cutting and sewing a wide variety of clothing items for men, women, children and youth. That same company is now making covers from heavy canvas and rubberized materials for equipment and machinery. The owner is now looking into the possibility of surgical gowns.

This is clearly an example of small business diversification. The resulting company is not only larger and stronger than it would have been had it stayed with dresses, it avoided a problem which many other small firms of this type experienced with inexpensive imports of dresses and blouses from the far east.

Our point is that small businesses can also pursue diversification efforts and should do so, because it is sound business sense! It can and does happen every day. A building contractor we know uses his crews to build dog and pet houses and prefabricated outbuildings when the weather is bad or the work is off. A real estate broker we know is now selling property insurance. An accounting service company which began with a general purpose computerized accounting system is now handling payroll and has acquired several specialized systems including one designed especially for gas stations. One gas station operator we know is now handling fuel oil. Another has built a convenience store. A convenience store operator used part of the land on his site to build a self service car wash. Virtually all businesses can find opportunities to expand products, services or markets with a little planning and effort.

Key Employees

Deciding in advance what you will do if you are faced with the loss of a key employee is just common sense. Taking steps to minimize the risk of such a loss means paying attention to compensation policies and implementing pension and profit sharing plans. That will help to be sure that you do not lose the employee to another company.

You should also take steps to minimize the impact of the loss of a key employee by acquiring life insurance on key people. Furthermore, you should plan for management succession by continually grooming new people for key positions. That way if you do lose a person to competition or to death, another employee will have been prepared to take over the duties. Needless to say, these last steps apply to yourself as well. What will happen to the business if you die or suddenly become incapacitated? Beyond the obvious effect that would have on your family, there is the business to consider. Countless small businesses depend so heavily on the owner that even a brief loss of that person could destroy the business. More than one small business owner has recuperated from a heart attack to discover that the business did not survive! You owe it to yourself and to your business to be sure that it can weather the loss of any person, including yourself.

Written Plans

How do you handle operational risks? You try to visualize all the things that might happen and you make plans to try to avoid as many as possible and to minimize the effects if the worst happens. Plans to deal with these risks should be made in writing and reviewed at least annually. Operational risks never go away and conditions never stay the same.

PROPERTY RISKS

Property risks are the type which most people immediately think of when risk management is mentioned. Most of these risks can be covered by insurance. They include the potential destruction or loss of one or more of the physical assets of a business. This goes far beyond fire insurance. Risk management of property hazards requires taking steps to minimize the risk of loss, insuring the losses and planning for recovery of the loss.

In order to minimize the risks, you must first carefully identify what they are. For example, safe construction, the removal of fire hazards and a fire prevention program can reduce the risk of fire, but how do you reduce the risk of shoplifting? Yes, the loss of inventory through shoplifting is an example of property risk. Natural disasters are simply the most obvious risks. Property risks include robbery and theft by employees as well.

Security Systems

Security systems, especially cameras can help deter theft. Employee theft is especially vulnerable to camera security. One owner of a convenience store we know installed a camera system above the cash register to deter armed robbery. Even though there was never such an attempt, shoplifting losses went down by half in the first month! That made the owner suspicious because the camera only had a limited field of vision and the film never captured any suspicious scenes. He installed other cameras including one in the storeroom which was off limits to customers. Shoplifting losses almost disappeared! Clearly, much of what he thought were shoplifting losses were really incidences of employee theft.

Other steps which can be taken include sensible locations. Part of the site location process described in previous chapters should generally be to avoid areas subject to high crime rates or else to make plans to minimize risks in areas subject to crime. Layout of the store, mirrors, cameras, and electronic sensing tags for merchandise are possible strategies.

Cash Protection

One of the most important strategies of all is the protection of cash. Surely you have noticed gas stations and convenience stores with signs which indicate that night staff do not have combinations to the safe. In addition, computerized price look-ups built into the cash registers and product code sensors and light wands help protect against accidental and deliberate mistakes in merchandise sales. Something as simple as requiring cash to be removed from the register whenever it exceeds a specified amount can be effective. Daily bank deposits of cash and additional deposits when cash exceeds a certain level are good ideas. Of course, procedures for handling that cash and for record keeping associated with it are also mandatory. Professional assistance can be useful to design internal controls to minimize cash risks and many other types of property risks as well.

Computer Security

An extremely disturbing form of property risk that has been born of the information age is the risk to data files and automated equipment. Records may well be the most valuable of all physical assets of a business. What would happen to a business if it suddenly lost all of its records? How would it collect its accounts receivable? Know which bills and statements it owed? Comply with statutory requirements to file sales tax returns, employee withholding statements, income tax returns? Some of the most spectacular losses businesses have ever experienced have come in the last few years in the form of computer fraud. This area is so sensitive that sensible risk management requires a separate security and disaster plan just for computer based information systems.

Losing It All

Safeguarding physical assets is an exercise in imagination. You must strive to identify what the potential hazards are for the resources of your particular business and plan for the reduction and minimization of those risks. Don't forget the ultimate risk: that of the loss of everything. Even if sufficient insurance coverage exists to permit the rebuilding of a business that has lost all of its physical assets, how does that take place? In an *Inc.* article a few years ago, a small business owner detailed his efforts to rebuild a business which had lost all of its assets to a major fire. The effort was a success, but only due to the owner's extraordinary perseverance. He recommended that every business have a written contingency plan which outlines how rebuilding will take place.[64]

CUSTOMER CENTERED RISKS

Most people think of customer centered risks as revolving around suits for injuries received on the premises. This is a clear risk, but one which can generally be covered by insurance.

Customer theft in the form of shoplifting is part of the property risk area. In reality, the greatest risk associated with customers is that of product or service liability. Originally this risk was associated principally with products, but recently, court precedents have moved its impact into the services field as well.

Product Liability

In general, the courts have held in ***product liability*** suits that a product must be fit for the purpose for which it was designed. That means that if a rope sold as clothesline rope breaks while a purchaser of that rope is using it for mountain climbing, the producer has no liability. But if a rope is designed and sold as a mountain climbing rope, then it must be able to stand up to reasonably anticipated rigors or the producer will be liable. ***Product liability suits*** have frequently been news producers in the last few years because of the size of the awards and settlements which have been made and the tendency for class action suits to grow out of product liability claims. A ***class action suit*** is one which is brought on the part of a group of customers or injured parties. In a broader sense, these actions can be brought by people who are not customers of a business. If a manufacturing plant explodes and people living nearby are injured, then the business owning that plant may be found liable far in excess of its insurance coverage.

Services, like products, must be provided with reasonable competency. Medical malpractice suits have never been more common than they are now and services of all kinds are increasingly being brought under product liability expectations. Accounting firms are being sued with ever increasing frequency by parties claiming injury as a result of reliance on financial statements prepared by the firms. The trend shows every sign of intensifying.

Don't make the mistake of thinking that you are free from liability because you are a retailer or wholesaler. People in these businesses frequently think that product liability falls only on the manufacturer of the goods they carry. That is not true! Courts have frequently held that retailers are liable as well as manufacturers.

How do you reduce the risk of product or service liability claims? It requires a sincere and concerted effort to provide quality products and competent services. It requires restraint in advertising programs and free communication with customers about product or service limitations. It requires an effective training program for employees about the way in which products and services are to be represented to the public, and training or education efforts aimed at customers to assure competent and proper use of the company's products or services. It requires constant vigilance on the part of the management of a business to ensure that short term profits never become so important that short cuts or unacceptable risks may be taken. It requires planning on a continuing basis to be sure that risks are minimized and to prepare actions to be taken if a disaster occurs. We will have more to say on this subject in the chapter on business law.

Accounts Receivable

Another aspect of customer related risk is the risk of nonpayment on accounts or notes receivable. If your business has accounts receivable, then it is inevitable that some loss will occur on those accounts. The difference in acceptable and unacceptable losses is frequently the result of planning. The business should develop lending and collection policies and set aside reserves to cover losses. There is a thin line which must be walked in accounts receivable: a credit policy which is too tight will lose sales; a credit policy which is too loose will lose too many accounts. Finding where you should be in that continuum is challenging and difficult. Constant monitoring of the credit practices and experience and adjustment of the policy is the only plausible approach to solving the dilemma.

Adequate training of the people who will be extending credit and the people who will be collecting accounts is a must as is a sound plan for how and when collection efforts will begin and end. *Trade credit* is by far the largest source of funding in the business world. It exceeds bank financing and bond and equity financing combined. Even large firms are frequently guilty of *riding* their accounts payable when times are tough. All the sales in an industry will not help a firm if it is unable to collect those sales. Cash flow is infinitely more important than profits in the survival of a small business. Planning is crucial to determine how cash flow can be maximized through the credit practices of the business.

EMPLOYEE CENTERED RISK

Many of the risks which revolve around employees could also be classified as operational risks. For example, in a prior section, we talked about the risk of losing key people. Other types of employee risks also involve property. Employee theft is something which is distasteful to consider, but is a very real problem in the business world. Due to a reluctance to report employee theft, no one knows the true extent of the problem. Many experts believe it to be far greater than the sum of all shoplifting and burglary in the country! Internal control procedures are vital.

Controls for Employee Centered Risk

Specific controls which might be considered to minimize employee risk include cash controls, which we discussed above, key controls, physical inventories, trash control, etc. Locks, strong effective locks, are an obvious control device but small business owners frequently make no effort to control the storage, location, or duplication of the keys themselves. Locks do no good if the keys or their duplicates are readily available. You will need a system for checking out keys on an as needed basis to responsible employees and a system for keeping those keys secure at other times. Physical inventories or counts of merchandise at unannounced times can be an effective device.

Trash controls are an area which is easily overlooked. There are two uses of trash which have potential damaging effects. First, there are documents and papers which are thrown away which present possible problems. Not only will documents containing your computer system passwords be dangerous, but so will papers which identify your suppliers, your customers, your employees, the location and arrangement of your business and warehouse, hours of operation, security arrangements, etc. The list goes on! Clearly, you need to condition people not to throw away documents or papers. They should be shredded. Shredders are inexpensive and can be valuable additions to a security system.

Secondarily, trash represents a tremendous opportunity for employee theft. If one of your people takes an item of value, he or she may simply hide it in the trash! If it is discovered before the trash is thrown away, well it would be hard to link to any individual and it could have been an accident. More likely, no one looks through the trash, so the container is dumped outside for the trash collector to pick up. The employee comes back at night and retrieves the stolen item. What can you do about this? Don't make trash cans readily available. All the papers and documents should be shredded so one container can be set aside for this purpose. Other trash containers will be required in restrooms and lounges, of course, but don't put trash cans in other areas. Assign one person the job of emptying trash containers and make that person aware that trash can be used to conceal theft. Finally, don't leave trash outside for pick up. Store it inside the building and arrange to have the trash taken directly to the truck during working hours.

By far the most important and effective control for employee centered risks is the careful selection, training and supervision of employees. In fact, in a previous chapter, we indicated the first rule of internal control is the hiring of honest, capable people. This puts more emphasis on the hiring process. If people were honest in the first place, and they are well trained and they are well compensated, they are less likely to be a problem.

Bonding of employees who are in sensitive positions can be accomplished through your insurance company. This will protect against their theft or fraud. Still other employee risks impact the firm's records and a major portion of the security planning for the computer based information system must deal with protection from breaches of security or confidentiality by employees. Also employees and the work they do affect customer relations and may well impact a business' ultimate liability for customer injuries or claims. Good supervision by competent managers will go a long way toward minimizing these risks.

Finally, employee risks involve loss of production through strikes or work stoppages and loss of income through such devices as ***sweetheart sales*** which are sales of items by cashiers at below price. This can be a serious problem, especially if you use young and inexperienced cashiers who must frequently ring sales for friends and peers. Mechanical devices, though expensive, and training and supervision can help to minimize the latter problem, but good employee relations are required to reduce the risk of work stoppages.

Polygraphs

Before we leave the subject of employee risk, we must talk about polygraph testing. This is a popular and visible technique which many retail firms employ. However, polygraphs have come under attack in the last few years because they have not always been proven reliable. In fact, many states now have laws which prohibit their use. There have been many examples in which employees have been discharged on the basis of polygraph tests and later won court suits as a result. Furthermore, reports about the effectiveness of polygraphs in preventing employee theft are mixed. In short, polygraphs are not a panacea! That means that their use does not guarantee employee honesty. Consequently, we strongly recommend against their use except in special industries and circumstances. For most small businesses, polygraphs are an expensive and not necessarily effective device which promises problems in the future. If you do intend to use polygraphs, be sure to obtain legal advice first and to follow careful procedures as outlined by professionals.

Workmen's Compensation

A business is responsible for providing a safe working environment for its employees and in some industries such as mining and textiles huge awards have been made by courts to employees who have sustained injuries related to their work. All states have enacted ***workmen's compensation insurance laws*** which provide for a schedule of payments to be made for employee injuries sustained in work related activities. That means that the business is liable for employee injuries on the job!

Superficially, it seems that risks of employee injuries are easily covered by insurance, but courts have gone beyond workmen's compensation coverage when they determined that hazards exist which should reasonably have been eliminated. For example, if a part of an underground mine was deemed to be unsafe and the owner took no action to correct the problems, then any employees injured could well receive court ordered compensation far beyond the level of workmen's compensation coverage. If a machine were improperly installed, or security panels were routinely left open, an employee injured by that machine could also win an award in excess of insurance coverage. Don't make the mistake of minimizing these risks as being associated only with dangerous occupations. If you run a bookstore which requires a ladder to reach the top shelves and that ladder is unsafe, watch out!

In essence, workmen's compensation laws and court precedents say that an employer has an obligation to provide a workplace and working conditions which are reasonably safe. Part of the risk management planning should be attention to the work place and working conditions to be sure that all reasonable precautions are taken and that safety is a continuing objective in all activities.

Employee Relations and Quality Circles

Perhaps the strongest insurance against employee centered risks in a business is an open relationship based on mutual respect between the owners and the employees of a firm. No one is in a better position to witness the development of problems of all types than the employees. If channels of communication are established which permit the communication of developing problems and an atmosphere is established which recognizes the value of that communication, then potential problems can be headed off at an early stage.

This concept is at the heart of the *Quality Circles* which have been developed in many large organizations and which have received so much press in recent years. The quality circle approach organizes employees in small groups who meet periodically to discuss their work and ways to improve it, improve products, improve output, reduce costs, etc. Many such programs have resulted in tremendous savings to the participating businesses, but more importantly, such programs can result in more concerned and caring employees and more rewarding work experiences. Whatever the method used, the fostering of an attitude of interest in the business and a belief that suggestions will be heard by management should be prime goals of any risk management program.

INSURANCE

Insurance can be exceedingly complex as well as expensive. The kinds of coverage available and the variety of policies which exist mandate the use of an expert to obtain a sensible insurance program. Many insurance companies specialize in particular hazards. That fact coupled with a natural desire to minimize policy premiums means that an independent agent is probably the best source of insurance assistance and coverage. An independent does not work for an insurance company. Such people are independent businesses themselves who have licenses to write coverage with a variety of insurance companies.

INDEPENDENT AGENTS

At an early point in the establishment of a new venture, you should establish a relationship with an independent insurance agent and develop a comprehensive insurance plan to protect the business. Just as selecting an attorney and a CPA is an important step, so too, is the selection of an insurance agent. You should interview several agents, discuss your plans, and find out about the agents' backgrounds and areas of expertise. Your goal will be to develop a continuing relationship with an agent who is knowledgeable in the kinds of risks which exist in your industry and who is willing and competent to assist you in a comprehensive risk management program. The best deal is not necessarily the lowest cost. For example, almost all fire insurance policies are written with a co-insurance clause.

CO-INSURANCE CLAUSES

If a policy specifies a co-insurance portion of 80% of the property value, then potential claims will be affected by that percentage. If you fail to insure property for its full value in an effort to reduce premiums, then that failure will affect coverage. A loss of $50,000 on a building valued at $100,000 but which was insured for $60,000 will only be covered at $30,000 (Since the building was insured at 60% of its value, the loss will only be covered at 60%). Had the building been insured for $80,000, or 80% of its value, the loss of $50,000 would have been fully covered. With the variety of coverage available for any given hazard and the flexibility in underwriting, cost can be extremely misleading. What you need is a person with whom you can work, in whom you have confidence and who takes a vital interest in your business.

TYPES OF INSURANCE

There are numerous types of insurance coverage beyond the life insurance which we all think of when we think of insurance. Among these are fire insurance and its related lines of coverage for natural disasters of all types. This type of coverage can also include business interruption protection which will cover lost profits during the time that a business is unable to operate due to a covered hazard. *Casualty insurance* refers to protection against theft, protection for automobile collision and related liability, protection for glass breakage and accident and health insurance as well. *Marine insurance*, so called from the days when virtually all shipping was conducted by water, provides protection for goods during shipment from place to place regardless of the method. There is a type of marine insurance which can protect goods and assets regardless of where they are located. Such coverage is especially valuable in an industry in which assets must be stored at unprotected sites, such as the construction industry. It is even possible to obtain *credit insurance* which will provide protection against abnormal losses on accounts receivable. This coverage generally protects only against losses which are the result of a customer's failure to pay due to unusual circumstances such as a natural disaster. Finally there are *fidelity* and *surety bonds* which protect a business against dishonesty on the part of its employees or from breach of contractual responsibility on the part of another firm or individual with whom you have dealings. Table 1 is a listing of various types of insurance coverage which are available.

Any or all of the types of insurance discussed above may be necessary for a given business. As you can see, it is entirely too complex for anyone to handle without professional assistance.

That's why we do not recommend that you attempt to buy the cheapest policies available from various agents for various aspects of your insurance plan. You need one agent who can handle everything, who is an expert in small business insurance and who will protect your interest. Your independent agent should be capable of assisting you in obtaining all of the types of coverage as well as advising you as to the trade-offs between self-insuring and premium expense. Spend some time finding such a person. It will be time well spent.

Table 1

Types of Insurance and Coverage

- *Fire Insurance* -- losses due to fire and lightning

- *Extended Coverage Insurance* -- losses due to windstorm, hail, explosion, riot, aircraft, vehicle and smoke

- *Business Interruption Insurance* -- losses due to expenses incurred while rebuilding after a property loss

- *Casualty Insurance* -- losses to automobiles and in automobile accidents

- *Liability Insurance* -- losses from accidents suffered by people who come in contact with the business

- *Marine Insurance* -- losses to goods in transit

- *Crime Insurance* -- losses due to burglary, robbery, employee theft

- *Workmen's Compensation Insurance* or *Employer's Liability Insurance* -- losses due to employee injury

- *Life Insurance* -- losses due to death

- *Health Insurance* -- losses due to medical treatment

- *Disability Insurance* -- losses due to inability to work

- *Fidelity Insurance* -- losses due to employee theft or fraud

- *Surety Insurance* -- losses due to failure of a business to properly complete a contract

---

Table 2
Risk Management Contingency Plan Checklist

I.   Identify all business risks
      A.   Operational Risks
            1.   Economic downturn
            2.   Change in market conditions
            3.   Change in competition
            4.   Change in product/service viability
            5.   Death or loss of key people
            6.   Your own death or incapacitation
            7.   Loss or compromise of records (Security/disaster plan for Computer Systems)
      B.   Property Risks
            1.   Natural disasters
            2.   Theft or vandalism
            3.   Shoplifting
            4.   Obsolescence
      C.   Customer Related Risks
            1.   Liability for injuries
            2.   Product/Service liability
            3.   Credit losses (Credit and collection policy and training for people)
      D.   Employee Related Risks
            1.   Employee theft and employee injuries
            2.   Work stoppages
            3.   Internal control procedures
            4.   Employee relations
II.   Steps to minimize risk or exposure
      A.   Operational Risks
      B.   Property Risks
      C.   Customer Related Risks
      D.   Employee Related Risks
III.   Insurance Portfolio
      A.   Independent agent
      B.   Risks to be self-insured and risks to be insured
      C.   Listing of all insurance policies and coverages
      D.   Procedures to prevent lapse of coverage
IV.   Contingency Plan
      A.   Actions to be taken in the event of occurrence of any of the events identified in I.
      B.   Actions to be taken in the event of the total destruction of the business

Self-insuring refers to the assumption of a risk by a business without the involvement of an insurance company. Many large businesses decide to self-insure one or more aspects of their operations because they believe it to be cost/benefit justified. The issue which a small business owner should keep in mind is that an unrecognized or overlooked risk is a self-insured risk. Small businesses can seldom afford that!

CONTINGENCY PLAN

The final outcome of the risk management planning process should be an insurance portfolio and a ***contingency plan*** which identifies the risks of the business, the steps to be taken on a continuing basis to minimize those risks, and the actions to be taken in the event of a partial or total loss from any of the risks. The plan should be in writing and should be developed in conjunction with your insurance agent. The plan should also be reviewed periodically, at least annually, to be sure that as the business changes its contingency plan changes with it. Table 2 contains a check list for the risk management contingency plan. Effective risk management is an extension of the planning process. For a small business with limited resources, it is an area which cannot be overlooked.

SUMMARY

Risk management is the science of identifying the risks inherent in a business venture, taking steps to minimize those risks, insuring those risks which are appropriate to insure, and preparing a contingency plan to deal with potential losses.

There are four major groupings of risk in a business: operations, property, customers and employees. Operational risks are generally not insurable. They are managed by being aware of factors which can affect a business, structuring to avoid as many effects as possible, and preparing a plan for dealing with those which cannot be avoided.

Property risks can generally be insured. Be sure to consider the risk to data files and automated equipment. Sensible risk management requires a separate security and disaster plan for computer based information systems.

Customer centered risks revolve around suits for injuries, which can generally be covered by insurance, risks of nonpayment on accounts and product or service liability. Reducing product or service liability requires a sincere and concerted effort to provide quality products and competent services. It requires planning on a continuing basis to ensure that risks are minimized and to prepare actions to be taken if a disaster occurs.

Some employee centered risks are covered under operational or property hazards. Others impact records and a major portion of security planning for computer systems must deal with risks involve loss of production through work stoppages and loss of income through *sweetheart sales*, etc. Insurance and bonding can cover some of these risks as can internal controls. But the strongest insurance against employee centered risks is an open relationship based on mutual respect between owners and employees.

Insurance can be complex and expensive. The best approach is to establish a relationship with an independent insurance agent early in the life of a business and develop a comprehensive insurance plan.

The final outcome of the risk management planning process should be an insurance portfolio and a contingency plan which identifies the risks of the business, the steps to be taken on a continuing basis to minimize those risks, and the actions to be taken in the event of a partial or total loss.

QUESTIONS, EXERCISES AND CASES

QUESTIONS:

1.   What are the elements of risk management?
2.   Name the four major groups involving risk and explain how the risks for each category can be minimized.
3.   What are the elements in operational risks and how might those risks be minimized?
4.   What form of property risk has caused the greatest losses in recent years? How can those losses be avoided?
5.   What is the greatest risk associated with customers?
6.   Why are accounts receivable an area of risk?
7.   Why is cash flow more important than profit in the survival of a company?
8.   What are some of the elements of employee centered risk?
9.   What is the strongest insurance against employee centered risk and why?
10.   Describe the concept of Quality Circles and how this approach can help organizations.
11.   Name the various types of insurance available and explain why they are important to a small business.
12.   What are the results of risk management planning?
13.   What are the major steps in a contingency plan and why is one important to small business owners?

DEFINE THE FOLLOWING TERMS:

1.   risk
2.   insurance
3.   risk management
4.   operational risks
5.   property risks
6.   customer risks
7.   employee risks
8.   product liability
9.   trade credit
10.   sweetheart sales

11.   insurance
12.   co-insurance
13.   casualty insurance
14.   marine insurance
15.   credit insurance
16.   fidelity and surety bonds
17.   self-insured risk

EXERCISES:

1.   Visit with several independent insurance agents and decide on the best coverage and the most inexpensive coverage available to you. Write down the pros and cons of each program.

2.   Develop a contingency plan for your business using each of the steps outlined in the text.

CASE

George was a genius when it came to computers and John was naive. George presented himself to John one day when John was at his wit's end. He had to take a financial statement to his bank that afternoon and his secretary was out sick and he didn't know how to operate the computer. As John was busily swearing at the dumb machine and wondering why he had ever let himself be talked into such a contraption, George walked in and saved the day.

George had heard that a new money order company had recently opened and was looking for employees. He had a partial degree in computer science meaning that he had dropped out of school before completing his degree because he still had 30 hours of what he felt were silly requirements. After all, he was good and he knew it. He didn't need a degree to tell him how to program. He'd been doing that since he was fifteen.

George was able to give John his financial statements in time for his meeting with the bank, so John hired him on the spot. John thought it would be great since Amy, his secretary, had been trained on the accounting program, but was not comfortable with it. George would assume her duties.

George insisted after several weeks that he could modify some of the existing programs to be more effective and give different reports. John, not really understanding the capabilities of the computer anyway, agreed to the modifications. Whatever George wanted to do.

Six months later, the bank called John and told him of an overdrawn account. According to John's record, he had $250,000 in his account; but according to the bank, John had ($50,000). John said that there must be some mistake because he had a $50,000 line of credit which he hadn't touched.

John told George of his troubles and George said that he would check into the matter on the computer while John tried to work with the bank. While John was gone, George erased several transactions which indicated money orders in the name of Jason George and implanted code which would erase all transactions if a listing of accounts was demanded.

On returning to his office, John found that George had gone out for a late lunch leaving a note that everything had been taken care of. When George did not return, John asked Amy to run a listing of all accounts for the bank to trace the discrepancies. She did. John never knew what hit him.

1.   What is the chief problem in this situation?
2.   What kind of background check should have been done before turning over sensitive data to a stranger?
3.   What should a manager do about security procedures?
4.   Develop a contingency plan for this company.
5.   What steps might have been taken to turn this disaster into a survival?

CHAPTER EIGHTEEN

INVENTORY MANAGEMENT

CHAPTER OBJECTIVES

Upon completion of this chapter, you should be able to:

- Explain the role which inventory plays in the determination of profit for a company;

- Describe the cash to cash cycle and its significance for inventory management;

- Explain the purchasing process and the effect of purchase discounts;

- List the various methods of inventory accounting;

- Describe and calculate economic ordering quantity;

- Demonstrate the role which computers can play in providing support for effective inventory management; and,

- Explain the principles of inventory budgeting and control.

INVENTORY MANAGEMENT

INTRODUCTION

In a retail or wholesale business, few things can be more important than an effective management of the inventory. Plautus, a Roman scholar, understood the basics of the problem 2,000 years ago. He said, *It is necessary to entice the buyer to unsalable wares; good merchandise easily finds a buyer...* Today, we know that the merchandise must be desirable to the buyer in order to be salable. In the modern world, the problem has become infinitely more complex. Effective *inventory management* must now encompass not only the stocking of salable merchandise, but must address the stocking of proper amounts of merchandise, adequate controls over that merchandise, its purchasing and control. The consequences of failure in any of those areas can be catastrophic to a small business because those factors dictate not only salability of inventory but its cost as well. A small business really exerts little control over the selling prices of its products. Those are set by the competition. Consequently, profitability is largely a function of cost control. In this chapter, we will address the aspects of inventory planning in a small retailer or wholesaler: from determining stock levels and order quantities to inventory accounting and control.

INVENTORY

Inventory consists of goods held for sale in a business. In a retail or wholesale business, the inventory typically is the largest asset representing the largest investment in the firm. Inventory is the major source of revenue for the business and the major source of expense in the business. Consequently, inventory management is the determinant of success or failure.

Inventory can take several forms. In a retail/wholesale business, inventory is typically finished goods; goods ready for use by the purchaser. In a manufacturing business, there are typically two additional forms of inventory: *raw materials*, which are products waiting to be converted into finished goods; and *work in process*, which represents those goods which have not yet been completed but are in the process of being converted from raw materials into salable form. In this chapter, we will focus on finished goods. In a later chapter we will discuss production management in small manufacturing firms.

Inventory can be displayed for customers to see and examine or it can be stored in a warehouse awaiting shipment to a buyer or movement to a display. We generally think of retailers as having inventory on display for customers and wholesalers as holding inventory in warehouses for shipment in larger quantities to purchasers which have been sold by traveling sales people. Nevertheless, both retailers and wholesalers can, and frequently do, have inventory held in both display and storage. The display of inventory costs more than its storage because the location of the store or display site and the furnishings and fixtures which are used for display create more expense. Warehouses can be located in less expensive areas and require no amenities beyond those required to protect the inventory, consequently, they cost less. That difference, plus the difference in sales quantities results in pricing which is higher for a retailer. Retailers typically expect to sell very small quantities of any single item, frequently single quantities, while wholesalers generally expect to sell in large quantities.

The difference is blurred by firms which specialize in wholesale situations but act as retailers. Firms of this type sell to other businesses which will use the products to complete their own business, but sell in small quantities. Automobile parts houses are an example. Such firms have generally larger occupancy and display costs than one which uses warehouses only, but have less cost than firms which seek out end users as customers. There are other types of firms, such as mail order firms, who appeal to end users like retailers do, but use warehouse and low cost sites like wholesalers. The only impact which the type of firm has on inventory management is in the quantities of inventory which must be stocked.

If the business does not depend upon display of merchandise for sales and can obtain short shipping times for merchandise from suppliers, then the quantity of inventory stocked can be minimized. Mail order firms and catalog stores, as well as many wholesale firms, have such conditions. For stores of this type, the inventory management is much simpler. In fact, most of the inventory planning will revolve around obtaining and maintaining dependable sources of supply, preparing sales materials such as brochures and catalogs, and the marketing effort itself. There are other types of firms which are able to rely primarily on inventory which they do not own. Inventory owned by the supplier, but held for sale by the vendor is termed ***consignment inventory***. Many retailers handling crafts are able to obtain inventory from the makers on a consignment basis, for example. Such firms are really conduits for the product and earn what are really sales commissions. The management of such firms has no aspects which are unique to inventory, consequently, we will not focus on such firms in this chapter. Here, we will be interested in those firms which must purchase and maintain major portions of the inventory which they will sell. Whether the sales effort is wholesale or retail, the inventory management is the same.

THE CASH TO CASH CYCLE

Cash is required to purchase inventory and its sale produces cash. This is called the ***cash to cash cycle*** and is illustrated in Table 1. As the table shows, inventory is purchased, creating accounts payable which must be paid using cash. Then inventory is sold, creating accounts receivable which must be collected to yield cash. Part of that cash is profit, that portion which represents the mark up or gross profit on the inventory items. Regardless, the resulting cash is available for use in the business. The primary need for cash in a retail or wholesale business is the acquisition of inventory. The sale of inventory, therefore, generates cash for the replacement of itself as well as cash for the payment of salaries, wages and other expenses of the business. This is what is meant when people talk about *cash flow*. You can see how a disruption in this cash flow is caused by inventory which does not sell.

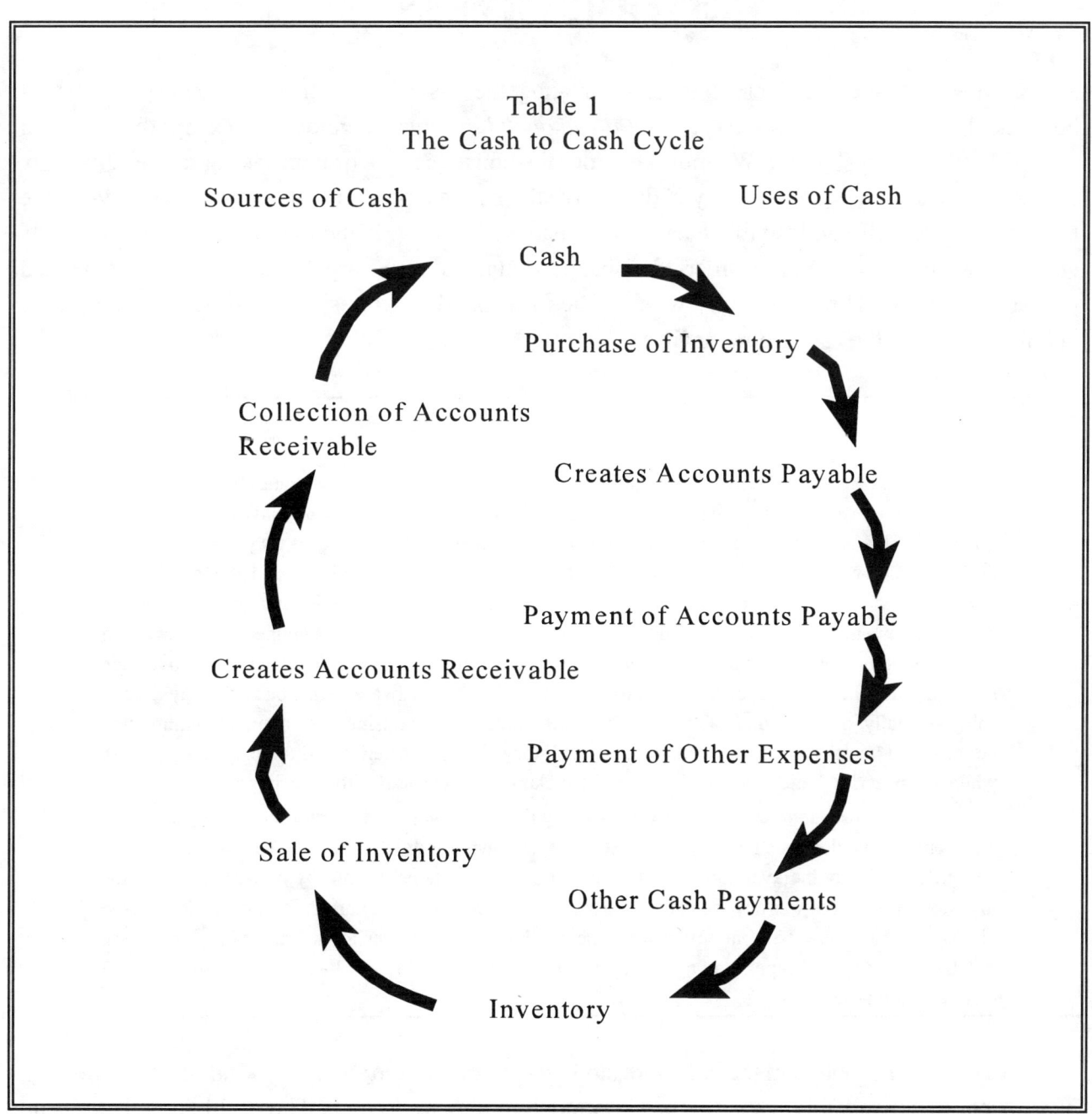

Table 1
The Cash to Cash Cycle

As the table shows, cash and inventory are at opposite points on the cash to cash cycle. Consequently, items which do not sell, consume cash but do not generate any. They just sit at the bottom of the cycle! A business can survive indefinitely without profits, but a business without cash flow will die in short order!

STOCK LEVELS

The first issue of concern in inventory management is the quantities of inventory which will be stocked. The old adage, *you can't sell it if you don't have it* is the guide here except that we need to modify the saying slightly. We must consider the consequences of not making a sale. Just how serious are those consequences? If you don't have the item a customer wants in stock, will you lose that one sale or will you lose that customer's business forever? Is the item such that a reasonable customer would wait for you to order it? What percentage of your target market could be expected to want this item? How frequently would it be in demand? No business can be all things to all people. Consider the case from our files.

A CASE FROM OUR FILES

The consultants had visited the premises of a hardware store. In reviewing the details of the business with the owner, the inventory was assessed. The owner had picked an unusual methodology for tracking his inventory. He placed different colored stickers on the objects as they were placed on the shelves. For example, white indicated merchandise purchased in 1985, red in 1986, and blue in 1987. A good system one might assume since the store was not computerized, but in reality one could see that the white stickers far exceeded the blue meaning that that stock had been there for a very long time without moving. When questioned about the concept of having sales to rid oneself of over-age inventory, the client responded that sales weren't necessary on hardware items, because they always sold eventually. In fact, hoping to impress the consultants with his business acumen, he claimed that not only did he not have sales on his regular inventory items, he often raised the price on that item when a new series came in at a higher price. He claimed that it helped the profit margin.

Obviously another problem overlooked by this client was when to reorder and what. When questioned about the basis for his reorder decisions, the owner indicated that he *eyeballed it* and was also influenced by the availability of discounts on quantity sales offered by his suppliers. If the inventory in the store was any indication, the suppliers were many and varied. Not only did he have almost any hardware item one might want, he had hand tools, power tools, gardening equipment, fertilizer, seeds of all types, and a large array of housewares. He even had chains available in 12 different link sizes.

The major problem in the hardware store was an attempt to stock any kind of hardware item anyone could conceivably want. It costs too much money to do that. The problem is that unsold inventory must be paid for just like inventory which is sold, as is illustrated in the cash flow cycle in Table 1. Now think about where the money comes from to pay for inventory which is not sold. It must come from cash injected into the business by the owners or by creditors. That is, the only sources of cash are sales of inventory, or loans and investments by owners. If cash is not available from one of those sources, then one of the others must be used to provide the cash. If there is no more cash available from owners and if the business is unable to borrow any more money, then it will find itself unable to meet the payment obligations on payables, loans and expenses. This is what is meant when people refer to *cash flow problems*. Such problems can destroy a business!

The issue for inventory management becomes balancing the need to stock inventory against the cash which will be available to pay for it. The best approach is to establish a budget for inventory and stick to that budget. In the budgeting chapter, we talked about inventory budgets and tying them to sales forecasts. The first step is to calculate the inventory turnover rate. This is the ratio of cost of goods sold to inventory on hand. You can calculate the number for your business by dividing cost of goods sold by average inventory

$$(\text{Cost of Goods Sold}/[(\text{Beginning Inventory} + \text{Ending Inventory})/2]$$

If the business does not have enough history for a calculation, the industry average for inventory turns can be used. The second step is the calculation of the cost of goods sold ratio. You can calculate this number by dividing cost of goods sold by sales (Cost of Goods/Sales). Again, an industry average can be used if the business has no history. Next, you must forecast sales, month by month, for the period of the budget; normally one year. Armed with this information, the preparation of an inventory budget is simplistic. Consider the example on the following page.

The budget for inventory investment level can be used to determine the amount of inventory to be purchased, as we will discuss in the following sections, but the budget is for the total dollar amount to be invested in inventory. It takes considerable work and know how to convert that information into quantities of the specific components of inventory. It would be simple if you carried a single product, because you would simply have to divide the budgeted amount by selling price. Few companies carry a single product. In the early days of the business, you will probably have to rely heavily on advice from your suppliers and vendors. Proper record keeping on sales experience will provide you with much better insight into the problem. Be sure to always subject the recommendations of suppliers to a healthy dose of common sense. Grits just do not sell as well in Michigan as they do in Georgia! If you deal with established, reputable suppliers, then chances are that the advice they give you will be sound. Such suppliers will be interested in obtaining your business over the long term rather than for a single sale. Nevertheless, you should begin keeping records immediately so that you will be able to evaluate your inventory makeup without help from suppliers. That will be necessary, because the needs of every business are different. Your supplier cannot be expected to keep track of your individual inventory movement history. You must do that for yourself. We will talk about inventory record keeping procedures later on in this chapter.

Example of Ending Inventory Budget

Sales Forecast:	January	$5,000	Desired Inventory Turnover	8.0
	February	4,000	Cost of Goods Sold	65%
	March	3,500		
	April	5,000		

Cost of Goods for:	January	$3,250	($5,000 X .65)
	February	2,600	($4,000 X .65)
	March	2,275	($3,500 X .65)
	April	3,250	($5,000 X .65)

Months in the Year/Inventory Turnover = 12 months / 8.0 = 1.5 months
Desired Inventory at any point in time is the next 1.5 months of Cost of Goods Sold

Inventory needed at December 31:	January Cost of Goods	$3,250
	½ of February Cost of Goods	1,300
	Total Inventory at December 31	$4,550
Inventory Needed at January 31:	February Cost of Goods	$2,600
	½ of March Cost of Goods	1,138
	Total Inventory at January 31	$3,738
Inventory Needed at February 28:	March Cost of Goods	$2,275
	½ of April Cost of Goods	1,625
	Total Inventory at February 28	$3,900

The final topic we need to address in this section is desired minimum stock level. In order to facilitate purchasing and protect yourself from stock outs, you will need to establish a minimum number of items to be held in inventory for each component of inventory. This number is a function of demand for the item and lead time or shipping time for the item. We will talk about setting the desired stock level in more detail in the section for economic ordering quantities.

PURCHASING

Once you have established the inventory budget, you must purchase the items necessary to maintain the budgeted levels. Determining the dollar amount of such purchases is simple. It requires that you remember the formula for calculating the cost of goods sold.

	Beginning Inventory
+	Purchases
	Cost of Goods Available for Sale
-	Ending Inventory
	Cost of Goods Sold

If we leave out the intermediary step, the formula is simply Beginning Inventory + Purchases - Ending Inventory = Cost of Goods Sold, or $BI + P - EI = CofG$. Using the data from the last example, we can calculate the amount of inventory which must be purchased during January:

Example of Purchases Budget

Sales Forecast:	January	$5,000	Desired Inventory Turnover	8.0
	February	4,000	Cost of Goods Sold	65%
Cost of Goods for:	January	$3,250	($5,000 X .65)	
	February	2,600	($4,000 X .65)	

Inventory needed at December 31:	$4,550
Inventory Needed at January 31:	$3,738

Beginning Inventory (December 31)	$4,550
+ Purchases	?
- Ending Inventory (January 31)	$3,738
Cost of Goods Sold for January	$3,250

Solving for Purchases: $BI + P - EI = CofG$

$P = CofG + EI - BI$

Cost of Goods Sold for January	$3,250
+ Ending Inventory (January 31)	$3,738
- Beginning Inventory (December 31)	$4,550
Purchases Budget for January	$2,438

Cost of Goods Sold for February	$2,600
+ Ending Inventory (February 28)	$3,900
- Beginning Inventory (January 31)	$3,738
Purchases Budget for February	$2,762

As in the case of the establishment of the inventory budget, the purchases budget is an indication of total dollars which can be used to acquire merchandise, but does not tell you how much of each item in inventory to buy. That information must come from your record keeping on inventory movement. Nevertheless, the process yields a budget for inventory purchases which can be an invaluable aid to preventing cash flow problems from developing. Of course, the budget must be adjusted each month as the sales forecast is adjusted. Each month you should compare the forecast to actual results, adjust the remaining months of the forecast and add another month to the end. Many managers have found automated spread sheets like Quattro, Excel, Lotus, or any one of dozens of other fine programs to be a valuable aid to inventory and purchases budgeting as well as other types of budgeting. We will have more to say on this topic in a later section in the text.

PURCHASE DISCOUNTS

When merchandise is purchased from a supplier, a discount for prompt payment is often extended. These discounts can represent major savings opportunities. ***Trade credit*** is one of the most frequently used forms of credit in business. The amounts extended each year by suppliers to their purchasers in the form of accounts payable easily exceed the total amounts borrowed from banks. Consequently, it is important for the long term viability of a small business to maintain a healthy credit rating from suppliers. If a small business develops a reputation for slow payment on trade accounts, it can find itself with a highly limited number of suppliers willing to deal with it and/or saddled with cash on delivery terms for its inventory. Neither of these is a desirable outcome, consequently every small business should make it a practice to always pay accounts payable within the terms granted by the supplier.

Supplier terms are quoted with the percentage of any discount available and its time limit first and the ultimate due date quoted last. For example, 2/10 net 30, a common trade credit term, means that a 2% discount is available for payment made within 10 days of the bill with the balance due in 30 days at the latest. Other terms could be 2/10, 1/20 net 60, which means a 2% discount is available for payment in 10 days, a 1% discount for payment in 20 days, but the balance is due no later than 60 days. If terms are quoted net 30 or net 60, that means that no discounts are offered and the balance is due in 30 or 60 days.

As we discussed above, failure to pay within the net period can damage the credit standing of the firm. With that in mind, if a firm fails to take advantage of a purchase discount, the cost could be extreme. Consider terms of 2/10 net 30. If you fail to pay within 10 days, then you will lose a 2% discount. Since you only gain a 20 day grace period (30 - 10), the effect is that you are paying 2% interest for a 20 day loan. We can convert that to annual interest rates so that we can compare it to bank loan rates by examining how many 20 day periods there are in a year. If we use 360 days for a year to make it simple, then there are 18 periods (360/20 = 18). Consequently, the annual interest rate is 18 X 2%, or 36%! That's a high cost! If the terms were 1/10 net 60, then we would be paying 1% interest for a loan of 50 days duration (60 - 10). The annual equivalent rate would be 7.2% (360/50 = 7.2; 7.2 X 1% = 7.2%). That's not a bad borrowing rate! The process of converting discount terms into annual interest rates is always the same: find the grace period which is built into the terms; divide that into 360 days; and multiply the result by the discount percentage. The formula looks like this:

Annual Interest Rate of Discount Failure = Discount Rate X (360/Days in the Grace Period)

You need to keep the discount in mind and always calculate its true cost in annual terms so that you will know the real cost. In some situations, it could pay to arrange a bank line of credit to permit discounts to be taken on trade credit.

INVENTORY ACCOUNTING

There are three basic methods which can be used for inventory accounting: the *specific identification*, *periodic* and *perpetual* methods. As the words imply, the *periodic method* involves counting the inventory at various points in time while the *perpetual method* involves keeping a running tally of inventory. *Specific identification* means recognizing each individual item in inventory and is only suitable for firms with a small number of inventory items. For many years, the periodic method was far and away the dominant procedure in small businesses because of the difficulty of keeping track of every inventory transaction. Recently, the reduced cost of microcomputers and inventory control systems have been changing that, but the periodic system is still popular with many small businesses because of its ease of use.

The inventory shrinkage problem can be severe for small firms. If a business depends heavily on part time and/or high turn over employees, carelessness, theft, sweetheart sales, etc. can be a real problem. *Sweetheart sales*, for example, occur when a cashier rings a price on an item for a friend which is less than the actual price or fails to ring the item up at all! The amount of inventory shrinkage cannot be determined without a physical count. Even then, it may be difficult if a firm has not kept good records. Any time the gross profit margin seems to be shrinking unduly and there are no sales or markdowns to justify it, shrinkage may be the culprit.

PHYSICAL INVENTORY

Regardless of which accounting method is used, the inventory must be subjected to a physical count at least once each year. This process is called a *physical inventory*. Tax rules require at least one physical count per year or some businesses might never count their goods. The tax requirement is not the basis for the need for a physical inventory. Inventory is subject to loss, damage, spoilage, theft, and a wide range of such problems which make it necessary to examine everything in inventory periodically to determine how much *shrinkage* has taken place. The inventory records must then be reconciled against the results of the count. The extension or pricing of the items occurring in the count can be handled under several different methods.

Anyone who has worked for a retailer or wholesaler is familiar with the physical inventory and can tell stories about the problems involved in such a count. In recent years, equipment has been developed which makes the process a bit easier. Chief among these is a portable device which permits the inventory identification number to be keyed in and stores a running count of the items for each number. The device can then transfer the data to a microcomputer to allow a physical inventory report to be produced. Even with such devices, the physical inventory remains a major problem.

Most people view the physical inventory as being a time when everything else is shut down and everyone pitches in to count. Actually, the requirement for a physical inventory can be accomplished piecemeal. That is, one department or division or category of inventory can be counted at one time and other categories counted at another time. One good approach is to schedule a physical inventory for the end of every month with a portion of the inventory to be counted each month so that all will have been counted by year end. Exactly where and what is to be counted should be kept secret until the count starts to prevent employees from tampering with the merchandise. By the same token, a surprise inventory taken periodically is a good device to discourage employee pilfering or to uncover the source of problems which a division, department or area is having.

When a physical inventory is conducted, the people making the count should not have access to records which indicate how many items are supposed to be on hand. The theory is the same as underlies the use of a blind copy of the purchase order for the receiving department to use in verifying the quantities of merchandise received. Not only does having a quantity available for an item make it possible for an employee not to count that item or to hide a shortage in that item, it can create errors in the count itself. Consider, if an employee is asked to count a shelf which is supposed to contain 152 cans of black eyed peas, the probability is much greater that the employee will come out with 152 cans. It is just human nature! A distraction during the count, a momentary mental lapse in concentration can easily be reconciled by comparing the results of the count to the number which is supposed to be there. Now, if the employee has no idea how many cans of black eyed peas are supposed to be on the shelf, then the chances are much greater that the employee will take care to make an accurate count. The reasoning is straightforward. If I am asked to count the peas, I know that my count will be compared to the records. If my count does not agree with the record when it is compared later on, I might be asked to recount the peas!

GOODS IN TRANSIT

One thing which frequently gives people a problem in the physical inventory process is the handling of items which are in shipment. Both items which have been purchased, but not yet received, and items which have been sold, but not yet delivered present a problem. The issue is, should these items be included in the inventory count or not? The resolution is based on the shipping methodology. If items are shipped ***FOB destination***, then the purchaser does not own the items until they arrive at their destination. ***FOB*** is an old term which dates to the days when everything was shipped by water and stands for Free on Board. If items are shipped ***FOB shipping point***, then the purchaser owns the items as soon as they leave the seller's place of business. It is an important distinction because the risk of loss goes with ownership. Whoever owns the items while they are in transit assumes the risk of loss and must ensure that adequate insurance coverage has been arranged. When we take a physical inventory, we must include all items which we own. Therefore, if we have sold any items under *FOB destination* terms those items should be included in our count unless they have been received by the buyer. If we have purchased any items *FOB shipping point*, then those items should be included in our count even if we have not received them.

SPECIFIC IDENTIFICATION

As we mentioned above, specific inventory accounting is a method which is used by firms with a small number of inventory items. It is used by automobile dealers, mobile home dealers, heavy equipment dealers, recreational vehicle dealers and similar firms. If the relative cost of each item of inventory is high, then specific identification is the best method to use in determining profits.

Under specific identification, each item in inventory has a separate record which will show the date acquired, amount of cost and any other pertinent information. Each car on a car dealer's lot has a file which contains that information. The cost of the item and the pricing policy of the firm is used to set a price for the item. In industries which use specific accounting, it is common for bargaining to take place on sales, consequently, the actual price accepted for an item is frequently not the original price. You can see why it is crucial in such a business to know what the real cost of the item under negotiation is so that it won't be sold at a loss. Also, profit margins vary item by item because of the bargaining. That means that the cost and price of the individual units sold must be accumulated in order to prepare a financial income and expense statement for the firm.

Some types of businesses mix specific identification with the other inventory accounting methods. For example, a jewelry store will probably want to keep separate records on diamond or other expensive pieces, but will not need such detail on the lower priced costume jewelry items. ***Specific identification*** is a good choice for accounting for any inventory item which is costly relative to the rest of the items in inventory, or which is unique or requires special handling or marketing such as price bargaining.

PERIODIC INVENTORY ACCOUNTING

In periodic inventory accounting, records relating to purchases and sales of inventory are not kept on a unit basis. The dollar values of the transactions are stored in general ledger accounts which are reconciled against the physical count of inventory on hand periodically. Frequently, this reconciliation is conducted annually as part of the fiscal year end process of completing the company's tax return. Quite frequently the reconciliation is strictly financial with no effort made to reconcile quantities at all. The accounting is simplistic but a major disadvantage occurs in that you can never know what the true situation of your inventory is until you count it. Interim financial statements at month ends and quarter ends must be prepared using an estimate of inventory costs. These can be, and frequently are, quite wide of the mark!

Purchasing decisions under a periodic inventory system are made using the **eyeball** or **bin** system. What that means is that the manager must periodically examine the inventory on display and/or in the warehouse. When the quantities look too low or the bins look too empty, more items are purchased. A more sophisticated approach is to establish a minimum stock level desired for each item in inventory. This information is either recorded for reference by the manager when considering purchases, or posted on the shelves or bins where the inventory is kept. Frequently, the postings will be coded and located unobtrusively so as to prevent customers from noticing the information. Under the minimum stock level approach, the manager examines the inventory every day and reorders those items which have dropped below the desired stock level. Does this sound simple? The process is simplistic, but in practice it can be quite time consuming, laborious and filled with error. Consider *eyeballing* 15,000 different items of inventory! The major problem with the process is the absence of any information which will aid in adjusting the established minimum stock levels. The manager can and will change stock minimums if he or she becomes aware that the minimum is too low because frequent stock outs occur. That process leaves much to be desired! Worse, the manager will seldom have occasion to notice when the minimum stock levels are too high, because that is not the kind of information which becomes available without deliberately searching for it. Consequently, the inventory will frequently consist of too much of the slower moving items and too little of the rapidly moving items and will be slow to change as the demand for the various items changes.

GROSS PROFIT METHOD

One of the popular techniques for estimating the inventory is called the **gross profit method**. It requires an historic estimate for gross profit ratios. Consider an example using the gross profit method. The general ledger account for inventory will start the year off with the correct value of inventory at last year end because a physical count had to be performed. The general ledger account for purchases and for sales will start the year off with a zero balance, as do all revenue and expense accounts. The total dollar value of all purchases during the year will be debited to the purchases account (the credit will go to accounts payable or cash). Let's assume that the year end is December 31, as is normal for most small firms. In the following example, the information is taken from the records for purchases and sales.

Example of the Gross Profit Method for Estimating Ending Inventory

	Inventory	Purchases	Sales	Historic Gross Profit Margin
January 1	$5,000	$ 0	$ 0	40%

Purchases:			Sales:	
January 5	$ 250		January 3	$ 750
January 9	325		January 10	1,200
January 15	475		January 17	925
January 21	150		January 24	575
January 30	300		January 31	550
Totals for the month	$1,500			$4,000

To estimate the financial results for January:

Sales		$4,000	100%
Cost of Sales			
Beginning Inventory	$5,000		
+ Purchases	1,500		
Cost of Merchandise Available	$6,500		
- Ending Inventory	?		
Cost of Goods Sold		$2,400	60%
Gross Profit		$1,600	40%

Ending Inventory must be $6,500 - $2,400 = $4,100

Sales		$4,000	100%
Cost of Sales			
Beginning Inventory	$5,000		
+ Purchases	1,500		
Cost of Merchandise Available	$6,500		
- Ending Inventory	4,100		
Cost of Goods Sold		$2,400	60%
Gross Profit		$1,600	40%

As you can see from the example, the gross profit method simply involves calculating gross profit as a percentage of sales using an historic average, then backing into calculations for cost of goods sold and ending inventory. The accuracy of the method depends on the accuracy of the average gross profit ratio. If a firm has few price changes during the year either in inventory purchases or in sales prices and has few inventory items lost through theft, breakage or spoilage, then the gross profit method will be close to the actual results. Unfortunately, few companies have such a stable situation. A more involved, but more accurate estimation device for use when prices and costs vary is called the retail method.

RETAIL METHOD

The ***retail method*** requires the purchases to be captured both in terms of cost and in terms of retail sales value. In addition, price markups which will occur when sales prices are increased for any reason must be captured as must price markdowns which occur for sales, etc. If either price markups or markdowns are canceled during the month, the amount of cancellations is also required. It sounds complex, but it is really just more record keeping. With a computer system, it is not all that difficult. When the debit is made to the purchases account, the bookkeeping clerk must calculate the retail sales value of the merchandise which has been purchased. That's not hard because the clerk will know what the markup policy of the store is for each item purchased and will know what the items purchased were. For example, if the store marks up everything 50%, then the retail value of purchases will simply be 50% more than cost. If markups vary by type of merchandise, which is more often the case, then it is a little more work, but still simply a process of calculating sales price item by item. Someone must do this anyway in order to put price tags on the merchandise!

The rest of the accounting revolves around markups and markdowns. Say the store decides to put a section of merchandise on sale. Then as new price tags are placed on the merchandise, someone must keep track of the total amount of reduction in sales prices which has occurred. Think about carrying a calculator with you while changing the price stickers on the merchandise. Every time you mark an item down, add up the amount of the price reduction. If you cancel any of the markdowns, for example on any items left over after the sale, just add up the price increases as you put the old price stickers back in place. If you had a general price increase store wide, you would add up the additional price increases for each item as new price stickers were affixed. If any of those markups were later canceled, you would just add up the amounts of price reductions. At the end of the month, you will have a total for inventory purchases at cost and at retail, a total for price markups and markup cancellations, a total for price markdowns and markdown cancellations, and, of course, the amount of sales.

You can find the net markups by subtracting markup cancellations from markups and the net markdowns by subtracting markdown cancellations from markdowns. You will also have the ending inventory value for last month both at cost and at retail. That will become the beginning inventory value for this month. To find the ending inventory value at retail is a straightforward reduction of the retail value of merchandise available for sale from the sales. Converting that to a cost basis is accomplished using the ratio of inventory available for sale at cost to retail. An example will make the process easier to see. Walk through the following numbers carefully and the calculations will make more sense.

Example of the Retail Method of Estimating Ending Inventory

	At Cost	At Retail
Beginning Inventory	$5,000	$12,600
+ Purchases	7,500	10,575
+ Net Markups	---	425
Merchandise Available for Sale	$12,500	$23,600
Sales	$9,950	
- Net Markdowns	450	
Net Sales	$9,500	

Ending Inventory at Retail must be:

Merchandise Available for Sale at Retail	$23,600
- Net Sales	9,500
Ending Inventory at Retail	$14,100

To Convert to Cost Basis:

Merchandise Available for Sale at Cost	$12,500
Merchandise Available for Sale at Retail	23,600
Cost/Retail Ratio = $12,500/$23,600 = 53%	
Ending Inventory at Retail	$14,100
Ending Inventory at Cost (53% of $14,100)	$ 7,473

Now we can complete the income statement:

Sales		$9,500
Cost of Sales		
Beginning Inventory	$ 5,000	
+ Purchases	7,500	
Cost of Merchandise Available	$12,500	
- Ending Inventory	7,473	
Cost of Goods Sold		$5,027
Gross Profit		$4,473

The retail method yields a more accurate estimate of the value of ending inventory, but it is still only an estimate. As in the case of the gross profit method, we cannot know what the results of operations really are until a physical count is taken and the value of the inventory is extended.

PERPETUAL INVENTORY ACCOUNTING

In *perpetual inventory accounting*, a continuous running count of every item in inventory is maintained. If a manual system is used, a ledger card will be created for each item in inventory. As new items are purchased, the date, purchase price and number of units will be recorded on the ledger card for each item purchased. As the items are received, the total number on hand is increased. As items are sold, the date and number of items sold are posted on the ledger card for each item sold and the total number on hand is decreased. As you can see, a manual system will only work if the number of inventory items is not too large. It is not uncommon for an auto parts house to carry 25,000 different items of inventory. A small hardware store can easily have 15,000 items in inventory. Manual systems just don't work with that many items! Fortunately, low cost microcomputer systems are available which will perform the same function with no work beyond the normal requirement to count and record inventory receipts and to ring up on a cash register individual items sold.

Perpetual accounting does not eliminate the need for a physical inventory. Items must still be counted in order to determine inventory shrinkage, but under perpetual accounting, we can have a number for comparison to a count which can help to identify and pinpoint problems. If, for example, we post broken, damaged and spoiled items to the system as they are removed from inventory, then the only source of shortages which should remain are errors in receiving, errors in selling and theft, either by employees or by customers. If shortages are severe, then you have an idea where to focus efforts on correcting the problem. If any of the areas are less likely than others due to control procedures, then the source of shrinkage can be pinpointed. This can be a significant advantage in inventory management over the periodic method.

Reordering information is available from the inventory records under perpetual accounting. The records will not only permit minimum stock levels to be pinpointed as they are reached item by item, but the records can show items that have already been ordered but not yet received. This can prevent duplicate ordering. Perhaps the greatest contribution to inventory purchasing which can accrue to a perpetual system is the ability to adjust minimum stock levels based on experience. The inventory records not only show the quantities on hand and on order at any given point in time, but they show inventory transactions item by item. As the volume of demand for an item increases, the transactions for that item will reflect that change and the stock levels can be increased. As the volume of demand for an item decreases, the transactions for that item will reflect that change as well so that the stock minimum can be decreased or the item eliminated from inventory completely. The transactions records can aid in determining which items would best benefit from sales or promotional pricing and marketing schemes. With a little imagination, there is almost no limit to the information available from perpetual inventory records! From cross selling opportunities to effectiveness of sales and marketing campaigns; from the impact of commission levels to the effect of store display locations; from the relative value of individual sales people to the identification of target markets; all that and more can be determined from a good perpetual inventory accounting system. With the advent of affordable, automated inventory systems, we wonder why periodic accounting continues to exist!

ECONOMIC ORDERING QUANTITY

One of the most talked about aspects of inventory management is the determination of the most economic quantity of inventory which can be ordered. Called the *EOQ*, the number is a function of the costs of placing inventory orders, the costs of holding items in inventory and the demand for inventory. In essence, the *EOQ* model seeks to find an optimum relationship between all of these factors. Table 2 displays a graph of costs.

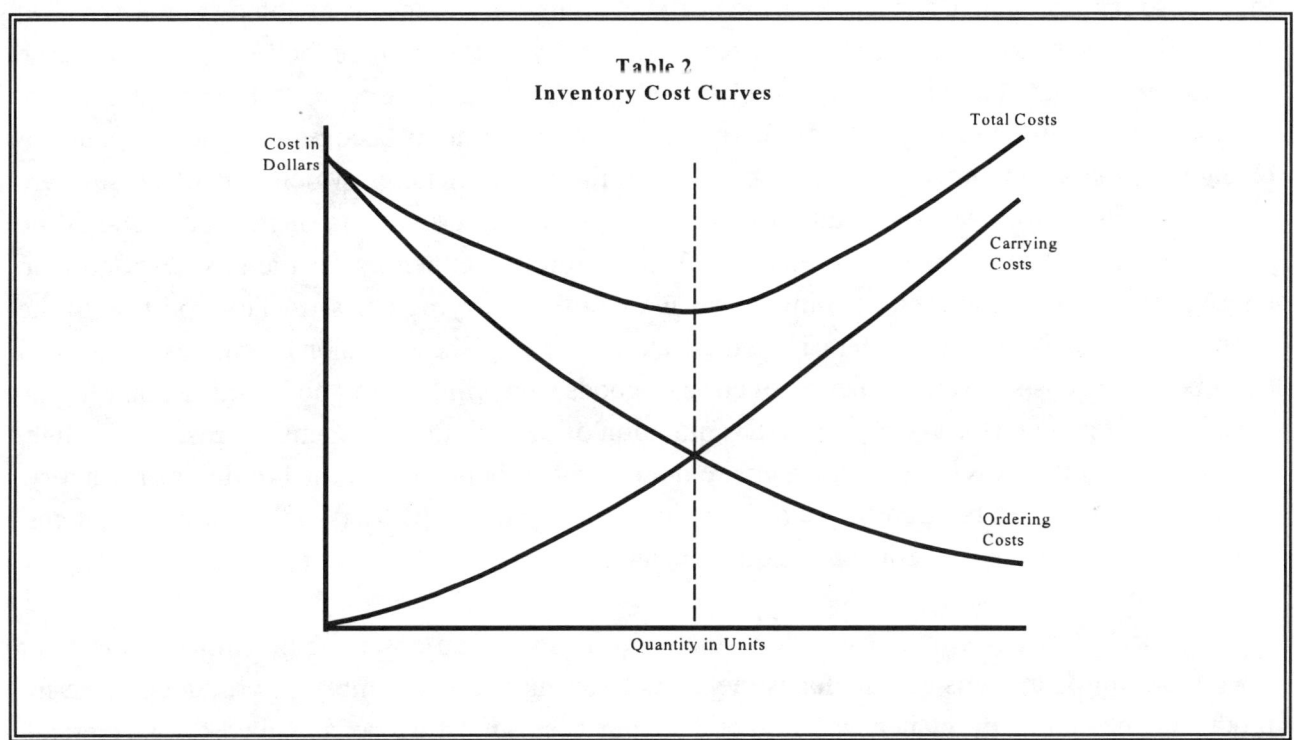

Table 2
Inventory Cost Curves

Notice that the total cost curve is simply the result of adding the numbers on the other two cost curves together. That means that the low point on the total cost curve will occur at the intersection of the other two curves. Finding where this point is in terms of the number of units for an item of inventory is what *EOQ* is all about.

In order to be able to calculate an *EOQ* for your business, you must accumulate data to be able to predict demand for an item. The sales forecasts which we have talked about preparing must be converted to sales in numbers of units. You will need the forecast for every item for which you intend to calculate an *EOQ*. Not every item in inventory will require an *EOQ* because many of them will move very slowly. You will probably find that 20% or less of the items you stock will account for 80% or more of your sales volume. *EOQs* for those items can reduce costs significantly. The remaining items should also have *EOQs*, of course, but are not as critical and the calculations can therefore be postponed. Generally, *EOQs* are calculated for a year at a time, although shorter periods are possible. The demand figures should be for the period you intend to use. If that is to be a year, then the demand should be for one year. We will assume that all numbers are for one year. If you have forecast sales, then cost of goods sold can be forecast as a percentage of sales and the number of items to be sold can be found by dividing the cost of goods sold by the expected unit price.

Carrying costs must also be calculated per unit. **Carrying costs** are the expenses which inventory creates. These costs can be difficult to calculate, especially on a per unit basis because they are so far reaching. Carrying costs include such things as storage costs, interest on loans used to purchase inventory, insurance costs, taxes on inventory and on storage facilities, rental or lease costs for warehouses, and inventory shrinkage whether from loss, damage, theft or other sources. Obsolescence could be a major cost of carrying inventory. If items become worthless because of changes in markets, competition or demand, then the value of items which cannot be sold are carrying costs as well. In short, all costs associated with the possession of inventory should be captured. It may be simpler for a small business to forecast expenses for the business and then aggregate all those which relate to inventory and call that carrying costs. A large portion of the expenses of a retailer or wholesaler can be traced to inventory. The exclusion of salaries, wages and other personnel costs, and the omission of costs of goods sold will leave a good starting point for the calculation of inventory carrying costs. Examination of the remaining expense items, line by line, should permit you to exclude costs which are not clearly associated with the holding of inventory. What remains can then be apportioned over the inventory items on the basis of the numbers of items, dollar value of items, or bulk or space requirements for items. What we want is an average carrying cost for each item in inventory.

The last cost we must estimate is the cost of placing an order for inventory items. For manufacturing firms, this cost includes the cost of setting up an assembly or production line for producing the item. For retailers and wholesalers, this cost is mostly a personnel cost. The clerical, accounting and managerial time spent in preparing and processing a purchase order is the major component. These costs can be difficult to estimate as well. A good approach is to track the preparation of several purchase orders for various items and allocate costs based on the results. For example, tracing the preparation of a purchase order might show one hour of clerical time, one hour of accounting time, and a half-hour of managerial time. Don't forget to include the time involved in receiving and paying the purchase order as well as its preparation. Once the time has been estimated, you can assign costs based on average wage rates for the people involved. The resulting number should have a percentage added for the costs of paper, postage, computer time, and employee fringe benefits as well as a factor for those things which you forgot to capture. An average of the costs involved in several orders should yield a fair approximation of the ordering costs.

The *EOQ* can now be determined. We will use the cost and demand estimates with the following formula which has been derived mathematically from the cost curves relationships depicted in Table 2.

Formula for Calculating Economic Ordering Quantity

Economic Ordering Quantity = Square Root[(2 X Demand X Ordering Cost)/Carrying Cost]

$$EOQ = \text{Square Root}(\ 2\ D\ O\ /\ C\ )$$

D = Demand for the item for the entire period

C = Carrying cost for one unit for the entire period

O = Costs of placing and processing one order

The use of the formula just involves plugging in the numbers:

Assume:	D = 5,000 units per year
	C = $1.50 per unit per year
	O = $10.00 per order

Then:	EOQ	=	Square Root(2 D O / C)
		=	Square Root{(2 X 5,000 X $10.00)/$1.50}
		=	258 units

Once the *EOQ* has been calculated, it indicates the optimum number of units to be purchased in each order. Notice that the *EOQ* must be calculated for each item in inventory because the demand will vary for each item. The order and carrying costs can be calculated for the inventory as a whole. Any error which results from that will be minimal because the dominant number in the calculation is the demand for the unit.

DESIRED STOCK LEVELS

To put the *EOQ* into operation, as the desired minimum stock level for an item is reached, a purchase order should be prepared for the *EOQ* for that item. We talked about stock levels in an earlier section of the chapter, but we delayed the specifics until now. The actual numeric stock level which is decided for each item in inventory can be derived from the predicted demand for that item and the length of time it takes to get resupply. In the example above, there was an annual demand of 5,000 units. If it takes 10 days to receive merchandise after it has been ordered, then you could never let your stock drop below a ten day supply. If the demand for the item were uniform throughout the year, we could find a number for that 10 day supply by simply taking the annual demand, dividing by 360 days and multiplying by 10 days. That would be 139 units (5,000/360 = 13.9 units per day; 13.9 X 10 days = 139 units). Of course, the demand for the item will not be uniform; almost everything has seasonal variations. Nevertheless, 139 units is probably a good starting point for choosing a safety stock level. We can adjust that as we gain experience from our record keeping activities. We could choose simply to adjust the number during the peak sales season each year by increasing it. If one month of the year represents twice as much sales volume as the others, then we could double the safety stock number. Of course, if we had months which had only half the normal sales volume, we could cut the safety stock level in half. *Safety stock levels* or desired inventory levels do not have to remain constant all year long. They can, and generally should be adjusted to reflect seasonality.

The *EOQ*, in combination with a desired stock level can make inventory management simpler as well as reducing the costs associated with inventory. Both require a sales forecast for the numbers of units to be sold for each item in inventory, as well as considerable additional calculations. Nevertheless, after the calculations have been prepared one time, future calculations will be simplified, and the time spent is easily justified. Not only will dollars be saved, managerial time spent in inventory management will be reduced overall! You will find that managers who do not use *EOQs* and safety stocks spend more time on inventory because they are really drifting around in the dark!

INVENTORY CONTROL

The elements of inventory management which we have discussed so far are technical aspects of inventory control. The more general aspects are decisions concerning what we intend to stock and from whom we intend to buy it. The initial decision about the extent of inventory, both in terms of which items to stock and the number of items to stock, can be aided by advice from good suppliers. How do you find good suppliers?

SUPPLIERS

The reference librarian in the library can point you to directories of suppliers for virtually any items you can imagine. The yellow pages of the telephone book for your town or for the nearest large city can provide lists of suppliers for a surprising array of items. In order to select the actual suppliers which you want to use from the lengthy lists that such research will yield, you need to look beyond price. A telephone call to any of the suppliers will result in catalogs and price lists as well as information about payment discounts, quantity purchase discounts, freight and shipping expenses, and delivery times. All of those factors are important, of course, and your first step should be to consider the costs of purchasing and obtaining inventory. Don't overlook freight and shipping expense. The actual cost of getting inventory items in place for sales purposes is the relevant cost. Be sure to examine quantity discounts for the volume levels which you anticipate for your business initially and over the first year or two of operations. Such discounts can be a major factor in inventory costs. Lead time is also an important consideration. If the lowest cost supplier is located 2,000 miles away, not only could shipping costs make the supplier impractical, but delivery times could be so long as to make the supplier undesirable. If your business is one in which drop shipping to customers is possible, be sure to explore this with the suppliers. ***Drop shipping*** means that customer orders are shipped directly to the customer from your supplier's warehouse.

A good system for evaluating potential suppliers is to prepare a list of suppliers from the yellow pages and from library references which have acceptable price and shipping characteristics. The companies on this list should be asked to provide you with names of some of the companies with whom they deal in your industry. You should call some of their customers to determine whether they are satisfied with the supplier. Don't forget to call the Better Business Bureau in the cities in which those companies do business to see if anyone has lodged a complaint about the supplier. Pay particular attention to firms in your area and any of your direct competitors who will talk to you. This process should result in shortening your initial list somewhat.

The second phase should involve talking to sales people in the remaining companies on your list. You are going to want a lasting relationship with your suppliers so you will need to be able to get along with the sales people and the office staffs of the suppliers. Also, the willingness of the sales people to help you in getting started and during the growth of your business will be important factors. Finally, the suppliers' credit policies will be an important factor. Many firms are unwilling to extend credit to new small businesses. An enlightened credit policy will be a tremendous asset to your firm. If you can find a supplier with such a policy, consider the advantage it will provide you in terms of cash flow.

You should not try to narrow the list to a single firm. Hopefully, you will be able to find several suppliers who can meet your needs and with whom you can work. You should make purchases from all of these and keep close track of the results. Any unsatisfactory experiences should be noted. Gradually, you will probably develop a relationship with one or two suppliers which is sound and satisfactory. As time goes on, you will be approached by the sales people of new suppliers. You should remember the problems you had in start-up and consider these new firms because new entrants and competitors can well result in stronger, cheaper, more helpful suppliers. The process of finding suppliers and establishing mutually agreeable relationships with them is a never ending job. For a firm with multiple products, multiple suppliers is almost always the rule.

Constant attention and monitoring of the relationship with suppliers can be rewarded with a relationship which is invaluable. Since inventory is the source of revenue for a retailer or wholesaler, time spent on inventory supply is easily justifiable.

We need to make one more comment about suppliers. Many small firms have route suppliers call on them and replenish their inventory. The process is usually to allow the route driver to remove outdated merchandise and replenish the stock right there in the display area. This sounds like a really good deal, because the supplier does all the work! It's a fine process in general but it can present problems. You must remember that the supplier wants to sell and will inevitably have some items which sell better than others. The fast moving items are easily disposed of, while the slow moving items take more work. There is a great temptation on the part of commissioned route sales people to stock your shelves heavily with slow moving goods in the hopes that someone will buy them. You can't afford to let that happen. Too many small business owners turn the inventory restocking over entirely to route drivers. You must monitor sales for these items just like you do for any other inventory items.

INVENTORY SELECTION

Early on in the chapter, we talked about the mistake of trying to be all things to all people. No business, regardless of its size, can afford to stock items which appeal to everyone. One of the most important decisions which a retailer/wholesaler can make is the determination of the inventory items to be stocked. This decision revolves around the target market to which the company appeals. Even then, the range of items stocked would be too large if we were to try to satisfy the entire market. After a little experience in business, if you have kept good records of inventory movement, you will find that a minority of the inventory items you stock constitute the majority of your sales. The rest of the items, which may well be 80% or more of the total number of items carried, are carried as a convenience to your customers. You cannot eliminate all of these items because the goodwill of your customers is required for success. How do you make the final decision?

After a company has been in business for a while, the elimination of unprofitable inventory items is possible. A perpetual inventory accounting system will show clearly those items which are not carrying their own weight. With periodic accounting, this is more difficult, consequently, we recommend that everyone use a perpetual inventory accounting system. The owner or manager should review the inventory movement data every month. When items appear sluggish, the safety stock levels which are used for reorder should be reduced as should the *EOQs* for that item. If no complaints are received from customers and if sales performance does not suffer, then the levels of safety stock and *EOQ* can be reduced again. After several months of this kind of monitoring and adjusting, the item may be eliminated from inventory completely. This process will protect you from major shocks as it is gradual and allows you to watch for any unfavorable results. If problems begin to develop, you can easily reverse the process.

The decision about new products to stock comes from supplier recommendations, customer requests, and decisions about changes in the business or diversification plans. All of these should be approached in a reverse fashion from the elimination procedure. That means that new items should be added with small initial quantities and built to larger and larger quantities on hand as time goes by and experience warrants. As in the case of eliminations, this process will avoid major shocks to the business.

The process described above for inventory adjustment is recommended as a general approach to market changes over time. If major changes in markets, demand or competition occur, then more dramatic and more rapid adjustment may be necessary. But you should be aware that rapid change in inventory makeup carries with it significantly more risk than does a slow, regulated adjustment.

None of this answers the question of establishing inventory makeup when little or no experience exists. In such instances, the first step should be a detailed examination of the stocks of direct and indirect competitors. If possible, you should personally tour your competitors and make notes about the extent of their inventories. In addition, the advice of suppliers can be a valuable input to the decision. The tendency of most new ventures is to stock too much and too broad an array of inventory, assuming that later downward adjustment can be made. It is true that downward adjustment is easier than upward, but far too many businesses expend too much capital on inventory that does not move to be able to recover from the error. The best approach is to establish a budget for the dollar value of inventory based on expected sales and to stick to that budget. Tell your suppliers how much money you have available to spend and ask their advice as to the best way to spend it. Compare various inventories which your budget can support to those of your competitors. Make sure you stick to the budget. Customers will understand the growth and expansion of inventory in a new and growing business if you make an honest and sincere effort to respond to their needs. Don't be drawn into the all too frequent mistake of spending more than you can really afford!

THE ROLE OF COMPUTERS

How many times in this chapter have we mentioned record keeping? Certainly we have talked about it enough to give you the impression that you are going to be spending all your time keeping records on inventory. Record keeping is important. Virtually none of the procedures for inventory management which we have discussed could be accomplished without records. However, the physical job of maintaining the kind of detail you need on each item of inventory is probably beyond the capabilities of a manual system. Several times in this chapter we have talked about microcomputer based systems and the possibility that they could help you. There are many such systems available which have inventory and point of sale capabilities. If inventory is to be a significant aspect of your business, you will probably need such a system. Don't be fooled into thinking that you can buy a $200 software package which will handle your needs. You can't.

Microcomputer based systems can handle the inventory valuation, but that is of small value from a managerial perspective. You will need a system which can provide you with the kind of detail which we have discussed in the various sections of the chapter. That is, a system which can produce information like that displayed in Table 3 for each item in inventory. In addition to data of this type on a per unit basis, the system should capture purchase information which will permit the calculation of inventory values on various bases. Further, it should be able to produce reports on demand with user designed contents and be able to produce physical inventory sheets.

Table 3 is not a complete list. Rather it is suggestive of the kinds of information which could be useful from a managerial perspective. You should make a list of the kinds of information which you consider valuable before beginning the search for an automated system.

Table 3
Inventory Data Desired

Quantity on hand, on order by supplier, on back order by supplier

Suppliers, addresses, payment terms, quantity discounts offered, delivery time required

Preferred supplier, back-up supplier

Selling price, unit cost, minimum stock level, EOQ

Discounts available for various classes of customers

Quantity sold for each month for the current year and for last year

Quantity lost in inventory shrinkage by month over the last two years

Date of the last physical inventory

Location of items in storage or on display

Special considerations, i.e.,
       carried for customer convenience,
       delivered by route suppliers,
       exclusive rights,
       minimum sales requirement, etc.

Point of sale inventory systems are those which are connected to, or based on, sales registers. This is, a point of sale system is capable of updating inventory files from the sales register as a part of the sales process. These systems can also be designed to look up and display prices based on stock numbers keyed in by clerks or read by light wands. Although more expensive than other types of inventory systems, point of sale systems are extremely valuable not only from the perspective of inventory management, but as an internal control device to safeguard assets and ensure correct pricing. Don't forget that such a system creates more opportunities for theft or embezzlement, consequently, the files and the machines should be secured.

With the level of sophistication and ease of use which many of the modern microcomputer systems display, more and more small businesses are able to justify their use. For a firm whose success hinges on inventory management, automation may be the only viable method of generating adequate managerial information.

SUMMARY

Inventory consists of goods held for sale in a business. In a retail or wholesale business, inventory represents the largest single investment and the major expense, therefore its effective management will affect the success of the business.

Inventory may be displayed or warehoused. If displayed, the cost is greater because of the necessity of creating an image that enhances the product and makes it more desirable. When stored, the concern is protection not enhancement, thus the cost is less.

The cash to cash cycle is so called because cash is required to purchase inventory and its sale ultimately produces cash not only for the replacement of inventory but for payment of salaries and other operating expenses.

The issue of how much inventory to stock involves balancing the need to stock inventory to support sales against the cash which will be available to pay for it. The best approach is to establish a budget and stick to it. The budget will be in dollars rather than indicating the actual numbers of each item to purchase. Experience is a good teacher and tracking sales will help you to become more proficient in detailing the purchases.

The three basic approaches to inventory accounting are the specific identification approach and periodic or perpetual methods. Specific identification means recognizing each individual item and is generally suitable only for firms with a relatively small number of inventory items or items of a high value. The periodic method involves counting the inventory at various points in time while the perpetual method involves keeping a running tally of inventory items.

Regardless of which inventory accounting methodology is chosen, there must be a physical count once a year. It is important not only from a tax perspective but is a benefit to the business in identifying inventory shrinkage.

A problem in physical inventory is how to handle items in shipment. If the items are shipped FOB destination, then the purchaser does not own the items until they are received. If the inventory is shipped FOB shipping point, it belongs to the purchaser immediately upon leaving the seller. Ownership determines how goods should be handled in inventory counts.

The specific identification method may be used for some or all items, especially those which have great value. Inventory replacement is generally simple because small numbers of items are involved. With periodic inventory accounting, the eyeball or bin approach may be used for replacement purposes. The best approach is a minimum stock level; however, this approach could be difficult without a computer if the business handles large quantities of inventory. Perhaps the biggest contribution to inventory purchasing from a perpetual system is the ability to adjust minimum stock levels based on experience.

Since the inventory is only counted infrequently, monthly financial reports require an estimate to be made of the inventory value. One of the most popular techniques for estimating the inventory is the gross profit method. This method involves calculating gross profit as a percentage of sales, then backing into the calculation for the cost of goods sold and ending inventory. A more involved and accurate method used when prices and costs vary is the retail method. With this methodology a record for inventory at both cost and retail is required.

The economic ordering quantity is a number which is a function of the costs of placing orders, the costs of carrying items in inventory and the demand for inventory. Not every item needs to have an EOQ calculated because 20% or less of the inventory items generally account for 80% or more of the sales volume.

Desired stock levels are a result of the EOQ evaluation. Once the number of units for a specified period is determined, the desired stock level is achieved by considering the demand for the item and the lag time required for that order to be filled.

Inventory control involves all the decisions which affect inventory from the managers's perspective: what to stock and from whom to buy. Suppliers are a good source of information. Reference librarians, telephone books, and traveling sales people are possible sources for suppliers.

Microcomputer based inventory systems are available which will handle items on a perpetual basis, provide data to support physical inventories, and establish values for inventory and costs of goods sold. Point of sale systems can handle price look ups and update inventory records as items are sold.

QUESTIONS, EXERCISES AND CASES

QUESTIONS:

1. What are the several forms of inventory?

2. Why is displayed inventory more costly?

3. What is the cash to cash cycle and why is it important?

4. What are the issues involved in inventory management?

5. Why is cash flow an important concept in inventory management?

6. Why is lead time an important consideration in ordering inventory? Explain.

7. What is trade credit and how does it work?

8. What are the three basic methods for inventory accounting and when do you use each type?

9. Why should the physical count date be kept secret?

10. What role can a microcomputer system play in inventory management?

11. What are point of sale systems and what value do they have?

DEFINE THE FOLLOWING TERMS:

1. inventory
2. finished goods
3. raw materials
4. work in process
5. consignment inventory
6. cash flow
7. economic ordering quantity

EXERCISES:

1.   The most difficult task in computing the EOQ is the gathering of the values to go into the formula. The easiest task is actually calculating the value of the EOQ. Given the following data, what is the economic ordering quantity for this situation:

       Demand is expected to be 7,500 units per year
       Carrying cost for one unit for one year is $2.25
       Costs of placing and processing one order are $15.00

ACTIVITY:

1.   Find in your local area a hardware store, an auto parts store, a microcomputer sales store, a shoe shop, a dress or clothing store and a household appliance sales store. What inventory accounting and valuation methods would you expect each to use? Ask the owner/managers of each of the stores what procedures they employ to handle inventory, including physical counts. Do these stores manage inventory in the manner you would expect? Are there improvements which you could see in their inventory management? If so, what are they? Present your findings to the class.

2.   As a class project, ask various members to choose one type of wholesaler or retailer to investigate with regard to inventory management. Have the students report the results and discuss the differences and their bases.

CASE

Jeremy Blackstone was the owner of a small record shop, RAX and TRAX. It sold records, CDs, and tapes. He had been in business a bit over five years and his business was doing well. He had been busy enough in fact that he had had to hire two local high school kids to work on Friday nights and Saturdays. Things were really popping! If business continued at this rate, he thought he might expand. A new site was coming open in the mall later this year which would allow him a bigger area. With more room he could display and sell stereos and CD players and the like. He needed to make a decision soon. But if the customers were any indication, this month sales were going to go out the ceiling. Obviously the two kids he had hired had influenced all their friends to come.

When the month end closeout for June was finished, Jeremy was in a quandary. He had, as was his habit at this time of year, conducted his semiannual physical inventory. At other times during the year he estimated inventory using the gross profit method. Now that he had a count, something was wrong. His gross profit margin was down significantly from its established level. Sales were up, but his profits were actually flat despite that rise! He had been experiencing a gross margin of about 30% except when he held a sale. There hadn't really been a sale since last Christmas and he didn't remember making very many markdowns. Surely, he thought, there must be some mistake.

1. What did the physical inventory tell Jeremy?
2. What is a possible explanation for the declining gross profit margin?
3. What calculations can he perform to determine the possible problem?
4. If "sweetheart" sales are taking place, how could they happen?
5. What precautions could Jeremy take to both discover the problem and prevent it from recurring?
6. If Jeremy were to institute a Point of Sale computer system, could sweetheart sales still occur? How?

CHAPTER NINETEEN

ACCOUNTS RECEIVABLE MANAGEMENT

CHAPTER OBJECTIVES

Upon completion of this chapter, you should be able to:

- Explain the importance of credit;
- Distinguish between the alternatives in credit sales;
- List three different kinds of accounts which can be used to support credit sales and when each is used;
- Explain how the credit decision is evaluated;
- Describe the four Cs of credit and how they affect the credit decision;
- Explain what information is captured on a credit history;
- Distinguish between the extension of credit to individuals and businesses;
- Discuss how to manage credit and delinquency;
- Describe the methods for accounting for bad debts; and,
- Explain the methodology of collections for bad debts.

ACCOUNTS RECEIVABLE MANAGEMENT

INTRODUCTION

All business is based on trust. No where is this more evident than in the practice of extending credit to the purchasers of goods and services. *Credit* is reversed savings. It permits people to acquire and enjoy things while they save the money to pay for them. In the absence of credit, we would have to save first, accumulate the cash necessary to purchase the items we desire, then buy them. Credit lets us buy first and pay later. Emerson said, *Trust men and they will be true to you; Trust them greatly and they will show themselves great.* The experience of most businesses indicates that he was right. The vast majority of people retire their debts promptly and properly. This has been the case since credit was invented.

Some say that the first evidence of credit was the purchase of seeds to be repaid out of the harvest by Chinese farmers 4,000 years ago. Clearly credit was well established by the time of the Phoenicians and had become a prime fact of business life by the time of the American Revolution. Originally, this credit was reserved for use between businesses. But, by the middle of the 1800s, credit began to change the lives of consumers. The Singer Company's well known entry into consumer installment sales made it clear that business had changed for good. By the turn of the century, consumer credit was well established. In modern times the use of credit has become so widespread that the use of cash is the exception rather than the norm. In many industries virtually all sales are made on credit while the use of credit cards is making inroads into the traditionally cash oriented industries of food service and consumables.

The growth of credit has brought special problems especially for small businesses who are more dependent on their cash flows for survival. Despite Mr. Emerson's encouraging words about trust, we know that some people will not pay their debts while others will experience difficulty in paying them. It is true that these people constitute a minority, but for a small business with limited capital, a loss of only a small percentage of credit accounts can be devastating. In this chapter we will address the effective management of the credit granting and collecting process. We will examine the hows and whys of credit extension as well as monitoring and collection of those credits.

ACCOUNTS RECEIVABLE

Accounts receivable mean trade credit or extended payment terms for goods and services purchased from a vendor. Increasingly people use the term to describe sales on credit. There is a major difference between trade credit and other types of sales on credit. That difference is in the supporting documentation.

Trade credit is generally supported solely by a purchase order or invoice. This is the most prevalent type of credit between businesses. Credit extended to consumers is not generally trade credit. Other types of credit sales have a note or contract of sale which specifies the payment terms, amounts, etc. This practice is more common when extending credit to consumers. A *note* is simply a document which recognizes a specific debt and repayment obligations. This can make a difference if an account *goes bad*. In the event of a bankruptcy, trade creditors will be treated as general unsecured creditors. That is not a desirable position as it is one in which losses generally occur. Credit evidenced by notes can receive more favorable positioning and may even be permitted a lien on assets. *Lien* simply means that a particular asset is pledged to secure a loan. In the event of nonpayment, the asset can be repossessed. Secured creditors are generally in a stronger position in a bankruptcy situation.

Frequently, industry practices make it impossible to avoid trade credit if you wish to be competitive. If a major purchase is being made, or a large item is being sold, then you should make every effort to handle such sales under contract. In all probability you will be unable to completely avoid trade credit. Consequently, at the first sign of delinquency on trade accounts, every effort should be made to convert the debt to one evidenced by a note and secured if possible. This is no guarantee of a stronger position because bankruptcy courts can set aside contracts which occur within 120 days of a bankruptcy under certain conditions. Nevertheless, an obligation spelled out by contract always puts the creditor in a stronger position.

CREDIT SALES ALTERNATIVES

No one would sell on credit if it were possible to avoid it because of the problems and risks involved. However, general business practices in most industries make sales on credit mandatory in order to be competitive. Credit cards are one alternative to credit sales but are not available to every industry. Other devices used to avoid problems with credit sales include financing through outside firms and factoring of accounts.

CREDIT CARDS

Many firms accept credit cards as a substitute for carrying their own accounts and in many industries this is an acceptable alternative. The advantage to *credit card sales* is that the risk of loss can be greatly reduced and the speed of collection can be greatly increased. If you follow proper procedures for credit card acceptance, checking stolen and lost card lists, requiring identification, and calling for authorization on larger purchases, then the risk of loss is dramatically reduced. Lists of stolen and lost card numbers is regularly provided by credit card firms and can even be obtained in machine readable format for use in a computerized checking scheme. The major credit card firms maintain 24 hour telephone service for use in authorizing purchases. A call to the proper center will result in an authorization code number which guarantees that the store will collect its money when the charge is received by the company. For firms with a low volume, these calls can be made by telephone. For larger volumes, electronic card readers are available which will automatically validate the purchase. With proper procedures, losses on credit card purchases can be lower than losses on bad checks. Of course, all this costs money and the main disadvantage of credit card sales is that the card sponsors charge a fee for handling the transaction.

Credit card fees vary from 1% to 7% of the sales amount and are generally based on the volume of transactions which a firm generates. Small firms can never qualify for the volume discounts because of their size and so can generally expect to pay 4% to 5% fees. Since the fee comes off the top and is simply withheld from the amount of the purchase by the card sponsor, that is a direct reduction in the contribution margin. If the margin was 50% before the credit card charge, a 5% fee would make the margin 45%. We discussed the impact of a change in the contribution margin in the chapter on breakeven analysis. It can be devastating! Some firms, especially gasoline stations which have a large volume of credit card sales, have recently begun to offer discounts for cash purchases. Consumer reaction to such discounts has been mixed, but the incentive for the discount is clearly to reduce the impact on the contribution margin. It is doubtful that discounts for cash purchases will become a viable solution to credit card fees for most industries. Consequently, most people will simply have to face the cost. Despite the magnitude of the fee, it could well be less expensive than running accounts receivable. Not only is the charge off potential greatly reduced, but there is no need for a collection department which can be extremely expensive. Therefore, credit cards are frequently a viable alternative to credit sales.

We indicated earlier that the collection period for credit cards could be much less than for accounts receivable. In a few industries, notably gasoline sales, credit card charge slips can be used as cash to pay for purchases, but most charge sales have to be handled through a collection procedure. Bank cards are generally handled through a special credit card account to which charge slips are deposited. A rapid collection process follows after which the proceeds, net of charge fees, are available for use by the company. The collection period can range between one and seven days and in some instances can be handled as checks with the cash available upon deposit but with charge backs of bad charge slips a possibility.

Nonbank cards generally require processing by mail. Charge slips are bundled by the company and a recap sheet prepared after which the package is mailed to the collection center of the card issuer. A check, net of charge fees, is returned to the business by the card issuer. This collection period runs from 7 days to 30 days from the date of receipt of the charge by the issuer. In either event, the collection period for credit card sales can be much more rapid than for ordinary accounts receivable.

FINANCING ARRANGEMENTS

Financing through outside firms is frequently used for large ticket items such as automobiles, but can be a viable alternative for many smaller purchases. A variety of products and services from musical instruments to dental services can be financed through local banks or finance companies. Arrangements can be made whereby the business receives cash from the lender in the amount of the purchase and the purchaser receives an installment loan from the lender. Most lenders have a minimum amount which they are willing to finance but this minimum can be as low as $500. Lower limits can sometimes be arranged if a larger volume of transactions can be assured.

In outside financing arrangements, lenders frequently wish the business to take a recourse position. **Recourse** simply means that the business retains some form of liability for the performance of the purchaser on the loan. The level of liability can range from ***full recourse*** which means that if a purchaser refuses to pay, the business must pay off the lender, to ***limited recourse*** which involves a dollar or percentage limitation to the liability of the business. Where products are involved, such contracts can also be handled on a ***full repurchase*** basis which means that the business must buy the collateral back from the bank in the event of repossession, or a ***limited repurchase*** in which the business guarantees a minimum price for repossessed merchandise. The difference in repurchase and recourse is that for the former, the lender must handle repossession while for the latter the business must handle repossession if it occurs.

Even though outside financing arrangements may not reduce risk, they can speed up collections and reduce, if not eliminate, the need for a collection staff. Consequently, financing can frequently be a viable alternative to normal accounts receivable. A business interested in such arrangements should explore the possibility with its local bank. Even if the bank is not interested, it will be able to steer a business to a potential finance company.

FACTORING

Factoring is the sale of accounts receivable to a bank or finance company. Under a factoring arrangement, sales are made on accounts receivable in a normal fashion, then these accounts are sold to a lender under a prearranged contract of purchase. The accounts can be sold *en masse*, all of them, or selected accounts can be sold. The lender pays cash for the accounts upon receipt thereby speeding up the collection period. A charge is deducted from the amount of the accounts purchased to compensate the lender. This charge can range from 4% to 15% depending upon the volume of accounts which a business sells and the quality of the accounts in terms of credit risk. As in the case of credit card sales, small businesses are at a disadvantage because of their size and can frequently pay 10% or 12% in factoring fees. In many instances, factoring can cost so much that it wipes out the profit! In addition, most factors are unwilling to purchase accounts on a nonrecourse basis. That means that some liability, in many cases full liability, for the collection of the accounts still rests with the business. Unless a favorable factoring fee can be arranged, this is frequently not a viable alternative for a small business. It can be useful for periods of extreme cash flow problems or as a tool for working a company out of financial problems. If you are interested in factoring, discussions with your local bank should reveal their interest, if any, or the names of finance companies who involve themselves with factoring.

TYPES OF CREDIT

There are three different kinds of accounts which can be used to support credit sales. These are open accounts, revolving accounts and installment accounts. We need to talk about each of these and how they function for a business. It is possible for combinations of the types of credit accounts to be used and for various approaches to occur which will result in a wide variety of possible credit accounts. We will concentrate on the basic approaches which make up the various accounts.

OPEN ACCOUNTS

An *open account* is the most frequently encountered form of sales credit. In an open account, a customer may or may not be reviewed for credit extension. If a review is performed, then a credit limit is established, otherwise, each sale is handled individually. An open account is simply an extended payment option for a single purchase. The terms of payment frequently include discounts for early payment and are expressed in standard terms which describe the discount and due date. Table 1 displays examples of open account terms. Finance or service charges are frequently added to amounts which are not paid when due. If such penalties are assessed, then some indication will generally be made on the face of the invoice or bill which is sent to the customer.

As you can see from the table, there can be an almost unlimited variety of payment terms on open accounts. Discounts may be offered to encourage early payment of the account. Frequently, industry practices make the offering of payment discounts mandatory in order to be competitive. Nevertheless, payment discounts can be expensive and you should be aware of the impact which they have on contribution margins. If you offer a 2% discount and all of your customers take advantage of it, the effect will be a 2% decrease in the contribution margin. If half of your customers take advantage of it, the effect will be approximately a 1% decrease in the contribution margin. Many companies are willing to forego the added margin in order to speed up the collection of accounts and thereby improve cash flow.

One problem which frequently develops associated with payment discounts is customers who take discounts but pay outside the discount period. Many small businesses are reluctant to risk angering customers by asking for the discount back when it has been improperly taken. Sometimes a discount is taken improperly by accident or oversight, but the consistent failure to observe payment terms should not be tolerated. A courteous but firm notification that the terms are expected to be honored followed by a consistent enforcement of those terms should not anger anyone.

Table 1

Open Account Payment Terms

Terms	Explanation
Net 30	Balance due within 30 days, no discount for early payment
2/10, net 30	2% discount if paid within 10 days of the date of the bill, balance due within 30 days
2/10, 1/20, net 60	2% discount if paid within 10 days, 1% discount if paid within 20 days, balance due within 60 days
2/10, net 30, ROG	2% discount if paid within 10 days of the receipt of the goods, balance due within 30 days of the receipt of the goods
2/10, net 30, MOM	2% discount if paid within 10 days of the middle of the month, balance due within 30 days of the middle of the month
2/10, net 30, EOM	2% discount if paid within 10 days of the end of the month, balance due within 30 days of the end of the month
MOM	All purchases will be due on the 15th of the month
EOM	All purchases will be due on the last day of the month
COD	Payment will be collected at delivery

REVOLVING ACCOUNTS

A *revolving account* is a line of credit which permits purchases to be made on account up to the credit limit. Regular payments, usually on a monthly basis, are required. The payments are generally established as a percentage of the outstanding balance but have a minimum amount specified. For example, the account terms might require a monthly payment of 10% of the balance due or $25, whichever is greater. The percentage used is calculated based on the maximum period which the business wishes to wait for payment. Credit cards are examples of revolving credit. In order for a business to offer revolving credit accounts to its customers, a formal credit policy must be established. Procedures will be required to review applications for credit and to establish credit limits. We will talk about credit evaluation in the following section. After a credit line has been approved, a contract between the customer and the business is required which spells out the terms of repayment and explains the way interest charges are calculated and the interest rate which will be used. This contract must be carefully prepared because revolving charge accounts are governed by the Fair Credit Billing Act. Generally, an attorney will be required to prepare a contract which meets the requirements of the law and still protects the business. The maximum amount of interest which can be charged on these accounts is set by state usury laws which is another reason for involving an attorney in the preparation of the contracts.

Revolving accounts can be a lucrative business if properly handled because of the potential to produce profits from the interest charges. This is why so many large department stores offer their own credit cards. However, for a small business, revolving accounts should generally be avoided. In order to handle such accounts, a business will require a credit department to manage the credit granting process and oversee the use of credit. The business will also require a collection department to handle the billing and payment collection process and to oversee delinquency control and the management of slow paying accounts. We will talk about that process in a later section. Like any other function, revolving credit activities should be subjected to breakeven analysis before a business decides to get involved. Most of the costs associated with maintaining a credit and collection department are fixed expenses. This means that the breakeven point is higher in terms of volume, although profits will accumulate faster once the breakeven point is passed. Nevertheless, few small businesses can generate sufficient volume of revolving charges to reach breakeven. Consequently, revolving charges are not generally a viable option.

INSTALLMENT ACCOUNTS

The final type of credit account which we will discuss is the *installment account*. These accounts are generally used for larger purchases. They function exactly like the outside financing which we discussed earlier, but the business holds the credit contracts and collects the payments itself. In an installment contract, a single purchase is involved. A down payment of 10% to 30% will be required on the purchase and the remainder will be financed over a period of time. The balance financed is subject to finance charges which must be spelled out on the face of a contract between the buyer and seller and is regulated by state usury laws. The disclosure of finance charges is required by the Truth in Lending Act. This complexity means that a contract which has been approved by an attorney will generally be required. The balance is generally payable in monthly installments, while the contract term can run from a few months to 4 or 5 years.

The contract usually provides the goods purchased as collateral to secure the future payments, although installment contracts are frequently used to finance the payment of services as well as goods. If goods are involved, the contract can take one of two forms: a conditional sales contract; or a security agreement or chattel mortgage. The last two terms mean the same thing but are used in different states. A *security agreement* or *chattel mortgage* pledges a specific item or items as collateral. The purchaser owns the items, as title to the items is passed at the time of sale, but pledges that in the event of nonpayment of the contract, the items will be returned to the seller. If nonpayment occurs, a condition called *default*, and the buyer fails to return the property, the seller can take court action to repossess the goods. A *conditional sales contract* functions in exactly the same way except that title to the items purchased does not pass to the buyer until the contract has been paid. A seller has a stronger legal claim under a conditional sales contract and can generally take a repossession action without having to go to court. The selection of which form to use as well as appropriate documents and contracts is a legal matter and therefore requires the assistance of an attorney.

Like revolving credit accounts, installment accounts can be profitable given sufficient volume. They also require credit and collection efforts which can be expensive. Most small businesses lack the volume to be able to justify the use of such accounts. A breakeven analysis examining the costs and income which an installment credit activity can generate should be conducted before any business undertakes the task.

THE CREDIT DECISION

In order to ensure that credit is only extended to customers who are honest and who can and will pay their bills, an evaluation must be made. This evaluation involves both the integrity and financial strength of the customer. Both are required for a satisfactory credit relationship. That is, a customer must be both willing and able to repay the debt before credit is extended. Judging a business rather than an individual is somewhat different. We will talk about extending credit to people first and will then discuss credit for business customers.

THE FOUR Cs OF CREDIT

The four Cs of credit refers to the evaluation of the customer and the risk of nonpayment which that customer represents. The four Cs are: *character*, which refers to the honesty and integrity of the customer; *capacity*, which refers to the financial strength of the customer with regard to the ability to repay the credit; *capital*, which also refers to financial strength but in regard to the ultimate collectability of the credit; and *conditions*, which refers to a host of factors which can affect the credit decision.

Character

The character of a customer is the single most important aspect of a credit decision. It is also the most difficult factor to assess. Most people fall back on the leopard simile which talks about the difficulty a leopard has in changing its spots. In credit, this means that a customer which has handled credit well in the past will likely do so in the future. Past credit payment habits can be learned through a review of the customer's credit history. We will talk about sources of credit history in a moment. In a bank, credit officers are trained to use a personal interview to assess the character of a customer, but many people find that to be an art rather than a science.

We are reminded of a bank loan officer we knew who had the highest delinquency rate in the bank. This officer also had the highest production of loans which is not remarkable when you compare that to his delinquency rate. It means that he made more loans each month than any other loan officer in the bank but more of his loans appeared on the delinquency reports each month than for any other officer. What is remarkable, is that Bob had the lowest charge off ratio in the bank. That means that fewer of his loans ultimately lost money for the bank than those of any other loan officer. ***Charge offs*** occur when a loan cannot be collected or when a repossession is required in which the collateral does not bring enough to pay off the loan. Furthermore, Bob's customers were extremely loyal. They would not deal with any other loan officer and when called by a collection agent because of delinquency, they would reply that they would talk to Bob about the problem. We asked Bob about his loans and their unusual characteristics and he simply replied that he made loans to honest people whether they had had problems in the past or not. He was sure that his people would pay him when they could. That is exactly what they did: they did not pay the bank, they paid Bob! Frequently when pressed by a collection agent, a customer would say, *Tell Bob I'll pay him when I can.* The records clearly showed that Bob's customers did exactly that.

Few of us have the sixth sense that Bob had about people and so credit history plays a major role in judging character. That's sad because it leads to the frequently heard complaint that *you can't borrow money if you never have borrowed any*. People who have never used credit have no credit history. This makes it especially difficult for young people to obtain their first loans.

Capacity

The capacity to repay a debt refers to a customer having enough income to be able to handle the payments. This is a function of available income which means income after existing obligations are met. We must look at income after taxes are withheld, payments required on existing debts, and payments required for housing. The difference between these is the amount of income which a person has to cover food, insurance, medical and other expenses and repay a new debt. Rules of thumb have been developed which indicate that a person has the capacity to repay a debt if all payments, including the ones on a new debt, are no more than 30% to 45% of income. The exact percentage varies from firm to firm. This leaves the majority of income to cover living expenses. Living expenses can surely be expected to consume the majority of any person's income. Another method of judging capacity is to use credit history. If the customer has successfully handled a debt in the past with similar payments to those we are considering now, then chances are that the customer will be able to handle them again in the future.

A second aspect of capacity is judging its reliability. Since the debt which we are considering will be paid out of future income, we are more interested in what that will be than what the past income has been. ***Stability of income*** is generally measured by the length of time a person has been employed and the reliability of that employment in the future. The longer an individual has held a job, the more likely it is that he or she will continue to keep that job in the future. The higher the skill level required in a person's job, the more likely it is that those skills will continue to be needed in the future.

Capital

The third of the four Cs of credit is capital. This refers to the financial strength of a customer. A personal financial statement will show the value of the assets which an individual owns and the amount of debts or liabilities which exist. The difference between these is called ***net worth***. The larger the net worth, the stronger a person is financially. The make up of net worth, that is the assets which are owned, is also a factor since some kinds of assets are more liquid than others. Stocks, bonds and investments are more liquid than is real estate. In addition, the appropriateness of the values set down for the assets is a factor. For most people, a home is the major asset. This is also a difficult asset to value without a professional appraisal which is not usually possible in credit decisions because of the time and expense involved in obtaining one. Few people have the skill to be able to properly value their homes, consequently, dates of purchase and purchase costs as well as tax assessment values are frequently requested. This information can be used to determine whether the value an individual places on a home is realistic. Other questions can be asked on a financial statement for the same purpose; make and model of automobiles; specifics about investments; etc. Also, information about life insurance and wills can help to assure that capital will continue to exist even in the event of the death of the customer.

Some people substitute *collateral* for capital in the four Cs when a major asset is being acquired. For example, if an automobile is being purchased, its value can be used to secure the credit. If a sufficient down payment is obtained, then the asset will not depreciate in value faster than the debt is retired. Other items such as refrigerators, freezers, musical instruments or other durable goods can be assessed in the same way.

Conditions

The fourth of the Cs of credit is conditions. This refers to any conditions which might affect a loan and requires anyone who is judging credit applications to be well informed. A condition which could affect a credit decision is an economic recession which could affect a customer's income or employment, or a decline in an industry which will result in layoffs in the company in which a customer works. Other kinds of conditions which will affect a credit decision concern the business extending the credit. If our business is suffering a decline in sales, then we might be inclined to accept more risky credit accounts in an effort to increase sales. If our past experience in collecting credit accounts is poor, we might want to tighten our credit policies in order to reduce the problems. The reverse of these things could also occur. Almost anything can affect a credit decision from a new highway which will claim the land on which an employer is located to a change in import rules which will affect the strength of an industry competing with foreign firms. Evaluating the conditions which affect a given credit decision is the job for a knowledgeable, well informed, insightful person.

CREDIT HISTORY

We indicated that credit history is an important part of evaluating the character and capacity of a customer. Sources of information about a person's history come from disclosures which are made on a credit application and from the Merchant's Association. The credit application should ask for the names of firms with which a customer has had credit dealings in the past as well as those to which money is currently owed. We can call those firms on the telephone and ask about how well a customer has handled his or her credit. In addition, there is a Merchant's Association or Credit Bureau in every major city in the country. These firms keep credit history information on file and provide it to members and customers for a fee. They will also undertake a current investigation of a customer and call the references which appear on the credit application, as well as credit bureaus in other cities in which a customer may have lived to provide an up to date picture of the credit history. This level of information obviously costs more and takes longer than a simple check of the files of the bureau.

Credit history will show types of credit, O for open accounts, R for revolving accounts, I for installment accounts, high credit, amounts of payments, balances outstanding, and promptness of payments received. Promptness will be shown as a number from 1, meaning all payments received on time, to 2, meaning some minor slowness in payments occurred, up to 9 which indicates that a charge off occurred. We will want to place more emphasis on credit types and amounts which approximate the credit which we are considering extending, but the overall history is important as well because it reveals the general approach which a customer has taken in dealing with debts in the past.

EXTENDING CREDIT TO BUSINESSES

When we extend credit to businesses rather than individuals, the factors involved are the same, but assessment is somewhat different. For example, the character of a business is a more nebulous concept than for an individual. The character of a business is actually that of its management. A business does have credit history which we can examine, but if there has been a change in the top management of a firm, then we should keep that in mind because it could signal a change in the character. Credit history for a business is not normally available from credit bureaus. The firm of Dun and Bradstreet (D & B) functions as a credit bureau for businesses and can provide the same information about credit history for businesses as we described for individuals. D & B also can provide information about the management of a firm and the backgrounds of its officers as well as financial statements for the firm. D & B services generally cost more than those of a local credit bureau.

The capacity and capital issues of a credit decision for a business come down to evaluating financial statements. Ratio analysis and interpretation of financial statements can be complex and generally requires a high level of training in finance and accounting. Few small businesses possess the expertise to be able to handle in-depth financial analysis. A Dun and Bradstreet report will include some financial analysis but is generally a lessor part of the report than is credit history. In the financial analysis chapter, we talked about conducting ratio analysis on your own business to determine its financial well being. The same kinds of techniques can be applied to the statements of a customer in a credit decision. If a major credit is being considered, one which could damage the company significantly if it were made incorrectly, you should consider having your CPA examine the statements of the business for you. Otherwise, the tools in the financial analysis chapter should be sufficient.

CREDIT AND DELINQUENCY MANAGEMENT

We have made several references to credit and collection departments in this chapter. Large firms that extend credit do have such departments, but most small firms do not. If you intend to extend credit you must at least have an office or a person who is responsible for making the credit decisions on customers, a process which will ensure the timely collection of accounts, and a policy which can be used to manage the credit activity. This is generally done by establishing credit and collection responsibilities, assigning them to an employee or a manager, and by preparing a written credit policy.

CREDIT POLICY

A *credit policy* should be prepared by, or at least approved by, the owner of the business. The policy should spell out information which is required to support credit applications, assign responsibility and authority for processing credit requests and for monitoring and collecting credit accounts, and establish guidelines for the credit activity. Guidelines could include such things as minimum and maximum amounts of credit which will be considered, levels of financial strength and types of credit history which will be required, amounts of credit which a given person or manager will be authorized to extend, and timing and type of contact which will be made on delinquent accounts. Any major credits, those which could severely damage the company if a default occurs, should require the owner's approval. The credit policy should be in writing and should be reviewed periodically, at least annually, to ensure that it is appropriate in the changing environment of the business.

CREDIT EXTENSION

An application should be required on all credit accounts. The application can be prepared by sales people or by the customer, whichever is desired, but key information required in assessing the four Cs of credit should be included. The application form should include information about addresses, telephone numbers, employment, income, bank accounts, etc. You can easily adapt an application form from the one used by your local bank. Alternatively, most software packages which handle receivables will include a basic data form which is generally adequate. After an application has been prepared, and after we have a desired credit amount, an investigation should be undertaken. Even on very small credit requests, a basic investigation should be conducted. For an individual, this should include verifying the employment, employment dates, position and income levels by telephoning the employer. A basic check of the files of the credit bureau or of Dun and Bradstreet should be conducted. If the credit desired is a larger amount, then more up to date credit history should be required. This can be purchased or can be developed by telephoning credit accounts directly. For a business, a financial statement should always be required; several years worth of financial data if the credit is a large one. A large credit to an individual should be accompanied by a personal financial statement. Personal financial statements include lists of assets and liabilities. Again, you can adapt such a form from the one used by your local bank. Once the information has been gathered, a responsible person should evaluate it and make a credit decision.

A popular approach to evaluating credit is the use of a checklist. A customer is given so many points for holding the same job for a specified time, for living in the same place for a specified time, for owning rather than renting a home and for holding a job with specified skill levels. These are factors which measure stability. Points can be awarded for the kind of credit history which a customer has to measure character. Other points are awarded for amounts of income, for the percentage of income which is available to cover debts, and for the amount of financial net worth. These are factors which measure capacity and capital. Finally, points may be awarded for the amounts of down payment or any other factors desired. Table 2 displays a sample of a credit checklist. After all the points have been awarded and added up, the total is compared to one which has been established as part of the credit policy. If the points are less than the policy level, then the credit is rejected. If the points are equal to or greater than the policy level, then the credit is approved. This process permits less skilled people to handle credit approvals, but can result in many good accounts being rejected if the policy level is set too high. Consequently, many firms have rejections referred to a manager for a second look before the credit is turned down. This permits the checklist to be used for all strong credits thereby reducing the workload for the credit manager in credit approvals. Another advantage of the checklist system is that it permits a stronger level of control over the credit extension process. Therefore, when credit experience or other factors indicate that policy needs to be changed, it can easily be done. A higher score can be required to tighten credit approvals, or a lower score to loosen credit approval. You should be careful to keep in mind that any credit scoring system, regardless of its sophistication, is a poor substitute for human judgement. Consequently, careful and continuous monitoring of the system and human review of large credits and marginal applications is a must for the effective application of the system.

Table 2: Credit Scoring Sheet			Score
Applicant's Age	Under 40	20 points	_____
Age:_____	40 to 44	28	_____
	Over 45	40	_____
Years at Address	Under 3 ½	16	_____
Years:_____	3 ½ to 7 ½	29	_____
	Over 7 ½	36	_____
Time on present job	Under 1 ½ years	16	_____
Years:_____	1 ½ to 3 ½	22	_____
	3 ½ to 6 ½	27	_____
	Over 6 ½	39	_____
	Homemaker	22	_____
Home	Renting	15	_____
Address:_____	Buying	40	_____
Bank Accounts	None	16	_____
Bank:_____	Checking/savings/loan	22	_____
	2 of the 3	28	_____
	All 3	40	_____
Credit Card	None	18	_____
Cards:_____	Department store	31	_____
	Major card	50	_____
Automobiles	Less than 1 year old	55	_____
Auto:_____	1 year old	42	_____
	2 years old	30	_____
	3 years and over	16	_____
Annual Income	Under $25,000	16	_____
Income:_____	$25,000 to $35,000	22	_____
	$35,000 to $45,000	23	_____
	Over $45,000	28	_____
Credit Bureau Report	No Record	8	_____
Ratings:_____	Slow	-23	_____
	1-2 Satisfactory accounts	13	_____
	3 + Satisfactory accounts	18	_____
		Total Score:	_____

MONITORING

Monitoring of a credit activity means more than tracking of delinquency. Of course, a continuous monitoring of delinquency is necessary because some payment failure is inevitable. Reports of numbers of delinquent accounts and of dollar amounts of delinquent accounts should be prepared regularly; at least monthly. These reports should detail the numbers and percentages of delinquency by time. Accounts should be shown in 15 day accounts, 30 day accounts, 60 day accounts, 90 day accounts and over 90 day accounts. That is, accounts which have payments which are 15 to 29 days late, 30 to 59 days late, 60 to 89 days late, etc. This is called an *aging of the accounts*. In addition to showing the number and dollar value of accounts in each category and the percentage of accounts and percentage of the value of accounts in each category, the report should show the number and percentage of accounts which have been contacted and which have made promises to remedy the delinquency. It should also show charge offs or actual amounts lost and any accounts referred to a collection agency as well as any amounts recovered on accounts which have been charged off in the past.

Monitoring of this information each month will reveal seasonal patterns which exist within the collection of your receivables and will provide trends which can be examined to evaluate the effectiveness of collection efforts. If, for example, delinquency percentages for December are higher than usual for a December, then credit extension or collection efforts are being less effective than in the past. Don't forget that economic conditions or other environmental factors will affect delinquency as well as the internal efforts of the staff. Also, remember that a decline in delinquency is not necessarily good. A certain amount of delinquency is normal; what that amount is differs for each business. If your delinquency rate drops below a normal level for your business, then it can mean that the credit policy is too tight and sales are being lost. It could also signal a problem in the reporting.

We knew one collection manager who was fired after the internal auditor for the firm noticed an unexplained decline in delinquency over a period of two years. The manager had received great praise and several raises in pay as a result of that decline, but the auditor became suspicious when his review of the collection department failed to turn up any significant changes in the collection practices. A thorough investigation and a careful monitoring of the manager's activities followed. It was discovered that the manager was extending the due dates of accounts in the computerized system so that they would not show as delinquent. The sad thing was that a recalculation of the true delinquency over the last two years showed that the manager had really been doing a fine job.

In addition to aging and delinquency reports, monitoring of the credit activity requires us to examine the credit sales and their trends. Since receivables arise as a result of credit sales, the credit granting and approval process will affect both collection of accounts and amounts of sales recorded. Effective management of the credit activity means balancing the losses and expenses associated with receivables with the loss of sales. If we minimize delinquency and charge offs, we may well be damaging sales. If we lose more money in sales than we save in charge offs and collection costs, then the business will be hurt. The comparison cannot be made directly with sales dollars because of the cost of goods sold and other variable expenses. The comparison must be made to contribution margin. The process requires the constant comparison of delinquency reports to credit and overall sales reports and contribution margins.

Finally, monitoring refers to the process of overseeing the collection effort itself. When an account defaults in payment, then the chances are that no money will be received on that account unless someone in the collection department contacts the customer and tries to arrange for payment. We will talk about collection efforts in just a minute, but the point here is that someone must monitor the collection activity itself. Records of all collection efforts must be made and review of those records on a regular basis must occur to ensure that timely, effective contact with delinquent accounts is being made. Collecting accounts is generally considered to be one of the most unpleasant of duties in the business world. Nevertheless, it is necessary and a critical part of successful business operations. Consequently, the monitoring of the unpleasant task is vital.

BAD DEBTS

When accounts cannot be collected, they are called *bad debts* and must be removed from the books. This involves a reduction of revenues because the sales associated with the bad debts have already been recognized. The sales were recorded when the sale was made. If the account cannot be collected, then an expense or a decrease in sales must be recorded and the account must be removed from the books because it is no longer an asset. There are two methods of accounting for bad debt expense. The first and most popular method is called the *direct write off method*. In this process, an account is simply charged off as an expense when it is determined that the account cannot be collected under ordinary means. The method is popular with small businesses because of its simplicity. Many firms simply write off bad debts at the end of the year. Many of these firms also write off only accounts which have declared bankruptcy or which are very old. Bankrupts should be charged off, of course, because there will be little recovery, if any, on such accounts. It is a mistake to hold old accounts for an excessive period before charging them off because it distorts the true charge off experience of the firm. Accounts should be regularly removed from the books at the end of each month as they are determined to be uncollectible with ordinary means. They can always be reinstated if payment is ultimately received, but failure to remove them in a timely fashion will make the delinquency report incorrect both in terms of charge offs and in terms of delinquency. Until the accounts are charged off, they will show as delinquent, thereby confusing two sections of the delinquency report.

The second method of accounting for bad debts is called the *reserve method* and is the preferred method by accountants and larger firms. In this method a percentage of credit sales or accounts receivable is set aside each year to cover bad debts. The percentage used is based on the experience of the individual firm and could range from 1/2% to 3% of credit sales. If expressed in terms of a percentage of receivables, then the percentage could range from 0% of the 30 day accounts at year end to 50% of the 90 day accounts. Generally, the amount will be calculated using an aging of year end receivables. Regardless of the method used to calculate the bad debt allowance, the amount determined is shown as an expense and as a reserve for uncollectible accounts on the balance sheet. The accounting entry is a debit to an expense account called bad debt expense and a credit to the reserve account. The reserve account will subtract from assets on the balance sheet and net receivables will show on that document much as accumulated depreciation is subtracted from long lived assets to arrive at a net investment. When accounts are determined to be uncollectible, they are removed from the asset account for receivables and charged against the reserve account. That means that the actual charge off of an account does not affect expenses or sales. This process is preferred by accountants because the bad debt expense is recorded in the same year as the sale was recorded thereby matching the two. Any error which is made in estimation of the amount of bad debts is taken care of at the end of the year by adjusting the amount of bad debt expense to be recognized for the next year.

Just because an account has been written off as a bad debt does not mean that collection efforts should not continue. Collection agencies are firms which will undertake to collect accounts which you have failed to collect. Such firms charge a percentage of amounts recovered as a fee. These fees can range between 25% and 50% of the amount collected. That seems a high cost, but the alternative is generally the loss of the entire amount. The use of a collection agency is generally a last effort. However, waiting too long to turn an account over to an agency can result in the failure of the agency to recover any money. Consequently, the collection department should be constantly aware of **chronic accounts**; those which consistently break promises to pay and which are consistently delinquent. When the amount of collection effort on such accounts becomes extreme, consideration should be given to turning them over to a collection agency. The more typical pattern is for a firm to turn over accounts which are 3 to 5 months delinquent and which have had no activity during that time. It may well be too late to recover anything without litigation after that long a period of inactivity.

Litigation is always possible as a collection device, but it is an expensive and time consuming process. It is usually practical only on larger accounts. There is a small claims court which can be used without an attorney for small amounts. The costs of using this court are small, but it does require an investment of time. Many businesses feel that the time which a small claims court will require cannot be justified by the amounts involved. Nevertheless, it is an option which should always be considered for accounts which refuse to pay.

When money is received on accounts which have been charged off, the handling of that money must be carefully monitored. Since there is no account on the books to support the receipt of such payments, it is simple for a person to embezzle the funds. Consequently, careful controls must be set up to handle the processing of such transactions. The preferred method is to **reinstate** *the account*. That means to put the account back on the books as an asset. Then payments can be recorded against the accounts. Payments of this type are commonly received from accounts referred to collection agencies and on accounts for people who have declared bankruptcy and who have been ordered by the court to pay a percentage of their obligations.

COLLECTION PROCEDURES

Collection procedures refer to the methods used to encourage customers who are delinquent or in default on their accounts to pay their debts. In general, these procedures simply require someone to ask for payment and then to check to see that the payment is received. The customer can be contacted about payment by letter, by telephone or in person. It is extremely expensive to employ collection agents to physically call on delinquent accounts, consequently, virtually no small businesses use such techniques. However, if sales agents or other employees of the business call on customers, then these people should be made a part of the collection effort. When a sales person calls on a business which is delinquent, then the agent should know the situation and should ask for payment as part of the sales call. If consistent delinquency occurs, then the agent should make the customer realize that future sales will be restricted or tighter payment terms will be enforced. In addition, sales agents and other traveling employees of the business should be used to call on delinquent accounts which are located along the route to be traveled. A firm, courteous discussion of a customer's delinquency in a face to face interview is the strongest possible collection effort. Involving the sales agents in the collection effort also makes it clear to those people that delinquency can and will damage sales commissions. It makes the sales people more attentive to the overall operations of the firm.

LETTERS

Letters to delinquent customers are the most well known and broadly used collection effort. Consequently, they tend to be less effective than other methods of contact. Nevertheless, they are useful for customers who have honestly forgotten about payments or due dates. That means that letters need to be sent early in the collection process. A computerized system with the capability of preparing delinquency letters is a must if there are large numbers of accounts to handle, because letters should be sent at a point no later than 15 days of delinquency. Additional letters can be generated at other times, but the 15 day contact is important to head off serious problems. If a customer has forgotten to make a payment and is not reminded for 30 days, then two payments are now due and it becomes more difficult for the customer to handle the debt. Consequently, early contact is important. This first letter should be courteous and should be a reminder of payment. Many good accounts, if not all accounts, can be expected to overlook a payment from time to time.

If you are excessively harsh or rude in the reminder letter, you can do great damage to the long term relationship with the customer.

Many books detail a series of collection letters, each more insistent and stronger than the last, which should be sent over a period of time to delinquent accounts. We feel that such effort is largely wasted. If a customer is having payment problems on your account, then that customer is probably having problems on other accounts as well. Consequently, a delinquent customer is frequently bombarded with collection letters from a variety of sources. Such letters are frequently ignored or even destroyed unopened. If a customer gets more than 30 days delinquent, someone needs to talk to that customer to find out what the problems are and what can be done to eliminate the delinquency.

THE TELEPHONE

The telephone is probably the most efficient collection device ever invented. It permits the next best thing to a face to face interview with costs which approximate letters. A strong collection department will make a telephone contact with every customer who reaches 30 days of delinquency. That contact should be made earlier on accounts which have a history of delinquency. The collector should be well trained to be courteous and helpful, but firm. If customers can not be reached during the day, then collectors should be employed to work in the evenings. If a customer cannot be reached by telephone, then immediate steps need to be taken to find the customer and protect the business.

Telephone collectors should not simply call people and ask for payment. If a reminder letter has been sent, then the customer realizes that the account is delinquent. Continued failure to make payment must be the result of a financial problem. The telephone collector should make every effort to determine what that problem is and what can be done about it. This takes a genuine interest in the customer. A poorly trained collector will simply get promises that the *check is in the mail* or that *it'll be mailed next week* or other statements which are made simply to terminate the conversation. A well trained collector will never ask for payment, but will ask what is wrong; will assure the customer that past business is appreciated and that future dealings are desired; that the business is willing and anxious to adjust payment schedules to meet temporary problems; that the customer is valued and that the delinquency is viewed as a joint problem which can and will be cured. Payment schedules can be adjusted to accept smaller amounts on a weekly or other basis until the delinquency can be eliminated. The telephone collector should strive to end every call with an understanding of exactly when and how much payment can be expected. Remember, it is true that many good customers experience temporary problems. A strike, job layoff, unexpected illness, breakdown of an automobile, dental expenses, or any one of an unlimited number of occurrences can disrupt your customer's income temporarily. When the problem is over, those firms which have displayed a helpful attitude toward the problem and the delinquency can expect to have a stronger, more loyal customer in the future.

FOLLOWUP

The secret to telephone collection, or any other collection effort, is followup. In order for specially arranged payment terms to be effective, a collection agent needs to check to see that payments have been made as agreed and must call the customer as soon as a promise has been broken. The same collector needs to deal with a customer throughout the length of a delinquency so that a personal relationship can be developed. The assigned collector must make records of agreements and promise dates and must maintain a file of promises by date. Daily, the collector must check the date file against payment records and as soon as a promise is broken, call the customer again. If the promise is kept, but the amount of payment is less than agreed, a second call should be made anyway. This second call should not wait! If a payment was to have been made on Tuesday, then the call should be made no later than Wednesday! Delinquent accounts must be encouraged to speak truthfully and to honor commitments. If unexpected problems complicate a payment, then the customer should call the collector and make that information known. The only way that such a relationship can be cultivated is for a rapid and consistent followup to occur throughout the period of delinquency.

THE IMPACT OF CREDIT ON SALES

We indicated at the beginning of this chapter that no one would extend credit to customers unless forced to do so by competitive pressure. It is certainly true that no business can expect to be successful if it is not competitive. Being competitive frequently means more than price; hours of operations, location, services and credit terms are frequently a part of the requirements. Nevertheless, you should have a clear picture of the impact which credit has on your sales and profits at all times. We have discussed how a credit policy can increase or reduce sales by being too tight or too loose. We have discussed how losses on credit accounts are to be expected, how they impact profits, and how those losses and collection costs need to be weighed against contribution margins to determine overall effectiveness. Considering all that, you should also examine the effect which credit has on the firm's strategic posture. Many businesses survive and do well while refusing to handle any credit accounts at all. These businesses are ones which have developed a strategic posture which is consistent with cash sales. For example, many discount or factory warehouse retailers require cash or credit cards but have an image of being low price stores. As a matter of fact, credit accounts were developed in exactly the same way. A growing number of businesses began to offer credit terms as part of a plan to gain a competitive edge and as part of their strategic postures. The pendulum has not swung back the other way, but it could. The important point to remember is that credit activities need to be consistent with your firm's image. If the image is low cost, no frills, then credit may not be required. If the image is high quality, high service, exclusive products/services, then credit may be required. As in all other aspects of your business which impact customers, your credit policies must be consistent with your strategic posture.

SUMMARY

Since all business is based on trust, nowhere is this more evident than in the extension of credit. Buy now and pay later is today's creed. Credit was first recorded as a practice 4000 years ago but has probably been possible in some form since the advent of tribal living. While traditionally credit was limited to business, the introduction of the credit card has made users of us all.

Yet with the growth of any element, the rapid growth of credit has brought with it special problems, especially for small businesses who are more dependent on their cash flow for survival. These problems deal with the possible loss from those who cannot or will not pay and the costs of effective management of credit from the granting to the collecting process.

Accounts receivable, trade credit or extended payment terms for goods and services purchased from a vendor have been discussed. Credit sales to consumers are another means of extending credit. Methods to limit the liabilities of your business when extending credit are the use of credit cards, financing through outside firms and the factoring of accounts.

There are three kinds of accounts which can be used to support credit sales. They are open accounts, revolving accounts, and installment accounts. The advantages and disadvantages of each of these accounts as they apply to small businesses have been examined.

Extending credit may be necessary to businesses as well as people. Judging their ability as well as desire to repay is a difficult process which requires some experience. There are four Cs of credit: character, which refers to the honesty and integrity of the customer; capacity, which refers to the financial strengths of the customer with regard to the ability to repay the credit; capital, which also refers to financial strength in regard to the ultimate collectability of the credit; and conditions which refer to a host of factors which can affect the credit decision.

Credit history is an important part of evaluating the character and capital of a customer. Information may be learned not only from the credit application but also from the Merchants' Association or Credit Bureau. Credit histories will show types of credit as well as promptness of payment.

Credit extension to businesses is similar to that of individuals but the assessment is different. The character of individuals is easier to assess than the character of a business. The business' character is a reflection of its management. Dun and Bradstreet functions as a credit bureau for businesses and provides information about credit history. The capacity and capital of a company is evaluated by analyzing its financial statement and the conditions which affect it are functions of its environment.

The management of credit and delinquency is important to the success of a small business. A credit policy should be prepared by and approved by the owner. It should spell out procedures and guidelines for the processing of applications, the granting of credit, and the monitoring of the collection of accounts.

Credit extension mandates a formal application whether from an individual or business with substantiating documents such as financial statements if a large amount of credit is desired. The credit may be evaluated according to a checklist with points assigned for various factors such as longevity in a particular situation.

The monitoring of delinquency is necessary if credit is extended. Not only does the monitoring of credit activity show aging and delinquency and the collection of accounts, it requires us to examine the credit sales and their trends.

There are two methods of accounting for bad debt expense. The most popular is the direct write off method. In this process an account is simply charged off as an expense when it is determined that the account cannot be collected under ordinary means. The second method of accounting for bad debts is called the reserve method and is the method preferred by accountants and large firms. In this method a percentage of credit sales or accounts receivable is set aside each year to cover bad debts.

After bad debts have been written off, the collection process may continue. Collection agents may be hired to pursue the delinquent accounts or litigation may be initiated on large accounts. If the collection process is successful, the account should be reinstated and controlled for the period of time payments are received.

Collection procedures refer to methods used to encourage customers who are delinquent or in default on their accounts to pay their debts. The collection effort may be aided by salespeople, a collection staff member or other employee who gets in touch with the delinquent account in person, by letter or by telephone and then follows up on promises to pay.

The ability of a business to be competitive can dictate its survival. Involved herein, also, is the company's strategic posture. Remember that credit activities need to be consistent with the firm's image. If the image is low cost, no frills, then credit may not be required. If the image is high quality, high service, exclusive products/services, then credit may be required. Thus the effective management of a company's accounts receivable is necessary for its survival.

QUESTIONS, EXERCISES AND CASES

QUESTIONS:

1.　　How could the extensive use of credit cards affect the survival of small businesses?

2.　　What are three methods for limiting the risk in the extension of credit to consumers?

3.　　With what problems are trade credits associated?

4.　　Why is factoring not generally viable for a small business?

5.　　What are three kinds of accounts which can be used to support credit sales?

6.　　What are the four Cs of credit?

7.　　What is the single most important aspect of a credit decision?

8.　　What are the two methods of accounting for a bad debt?

9.　　What are the advantages of having a checklist in making the credit decision?

DEFINE THE FOLLOWING TERMS:

1.　　accounts receivable

2.　　factoring

3.　　lien

4.　　note

5.　　recourse

6.　　trade credit

EXERCISES:

1.   Using the checklist in the text, role play several loan applicants being interviewed by one or several bank officers concurrently. If concurrently, have a loan officer's meeting following the applications to discuss each application. How does the checklist make the decision easier? Under what conditions might it be essential that such checklists be used? Should there ever be any exceptions made to the evaluation by checklist? What other considerations might there be in evaluating a credit application which may not be included on the checklist?

2.   The situation is this: several accounts have been delinquent for a period of 30, 60 or 90 days. Have the collection manager demonstrate the collection techniques he would use in each situation. The collection manager may role play as if he were instructing new people in the collection department as to how they should do the job or as a collector himself with others playing the role of delinquent accounts. Which techniques are most adequate in which instances? What attitude is important for the collection personnel? What could be the results of an abrasive personality in this situation? Would you do well in this job or not? Many bankers must go through a trial period in this position in the bank as training for their jobs as loan officers, why do you think that this is a good idea?

CASE

Mr. Peabody was a local attorney specializing in Real Estate. He was well known in the community and had several loans with a very small local bank. He had his house, business, a business for his wife, leasehold improvements on his office as well as his cars financed with them. He, in addition, had his business accounts there.

As all busy people, he was occasionally late with a payment but was never really delinquent until one day the bottom dropped out. The bank was frantic because Mr. Peabody's trust account was overdrawn by $20,000. This couldn't happen. Trust accounts are sacred. A real estate *trust account* is an account set up by attorneys to safeguard the money in real estate transactions prior to closing at which time it is disbursed and typically is a sizeable account.

Mr. Peabody was immediately contacted. He told a woeful tale about his trusted secretary forging his signature on a check on that account in that amount. It was a clear case of embezzlement according to Mr. Peabody. His secretary had stolen from him and run away. Mr. Peabody had to make the money good. If he didn't come up with the $20,000 immediately, not only would he be in serious trouble but his professional reputation would be ruined. Since the bank was concerned about the situation, they loaned him the money to make up the deficit.

But Mr. Peabody's duplicity was not long in revealing itself. His other loans began defaulting and he was unavailable. His wife was filing for a divorce and was as interested as the bank in knowing of his whereabouts. The office was closed and the bank started procedures to repossess the assets which were held as collateral for his many loans. What a nightmare for the bank! Discussions with Mrs. Peabody further clouded the issue of how guilty the bank may have been in covering the overdraft for his real estate account, when they learned that Mrs. Peabody was naming Mr. Peabody's secretary as a co-respondent in her divorce action. Of course, neither was available for questioning.

1. Clearly there was some fault in the bank in making a loan to cover an overdraft of this type rather than reporting it, but one of the problems is that professional people are usually not examined quite as closely as other credit applicants by lenders. Also there was not a clear accounting for all of the outstanding loans made to Mr. Peabody. With computerization, this is not as much of a problem, but what steps might the bank have taken in the loan process and credit history process that might have alleviated some of their later problems with this account?

2. What methods should they have taken to collect on the delinquent accounts?

3. If you had been involved with Mr. Peabody's credit decision, what would you have done and when?

4. What can now be done to enable the bank to recoup it losses?

CHAPTER TWENTY

FINANCIAL MANAGEMENT

CHAPTER OBJECTIVES

Upon completion of this chapter, you should be able to:

- Explain the types and sources of financing for small businesses;

- Discuss the advantages and disadvantages of common and preferred stock;

- Distinguish between the different types of loans available to small businesses;

- Describe the role of debt in risk management;

- Explain the difference between long and short term loans;

- Identify the two sources of cash flow in a small business;

- Describe the role of retained earnings in small businesses;

- Discuss the importance of maintaining a sound bank relationship;

- Explain the impact of growth on a small business; and,

- Describe the importance of financial planning to a small business.

FINANCIAL MANAGEMENT

INTRODUCTION

When we talk about finance most people think of loans and debts. *Finance*, however, consists of all sources of funding available to a business. There are only two such sources: *debt* and *equity*. The principle difference between the two is that *debt* must be repaid while *equity* does not have to be repaid. That means that debt gives greater operational problems for a small business than does equity. Equity can create problems in control and can be highly expensive in that dividends or returns must be continually paid to equity holders, but the failure to repay debt can result in the bankruptcy of a business. In most states, as few as three unpaid creditors of a firm can force that firm into bankruptcy.

The United States economy is truly based on credit. Virtually every year new records are set for the highest ever debt levels of the nation, of businesses and of consumers. Debt has become so thoroughly ingrained in the economy that virtually no small business can effectively survive without access to credit.

Most of our focus in this chapter will be on debt because of its importance to a successful operation. Thomas Carlyle said, *There are but two ways of paying debt: increase of industry in raising income, increase of thrift in laying it out.* Carlyle's words are of particular importance when we consider debt management. As he said, there are only two ways that debt can be repaid. One is through an increase in revenues and the other is through a reduction in costs. This means that debt can only be justified when its use can result in one or the other circumstances for its repayment. Any other use of debt will cause problems because other actions will have to be taken for its repayment.

TYPES AND SOURCES OF FINANCING

As we said earlier, financing can be obtained through debt or equity. *Equity* refers to funds invested in a business by its owners, regardless of whether a firm is a proprietorship, partnership or corporation. In recent years new vehicles for equity investment have been developed to make raising money from investors easier.

LIMITED PARTNERSHIPS

In the area of partnerships, the concept of limited partners has been developed. A *limited partnership* is a firm with two classes of owners: general partners and limited partners. A *limited partner* is closer to a shareholder in a corporation than a partner in a partnership. In fact, the SEC treats limited partner shares as though they were stock certificates for regulation purposes. A limited partner invests money in an enterprise by purchasing a certificate. Thereafter, the investor shares in profits or losses and cash distributions on a basis established by the partnership certificate. Since the firm is generally taxed as a partnership, it pays no tax, the limited partners must report on their personal income tax returns their share of profits or losses. Distributions of cash over and above profits reduce the tax basis of the partners' investment in the business. After that basis is reduced to zero, that means 100% of the partner's investment in the firm has been returned, any further distributions are generally taxed as capital gains. Consequently, a limited partnership can have favorable tax treatment. Nevertheless, limited partners have no control or participation in the management of a firm. The general partners of the firm will exercise management control and make all decisions. For this reason, a limited partnership is frequently used as a device for raising equity capital rather than an organizational format.

For small businesses the limited partnership approach can be worthwhile. Several small ventures with which we are familiar have used this vehicle successfully. However, the process can be complex because we are dealing with an area which is highly regulated. Consequently, we recommend that you obtain professional assistance in preparing limited partnership fund raising efforts. You will need an attorney who has experience in this area as well as a CPA firm to prepare a prospectus. Of course, the use of professionals will raise the cost, consequently, limited partnerships are probably not worthwhile unless you intend to raise substantial sums, say $250,000 or more.

STOCK

In the corporate field, there has been an unbelievable variety of investment instruments or securities developed. These range from different classes of common stock to preferred stock, preference stock, stock rights, options and warrants, convertible bonds and instruments of all kinds, etc. To understand all these types of securities, we must recognize that the holders of **common stock** are the true owners of a corporation. These people share in the profits of the business through dividends or distributions of income and share in the management of the firm through election of a board of directors. The common shareholders are generally equal regardless of the cost of their stock. Each share of stock is entitled to one vote[65] and is entitled to a pro rata share of income based purely on the number of shares of stock outstanding. Originally, this was the only form of equity available for a corporation. Because people wanted to use equity for the purposes of raising money but without losing control of the company, other forms were invented.

It is now possible to have more than one class of common stock: one class which has voting rights and one or more other classes which cannot vote but do share in income. In addition, there is **preferred** and **preference stock**. These securities generally take preference over common stock in terms of distributions of income but have no voting rights. The dividends which are paid to preferred and preference stockholders are generally stated in terms of an interest rate so that there is a guaranteed return. In the event of bankruptcy or liquidation of the firm, these shareholders take precedence over common shareholders for any capital left after creditors are paid.

Common and preferred stocks of various types are frequently used as financing vehicles for small businesses. Family, friends, associates, employees, etc., can generally be offered stocks as investments with good success for the business. If you wish to approach outsiders, you must be more careful because the SEC regulates stock offerings. In a previous chapter, we talked about small offerings which avoid the SEC registration requirement. Those are the approaches which small firms generally take, but they require professional assistance to ensure regulatory compliance.

Rights, *warrants* and *options* are devices which entitle the holder to acquire stock in a corporation. Small business corporations seldom make any use of these securities because their value is generally based on the availability of a market for securities such as a stock exchange. *Convertible securities* are generally types of debt which can be converted to equity under certain circumstances or at specified times. These are also seldom used in the small business world.

PERMANENT FINANCING

Stock certificates of all kinds and *limited partnership certificates* are considered *permanent* financing because the investment in the business never has to be repaid. Preferred and preference stock frequently have *call options* built in which permit a business to repurchase the stock under certain conditions thereby effectively repaying the investors, but those options are not generally mandatory. Since the investment does not have to be repaid, there is less risk associated with equity financing. The other side of this coin is that the investors in equity have to be paid shares of income as long as the business exists. In addition, these payments, called *dividends*, are not tax deductible. That means that equity financing can be quite expensive in terms of the amount of cash which must be invested in the financing each year and over the long term. You frequently hear of large corporations which pay no dividends on their stock thereby avoiding this cash drain, but that is not normally possible for a small business. Holders of stock in large businesses have the stock markets available as a place to buy and sell stock certificates. Profits can be made in the markets through those sales. Such markets are not generally available for a small business, consequently, stockholders in small firms look to dividends for the returns on their investments.

GOING PUBLIC

Finally, the absence of stock markets for small businesses and the complexity of SEC rules governing stock and equity sales makes finding equity investors difficult for a small business. You frequently hear about small businesses *going public*. Such firms have made the jump from small, closely held corporations with a small number of shareholders, to corporations whose stock will be traded on some stock market and therefore be available to anyone who wishes to buy it. This is a dream for many small business owners because it marks the entry of a business into markets which make equity financing a viable option. Unfortunately, very few small firms ever make the jump. It requires a tremendous amount of capital to pay the professional fees to CPAs and attorneys for the development of the initial stock offering and for the necessary filings with the SEC. Nevertheless, going public remains the only really effective approach to consistently obtaining equity financing.

If you have dreams of taking your operation public, you should plan carefully for that event. Professional advice will be required not only to structure the offering in accordance with legal guidelines, but to protect yourself and the interest of other owners in the firm.

TRADE CREDIT

People frequently overlook trade credit when they talk about sources of financing. Perhaps this is because it is so obvious. Nevertheless, ***trade credit*** is a tremendous source of financing for a firm, regardless of its size. In reality, the amount of trade credit issued each year by the businesses in the country exceeds the amount of all other types of borrowing. Trade credit, as we have discussed in previous chapters, arises by purchasing inventory, merchandise, supplies or other goods on account from a vendor. The terms of trade credit range from a few days to several months and are generally established by industry practices. If trade credit were not available, then cash would have to be used for all purchases. Such a requirement would put tremendous numbers of small firms out of business!

Trade credit is frequently issued with discount terms for early payment of the obligation. In a previous chapter, we explained how those cash discounts could be converted to annual percentage rates. The process was simply dividing the grace period or extended payment period into 360 days and multiplying the result by the amount of the discount. For example, 2/10, net 30 day terms mean a 2% discount is available if paid within 10 days, but the balance is due in 30 days at the most. For these terms a 20 day extended payment period exists (30 - 10) and there are 18 such periods in a year (360/20). That means that the annual percentage rate which would result from not taking the discount is 36% (18 X 2%). The other side of the coin is that the 10 day payment period amounts to free credit. It may be that the cost of not taking cash discounts is too high to be able to afford, although that is not always the case. If a firm gets into trouble and is unable to obtain other types of financing, then the cost becomes less important. Under normal circumstances, the discount period may be all that is available, but it is still a source of credit.

LOANS

When we talk about financing, most people think of loans. There is a tremendous variety of loan arrangements which can be made. Prominent among these are revolving credits and term loans.

Revolving credits are amounts which are set aside by a bank or other lender which can be used on an as needed basis by a business, repaid and then used again.

Lines of Credit

A *credit card* is a line of credit for an individual. A specified amount is established as the maximum which can be borrowed. Thereafter, the borrower can use the credit whenever desired. Payments must be made regularly, but when the line has been reduced below the maximum, more funds are available for borrowing.

For businesses, *lines of credit* are generally issued for a year at a time. A firm will request a specified amount of credit which is usually supported by a cash budget. The line is intended to cover timing problems in the cash flow of a firm, not for expansion or other purposes. Needs of this type are called *working capital requirements*. The approved line can generally be drawn by simply writing a check or by telephoning the bank to ask for an advance to be deposited to the checking account. At the end of a year, the line is generally required to be completely repaid before it is extended for another year. This last requirement is used to ensure that the funds are used strictly for temporary cash needs. Total repayment of the line would be difficult or impossible if the funds were used to finance anything other than short term cash flow requirements.

Lines of credit may be secured or unsecured, that is it may have collateral pledged or not. The owner of a small businesses is frequently asked to *endorse*, *co-sign* or *guarantee* the line. Any of these actions simply makes the owner personally responsible for the repayment of the debt. This precaution is frequently required by lenders because a small business is generally totally dependent upon its owner for success.

A revolving line of credit can be an extremely valuable type of financing if properly managed. Almost every company will experience cash flow variations which can cause extreme problems in the short run. Lines of credit are ideal solutions for such problems. It is virtually impossible for a small business to obtain such a line however, unless good budgeting techniques are used in the business. All banks prefer, and most demand, that lines of credit be supported by cash flow budgets which show when and how much will be needed as well as when and how much will be repaid. One word of caution is due here. Never use a line of credit for anything other than short term cash flow deficits. If you follow that rule, a line of credit can make managing a business easier and more pleasant.

Many small businesses do not use revolving lines. Instead, 30, 60 or 90 day notes are used. These may be unsecured or secured and may require owner guarantees, just like other loans. These short term loans can serve the same purpose as a revolving line, but the bank has total control over each transaction and whether the note will be required to be paid at maturity or will be renewed. Should the bank become disturbed over economic or other conditions or an interim financial statement or any other change in a business, it will probably not be willing to renew notes or advance any further amounts. Consequently, these short term notes are not a viable vehicle for financing. Their popularity is a result of the absence of budgeting activities among small businesses. Banks will make 90 day loans supported only by a financial statement and a verbal description of need. A line of credit generally needs more. We highly recommend that you avoid short term notes. Do the budgeting necessary and use lines of credit. The results will be much more desirable.

Term Loans

For needs other than those of a cash flow nature, ***term loans*** of all types can be used. These loans have maturities from 1 to 10 years although banks tend to prefer the shorter periods. Anything over 5 years is unusual. Term loans are generally secured. That means that some of a firm's assets are pledged as collateral. Accounts receivable, inventory, furniture, fixtures, machinery, equipment, vehicles, etc., can be used as collateral. Term loans are generally installment in nature. That means that a specified amount of payment is required each month during the life of the loan. Because the loan repayment is fixed, budgeting the cash to cover the requirements is possible.

Term loans are used for a variety of purposes but most frequently for the financing of purchases of long lived assets. They are one of the most frequently used financing vehicles for small businesses. They frequently have higher interest rates than short term notes because the risk factor for the lender is greater with a longer period for repayment. Guarantees from the owners are frequently required as well.

Commercial mortgages are term loans which are secured by real estate or buildings. These loans generally have maturities from 10 to 20 years. Owner guarantees are frequently required for these loans as well as the other types. Mortgages are generally used to acquire land, build buildings, make renovations or major repairs, etc. It is possible for a mortgage to be acquired on a building alone when the land under it has a long term lease. Frequently, a business will be able to obtain lease terms for urban land of 10, 20 or 30 years, but will be unable to buy that land. In such cases, a mortgage can be acquired to finance the construction of a building with the lease assigned and a lien on the building conveyed to the lender.

Bonds

Bonds are debt securities which are sold to investors just as stock certificates or limited partnership certificates. Large firms use bonds, which are generally secured by assets of the business, or ***debentures***, which are not generally secured, to raise debt capital. These securities will have specified interest rates and maturity dates and will be sold in financial markets. This approach is not generally feasible for a small business because it really requires access to a financial market to be effective. Those firms that make the leap to public corporations can use bonds and debentures, but most other firms cannot.

Table 1
Sources and Uses of Capital

Sources of Capital	Uses of Capital	Form of Capital
Personal Funds and Savings	Start-up Capital	Equity
		Long Term Debt
Family and Friends	Start-up Capital	Equity
		Long Term Debt
Partners, Friends, Business Associates	Start-up Capital	Equity
	Expansion Capital	Long Term Debt
Private Investors (Need professional assistance)	Start-up Capital	Equity
	Expansion Capital	Long Term Debt
Venture Capitalists	Start-up Capital	Equity
	Expansion Capital	Long Term Debt
Small Business Investment Companies	Start-up Capital	Long Term Debt
SBICs and MESBICs chartered by the SBA	Expansion Capital	
State sources (State Business Assistance Office)	Start-up Capital	Long Term Debt
	Expansion Capital	
Local Development Companies	Expansion Capital	Long Term Debt
Industrial & Business Development Agencies	Expansion Capital	Long Term Debt
Federal Sources	Start-up Capital	Long Term Debt
Small Business Administration	Expansion Capital	
Department of HUD		
Department of Commerce		
Farmers Home Administration		
(directory available from Printing Office)		
Banks	Start-up Capital	Long Term Debt
Independent, SBA Certified, and	Expansion Capital	Short Term Debt
SBA participating	Working Capital	Lines of Credit
	Commercial Mortgage	
	Equipment Purchase	
Savings Banks and Mortgage Companies	Start-up Capital	Long Term Debt
	Expansion Capital	
	Commercial Mortgage	
	Equipment Purchase	
Insurance Companies	Start-up Capital	Long Term Debt
	Commercial Mortgage	
	Equipment Purchase	
Finance Companies	Start-up Capital	Long Term Debt
	Equipment Purchase	Short Term Debt
	Working Capital	
Stock Offerings (Public or Private)	Start-up Capital	Equity
	Expansion Capital	

Sources of Financing

Loans can be acquired from banks, finance companies, insurance companies, mortgage companies, savings and loan associations, venture capitalists, private investors and individuals. Loans can be obtained from federal, state and local governments and agencies or can be partially or fully guaranteed by such agencies. We talked about these sources at length in a previous chapter. For a small business, access to future credit can frequently be as important as good terms and rates on a loan. That means that obtaining a loan, of any sort, is not simply a matter of choosing the lender with the longest maturity and the lowest interest rate. It may well be worth a little higher rate and a shorter term if the result is the development of a borrowing relationship which can help the firm in the future. Building a good relationship with a lender is vital. Taking some business away and bringing some business to a lender is not normally a good way to cultivate such a relationship. We will talk more about this in a later section on bank relations.

Table 1 is a recap of the sources of funding and their typical use in small businesses. We examined the start-up capital issue previously. In this chapter, we have focused on expansion and working capital, commercial mortgages and equipment financing. Expansion loans indicated in the table are generally a combination of working capital and equipment or fixtures purchases. That is, some portion of the loan is expected to be used to handle the short term needs associated with growth of the business. In the next section, we will examine the differences and roles of short, long term and permanent financing.

THE ROLE OF DEBT IN RISK MANAGEMENT

How much debt should a business have? Which is better: short term debt or long term debt? These are difficult questions because there is no one answer. Like most things in business, it depends on the industry, conditions, competition, and the desires and preferences of the owner(s) of a business.

DEBT VERSUS EQUITY

There are three factors to consider about debt or equity financing. These are risk, cost and availability. The availability issue frequently makes the decision for a small firm. That means that equity financing is frequently not a viable option for a small firm outside its start-up as we discussed in the previous section. Consequently, small firms frequently depend totally upon debt for their financing needs.

Even if equity financing is not available, you need to be aware of the impact of debt on a firm's risk. The greater the debt level in a firm, the higher the risk to which that firm is exposed.

This is simply because the more money a firm is obligated to repay, the harder it is for that firm to handle the repayment. Failure to honor debt obligations will destroy a firm. Like all risk issues, however, there is a return tradeoff. Table 2 displays abbreviated financial data for three firms which are identical in every way except the proportion of debt financing which they use. Notice how the debt leverages up the return on the owner's investment in the firms. Because of this leveraging effect, debt levels are termed *leverage*. We say that a firm is highly leveraged, meaning that it has high levels of debt. Leverage refers to the relative amount of debt which a firm has compared to the amount of equity.

	Table 2		
	Debt Versus Equity Financing		
	Firm A	Firm B	Firm C
Total Assets	$100,000	$100,000	$100,000
Total Debt	25,000	50,000	75,000
Total Equity	75,000	50,000	25,000
Profit before Interest	15,000	15,000	15,000
Interest on Debt (10%)	2,500	5,000	7,500
Profit before Taxes	12,500	10,000	7,500
Taxes (30%)	3,750	3,000	2,250
Net Profit	8,750	7,000	5,250
Return on Equity:			
Net Profit/Total Equity	12%	14%	21%

The higher the leverage is in a firm, the lower its equity, consequently, the higher its return on investment. This is true so long as the interest rate for the debt is less than the profit margins. If interest rates exceed profit margins, then undesirable results will follow. Of course the risk also goes up with the returns. Judging how much debt is too much is largely a function of a firm's ability to repay the debt or its *debt servicing* capacity. In a previous chapter we talked about financial analysis and discussed ratios which can be calculated to evaluate a firm's debt capacity. We also discussed how comparisons of various ratios, including the debt ratio could be made to industry averages to determine how a firm compares with its peers.

The cost issue of the debt equity trade off is complicated by income taxes. The interest paid on debt is tax deductible. That means that a profitable firm in a 30% income tax bracket will actually pay only 70% of the interest charges on a loan because the remaining 30% of the interest will be saved in income tax reductions. All of the dividends paid on equity must be paid after tax, as we have discussed, so there is no corresponding reduction. In addition, debt is eventually repaid in full, while equity investments are generally permanent. Consequently, the after tax cost of debt is generally less than the cost of equity.

This is not the whole picture. In previous chapters, we have stressed that cash flow is really more important to a firm than profits. Dividends on equity do not have to be paid when there are no profits or when cash is not attainable, but loan payments must be made regardless of profitability or cash levels. In addition, the principal must be repaid along with the interest on a loan. Principal repayments do not show as an expense, but they do constitute a cash drain. This is the real reason that the risk level increases with the debt level. The impact of debt on cash flows must be assessed and it is this impact which is the real cost of debt.

SHORT TERM VERSUS LONG TERM

Another factor in the management of debt is the mix between short term debt and long term debt. Revolving credit, trade credit and notes payable are all short term credit obligations. Term loans and commercial mortgages are long term debts, although that portion of the loan which must be paid during the next fiscal year is actually a short term obligation as well. It shows on the balance sheet as current maturities of long term debt. The issue of which is better, short or long term, revolves around the source of funds for repayment.

There are really two sources of cash flow in a business: the liquidation of current assets and profits. Profits are funds left over after expenses have been paid and can be used for debt repayment or distribution to the owners or any other purpose which a firm desires. But if we take a short term perspective, the collection of accounts receivable will produce cash. That cash could be used to repay debt. You could argue that both sources of cash flow are really one in the same and that strictly speaking is true. However, if we view them as distinct sources, we can better balance short term and long term debt levels in the business. From a different perspective, we can say that long term debts are never actually repaid, but are reclassified as short term debts which are then repaid. It sounds like and it is a circular argument. Viewing the sources and types of debt as distinct simplifies everything and makes evaluation of the firm's debt level and debt mix possible.

Short term debts should be repaid from the liquidation of current assets. Therefore, if the level of current assets goes up, the amount of short term debt we can handle will go up also. This is a working capital concept. In a previous chapter we explained that *working capital* is the difference between current assets and current liabilities and indicates the resources which the firm has to support its day to day operations. So long as we maintain an appropriate balance between current assets and short term debt, the firm will be able to handle its obligations. Long term debt should be repaid from profits. So long as the relationship between profits being generated and long term debt is appropriate, the firm will be able to handle its obligations.

The trade off between short term and long term debt comes about because of the fluctuating nature of short term assets. Table 3 displays a growth curve for short term or current assets and long lived or fixed assets such as plant, property and equipment. The growth curve demonstrates how the assets must grow to support sales growth, but that current assets behave in a *sine wave* fashion. We demonstrated this same up and down pattern when we developed the cash budget in a previous chapter and it was the cause of the fluctuating cash flows.

Fixed asset growth follows a step function, as we have discussed. You cannot acquire half of a machine. Consequently, when sales grow beyond the firm's capacity, another block of fixed assets must be acquired.

The graph shows current assets going up and down with the seasonality of the business. As those assets go up, short term debt is needed to finance that growth. As those assets go down, cash is generated which should be used to repay the short term debt. The growth in fixed assets, on the other hand, is more constant and these assets do not generate cash directly, although they do support sales. The building which a firm occupies or the machines which it uses in its business do not generate cash but they do make it possible for sales to be made. Consequently, it would be foolish to acquire fixed assets with short term debt because there will be no cash generated by those assets for repayment. Long term debt should be used to finance the fixed assets and the source of funds for its repayment is profit or cash flow from current asset liquidations which is not required to cover short term debt.

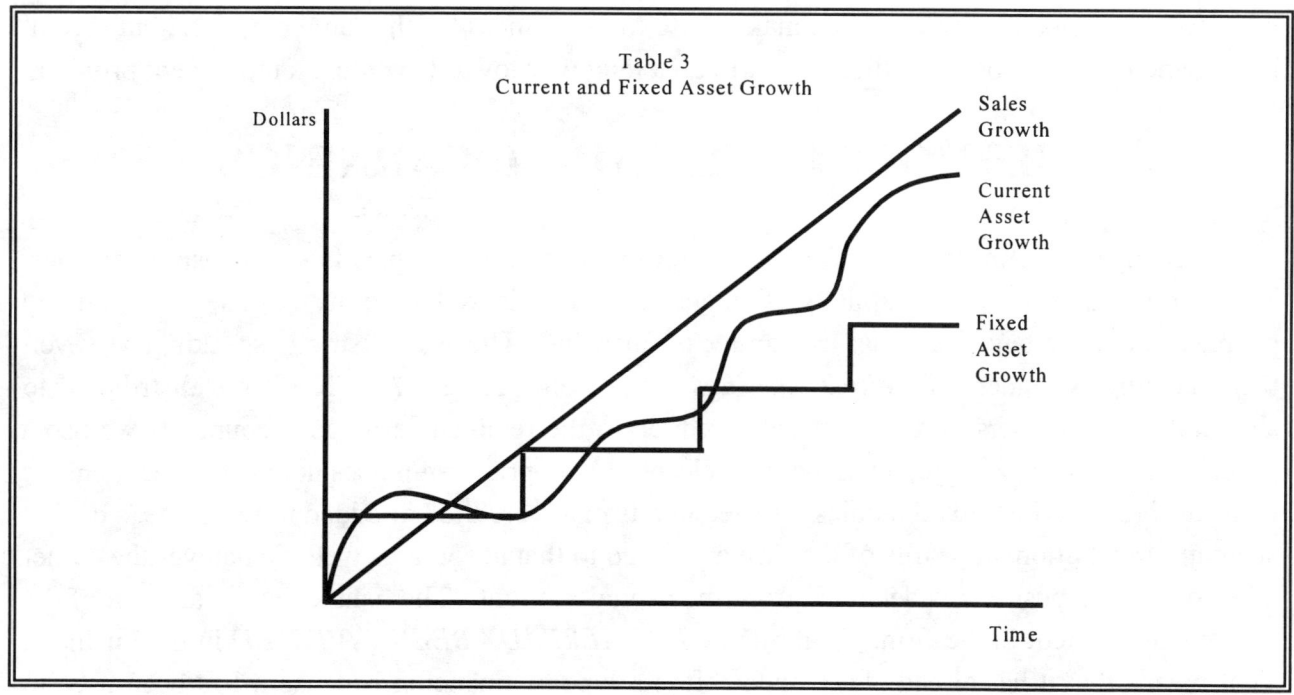

Table 3
Current and Fixed Asset Growth

It is possible to finance short term assets with long term debt, but that is also not usually wise, because after the assets have been liquidated, the debt will still remain. A drain on future profits will result despite the fact that only a very short period in the firm's life is improved by the debt. To finance a major expansion of a firm usually does require financing some short term assets with long term debt, because the firm wants to achieve a higher level of sales without having working capital problems restrict the growth.

For normal financing needs, working capital, equipment acquisitions, etc., it makes more sense to balance the use of debt: short term debt with short lived assets; long term debt with long lived assets. A portion of the current assets can be considered to be permanent because the inventory and receivables and other components of current assets will never actually be reduced to zero. The graph of current assets clearly shows that. Treating the permanent portion of current assets as long lived and using long term debt to finance it can make sense. This is really the justification for inclusion of working capital in an expansion loan. It can improve the operating cash flows of the business and make life easier. There is a danger however, in overestimating the permanent level of current assets. If that happens, we will simply be trading short term cash flow for future cash flow and problems will develop for the firm in the future.

There is one other source of funds which can be used to repay debt which deserves mentioning. That is other financing. Equity financing can be raised and used to repay debt. Debt can be used to repay debt. That means that a term loan can be used to retire short term credit or a loan can be renewed, that is the maturity extended. When debt is used to repay older debts, we are simply postponing a problem. Individuals do this frequently when they get into financial difficulties with loan consolidation loans. It can make sense for a business for the same purposes, but careful management of the debt in the first place will go a long way toward avoiding a repayment problem.

THE ROLE OF RETAINED EARNINGS

Many people are confused by the role which retained earnings play in small business finance. They show as an entry in the capital section and so are considered as equity. Consequently, many people talk about retained earnings as a source of financing. This is true, strictly speaking, however, the financing is hidden. ***Retained earnings*** come from profits. Any profit not distributed to shareholders or owners of a firm will be credited to the retained earnings account. If we use a proprietorship as an example, it will become clearer. A proprietorship does not have an account for retained earnings. Instead all monies invested in a firm are credited or added to the owner's capital account. In addition all profits of the firm are added to that account as well. Whatever the owner takes out of the business is deducted from the capital account. The balance is the amount of the owner's investment in the firm. That money *HAS ALREADY BEEN INVESTED* in the business. That means that it has already been spent. It is a type of financing because it has been used to acquire assets or repay debts, etc., but it is not a future source of financing. It is much like trade credit in that it arises on a daily basis as part of the business operations and is used on a daily basis and spent on a daily basis. Retained earnings in a corporation are exactly the same. They do not constitute a source of unused capital or future financing. Instead, they are simply evidence of the amounts of money which the owners have left in the firm and which have been used in the firm in the past.

MAINTAINING BANK RELATIONS

Any business which experiences seasonality or which is growing rapidly will require frequent access to credit. We have discussed how the fluctuations in current assets resulting from seasonality will create short term borrowing needs. The long term growth of sales will also create borrowing needs to finance the fixed assets which must be acquired to support the growth. Before the sales can grow, the capacity of the firm must be expanded. If we are operating at capacity in the present facilities, then no more sales can be made until capacity is expanded. That takes cash to finance the expansion. The money cannot come from operations, because sales have not yet expanded. Consequently, the funds must come from debt or equity financing. Since equity is frequently not viable, the conclusion is that term loans will be needed to support the growth.

Despite all the various sources of financing that exist, your local bank remains the most important single source because of the speed of possible response to credit needs. When a strong relationship has been established, there are no sources of credit which can react as fast as a bank. Consequently, developing and maintaining that strong relationship is important.

Banks actually make most of their money on businesses through deposits not through loans. That sounds strange because interest is charged on loans, but numerous studies have demonstrated its truth. All of the loans and other investments which a bank makes are supported by its customers' deposits, therefore, no income is possible without those deposits. In reality, this is the primary reason for the difficulties which small businesses encounter in bank relations: they simply do not have large enough account deposits to make them as valuable to the bank as larger firms.

There are two schools of thought about developing bank relations. One school says, *Don't put all your eggs in one basket, develop relations with at least two banks.* Another school says, *Banks don't like to share business with other banks so be loyal.* Both have some validity. It is true that banks prefer not to share a banking relationship with other banks. That means that you will have a stronger relationship if you do all of your business with a single bank. That means all checking accounts, credit card accounts, investments and loans for both the business and for the owners of the business. However, if the banking officer which you come to know leaves the bank or transfers to another town or if any changes occur inside the bank, it is possible for you to experience problems with loan requests. People who ascribe to the two bank approach have often experienced such problems in the past and have sought to avoid such problems in the future. However, since deposit balances are so important to a bank relationship, using two banks will inevitably lower your value to each bank. What can you do?

We recommend that you use a single bank until such time as the business grows to a point that it generates deposits which can support multiple banking relationships. That means that in order to avoid potential problems, you need to choose the bank carefully and strive to keep current with what is going on inside the bank. Far too many people make the choice of a bank based solely on convenience. The bank with the closest branch to their businesses are selected. It is wiser to visit every bank in town, talk to the lending officers, find out if there is experience in your industry in the bank, develop a relationship with the banking officers who will be supporting your accounts. If a bank has no lending experience with firms in your industry, it is going to be less supportive of your needs. Banks tend to specialize and lending officers employed by banks tend to specialize even more. Find an individual with whom you can talk, who is responsive to your needs, understands your business and is willing to take the time to become acquainted with your operation.

Your banker needs to have a sufficient lending authority to be able to handle your needs. Bankers are assigned a lending limit based on experience and longevity. If the officer you cultivate cannot approve your loan requests, then much of your efforts will be wasted. This frequently happens to small firms. They develop a strong relationship with the branch manager of the closest branch never realizing that all of their loan requests will be approved in the main office downtown.

Determining whether a bank officer has a loan authority which can cover your needs can be difficult. Bankers will frequently avoid such inquiries by saying that the loan committee makes the actual decisions. The ***loan committee*** is a group of loan officers who meet periodically to approve very large loans and loans which are beyond the credit limit of an officer. In some very small banks, virtually all loans must be approved by the loan committee, but in most banks the majority of small business loans are small enough relatively speaking that individual officers can approve them.

As a general rule, if your loans have to be approved by committee, you are in trouble. There is no way that all of the members of a committee can know you personally. That means that the decision will be based on cold, hard facts, like your financial statements and the bank's assessment of economic conditions. Your lending officer will generally be able to make a presentation to the committee in your behalf and can support your needs, but the value of that support is a function of the internal politics of the bank. That means that the relative power and prestige of your loan officer will affect the committees' reaction to his or her support. Not only that, it is much easier to make a negative decision in a group. It's just human nature to want to avoid unpleasant situations. When a group makes a decision, then the lending officer is absolved of responsibility.

This is one of the major reasons that it is so hard for an individual to obtain the loan necessary to start a business. There has been no relationship established with an individual and the amount of such loans are frequently so large that they require committee action. What all this means to you is that you should avoid a bank if it is going to shuffle all of your loan requests off to a committee for action. Go somewhere else! If you cannot find a bank in which an *individual* can handle your needs, then at least make sure that the person you cultivate inside the bank is a permanent member of the loan committee.

How do you learn all this information about a bank? It takes patience and persistence in visiting and interviewing bankers. Don't concentrate on branch managers. Go to the main office and ask to see people in the commercial or business lending area. Pick up a copy of the bank's financial statement, they will be laying on almost everyone's desk, and read the names and positions of the officers. Pick out someone in commercial lending to see. Ask people direct questions. Make them understand that these are issues which will influence whether you do business with the bank or not. Make them understand that once you settle on a bank you will bring all of your personal and business accounts to them and you will deal with them exclusively. Find out how the loan committee works. If the individual you're talking to cannot handle your needs, ask who can and then go see that person. In short, pay as much attention to choosing and developing a banking relationship as you do to the selection of any other professionals with whom you deal.

You need a banker who will visit your business and spend time getting to know you and your managers and understanding your markets, suppliers, problems, etc. After you have found such a person, keep the contact alive! That means providing monthly financial statements to the bank, whether they request them or not, visiting with your banker regularly, whether you need something or not. You want to develop such a sense of loyalty that your banker will keep you informed of pending changes within the bank which could affect your firm. You also want the banker to develop such a feel for your operation that he or she will know when and how you need money as soon as you do. That means being open with the banker. The monthly financials will help but you should make it a point to discuss potential changes and developments in your business whether those are positive or not. One of the strongest actions you can take is to institute a budgeting process and send copies of the monthly budget to the bank. This will not only keep the banker informed as to the projected developments but will force you to do a better job of budgeting.

THE IMPACT OF GROWTH

We talk about growth in businesses as if it were the primary, overriding objective of every firm. The truth is that growth which is unplanned and too rapid can kill a firm. The problem with growth is that you must have the people, systems and resources in place to handle the increased volume. If you don't, then it becomes a constant battle of trying to keep up. That is a battle that's hard to win. The larger a firm becomes, the more important it is to have good systems for handling sales, record keeping, merchandise, etc. The systems are as important as the people. If there are no systems for keeping track of things, then no one will know what is happening or be able to keep up with what is required. Systems require planning. People and resources require money. The time and money must be planned and managed as well as the added sales, or the firm will lose. Our client in the case from our files note lost what promised to be a strong, healthy business because he would not or could not do anything but sell. The owner of a business must be a manager. There is no one else to worry about organization or planning.

A CASE FROM OUR FILES

We were called in to assist the client in obtaining a loan. They wanted us to help prepare an SBA loan package because they had been turned down by every bank in town. There were two owners, 50%/50%, both young men in their late twenties. They had been in business for about a year and a half. We worked with them for almost a full year. Their sales growth was phenomenal. The first year of operations, sales were $40,000. The second year, sales were $170,000 and the first two months of the third year, sales were $70,000. That was really the whole problem.

The business had been strictly retail for most of its first year. They sold pottery, baskets, macrame and craft items and supplies, wicker and rattan items and a large assortment of imported gift and novelty items. The retail store seemed to do well. They had started the business with an SBA guaranteed loan through a local bank and they made money the first year.

Then one of the partners discovered wholesale. Dan was approached by several small dealers at a show. It seems that his wicker and rattan items were popular but hard to find. He agreed to wholesale some of it. In less than four months he had become known nation wide. Seems he had the best prices in the country. At the time we came in, the business was sitting on $60,000 of wholesale orders which it couldn't fill because it didn't have the money to buy the merchandise. They needed a loan, quickly!

Burt wasn't too happy with his partner. They had been friends since high school, but Burt had doubts about how much profit they were actually making on all these sales. They had to rent a warehouse to process the stuff and hired 2 or 3 more people to try to keep up with it. We wondered about profits too. Dan was too popular. During our first visit with him he was interrupted by telephone calls from buyers 6 times in one hour. He sold everyone of them something.

The accounting system was a mess. They had hired an accountant to prepare the year end statement for the last year and intended to do that again. There was a clerk who was posting records in house, but no one had any idea what the inventory looked like. The sales weren't even separated between wholesale and retail. The P&Ls which they were preparing showed a profit, but Dan was the only one who believed it was true.

We tried to talk them out of a loan application. We said that would only postpone the problem. They had to get things under control before they got entirely out of hand. Dan wouldn't listen. We did prepare a loan application, but it was turned down after 4 months of trying. Dan continued to sell. Things got worse.

They hired a person to be the bookkeeper. We set up the books, but it didn't seem to work. The bookkeeper couldn't get the transactions down. Dan was too busy to tell her what he had done. He was buying and selling by phone with no records. Bills and invoices would come in and no one knew where the stuff was. Some of it was drop shipped. The warehouse was a mess. It wasn't safe to go in the place. Rattan furniture was stacked so high that it looked ready to fall over any second. Dan kept selling.

We tried to get him to slow down. He wouldn't listen. There was no money to meet payroll. Burt had enough and quit coming in. He wanted Dan to buy his stock. We said its easy to slow down, just raise prices! Not only will your growth slow down but you'll be generating more money with each sale. Dan wouldn't listen. Some guy in the bank lent him $8,000 using some accounts receivable as collateral. That got him through the end of the year.

A CASE FROM OUR FILES (continued)

We tried to rush the end of the year financial statement so that Dan would see the real problems. The accountant couldn't figure out the books. We never did see the actual statement for that second year. The internal records still showed a profit, but the inventory levels were ridiculous. Dan kept selling.

People started suing. Actually, we discovered that they had been for some time. Dan finally told us that he had some suppliers who hadn't been paid in a year. When they cut him off, he just found another one and kept right on. These guys were in Spain and all over. We couldn't believe they would sell on credit to someone they never heard of, but Dan was a born salesman.

Things got so bad that Dan began to listen. He laid off most of the people. Burt wasn't talking to him anymore. It looked like it was too late to save much. We told him it was either stop selling or bankruptcy. He was listening. Then the phone rang and Dan sold $20,000 worth of stuff he didn't have. When he got off, he told his bookkeeper to write checks to pay off three of the suppliers. He wanted to buy from them again to fill this order. She said there was no money in the bank. He said, yeah, but it'll get me a couple of weeks. We walked out. We heard a few months later that he was bankrupt. We weren't surprised. We never saw anyone who worked harder at failing.

How can you avoid growth problems? The answer is plan. Use the budgeting processes we have discussed. Make arrangements for the financing to support the growth in resources and people needed. Set up systems to handle the growth. Don't let the growth get out of hand! If it starts going faster than you can handle, raise prices. If that doesn't work, raise prices again. You can always drop the prices back when you get a handle on things. Don't be afraid of losing out permanently because of higher prices. If you do lose some accounts, that is preferable to losing the business.

FINANCIAL PLANNING

Financial planning is a phrase which has gained popularity in recent years. From a narrow perspective, it is the process of arranging the financial support for a company's needs. The tools are budgeting and financial analysis. From a broad perspective, much of what we have discussed in this book could be considered financial planning. Almost everything we do in a business has a financial impact: from determining salary levels for employees to deciding how much capacity is required in our fixed assets; from establishing minimum cash levels to determining prices. The important part of the phase is *planning*. Throughout the text, we have stressed the need to plan. In an *Inc* article, Bruce Posner says that planning is just another word for good management.[66] The success stories of entrepreneurs who made a fortune with *seat of the pants* management are examples of *pure, dumb luck*, Posner says. The truth of the matter is that the failure to plan is to doom a firm to a mediocre existence if not to absolute failure.

In the realm of finances, planning requires attention to the sources and uses of financing alternatives, and the maintenance and cultivation of financing relationships which can be used in the future. There are no mysteries or magic formulae. Planning is simply work. It is a manager's work. It is the one thing which an owner must do and it is the thing which separates weak businesses from strong. All of the talk about firms which fail due to cash flow problems, inadequate capital and all the rest, are really stories about firms which did not plan. The primary message of this book and of all of the literature about successful small business management is to *PLAN* is to *SUCCEED*.

SUMMARY

Finance consists of all sources of funding available to a business. There are two such sources: debt and equity. The principal difference between the two is that debt must be repaid while equity need not. Therefore, debt creates greater operational problems for a small business. Although equity can cause control problems and can be expensive, debt can bankrupt a business.

How much debt a business should have depends upon the industry, conditions, competition and the desires and preferences of the owner. However, there are three factors which impact debt: risk, cost, and availability. Nevertheless, availability frequently makes the decision for a small business.

The cost factor involved in debt and equity is complicated by income taxes. The after tax cost of debt is generally less than the cost of equity, but its real cost is the impact on cash flow. Dividends do not have to be paid when there is no profit, but repayment of debt must be made regardless.

A major factor in the management of debt is the mix between short and long term debt. The issue of which is better revolves around the source of funds for repayment. There are two sources of cash flow in a business: the liquidation of current assets and profits. The most sensible policy in general is to use short term debt to acquire short lived assets and to use long term debt to acquire long lived assets. Short term debt will be repaid from liquidations, while long term will be paid from profits.

Retained earnings are often mistakenly considered sources of funds. However, they are simply evidence of the amounts of money which the owners have left in the firm and which have been used in the firm in the past.

Any business which experiences seasonality or rapid growth will require frequent access to credit. Consequently, it is important to find and develop a relationship with the right bank and the right person in the bank to meet your needs.

Growth is typically a primary goal for small businesses and is to be admired because it reveals success. However, unplanned and too rapid growth can and will kill a business. The solution is planning which is the ultimate task of the manager.

QUESTIONS, EXERCISES AND CASES

QUESTIONS:

1. What are the two sources of funding available to a small business?
2. What is the difference between the two sources mentioned above?
3. In what two ways may debt be repaid?
4. How does a limited partnership work?
5. What are some of the investment instruments available to a corporation?
6. How do dividends work in preferred stock investments?
7. What is the difference between common and preferred stock?
8. Why is it difficult for small businesses to find equity investors?
9. Why is trade credit such a good source of funding for small businesses?
10. What are the various loans available to small businesses?
11. What are the three factors to consider about debt or equity financing?
12. Explain the relationship between debt and risk.
13. What are the two sources of cash flow in a business?
14. For what should long and short term loans be used?
15. What is the role of retained earnings in small business finance?
16. How does one establish a good bank relationship?
17. Why is it necessary to investigate the bank and loan officer before making a decision on who should handle your loan requests rather than just adhering to the policy of convenience of location?
18. With how many banks should you establish a relationship and why?
19. Why can unplanned and too rapid growth kill a small business?
20. What is the primary illness which kills small businesses?

EXERCISES:

1. Make an appointment with a local bank loan officer, in the main office preferably, and ask questions about evaluating a small business that wants to make a loan. Are there different guidelines for long and short term loans? How does the banker feel about small businesses in general? Does the banker make client calls? Upon whom? Evaluate your impression of the visit for the class. Would you consider this banker for your own if you were involved in a small business?

2.   Go see a small business owner and ask how that person chose a banking situation and why. Don't be surprised if they tell you that they have more than one bank. Ask them why if such is the case. Ask them also if they have ever considered a different banking relationship and why?

3.   Consider the area. Have you ever watched a seemingly thriving business suddenly close its doors? Do you know why? If you can question someone involved with the business perhaps you can discover what caused the failure? Was it growth? What could you have specifically recommended to the owners given the chance?

CASE

Trey Ensley and Jason Fairchild were called in to help a local business. They were surprised by the call because all around the town, the scuttlebutt was that Strips and Straw was astoundingly successful. They had opened their doors five years ago when they decided to turn a hobby into a business. Jane and George Cleveland had been making baskets and chairs and anything wooden for a number of years. George had learned the craft from his father and grandfather who had used the skill to get them through the bad times when they were out of work at the mill. George had learned really just by being the errand boy for them and had picked up the trade quickly. He had a way with wood really that the others envied. He could see a plan in his mind and transform that image into reality.

As was the custom in the mountains, George had married just out of high school and both Jane and he had gone to work at the local mill. Jane was employed in the bookkeeping area and George was on the loading dock. For relaxation, George still worked on baskets and wooden furniture. Jane found that she had a talent for painting designs and embroidery, so many evenings found them in front of the fire making things for their friends and family.

They went into business by happenstance as it were. George hurt his back on the job and had to leave on disability. His injury was such that he could no longer lift heavy burdens, but he wasn't qualified to do anything else. Jane's job was also in jeopardy. The mill where she worked was being forced to relocate and her job was also running out. What could they do?

During George's convalescence, he had worked on weaving baskets, because that kept him occupied while he was unable to be up and around. Friends had hit upon a perfect way to help them out by asking George to make baskets for them for gifts. This brought in some income and the demand increased.

When Jane's job was finally phased out, she began helping George with the woodwork while she looked for another job. Everyone liked the Clevelands, but the jobs were scarce. So more and more time was spent in what they perceived as a hobby.

One evening they decided after a frustrating day of looking for nonexistent jobs, that they were working and making an income already. A friend of theirs had asked them to make some baskets and wooden products on consignment for his craft shop and everything had sold quickly. He had asked for more. In fact, he had asked for one hundred more over the next three months.

Jane and George wanted to give their business a name and decided on Strips and Straw. The next few years were busy but happy and then their work really caught on. They had shown their wares at several craft shows and the orders were really coming in. In fact, they had more orders than they had supplies or time. They were working out of their house and already there was no room to walk and work was becoming impossible and yet the demands on their time were incredible. They had decided to open a store. They needed a loan and they needed advice. Things were getting out of control. They were six months behind in orders and even though their expenses had been reasonably low, they were finding it hard to actually ship their finished products. They had purchased a large supply of material because they needed it to finish up their last order. They had not received payment for the order because the contract called for payment on delivery, yet they had to pay for the material on receipt. At the rate they were going, they weren't going to be able to make that delivery. So they called Trey and Jason for help.

1. What are several problems which Strips and Straw is currently facing or will soon face? What kinds of decisions will they be forced to make?

2. What advice can the consultants give Jane and George?

3. What do you suppose their prospects are for getting a bank loan to tide them over? What will they need to prepare to show to a lender?

4. What kinds of things should the Clevelands have done in prior planning for such an occasion?

5. What are some possible sources of funding for the Clevelands?

6. Discuss how the business can be saved.

CHAPTER TWENTY ONE

PRODUCTION MANAGEMENT

CHAPTER OBJECTIVES

Upon completion of this chapter, you should be able to:

- Explain what manufacturing is;

- List the types of production;

- Explain the concept of risk and return;

- Explain the steps in production planning;

- Describe *just in time inventory* policies and when they will apply;

- Explain the concept of product control and to what it refers; and,

- Describe management's role in control and production.

PRODUCTION MANAGEMENT

INTRODUCTION

Thomas Carlyle said, *Man is a tool using animal..., without tools he is nothing, with tools he is all.* When he distinguished humans from animals through tool use, Carlyle was probably thinking about the use of simple hand tools. During his day, sophisticated machinery was virtually unknown. Nevertheless, machines are tools and the modern application of machines has been the dominant factor in the rise of civilization. The Industrial Revolution was largely brought about by the development of machines and manufacturing processes. Today, only a tiny fraction of the world's population is untouched by manufacturing and that percentage shrinks each year. The first step which emerging nations must take to make themselves part of the world community is the development of their manufacturing processes. You have probably read about the decline of manufacturing in the United States and the rise of service industries; about how we are shifting away from a production orientation. It is true that the number of manufacturing and blue collar jobs is shrinking and the number of clerical and white collar jobs is growing; it is true that firms in the services industries are making great strides and that many such firms now are named in the *Fortune* list of the 100 largest firms in America when once that list was totally dominated by manufacturing firms. Nevertheless, the production of goods is and always will be a mainstay of business. No economy can exist without manufacturing, no business can survive without products, tools and machines produced by manufacturers, no standard of living can be maintained without the products and goods produced by manufacturing. The only thing that has truly changed is that manufacturing has become an increasingly complex and competitive business. The management of manufacturing firms must become increasingly sophisticated in order for their firms to remain competitive.

None of this means that small businesses cannot enter and succeed in manufacturing. It is true that the majority of small business ventures are in fields other than manufacturing, but that is predominantly because of the entry barriers. It takes a great deal more capital to start a manufacturing operation than it does to start any other type of venture because of the initial investment required in plant assets. Since small businesses are almost universally plagued by capital shortages, it follows that fewer small firms venture into manufacturing. Nevertheless, there are many, highly successful small firms engaged in manufacturing. In fact, some of the greatest opportunities for new ventures exist in the area of manufacturing. Such firms are frequently the site of the development of new products, new methods of production and innovative operations. Like their counterparts in other industries, small manufacturers are a mainstay of the US economy and a vibrant part of American business. In this chapter, we will address the key aspects of production planning and control which are required for a small manufacturing operation to succeed.

MANUFACTURING

In general terms, ***manufacturing*** is the process of converting raw materials into usable products. To raw materials are added labor and capital to transform them into salable units. Success in such an operation involves the effective management of the resources of money and people and effective control of their combination through a production process. We have talked about human resources management and financial management, consequently, we will focus here on the management of the production process itself.

There are many types of production. The one most people think of when they think of manufacturing is a process system. In a ***process system***, a homogeneous product is produced in a continuous operation. ***Homogeneous*** means that the individual units of product cannot be distinguished from each other. A good example is a cement manufacturing plant. Raw materials go in one end in a continuous stream and cement comes out the other end, also in a continuous stream. There are special problems associated with the management of a process system, as is the case with other types of systems. ***Job order systems*** are polar opposites of process systems. In this type of production, no two units of output are the same. A manufacturer which produces a unique product to customer specifications is an example, such as a custom designed, machine tool producer. Of course, few firms are ever clearly involved in one or the other types of operations. There are differences in cement! It may take a chemist to identify different types of cement, but engineers specify characteristics of cement which they require for the kinds of projects they build. In addition, one of kind orders frequently develop repeat opportunities. The first order for a space shuttle was a custom designed product, but the second shuttle was not!

One of the main differences between manufacturing operations is the use of ***subassemblies***. Many manufacturing firms are really assemblers because they purchase everything they need in the form of completed subassemblies from other manufacturers and then assemble the parts into a finished product. Many computer manufacturers operate in this fashion. Other firms start with totally raw materials and carry through to a finished product. Oil refining is frequently done like that. Still other firms stop at various points along the way. These are the companies which produce the subassemblies used by other manufacturers. Still other types of firms purchase completed products and then make modifications. Firms which produce custom vans, automobiles and the like, generally buy a completed vehicle and then convert it in their plants. As you can see, the combinations possible between these types of approaches are limitless!

RISK AND RETURN

Before we talk about the management of production, we need to say a few words about the risks and returns associated with production. Because the machinery and plant required to manufacture a product tend to be highly specialized, the impact of failure is high. If a retailer fails to make a go of one of its products, it simply drops that product. If a manufacturer fails to succeed with one of its products, there may be equipment and facilities which cannot be used for other purposes. The market for used, special purpose equipment is small! The manufacturer stands to lose a great deal. That's why assembly has become so popular in recent years in high technology businesses. If we are buying subassemblies from other manufacturers, then conversion to another product is simplified if the market for what we are producing changes. The risk is shifted backward to the firm producing our subassemblies. This has become extremely popular in recent years and is often called **outsourcing**. Of course, if we subcontract or outsource our fabrication, we won't make as much money, because the subassembly manufacturers are charging us for the cost of production plus a profit margin for themselves. Risk and return are almost always commensurate with each other. The point which you should keep in mind is that your manufacturing business can manipulate its risk/return tradeoffs by subcontracting parts of the production process and/or by buying more and larger subassemblies. The choice should not be made blindly, but should be made only after a careful evaluation of the alternatives.

PRODUCTION PLANNING

Production planning consists of the designation of raw materials required for production, the selection of machines and labor skills to be used in production, the specification of volume of output and the acquisition of material and labor required to achieve that output, and the timing required for each phase of the operation. The first part of planning is the design phase. Here is where you must decide how you will build each product which you produce. What raw materials are required, what subassemblies will be used, and how the fabrication will take place. The outcome of the design planning will be a bill of materials and a work layout. The *bill of materials* is a list of the specific items and quantities required to produce one unit of output. It is the basis for raw materials inventory management which will be conducted in much the same way as retail inventory management which we discussed in that chapter. The *work layout* details the fabrication steps: what must be done to convert the raw materials to finished goods; whether the step will be done by machine or by hand; the order in which steps must be completed; and how the work will flow through the fabrication process. The work layout can be a lengthy document if the fabrication process is complex. Each stage in manufacturing must be detailed and described. This is where you say *part A is attached to part B* and describe how the attachment is accomplished; by hand, by machine, welded, bolted, etc. In addition, the work layout must specify how all of the steps in fabrication fit together. If two parts must be put together to form a subassembly which will be added just before the fabrication is finished, then the work flow must be planned to ensure that the needed subassembly is ready when the rest of the production has been completed.

DESIGN PLANNING

To visualize design planning, think about the manufacture of automobiles. There are thousands of parts involved in the bill of materials and there are hundreds of subassemblies which will be used in production. If the assembly line approach is used, then multiple assembly lines are required so that a continuous stream of subassemblies are ready to be added to the units in process at the correct time. The main assembly line starts out with the construction of the frame of the automobile, but simultaneously another assembly line must be preparing the engines to be attached to the frame at the correct point. The same is true for the fabrication of the automobile bodies. Still other items from the bill of materials must be provided in a continuous stream to the correct point in the work flow: seats, windows, tires, batteries, and a host of other items. The efficiency of the operation is, in large measure, a result of the planning which has been done. Whether you are building a product as complex as a car or not, the process is the same for your operation.

The best approach to the work layout is to start with the finished product and disassemble it on paper and in detail. Use graph paper and design the working space to scale at the same time. The space requirements will be a function of the number of people required to perform the operation, and the size and number of machines required. Be careful to locate sources of supply of raw materials and subassemblies properly. Place storage bins or tables or storerooms so that parts required will be close at hand to the operation in which they will be used. Locate assembly areas for phases of the operation which can be carried out simultaneously so that the subassemblies will flow into the main production smoothly. Make access to the storage areas easy for stocking purposes. Be sure to include inspection stations for quality review and control. This process is outlined in Table 1.

The result looks like a big flowchart. That's exactly what it is! It will not only show the work flow, but will show the size and layout for the building you will need. Once the layout has been completed, if there are restraints, such as the size and shape of a particular building which you wish to use, you can make adjustments to the flowchart to fit the process into the facility and determine modifications which must be made or special requirements such as wiring, water connections, etc. Be careful not to allow adjustments to snarl the work flow. If an existing facility is totally unsuitable, it will be better to find an alternative than to disrupt the work flow by forcing it to fit. Remember, the efficiency of the production will reflect the planning of the work flow and that efficiency can make the difference in profit or loss.

We have so far assumed that the units in process will move through stages where work is done. In some manufacturing processes, the product does not move because of its size. Aircraft manufacturing is an example. In such a situation the work flow diagram should show production and fabrication teams together with their equipment, raw materials and supplies, moving in and out of the product. The result is still a flowchart, but the items moving are employees and material. The key factors are: the minimization of movement of equipment; arranging for delivery of material to the proper location at the proper time; and, to minimize interference of crews with each other. An added detail is the removal or relocation of equipment when it is no longer needed.

Table 1
Work Layout Procedures

I.   Begin with finished product
    A.   Disassemble on paper
        1.   List all subassemblies
        2.   List all materials (include subassemblies)
        3.   List all supplies (glue, lubricants, etc.)
        4.   Describe labor procedures
            a.   number of people
            b.   duration of labor procedure
        5.   Describe machine procedures
            a.   number and size of machines
            b.   duration of machine process
        6.   Draw a graph or diagram of manufacturing steps

II.   Layout production process
    A.   Determine space requirements for each step
        1.   Space required for machines
        2.   Space required for people
        3.   Space required for material
        4.   Space required for supplies
    B.   For each step in graph or diagram
        1.   Draw a floor plan-to scale using graph paper
        2.   Locate machines and people on floor plan
        3.   Indicate points where materials and supplies must be injected into process
        4.   Determine what materials and supplies are needed at each point
    C.   Determine material and supply similarities between steps

III.   Layout plant
    A.   Draw a floor plan which aligns production steps so that common material and supply input points are located close to each other
    B.   Locate subassembly steps so that they feed into assembly steps appropriately
    C.   Locate storage bins or table or storerooms so that materials and supplies will feed into appropriate steps
    D.   Arrange access to assembly process and storage areas to ease the transfer of goods and restocking of materials and supplies
    E.   Locate inspection points for quality control

When you are done, the result will be a plant layout diagram and a written description of each operation in the fabrication process. Table 2 is an example of a very simplistic plant layout. It shows raw material coming into the process, where it is staged for production, where work is accomplished, how subassemblies flow into the main assembly process, and where quality checks occur.

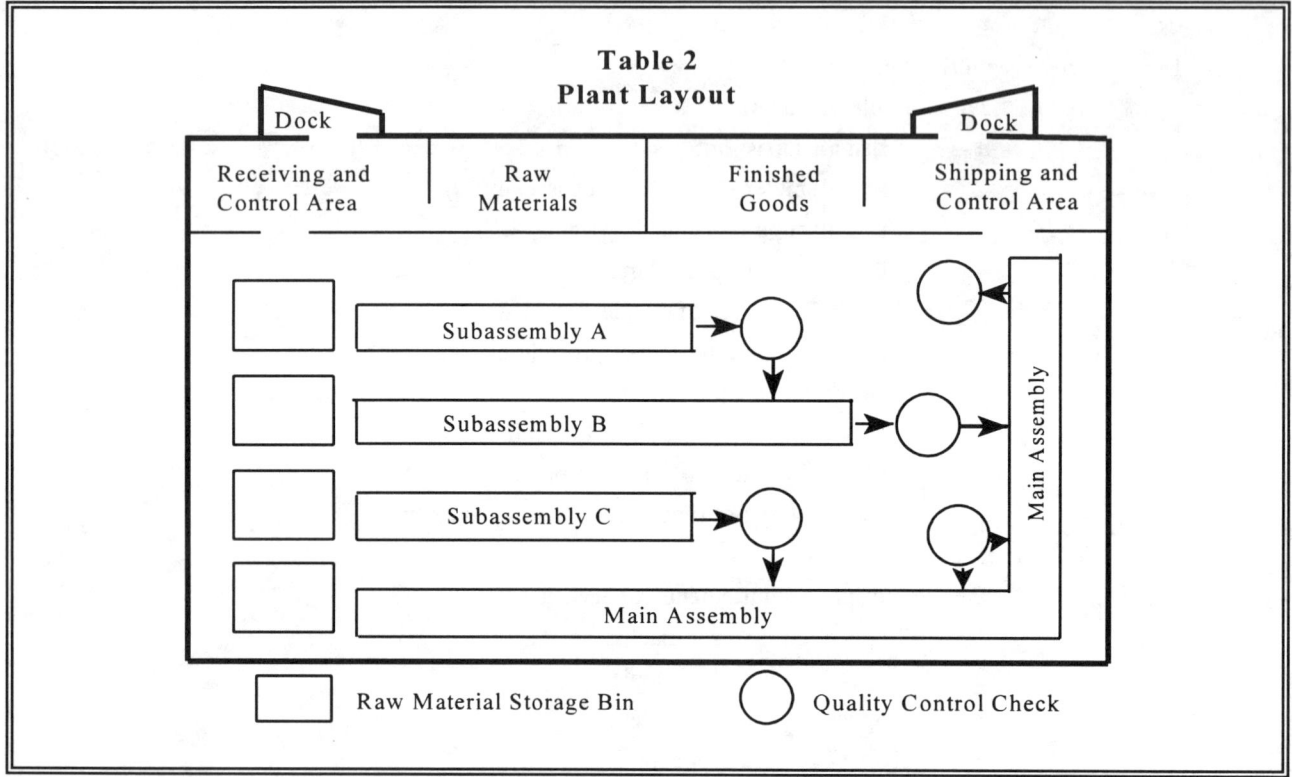

The description of each block in the work flowchart should explain what is done in that cell. This will not only provide a guide for supervision of the work, but will form a basis for specifications of skills and training required for the people to be employed. You should also devote some attention to estimating the amount of time which will be required to complete each step. This will be an ongoing problem, because the labor times will vary with skill levels and experience, but the initial estimates should be made at the time the work flow is laid out so that labor cost estimates can be prepared.

The design work is not completed when the flowchart is done. It will be difficult and expensive to change the work flow once it has been established, so you need to be as careful as possible. Nevertheless, the actual flow of work through the plant should be constantly monitored and if changes need to be made to streamline the process they should be. Get the people involved who are working on the production line and first line supervisors. Make sure that the layout is effective and efficient. Attention to the work flow will pay off in profit margins!

PRODUCTION SCHEDULING

The second phase of production planning consists of volume scheduling and is an ongoing need. The desired objective is to produce the correct number of items for sale as the demand for those items dictates. If you produce less than is needed, then the demand for higher levels of production can result in adding overtime wages or excessive errors, too much rework and poor quality as people try to find short cuts and push for higher output. All of these factors cause greater expense. In addition, if quality falls, permanent damage to the firm's image can result. If you produce more than is needed, then excessive inventories of finished goods develop. That creates problems in storing and handling inventory and raises inventory carrying costs. The answer, it seems, is to prepare a sales forecast and then to produce the correct amount of product to cover the forecast. There are two problems. The first is the difficulty of preparing a sales forecast. As we have discussed previously, the sales forecast is less accurate, the farther in advance it is prepared. That means that the sales forecast must constantly be adjusted to reflect changing conditions. This is less of a problem for a manufacturer which has a short production time, but can be a major problem for a firm which has a lengthy production phase. The second problem is in varying the production process itself. The skill and training levels required for manufacturing workers means that they are expensive and difficult to replace. That means that you will not be able to afford to have large amounts of idle or unproductive time in the work force, but neither will you be able to lay workers off for short periods as demand fluctuates. Changing the pace of production is not normally feasible either, because of the problem of maintaining quality and controlling rejects. If the pace of production is constantly going up and down, then errors, mistakes and oversights will be magnified. The workers won't be very happy either, especially if the compensation plan includes production incentives.

One approach to production scheduling is to determine the desired pace of production and then forecast sales. Now the inventory of finished goods is used to balance the two numbers. Consider an example. Assume that desired production is 10,000 units per month and sales forecasts are for 9,000 units per month over the next 3 months with an increase to 12,000 units for the 4th month. If you produce 10,000 units per month over the entire 4 months, then you will satisfy the forecast because 1,000 units will be added to inventory each of the first 3 months. Then, the extra 2,000 units needed in the 4th month can come from inventory, leaving it with 1,000 units left to carry forward to the 5th month. Most manufacturers make more than one item, consequently, the production planning is a matter of juggling the fabrication process between products. Since a new set up of the production line is required to change products and since that is a time consuming, expensive proposition, the production runs for each product need to be as long as possible without creating unreasonable inventory levels. Major changes in production volume beyond that possible at desired capacity are achieved by shifting workers from one task to another, by changing the number of shifts working, by scheduling overtime production, by buying larger quantities of subassemblies or contracting portions of the work out to other firms. All of those alternatives are expensive, consequently, the planning strives to minimize them. Of course, storing inventory is expensive also, but is generally less costly than the alternatives for production increases. Our main concern will be to prevent the inventory levels from becoming excessive.

This was one of the main problems for Chrysler before the coming of Iaccoca. Chrysler regularly built up large inventories of the various models of cars it manufactured before it retooled to produce different models. The other major car manufacturers had abandoned this practice, but Chrysler continued it. As Murphy's law predicts, when the market for large, high gasoline consumption cars dried up, Chrysler was left with thousands of unsalable vehicles. It actually had to rent large vacant lots to store the automobiles which dealers would not buy. Iaccoca not only changed the company's strategic competency by focusing on smaller, more efficient cars, he changed its production scheduling policies to protect it from excessive inventories in the future. The turnaround of Chrysler, hampered as it was by a myriad of other problems and inadequate capital, was a milestone in management history.

JUST IN TIME INVENTORY MANAGEMENT

In some industries, the problems of production scheduling are reduced by the willingness of purchasers to wait for products. In such industries, a ***just in time*** scheduling system is possible. Just in time (*JIT*) inventory policies have been gaining popularity in recent years because of the increasing use of automated scheduling and production control systems. Under *JIT*, the idea is to eliminate inventories. Production output is scheduled to coincide with projected shipping dates so that items are shipped directly to purchasers as they roll off the assembly line. Under conditions of stable demand or industry acceptance of longer lead times for shipment of purchases, *JIT* is a viable tool for reducing the cost of production. If demand fluctuates widely so that forecast of sales is difficult or if purchasers demand immediate delivery of their purchases, then *JIT* cannot work for production scheduling, although it can function for raw materials acquisition. If your company is a producer of consumer goods, then the demand characteristics are less likely to be as predictable as would be desired. If you sell to other manufacturers who use your products in their own manufacturing, then stability of demand is more likely to occur. In fact, your customers may desire to use a *JIT* approach to buy their purchases from you!

A manufacturer must manage raw materials inventory as well as finished goods inventory. An alternative to the practice of inventory management which we discussed in that chapter is the application of just in time inventory control to the raw materials. The objective of the process is to have sufficient raw materials arrive at the factory to support the production which is taking place, thereby eliminating the need to store large quantities of raw materials. In order for *JIT* to work for raw materials, the sources of supply must be dependable and lead times for the receipt of purchases must be predictable. If the industry is subject to problems in supply or to undependable shipping and transportation of goods, then *JIT* cannot work. Remember that both the ***source of supply***, that is the firms from which you purchase goods, must be dependable, and the ***lead time***, which is dependent on the firms which transport the goods from suppliers to your factory, must be predictable. If your raw materials are acquired from manufacturers in third world companies where political and economic conditions make suppliers undependable or if your goods are shipped by ocean freight in which arrival times are undependable, then you will probably have to accumulate at least basic levels of raw materials to prevent the production from being disrupted. If the potential for strikes among shippers or handlers or manufacturers of your goods is high, then you need plans for alternatives or you will require some level of raw material inventory maintenance. Many small firms discovered the danger of sole source reliance during the recent United Parcel Service strike. If *JIT* is possible, then it is vastly preferable to the other alternatives.

The bill of materials provides a listing of raw materials and subassemblies which must be acquired outside the company. The production schedule predicts the volume and rate of manufacturing. This information can be combined with lead time information on each item to be purchased to produce a series of orders for raw materials which will arrive at the plant in time to support manufacturing without a build up of inventory. If the bill of materials is lengthy, if lead times vary greatly by item, or if multiple raw material injection points into production exist, then the purchasing of raw materials can be extremely complex. From a practical perspective, it is extremely difficult to conduct a just in time inventory policy for raw materials without a sophisticated computer based system. Such a system can frequently be justified in the cost savings which can result. Just as economic ordering quantities, *EOQs*, were a step in reducing inventory costs, *JIT* is a larger step. Most suppliers who are dependable enough to permit *JIT* will willing cooperate in the implementation of the process. Although more orders occur under *JIT*, the overall supply of items by vendors takes on desirable characteristics for their companies as well. Remember that the vendors are manufacturers also. That means that they are plagued with the same problems in production scheduling that you are! Shipments under a *JIT* plan to your factory from their factories can provide the stability required to improve efficiency of their production. That means that they may be willing to make pricing concessions which can equal or exceed the old quantity discount which you would have received under *EOQ* inventory management. That cost reduction, combined with the virtual elimination of inventory carrying costs, and the minimization of inventory handling costs can mean great savings.

If *JIT* policies can be applied to production scheduling, then additional savings can occur in the form of more efficient production methods, higher quality of output, reduced set up costs, and the virtual elimination of finished goods inventory carrying and handling costs. As in the case of *JIT* raw materials inventory policies, *JIT* for production requires a dependable forecast of the demand for items and the dates such items must be shipped. Again, balancing the shipment times or lead times for delivery, the production time for fabrication, and the units required by various purchasers is an extremely complex process. An automated system is really required.

PRODUCTION CONTROL

Production control consists of the management of the flow of raw materials through the plant, the application of labor and machinery to the raw material, the flow of finished units and units in process through the plant, and monitoring of the quality of production. Much of the problem of handling raw material and finished goods is eliminated with a just in time inventory policy. Under *JIT*, the management is limited to receiving raw materials and shipping finished goods. If a *JIT* system is not used, then you must address the flow of raw materials from the receiving station to the storage locations, and the movement of those inputs from storage to the production line at the time required for use. Finished goods must be removed from the production line at completion and transferred to a storage location from which they will be removed for shipping when sold. Raw materials really follow the control patterns for inventory management. In the case of a manufacturer, the production schedule and the bill of materials dictates the quantities of items which will be required over time. This takes the place of converting sales forecasts to numbers of units of inventory. Using inventory monitoring procedures, minimum stock levels and economic ordering quantities, the raw materials must be kept flowing to production. As in the case of retailers, the raw materials can be tracked on a periodic or a perpetual basis. They must be subjected to physical inventory at least once each year and the ending inventory must be valued using *FIFO, LIFO*, or *average* techniques. Exactly the same things are true for finished goods inventory. In addition to controlling production, a manufacturer has two complete inventory systems which must be monitored! All this is another strong argument for *JIT* inventory policies whenever they can be used.

The other aspect of production control is the management of the fabrication process itself. There are two aspects to this management: the control of the flow of physical units and work; and the monitoring of costs associated with that flow. The *physical flow* refers to the introduction of raw materials into the fabrication process, the application of labor to the production, the movement of units in process from work station to work station and the maintenance of desired quality levels.

THE FLOW OF PHYSICAL UNITS

The design planning produced a flowchart of the work stations, a description of the work to be completed at each station and an outline of the flow of raw materials and subassemblies into the production process. All that was just a plan. In order for it to work, it has to implemented. The supervisors of the production process must oversee the actual work and ensure that the plan is carried out. The two inputs to production involved are labor and raw materials. The control over raw materials flow is shared by the people who handle the purchasing of raw materials and those who manage the use of raw materials. If either falls down, production will suffer. Purchasing control has been discussed previously, so we will concentrate on the control over the use of raw materials.

The design plan will show how raw materials should flow into production. One of the production supervisor's duties will be to see that the flow occurs. That individual should constantly monitor the bins, storage tables, shelves or storerooms in which raw materials begin their journey down the production line to ensure that the flow is not disrupted. Generally, the supervisor should take custody of the raw materials at the injection point. This custody should take the form of a signature of release for the raw materials from storage or from receiving. A document, generally called a ***requisition form***, shows the quantities and description of items which have passed to the control of the production supervisor. Thereafter, the supervisor will be concerned with observing the use of raw materials to ensure that the items are properly handled and that excessive breakage, waste or damage does not occur.

Control over the people doing the work is an exercise in human resource management. We talked at length about that in an earlier chapter. The production supervisor will be responsible for maintaining desired production levels and for monitoring the hours worked by the various people under his or her supervision. If production incentives are incorporated into the payroll plan, then the supervisor must capture the information necessary to make the incentive plan work. Of course, all this must be done while maintaining morale and quality of work. No easy job! Good first line supervision is crucial to effective production control.

The supervisor is responsible only for quantities of inputs. The costs of inputs are beyond the ability of the supervisor to control. Costs of raw materials are affected by purchasing and wage rates are set by management levels above the supervisor, although both of these costs can be influenced by the supervisor. Recommendations concerning quality levels of raw materials and performance levels of employees will have an effect on the ultimate costs of the inputs. Ultimate responsibility, however, rests with other management people.

QUALITY CONTROL

The supervisor is also responsible for the quantity and quality of output. He or she is charged with achieving the production goals and must accomplish that without sacrificing quality. Both quantity and quality of output is influenced by the quantity and quality of inputs. If inferior raw materials are purchased, inferior products will result. If poorly trained or incompetent people are used on the production line, inferior products will result. A first line supervisor will have little control over either of these occurrences, consequently, we must be careful to ensure that problems with output are within the ability of the supervisor to control before placing blame or taking corrective actions.

Quality control is not well understood. Most people tend to think of it as a technique for insuring that no errors occur in production or a way of assuring that all items produced are perfect. In reality, it is a management process devoted to the maintenance of an established level of product performance. Perfect products can never be consistently produced. Even if that were possible, it might not be desirable because of the costs of production. There are two aspects of quality control. One is the proper completion and construction of the product. Quality control procedures must be designed to totally prevent improper construction or fabrication. Such items cannot be sold because they are defective. If quality control procedures allow an excessive number of defective units to slip through, then the company will be damaged. It will have to replace defective units sold, or refund purchase prices. It may also suffer damage to its reputation which could affect sales in the long term. The second aspect of quality has to do with product performance: how well a product stands up under its intended use. This aspect of quality is subject to determination.

Control over defective units requires inspection stations to be set up along the production line so that items can be examined at crucial points. The location of the inspection station will have a major impact on its effectiveness. If fabrication results in interior components being enclosed in a shell, engine or body, then it will be impossible to inspect those components after they have been enclosed. Inspectors can check every item in production or take a sampling of items. It will obviously cost more to check every item than it will to check every 25th item. The decision about frequency of inspection is a function of the impact of errors. If we are filling 5 pound bags with dog food, then the impact of a error which results in putting 4.75 pounds in a bag is much less than would be the impact of putting 3 screws in a package which needs 4 screws for use in assembling a bicycle. In the former case, the error would probably go unnoticed by the consumer. In the latter case, we might get called by an irate consumer at midnight on Christmas Eve!

Quality control inspectors should not normally work for the line supervisor so that they will be less likely to be influenced in their reports. Since they are evaluating the work of the supervisor, they should report to a different manager or to the manager above the supervisor. Of course, defective units should be pointed out to the supervisor as they are found so that repair or rework can be accomplished.

The owner of a manufacturing firm must decide what level of performance quality is acceptable. This is generally a function of demand. For example, in the pharmaceuticals industry, an exceptionally high quality of output is required because the purchasers of the drugs and chemicals will be using them to treat human illnesses. On the other hand, a company manufacturing umbrellas will have a much lower quality level required. In fact, the relative sales value of the umbrellas will affect the quality control. For umbrellas which are intended to retail for $5.00, a much lower level of performance quality is required than for umbrellas which are intended to retail for $40.00! Performance quality is affected by inputs as well as fabrication. If lessor quality raw materials are acquired, or less skilled employees are utilized, lower quality products can be expected. Of course, those products will cost less to produce! Errors in fabrication can also affect performance. To consider the umbrella example again, if the fabrication process results in an inferior job of attaching ribs to cloth, then the item may not be caught as a defective item because it does work at the point the item is completed. Nevertheless, the umbrella will be inferior in that it will survive only a small number of uses before coming apart.

Performance quality cannot be measured by inspectors on the production line. Instead, products must be subjected to performance tests. The general approach is to select a sample of units and subject those to a variety of tests designed to monitor performance under simulated conditions. Sometimes commercials for products are designed to show performance testing as a way of building consumer confidence. We remember one such commercial in which a car door was being opened and closed by a mechanical hand while the announcer was saying that the door was subjected to 50,000 openings! We just hoped that the car in the commercial was not the one that we had bought!

Like quality inspectors, the performance testers must not report to the people who are responsible for production. In the case of inspectors, the reporting could be to the supervisor's boss because the supervisor had control over defective items. In the case of performance, the purchasing manager, the supervisor, the manager responsible for employee training, and a host of other people can have an impact on the product. Consequently, performance checkers generally report to a high level of management such as the plant manager or the owner.

Quality control is an important part of the production process because purchasers demand products which perform as their cost indicates they should. If there is a perceived gap in that match up, then over the long term, the producer will suffer. Effective quality control is not just a function of production. It requires attention from every manager in the organization on a continuing basis.

SUMMARY

Machines are tools and the modern application of machines has been the dominant factor in the rise of civilization. While it is true that service companies are proliferating in the U.S. today, one must remember that the production of goods is and always will be the mainstay of business. No economy can exist without manufacturing; no business can survive without products, tools and machines produced by manufacturing; no standard of living can be maintained without the products and goods produced by manufacturing.

While most small businesses are not manufacturers, it does not mean that they cannot succeed. The only real limitation is the necessity for a large amount of capital required at start-up.

Manufacturing is the process of converting raw materials into usable products. To raw materials are added labor and capital to transform them into salable units.

There are several types of production. One type is the process system whereby a homogeneous product is produced in a continuous operation. Another type of production is the job order system. In this type of production, no two units of output are the same.

One of the main differences between manufacturing operations is the use of subassemblies which can speed up the process of production considerably. Some concerns use no subassemblies and begin with the raw materials while others use partial assemblies in various phases of the operation.

Inherent to the manufacturing firm as to other businesses is the concept of risk and return. Manufacturing companies are especially susceptible to risk because of the size of the operation. Also, the greater the use of subassemblies in a manufacturing operation, the lower the risk.

Production planning consists of the designation of raw materials required for production, the selection of machines and labor skills to be used in production, the specification of volume of output, the acquisition of material and labor required to achieve that output, and the timing required for each phase of the operation.

Production control consists of the management of the flow of raw materials through the plant, the application of labor and machinery, to the raw materials, the flow of finished units and the units in process through the plant and monitoring of the quality of production.

Control is especially important if *JIT* inventory management is not possible. The other aspect of production control is the management of the fabrication process. This involves control of the flow of physical units and work and the monitoring of costs associated with the flow.

Another important control is quality control. Both quantity and quality of output is influenced by the quantity and quality of input and should be kept in mind by the manufacturer. Those persons charged with the task of quality control should be autonomous and free of the production process so that the temptation to pass certain imperfect items will not be a problem. The owner must decide what level of performance and/or quality is acceptable and ensure that those guidelines are maintained.

QUESTIONS, EXERCISES AND CASES

QUESTIONS:

1.   What do the terms manufacturing and production mean and to what do they apply?

2.   What are the two types of production?

3.   How do risk and return tradeoff?

4.   Explain the steps in production planning.

5.   Why are Just in Time inventory policies not always possible?

6.   What are the various functions involved in production control?

EXERCISES:

1.   Assume that you have been hired as a consultant to help with the plant layout requirements for a furniture manufacturer. How would you design the plant for such a company if fifteen pieces had to be assembled and then shipped? What other considerations might arise or questions might you be asked when presenting your design?

2.   If there are any small or even not so small manufacturing companies in your area, perhaps you could with the help of your instructor take a tour of the facilities and note the plant layout and evaluate their operation when you return to class.

CASE

Ralph Hobbs and his wife ran a small manufacturing firm. They employed thirty part time employees to cut and sew garments. There were ten sewing machines and twenty long tables equipped with patterns, shears, pins, needles and thread. Mr. Hobbs was not only the supervisor of the operation but also the one who laid out the work for each station and tracked inventory. Having part time employees, he was exempt from fringe benefits, but it also meant that the same employees worked at very different times. However, the ladies were encouraged to make production and were paid on that basis. For example, the cutting of sleeves might be worth $.20 a sleeve with production being 25 sleeves per hour. When that task was finished, the same employee might move to cutting legs or even to sewing sleeves. Operating the machines earned more money and so was frequently a source of contention among the ladies employed there. Mr. Hobbs had tried an equal time sharing technique for the machines, but some of his ladies did not do well on the sewing machines. The same was true for the pressing machine which was not as popular because of the heat.

Payroll was a nightmare which was handled by Mrs. Hobbs and took her a whole day to figure the production and then write the checks. At the end of each day, the ladies would turn in the stubs which showed the amount of work done at which cost. The bookkeeper would then enter those stubs on a giant spreadsheet she kept listing the employee's name, the day of the week and what had been done by that person on that day.

Because of the part time situation with the employees, production varied from week to week, but Mr. Hobbs tried very hard to finish the orders as they came in and to ship them out on or before their due date. Because he wanted to increase his business, he knew that he must take in more orders, but that would require hiring more part timers or taking on some of his existing staff full time. Most of his employees presently were middle aged women who were working merely to supplement their husband's income and seemed reluctant to give up their free time unless the full time position paid much more.

Mr. and Mrs. Hobbs had talked about how they could expand their business and take in some of the contracts they had let pass because of the size of their operation. If they really wanted to be successful, they were going to have to expand their operation. They had started out small doing much of the work themselves. With help from family they had expanded until even they could not do all the work. The growth had been sporadic with a large turnover in employees. Those employees who had come to them and wanted to earn a good living had left them to go to work at a mill in the next town and those others who weren't as qualified had stayed.

As you can see, the Hobbs have several problems they need to overcome if they want to expand their business. Take each problem and discuss what can be done to help the Hobbs became very successful through expansion. Prepare a plant layout chart for the operation. How could you take the Hobbs from a marginally successful company to a very strong company?

PART SIX

SPECIAL TOPICS

CHAPTER TWENTY TWO

INTERNATIONAL OPPORTUNITIES

CHAPTER OBJECTIVES

Upon completion of this chapter, you should be able to:

● Describe international markets and how a small business can gain access to them;

● Discuss exporting and importing and the special problems involved in such businesses;

● Explain how to make contacts with potential markets and buyers for your products internationally; and,

● Plan and manage an international marketing effort.

INTERNATIONAL OPPORTUNITIES

INTRODUCTION

International marketing is one of the oldest aspects of business. In the age of the Phoenicians, 3,000 B.C., international trade was well established. In fact, much of the exploration of the world was a direct result of the search for new markets and new sources of supply. Small businesses have been leaders in international trade as they have been in business since those earliest days. The Phoenician traders were family businesses intent more on profits than in the spread of culture. Columbus, himself a merchant and small business owner, sailed to America in hopes of finding a shorter route to the Indies which were a major source of spices and trade items. His discovery of America was just an accident! In a large sense then, America is a product of small business!

The role of small business in *international trade* is not just a foreign phenomenon. In fact, when this nation was founded, 200 years ago, Yankee traders were well established in foreign trade. U.S. small businesses were sending ships to Europe and to the Far East to trade American products for local goods. In fact, these international small business operators drove the country to second place behind the already well established empire of Great Britain in trade with China![67]

Beyond discovering countries, small businesses have driven modern improvements in transportation and communication because they have been trying to improve access to markets and sources of supply. International areas have long been prize specimens of both markets and sources of supply. In addition, tensions have been easing between the United States and other powers providing a more open environment for trade. As a result of these improvements, international access and trade opportunity is greater today than at any time in history. We've already established Kentucky Fried Chicken in China and Pizza Huts in Russia! It is logical and proper that small business should take its share of these new markets.

MISCONCEPTIONS IN FOREIGN TRADE

Far too many owners of small businesses view international business as the playground for large firms. They don't even consider the possibility of doing business across national borders because they think it too complex, too expensive, or too difficult. Nothing could be farther from the truth. As we have mentioned in prior chapters, the overwhelming majority of firms in the United States and throughout the entire world are small businesses. Just as they dominate business in their own countries, these firms have the potential to dominate international trade. Many of the firms involved in such trading are small businesses. It is true that within the United States, most of the firms involved in international business are larger firms. This is truly a result of interest, not because of any barriers to trade. Those small business owners who have taken the time to learn about international trading opportunities have reaped rich rewards for their efforts.

A CASE FROM OUR FILES

The client called us in to help him in preparation of an application for insurance on an international trade. He wanted to insure against the default of his customer in the event of a political problem in the country. We said we would be glad to help him and set up an appointment to meet with him and go over the particulars.

When we got to his place we were surprised to find the man and his wife alone in a rather run down warehouse half filled with lumpy looking bags. They were located in a small town in central Georgia. There were no other employees besides the owners. They had a couple of desks and a filing cabinet in one corner, a coffee pot and a telephone. It was not a very impressive place.

When we began to look at the application for insurance, we were really impressed by how sharp these people were. Their records were in order, they understood what was needed, and they were ready to go. Actually they didn't need us!

Naturally we had to know what kinds of products were being sold in order to complete the package. We were amazed to find out that they were selling rags! We said, *What do you mean, you're selling rags!* They said, *They're rags. Just rags. We discovered that a lot of countries in South America and in Asia don't have enough textiles to be able to provide clothing requirements and so there is a need for rags. They need them for cleaning and wiping up in manufacturing plants, they're really in demand. All we had to do was find out how much they were willing to pay, what it would cost to ship them, and then find a supply cheap enough to make a profit. It was easy! We sure couldn't do this domestically, because there must be a 1,000 firms selling rags by mail order and every other way! Over there, we're all alone.*

At first we couldn't believe it, but there was a half warehouse full of laundry bags of rags just waiting to be shipped. When they were sold, they were trucked out to a port on the Atlantic and then went by ship to the country of destination. They had all kinds of suppliers and they were certainly making money. They didn't have any employees because they didn't need any, and they didn't see any sense in wasting rent on a better facility. We had to admit that it was a first class operation!

Were you surprised to find that the business in the note from our case files was selling rags? The range of products which is in demand in countries around the world is absolutely staggering. In reality, every product which is in demand in the United States is also in demand elsewhere. All that is required is the foresight to look for a market.

More and more small business are doing so. In fact, a survey published in *Inc.* magazine reported that exports are growing four times as fast as the gross domestic product which is a general measure of economic expansion in the United States. Even more exciting is the fact that only half of that phenomenal grow in exporting came from the nation's largest firms.[68]

One of the most pervasive myths about foreign trade is that it takes a long time to establish sales and develop profitability. Although the performance of an individual company cannot be predicted, a survey conducted by *Inc.* indicated that over 60% of respondents were profitable within one year of beginning international operations.[69]

INTERNATIONAL MARKETS

Markets exist around the world for every conceivable product and service. In fact, the vast majority of the potential market are small businesses, themselves. That means that a U.S. small business owner actually has an advantage because foreign firms will prefer to deal with businesses of their own size who can better understand their problems and needs.

A great deal is heard about the problems of international finance and the instability of foreign governments and cultures and language barriers. The reality is that such problems are not barriers to doing business. Clearly, international customers are going to want credit terms on their purchases just as domestic firms do. Clearly, there will be differences in monetary exchange rates which have the potential to wipe out profits. It may even be that a political climate is such that business is jeopardized by the instability. All of that can be handled by insurance. Language problems can be handled by using intermediaries who will buy and resell. All that is really required is the interest and a bit of research. The Federal government is keenly interested in fostering international trade and has a tremendous range of assistance services available.

GOVERNMENT ASSISTANCE PROGRAMS

In 1987, the ***Interagency Task Force on Trade*** was created to better serve small businesses in the area of international trade. The Task Force was established as a response to the 1986 White House Conference on Small Business. The Conference found that there was a bewildering array of federal programs which were not well known, but which could provide valuable assistance to small firms which wanted to get involved in international trade. The Conference recommended that a central office be created which would act as a clearing house for information.

The federal government was anxious to do something to get more small firms involved because of the tremendous potential that these firms have for alleviating the international trade deficit. Because our nation is dominated by small businesses, large firms cannot be expected to produce enough exports to balance the huge imports which other countries are pushing so successfully to American consumers. Small businesses could easily wipe out the trade imbalance if they could be persuaded to get involved. Consequently, with thoughts of the original Yankee Traders, the government created the Task Force to encourage, aid and support small firms who wish to export.

The Export-Import Bank of the United States, headquartered in Washington, D.C., is the central contact point for federal assistance in exporting. The bank offers training seminars, and publishes a host of guides, brochures and aids. The bank has regional offices and assigned business development officers for each state. These people can serve as resources to help any interested business get started in, or expand an exporting venture. The bank maintains a web page which has the most current information, dates and times of upcoming seminars, names and addresses of business development officers, and a host of transfers to various sites of interest and value to prospective and active exporters. Its web address is:

---

www.exim.gov

FINANCIAL, CREDIT AND INSURANCE ASSISTANCE

Most small business owners think that credit and insurance are the major stumbling blocks to international trade. The Export-Import Bank of the United States has a variety of programs which can alleviate this problem. The Export-Import Bank can lend at competitive rates to small businesses to finance export sales. It can also guarantee loans made by local banks to firms involved in exporting. The bank will guarantee loans made to foreign firms who are buying U.S. goods and services. It also has an insurance plan. The Foreign Credit Insurance Association is a subsidiary of the bank and it offers insurance policies which protect U.S. firms from nonpayment of foreign customers. Special policies are available for small businesses which can guarantee that the business will not lose in the event of nonpayment by a foreign customer due to commercial or political problems.

Federal agencies offer a tremendous range of financial services to small businesses. Any firm interested in pursuing international trade has available programs which can alleviate most of the problems and fears of default and nonpayment. They can also provide assistance in protecting against loss due to currency trading fluctuations. Information on all of the loan and insurance programs is available on the Export-Import Bank home page, listed above.

In addition to federal efforts to aid small firms, most of the states have established offices and programs to assist small firms. Many states provide much more than simply information; they provide money! Some states provide loan guarantees, while others offer direct loan programs. The Small Business Administration maintains a list of web site referrals which can help you find information on your particular state. In addition, the SBA home page has a link to a directory of all state and federal agencies maintaining web sites which might be of interest to small businesses in a wide variety of areas. The SBA web address is:

---

www.sbaonline.sba.gov

MAKING CONTACTS AND FINDING MARKETS

The final barrier to international trade is finding a market and a buyer in a foreign country. Federal assistance programs and some of the state programs can help in this area as well. The International Trade Assistance (ITA) office is a division of the U.S. Department of Commerce. This agency offers a host of assistance programs. Among these are market surveys and identification of foreign distributors who will buy and distribute your products. Many services are free, others are available for a small fee. The ITA will investigate any country you choose for any product you choose and provide you with a list of qualified agents and distributors who are interested in your products. The agency will also put you in contact with those people and help you to begin working with them. You can also can get an in-depth study on the best foreign markets for a product or a group of products for an entire country. Table 1 is a partial list of ITA services available to small businesses.

Table 1
International Trade Assistance

- Analyze foreign markets
- Find representatives and buyers overseas
- Gather data on specific export opportunities
- Identify foreign prospects who want to represent a product
- Provide sales leads from overseas firms
- Prepare custom background reports on potential trading partners
- Provide personal counseling to exporters

As Table 1 indicates, the ITA is a goldmine of information and assistance to any firm interested in selling its products or services overseas. It, like all of the other agencies, makes a special effort to assist small businesses and first time exporters. For more complete information, check its web page:

---

www.ita.doc.gov

GETTING INVOLVED IN INTERNATIONAL TRADE

As the preceding sections show, the federal government has numerous programs and agencies which are ready and willing to help any small business get involved in international trade. The reasons for this are self-serving. The Export-Import Bank has estimated that each billion dollars of exports is worth 30,000 jobs in the United States. They also believe that at least 18,000 more small businesses could produce $4.5 billion in exports within the first year through simple education. The potential for the long run is absolutely staggering. Small businesses really do have the potential to dominate the international markets. All that is really required is interest!

Inc. recommends that one way to break into exporting is to begin selling to American operations of foreign firms. It is only one short step from there to selling to their domestic operations.[70] Of course, one of the most popular approaches to selling overseas is the use of another firm specializing in exporting. Exporters are firms who use their contacts to find markets for your products. These firms charge a commission for the sales they produce but can provide a variety of services from fax machines to translation to advice about product modification. ***Facsimile machines*** can be a very important aspect of international trade because they permit written communications in languages foreign to the parties, and written communications are more comfortable for people dealing in foreign languages. Most exporters are also engaged in importing so they can be good sources of supply as well. You can also attend international trade shows and conferences. Many of these are held in the United States each year. Not only can you find contacts, you can find exporters at these shows as well.

We highly recommend that every small business owner explore the possibilities of international sales. You might just find that it is easier than doing business in the United States because the competition is lower! Large firms are not interested in pursuing what they consider to be small markets. A market like that can be quite large to a small business. In addition, most small business owners in the United States have not yet had the interest to get involved. That provides a tremendous opportunity for aggressive and forward thinking small firms. Yet as in all enterprises, the key to success in international trade is *PLANNING*.

SUMMARY

It is popularly believed that international business is complex and difficult and filled with risk of nonpayment and other problems resulting from political and commercial instability. Consequently, a small business cannot hope to get involved in it. In reality, this is not the case. Many small businesses are successfully running international operations.

The White House Conference on Small Business held in 1986 recognized that many more small businesses had international prospects. They also recognized that many federal assistance programs existed but were not well known. Consequently they recommended that the Interagency Task Force on Trade be developed. It has published a guide for exporters which is invaluable to any small business wishing to pursue international trade.

A tremendous variety of federal assistance programs exists which are designed to aid small businesses in international trade. These agencies can provide assistance in financing and in credit. They can provide insurance to protect against nonpayment from commercial or political sources. They can locate markets, customers, buyers and representatives, and they can provide advice and counseling to a small business. Services from these agencies are often free or have an extremely low cost. In addition a tremendous number of publications are available which spell out how to get involved in international trade and which can support an international operation.

Any small business can get involved in international trade if its owner has the interest to investigate possibilities. A small business can find itself in a superior position internationally because most of the firms it deals with will also be small firms. In addition, the level of competition may well be lower.

QUESTIONS, EXERCISES AND CASES

QUESTIONS:

1.   Why have small businesses felt that only large companies could experience international trade?

2.   How might the high tech industry have facilitated the possibility of international trade for small businesses?

3.   Would you consider entering an international market for your product/service? Why or why not?

EXERCISES:

1.   Visit the Small Business Development Center closest to you and gather any pertinent information regarding the international market or write or call the agencies listed in the text to further your knowledge of the international prospects for small businesses.

2.   Include in your business plan the opportunity for internationalizing your business if your product/service lends itself to such an expansion. Don't limit yourself.

3.   After reading the chapter on ethics, discuss what limitations might be imposed on international trade in the interest of foreign relations, national security, and ethical considerations.

4.   Log onto the Export-Import Bank's web site (www.exim.gov) and explore the links to other agencies and sites of interest to an exporter. Prepare a class report of your findings.

CASE

Guy Rambois was an interesting individual. He had asked us to advise him about the start-up of a small business. He had worked in Nigeria for a number of years as a missionary on a training mission for his church and had developed many friendships while there. He was presently working part time at a local technical college teaching various classes. Yet he wasn't satisfied. He wanted to do something not only more exciting but more profitable.

Although he had been back in the States for three years, he had maintained his friendships with the people of Nigeria and had even tried his hand at trade on a small scale. He had brought back with him on each of his trips, several types of souvenirs representing the African culture and his friends had asked to purchase them. He had sold his souvenirs and contacted his friends in Nigeria to send him more. They did and he sold those items quickly as well.

His African friends had now asked him to return the favor by sending them goods such as books, paper supplies, tapes, records and a variety of American products. The demand was growing to the point the Guy had decided to use this export prospect as a means of livelihood. The demand for American products was growing among his acquaintances in Africa and no one seemed to be responding to their needs.

1. Where could Guy go for real start-up information for his new venture?

2. What types of goods might he export?

3. What political unrest in neighboring countries might give him pause?

4. Develop a plan for Guy for marketing, finance, and inventory.

5. Would any ethical considerations arise from the difference in culture, environment, or attitudes?

CHAPTER TWENTY THREE

SMALL BUSINESS LAW

CHAPTER OBJECTIVES

Upon completion of this chapter, you should be able to:

- Discuss the Uniform Commercial Code is and understand its significance;

- Define torts and how claims are brought and settled;

- Describe the intentional torts of defamation, assault and battery, false imprisonment and fraud; and how to avoid potential claims for intentional torts;

- Describe the tort of negligence and how claims are brought and settled;

- Explain duty and due care and how to plan for minimization of liability under claims of negligence;

- Define warranties, express and implied;

- Discuss contract law and agency law and know the elements required for an enforceable contract;

- Explain the importance of copyrights, patents, trademarks, and trade secrets and the levels of protection they provide; and,

- Describe the contents and differences among Chapters 7, 9, 11, and 13 of the Federal Bankruptcy Act.

SMALL BUSINESS LAW

INTRODUCTION

A full and complete treatment of ***business law*** is beyond the scope of this book. However, there are certain aspects of the law which affect all prospective small business owners. We have termed these aspects, Small Business Law, although the law does not actually make special dispensation for small businesses. Because it is a pervasive issue and one which affects every small business owner in the country every day, we feel that we would be remiss if we failed to present an overview of the more basic aspects of business law. All people planning on a career in small business should pursue a more detailed study of this topic because every aspect of the operation of a business is affected by the law. Businesses, just like people, are subject to the law and are responsible for their actions. This means that a small business owner is not only responsible for obeying the law personally, he or she is also responsible for ensuring that the business obeys the law as well.

Please be aware that this entire discussion is general in nature. Not only are legal issues exceedingly complex, they are frequently situation specific. That means that the law takes into consideration all circumstances surrounding an event. A small business owner must consult with an attorney in establishing business policies and practices in order to be well advised. Such a consultation goes beyond using an attorney in establishing the business. Legal advice will be needed on an ongoing basis. A wise business owner establishes a relationship with an attorney early and consults with that attorney frequently.

THE UNIFORM COMMERCIAL CODE

The principal body of law which all small business owners are expected to know is the ***Uniform Commercial Code***. Developed in the 1940s, as an approach to standardize the way various states dealt with merchants, the Code has been adopted by every state, although there are minor differences between the states on some issues. The most important aspect of the Code, or *UCC* as it is frequently called, is the requirement that all merchants be familiar with its contents. Under the Code, every small business owner in the country who sells a product is a ***merchant***. Furthermore, a seller of services can be a merchant in some instances. Even if not classified as a merchant, a small business owner will be affected by Code provisions because they cover negotiable instruments, which includes most personal and business checks, letters of credit, documents of title, bank deposits and collections, and a host of factors which will occur every business day. The end result is that you must become familiar with the Code if you intend to go into business.

The Code covers sales and contracts of sale of goods in general. The important aspect about this component of the Code is that it has the capability of overriding some aspects of common law. For example, under normal contract law, which we will discuss later, an offer and its acceptance must be exactly alike in terms of their provisions. Under the *UCC*, changes and conditions to the original contract can usually be made freely and without concern for contract validity. The code also requires that sales contracts in excess of $500 be written in order to be enforceable.

Obviously, a full discussion of the Code is beyond the scope of this book. Fortunately, the Code is readable and understandable without a legal education. We highly recommend that you obtain a copy, read it and become familiar with it. The Code can be obtained in many bookstores. In fact, there are books and texts available which contain the Code, comments and explanations of aspects of the Code and differences between the states, when those occur. Refer to the *Books in Print* carried by your local bookstore if they do not carry copies of the Uniform Commercial Code.

TORTS

Laws designed for the protection of an individual's rights to person and property are called **tort laws**. A **tort** is a civil or private wrong, other than breach of contract. We will examine contracts in the following sections. Torts are important in small business management because a court will grant an action for damages when a tort has been proven. This action, called a **remedy**, is usually monetary in form. Torts are different from a crime. Table 1 displays the primary legal differences.

Table 1
The Differences in Torts and Crimes

	Crimes	Torts
Who is wronged	Society	An Individual
Who brings suit	The People action by the District Attorney	An Individual action through litigation
Burden of Proof	To a Moral Certainty "beyond reasonable doubt"	Preponderance of Evidence 51%
Punishment	Incarceration, Fines, etc.	Restitution or Monetary Damages

As the table indicates, a ***crime*** is a violation of a law which affects society. Prosecution of such violations is the responsibility of a ***District Attorney***; a person appointed in every city or county of the country for the purpose of pursuing people suspected of wrong doing. The burden of proof in a court action involving a crime is ***to a moral certainty***. This means that a jury or judge must be convinced of guilt beyond a reasonable doubt. The punishment for crimes can include prison terms, fines, assignments to perform public service, etc.

Torts are violations of laws which affect an individual. Court actions in tort cases are brought by the individual who has been wronged in the form of litigation. Juries or judges in these cases need only be convinced that the ***preponderance of the evidence***, or the majority of the evidence, supports the claim of wrong doing. Punishment in such cases is usually restitution in the form of monetary awards for damages.

Torts can result from an intentional act. These will be addressed in the following section. Torts can also result from negligence, which is a far more serious problem for small business owners.

INTENTIONAL TORTS

The most common ***intentional torts*** are defamation, assault and battery, false imprisonment and fraud. We will examine each of these individually and will focus on the best way to avoid problems for your business and yourself.

DEFAMATION

Defamation means maliciously attacking an individual's name or reputation. The word ***malicious*** in this context implies that the attack on the individual is unfounded and is intended to cause harm to that person. Oral or spoken defamation is called ***slander***. ***Libel***, the other form of defamation, is in written form.

As is always the case, the best defense against defamation is to avoid it in the first place. You should be careful about making statements about your competitors, suppliers, customers, employees, or other people. The best advice is simply to never say anything negative about others, even if you are convinced that they have wronged you. This is just good business sense. In the first place, you should never reveal any personal information you might have access to because it violates a person's privacy. It will also brand you as a gossip. In addition, revealing information of a negative nature will not improve your position. Negative statements do not win customers nor enhance your own reputation. You can only improve your position through performance, not by attacking others. The rule to follow is simple; *if you can't say something positive about a person or a business, don't say anything at all.*

PERSONNEL REFERENCES

Giving personnel references can be a problem if the individual in question has not performed well. If a prospective employer of a former employee calls for a reference, you clearly cannot lie. That would be an unethical act. However, if you go into any detail with respect to unsatisfactory performance, you may be opening yourself to a defamation claim. The best practice is to simply say, *It is against our policy to make any statements about employees. We will verify only length and time of employment and positions held.* There is nothing wrong with verifying that kind of factual information, but you should only verify it to a legitimate party, not volunteer any information that they do not have. You should ensure that neither you nor any other employee reveal any information of a personal nature or give any negative information about any person who is or who has ever been associated with your business. Most employers will not even verify salary data and we recommend that course of action for you. Say nothing beyond a verification of employment term.

If you have an employee that you would really like to support in obtaining a new position, it is best to handle that through a personal letter of recommendation. You can make it clear to all employees that the company's policy is not to reveal or verify any information beyond employment dates and positions. Then, if an individual wishes to ask you for a recommendation, you can handle that with a personal letter, or you can refuse to write such a letter if you do not feel that you can in good conscience recommend the person.

ASSAULT AND BATTERY

Assault is placing an individual in fear of immediate bodily harm. The fear must be reasonable and it is this reasonableness which must be proven in court. The use of threatening words or actions can constitute assault. Pointing a loaded gun is clearly assault. *Battery* is the intentional touching of another person without that person's consent. Battery is the actualization of assault. We normally think of battery as striking a person, but the contact need not be that violent. Simply shoving a person or other less violent contact can be battery.

Obviously, the best defense is avoidance of conflict. Be wary of losing your temper and walk away from potential arguments and conflicts. Nothing is ever settled in a shouting match, anyway! Cultivate this attitude among the people in your business. If you lead, they will follow, so you need to set the example in this as well as all the other areas of concern.

FALSE IMPRISONMENT

Individuals have a right to freedom and movement. Holding someone without their permission or without *just cause* constitutes *false imprisonment*. This can be a real problem for small businesses when an act of theft, embezzlement or bad check writing occurs. Some states do allow reasonable detainment of suspected shoplifters or lawbreakers. However, determining what is reasonable is difficult. Not only that, there is the possibility of assault or battery as well as false imprisonment if you or your employees attempt to take action in a case of suspected theft or other wrong doing.

What can be done to protect the business? You should discuss the issue with your attorney and establish a policy and procedure for the business to cover incidences of suspected shoplifting, theft or other wrong doing. You need to establish that policy in writing, be specific with respect to actions which will be taken, and have your attorney review and approve it. Then you must ensure that all employees are familiar with the policy and know what to do when they suspect someone of a crime. The policy should be reviewed by your attorney periodically, to ensure that it remains current. It should be discussed with your employees on a regular basis, especially those who come into contact with customers, to ensure that they understand and are complying with the policy.

FRAUD

Perhaps the best known of the torts is *fraud*. However, it is not generally well understood among small business owners. The tort of fraud is complicated and an incidence of fraud is difficult to prove in court. Legally, there are six elements involved in the demonstration of an incidence of fraud. In other words, a court must be convinced that each of six different actions occurred in order to accept an allegation of fraud. These six factors are listed in Table 2, below. The table talks about the parties to a claim of fraud using legal terms. If an individual brings a claim of fraud or other legal wrong doing in a court action, that person is called the *plaintiff*. The individual who is accused of the wrong doing is called the *accused*.

As the table indicates, there must have been an intent to deceive a person in order for fraud to occur. It can be difficult to prove intent. Nevertheless, careful attention to the claims made in writing or made verbally by sales personnel or other employees is a must for effective avoidance. Everyone needs to be careful about what they say to a customer.

The concept of a material fact is more straightforward. In essence, any information which a reasonable person might be expected to consider in reaching a decision is material. In business, material facts or information are used all the time. Every statement made by a sales person or other individual representing your business to a customer could well be a material fact.

Avoidance of potential fraud makes sound business sense, despite the fact that it is difficult to prove in court. Even if a customer or other person dealing with your business does not bring a claim of fraud against you, your reputation will be damaged if that individual feels that you or your people misrepresented a product or service. Misrepresentation need not actually occur in order for there to be a problem. If a customer perceives that a product or service has been misrepresented or even poorly represented, the damage to the company will be done.

Table 2
The Elements of Fraud

1.   There was intent to deceive.

2.   There was misrepresentation of a *material fact*, or an important factor in the plaintiff's action.

3.   The accused knew the representation was false.

4.   There was intent that the plaintiff would act in reliance on the false fact.

5.   The plaintiff did rely on the false fact and it was reasonable to do so.

6.   The plaintiff suffered personal or financial injury and can prove that loss.

Careful attention to training of people who will represent the firm to customers and others is the best strategy to avoid misrepresentation. Whenever possible, especially in the case of services to be rendered, a contract between your firm and its customers is a sound procedure. Spell out everything in writing and there is less likelihood of misunderstandings. Be sure to have your attorney review all contracts.

NEGLIGENCE

As we indicated earlier, a tort can occur from negligence. This is an extremely important aspect of law for a small business owner because of the contact with so many people inside and outside the business. The concept of negligence is not easily understood. To demonstrate what is involved, consider a claim of negligence. In a successful action for **negligence**, four things must be proven: the duty, the breach of the duty, causation from the breach, and the actual injury. What all this means is that a plaintiff must have incurred an injury as a result of a failure of the accused to behave properly.

In defining duty, courts have traditionally used the actions of a fictitious person, a reasonable, prudent person, to determine if an individual behavior in a certain set of circumstances was acceptable. A reasonable, prudent person owes a duty of *due care* to others, particularly to those who are foreseeably in risk of some danger. Due care means taking reasonable precautions to protect others.

People visiting the premises of a business are divided into three categories: invitees, licensees, and trespassers. A different standard of duty is owed to each of these three classes.

Invitees are persons present through the express or implied request of the owner for social or business related purposes. The business and its owners have a duty to provide reasonably safe premises to all invitees. *Licensees* are those persons allowed to frequent premises for reasons relating to their own businesses, purposes, or conveniences. The owner owes a lesser degree of duty to licensees. That duty is to refrain from being actively negligent. *Trespassers* are people who enter without permission from the owner. Trespassers are owed no duty except to refrain from their willful injury. These levels of duty and the determination of due care are complex to establish and understand. The simplest approach is probably to examine how a **breach of duty** is established.

To prove a breach of duty, a plaintiff must show that the accused failed to execute the due care of a reasonable, prudent person. Some cases which appear inherently negligent do not require comprehensive proof.

Proof is often aided by the doctrine of ***res ipsa loquitur***, meaning *the thing (or act of negligence) speaks for itself.* If an individual sustains an injury which would not ordinarily occur unless some other person was negligent, this doctrine can be applicable. The only other tests which must be met are that the injured party did not contribute to his or her own injury and that the injury was caused by a device within the control of the accused.

Injury is the simpler concept. Simply put, if no physical or financial harm results from an individual's actions, no matter how reckless those actions are, he or she may not be sued for negligence. *Causation* is the more complex and crucial element of proving a breach of duty, and therefore supporting a claim of negligence.

There are two types of causation: actual cause and proximate cause. *Actual cause* is an obvious cause; an automobile strikes a pedestrian. *Proximate cause* is cause from a natural, continued sequence that is unbroken by any efficient, independent, or intervening cause. This is an extremely difficult concept. It is really decided on a case by case basis after consideration of all factors leading up to an injury. In essence, the law attempts to decide whether it is reasonable for an accused to be held liable for an injury.

Negligence claims all revolve around whether a business owner has provided reasonably safe premises for the various parties who will come into contact with the business. Consequently, the best preventative measure is to practice concerned management of the premises. Consider what possible dangers may exist on the company's premises and what the best way to protect people from those dangers are. Posting signs will frequently *NOT* be adequate. Proper use of barriers, shielding, safety equipment, security precautions, etc., is a wiser course. If you have a business in which potentially dangerous or harmful conditions can exist, you will be well advised to discuss the situation with your attorney and take precautions.

Proof of negligence can be difficult or impossible if the defendant can prove that the plaintiff assumed the risk. Assumption of the risk applies in cases where the plaintiff realized the risk involved but proceeded to act anyway. A potential problem with this philosophy is children!

Children represent a special case in potential negligence claims because they are not capable of understanding and assuming risk. Everyone is aware that if a child falls into a swimming pool that has no fence or barrier around it or crawls into an abandoned refrigerator which has its door intact, the owner can be sued for negligence. Businesses must be especially careful because their premises may be attractive to children because of the premises, equipment, inventory or machinery. The law expects a reasonable, prudent person to anticipate the actions of children. This can sometimes be difficult to do!

CHILDREN AND ATTRACTIVE NUISANCES

Our earlier comments about making the premises reasonably safe can be echoed here with a stronger need for caution in some circumstances. If there is any aspect of the premises which might be interesting or attractive to children, then you will need to make an heroic effort to make the place secure. Signs clearly will not be acceptable! In fact, some aspects of normal security can themselves be attractive to children. Consider the case of guard dogs used to patrol inside a fence at night. Children are frequently attracted to animals, consequently, you should anticipate that a child might reach through a fence to pet a dog. If that child were injured, you could be liable. Furthermore, blocking access to a dangerous area with a fence might not be adequate. A fence that represents a barrier to an adult may well not be a barrier to a child. In fact, the fence itself could be an attractive nuisance!

It should be clear that security precautions themselves must be reviewed in order to protect yourself. Be sure to consult your attorney before you install any type of security and pay particular attention to blocking access to little people and safeguarding people who might have no concept of danger.

WARRANTIES

The function of a warranty is to establish the characteristics and level of quality the purchaser can expect of the good or services being acquired. *Warranties* are part of a contract for the sale of goods. There are two basic types of warranties: expressed and implied.

An *expressed warranty* is communicated from the seller to the buyer in writing or orally. There are two legal buzzwords applicable to expressed warranties: quantifiable and relative. Quantifiable statements will be treated as facts. For example, if a real estate broker says the roof doesn't leak, the statement would be treated as a warranty. Relative statements are treated as opinion or supposition. A statement such as *good roof* would not constitute an express warranty. The wording is extremely important. Many small business owners frequently make statements that could be warranties without realizing what they are doing.

Implied warranties are a part of the Uniform Commercial Code. Under the Code, there are four types of implied warranties. These are displayed in Table 3, along with their meanings.

Table 3	
Implied Warranties	
Type	Meaning
Title	Requires the goods to be of clear title No liens or claims against the goods
Infringement	The seller must protect the buyer from claims by third parties (usually applies to patents)
Merchantability	Goods sold must be fit for the customary purpose for which they are used. They must be safe for that use, they must be adequately contained, packaged, and labeled, and conform to any facts or promises on the label.
Fitness for Purpose	The goods must be fit for the purpose for which they are intended. The buyer is entitled to rely on the seller's skill or judgement to select or furnish suitable goods

It is the fitness for purpose and merchantability which has potential problems for small businesses. Far too many retailers and wholesalers think that implied warranties are only applicable to manufacturers. That is not the case! You must make sure that you are familiar with the products you sell, establish their quality, understand their uses and purposes, and advise your customers as to those uses as well as the quality of the item.

PRODUCT LIABILITY

Product liability deals with situations where no warranty protects an injured buyer. In this case, remedies are available through the negligence or liability aspects of tort law and liability of a business will be established in accordance with tort requirements. In essence, manufacturers and/or sellers may be held accountable because of negligence in the manufacturing, designing, or packaging of products. This takes us back to the exercise of *due care* which we discussed in the earlier section.

Strong quality controls are the best defense against product liability as well as attention to fitness of purpose and proper use and care of the item.

There is even stronger concern for makers and sellers of goods that are imminently or inherently dangerous. Businesses involved with these items are subject to strict liability even though there was no lack of due care in the manufacture or sale of the item. If you make or carry such products, be sure to consult with your attorney early and on a regular basis!

Table 4

The Elements of a Contract

1.	*Offer*:	a proposal made by one party to another to enter into a contract. An offer may be oral, written, or implied from the facts but it MUST be made with intent to enter into a contract.
2.	*Acceptance*:	another party, the offeree, must accept the terms of the offer in the manner requested by the offeror. Unilateral acceptance is constituted by an act of substantial performance of the contract. Bilateral acceptance can be made orally or in writing and specifies how the offer can be accepted.
3.	*Consideration*:	something which is given in exchange for a promise in the contract. In short, the offeror bargains for and receives something in exchange for his or her promise. In bilateral agreements, the mutual promises can serve as consideration. In a unilateral agreement the act performed can be the consideration.
4.	*Capacity of the Parties*:	the ability of individuals to enter into a contract. In general, mentally incompetent or intoxicated persons or minors lack contractual capacity. Although they may enter into and fulfill contracts, a person without capacity may avoid or discharge any contract to which he or she is a party.
5.	*Legal Objective*:	must be based on a legal act or promise. Contracts made with an illegal objective are void contracts.
6.	*Proper Form*:	Oral contracts may be acceptable, but written form may be required for some categories of contracts.

CONTRACT LAW

A *contract* is a legally binding agreement made by two or more competent parties containing a promise or set of promises to perform or refrain from performing some act or acts. In other words, a contract is a set of promises which can be enforced by a court. It must have been made between two or more people who are legally capable of handling their own affairs. That means that none of the parties is a minor or a mental incompetent, etc.

Contracts can be written or oral. In order to be legally binding a contract must fulfill six elements. These are displayed in Table 4.

As the table shows, any attempt to enter into a contract is not effective in the absence of consideration. Consideration is the element that is usually lacking in quasi-contracts. There are some things that can not be consideration. The more common ones are: gifts, acts which are duty bound, past consideration, and moral obligations. Employers often promise raises on the basis of *faithful service in years past*. These promises are not real because past service cannot be a stipulation of an agreement.

There are several types of contracts that are thought to be so important to the parties that a written contract is required to show evidence of intent. Some of these involve estates, bonding or surety and marriage contracts. Several other types affect small businesses every day. These are contracts which cannot be performed in one year, i.e., a long term contract; an agreement for the purchase or sale of an interest in land; or an agreement for the sale of personal property over a certain amount, $500 in most cases. For contracts involving these situations, oral agreements are not enforceable. Further, a written contract must be in proper form and contain proper information for it to be enforceable. This requires legal advice. You should refer the development and review of all written contracts to your attorney.

Contracts can be classified from several perspectives. Table 5 illustrates a classification of contracts and their characteristics. Note that the categories are not mutually exclusive. That means that a contract does not necessarily have to be one or the other of the types indicated. A contract may have characteristics of one or more types.

Note that a *quasi-contract* is not a contract but may be enforceable. Generally, a quasi-contract can be enforced if the four elements listed in Table 6 exist. Clearly, the strongest situation is to utilize contracts appropriately rather than depend on the enforceability of a quasi-contract. Many small business owners fail to make and use contracts, even for purchases or sales which are large enough to require them. This failure results from a lack of understanding of the legal ramifications. We cannot overstress the necessity for a close working relationship with an attorney and attention to legal issues. Businesses, including small firms, are being sued on a ever increasing basis.

Table 5

Classifications of Contracts

Category	Contract Type	Characteristics
Formality	*Formal*:	Formal contracts must be in a specified format to be enforceable. Two examples of formal contracts are checks and promissory notes. Wording is important.
	Informal:	Generally referred to as simple contracts. They require no particular format or wording.
Parties	*Unilateral*:	A promise in exchange for a specific act, such as an agreement to pay a specified amount for a specified job. Performance of the act constitutes acceptance of the offer.
	Bilateral:	A promise in exchange for a promise, or mutual promises. Each party promises to perform an act contingent upon other factors.
Compliance	*Executed*:	Have already been performed. That is, both promises have been met. If one of the promises has been satisfied, the contract is partially executed.
	Executory:	Promises have yet to be performed. If one promise has been satisfied, the contract is partially executory.
Intent	*Express*:	The parties set forth their intentions and promises specifically and definitely. The contract may be written or oral.
	Implied:	Its existence must be inferred from the actions and conduct of the parties.
Validity	*Valid*:	Contains all the necessary elements of a contract and is therefore easily enforced by the courts.
	Void:	Not a contract because it is lacking in one or more of the legal requirements. A void contract is a contradiction in terms, but is frequently used.
	Voidable:	A contract that can be canceled by one or both of the contracting parties. Contracts made under duress or fraud are voidable. A contract with a minor is voidable at the minor's option.
	Unenforceable:	A valid contract which cannot be enforced due to the operation of the law. For example, immunity from collection as a result of bankruptcy or statute of limitations.
Quasi-contracts	*A legal fiction*:	It lacks one or more of the elements of contracts. A legal fiction that courts will sometimes enforce as a contract to prevent the undue enrichment of one party at another party's expense.

Table 6

Elements of Enforceable Quasi-contracts

1. Plaintiff conferred a benefit on the defendant; and
2. Plaintiff expected to be paid; and
3. Plaintiff was not meddling in another's affairs; and
4. To allow the defendant to retain the benefit would result in undue or unjust enrichment.

AGENCY LAW

An *agent* is a person who represents another person in a business transaction. That means that your employees will generally be agents for you. This is a serious matter because of the potential liability which exists. The general rule is that you will be responsible for any damages or injury which an employee causes so long as that person is performing his or her duties. In fact, a temporary employee, a part time worker, a delivery agent, or even a friend who volunteers to perform some service for you can be your agent. The impact of this aspect of agency law makes the internal control aspect of hiring competent people and training them for their jobs even more important.

LIABILITY FOR CONTRACTS

Another aspect of agency law is the ability of an agent to bind the company. An agent can enter into contracts with other parties on behalf of the company. That means that you can be forced to comply with an oral or written contract established by an employee. In general, you will be liable for contracts of employees in any of the situations outlined in Table 7. The owner of the business will be the principal and the employee will be the agent as described in the table.

As you can see from Table 7, you must be extremely careful to avoid the appearance of authority which does not exist if you wish to protect the business. Ostensible and apparent authority are the most dangerous aspects. You should develop personnel and supervision policies and practices to ensure that employees who are authorized to perform tasks are identifiable by third parties. You will need the assistance of your attorney to accomplish this.

INDEPENDENT CONTRACTORS

Independent contractors are not employees and therefore are not agents. In general, the difference between an independent contractor and an employee is the degree of control which you

Table 7
Agent Authority

Express Authority: Principal authorizes agent to perform a task or enter into a particular contract; An agent has the power to enter into a contract for the purchase of an item when directed by the principal to do so.

Ratification: Principal approves an unauthorized act of an agent at a later date; An agent enters into an unauthorized contract, but the principal decides to accept the terms of that contract, anyway.

Incidental Authority: An agent is authorized to perform tasks or enter contracts necessary to carry out his or her assigned duties; A department manager has the power to enter into a contract of employment with an individual needed to work in the manager's department.

Implied Authority: An agent has authority based on his or her assigned position in the business or based on past dealings with a third party; A purchasing agent has the power to enter into contracts with established suppliers of the business for the purchase or items normally acquired.

Emergency Authority: An agent has the authority to respond to emergencies; An agent supervising the construction of a building has the power to enter into a contract for the purchase of equipment required to respond to an emergency situation.

Apparent Authority: A principal implies that an agent has the power to enter into a contract by his or her conduct toward a third party; An employee is undergoing a trial period of employment before being granted express authority to enter into sales contracts. The principal accompanies the agent and implies to a customer that the agent has the power to enter into a sales contract by introducing the agent as a sales representative of the company. The agent later returns to the customer and enters in a sales contract. That contract can be binding on the principal.

Ostensible Authority: A principal permits an agent to represent to a third party that contract power exists; A sales agent calls on the principal who allows an employee to represent himself as an agent authorized to make purchases for the business. A contract between the sales representative and the employee can be binding on the principal.

have over their actions. If you have the right to direct a person to perform a task *AND* the right to control how the task is done, that person is an employee. You don't actually have to control how the task is done, it is enough simply to have the *RIGHT* to control how it is done.

If you have the right to direct a person to perform a task and you do *NOT* have the right to control how the task is done, that person is an independent contractor. These people are expected to rely on their own expertise to determine how to accomplish a task. It is an important distinction not only because an independent contractor cannot be an agent, but because they are not employees for tax purposes. That means that payroll taxes and social security taxes are not required for independent contractors.

BANKRUPTCY

Bankruptcy is not a pleasant topic for consideration. Nevertheless, thousands of small businesses file for or are forced into bankruptcy each year. In fact, the number of bankruptcies has been growing annually and shows no signs of slowing in the near future. It is wise to understand something of how the law functions in this area.

When America was colonized, many of the immigrants were fleeing debtors' prisons. The nation's founders wanted to avoid the possibility of such treatment, consequently, the Constitution includes an authorization for Congress to establish uniform laws on bankruptcies. Several laws have existed throughout the nation's history, but the *Bankruptcy Reform Act*, established in 1978 and amended in 1984, establishes the legal aspects of bankruptcy in the United States.

The law established a separate court system to hear and handle bankruptcy cases. The Act has four major sections which are called chapters. These are Chapters 7, 9, 11 and 13 and they dictate how liquidations, municipal debt adjustments, reorganizations and individual debt adjustments must be handled. Chapter 9, municipal debt adjustments, is of little interest to us since it is relevant only to incorporated cities and towns.

CHAPTER 7

Chapter 7 proceedings involve a straight liquidation. That means that an individual or a business has its assets sold off and the proceeds paid over to its creditors. If any residual funds remain they are the property of the debtor, but any unpaid debts are discharged by the court. Contrary to popular belief, the law does not require a debtor to be insolvent. In other words, you do not have to be in a position of inability to pay debts to file bankruptcy. In practice, this led to some misuses, consequently, the 1984 amendment gave courts the power to assess the need of a debtor to seek relief from creditors. If the court decides that the filing would result in abuse, the bankruptcy will not proceed.

A business or individual can voluntarily file for bankruptcy or can be forced into bankruptcy by creditors. If a debtor has 12 or more creditors, then three of them are all that will be required to force a trial. If a debtor has less than 12 creditors, only one creditor is required to force a trial. The creditors must have an aggregate claim against the debtor of at least $5,000 and those debts must not be secured by collateral. Farmers are specifically exempt from an involuntary proceeding, but most other types of small businesses have no such protection. Of course an involuntary petition simply forces a trial, not a bankruptcy. The court will decide whether a debtor is bankrupt.

The possibility of an involuntary petition for bankruptcy can be especially dangerous for a small business which is not a corporation, because personal assets may be available to creditors. We discussed this issue previously and it is one of the reasons we recommend the corporate form.

In the event of a Chapter 7 bankruptcy the debtor is permitted to keep some property. The surprising thing is that the amount of property which can be protected is determined by state laws despite the fact that the bankruptcy laws are federal. There are wide differences between the amounts of property protected in the various states. Consult with your attorney for more relevant information.

CHAPTERS 11 AND 13

Chapter 11 of the bankruptcy code is designed to support the reorganization of a corporation so that it can continue to exist. *Chapter 13* is the counterpart for individuals. Both chapters establish a payment plan for creditors with the anticipation that the debtor will be eventually be able to pay creditors in full. The advantage of these chapters over Chapter 7 is that they permit the business to continue to exist and they force creditors to cooperate. The same rules about involuntary petitions for bankruptcy apply to these chapters as for Chapter 7.

Chapter 11 and 13 proceedings require that a debtor prepare a plan which will permit the debtor to avoid a liquidation and at the same time satisfy the claims of creditors. When the bankruptcy proceeding is first filed, the court will issue an order of relief which will stop creditors from attempting to collect from the debtor. The debtor will now have 120 days to propose a plan. If the debtor fails to do so, any interested party, a creditor, a stockholder, a trustee, etc., can propose a plan. Further, the court must be satisfied that the plan is feasible and is fair to all parties. Otherwise, a new plan may be considered or the debtor may be forced into a Chapter 7 liquidation.

Obviously, the details of a reorganization or payout plan and the factors involved in handling a bankruptcy petition or response require legal advice. This is particularly true for small firms because of the difficulty in separating business assets from personal assets. Even if a business is incorporated, the owner will generally be asked to personally guarantee loans from banks and most other lenders. Trade credit will generally be limited to a corporate liability, but those guarantees make personal assets available to the lenders as well as corporate. Small business owners generally have no choice in the matter of guarantees because they are such an established practice among lenders.

The result is that a business which is experiencing difficulties should seek legal counsel early and explore possible options. Bankruptcy may be a last resort, but if it becomes necessary, early planning with the aid of an experienced attorney can make the difference between a survivable and a disastrous outcome.

INTELLECTUAL PROPERTY RIGHTS

Small businesses are frequently involved with creative processes and consequently need protection for their ideas. Although limited in scope and effectiveness, there are several areas of protection available under federal law. These include copyrights, patents, and trademarks. We will examine each of these in turn and close with a discussion of state and common laws that protect trade secrets.

COPYRIGHTS

A *copyright* grants an exclusive right to sell, publish, or reproduce a book, computer program, catalog or directory, song, work of art, or similar item. Even such items as advertising copy may be copyrighted. Protection generally lasts for the lifetime of the creator plus fifty years. Copyright is held either by the author of the work or by an entity, such a s a publisher, that the author has agreed may assume the copyright. In the case of works made for hire and certain other works, the duration of the copyright is 75 years from publication or 100 years from creation, whichever is shorter. Copyrights are granted automatically upon the creation of any copyrightable item. However, if you wish to make a copyright enforceable, it generally must be registered with the Library of Congress. In some commercial instances, registration is required. Registration is a simple process and is not expensive. Currently, registration fees are $20. Copies of the copyrighted material must be deposited with the U.S. Copyright Office, Library of Congress, Washington, DC. That office will provide copies of the copyright registration form and will assist you in filing the copyright registration.

Copyrights provide passive protection. That is, the holder of a copyright must bring a claim of copyright violation in federal court and must demonstrate to the court's satisfaction that a violation of copyright has occurred. For most small businesses, this self policing is not feasible. Furthermore, copyrights protect the *expression of ideas*, not the *ideas themselves*. This is an important distinction as Apple found out when it sued Microsoft for infringing on its graphical user interface design. The outcome of that litigation made Microsoft the king and left Apple in danger of failure. Consequently, sound legal advice is a must in order to maintain copyright protection.

PATENTS

A ***patent*** is a protected monopoly given to the inventor of a device or a process. The monopoly lasts for 17 years, although design patents can be granted for shorter periods at an inventor's discretion in order to protect the development phase of a patentable product. Patents and their regulation are handled by the U.S. Patent and Trademark Office and the Court of Customs and Patent Appeals.

In order to obtain a patent, you must have a device or process which meets one of the following definitional requirements. If your device or process fits the definitional requirement, it must also qualify under three conditional tests to be able to obtain a patent. Table 8 displays the requirements to obtain a patent.

Table 8
Requirements for Obtaining a Patent

Defintional Requirements:

- a new process or method of doing or building something;
- a new machine;
- a new manufacturing technique;
- a new composition of matter; or,
- a new and useful improvement on any of the other aspects.

The device or process must also be:

- useful;
- novel; and,
- not obvious to a person of ordinary skill in the industry in which the patent will exist.

Obtaining a patent is a lengthy and complex process often requiring two or more years of work. In addition, a registered patent agent or attorney is a must. A list of the more than 11,000 registered agents can be obtained from the U.S. Patent Office in Washington. Although the filing fees are not extreme, the legal fees can be. Not only is the application complex, a search of existing patents is required. Expert assistance is generally required to handle the search and to analyze the findings.

As in the case of copyright, the holder of a patent must bring action against others who infringe upon the invention. This can often be a lengthy and expensive process and requires legal assistance. However, the protection can be stronger than that provided by a copyright. If the patent has been properly prepared, imitators will not be able to make minor modifications to avoid liability. Clearly, the field of patents is complex. Anyone considering a patent should seek legal advice early about the viability of the idea and the level and cost of protection it affords. If the decision is made to proceed with a patent application, a registered agent or attorney should be consulted.

TRADEMARKS

A ***trademark*** is a protected mark or symbol that identifies a particular product, brand, or company. Such marks can be registered with the U.S. Patent and Trademark Office in order to prevent others from using the same mark. Trademark protection can even extend to packaging or ***trade dress***. That is, imitators will not be able to offer competing products in similarly shaped, sized, or colored packages to try to mislead consumers.

As in the case of patents, the application for a trademark must demonstrate that the mark is unique. Phonetic, deviate, or unusual spellings of common terms cannot be registered, nor can you register generic names. A variety of registrations are available. In addition to the trademark, you can register a service mark symbolizing the services offered by a business, or a logotype, which is simply an identifying symbol.

The owner of a registered trademark or service mark must protect the symbol through litigation aimed at violators to prevent losing the protection. Our language today is filled with generic terms that were once trademarks: escalator, cellophane, and thermos, to name a few. If the owner fails to protect the symbol it can become a generic name, and no longer subject to protection. This is why the Coca Cola company tries so hard to protect its trademark, Coke. When wait staff reply to an order for a coke, *will a Pepsi do*, they are responding to pressure from the Coca Cola company to protect its trademark. As is the case with all intellectual property rights, the responsibility for protection and enforcement rests with the owner.

TRADE SECRETS

Unlike the previous types of protection, ***trade secrets*** are governed by state and common law. In fact, a series of doctrines including trade secrets, unfair competition, and misappropriation can serve to protect a small business. No public registration is required, however, strict secrecy must be maintained to ensure that a claim can be successful.

In general, any device, process, or knowledge that has the potential of competitive advantage for its holder can be a trade secret. Table 9 outlines the facts which the courts consider in determining whether a trade secret exists. These are important facts to know, because if a trade secret exists legally, then it can continue into perpetuity. That is, it can last as long as the information continues to afford a competitive advantage.

Table 9

Facts in Determining the Existence of a Trade Secret

1. How valuable is the information to the business and its competitors?
2. How broadly is the information known outside the business?
3. How broadly is the information known inside the business?
4. What steps have been taken by the business to ensure secrecy?
5. What is the cost or effort involved in developing the information?
6. How easily can the information be duplicated by other businesses?

Clearly, legal advice is required in order to develop and establish procedures that will enable a firm to protect its trade secrets. Some of the steps which an attorney might recommend are displayed in Table 10.

Table 10

Steps to Protect Trade Secrets

1. Nondisclosure, noncompete, or confidentiality agreements with employees
2. Physical segregation of employees and limited access to development and storage areas and records of the business
3. Licensing agreements to accompany sales
4. Proprietary labels for records and products
5. Entry and exit interviews with employees and agents

Even if a trade secret has not been established, some actions are flagrant enough to be covered under unfair competition or misappropriation doctrines. For example, if an employee takes a customer list, quits the company, and begins to call upon those customers for a new employer selling similar goods, legal action may be available. As in the case of the other types of protection, legal advice is required when you think a violation has occurred.

SUMMARY

A full treatment of business law is beyond our scope, but everyone planning a career in small business should become familiar with business law because it affects every aspect of business. You should consult with an attorney to establish business policies and practices on an ongoing basis.

The principal body of relevant law is the Uniform Commercial Code, adopted by every state with minor differences. The code requires that all merchants be familiar with its contents. It governs negotiable instruments, sales, and contracts for sale of goods.

Laws protecting an individual's rights to person and property are called tort laws. A tort is a civil or private wrong and can result from an intentional act or negligence. The most common intentional torts are defamation, assault and battery, false imprisonment, and fraud.

Defamation is maliciously attacking an individuals's name or reputation; in oral form, it is slander; in written form, libel. The best defense is avoidance; be careful about making statements about competitors, suppliers, customers, employees, or others.

Giving personnel references can be a problem. The best practice is to simply say, "It is against our policy to make any statements about employees." Do not verify salary data. Say nothing beyond a verification of employment term.

Assault is placing an individual in fear of immediate bodily harm. The use of threatening words or actions can be assault. Battery is the intentional touching of another person without consent. The contact need not be violent. The best defense is avoidance: walk away from potential arguments.

Holding someone without their permission or "just cause" constitutes false imprisonment. With your attorney you should establish a specific, written policy and procedure to cover suspected shoplifting, theft or wrongdoing, and ensure that employees know what to do if they suspect someone of a crime.

The best known tort is fraud, but it is complicated and difficult to prove in court. Among other things there must be an intent to deceive, a misrepresentation, and actual personal or financial injury. Avoidance of misrepresentation makes sound business sense because of its potential impact. If a customer has even the perception of misrepresentation, it will be damaging. Careful attention to training of people is the best defense.

A tort can occur from negligence. In general, a plaintiff must have incurred an injury as a result of a failure of the accused to behave as a reasonable and prudent person. The best preventative is concerned management of the premises. Consider possible dangers and the best way to protect people from those dangers. Children present a special case. The law expects a reasonable, prudent person to anticipate the actions of children.

An expressed warranty is communicated in writing or orally. Many small business owners frequently make statements that could be warranties without realizing it. Implied warranties exist under the Uniform Commercial Code. In general, a product must be salable and fit for the purposes for which it is intended. You must be familiar with the products you sell, know their quality, uses and purposes, and advise your customers accordingly.

Product liability deals with situations where no warranty exists. Manufacturers and sellers may be held accountable for negligence in manufacturing, designing or packaging. Strong quality controls are the best defense.

A contract is a legally binding agreement between competent parties. It can be written or oral and must include an offer and an acceptance, and consideration must be given. Some contracts must be written: estates, bonding or surety and marriage contracts, long term contracts, an agreement for the purchase of land or personal property over $500.

An agent is a person who represents another in a business transaction. You will generally be responsible for any damage an employee causes as long as that person is performing his or her duties. Hiring competent people and training them for their jobs is important.

An agent can enter into contracts on behalf of the company. You can be forced to comply with an oral or written contract made by an employee. You must be careful to avoid the appearance of authority that does not exist. You should develop personnel and supervision policies and practices to ensure that employees who are authorized to perform tasks are identifiable by third parties.

Independent contractors are not employees of agents. If you do not have the right to direct a person to perform a task and the right to control how the task is done, that person is not an employee. Aside from agency considerations, it is an important distinction because an independent contractor is not an employee for tax purposes.

Small businesses frequently need protection for their ideas. A copyright grants exclusive rights to a book, computer program, catalog or directory, song, work of art or similar item for the lifetime of the creator plus fifty years. A copyright holder must bring a claim of infringement in federal court and demonstrate to the court's satisfaction that a violation has occurred.

A patent is a monopoly given to the inventor of a device or process that is useful, novel, and not obvious to a person of ordinary skill in the industry. The patent lasts for seventeen years, although design patents can be granted for shorter periods. The holder of a patent must bring action against others who infringe upon the invention.

A trademark is a protected mark or symbol that identifies a particular product, bank or company. The owner must protect the symbol through litigation to prevent losing the protection.

Trade secrets are governed by state and common law. In general, any device, process, or knowledge that has the potential of competitive advantage for its holder can be a trade secret. Trade secrets can continue as long as the information continues to afford a competitive advantage.

The Bankruptcy Reform Act of 1978, amended in 1984, established a separate court system to hear and handle bankruptcy cases. The act has four major sections: Chapter 7, 9, 11, and 13. Chapter 9 covers municipal debt adjustments. Chapter 7 covers a straight liquidation: the assets are sold off and the proceeds paid over to the creditors. Chapter 11 covers the reorganization of a corporation. Chapter 13 is the counterpart for individuals. These chapters establish a payment plan for creditors with the anticipation that the debtor will eventually pay creditors in full.

A business or individual can voluntarily file for bankruptcy or can be forced into bankruptcy by creditors, although farmers are specifically exempt from an involuntary proceeding. An involuntary petition simply forces a trial, not a bankruptcy. The court must always decide whether a debtor is bankrupt.

QUESTIONS, EXERCISES AND CASES

QUESTIONS:

1.   Why is the Uniform Commercial Code important to small businesses?

2.   In what ways are torts different from crimes?

3.   Why is it important not to give references, either good or bad, about previous employees?

4.   What would happen if an employee were dismissed from a firm and that firm was called for a reference? What should the owner/manager do? Why?

5.   What laws might apply in a case of shoplifting? Why must the business be especially careful?

6.   What is fraud? Can you think of some examples of fraud?

7.   What would happen if a microwave was purchased which gave off radiation? Under what legality would this apply?

8.   What is a quasi-contract and when would one be used?

9.   What is the difference between an independent contractor and an employee?

10.   Why is the concept of agency so important to small businesses?

11.   What are the four chapters of bankruptcies and which apply to small businesses?

12.   What are the five types of authority given an agent?

13.   Which authorities are the most dangerous to a small business?

14.   Why could it be said that copyrights are easy to get but difficult to sustain for small business owners?

15.   How are patents and copyrights different?

16. Is a copyright or a patent more likely for a small business owner to acquire and why?

17. What is a trademark? Name a few that have become household words. What trademark would you like to protect?

18. What trade secrets might a small business have?

19. What can be done to protect small business from losing their trade secrets?

20. Under what conditions may a business or individual be forced into bankruptcy under Chapter 7?

21. Why should small business owners be aware of bankruptcy laws?

22. Which bankruptcy chapters would cover each of the small business organizational types?

23. Define the following terms:

    a.   tort
    b.   defamation
    c.   negligence
    d.   fraud
    e.   attractive nuisance
    f.   quasi contracts
    g.   ostensible authority
    h.   bankruptcy
    i.   agency law
    j.   apparent authority
    k.   warranty

EXERCISES:

1. Go to your library and check out the Uniform Commercial Code. Read about the particular rules and report back to the class.

2. Ask a local attorney who deals with small business, or a business law professor to come to your class and talk to you about the laws which can apply specifically to small business.

CASE 1

It was nearly seven and sirens were screaming into the work site on Vine and Elm. A child had fallen under a sub flooring in the building which was being constructed. Several children had been chasing each other around the fence surrounding the site, when they discovered that the earth had fallen away from the base on the back side following several days of rain. They had great fun slipping back and forth under the fence for about an hour and then two got rather adventuresome and decided to explore the site. The workers had left for the day and had pulled away the plank used to cross the threshold into the main approach to the building. The kids eager to see inside found a plank and laid it across the doorway and did not seat it securely. As the young boy was edging across the plank to the doorway, his weight caused the board to sag and fall, tumbling him into the sub flooring below. He was trapped and shaken up by the fall. Frightened, his friend ran for help.

1.   What legal situation is presented above?
2.   Of what is the company guilty? Why?
3.   What can be done now?
4.   What should have been done previously?

CASE 2

Mark Wheelen has just been fired from the RYC Loan Company. Fred Hankamer, the owner, has discovered that Mark has been embezzling funds through a computerized accounting scheme over which he had been given control three years ago. Fred is devastated, not just by the amount of money he lost but even more by the thought that Mark whom he had come to treat as a family member had for the last six months written himself $250,000 worth of checks to a fictitious account.

Mark was dismissed immediately but no charges were filed against him when he claimed hardship had made him to it and he had promised to pay Fred back. Fred wanted to believe Mark and hated to see him convicted and even more hated to have everyone know of his lack of internal controls which had allowed the embezzlement to occur. Fred truly felt that in large measure he was to blame for Mark's behavior.

Three weeks later, Fred receives a call from ZYT Credit Company. Mark has applied for a job in their computerized accounting area and has listed RYC Loan Company as the name of his last employer. What should Fred do?

1.   Why is Fred correct in feeling that he was to blame for Mark's behavior?
2.   What should Fred do about the reference call by ZYT Credit concerning Mark?
3.   What would you have done in this situation had you been Fred and why?

CASE 3

Jacob Zell is a born salesman. He has been hired to sell commercial spots on the local cable channel. He has had many years of experience in sales and has sold everything from shoes to computers. He could sell snow to Eskimos and tickets for the river Styx.

Tom Bradley was delighted to have the opportunity to hire Jacob away from his last employer. He was selling microcomputers and was doing extremely well according to all accounts.

Tom was amazed! Jacob had sold 50 slots in his first month and yet his closest competitor had only sold 20. Boy, if Tom could only find a few more salespersons like Jake, he could expand into other areas.

Three months later, however, Tom was bewildered. Jake was still making fantastic sales, but they weren't sticking. Tom had just hung up the phone from his last frustrated customer, who had said that Jake had promised that he could have his spot during the nightly news and it still had not appeared. Tom tried to explain to the unhappy client that there were only a few slots available for those times and that previous customers had already bought those spots months ago and still had them retained.

In an effort to appease the customer, Tom suggested that as soon as the present contract for one of the current customers was complete that he personally would put the client into that time slot. What else could he do? Frustrated he answered the phone again and listened to a similar complaint.

1. What has Jake done to harm the business?
2. What can Tom do about it? In what manner is he accountable?
3. Why do you suppose that Jake has been in so many different jobs over the years?
4. What should Tom do about Jake?
5. What are the potential legal implications in the case?

CHAPTER TWENTY FOUR

ETHICAL CONSIDERATIONS

CHAPTER OBJECTIVES

Upon completion of this chapter, you should be able to:

- Discuss the concept of ethics as it applies to small business;

- Distinguish between legal and ethical issues;

- Discuss the social awareness of ethics in the small business arena; and,

- Design a formal development plan for your business with an ethical base.

ETHICAL CONSIDERATIONS

INTRODUCTION

Ethics is a term which seems to create an avoidance syndrome. Just as many of us have very deep feelings about what is right and what is wrong, many of us dislike discussing issues very close to our hearts with other than our closest friends and family. Yet such avoidance has tended to prevent resolution of issues in society which can impact our lives and the success of our businesses. Can ethics be taught? Or is it a birthright which is unchanged? No matter what your attitude, the important issue is to share with your employees your expectations and your perception of theirs.

WHAT IS AN ETHICAL SITUATION?

Just because a business is small does not mean that it is not subject to ethical issues. What happens, for example, if a small business has ten microcomputers and one copy of a software package that claims that no copies can be made except for backup copies, and yet quickly the business discovers that multiple people need access to the software? The manager chose not to purchase a site license because he wasn't even sure the package would be used and indeed it wasn't for some time. Yet once the employees became familiar with the package and its capabilities, they all found uses for it. Technically, it is illegal to violate the copyright, yet how many businesses have rationalized that the one copy was purchased by the business and it is the same business after all, so why buy additional copies? Does this then become an ethical as well as a legal issue?

The situation outlined in the note from our case files may or may not be common, but it is possible. On the surface this is not a legal issue, but it is an ethical one and it is damaging not only employee morale but the company's image. If no one is really hurt, does that make it right? This brings us to the question of ethics and the role it plays in small businesses.

WHAT IS ETHICS?

Ethics has an ambiguous meaning. Webster defines it as ...*the study of the standards of conduct and moral judgment*.[71] Many organizations have their own ethical codes which in effect outline the acceptable conduct for their professions such as the Association of Accountants (AICPA) and the Association of Computing Professionals (ICCP). These associations rescind membership in situations where individuals have been found in noncompliance and the individuals may be subject to imprisonment and/or fine from a legal perspective as well. Yet what is ethics to the general populace? Do they have written guidelines for their behavior? Of course not, but should they?

A CASE FROM OUR FILES

Jim came breezing into the office whistling a merry tune on Monday morning. He had played golf on Saturday with the parts supplier for the office equipment and was thrilled with his play. Mary Anne was delighted that her boss was happy because Mondays were usually bad days, catching up on the weekend orders. Also today was the day that the owner came in to touch base and she was never sure what he would ask to see.

The company was ABC Office Services and they sold not only office supply materials but computer components and software as well. Mary Anne liked her job, but she was often frustrated with Jim who seemed to never be able to make up his mind about purchases from the suppliers. One minute, he was making out a large purchase order for one supplier and the next telling her to cancel that order and instead go with another supplier. His indecision made constant paperwork for her and record keeping was a nightmare. Also she had to answer the telephone which brought complaints from frustrated suppliers when the order changed.

She was thinking seriously about quitting her job when Jim arrived in such a good mood on Monday. Yet she wondered how he could be so cheerful when Mr. Durant was due at any time, so she asked about his weekend.

Jim was so thrilled with himself that he told her about the new set of golf clubs that Hagmore Supplies had given him for his last two orders of ribbons and carbon paper. He also claimed that they had promised him a weekend at Las Vegas if he would bring them a larger order for their machines. Mary Anne was amazed. They had always used Dunbar Services for their machines because of the quality of their machines and their reputation for service. The changeover would cause some problems.

Later in the day, Mr. Durant stopped by Mary Anne's desk and said that he would be opening another branch office in the nearby town. He wanted a list of the suppliers and copies of all purchase orders for the last year. He was going to use the information to find out what sort of start-up inventory he could expect and who would give them the best deal. Mary Anne gave him the information requested and he studied it that week. On Friday he came back in and was furious. *Why have we changed suppliers constantly? Why haven't we developed a relationship with any particular one and why when I tried to call Dunbar yesterday to get estimates were they so unfriendly? We have always had a good working relationship with Dunbar and now they act as if they don't want our business. Do you know why?* Durant demanded.

Mary Anne was in a quandary. She had caught on to the fact that Jim was vying for the highest personal premium in his decision about suppliers. After all, it wasn't his money, but it was his trip, his golf clubs, his portable bar, his tickets for the plays, etc. How much difference could there be in paper or ribbons? So it cost the company a few dollars more on each order, they could afford it and this was a great method for improving his perquisites.

Mary Anne was concerned because she had worked for the company longer than Jim had and felt that she had always been treated well. What could or should she tell Mr. Durant about the premiums paid by the suppliers to Jim for their orders?

Everyone can understand and accept the ethical issue relating to the standards of conduct because they are written, acknowledged and accepted by those who join professions requiring such compliance. But how does one define moral judgment? Again Webster claims that **moral judgment**[72] deals with the ability to make the distinction between right and wrong. If everybody does it, does that make it right?

The fast pace, constant competition, global quality, and diversification of our business arena today has seemed to cause a blurring of those distinctions between right and wrong. It seems today that the world and its concepts are various shades of gray rather than the black and white of the past. Can we blame our ability to communicate and trade internationally? When we were isolated, lacking sufficient technology for rapid communication, we didn't know what our competition was doing until we saw it. We were not able to have a small business in Kansas with international outlets. But high tech has brought with it changes in the psyche of the business owner. In order to compete and survive, some have turned ruthless, not illegal. But what does that do to the moral fiber of our country? Remember that small businesses and the men and women who own them are the backbone of our nation; the reason for its survival. So what happens when issues important to us as individuals start becoming ethical issues in various shades of gray?

Each time a person does one small thing with which he or she is uncomfortable, that makes it easier to rationalize the next time the opportunity presents itself. Until very soon, that person would hardly recognize himself or herself as the same individual of a few years ago. Has this change been prompted by our international endeavors which have different standards of conduct or have we been steadily eroding our values in the name of competition? We trust that this is not true for you or for many others, but more and more the news beings us items of fraud, embezzlement, illegal transfer of technology, etc. These items make headlines, but each of us may be faced with dilemmas of smaller scale every day. What should we tell our bosses about using the computers for personal accounts; using office supplies for our children's homework; doing our own work on company time and using company resources; implying company support for personal promises; using the petty cash for lunch without repaying; filling up with gas at the company pump and not leaving a record?

SOCIAL AWARENESS OF ETHICS

Morrie Helitzer, publisher of *New Accountant*, asked the question, *Does Mr/Ms. Clean Exist?* He states: *A great foe of sound, ethical business practice, or of sound behavior in general, is indifference. The notion that our actions, or inactions, don't much matter, paves the road to disastrous outcomes. What we do and how we do it does matter. As an employee, an employer, a shareholder or a member of the public, you and I are cheated--or cheat the others--when we break the rules.*[73] Much of his discussion was prompted by the fact that firms who have been given the seal of approval by auditors have subsequently been found guilty of various infractions, some major and some minor. He also notes that the cleanest of us may have areas in which we are not 100% pure.

Ethical considerations are quickly becoming an issue for us today as we see cases of insider trading, malicious hacking, and viruses let loose on the nation's computer networks. Longnecker, McKinney and Moore surveyed both large and small businesses and presented them with ethical vignettes concerning such issues as padded expense accounts, environmental pollution, faulty investment advice, foreign business payoffs, hiring a key employee of a competitor, collusion in bidding, gifts to purchasing agents, favoritism, discrimination, misleading advertising, etc. They discovered that in some areas small firms appeared more tolerant than larger firms and speculated that this was true in areas where there was more involvement on their part and where there was less rigor in the controls of the firm. Longnecker et al. remarked that small businesses are of less formal structure and may have looser controls than larger firms which might account for some of the differences recorded.[74] Perception indeed seems to be a factor in ethical decisions.

DISTINCTION BETWEEN ETHICAL AND LEGAL

What is the difference between legal and ethical issues? Legal issues are very much like the codes of conduct mentioned earlier. *Legal* means that an action is in conformity with the law.[75] Laws are written mandating what is constituted as right or wrong and punishments are described for enforcement of those laws. Because the breaking of legal codes can lead to specified punishments of the person, most people try to conform and see that others do likewise. But what about ethical issues which may only mark the soul and have no outward appearance? Ethical issues may relate to legal ones, but this is not a given. Codes of right and wrong which have been mandated by laws are typically enforced, but moral judgment calls are not so well delineated. Taking bribes in a foreign country or *greasing palms* may be an accepted practice in other parts of the globe, but it is not an accepted, legal practice in the United States. Do companies who deal internationally forget where they are at times? We don't think so. Accepted practices can be both ethical and legal.

ETHICAL ISSUES

If indeed social awareness of ethical misconduct is an issue, it is probably the result of the coverage given to companies who allow their sense of profit to outdistance their sense of right. How can computer companies knowingly allow high tech products to wind their way into the hands of the Iraqis? How can we produce software viruses that can destroy companies' records? How can we produce cheaper imitations of products for sale? How can we ban the sale of certain products in the US and then sell them abroad? Has our sense of fair play been replaced by our lust for the dollar? Surely not!

Quality and competency are other issues with ethical overtones. How can we be content with substandard products or services? Why are cars scheduled to disintegrate with the last payment? Where is our pride of workmanship? Should we not be able to expect a day's work for a day's pay? Should we not expect our doctors, our lawyers, our accountants, our consultants, our managers to have competency? These issues are important to our discussion of the ethics of small business. Many of our professional people are beginning to realize that they are in small businesses too. They must promote a service to a particular number of clients or find that they can no longer stay in business. Many professionals are going back to school to learn business topics, so they see not only a need for competency in their chosen fields but in business as well.

MORAL OBLIGATIONS

Small businesses are increasingly confronted with the moral obligations which relate to their chosen industry. Since the ethical attitudes of the business are a reflection of those held by the owner, the owner also feels the onus when an employee steps out of line. The owner has a moral obligation to provide a safe, comfortable working environment for his employees, which may soon mean the enforcement of restrictions of smoking; the provision for the safety of the employees; the provision of good, reliable services/products; the assurance of a quality environment and the maintenance of an ethical image for the company.

Perhaps our legal system has had to replace our consciences in recent years. Why else would companies be forced to go to court for manufacturing faulty and dangerous products; for giving erroneous and harmful advice; for causing harm through neglect or ignorance; for endangering the environment by polluting it; for trading secrets for money; for taking products which are not ours? Small business owners need not sell their souls to Mephistopheles to succeed. Success in their arena means creating the best product or service for the best price and making it available to the people. This is done through *PLANNING*, not through scheming.

DEVELOPING AN ETHICAL PLAN

What can you do? You have pressures. You have felt the twinges or witnessed the results of pseudoethical practices and have had to handle them as they arose. What can you do? The best solution is to plan. Many organizations who have struggled with these issues feel that the best approach is to set down standards of conduct. You can too. When you work out your business plan, stop and think about possible problems which could arise and address them in a written format. Decide on your usage of company resources: what is acceptable and what is not. Decide on how you deal with suppliers. Decide who has access to sensitive data on the computer. Decide on a job description for each employee. Decide how you are going to handle and credit innovations. Define ownership of products. Reward *watch dogging*, don't punish it. Explain that this is not carrying tales but working for everyone's success. But most of all, write down your standards and have them read as a part of the employment contract. And, you be the first to obey the rules! Granting exceptions is the fastest road to disaster, because then inequities are perceived and the edges get blurred.

There is a misconception that a business cannot be successful without condoning some unethical practices, but that is not true. Successful businesses cannot sustain profit without acting ethically, according to Duane Kullberg, because of their linkage between owners, employees, and customers.[76] As long as there is a recourse or an alternative, the customer will opt for fair treatment or fair product at a fair price.

Ethical issues are felt by some to be a personal assessment of right and wrong, so it becomes a taboo subject for discussion. Today we need open discussions about what is ethical, legal, and moral. We can no longer hide our heads in the sand and pretend indifference. It is our business, our life and our country which has a stake in our ethical decision making. Let's make the right decisions.

SUMMARY

Ethics are a standard of conduct which everyone must come to terms with individually and for his or her own enterprise. They are a standard which must be written down and passed to the employees as guidelines of acceptable behavior. Written rules of conduct can eliminate judgments which are often painful on the part of the owner.

Often the issues faced by a company have legal as well as ethical overtones. Be aware of the consequences of actions and ponder your decisions in light of how well you can live with yourself as the result of such an action. Let this serve as a guideline to ethical behavior. Just because an action is legal does not necessarily make it ethical.

The key to ethical consideration is awareness. Don't refuse to think about or decide upon possible courses of actions, because you feel that ethics are too personal. Be willing to delineate your expectations for yourself as well as others. Develop a written code of conduct to be applied in given situations and there can be no misunderstandings of what is right or what will be condoned by you or your company.

QUESTIONS, EXERCISES AND CASES

QUESTIONS:

1.   What is the definition of ethics? What is your definition of ethics? Do the two definitions differ in any substantive way?

2.   Can ethics be taught? Why or why not?

3.   What is the difference between ethical and legal behavior? Can you give some examples of legal but not ethical behavior?

4.   Why should there be social awareness of ethical attitudes? How does social awareness make ethical decisions easier?

5.   Why is it necessary to have a written plan signed off on by the employees of a small business?

6.   Is Jim's behavior in the situation presented in the chapter, ethical or unethical? What should Mary Anne do? What should Mr. Durant do? How would you solve the problem?

DEFINE THE FOLLOWING TERMS:

1.   ethics
2.   moral judgement
3.   legal
4.   pseudo-ethical

EXERCISES:

The following are situations with legal and/or ethical overtones. In some cases the problems have not been delineated, because problem identification is perhaps more important to success than problem solution. Define the potential problem as well as decide what would you do in each of the situations.

1.   Take both sides of the issue or divide into opponents and proponents within your groups. You are a Computer Information Systems professional. What is your stance on hacking and copying applications? What is your stance on those issues as a manager?

2.   You have just been given the position as principal buyer for the office supplies for your company. There does not appear to be a difference between suppliers except that one has a special catalog he carries in his briefcase with premiums that could be earned by purchasing from his company. Here is a set of golf clubs that can be yours if the company purchases only 200 boxes of paper.

3.   Your chief competitor has just come out with a new product just six weeks before yours was due to be released and it has many similarities.

4.   As a computer professional, you are asked to erase a transaction for a charitable contribution so the company does not exceed the cap on its income tax deduction for such contributions.

CASE

Norman was concerned that his company was losing money. The usual cash flow was not there and yet it seemed that it was business as usual. He ran a sheltered workshop which catered to the employment of handicapped individuals. It was the task of the workshop to use company cars to provide transportation to the clients and offer them some type of work activity at the site.

The orders had not changed, the number of employees had not changed and none of the expenses seemed out of line. So Norman called in a consultant to help him find the difficulty. If this situation continued, he would have to do something drastic.

The consultant asked for and received the financial records of the organization and at first seemed unable to find any points of discrepancy. Hal, the consultant, took his lack of findings to his supervisor and explained the difficulties at the workshop and his lack of findings. Hal's supervisor suggested that if all else failed and nothing was suggested by his first perusal of the records to try some reasonableness testing in various areas.

Hal did his reasonableness checks and found nothing out of line until he got to the item dealing with gasoline expense. After performing the reasonableness check on the gas, he found that the company vans were only getting one mile to the gallon. This item had been previously overlooked, because the vans were used to provide transportation for the handicapped clients and it was expected that there would be a large gas consumption. But could any vehicle still be on the road that got only one mile per gallon?

When Norman was told of the findings, he could not explain it and truly did not believe it. Hal then proceeded to observe the facility for several days and discovered that the employees who worked for the sheltered workshop were topping off the tanks on their personal automobiles at the facility's gas pump periodically and leaving no record of the transaction. Hal again reported his findings to Norman and Norman was appalled. He called his employees together and explained the situation to them. He discovered that the practice had started when some of the company vans had been in the shop and the employees had to use their own cars for transportation of clients. They had been reimbursed for their gas. Then a couple of times, employees would find that they were low and would give themselves enough to get to the station for a fillup.

What had started as a legitimate practice had become an abusive and unethical one. As new employees came on board and saw these practices taking place in the company, they perceived this as a job perquisite to which they were also entitled and so the financial impact of the company was not considered. When the employees were confronted with their behavior, they were not contrite! Rather, they reacted as if a fringe benefit had been removed which was their due.

1.	Why was it difficult to find the cause for the financial losses?

2.	What do you suppose prompted this behavior?

3.	Why do you think the employees did not react well to the disclosure?

4.	What would you have done in this situation?

CHAPTER TWENTY FIVE

SMALL BUSINESS SUCCESSION

CHAPTER OBJECTIVES

Upon completion of this chapter, you should be able to:

- Describe the importance of planning for succession;
- Identify the various contingencies for which the owner must plan to ensure successful succession;
- Identify the problems which could result from divorce;
- Explain the impact a change in management can have on a small business;
- List problems created even when succession is planned;
- Explain why contingency plans should be made for the disability of the CEO in a small business; and,
- Discuss how to deal with the problems which will arise when taking over a business.

SMALL BUSINESS SUCCESSION

INTRODUCTION

Like the Walrus in Lewis Carroll's famous poem, who said, *the time has come to talk of many things,* we find ourselves come to a time to talk of different topics. What concluding topics could be more important than the recognition of mortality. It has been said that the human race owes its speed of development and its pace of invention and innovation to the shortness of the lives of its members. There is a passage in Homer's Illiad, which says it best:

> *Like leaves on trees the race of man is found,*
> *Now green in youth, now withering on the ground,*
> *Another race the following spring supplies;*
> *They fall successive; and successive rise.*

> *Homer*
> *The Iliad, Book 6*

Like the leaves of Homer's tree each spring brings a new generation and each generation is filled with drive and ambition. That shortness of life drove mankind to develop writing so that knowledge might be preserved and the invention of writing freed each succeeding generation to blaze new trails building on the wisdom accumulated over the ages. It behooves each of us to make plans for the passing of the torch to the next generation in which our creations and our knowledge will live. That is the primary subject of this chapter.

There are special problems in small businesses both with passing a business along and with managing a business after its passing. How do you plan for *management succession*? How do you leave a business to your heirs? How can second generation management succeed? A special stage of this passing is involved in planning for the continuance of a business despite the failure of human institutions or the incapacitation of its management. This last refers to the problems and effects of divorce and of disability. What happens to the business when a marriage fails? What happens when the owner becomes disabled?

THE PROBLEM OF DIVORCE

One *Inc.* cover story article was entitled *Divorce, Entrepreneurial Style.* The author concluded that to plan for it could ruin your marriage but not to plan for it could destroy your company.[77] The reporter detailed several accounts of people so distraught about the potential loss of a business that they lost everything. One man was convicted of hiring a killer to murder his wife. Another was killed in an altercation with his wife about the division of a business. Many entered into dubious schemes involving salaries and under the table deals in an attempt to influence the valuation of a business for divorce settlement purposes. Others, both men and women, lost their firms to bankruptcy after a divorce. With the rising rate of divorces in the United States, a serious problem has emerged for small business owners.

Some of the states have community property laws which, in general, will treat a business as a marital asset in which case it is likely to be divided 50-50. Other states have equitable property distribution laws which consider economic contribution toward assets in deciding upon settlements. However, a number of states have passed the *Uniform Marital Property Act* which treats marriage as a partnership. Under that treatment, a business is likely to be divided on a 50-50 basis.[78]

Even if ownership of the business is not an issue, the emotional trauma of a divorce can destroy a small business owner's ability to concentrate and make decisions. Some owners have worked out divisions of businesses only to have the company fail during the transition period. In some companies in which both spouses were active, the parties have attempted to continue their business relationship in the interests of the company. It takes a very unusual couple to make that work!

The problem is that people don't think about such things as who owns what and how stock certificates are registered until a divorce occurs. Of course, it sounds heartless to arrange for the possible distribution of business assets and ownership while a marriage is healthy. Few people are willing to consider that a marriage might fail until it actually happens. Then it's too late! The best approach seems an honest appraisal of business ownership and planning for the best interests of both spouses and the business in the event of a breakup. After all, the parties to a divorce are not the only people affected when a business is involved. Employees, other owners or partners, lenders, suppliers and customers are also affected by a business which is hurt or destroyed by a divorce. Consequently, distasteful as it may seem, the wisest course is to discuss with your attorney the effect of various stock ownership options in the event of a divorce before that stock is distributed. As is usually the case, planning can prevent a host of ills, but it requires careful consideration of the contingencies.

THE PROBLEM OF CHANGE

It has become almost a cliche that small business owners can't let go of their companies. In fact, it has become so prevalent for small business owners to sell their stock to their children and stay on as manager, that the IRS has special rules governing such sales. The IRS doesn't like the fact that the proceeds from the sale are taxed at capital gains rates, which tend to be much lower than income tax rates, while nothing really changes. These *sham* sales are discouraged by IRS rules which can require that a small business owner sell 100% of his or her investment in the company and then never set foot on the premises again. One *Inc.* article detailed one family's successful efforts to get around IRS rules which would prevent the first generation management from continuing to be involved in the company.[79] Color Art, Inc. was successfully passed to the sons of the founders while the founders stayed on as consultants to the business. However, the founders did give up control. That is a hard thing for many owners to do.

The truth is that companies go through a life cycle just like people do. A problem frequently develops because during the start-up phase of a business, which can last from one year to 10 years, the skills required for success are entrepreneurial. That means that penetration of a market for a new firm requires innovative approaches. After a firm has passed start-up, it enters a growth and consolidation phase during which time it must establish itself as a permanent member of the competitive community. The skills required to consolidate gains and to see a firm through to its maturity stage are administrative skills. Many entrepreneurs do not possess such skills and consequently are forced out of their businesses by other shareholders, by venture capitalists or by lenders. The solution to the problem is self evaluation. A small business owner must recognize personal strengths and weaknesses and be prepared to acquire personnel with the skills necessary to handle the company as its needs change. Cultivate the expertise and share power and authority with the people who have it. That means sharing control.

Frequently, small business owners look to their children for such expertise. At least they say they do! Sons and, with increasing frequency in recent years, daughters are sent off to school and then brought into the firm at lower management levels. These young people are then brought up through the company with the purpose of giving them a broad based understanding of the business and its needs. In effect, they are being groomed to take over the firm. The problem is that the old hands are reluctant and frequently unable to turn over the reins of control. Billye Ericksen-Desaigoudar is an exception.[80] She is grooming 5 managers, including her three children, to take over her business and has taken pains to keep bankers, customers, suppliers and employees up to date on her plans. She has even set up a new board of directors to assist in the training the next generation will need. In a few years, she plans to sell the business to the next generation using the customary leveraged buy-out.[81]

Billye is able to carefully plan this transition because she has other activities which she wishes to pursue, including two other businesses which she owns. Perhaps the problem with other owners is that they have no such activities and are afraid of retirement and inactivity. Small business owners tend to be workaholics, as we discussed in the introduction to this text. It is much more difficult for someone like that to contemplate retirement. Perhaps the problem is with the degree of involvement many owners have with their businesses. Starting a business is a creative act and people can be fiercely protective and possessive about their creations. Many have difficulty even thinking about someone else making decisions which will affect the company. You don't have to totally give up a company to bring along a successor.

How about staying involved with the business as long as your health permits? That can be done, but even then problems can arise because of the next generation's desire to *do something important*. They quite naturally become impatient, want to try out new ideas, want to change things. The old hands frequently fear that change, fear the mistakes which could be made and the damage which could occur to their creations. But new ideas are the hallmark of small businesses and should be encouraged. Of course, there is risk, but new ideas can rejuvenate a company.

Consider the case of M. Jacob & Sons, a 100 year old family business.[82] Max Jacob, a Russian immigrant, started the business in 1882. Bottles were hand-blown and expensive and Max saw an opportunity to make money by collecting used bottles door to door in Detroit and then selling them to local breweries and other businesses. Despite stiff competition, the business grew and prospered and Max became the king of the used bottle business in Detroit. He brought his sons into the business in 1915. William became a salesman, Ben was the bookkeeper and Sam drove the horse drawn delivery wagon. In the 1920s, new technology made mass production of bottles possible. The Jacob brothers saw that the business had to change or die. They developed relationships with bottle manufacturers and became a distributor serving as the link between manufacturers and breweries and other users of bottles. They built a strong state wide business. Sales were $1 million in 1940 when Marty, Ben's son, came into the business. It continued to grow until the 1950s when breweries began to consolidate and to turn to cans. Sales dropped from $6 million to $3 million and the brothers were lost. Marty put the company into plastics. By 1977, the company was selling $20 million of plastic bottles each year to Michigan businesses.

Then the businesses started to move south and plants started closing. Sales slumped and Marty tried a host of ideas but nothing worked. His son, Joel, had come into the business in 1982 fresh out of college. Marty had made it clear that Joel would have to prove his worth or he would never take over the business and that nothing special was going to happen just because he was the boss' son. Joel hit the road selling. One day he noticed the plastic spray bottles in a K-Mart store had a poor lettering job and wondered about changing the company's emphasis to mass merchandisers. Marty was skeptical, the company had never sold to retailers before, but he told Joel to give it a try. Joel did. He landed the K-Mart account, then Frank's Nursery. They set up a division of the company to specialize in spray bottles and Joel ran it. He started using sales representatives instead of salespeople. By 1985, the firm was selling bottles nationwide through a network of representatives. It had been rejuvenated again.

Marty is pleased and proud, of course, but not totally comfortable. He sometimes feels that he has lost control and gets upset with Joel's constant ideas for change. He finds the enthusiasm draining sometimes. That's perfectly understandable. Marty was probably like that himself once upon a time, he just doesn't remember it.

The moral of the story is: if you want to stay involved with your business while bringing along a successor, do so! Just don't be afraid of new ideas and let your candidate have some freedom to learn to fly. Some things won't work, of course. Mistakes are inevitable. However, think back to the mistakes you made and how much you learned from them. Don't become so arrogant as to think that you will always be able to judge what will and will not succeed. The best thing you can do is ensure that any moves which you consider dangerous are always **hedged**. That means that you never bet the entire firm on a new idea. Be sure that the firm will survive even under the worst possible results. That way, the losses won't hurt as badly and the winnings may well rejuvenate the company. It will also allow you to get used to the idea of sharing control and eventually giving it up. It is also a great way to evaluate a successor!

THE PROBLEM OF MANAGEMENT SUCCESSION

You may remember reading in your introduction to management book that the first responsibility of management is to provide for succession. Large firms do this as a matter of course. The multiple levels of management which exist provide opportunities for new people to be trained and groomed for advancement. As their experience and knowledge grow, their responsibilities grow, so that there are always individuals who can be tapped to fill vacancies in management resulting from death, departure or retirement. The difference in small businesses is that there are fewer levels of management, and control is typically vested in a single person, or, at most, in a very small number of people. To groom a person for leadership in a small business means that the manager and any other owners must give up part of their control so that the new managers can gain the necessary experience to be able to take over the operation one day.

How do you do that? Like most things in business, it is done by planning. If a son or daughter or any other individual is selected as the **heir apparent**, then you must plan for the education and training of that individual. Your candidate for ownership or control must be identified and be a willing participant in the grooming process. What role will college play? Are some fields of study more important than others? What jobs and positions within the company are important for understanding the operation? How long should a person be apprenticed in those positions? How can you bring them into more responsible positions? How can you avoid problems with employees who might resent the *fair haired child*? This and a host of other issues must be dealt with and planned. There are no absolute answers because the needs of every business and every candidate will be different. One thing is constant, however: the need to bring your successor into top level management activities. The candidate should be exposed to the planning process itself at an early point and encouraged to help with the planning, budgeting and financial review. Ideas must be encouraged and the candidate must be allowed to develop and to demonstrate competency. At some point, authority must be delegated and the candidate must be allowed to make and follow up on decisions. A sound approach is to provide experience in running the business by having your candidate take over for you during vacations, sales trips, conventions, etc. These periods can gradually be lengthened as the candidate gains maturity and experience.

One word of caution is due at this point. The individual whom you choose to succeed you must want to succeed you. If you attempt to force a son or daughter to come into the business, both your child and the business will suffer. The one will be unhappy and, consequently, a poor manager which can destroy the other. Being a small business owner is hard work and has long hours. It is filled with risk and diversity. It can be rewarding but only to a person who enjoys the job. If your candidate does not truly want the job, then that person will not do the job well. If your candidate discovers, for whatever reason, that he or she really doesn't want the job after the training and grooming has begun, then change candidates.

The person you choose to groom for your successor need not be a relative. Many small business owners choose a promising employee to cultivate. You must choose someone, however, in your own self interest. Even if you care nothing for the prospects of the business surviving you, you must be concerned about it providing for your retirement and for it surviving a disability. You won't feel comfortable about retirement if you don't have capable hands in which to leave the business. In fact, you can't even take a vacation, spend time with your family, or find time away from the business unless there is someone who can be trusted to take care of it during your absence. You will be like the independent dairy farmer who could never take a day off because the cows had to be milked every day. You must find someone who can milk the cows, at least occasionally, and you must plan for the candidate and the cows to get used to each other.

THE PROBLEM OF DISABILITY

A large firm simply moves another manager into a slot if a person becomes disabled. A small firm may be able to do that with employees, but it cannot with the owner unless someone has been groomed for the job. It makes good business sense to cross train people so that they can cover for each other in the event of an emergency. You should do the same for yourself. You can cover your financial risks of disability with insurance, but you cannot prepare your business to survive your disability without planning.

Even a short period of disability can destroy a small business. If you should, through accident or disease, be unable to function as the manager for only a few months, what would the business do? Who would make decisions? Who would do the planning? Would you have a business to come back to after you recovered? A small business can never rest on its laurels. No matter how strong it has been in the past, no matter what its position now, a small business depends on its future management for survival. The market, competition and conditions are constantly changing. The business must be constantly changing also. Even a business in a stable industry with an established customer base will suffer from the absence of the owner/manager.

Not only are there numerous decisions which must be made daily, but the planning must be done by that person. This means that you must train and prepare people to be able to take over your functions to protect yourself. What if there is no one in the business who can do the job? What if there is someone, but it will be years before that person is sufficiently trained to do the job? You can provide income to be able to hire a competent manager through insurance. You can obtain disability protection insurance which will pay the firm money to be used for the salary of a good manager. It may be hard for the firm to find such an individual and you must appoint people to do the hiring in the event that you are unable to participate, but it is the only option available outside simply hoping that nothing bad will happen. At least you can be assured that your planning and budgeting records will be a valuable asset for anyone coming in to take over the operation. They will provide a sound foundation about where the company is, what it does, the strategic image it portrays as well as the goals and objectives you had established. We all hope, but statistics show that many of us hope in vain. It makes more sense to plan and prepare, then hope!

PLANNING FOR SUCCESSION

The first step in planning for succession is grooming a replacement for yourself as manager. However, there are other questions which must be answered. Principally, who will own the business in the event of your death? Who will manage it? What role will your spouse play? Do you plan to leave the business to someone who cannot manage it? If so, have you discussed the management of the firm with that person and made plans for that need? Do you have a will? What about life insurance? What will the estate taxes do to your business? More than a few people have had to sell businesses in order to pay the inheritance taxes because there was not enough cash in the estate to cover them.

It is vital that these factors be considered and contingency plans made. Not only is the survival of the business at stake, but the welfare of your family as well. A business acquaintance of ours had built a strong, healthy chain of automotive service firms specializing in automatic transmission and brake repair. The business was doing several million dollars per year in volume in some nine separate shops and was well established when he was tragically killed in an automobile accident. Like most small business owners, he had never faced his own mortality, consequently, he had made no plans for that contingency. His will simply left all assets to his wife since his two children were preschool age. Unfortunately, she had neither the business knowledge nor the time to be able to run the firm. What we all had thought was a healthy life insurance coverage disappeared quickly in business expenses and payments to suppliers while the operation began to rapidly decline. She hired a manager, but it was several months before one could be found. In the interim, several employees tried to help, but their knowledge of the operation was less than optimal. Bankers and other lenders began to press for payment when several substantial 90 day notes matured and there was no money to pay them. She was forced to sell the business, but because of its size and condition was unable to find a buyer for the operation as a whole. Each location was finally disposed of in separate deals. As you might imagine, the business did not bring anywhere near its value at the time of the accident. Most of the proceeds of the sale were consumed by bank notes, so that little was actually left when it was finally over. All of that could have been avoided with a little planning.

There are special problems to consider if there are other owners in the business. Are there family members or investors who have a stake in the operation but are inactive in management? In the event of a problem in your estate, such people are likely to exert influence in appointing a manager. Is that what you want? If you have a partner, do you agree on what will happen in the event of the death or disability of one of you? If you have a partner or co-owner who will take over the firm, what will happen to your family? Is there key man life insurance which can be used to buy out your family's interest? Does your partner have the same situation?

Have you done any estate planning? Even though you may not consider yourself to be wealthy, estate and inheritance taxes can be a significant burden to your family. One of the great needs of the estate will be cash or highly liquid assets. If these are inadequate, then the business or part of its assets may have to be sold under distressed conditions. It surely won't bring much that way. Do you know how much your business is worth? Its value will be part of your estate and you can be sure that the IRS will determine a value for it if you haven't. That value will have a major impact on the amount of cash the estate will require. You should talk to an attorney or estate planning specialist to protect your family and your business. This is not a one time action. You must regularly update your estate plans as the value of your business grows and other circumstances change. An annual review of your estate plans is a sound practice.

TAKING OVER A BUSINESS

There are special problems for a person who is being groomed to take over a business as well as for the new CEO of a business. If you wish to have a smooth transition and a healthy business, you need to be aware of these. Many of the problems can be minimized by the right approach on the part of the old management.

The ***heir apparent***, the young person being groomed to take over a business, can experience resentment from the other employees and managers of the firm. Phrases such as *that's the boss' idiot kid*, or *here comes our future boss*, have frequently been heard in the employee lounge. If the staff of a small firm have no confidence in your candidate, then his or her effectiveness, both on the present job and later as owner/manager, can be greatly harmed. These feelings of resentment spring from a natural feeling of superiority which most people have. They consider themselves to be more knowledgeable and capable than your successor and so they resent being forced into a subordinate position. They may dislike the prospects which your successor has for advancement. After all, that person is assured of rapid movement through the company and choice job assignments while everyone else has to work for those advantages. They may also resent the idea of a successor. It means that there is an established limit to their own ambitions. How do you fight these problems?

First of all, your candidate as well as the staff and employees need to know that nothing is guaranteed. No one will be permitted to succeed to the office of owner/manager without first demonstrating the ability to handle the job. You need to dispel the idea of choice jobs and rapid promotion by requiring that your candidate work harder than anyone else in the firm. The one overriding quality which your successor is bound to need is a capacity for hard work. You know that; your candidate should know it as well. Promotions may well be rapid in terms of time, but if they are always based solely on merit and demonstrated competence, then the resentment will be less. That competence must be real. Your candidate must rapidly become knowledgeable. You need it, the company needs it, and the candidate needs it in order to forestall problems with the employees of the firm.

A good part of the problems with other employees can spring from the attitude of your candidate. If that person is arrogant in speech, mannerisms or actions, then your staff and employees will react unfavorably. Your training must make it clear to your candidate that the future management of the enterprise means the management of its people and that their trust and confidence, or lack of it, will be the limiting factors on the effectiveness of that management. Your successor must win that trust and confidence through hard work, study and concern for the company and its employees. This sounds a little like a sermon, doesn't it? What it truly is, is psychology. People are managed by maneuvering them into *WANTING* to perform for the company. They cannot be *MADE* to choose the company's goals and objectives as their own. They must want to do so. They must also want to help bring along your successor. To accomplish that, both you and the candidate must work together. Both skills and knowledge must be developed, but also leadership ability must be cultivated. As the old saying goes, *You lead from the front. You can't push a chain, it must be pulled to get it anywhere.*

Even if you have the perfect candidate, an outstanding training and educational program and an enthusiastic and supportive staff, your successor will never be able to succeed if you personally do not let go. In a case in a previous chapter, we described a second generation manager who was unable to establish an effective inventory control program because of his father's continued involvement in the firm. Control had been relinquished and the son was the owner/manager and made most decisions. The problem was that the founder of the company made decisions also; decisions which were frequently at odds with those of his son. That happens more often than most would believe. It is one thing to give up control of a company which you founded and fought and sweated to establish, it is quite another thing to give up all power in that company.

We talked earlier about maintaining an involvement in a company after turning it over to a successor. There is nothing wrong with that action, however, both you and your successor should understand what that involvement will be. One thing it cannot be, is at odds with the role of your successor. The most valuable role you can play in a company after passing it on is as a senior advisor and consultant on policy matters. That is also the most rewarding role you can play from your perspective. The place to maintain an involvement is in the planning activities. You can truly make a continued contribution to the firm and its growth and development in that fashion. Nothing is more important than the goal and objective setting; the strategic posture development; the budgeting, forecasting and financial analysis; in short, the planning process. This is where a firm is made or broken, the future molded. It is the most difficult and challenging aspect of management and the hardest skill to develop. A new owner/manager who has an old hand to guide this effort is twice blessed. Not only will that involvement mean that counterproductive actions never occur, it will mean that planning will be stronger and more effective.

As any small business owner who has practiced planning activities will testify, planning can consume as much time as you will devote to it. In a typical firm, the owner/manager never has enough time for planning. That means that you can devote as much or as little time to planning assistance as you desire. Your continued involvement in the firm can be full time, half time or one weekend per month. Not only will that effort be useful to the firm, it can continue the training of your successor as you participate in the planning activities together. A more rewarding solution to the problem of continued involvement cannot be found!

There is a word of caution due here. The new ideas which we talked about earlier must be encouraged in the planning process. You must give your successor full input. Only in that way can the firm benefit both from your accumulated wisdom and experience and the fresh insight and enthusiasm of your successor. If you have done your job well, if you have cultivated a strong successor, then the give and take of the planning sessions can be the most fun you have ever had in managing the company. This is truly the secret of family businesses which succeed from generation to generation: the mingling of fresh ideas and approaches with the wisdom and insight of experience. It can also be the secret of a happy and long lasting career.

SUMMARY

No one likes to think of death nor plan for its contingencies. But planning for such an event is a very unselfish act. Even without a business' survival with which to contend, a spouse has to shoulder a large burden when a loved one dies. With the added stress of grief, why compound the suffering by precipitating financial insecurity in the form of business decisions? Plan for your loved ones as well as your business. If you have dreams of building a successful business for your family, don't allow it to be taken away from them by failure to plan.

The loss of a business is not predicated upon death only. It could also result from divorce or disability. If the owner/manager becomes ill or survives a debilitating accident, there may be long periods of time before the running of the business can be undertaken. Can it survive your absence even temporarily? It can if you have planned wisely.

Divorce is also not a popular contingency for which to plan. But in this age when almost three out of four marriages end in divorce, it is a contingency for which plans must be made and then pray that it doesn't happen to you. Working closely together in a business is sometimes hazardous to a marriage. Partners are often heard to say that they have no breathing space away from each other or they bring the stresses found in the business home with them. Just as it takes effort to have a successful business, so too, is effort required for a successful marriage. Perhaps planning for the contingency of divorce will strengthen a marital relationship by causing you to examine what could happen if the marriage were not successful. Planning again is an unselfish act. Not only is the business in jeopardy from a divorce, but so too are the employees, other partners or owners, and the customers.

Change in management from first to second generation is also an area for which plans should be made. Many founders find that they cannot really leave the business to those for whom it was intended. Children are sent to school or employed by the business in anticipation of coming into their own, only to find that the owner won't let them make any decisions.

Successful businesses which are not family oriented find that they have problems too in the same area. If a business is to grow over time, the owner/manager must relinquish some of the control to others. Many founders discover that they cannot grow in their management skills as the company grows with the result that the company does not achieve its potential or others take the company away through stock manipulations. The solution is to plan for growth and succession and to stick to your plans. Since start-up of a new business is a creative venture, and many small business owners put their very souls into its success, it is difficult to watch others take over and do things differently. The best solution when you pass the company on to your successor is to take over the aspects of the company for which operational management has no time. Be a consultant for the firm. Give the benefit of your wisdom, experience and expertise and help with the strategic planning of the company. In this way the company remains successful under second generation leadership and you continue to be useful.

Large businesses plan for succession naturally. However, when small businesses do likewise, problems can develop. Naming a successor can lead to jealousy and frustration if that successor is unwilling or incompetent. So be sure that you choose wisely and train well your successor.

On the other side of the succession coin are the problems related to the successor and how well he or she will fare when their succession is known. The attitude of the successor is vital to the success of the company. How well he or she can relate to the other employees is an important question. Your successor's competency should be without question.

Yet as in all else the emphasis has been on planning. Here, too, it is imperative. The life of your company depends upon it.

QUESTIONS, EXERCISES AND CASES

QUESTIONS:

1.   What are the problems associated with succession?

2.   How can the problems of succession be eliminated?

3.   Why do you suppose so many states are looking at the issue of property rights when a business is at stake in a divorce proceedings?

4.   Why does the CEO have difficulty in turning his company over to a successor?

5.   What problems do the successors have even when chosen early and groomed for the takeover?

EXERCISES:

1.   Go see several business owners and broach the topic of succession with them. Have they considered it? Are they planning to turn the company over to a son or daughter? What makes the son or daughter qualified to take over the business? Is there someone else who plans to take over? If so, when and how?

2.   Talk to a local attorney and find out what the divorce laws are that relate to a small business in your state. Perhaps the attorney can give you examples of what types of actions to beware of in making your contingency plans. What are the estate laws for your state? What happens if the owner does not leave a will?

3.   Share with the class any examples of how business succession was treated in the case of a death, divorce or disability with which you may be familiar. What would you do if you were a small business owner to cover these contingencies?

CASE 1

Betty Lynn and Dan Roberts were co-owners of a moderately successful book store in the Northern section of Atlanta, Georgia. They had been married for 6 years and in business for 5 years. The marriage failed and they decided to divorce. The problem is what to do with the business. The business is incorporated with each spouse owning 50% of the stock. Both of them want to keep the business and continue to operate it under its established name: Bell, Book and Candle.

Betty Lynn and Dan have discussed the possibility of continuing their business association after the divorce is final, but both of them are concerned that there will be too much strain for that to succeed. They might be able to sell the business, but neither one really wants to do that.

Each has offered to buy the other out using a leveraged buy-out arrangement. Neither one wants to sell because they both want to continue in the business. Both have been advised by their attorneys that they must reach an agreement soon or else the court is likely to force the sale of the business.

1. What would you recommend to the Roberts?

2. Could prior planning have eased this problem?

3. What kind of prior agreement would you have recommended?

CASE 2

Arnold Brackett, 26 years old, was the proud owner of a roofing company in a medium sized city in Eastern North Carolina. Arnold's father had retired a year and a half ago after setting him up as the owner and manager of the family business. Arnold's father had founded the firm more than 20 years ago and had built it into a strong, reputable, local contracting business specializing in roofing jobs for commercial buildings.

Arnold called in a consultant because the firm had not been performing well over the last couple of years. When the two consultants arrived at the business, they examined the books and the financial statements and determined that the business had lost sales and profits since the change in management. The business had done well for many years prior to that change.

Arnold explained that the problem was the economic conditions: housing starts were down and everyone knows how that affects the construction business. He needed some way to make the permanent staff more productive.

There was a core of employees who were employed full time, year round, because of their skills. The bulk of the employees were hired on a job by job basis. The core employees handled the supervision of the temporary staff and all of the details of completing a roofing job. One of the older men had been with the firm 15 years and handled most of the job bidding for Arnold. Since this core of people was basically nonproductive when the weather was bad or when a job was not underway, it created a great drain on the business.

Arnold had grown up in the business. He worked summers during high school for his dad. He had gone away to college after high school, but in his words, *That didn't work.* After a year and a half, he came back home and went to work in the business. His dad immediately made Arnold a supervisor and set out to teach him the roofing business. That was 6 years ago. Arnold had worked at every job in the firm and learned them all. All of the employees liked him.

During the interview, Arnold frequently became defensive. He was especially sensitive about the decline in the firm's performance since he had taken over control. His dad had retired for real and was unaware of the decline in the business.

The consultants developed a series of ideas to make the permanent staff more productive. These ranged from fabricating a variety of wooden products which could be sold in the local area, to diversifying the business into related lines of construction. Arnold didn't like any of them.

On the third visit, the consultants began to ask personal questions. What was it that Arnold really wanted to do with this company, what were his goals and objectives, where would he like to be in 5 years, etc? He replied, *I dunno, fishin' I guess.* One of the consultants asked Arnold if he enjoyed his job. Arnold replied, *No one likes roofing. It's a hot, dirty job and mighty hard work.* The second consultant asked why he was in the business if he felt that way about it. *My Dad always wanted me to take over the business some day. Every one knew I would.*

1. If you were a consultant in this case, what advice would you give Arnold?
2. Do you think Arnold's father did a good job of preparing him to take over the business?
3. What mistake do you think Arnold's father made in making his succession plans?

ENDNOTES

1.   Megginson, L.C., Trueblood, L.R. & Ross, G.M. *Business.* Lexington, Mass: D.C. Heath & Co., 1985, 4.

2.   Bursk, C.B. *The World of Business.* New York: Macmillan, 1963, 2.

3.   Driver, G.R. & Miles, J.C. *The Babylonian Laws.* Oxford: The Clarendon Press, 1955, 83.

4.   U.S. Small Business Administration. *SBA Rules and Regulations.* Washington, DC: U.S. Government Printing Office, 1978, 121.

5.   Standard Industrial Classification Codes and Size Standards, *Code of Federal Regulations*, Title 13, Section 121.601, 1994.

6.   *The State of Small Business: A Report of the President 1987.* Washington, DC: U.S. Government Printing Office, 1987.

7.   *The State of Small Business: A Report of the President 1993*, Washington: U.S. Government Printing Office, 1993, 48-51.

8.   *The President's Task Force on International Private Enterprise: Report to the President,* Washington, DC: Agency for International Development, 1984, 161.

9.   *The State of Small Business: A Report of the President 1993*, Washington: U.S. Government Printing Office, 1993, 48-51.

10.   *The State of Small Business: A Report of the President 1987.* Washington, DC: U.S. Government Printing Office, 1987.

11.   PC Greetings, *Independent Business, 5(2)*, March-April, 1994, 16.

12.   *The State of Small Business: A Report of the President 1987.* Washington, DC: U.S. Government Printing Office, 1987.

13.   *Small Business and Innovation.* Washington, DC: U.S. Government Printing Office, 1979.

14.   *The State of Small Business: A Report of the President 1992.* Washington, DC: U.S. Government Printing Office, 1992.

15.   Edwards, K.L. & T.J. Gordon, Characterization of Innovations Introduced on the U.S. Market in 1982, *The State of Small Business: A Report of the President 1985.* Washington, DC: U.S. Government Printing Office, 1985.

16.   Edwards, K.L. & T.J. Gordon, Characterization of Innovations Introduced on the U.S. Market in 1982, *The State of Small Business: A Report of the President 1985.* Washington, DC: U.S. Government Printing Office, 1985.

17.   Cooper, A.C. & F.J.G. Gascon, Entrepreneurs, Processes of Founding and New Firm Performance, in D.L. Sexton and J.D. Kasarda (Eds.), *The State of Entrepreneurship*, Boston: Kent, 1992, 308-309.

18.   Smith, A. *The Wealth of Nations*, Toronto, Canada: Random House, Inc., 1937.

19.   Kilby, Peter, Hunting the Heffalump, *Entrepreneurship and Economic Development*, The Free Press, 1971.

20.   McClelland, David, *The Achieving Society*. Princeton: Van Nostrand, 1961.
       McClelland, David, Achievement Motivation Can be Developed, *Harvard Business Review*, November-December, 1965.
       McClelland, David & Winter, D.G., *Motivating Economic Achievement*. New York: Free Press, 1969.

21.   Hull, D.L., Bosley, J.J. & Udell, G.G., Renewing the Hunt for the Heffalump: Identifying Potential Entrepreneurs by Personality Characteristics, *Journal of Small Business Management, 18(1)*, 1980.

22.   Liles, P.R., *New Business Ventures and the Entrepreneur*. Homewood, Il: Irwin, 1974.

23.   Rotter J.B., Generalized Expectancies for Internal Versus External Control of Reinforcement, *Psychological Monographs*, 1966.

24.   Liles, P.R., *New Business Ventures and the Entrepreneur*. Homewood, Il: Irwin, 1974.

25.   Hull, D.L., Bosley, J.J. & Udell, G.G., Renewing the Hunt for the Heffalump: Identifying Potential Entrepreneurs by Personality Characteristics, *Journal of Small Business Management, 18(1)*, 1980.
       Brockhaus, R.H. & Nord, W.R., An Exploration of Factors Affecting the Entrepreneurial Decision: Personal Characteristics Versus Environmental Conditions, *Proceedings of the Academy of Management*, 1979.

26.   Hornaday, J.A. & Aboud, J., Characteristics of Successful Entrepreneurs, *Personnel Psychology, 24*, Summer, 1971.

27.   Shapero, Albert & Sokol, Lisa, The Social Dimensions of Entrepreneurship, in Kent, C.A., Sexton, D.L. and Vesper, K.H. (Eds.) *Encyclopedia of Entrepreneurship*, Englewood Cliffs, NJ: Prentice Hall, 1982, 72-90.

28.   Shapero, Albert & Sokol, Lisa, The Social Dimensions of Entrepreneurship, in Kent, C.A., Sexton, D.L. & Vesper, K.H. (Eds.), *Encyclopedia of Entrepreneurship*, Englewood Cliffs, NJ: Prentice Hall, 1982, 72-90.

29.   Hornaday, J.A. & Tieken, N.B., Capturing Twenty-One Heffalumps, in Hornaday, J.A., Timmons, J.A. and Vesper, K.H. (Eds.) *Frontiers of Entrepreneurship Research*, Wellesley, MA: Babson College Center for Entrepreneurial Research, 1983, 23-50.

30.   Shapero, A. & Sokol, L., The Social Dimensions of Entrepreneurship, in Kent, C.A., Sexton, D.L. & Vesper, K.H., (Eds.) *Encyclopedia of Entrepreneurship*. Englewood Cliffs, NJ: Prentice Hall, Inc., 1982, 72-90.

31.   Peterson, W., Chinese Americans and Japanese Americans, in Sowell, T. (Ed.) *American Ethnic Groups*, Washington, DC: The Urban Institute, 1978.
       Light, I.H., *Ethnic Enterprise in America*. Berkeley, CA: University of California, 1972.

32.   Shapero, Albert & Sokol, Lisa, The Social Dimensions of Entrepreneurship, in Kent, C.A., Sexton, D.L. & Vesper, K.H. (Eds.), *Encyclopedia of Entrepreneurship*, Englewood Cliffs, NJ: Prentice Hall, 1982, 72-90.

33.   Hornaday, J.A. & Tieken, N.B., Capturing Twenty-One Heffalumps, in Hornaday, J.A., Timmons, J.A. and Vesper, K.H. (Eds.) *Frontiers of Entrepreneurship Research*, Wellesley, MA: Babson College Center for Entrepreneurial Research, 1983, 23-50.

34. Richman, T., The Entrepreneurial Mystique: An Interview with Peter Drucker, *Inc.,* October, 1985, 34.

35. Hornaday, J.A. & Aboud, J., Characteristics of Successful Entrepreneurs, in Baumback, C.M. & Mancuso, J.R. (Eds.) *Entrepreneurship and Venture Management*, Englewood Cliffs, NJ: Prentice Hall, Inc., 1975, 11-21.

36. Collins, D.F. & Moore, D.G., The Enterprising Man, *MSU Business Studies*, East Lansing, MI: Michigan State University, 1964.

37. Cooper, A.C., Technical Entrepreneurship: What Do We Know?, in Baumback, C.M. & Mancuso, J.R. (Eds.) *Entrepreneurship and Venture Management*, Englewood Cliffs, NJ: Prentice Hall, Inc., 1975, 42-53.

38. Dun & Bradstreet, *Failure Rates of New Business Ventures*. New York: Dun and Bradstreet, 1977.

39. Dun & Bradstreet, *The Business Failure Record*. New York: Dun and Bradstreet, 1981.

40. *Ford at Fifty*. New York: Simon & Schuster, 1953.

41. Chief Executives Typically Work 60 Hour Weeks, Put Careers First, *Wall Street Journal*. August 19, 1980.

42. Wozniak, S. Chips and Dips, *InfoWorld, 6(41)*, October 8, 1984, 50-51.
To Each His Own Computer, *Newsweek*, February, 22, 1982, 50-56.

43. Lynn, R. (Ed.), *The Entrepreneur*. London: George Allen & Urwin, Ltd., 1973, p. 50.

44. Emerson, R.W., lecture in 1871.

45. *The New Millionaires and How They Made Their Fortunes*. New York: Bernard Geis Associates, 1961.

46. *The 50 Great Pioneers of American Industry.*, Maplewood, New Jersey: Hammond, Inc., 1964.

47. Previts, G.J., The Accountant in Our History: A Bicentennial Overview, *Journal of Accountancy*, July, 1976, 46.

48. Winkler, J., *John D., A Portrait in Oils*. New York: The Vanguard Press, 1929, 67.

49. It is important to be able to convert markups based on cost into retail markups and vice versa. Markup based on retail is an important number because it is equivalent to the gross profit percentage. The process is simple if you remember that cost + markup = sales. Let MC be markup based on cost, MR be markup based on retail and C stand for cost. Now, MR = MC/(C + MC), or markup based on cost divided by cost + markup based on cost will equal markup based on retail. You can solve in the other direction also. Solving the above equation, MR = MC/(C + MC) for MC yields: MC = (MR X C)/(1 - MR)

50. Wojahn, E. Divorce, *Inc.*, March, 1986, *8(3)*, 55-64.

51. Dealing in Discounts, *Time.* February 15, 1982, 44.

52. Dahl, J., Opening the Financial Door, *The Wall Street Journal*, May 19, 1986, 1D ff.

53. Dahl, J., Opening the Financial Door, *The Wall Street Journal*, May 19, 1986, 1D ff.

54.   Hand, Learned, *Commissioner v. Newman*, 159 F. 2d 848 (2d Cir., 1947).

55.   Gomes, G.M. Excess Earnings, Competitive Advantage and Goodwill Value. *Journal of Small Business Management 26(3)*, 1988, 22-31.

56.   Coyne, K.P. Sustainable Competitive Advantage--What It Is, What It Isn't. *Business Horizons*, January-February, 1986, 54-61.

57.   Stoner, C.R. Distinctive Competence and Competitive Advantage. *Journal of Small Business Management, 25(2)*, 1987, 33-39.

58.   Stoner, C.R. Distinctive Competence and Competitive Advantage. *Journal of Small Business Management, 25(2)*, 1987, 33-39.

59.   155 Top Franchises in the US, *Entrepreneur*, 1996, October, 176-181.

60.   *The State of Small Business: A Report of the President 1993*, Washington, DC: U.S. Government Printing Office, 1993.

61.   *The State of Small Business: A Report of the President 1993*, Washington, DC: U.S. Government Printing Office, 1993.

62.   Dun & Bradstreet, *The Business Failure Record*. New York: Dun & Bradstreet, 1981.

63.   Chandler, A.D., *Strategy and Structure*. Cambridge, MA: The MIT Press, 1962.

64.   Joe Larson's Trial by Fire, *Inc., 3(12)*, December, 1981, 61-64.

65.   A deviation from this one vote policy is called *cumulative voting* and exists in several states. Under cumulative voting, a shareholder has the right to cast one vote for each position on the board of directors or all votes for one candidate for the board. For example, if a corporation had 15 members of the board, a shareholder could vote 15 times: once for each position available on the board. Alternatively, the shareholder could cast 15 votes for a single candidate for the board and give up his rights to vote for the other 14 positions.

66.   Posner, B.G. Real Entrepreneurs Don't Plan, *Inc.*, November, 1985, 129-135.

67.   The American Opportunity. *Inc.'s Guide to International Business*, Special Edition, Fall, 1988, 5.

68.   The American Opportunity. *Inc.'s Guide to International Business*, Special Edition, Fall, 1988, 5.

69.   Plotkin, H. Going International. *Inc.'s Guide to International Business*, Special Edition, Fall, 1988, 6-12.

70.   Egan, T. Home Court Advantage. *Inc.'s Guide to International Business*, Special Edition, Fall, 1988. 37-39.

71.   Ethical, Webster's New World Dictionary of the American Language, New York: The World Publishing Company, 1962, 499.

72.   Ibid, 956.

73.   Morrie Helitzer, Does Mr./Ms. Clean Exist?, *New Accountant, 4(1)*, September 1988, 2.

74. Longnecker, J.G., McKinney, J.A., & Moore, C.W. Ethics in Small Business, *Journal of Small Business Management, 27(1)*, January 1989, 27-31.

75. Op. Cit., Webster, 835.

76. Duane Kullberg, Right and Wrong: How Easy to Decide? *New Accountant, 4(1),* September 1988, 16-20,37.

77. E. Wojahn, Divorce, Entrepreneurial Style, *Inc.*, March, 1986, 55-64.

78. D.J. Freed & T.B. Walker, Family Law in the Fifty States: An Overview, *Family Law Quarterly, Vol 18(4)*, Winter, 1985.

79. J.P. Kahn, A Perfect Pass, *Inc.*, June, 1985, 68-71.

80. D. Fenn, The Family Plan, *Inc.*, April, 1986, 119-120.

81. A leveraged buy-out is a process by which the business funds its own purchase. That is, funds are borrowed from the business by the new owners and given to the old owners. Repayment of the debt to the company will come from future salaries and bonuses paid to the new owners. If necessary, the company can borrow the funds and pass them along to the new owners who repay the loan from salaries and bonuses. Alternatively, the stock of the business is pledged as collateral to secure a loan made by the new owners to fund the purchase from the old owners. The key in every variation is the funding of the payment from future business profits.

82. B.G. Posner, The 100 Year Old Start-Up, *Inc.*, September, 1985, 79-85.

INDEX